JEFFERSONIAN LEGACIES

JEFFERSONIAN LEGACIES

EDITED BY PETER S. ONUF

WITH A FOREWORD BY DANIEL P. JORDAN
AND AFTERWORD BY MERRILL D. PETERSON

UNIVERSITY PRESS OF VIRGINIA
CHARLOTTESVILLE, 1993

To the people at Monticello
then and now

THE UNIVERSITY PRESS OF VIRGINIA

Copyright © 1993 by the Rector and Visitors of the University of Virginia
First published 1993

Library of Congress Cataloging-in-Publication Data
Jeffersonian legacies/edited by Peter Onuf.
    p. cm.
    Includes bibliographical references.
    ISBN 0-8139-1462-0 (cloth). — ISBN 08139-1463-9 (pbk.)
    1. Jefferson, Thomas, 1743–1826—Influence—Congresses.
    2. United States—Politics and government—1783–1815—Congresses.
    3. United States—Civilization—1783–1865—Congresses. 4. Vir-
    ginia—History—1775–1865—Congresses.   1. Onuf, Peter S.
    E332.2.J48   1993
    973.4'6'092—dc20   92-43937

Printed in the United States of America

Contents

II. JEFFERSONIAN VISIONS

III. JEFFERSONIAN LEGACIES

Foreword

The fifteen essays in this volume are an outgrowth of a remarkable conference on "Jeffersonian Legacies," held at the University of Virginia in October 1992 as the opening event in the University's commemoration of the 250th anniversary of the birth of its founder, Thomas Jefferson. Revisionist in spirit, innovative in format, the conference sought new perspectives on the Jefferson legacy by measuring Jefferson's life and values against major concerns of the 1990s.

The six-day conference brought together a wide variety of individuals—academicians representing many disciplines but also policy makers and interested parties from the general public—for the purpose of exchanging ideas about the enduring qualities of a man born two and a half centuries ago. Three formal lectures were given, but most sessions were organized around panel discussions that provided ample opportunity for audience participation. Commissioned papers, which form this volume, were made available in advance but were not publicly presented, and their authors met in private seminars to talk about each others' work. Social occasions and a visit to Monticello provided additional opportunities for spirited conversation.

The conference was structured around central themes: Jefferson and rights, education, the democratic tradition, and race. Its core purpose was to consider critically what Jefferson thought, said, and did in these broadly defined areas of concern. The premise of the conference was that Jefferson's legacies—for better or worse—are directly relevant to some of the most crucial concerns of Americans in the 1990s. If women's rights and racial tension are burning issues today, what can be learned about them from Thomas Jefferson and how do Jefferson's words and deeds stand against modern sensibilities?

The conference was ingeniously structured to promote genuinely fresh thinking about Jefferson and his legacy. The list of participants did *not* include many leading scholars with established reputations as Jefferson specialists who had already had their say; conspicuous by their absence on the program were such names as Bedini, Cullen, Cunningham, McLaughlin, Matthews, and Sheldon, among others, while the role of the ranking Jefferson scholar, Merrill D. Peterson, was limited to a brief commentary at the conference's final session. To generate new ideas, conference organizers invited scholars distinguished for having written about other subjects in the eighteenth century or about other eras within American history to turn their attention to Thomas Jefferson.

Also participating were historians whose important research on Jeffersonian topics had not yet been published. Other voices heard were those of civil rights activists; a real estate broker; scholars from France, Russia, and the Ukraine; public officials; lawyers; a television journalist; museum professionals; and specialists in several academic disciplines, with up to a dozen panelists in some sessions, and lively audience participation in most. The result was an intellectual free-for-all, with polemical discourses, reasoned debates, brilliant insights, wild digressions, and even some egregious misinformation, all under the big tent of serious conversations about Thomas Jefferson. As organizer Peter S. Onuf noted, "It's hard to imagine a conference of this scope on any other American figure, or to think of anyone else whose life has such relevance to issues today." Critics who groaned about revisionist zeal, presentism, and a tint of political correctness missed the point of Jefferson's own standard: "We are not afraid to follow the truth wherever it may lead, nor to tolerate any error so long reason is left free to combat it."

The essays in this volume reflect the critical reassessment that marked much of the proceedings, and both the book and the conference will add detail and insight to the Jefferson literature. Necessarily eclectic, these essays are not intended to cover all topics of the conference but instead to suggest its scope and revisionist tone.

Joyce Appleby's contribution, the keynote address, sets the stage for her colleagues by exploring Jefferson's "complex legacy." Basing his political philosophy on "nature," Appleby says, Jefferson was a powerful enemy of monarchy, aristocracy, and all artificial distinctions; at the same time, however, nature sanctioned the exclusion and suppression of those who were "naturally" different.

The essays grouped in Part I, "Jefferson's World," focus on aspects of his private life: Jefferson's lifelong pursuit of religious truth, his membership in an enlightened, transatlantic "republic of letters," and the experience of living at Monticello—for Jefferson, his family, and his slaves. Paul K. Conkin suggests that Jefferson's religious "pilgrimage" was sustained—and profoundly limited—by his uncritical faith in reason; the enlightened friendship of reasonable men, Douglas Wilson shows, was the foundation of the great republic of letters to which Jefferson proudly belonged. In an imaginative effort to discover what "the first Monticello" meant to Jefferson, Rhys Isaac depicts Jefferson's mountaintop home in the years up to his wife Martha's death in 1782 as a "storied" mountain. The young Jefferson had absorbed many of these stories in his wide reading and told his own stories of domestic bliss and of political liberation, but he was never able to hear the stories of his own slaves. Jan Lewis also focuses on the domestic side of Jefferson's life, illuminating the importance of his "home"—and what we might call "family values"—in his political career and the tension between his private and public personas.

Slavery and race appear as themes in several essays, to Jefferson's discredit, and they are central to the contributions of Lucia C. Stanton and Paul Finkelman. Stanton works from an exhaustive study of the primary sources of slavery at Monticello and introduces for the first time an accurate and coherent picture of African-American life on the mountaintop and Jefferson's attitudes toward it, while Finkelman, collecting and analyzing more readily accessible materials, condemns Jefferson's failure to free his slaves and to be an authentic spokesman for the antislavery movement.

Part II, "Jeffersonian Visions," includes a variety of fresh approaches to familiar questions in the history of Jefferson's political philosophy and practice. Jack P. Greene reminds us of the importance of Virginia in Jeffersonian thought: the *Notes on the State of Virginia*, he argues, should be seen as a pivotally important contribution to a tradition of critical historical writing on the commonwealth that helped Virginians construct a positive collective identity. Stephen A. Conrad also emphasizes the importance of context: his rereading of the *Summary View*, the 1774 pamphlet that thrust Jefferson into national prominence, concludes that Jefferson saw the insufficiency of simply *talking* about rights and was primarily concerned with larger questions of justice and power. Jefferson's lifelong indebtedness is the focal point of original research by Herbert Sloan, whose essay uses a famous letter from Jefferson to Madison in 1789 to analyze the influence of Jefferson's debt on his political philosophy and private life. The political arena is also of interest to Michael Lienesch, who contends that Jefferson the partisan helped to invent a modern, liberal, pluralistic politics despite himself and despite his republican scruples about parties; John Lauritz Larson posits that Jefferson's constitutional scruples, nurtured in the fervid opposition of the 1790s, proved disabling when Jefferson and Madison sought to strengthen the Union later through internal improvements. In the concluding essay in this

section, diplomatic historian Walter LaFeber also explores the links between precepts and practices. But in this case, the verdict is more favorable: LaFeber argues that Jefferson's foreign policy, for all its notorious
shortcomings, was consistently responsive to a dynamic agrarian political
economy.

Appropriately, the volume is capped off in Part III with two essays on
"Jeffersonian Legacies." The essays in previous sections also consider legacies, sometimes explicitly, and thus prepare the way for a more systematic,
self-conscious review. Gordon S. Wood, the conference's closing speaker,
offers a provocative interpretation of the main themes in Jefferson's career,
as well as trenchant commentary on the Jefferson image in recent historical
writing. Wood also shows us how Jefferson in his later years reflected on
his own legacy, remaining to the end faithful to the democratic revolution
he had helped unleash—but had never fully understood. Scot French and
Edward L. Ayers then consider the Jefferson image—and legacy—in contemporary American culture. Concluding with a discussion of the Jeffersonian Legacies Conference, French and Ayers demonstrate that Jefferson's
reputation in the academic community and with the general public has
been inextricably bound up with our contemporary concerns about race.
Finally, in a brief afterword, Merrill D. Peterson, who so brilliantly deline-
ated the ways we have thought about Jefferson throughout our history in
his *Jefferson Image in the American Mind* (1960), responds to the previous
essays and offers his own views on some of the enduring legacies of Jefferson's life and career.

While the conference and essays allow fresh voices to be heard on aspects
of the Jefferson legacy, good and bad, at times they merely echo partisan
arguments about Jefferson's life and politics going back to his own era; in
other ways they provide a 1990s standard of judgment. The centrality and
complexity of Jefferson's ideas and career, his extraordinary versatility, his
gift of felicitous prose, and the exceptional corpus of letters he left behind
will assure that Jefferson will remain a fascinating and compelling subject to examine and ponder for edification and inspiration, for admiration
and admonishment, for generations to come. As Henry Adams observed
long ago:

> Almost every other American statesman might be described in a parenthesis.
> A few broad strokes of the brush would paint the portraits of all the early
> Presidents with this exception, and a few more strokes would answer for any
> member of their many cabinets; but Jefferson could be painted only touch
> by touch, with a fine pencil, and the perfection of the likeness depended
> upon the shifting and uncertain flicker of its semi-transparent shadows. [1]

It is the signal contribution of the conference and of this volume that "a few more strokes" have been added "touch by touch" to the enduring portrait of a universal man whose self-written epitaph, itself even standing alone, makes the case for a prodigious legacy: "Author of the Declaration of American Independence, of the Statute of Virginia for Religious Freedom, and Father of the University of Virginia."

DANIEL P. JORDAN

NOTE

1. Henry Adams, *History of the United States of America During the First Administration of Thomas Jefferson* (New York, 1891), p. 277.

Editor's Note

The Jeffersonian Legacies Conference was made possible by generous support from the Virginia Foundation for Humanities and Public Policy, the Curry School of Education, the University of Virginia Law School, and the Woodson Institute for African and Afro-American Studies. Melvyn P. Leffler, chair of the Corcoran Department of History, provided decisive leadership. Without the crucial and enthusiastic support of President John T. Casteen, the conference would never have taken place; without coordinator James Lewis's unflagging energy and commitment, it would not have been such a great success. Seminar moderators Drew McCoy, Armstead Robinson, Jennings Wagoner, and Ted White also did splendid service. Bob Brickhouse handled public relations skillfully. Many, many others, not the least our wonderful students, made important contributions: I wish I could list them all.

John McGuigan, formerly of the University Press of Virginia, suggested that Thomas Jefferson's 250th birthday should be commemorated with an appropriately scholarly volume. The Legacies conference was an outgrowth of that original interest. In the intervening months, Press director Nancy Essig and editor Dick Holway have enthusiastically supported this book project, pushing it through a radically accelerated and nerve-wracking publication schedule. Cornelia Wright kept us on the fast track with expert and timely copyediting. My thanks to them all and to an extraordinarily able and agreeable group of authors who delivered their fine essays in timely fashion. These essays embody the new perspectives that justified the conference.

The production of this volume has been immeasurably aided by the efficiency and dedication of the secretaries of the Corcoran Department of History: Lottie McCauley, Kathleen Miller, Elizabeth Stovall, and Ella Wood. I am grateful to all of them for their efforts.

Over the long course of organizing the conference and of conceiving and completing this conference volume, Merrill Peterson and Dan Jordan have been most gracious and supportive. My thanks for their insights and their excellent contributions.

The Jeffersonian Legacies Conference marked the debut of the Institute for Early American Studies, 1750–1860. This book is its first substantial product.

PETER ONUF
November 1992

Abbreviations Used in Notes

Boyd   Julian P. Boyd et al., eds., *The Papers of Thomas Jefferson,* 24 vols. to date (Princeton, N.J., 1950–)

Ford   Paul Leicester Ford, ed., *The Works of Thomas Jefferson,* 12 vols. [Federal Edition] (New York, 1904–5)

L&B   Andrew A. Lipscomb and Albert Ellery Bergh, eds., *The Writings of Thomas Jefferson,* 20 vols. (Washington, D.C., 1903–4)

LofA   Thomas Jefferson, *Writings,* ed. Merrill D. Peterson [Library of America] (New York, 1984)

Malone   Dumas Malone, *Jefferson and His Time,* 6 vols. (Boston, 1948–81)

PJM   William T. Hutchinson et al., eds., *The Papers of James Madison,* Congressional Series, 17 vols. (Chicago and Charlottesville, Va., 1962–91)

VMHB   *Virginia Magazine of History and Biography*

WMQ   *William and Mary Quarterly,* 3rd Series

JEFFERSONIAN LEGACIES

Introduction
Jefferson and His Complex Legacy

JOYCE APPLEBY

For many years I have, prompted by genuine curiosity, clipped references to Thomas Jefferson out of articles in the popular press. What is there about Jefferson, I ask myself, that connects so powerfully with every generation of Americans? How can his ideas continue to hold their buoyancy in the fluctuating currents of our public life? Why is Jefferson the only president whose name forms an adjective of general meaning? The words *Washingtonian, Jacksonian, Wilsonian* direct us to a past political regime. Only *Jeffersonian* circulates in contemporary conversations. "Let us return to our Jeffersonian origins," a Democratic presidential candidate exhorted a crowd in 1992, while a Republican pundit asserted that Ronald Reagan had been the most Jeffersonian president since Martin Van Buren—a point he embellished with Reagan's own recommendation that we "pluck a flower from Thomas Jefferson's life and wear it in our soul forever." In a recent *New York Times* article, Massachusetts governor William Weld described himself as a Jeffersonian. Just a few weeks later, we heard an anguished Jerry Brown demand of his party's delegates, "What would Jefferson think?" [1] Even what Jefferson did *not* do has grown more impressive with the passage of time. Of those queried in a *Wall Street Journal*–NBC poll, 31% thought that Jefferson had played the most important role in the Constitutional Convention. [2] To speak of Jeffersonian principles or Jeffersonian traditions is to point to pretty stable referents. But I probably need not belabor the point as we reflect upon Thomas Jefferson's enduring contributions on the occasion of his 250th birthday.

The theme of the Jeffersonian Legacies Conference, echoed in my title,

"Jefferson and His Complex Legacy," sets up the issues. It also brings to mind the lexicon from probate courts, with which Thomas Jefferson as a practicing attorney was well familiar. Legatees, bequests, contested wills, trustees, codicils, heirs, the disinherited, estates—the imagination trips over them all, eager to exploit the rhetorical possibilities in a discussion of the Jeffersonian heritage. But an irony presents itself immediately, for Jefferson set little store by inheritances. He would no doubt have been flattered by our conference, but he would probably have found the idea of a Jeffersonian legacy an oxymoron, for Jefferson distinguished himself from his contemporaries in opposing the mindless transfer of laws, ideas—even words—from one generation to another. The true Jeffersonian legacy is to be hostile to legacies.

But no more than anyone else has Jefferson been successful in controlling his admirers and detractors. And they, present company excluded, have been a mixed lot. As Merrill Peterson has taught us, Jefferson's reputation changed over time, reaching its nadir in the closing decades of the nineteenth century. The reasons for this precipitous decline are not hard to find. The Civil War had disclosed the pernicious effect of the states' rights doctrine ascribed to Jefferson; national reformers confronted problems that required more effective, not less active government; and the democratic values Jefferson had championed lost much of their charm when America's wholesome farmers had become defiant populists. It was hard then to do Jefferson justice, and even harder to celebrate him.

I was amused recently by an exchange of letters between Henry and Brooks Adams. Brooks had sent Henry a manuscript biography that he had written about their grandfather, John Quincy Adams. Evidently he had been highly critical of Jefferson, or so Henry thought. "For God Almighty's sake," he wrote his brother, "leave Jefferson alone!"[3] One wishes Henry had followed his own advice. And it certainly would have been wise counsel for Paul Leicester Ford, who edited a grand edition of Jefferson's papers in 1892. Introducing his ten volumes, Ford could barely be civil to Jefferson's memory. He retailed every nasty thing that had ever been said about Jefferson, telling readers that he had been charged with "contradictions and instability," "with hypocrisy, opportunism, and even lack of any political principles," to the embarrassment of "his most devoted adherents." Not counting himself among the latter, Ford struggled to find a justification for his editorial effort. He finally concluded that although Jefferson's character and conduct were filled with serious flaws, the people in some subtle way had understood him and realized that his controlling aim was neither national independence nor state sovereignty, but rather to secure for them "the ever enduring privilege of personal freedom."[4]

I agree with Ford. Freeing the human spirit was Jefferson's lifetime crusade. His felicitous expression of a natural rights doctrine crystallized the yearnings of many ordinary Americans, particularly those young men who had been stirred by the *double entendre* of self-government for which the Revolution was fought. But Jefferson went further as he imagined ways to bring into being the social world implied in that doctrine. Like other leaders of great popular movements—Luther comes to mind—Jefferson desired what many of his contemporaries desired, but he transformed that common wish into a clearly articulated possibility and marked out a course of action to turn that possibility into a reality. This enterprise covered many years, stretching from the inspired composition of the Declaration of Independence through the vigorous exercise of executive power a quarter of a century later. What I would like to examine is the intellectual scaffolding that Jefferson raised for that new social world, for I think his most enduring legacy, entailed on us in the name of nature, has been a particular understanding of personal freedom.

Jefferson's framing of an American political creed is largely invisible because he offered his opinions as propositions about nature, and we, his cultural heirs, have so received them. To recognize this involves the willing suspension of belief—not the willing suspension of disbelief that enables us to enter into the theatrical fictions of a play—but the willing suspension of belief that comes from deliberately detaching ourselves from the convictions we have about the past. To say, for instance, that Thomas Jefferson mobilized his contemporaries to strike down privilege and extend the ambit of free choice seems too obvious to warrant comment. To say further that he worked feverishly for seven years to stir his countrymen to exercise their power as awakened voters is to imagine Jefferson pushing hard on an open door, but in fact the positions of power in the newly constituted United States were held by men who were socially conservative and intellectually unadventurous. Many, including Vice President John Adams, drew their truths from a kind of secular Calvinism, an amalgam of wisdom drawn from the classics and the Bible. Men are prone to sin and society is subject to degenerative diseases, they stressed. The specialness of the United States lay not in signaling a new dispensation for the human race, but in offering enlightened statesmen an opportunity to apply the lessons of the past. According to these national leaders, when the American colonies separated from Great Britain, they freed themselves from the mother country's corruptions, but not from the pure model itself. Their history taught that order preceded and conditioned liberty and that gentlemen, filtered from the mass of the voters through fine electoral processes, could alone preserve that order. These Federalists, true sons of Englishmen, extolled personal freedom. It was the most cherished element of their heritage, a fact that presents us with something of a conundrum. If both the Anglophile Federalists and Anglophobe Jeffersonians prized liberty, what was at issue? Is the Jeffersonian legacy a codicil to our grand English inheritance or did Jefferson fundamentally alter the intellectual framing of personal freedom? I will argue the latter.

William Duane, a fiery Irish journalist with excellent radical credentials, described Jefferson as the best rubber-off of dust he had ever met.[5] The metaphor is apt because it was Jefferson's peculiar relation to the settled and stationary—those things that collect dust—that separated him from almost everyone of his peers in the Revolutionary elite. Natural rights philosophy did not represent for him, as it did for others, a learned discourse going back to the Stoics. Rather, it delivered a warrant to dismantle the old social order so that men (and strictly speaking it *was* men, alas), long alienated from their true natures, might recover them. A zeal for personal freedom did not divide the Revolutionary elite; it was the Jeffersonians' supporting arguments about human nature and society—the essential conceptual context created for personal freedom—that acted as the cleaver.

For Jefferson, like Thomas Paine, the implementation of natural rights required radical surgery on the traditional body politic. More urgently, the burden of old ways of thinking, of antediluvian conceits, of controlling institutions, had to be shed. Only liberation from archaic authorities of all kinds, in their view, would lift the dead hand of the past off the shoulders of the present generation. Paine stirred readers with the pungent prose of a Speaker's Corner incendiary. But Jefferson was no deracinated intellectual; he plotted his weight-lifting campaign within the bosom of America's ascendent Revolutionary elite. And his education made the job more complex, because the voices from dozens of venerable texts resonated in his head. He took on the task of reconciling his radical understanding of personal freedom with pervasive assumptions about order and justice.

Scholarly and philosophical—characteristics that often promote timidity—Jefferson boldly levitated himself out of his social milieu and trained his great learning on the real problem of liberty at the end of the eighteenth century: how to make good on the Enlightenment promise that men, born with a capacity for benign self-direction, could work out their own destinies and bring into existence a world that reflected the fulfillment of desire rather than a compromise with despair. Fired by this compelling social ambition, Jefferson put into circulation ideas about a different kind of freedom—one rooted in nature and accessible to reason, its workings explained by abstractions, its validation projected onto the future. Just how radical this departure point was can be judged by considering the English alternative of rights won by extracting concrete concessions from the Crown and implemented through the arcane processes of the common law.

The Jeffersonian idea of freedom did not accord with that of America's many evangelical Protestants or of the secular conservatives who made up the Federalist party. Both classical and Christian political theory viewed the state of nature in the unkind light that Hobbes made famous. Government offered a haven from the heartless war of all against all. When men sought to throw off authority, it was the Old Nick speaking through them. Even worse for traditionalists, free thought and insubordination seemed to go together. Early in the century Cotton Mather had lamented the fact that enthusiasm for order and law in nature went hand in hand with people's wishing "to approach God as an equal," a complaint one of Jefferson's opponents echoed with the observation, "Whenever modern philosophers talk about mountains something impious is about to be said."[6]

Our political scientists tell us that the Jeffersonians created the first American party system, but this hindsight obscures the reality. Jefferson's was not a party, but a radical political movement, mobilized to save the American Revolution from—excuse the anachronism—its Thermidorean reaction. When Jefferson threw off the constraints of his office—the year would have been 1793—and took his principles out of doors to an electorate unused to partisan politics he did what had never been done before. Yet this novelty that transformed American culture has been neutralized by a social scientific construct about party development.

In the years before his election in 1800, Jefferson and his allies had to create an image of a society that had never existed—one in which the unbounded area of voluntary association took precedence over the formal realms defined by public policy. The Jeffersonians' assertions about a natural ordering mechanism prompted skeptics to ask why this spontaneous order had not manifested itself earlier. The riposte to this challenge was to point out how the overbearing hierarchies of church and state had worked in tandem to suppress natural human potential, an answer that further undermined respect for the exercise of formal power. With great rhetorical virtuosity, they drew invidious distinctions between the artificial and the natural, the prescribed and the voluntary, the repressive and the liberating. George Washington reacted viscerally to the unprecedented phenomenon of ordinary voters forming political clubs to discuss state affairs. He dismissively spoke of them as "certain self-created societies"; in response, the Jeffersonians turned the whole nation into a political club. Repeatedly putting government itself on the defensive, they catalyzed voters so effectively that Americans ever since have talked about politics in Jeffersonian terms.

The liberal social order that Jefferson sketched involved a significant reworking of traditional ideas about time and nature. In classical republican thought, all change figured as contingency; time brought cycles of degeneration against which mere mortals labored in vain. Liberal discourse, however, embedded the idea of time in the dynamic concepts of process, development, and progress. The future would be fundamentally different because ongoing processes were actually transforming society. As strictly as any French *philosoph,* Jefferson marked his own age as a great divide. Writing to James Madison, he banished the legitimacy of force in international relations to "the dark ages which intervened between ancient and modern civilization."[7]

Logically, this expectation of inexorable improvement undercut the importance of past knowledge, an attitude Jefferson nicely epitomized when extolling modern forms of representation. "The introduction of this new principle of representative democracy," he said, "has rendered useless almost everything written before on the structure of government." And then, delivering the *coup de grâce* to classical learning, he added that this fact "in a great measure relieves our regret if the political writings of Aristotle, or of any other antient, have been lost."[8]

In language, too, Jefferson felt the past's heavy hand. If existing laws constrained each cohort of the living, how much more profoundly inhibiting was the conceptual vocabulary one inherited through language. Jefferson targeted the purist as the enemy of linguistic freedom. Dilating on two words he had just learned, purism and neologism, he announced, "I am no friend . . . to what is called *Purism,* but a zealous one to the *Neology* which has introduced these two words without any authority of any dictionary. I consider purism as destroying the verve and beauty of the language, while the other improves both and adds to its copiousness."[9]

Jefferson defined dictionaries as the repositories of words already legitimated by usage. Resorting to the metaphor of production, he called society the workshop for words.[10] His receptivity to neology, neologisms, and neologization—a neology he coined—was not shared by his friend John Adams, with whom he resumed a correspondence in old age. Upon receiving from Jefferson a three-volume work on ideology, Adams feigned ignorance of the word. "Pray explain to me this Neological Title! What does it

Mean? When Bonaparte used it I was delighted with it, upon the Common Principle of delight in every Thing we cannot understand. Does it mean Idiotism? The Science of Non Compos Menticism. The Science of lunacy. The Theory of Delerium. Or does it mean the Science of Self Love? of Amour propre?" [11] Thus Adams gently ribbed his friend's unflagging love of the new.

Jefferson and Adams read the same Enlightenment texts, but where they amused, consoled, and infuriated Adams, to Jefferson they represented a great magazine of ammunition with which to attack the smug Federalists and all others who emphasized the frailty of men, the better to exert power over them. Jefferson's great gift was as a synthesizer. He took several strands of liberal theory and braided them into a coherent rope on which to hang his reforms. Nature had already been pushed to the forefront of thinking about society by way of a complex trajectory that moved from Isaac Newton's cosmology to the French *philosophs'* theorizing about laws of social development. This naturalizing of social processes happened at the same time that nature itself was being reconceived as orderly and predictable. Where previously the term *natural* had referred to that which remained wild and unbridled, during the course of the eighteenth century the word became Newtonianized. And as nature became orderly, it became more attractive as a model for society. Social theorists raided the lexicon of the natural philosophers, drawing their analogies from the new physics. They spoke of immutable rights, inexorable developments, and natural laws, finding in nature a better order than the one offered by governments and constitutions. [12]

The Jeffersonian Republicans cast their longest shadow over American political thought by linking scientific rationalism to free trade. Jefferson's gifts as a synthesizer are again conspicuous. The new language of science had intruded farthest into the domain of society in matters economic. Observers of the burgeoning world trade were talking about natural laws that governed the flow of goods and determined their pricing. These writers detached commerce from its traditional association with government policy and reconstituted it as a natural system with its own ordering mechanisms. Jefferson saw the liberating potential in economic freedom, and he used this new science of economics to infuse both certainty and morality into his prescriptions.

For Jefferson, almost every moral question contained a scientific solution, at the very least a scientific-sounding solution. Reflecting on the population pressures from which his contemporary, Thomas Robert Malthus, had drawn such grim conclusions, he claimed with some hyperbole that

American crops grew exponentially. He envisioned great benefits from the fact that Europe was running out of food. Indeed, the fortuitous fertility of America's farm acreage enabled him to square the circle of self-interest and community welfare. "So invariably do the laws of nature create our duties and interests," he wrote the French economist, J. B. Say, "that when they seem to be at variance, we ought to suspect some fallacy in our reasoning." [13]

Again, while resisting a call for distributive justice, he invoked a general law: "To take from one, because it is thought his own industry and that of his fathers had acquired too much in order to spare to others who, or whose fathers have not exercised equal industry and skill, is to violate arbitrarily the free principle of association, the guarantee to everyone a free exercise of his industry and the fruits acquired by it." [14] Elsewhere he spoke of "the natural right of trading with our neighbors" and grounded property in "the natural wants" of men. [15] This way of thinking about the economy became so deeply ingrained in ensuing decades that concepts like the declining rate of profits and the iron law of wages could be treated as natural principles rather than imaginative ways of talking about a specific economic culture.

Two key abstractions—nature and freedom—owed much of their eighteenth-century reworking to changes wrought by the market. Speaking generally, we can see that one of the distinguishing features of a commercial economy is that its coercion is veiled. The apparently voluntary nature of its private transactions creates the illusion that participants are free to choose. The fact that people must earn before they can eat is a commonly recognized connection between need and work, but it appears as a natural link, embedded in the necessity of eating rather than coming from a particular social arrangement for distributing goods. Despite the fact that men and women must buy and sell in order to live, the voluntary aspects of the market remain most salient. The individual makes choices, takes risks, and either suffers or enjoys the outcomes of those decisions.

Economic enterprise in the eighteenth century had also promoted the individuality of ordinary white men by engaging them as single members of society and encouraging their self-definition as men endowed with rights to life, liberty, and the pursuit of happiness. If the realm of politics could be severely restricted, the Jeffersonians reasoned, men would live harmoniously, their competitive urges deflected into the broad avenues of an expanding private sphere. This formula calls to mind Samuel Johnson's observation that men are never so innocently engaged as when they are busy making money.

The market—again conceived abstractly—also suggested a different solution to the problem of order. Its capacity to enlist men in productive activities offered an alternative to overt social direction. In the presumed naturalness of market behavior lay the key to converting self-interest from a moral defect into an organizing principle of nature. As early as the Stamp Act resistance, mechanics in New York had rejected the gentry's patronizing notions about the limits of human rationality. Radical pamphleteers then had redefined reason as a normal capacity for looking after oneself that had been given to all men. What gentlemen denounced as debasing self-interest their inferiors hailed as a "universal law." [16] Self-interest could be infused with moral value just because its universal promptings suggested the uniform operation of a natural law, one, moreover, that linked freedom and equality. These themes were particularly prominent in Jefferson's campaign literature of the late 1790s, where the natural man of Christian drama was replaced by the natural man of an orderly universe. Individual freedom, so long hedged in by political and ecclesiastical authority, became the secret spring of a new liberal system because it could also put food on the table.

The market for the Jeffersonians, however, was never merely an economic system; it represented a new sphere of action for the unfolding of human potential. Under conditions of freedom, men would be lured from sloth by opportunities for self-improvement. They would choose their own goals and learn responsibility through the discipline of consequences. Like his hero, Francis Bacon, Jefferson longed to engage men's minds in reality and its practical imperatives. For him, the economic realm deserved respect not because it made men wealthy, but because it was part of the natural order which yielded only to correct responses—unlike politics, where the art of persuasion, if not outright cajolery, reigned supreme.

Throughout the eighteenth century, the market had forged an identity of interests among those attracted to the productive ideal and the personal initiatives it sponsored. Here was a form of materialism that touched moral as well as practical concerns because market participants had to suppress their passions and fantasies to attain their goals. The liberal formula, that government governs best which governs least, owed its empirical base to the American experience in the free enterprise economy which the Constitution so well protected. The widening scope of opportunity in the early nineteenth century engaged men's energies and confirmed their expectations about the blessings of liberty. The benign character of the American economy, with its owner-run farms and shops and its extraordinarily favorable ratio of natural resources to population, greatly enhanced the reputation of nature and gave credence to the idea that its laws were better than

those of legislators. Values associated with capitalism—an economic system—and liberalism—a set of beliefs about reality—merged to create the
deeply felt conviction that both owed their being to nature itself.

The exclusion of women, blacks, and native Americans from the liberal
crusade raises a provocative thought. Was there something in the Jeffersonian creed which licensed this? Far too large and important a presence in
Jefferson's world to be counted exceptions, these excluded contemporaries
bracket his undoubted iconoclasm. Their inclusion in liberal reforms was
not inconceivable, for others far less bold than Jefferson recognized their
capacity. A case in point is his Secretary of the Treasury, Albert Gallatin.
Worried about the pressing shortage of first-rate talents for government
office, Gallatin suggested naming women to certain posts, a proposal which
elicited this curt reply from Jefferson: "The appointment of a woman to
office is an innovation for which the public is not prepared, nor am I." [17]
Women, as he explained to several correspondents, were formed by nature
for men's need and pleasure.

Nature was also interpreted as similarly marking out blacks for a subordinate position in white society, as indicated by the oft-quoted passages in
the *Notes on the State of Virginia,* where Jefferson expressed "a suspicion" that
Negroes were inferior to the whites in the endowments of both body and
mind. [18] For native Americans, it was not innate inferiority but cultural
obstinacy which accounted for their disqualifying differences. Their unfit-
ness nonetheless led to a draconian conclusion. In 1780, Governor Jefferson
wrote the Revolutionary frontier leader, George Rogers Clark, "If we are to
wage a campaign against these Indians the end proposed should be their
extermination, or their removal beyond the lakes of the Illinois river. The
same world will scarcely do for them and us." [19] Despite his pronounced
environmentalism, Jefferson chose nature rather than nurture to explain the
apparently different behavior of women, blacks, and native Americans;
these differences placed them outside the liberal thrust of Jeffersonian
theory with its naturalizing and systematizing of social experience.

Here we see the underside of Jefferson's reliance upon the concept of
nature to decide moral questions. A mighty liberator in the face of historic
privilege, natural law doctrine raised its own form of exclusion. Indeed,
nature, when abstracted into a system of universals by the scientific imagination, could discriminate just as effectively as society. For Jefferson "the
immovable veil of black" he described in the *Notes* truly hid the African-
American slave, so much so that he could excoriate his Federalist opponents
for their debasement of ordinary men with lines that startle us: "Still further to constrain the brute force of the people, they deem it necessary to

keep them down by hard labor, poverty, and ignorance, and to take from them, as from bees, so much of their earnings, as that unremitting labor shall be necessary to obtain a sufficient surplus barely to sustain a scanty and miserable life." [20]

The assertion of an underlying uniformity in the face of conspicuous human differences had enabled the Jeffersonians to enlist nature in the war against hierarchical society. Claiming to interpret the laws of nature, Jefferson had created a complex intellectual tradition that linked the American nation to a grand human destiny, but the association of the right to life, liberty, and the pursuit of happiness with a uniform human nature bode ill for those deemed naturally different. Where traditional society recognized a variety of statuses, ethnic groups, and regional identities, Jeffersonians obliterated that variety in the celebration of all free men, except where, as Jefferson wrote, "the difference is fixed in nature." [21] It is not surprising that the antislavery movement that finally led to abolition came from America's Evangelical Christians who spoke the language of sin and damnation, not that of nature and rights.

The Jeffersonians won an overwhelming victory in 1800 with a polemic against their own inherited political culture. Accepting the challenge of implementing natural design, Jefferson turned himself into an agent of change—profound, transformative change in the social relations and political forms of his country. However stereotypical Jefferson's enlightenment faith, his opportunity to act upon his ideas as president of his country was unique. The course of American politics had not been set by the War for Independence, nor by the ratification of the Constitution. There were many possible futures in the exceptional situation of the new nation. Jefferson seized on one of them, imposing his will on the federal government and his spirit upon the American electorate.

Nothing could be further from the truth than the claim by Henry Adams that Jefferson in office outfederalized the Federalists. It errs in both directions: in misconceiving the profundity of Jefferson's reforms and in assuming that such ideologically tepid acts as the Embargo and the Louisiana Purchase contained the essence of Federalism. Noble Cunningham's examination of Jefferson as an administrator should scotch for all time the canard about his being a visionary without practical know-how. The thoroughness with which Jefferson exorcised the influence of his opponents still astounds. He removed a whole cohort of young Federalists from civil and military offices; he eliminated domestic taxes; he substantially reduced the national debt; he shrank the size of the bureaucracy despite the growth in population and territory; he hastened the conveyance of national land to ordinary farmers; and he replaced Federalist formality with a nonchalance in matters of etiquette that quite amazed foreign dignitaries. Not a symbol, a civil servant, or presidential initiative escaped his consideration as a tool in his dismantling of the "energetic" government of his predecessors. And after his two terms, Jefferson had the exceptional good fortune to be able to pass on his standard to two close political allies.

Looking back on the presidential campaign of 1800 from the safe shore of success, Jefferson reflected on the fundamental differences between the voters who had rallied around him and those who had supported the defeated president, John Adams. In a letter to Joseph Priestley, the famous English scientist then ensconced in rural Pennsylvania, Jefferson stressed that his opponents had looked "backwards not forwards, for improvement." They favored education, he said, "but it was to be the education of our ancestors," and he noted ruefully that President Adams had actually told audiences that "we were never to expect to go beyond them in real science." Rising to this handsome occasion for expatiating on the subject of change, Jefferson declared with great gusto, "We can no longer say there is nothing new under the sun. For this whole chapter in the history of man is new. The great extent of our republic is new. Its sparse habitation is new. The mighty wave of public opinion which has rolled over it is new." [22]

Writing years later to Adams, Jefferson unequivocally characterized their respective parties as "the enemies of reform" and its champions, the two sides splitting on the question of "the improvability of the human mind, in science, in ethics, in government." "Those who advocated reformation of institutions, *pari passu,* with the progress of science," he lectured Adams, "maintained that no definite limits could be assigned to that progress." [23] Still eager to define the differences in 1823, Jefferson summed them up in pairs: the guidance of experience or of theory; fear and distrust of the people as opposed to their "cherishment"; use of coercive economic and political power versus trust in the people's capacity to act in their best interests. His was the party of theory, democracy, and liberation.

Nothing is so hard to detect in the past as those novelties that have subsequently become familiar. The style and substance of the Jeffersonian program represented a dramatic rupture with established forms and expectations. Yet we can scarcely see the breakthrough. In our schoolbooks, Jeffersonian Republicanism was renamed "democracy" and depicted as a force of nature, a democratic tide. Far truer was Jefferson's own remembrance of the contest with his apprehensions that the Federalists might prevail. So completely did Jeffersonian ideals triumph in the ensuing years that it is hard for us to take seriously an opposition that looked longingly to the past for wisdom while actively propagating the view that the people lacked judgment and needed an upper class to direct the country's affairs. We have fallen into a way of viewing as a natural evolution what in fact was a sequence of historical events replete with human striving, worthy antagonists, and unintended consequences.

When that discerning Frenchman, Alexis de Tocqueville, visited the United States in 1831, he discovered the America that the Jeffersonians had envisioned a generation earlier. A natural environment had replaced a social order. The conventional connection between the nation's elite and its people had been snapped. Eagerness for private ventures had replaced ambition for public office. The ties that knit human beings into communities—those repetitions found in custom, habit, and routine—had been discarded in the competition for improvements and innovations. Americans, Tocqueville wrote, sought nothing so much as "to evade the bondage of system and habit, of family-maxims, class-opinion, and, in some degree of national prejudices." He then metaphorically described for his readers how aristocracy had made a chain of all the members of the community while democracy had broken that chain and severed every link of it. In the New World, Tocqueville noted, the individual man stands alone without hereditary friends or neighborhood solidarity.[24]

It's easy to call to mind which of Jefferson's convictions contributed to this outcome: "the rights of the whole can be no more than the sum of the rights of individuals," "by the law of nature, one generation is to another as one independent nation to another," and "the rights of one generation will scarcely be considered hereafter as depending on the paper transactions of another."[25] The most striking lines of all came with Jefferson's defense of the Jacobins in early 1793, when he reminded a friend in Paris that "the liberty of the whole earth was depending on the issue of the contest . . . rather that it should have failed I would have seen half the earth desolated; were there but an Adam and an Eve left in every country, and left free, it would be better than as it now is."[26] At that writing the Jacobins had not begun to desolate their enemies. Yet surely it must be the case that few practical men, entrusted repeatedly by their peers with positions of responsibility, have seriously entertained as many subversive ideas as Thomas Jefferson.

Jefferson's profound antagonism to the debasing effects of tyranny inspired his greatest lines of prose. He carried to his death his hostility to authoritarian doctrines, precedents, and officials. But Jefferson was more than a catalyst for the liberal opinions rife in the society, he was the live wire that made the connection between Enlightenment philosophy and

American public policy. For Tocqueville, the cause of America's distinctive democratic culture was not a political movement, but something passive— the equality of condition. So well had the Jeffersonians explained the work of nature that their own handiwork went unnoticed.

In retrospective we can see that Enlightenment thinkers marked out two broad avenues for the development of the human potential. The first was the study of nature in all of its manifestations, under the guidance of objective reason. The second was the replacement of authoritarian institutions with democratic governance. Ironically, the second enterprise succumbed to the triumph of the first. Interpretation of the natural order did not promote popular government, but limited government—a very different thing. Because the advances of science encouraged people to admire the natural more than the artificial, large areas of human activity which had traditionally been ordered by public authority were set free on the grounds that they were really a part of nature. Defined as natural, these domains of society were made private and, once private, were thought deserving of protection from government. Successful in perpetuating his pristine republican style of government for a quarter of a century, Jefferson laid the institutional foundation for limited government and the intellectual undergirding for Americans' suspicion of governmental power, even that exercised by the people.

Jefferson gave expression to one of the most attractive propositions of the American experiment: that political and economic liberty could eradicate the differences imposed by ignorance, superstition, and tyranny. Working together, economic and political liberty would serve each other's moral purposes as they reformed a world distorted by the accumulated abuses of the past. Access to economic opportunity and political participation would strip away artificial barriers, leaving men as men to prosper in a new era of equality. The future was the screen upon which Jefferson projected his faith in the unfolding of the human potential under conditions of freedom. This animating hope of American liberalism secured the loyalty of the poor for free enterprise and the patronage of the rich for democratic suffrage. Our own thinking still rotates within these round Jeffersonian categories. Highly moral in their genesis, they came to us as descriptions of reality.

We live in a world of "posts." The buildings going up around us are postmodern; our literary criticism is poststructural; our sociology postpositivist; our legal scholarship postrealist; our political science postbehavioral; the whole era postindustrial. Ours is clearly an age that knows where it has been and senses that it is no longer there. What deserves remarking about this "post" phenomenon is the self-aware activity of exploring what it means to be where one once was and is no more. Is it time to ask, are we now post-Jeffersonian? This is not an easy query to answer. As my opening remarks suggest, time has turned Jefferson into what he taught, a kind of ever-recurring principle for American reformers. His influence is responsible for keeping taut the tension between high aspiration and practical accommodation that characterizes Americans. Trying to keep faith with Jefferson has produced the familiar pattern of public disillusionment and reillusionment that is so striking to foreigners. His evocation of the values of freedom along with his "cherishment of the people" still stir the heart, but the head rejects the intellectual context he established in order to claim a new dispensation for mankind.

Another part of the Jeffersonian legacy is to cover its tracks. The concepts of time as process and change as development, which have dominated social thinking since the nineteenth century, have made it hard for us to see what was historically conditioned in the original fusion of democracy and capitalism. This linkage has raised formidable barriers to the public oversight of economic affairs. Should we wish to bring the political back in, areas lost to nature would have to be reclaimed for society. More worrying for our nation, wealth and economic power have steadily encroached upon the restricted ambit of politics. Indeed, the debility of our political system indicates that democratic forms have outlived democratic substance.

Jefferson never lost faith in the harmony of nature and the superiority of natural relations to political conventions. An article of that faith was the scientific character given to the social order, a proposition that has weathered the years less well than his ideals. The images and tropes of Jeffersonian naturalism discourage respect for government just as the language of science has nurtured biases against those who affront nature's uniformities. A telling sign of our postmodernity is that we have difficulty accepting Jefferson's arguments with their scientific gloss of universal truths, first principles, and immutable norms. The words that fill our public debates—pluralism, diversity, multiculturalism, relativism—point to different truths about the human experience. Jefferson developed a powerful rationale for his liberal reforms in the idea of a natural social order that reveals itself to scientific inquiry. Success long ago froze that rationale into an American creed. Should we continue to reason with outworn concepts of nature and truth? We can be certain of one thing—Thomas Jefferson would not have.

NOTES

1. *New York Times Magazine,* Aug. 23, 1992.
2. As cited in Denis Lacorne, *L'Invention de la république: Le modèle americain* (Paris, 1989), p. 21.
3. Paul C. Nagel, *Descent from Glory: Four Generations of the John Adams Family* (New York, 1983), p. 353.
4. *Ford,* I, p. xii.
5. *Works of John Adams,* II, p. 430, as quoted in Otto Vosler, *Jefferson and the American Revolutionary Ideal,* trans. Catherine Philippon and Bernard Wishy (Washington, D.C., 1980), p. 89.
6. Robert Middlekauff, *The Mathers: Three Centuries of Puritan Intellectuals,* 1596–1728 (New York, 1971), p. 295; Linda Kerber, *Federalists in Dissent: Imagery and Ideology in Jeffersonian America* (Ithaca, N.Y., 1970), p. 91, as quoted in Robert E. Kelley, *The Cultural Pattern in American Politics: The First Century* (New York, 1979), p. 122.
7. TJ to James Madison, Aug. 28, 1789, in *Boyd,* XV, p. 367.
8. As quoted in John Dewey, ed., *The Living Thoughts of Thomas Jefferson* (London, 1941), pp. 59–60.
9. TJ to John Waldo, Aug. 16, 1813, in *L&B,* XIII, p. 340.
10. As quoted in Dewey, ed., *Living Thoughts of Thomas Jefferson,* p. 9.
11. Adams to TJ, Dec. 16, 1816, in Lester J. Cappon, ed., *The Adams-Jefferson Correspondence,* 2 vols. (Chapel Hill, 1959), II, pp. 500–501.
12. See particularly the discussion of how Locke moved unself-consciously from a moral to a scientific meaning of natural law in William Letwin, *The Origins of Scientific Economics* (London, 1963), pp. 147–48, 176–81.
13. TJ to J. B. Say, Feb. 1, 1804, in *L&B,* XI, pp. 2–3.
14. TJ to Joseph Milligan, April 16, 1816, in *L&B,* XIV, p. 466.
15. As quoted in Dewey, ed., *Living Thoughts of Thomas Jefferson,* p. 72; TJ to Pierre Samuel du Pont de Nemours, April 24, 1816, in Dumas Malone, ed., *Correspondence Between Thomas Jefferson and Pierre Samuel du Pont de Nemours, 1798–1817* (Boston, 1938), p. 182.
16. Bernard Friedman, "The Shaping of Radical Consciousness in Provincial New York," *Journal of American History,* 56 (1970), pp. 789, 792.
17. TJ to Gallatin, Jan. 13, 1807, in Henry Adams, ed., *The Writings of Albert Gallatin,* 3 vols. (Philadelphia, 1879), I, p. 328.
18. TJ, *Notes on the State of Virginia,* ed., William Peden (Chapel Hill, 1955), pp. 138–43.
19. TJ to George Rogers Clark, Jan. 1, 1780, in *Boyd,* III, p. 259.
20. *Notes,* p. 138; TJ to William Johnson, June 12, 1823, in *Ford,* X, pp. 226–27.
21. *Notes,* p. 138.
22. TJ to Joseph Priestley, Jan. 27, 1800, in *Ford,* X, p. 146; as quoted in Dewey, ed., *Living Thoughts of Thomas Jefferson,* p. 102.
23. Cappon, ed., *Adams-Jefferson Letters,* II, p. 332.
24. Alexis de Tocqueville, *Democracy in America,* 2 vols. (New York, 1899), I, pp. 240–71.
25. TJ to Madison, Sept. 6, 1789, in *Boyd,* ed., XV, pp. 392–97; TJ to John Adams, April 25, 1794, in Cappon, ed., *Adams-Jefferson Letters,* I, p. 254.
26. TJ to William Short, Jan. 3, 1793, in Adrienne Koch and William Peden, eds., *The Life and Writings of Thomas Jefferson* (New York, 1944), pp. 321–22.

PART I

JEFFERSON

AND HIS WORLD

CHAPTER I

The Religious Pilgrimage of Thomas Jefferson

PAUL K. CONKIN

One brief essay cannot do justice to Jefferson's involvement with, knowledge about, and contributions to the elusive subject of religion. The literature on these subjects is already extensive, as it is on almost every aspect of Jefferson's life. Jefferson not only had experiences, matured beliefs, and nourished hopes that, by most definitions, qualify as religious, but he was also at various points fascinated with the subject of religion and read widely about various religions. He was very concerned with the role of organized religion in the new American republic and made important contributions to an always contested and never completely coherent constitutional protection for religious freedom. Religious issues were so pervasive and so important in his life that ignorance of them precludes any holistic or undistorted understanding of either his character or his thought.

The word "religion" is rich—and thus very ambiguous. Most people do not define the word carefully, and if requested to do so fill in a parochial content tied closely to their own traditions or beliefs. Those within the emphatically theistic Semitic religions tend to make belief in gods essential to being religious, thus excluding from the class "religion" such nontheists as early Buddhists. I have developed my own guidelines to religious phenomena, guidelines I use to bridge the gap between theistic and nontheistic religions. The defining content of a religion is one or more of the following: broad or solacing beliefs about reality, special and fulfilling types of experience, rituals or forms of worship, and highly sanctioned moral codes. Such beliefs, experiences, rituals, and moral codes are variously conducive to the attainment of wisdom or enlightenment, ecstasy or beatitude, mental or physical health, and thus worldly success and happiness or life beyond death. Institutionally, such beliefs, experiences, rituals, and codes are usually embodied in sacred texts, espoused by prophets or priests, focused upon shrines or temples, and sustained by organizations responsible for promotion, education, or proselytizing.

It is easy to fit Jefferson to this taxonomy. He nourished consoling beliefs about the universe and at times enjoyed a sense of wonderment and awe. He spent a lifetime agonizing over the foundations of morality. He sought types of wisdom, wanted a healthy mind, and always was confident of life after death, a belief that gave him consolation and also one that seemed necessary as a support for public morality. He turned, continuously, to inspired religious texts, those deriving from classical authors as well as selected parts of the Christian Bible. He honored religious teachers who did not use mystifications to gain illegitimate power, eventually believing Jesus the greatest of these. He appreciated the role of religious institutions. But he was very leery of any priesthood and had almost no involvement with any organized religious sect, possibly because he found the options available to him so uninviting.

Jefferson was born into a largely Christian society. Christianity, in all its complexity and variety, has some essential or defining beliefs. For understanding Jefferson, it is vital to divide these essential beliefs into two components. First, Christians are part of the broader Semitic tradition, rooted in the ancient Hebrew experience. Out of this came a basic, theistic cosmology. A masculine god created the world and all that inhabit it, and such a god also controlled or planned the history of his creation. Jefferson never doubted such a creative and providential god, even when he tried without success to understand the views of authentic atheists. This cosmology remained the foundation of his private religious beliefs and a support both for objective knowledge and moral confidence. He was so certain of his beliefs in such a creative god, in a planned and ordered universe, and in a divinely implanted moral sense in each person, that he assumed, quite incorrectly as we know, that such beliefs were universal, at the heart of all religions. When anyone challenged such beliefs, he easily and routinely referred to the evidences of design in nature and in the human mind. Such evidence made belief in a creative and purposeful god unchallengeable, self-evident.

The second major component of Christianity is not shared with the other Semitic religions. It involves not cosmological foundations but what might be called the distinctive Christian superstructure. This all relates to the status and role of Jesus of Nazareth. Christians believe that Jesus was the promised Messiah of the Jewish scriptures and that he came to establish a new scheme of salvation, a scheme first carefully elaborated by Paul. The Greek word for Messiah—Christ—even lent a name to a new religion. The new religion built upon and elaborated, in rich and soon diverse ways, the status and the teachings of Jesus. All versions supported a scheme of salvation that involved, at the very least, the late-Jewish belief in a bodily resurrection.

Jefferson, apparently very early in life, found most of this distinctive Christian superstructure unbelievable, save for the assurance of life after death. In the middle years of his life he affirmed the Semitic cosmology without the Christian superstructure, although not without some sense of loneliness in a society so assertively Christian. He was persuaded, in part by the strictures of orthodox critics, that his form of religious rationalism did not qualify as Christian, and thus he did not so profess. In times of stress and anxiety he sought inspiration and consolation not in Christian sources but in Stoic and Epicurean moral philosophers. Then, in a period stretching from the early 1790s until the time he became president, he discovered a minimalist, unitarian version of Christianity, most of whose tenets he could affirm. He remained a reasonably consistent advocate of such a unitarianism until he died. What follows are some details of this religious pilgrimage.

I

It is not possible to identify Jefferson's earliest religious beliefs. A natural reticence about such a personal issue as religion, and the loss in a 1770 fire of most of his early private papers, conspired to leave only a few tantalizing clues to his earliest religious experience. He grew up as a nominal Anglican, but the conditions of life on scattered plantations in the back country of Virginia, and the scarcity of clergymen, meant infrequent worship services in lonely chapels served by what amounted to circuit-riding ministers. It is simply not clear how much of the Christian version of salvation the very young Jefferson learned or internalized, at least up to the age of nine when he began boarding school. From nine to fourteen, when his father died at the home plantation of Shadwell in Albemarle, Jefferson spent a part of each year in Goochland County as a pupil of an Anglican clergyman, William Douglas, a Scotsman. Jefferson would later lament Douglas's deficiencies as a classical scholar but revealed nothing about his religious instruction. In these years Jefferson was nominally a member of the English Church, but what one cannot know is how deeply and how personally the conventional religious culture affected him. Perhaps even then he began to nourish doubts about the Christian scheme of salvation. In one later, rare backward glance, he said that he began doubting the Trinity doctrine in an early part of his life.[1] What is unlikely is that Jefferson affected the indifference toward religious issues that marked so many of his contemporaries. Early on, young Jefferson was serious, conscientious, and full of intellectual curiosity. Every subject fascinated him, including religion.

After his father's death, Thomas had to remain close to home. His subsequent grammar school education brought him for two years into the home, and under the tutelage, of another Anglican clergyman, the ex-Huguenot James Maury, who struggled to raise a large family on an inadequate minister's salary and serve the scattered chapels in his huge parish, which barely included Shadwell. Maury helped Jefferson master Latin and Greek and drew his later praise as a teacher. Maury was an accomplished preacher and a very devout man. Notably, both of Jefferson's teachers were on the Calvinist or evangelical or low-church side of Anglicanism, as would be Jefferson's later parish minister in Charlottesville, Charles Clay. Despite Jefferson's inability to understand Calvinist doctrines (he always resorted to crude caricatures), and his later bitter comments about Calvin, he was appreciative of the character and piety of these three Anglican clergymen with whom he had the most direct relationship. What is again unclear is how much these clerical mentors shaped his own religious beliefs.[2]

This leads to a question not resolvable by evidence. Did Jefferson really absorb, in any moving or involving way, the most broadly shared and general Protestant doctrines—a sense of an inherent alienation or sinfulness, a felt need for forgiveness, a reliance upon God's grace offered through the atoning role of the Christ, the Church as the ark of salvation, and the need for a continuing devotional life tied to worship, prayer, and the sacraments? If he did, then one has to posit a later crisis of faith, a traumatic period when he questioned or agonized about these doctrines, for it is clear that by the end of his college years he had rejected all of what he now saw as the mysterious and supernatural components of Christianity, or in brief, the whole Pauline scheme of salvation. What is not clear is when such a crisis occurred, if it did, or exactly by what process Jefferson moved through it.[3]

The other possibility is that he never, with any depth of understanding, absorbed this distinctively Christian outlook, even though he never doubted the Semitic cosmology that undergirded it. Thus, the easy but largely verbal confessions of youth slowly gave way to overt doubt when Jefferson was able to mature, articulate, and rationalize a reasonably coherent philosophy of life. If this is the case, then he simply drifted, without a period of rebellion and trauma, away from the conventional but never fully believable religion of his youth. This drift did not reflect indifference, but was rooted in serious reflection based on extensive reading.

The next stage in Jefferson's religious pilgrimage encompassed his years as a student at the College of William and Mary, his subsequent legal training with George Wythe, and his early career as a lawyer in the heady years just before the Revolution. In 1760 Jefferson came to Williamsburg to attend the College. He became part of a rather cosmopolitan culture, at least as reflected in the College faculty. His one nonclerical professor—William Small, professor of natural philosophy—had the greatest impact on Jefferson. Of the other two professors, one was dismissed after a year for laxity and overly convivial behavior, while the other, the president of the College, was an alcoholic. Such facts would not have boosted Jefferson's respect for the clergy, although his virulent anticlericalism developed later, triggered by vehement clerical opposition to his 1776 bill for religious freedom and a complete disestablishment of the Anglican Church in Virginia, and even more by the hostility and overt slander directed at him by orthodox ministers during the election of 1800.

Jefferson attended, how faithfully we do not know, the Bruton Church in Williamsburg, but it is clear that his attachment to the church was waning in these student and apprentice years. He moved in a circle of latitudinarian or rationalistic Anglicans, including his mentor in the law, George Wythe, and soon began copying in a literary diary or commonplace book extensive quotations from Lord Bolingbroke, the eloquent English advocate of a natural and "rational" as opposed to a revealed and superstitious religion.[4] For at least the next two decades, Jefferson's religious views departed in no significant respect from those of Bolingbroke. Bolingbroke helped account for Jefferson's very dismissive view of the Bible, an early affinity for a type of metaphysical materialism, and even a restrained and quite qualified respect for Jesus.

It is at this point that biographers of Jefferson have too often capitulated to the perspective of his contemporaries.[5] They see Jefferson's increasingly self-conscious repudiations of the Christian superstructure or of revealed religion as a whole as a retreat from, even a repudiation of, religion itself. This reflects the curious—and fatal—identification of a sub-class, Christianity, with the class, religion. Even in these relatively carefree years, Jefferson was already very serious about issues of belief. He was already a rigid, puritanical moralist, with exceptionally high expectations of himself and others. He wanted to find a ground for moral behavior. Even though he came to believe, under the influence of Scottish moral theory and particularly that of Lord Kames, that a creator god had implanted in all normal people a moral sense, an almost aesthetic appreciation of what is good in the way of behavior, he knew that the type of self-discipline, and at times the courage, to do right, to follow the dictates of conscience, was the pressing practical moral problem for himself and for others. He spent a lifetime trying to find the types of intellectual authority needed to support moral conduct, and always conceded that the most superstitious forms of religion might provide this for those who believed. Since he found such religions unbelievable, he had to find other intellectual props.

In my taxonomy, Jefferson was one who always saw, as the highest goal of a religion, a support for righteousness. People needed the authority, or the inspiration, to live up to basic moral imperatives shared by all people, whatever their cultural differences. Belief in a single, creative, providential god, and in some form of rewards and punishments after death, seemed essential because they were so directly relevant both to private and public conduct. In later years, and at the urging of Benjamin Rush, Jefferson increasingly tied such a theism (he usually called it deism) to the problems of a republican society. Without the centralized authority of a monarchy or of any public order based on hierarchy and command, it was even more imperative that people develop internalized supports for self-discipline. The authority of a god seemed essential for such self-discipline, a theme later developed by Tocqueville. Thus, Jefferson's moral or political perspective on religion reinforced his lifelong affirmation of what he saw as the unifying Semitic cosmology of Christianity, even as it undermined belief in the divisive elaborations upon this foundation reflected in various Christian schemes of salvation and in the pretentious, self-serving mystifications created by priests. Orthodox Christianity confused people and had led to all manner of historical strife and cruelty.

By his marriage in 1772, and his increased involvement with the developing struggle against the mother country, Jefferson had clearly moved to a form of religious rationalism. He would accept only beliefs that he believed essential to religion, and thus beliefs common to all religions—or what some have called religious essentialism. Even these simple beliefs were not, and would never be, completely coherent. Jefferson was always impressionable, open to the influence of a new book, variously under the sway of different friends. Yet the core would remain intact for the rest of his life. His leading principles tied him closely both to professed exponents of natural religion and to latitudinarian and rational Christians. By the prevalent understandings of Christianity in America, he was not a Christian. The basis of his faith was what he called "reason," a loaded and even demagogic word in his vocabulary. He believed that most of the content in all revealed religions was irrational, but that his minimalist belief in a creative and providential and morally judgmental god was rational.

Throughout his career, Jefferson used the word *rational* in at least three senses, plugging each one in according to need and context. When discussing Trinity doctrines, for example, he made the test of rationality internal coherence or logical consistency. He thus always declared the Trinity to be an irrational aspect of Christian orthodoxy, although he never probed deeply into more sophisticated Trinitarian arguments. His god was always singular and unified. In other contexts, rational meant verifiable cognitive propositions, those clear enough to be testable by evidence. He believed much of the history contained in the Jewish scriptures and in the New Testament was not confirmable, and thus suspect, most of all miraculous events. More important, he believed that all references to some realm of pure mind or spirit, beliefs that he usually attributed directly or indirectly to the baneful influence of Plato, were without operational meaning, vaporous, and thus beyond any type of proof. This early inclined him to what he eventually confessed, based on the early influence of Bolingbroke and Epicurus, and the later influence of Joseph Priestley and Destutt de Tracy—a type of metaphysical materialism or corporealism. These conceptions of "reason" usually served him as a tool of criticism, a means of rejecting or castigating popular religious "superstitions."

His third use of "reason" almost always served a positive goal. This involved all propositions that are intuitively certain, self-evident, indubitable. The chief of these was the necessity of a designer behind the ordered world of nature and the harmonious commands of conscience. Thus, to Jefferson, it was reasonable to believe in a creator god, but unreasonable to believe in a Trinity or to affirm miracles. Of course, one can see elements of self-deception in this appeal to "reason," and the demagoguery usually involved in appeals to such a bogus authority.

It oversimplifies Jefferson's religious views to reduce them to problems of morality, although his dominant approach to religion always began with the moral component. His theistic essentialism informed his political writings, guided him in a bitter but uphill fight to gain complete religious liberty in Virginia, and created for him a critical public relations problem as a politician. He thus early hid behind a principle—the freedom of each person to believe what one must in the area of religion, and the absence of any public interest in, or right to suppress, any private religious belief whatsoever (it is proper only to regulate the conduct that flows from such beliefs). He thus deflected all questions about his private religious beliefs. This tactic fanned wild speculations, but prevented an open airing of religious views sure to have offended most Christians and likely to have doomed his political career.

His battle for a full disestablishment of religion in Virginia had an enduring impact on Jefferson's own religious beliefs. The battle began with petitions from dissenters, primarily Presbyterians and Baptists. Jefferson fought for the bill, unsuccessfully as it turned out, in a bitterly divided legislative committee in the heady first year of the new and independent Virginia Assembly. In defense of his position Jefferson mined all the sources in his library or in Williamsburg, building a very broad and informed brief in behalf of complete liberty of conscience. He turned, with more careful attention than in his political writing, to John Locke, as well as to Milton and Shaftesbury. He sought all the information he could find about the early history of the Church, including the development of both hierarchy and canon. He cited the various heresies that the Church had suppressed in the past, all to make clear the impossibility of settling doctrinal controversies. In the process he probably for the first time learned about the enormous variety of doctrinal positions present in Church history, and with some precision detailed various then-heterodox positions about the Trinity, ranging from modalism (the belief that the three persons of the Trinity are only modes or expressions of a unified god) to Arianism (the belief that Jesus was begotten of God, and thus subordinate, but that he was both preexistent and divine) to Socinianism or unitarianism (a belief in the complete unity of God and the full humanity of Jesus). Notably, when Jefferson later recommended reforms for the College of William and Mary, the only religion-oriented subject he suggested for the curriculum was Church history. He found such a history confusing enough to be liberating; the messy episodes would lead students to question received dogmas.[6]

Another aspect of Jefferson's early religiosity is less open to the historian. From his college experience he gained an absorbing, lifelong interest in classical literature, most of all for Stoic and Epicurean moral philosophers. In the early years of legal practice, during his political apprenticeship in the House of Burgesses, and in the first years of marriage and the births of his daughters, he found solace and delight in such classical authors and prided himself on his linguistic skills in Greek and Latin. He added quotes from Cicero, as well as from Greek and Roman poets, to his commonplace book.[7]

Jefferson needed such consoling sources of inspiration. His youth had not been one of fame or even unalloyed success. As a student he was unusually serious, worked long hours, resisted most temptations to dissipation, and generally repudiated the more frivolous aspects of planter culture. He was extremely sensitive, relatively ill at ease in public speaking, suffered frequent and almost disabling migraine headaches, had a troubling and at times tense relationship with his mother, and proved inept in his early courtship of women, with both a sophomoric but unrequited romance and then improper advances to a married woman. His rejection of the more consoling and supportive aspects of Christianity, or those he believed to be superstitious, left him without the consolation of a church or other religious community. Yet, he needed support and developed what one could call a rich meditational if not devotional life, as evidenced by his meticulous copying of the most inspiring or helpful readings into his commonplace book, and even in his choices for what soon became an outstanding private library. He found in the ancient moral and religious philosophers, and particularly in Epicurus, the support he needed for his almost superhuman efforts at self-improvement and the courage needed to keep at his tasks. He also found in the less anthropomorphic theism of the Stoics a reinforcement of his core religious beliefs but without all the superstitious elaborations he still found in the Bible.

After the heady days of the early Revolution, he had a much deeper and more urgent need for such inspiration. His afflictions briefly rivaled those of Job. The death of loved ones seemed unending—his best friend in 1773, a beloved daughter in 1775, his mother in 1776. Then he suffered the frustrations of his problem-plagued tenure as governor, which ended in a lame resignation, a public investigation of his role during the occupation of Richmond by the British, and his near-capture at Monticello. This all embarrassed and embittered him, but was only a prelude to the early death of his beloved wife in 1782. This left him completely devastated, close to suicide. His disabling grief may have reflected some measure of guilt because of how often his political career had kept him away from home. A promised diversion—appointment to the peace mission in Europe—led to elaborate preparations for a trip that did not take place because of the early signing of the treaty. In these dark years, the worst by far in his whole career, he turned to his Stoic and Epicurean sources with desperate urgency. He needed the courage to go on living. Almost consumed by grief, he struggled to acquire control over his passions, to attain a tranquility of mind in the midst of constant suffering. He tried to discipline his will to accept the fortunes of fate or of divine providence in a period when he was almost overcome by a morbid, pessimistic, or even fatalistic mood.

In these dark periods, as he later confessed, he found the greatest solace in Epicurus. Eventually he would write a brief syllabus of Epicurus's teaching, an honor he also bestowed only upon Jesus. Epicurus helped him attain sanity and equanimity, strength and courage. Much later, when his concerns shifted back more exclusively to issues of righteousness or, in a larger sense, to policy, he acknowledged limitations in the self-centered, or parochial, moralism of the Greeks, and found a broader, more universal, more interior or heartfelt morality in the teachings of Jesus. Here were the tenets that best supported America's experiment with self-government. But he would not deprecate the ancients even then, and still found in them needed consolation and excellent guides to private meditation. He lamented the popular and false stereotypes of Epicurus, who was often dismissed as a hedonist or an atheist. Jefferson appreciated the modern effort to reevaluate Epicurus by the French atomist and philosopher, Pierre Gassendi, and used his collection of Epicurean writings as a guide. Such advocacy by a Roman Catholic scholar helped make Epicurus seem closer to Jefferson's own version of theism.

Epicurus believed in an eternal, material, atomistic universe as his first principle. He accepted an order of gods above humans but in no way involved with humans (Jefferson considered this polytheism superstitious but only a minor fault). Epicurus made virtue the foundation of happiness and utility the test of virtue. He wanted to avoid or overcome pain, and thus attain a tranquility of mind, which is what Jefferson long sought for himself. Epicurus, like many of the Stoics, tried to minimize desire, and thus frustration and pain, and to be temperate, courageous, and just. This ideal supported an abstemious and demanding faith, one that began with renunciation and a retreat from the cares of the larger world. It required great self-discipline, a virtue that appealed to Jefferson in the midst of his personal suffering. Finally, although unnoted by Jefferson, Epicurus retreated from the cares of the world to his own garden. Over and over again Jefferson did the same. He yearned for the peace and solace of Monticello, where he could indulge in conversation, music, reading, reflection, and all the arts of husbandry in his mountaintop garden.[8]

II

After 1789 Jefferson began to come to terms with Christianity. In France he became more widely informed about the varieties of Christian belief and also about often frightening forms of unbelief. This led him, as always, to repudiate sectarian strife, and to join Benjamin Franklin and others in dismissing all forms of dogmatism, for each was reared on unprovable presuppositions or imposed on fearful people by self-serving priests. In France, his anticlericalism flowered in all its near-paranoia, for Jefferson was always susceptible to conspiracy theories of one type or another. But in the midst of this iconoclasm, and after contact with French *philosophes* who carried such iconoclasm to extremes that threatened Jefferson's own religious certainties, he began a reevaluation of Jesus. He already knew something about unitarian Christianity, but now wanted to know more. An innocent letter, written in 1789, proved to be a turning point in his religious pilgrimage.

Because of several mutual friends, Jefferson became a friend and correspondent of Richard Price, the independent London minister. In his one extended visit to London in spring 1786, Jefferson dined with Price and attended at least one of his worship services. Price reflected a very liberal and Arian version of Christianity, had been a supporter of American independence and an admirer of new American constitutions, and provided a type of spiritual home for a group of English and visiting American scientists and intellectuals. It was in the circle that surrounded Price that Franklin and Joseph Priestley began their fruitful scientific collaboration. Abigail Adams came to love Price, and so did Jefferson. Had he been posted to London, he would have regularly attended Price's congregation. With the events leading to the French Revolution, Jefferson began sending Price frequent, detailed reports on political events in Paris, and as a footnote to such a letter on July 12, 1789, asked Price for reading material on Socinianism. Price obliged, sending Jefferson some pamphlets by Joseph Priestley, by then the leading spokesman for an emerging Unitarian movement in Britain and a close friend of Price, although always at odds with him on theological issues. Although Jefferson knew of Priestley's scientific discoveries, this was probably his first direct contact with Priestley's religious thought. He capitulated at once to the person who became, for the rest of his life, his most important religious mentor.[9]

In the next few busy years, Jefferson read all or part of Priestley's huge 1782 tome on the history of corruptions in the Church. The more he read, the more fully persuaded he was of all its main arguments. It gave him a new and enduring perspective on the teaching of Jesus and on the history of the early Church. In March 1797, when Jefferson traveled to Philadelphia for his inauguration as vice president, he met Priestley for the first time; as long as he was in the city he attended a series of sermons that Priestley gave before his new Unitarian congregation (the first in America). Incidentally, this is the only record of Jefferson ever gladly and regularly attending worship services.[10] Jefferson was, in a sense, Priestley's most distinguished convert to Unitarianism. He now chose sides from among the numerous alternatives offered by historic Christianity, in what seemed to mark the most dramatic and momentous shift in his long religious pilgrimage. A few of his friends, as they became privy to his newly clarified religious views, believed that Jefferson had experienced a religious conversion, that belatedly he had become a Christian.

The reality was more complex. In actuality Jefferson changed few of his core religious beliefs after reading and hearing Priestley. He did not even grasp, or accept, Priestley's more subtle doctrines, although Jefferson never realized this. He easily read his views into those of others that were close to his own, even as he always caricatured, sometimes unmercifully, the views of those who were his opponents or who profoundly disagreed with him. This tendency helps account for his many unfair, unnuanced, and shallow caricatures not only of Calvinism and Catholicism but of Judaism and Islam. Much more than he realized, his personal version of Unitarianism remained distinctive, amounting to little more than a grafting of some of Jesus's moral teachings upon the Semitic cosmology that had always formed the core of his philosophy. But in the charged political context of 1800, his "conversion" to Unitarianism served a wonderful role. It allowed him to affirm his own allegiance to the earliest, purest, and simplest form of Christianity, and to dismiss his purportedly orthodox opponents as deceived purveyors of a corrupted, paganized, Platonized religion that they incorrectly identified with the teachings of Jesus. This was a consoling tour de force, to say the least.

Space does not permit an adequate description of the religious views of Joseph Priestley. He was born in 1733 in a dissenting, Calvinist, latter-day Puritan family. Precocious, he advanced rapidly in school, early became a linguist, and when he was thirteen years old was deeply committed to religion. He completed his formal education at a dissenting academy (his religious views prevented him attending Oxford or Cambridge). By then, at the age of nineteen, he had already followed the fashions of the day and rejected the Calvinist doctrines of his family. He was on the way to religious radicalism. As a secondary interest, he began the serious study of mathematics and natural philosophy. He soon became the prototypical Renaissance man, with an interest in almost all intellectual subjects.

After college, Priestley sought and gained his first pulpit; he began to develop his radical theology even as he gradually became famous as a scientist. Encouraged by Franklin, he wrote the first history of electricity and, during a series of experiments on air, first isolated what we now know as oxygen. By 1767, when he became a minister to a dissenting congregation in Leeds, he had converted to Socinianism, or unitarianism. In 1780 Priestley moved to Birmingham for what would become the most fruitful and controversial decade of his life. Here he became minister of the New Meeting, possibly the largest dissenting congregation in Britain. In 1782 he was able to bring together much of his earlier controversial writings about Christianity from dozens of tracts or small books into one powerful two-volume polemic, *History of the Corruptions of Christianity,* the treatise that had the greatest influence on Thomas Jefferson. This publication raised a storm of controversy and triggered a long, famous intellectual duel between Priestley and Anglican Archdeacon Samuel Horsley. From these debates, or published letters, came much of Priestley's subsequent doctrinal writing, including a four-volume *History of Early Opinions Concerning Jesus Christ,* volumes that Jefferson claimed to have read over and over again.[11]

By 1790, the vehement condemnations of Priestley by the orthodox gained a new and sinister political content. As one would have expected, Priestley enthusiastically endorsed the early French Revolution. He was the most prominent member of a radical circle in England, one that had long pushed for the repeal of the Test Act and for a complete separation of church and state. His close friend and later Jefferson protégé, Thomas Cooper, a scientist, journalist, and political economist, helped form a pro-French Constitutional Society in Manchester in 1790, a society that held dinners on July 14 to celebrate Bastille Day. During the next year Priestley helped form a similar society in Birmingham, and this group in turn made elaborate plans for a July 14 dinner. With the semiofficial blessings of local authorities, and egged on indirectly by orthodox ministers, a mob gathered to disrupt this dinner. It arrived too late: forewarned of violence, Priestley had not attended. But the mob burned his church, then moved to his home and laboratory, destroying both, and announced its intent to kill Priestley. He had to flee the mob with only a few manuscripts and books, eventually to take refuge in London. He never lived again in Birmingham. Instead, as political tensions grew in Britain, he made plans to join two of his sons in America. Cooper also fled to America. By now Priestley was dismayed with the course of the Revolution in France, but suffered in England when the French tried to honor him and even elected him as a delegate to their National Convention (he declined). Through successful legal action, he won major damages from the local government in Birmingham and used part of this to settle with his land-speculating sons at Northumberland, Pennsylvania, in 1794. On arrival in America he was greeted as a martyr and hero. Few men of such fame had chosen to immigrate to the new nation.

Priestley summarized his mature religious views in the *Corruptions*. He wanted to restore the early, primitive Jewish church, one uncorrupted by Greek and pagan ideas. The two great corruptions (he actually listed hundreds of corruptions in both beliefs and forms of worship) involved two noxious and related doctrines—the Greek concept of a separate soul or spirit, and the orthodox doctrine of the Trinity. Priestley wanted to restore the corporealism or materialism of the ancient Jews, a materialism he believed essential to any mature religion. He rejected Arian views of Jesus (divine, preexistent, and immaterial) as emphatically as Trinitarian ones. To him, Jesus was simply a human with a special mission, a mission that required a human messiah (the standard Socinian view). Since Priestley rejected any spiritual substance, he had to reject any concept of incarnation. This, in turn, led him to reject all versions of a substitutional atonement. Jesus lived an exemplary life, taught us our duties, but above all rose from the dead. The resurrection was central to Priestley, for it gave promise that righteous humans who die and decay (no immortality), can also come back to life in the coming kingdom (since eternal torment makes sense only for disembodied spirits, Priestley saw the wages of sin as death, not some perpetual hell). These doctrines (materialism, soul sleep, a literal resurrection, and no eternal punishment) were close to those of an earlier Thomas Hobbes and at the heart of later Adventist Christianity. Priestley also had a profound sense of divine providence (a type of necessitarianism), but he spent most of his writing trying to demonstrate the errors in the existing orthodox churches. With some looseness, and sophistry, he tried to establish the unitarian origins of the Church, and thus lambasted the Greek mysteries, the pagan influences, that corrupted the simple beginnings. These arguments, including the materialism, proved completely persuasive to Thomas Jefferson, largely because they coincided so well with his existing beliefs.

Jefferson did not accept all of Priestley's doctrines and misunderstood others to which he verbally assented. Yet he remained innocently unaware of how selective was his use of his new hero's writings. He would never utter a deprecating word about Priestley. When John Adams teased Jefferson about what he perceived as the less commendable doctrines of Priestley, particularly his sense of a fully controlling divine providence (Adams playfully termed this predestinarianism, when in fact Priestley did not believe in election to salvation), or his belief that the human identity dissolved in death only to be brought back to life at the resurrection (soul sleep), Jefferson claimed to be unfamiliar with such beliefs (actually, he was familiar with both, but Adam's choice of labels threw him off).[12]

Adams was correct in one sense. Jefferson never tried to unravel the implications of materialism, or necessitarianism; he always shied away from metaphysical puzzles. Even Priestley had difficulty maneuvering around the conundrums of this doctrine, one that seemed necessary if one believed in a sovereign god and the rule of law in nature. Jefferson escaped the burden of reconciling a sovereign deity with human freedom by the simple expedient of ignoring the issue of sovereignty and by refusing, at any time in his life, to work out a true theology, in the sense of a coherent image of God and a vindication of his ways in the world. Priestley made clear that divine providence is not inconsistent with human freedom, and in this relied upon arguments familiar to Calvinists. This satisfied Jefferson, who at times reflected a resignation and fatalism that exceeded even Priestley's.

The soul-sleep doctrine was simply a necessary implication of any denial of mental or spiritual substance. Without such, immortality is inconceivable and life without a body impossible. Jefferson affirmed the materialism, and even more than Priestley hated the idea of immaterial beings, such as angels and demons, but simply was not concerned with the detailed fate of individuals at the time of death. He took the substance of Priestley—there will be life after death with both punishment and rewards—but tended to ignore the implications. In these areas Jefferson did not so much dissent from Priestley as refuse to follow a determined scholar and an able dialectician into murky terrain.

One major issue did clearly separate Jefferson and Priestley; both were aware of this difference and corresponded about it. Priestley thought it a vital difference; Jefferson thought it of minimal or no significance whatsoever. The issue was the old one—the status of Jesus. Priestley believed, with some compelling evidence from patristic sources, that the earliest Jewish Christians had believed that Jesus was fully human, born in a normal way in Bethlehem, the son of Joseph. But he, along with all early unitarian reformers, including Socinus, believed that Jesus was the Messiah promised by the prophets and that God selected him for his redemptive role. He was a human with a divine role, not a divine person or god. Priestley believed that Jesus's teaching, his preternatural wisdom, his commanding personality, his miraculous works, and above all his resurrection vindicated his special role as the divinely appointed savior of humanity. Although an early textual critic of the scriptures and in no sense a biblical literalist, Priestley had no doubt that God revealed his will in the Bible, and thus he claimed the authority of divine revelation for his unitarianism. Priestley, following Newton, was particularly fascinated with the apocalyptic sections of the Bible. With some tensions, he even tried to fit Paul within his unitarian understanding of the early Church, whereas Jefferson saw Paul as the first great corrupter of the teaching of Jesus. In all these views Priestley was not far from other Christians, and was a devoted minister of a liberating gospel. He deplored non-Christ-centered religions, and believed faith in the Christ a condition of membership in the Church, which he loved and served faithfully until his death in Pennsylvania in 1804.

When, in 1803, Jefferson sent to Priestley his syllabus on the merits of the doctrines of Jesus, Priestley immediately noted what was absent—any confession that Jesus was the Messiah. Jefferson, in his covering letter, anticipated this concern, and noted that his syllabus would omit the issue of Jesus's divinity or the source of his inspiration. Priestley knew what this omission meant—that Jefferson shared with him the belief that Jesus was not divine, but also, contrary to Priestley, believed that Jesus was not divinely inspired, not an agent of God in providing the means of human redemption. From all the evidence, Priestley read Jefferson correctly. Nothing in any of his writings suggest that he really believed that Jesus was the Messiah, or that God so intervened in human history as to appoint special agents to effect salvation, or that the Bible was inspired, or that Jesus rose from the dead. Such direct divine initiatives or interventions would shift the issue of deserved salvation away from virtue to belief, or trust, or discipleship, and thus lead to a less-than-universal standard. Even in the attenuated form of English Unitarianism, the path to salvation would be sectarian and exclusive. For Jefferson, this sectarianism in Priestley was a minor, forgivable lapse, comparable to the polytheistic deities in an otherwise sublime Epicurus. For a concerned Priestley, who had hoped to be able to bring Jefferson fully into his rigorously restored Church of Christ, this difference had profound significance. Priestley died with troubling doubts that his friend Jefferson was really a Christian, or that he was assured salvation, although Priestley would leave judgment to God and hope for mercy.[13]

What Priestley gave to Jefferson was a soon-fixed view of church history. Even as Jefferson slighted or ignored many of Priestley's positive doctrines, he accepted without question all the corruptions that Priestley identified, and these encompassed most of the dogmas and practices of both Catholics and Protestants. From 1800 on, in what now became Jefferson's quite frequent writings about religion, almost all of his negative comments about orthodoxy—a virtual litany of abuses—came directly from Priestley. He used Priestley as his guide in part because Priestley was a famous scientist and a learned scholar. His books included numerous quotations from patristic sources, and on some issues reflected new departures in biblical scholarship. Thus, his judgments seemed much more weighty and objective than the more abstract reflections of a Bolingbroke or the iconoclastic ridicule of a Thomas Paine. More important, they were such as to retain not only the Semitic core (Bolingbroke and Paine did this), but the centrality of the Jesus of the gospels as distinct from the god-man soon manufactured by paganism-influenced priests.

As was so often the case, Jefferson was all too gullible. His enthusiasm led him to accept Priestley uncritically. In religion, as in his political thought, Jefferson tended to paper over the problematic or inconsistent elements in the thought of his heroes, and thus always ended up with such an eclectic mix of ideas as to defy systematic ordering. He was a creature of mood and sentiment much more than a rigorous thinker. Had he bothered to read Priestley's English critics, particularly Horsley, he would have recognized how loaded was Priestley's narrative. Priestley arbitrarily selected among sources, and worst of all reared vast speculations upon very limited evidence. His case for the significance, and endurance, of early unitarianism was drastically overstated, although not more so than conventional defenses of Trinitarianism. John Adams, much more skeptical and critical of anything he read, knew this and gently chided Jefferson for not having read Priestley's debates with Horsley. Adams also sensed an unjustified metaphysical dogmatism in Priestley's materialism, a negative opinion shared by Richard Price.[14]

III

In the election year of 1800, Jefferson decided to reveal some of his maturing religious views to a few close friends. The word "campaign" hardly fit the events before the voting in the fall of 1800 (neither Jefferson nor Adams openly sought the office), but the supporters of both Adams and Jefferson broached new extremes in vilification, with Adams's supporters often making Jefferson's purported infidelity their clinching accusation. Such attacks hurt a sensitive Jefferson who, despite his stoic effort to attain detachment and tranquility, always agonized about unfair slander and could never quite forgive those who originated it.

Jefferson had for years argued that religious beliefs were private matters. He consistently refused, on the grounds of high principle, to state his own or to argue with anyone in print. He maintained this posture until his death and shared his deepest religious insights with only such close friends as Benjamin Rush or, much later, John Adams. In each case he prescribed secrecy and often asked a return of written platforms. He never granted permission for the publication of his religious reflections under his own name. Yet however much he persuaded himself to accept this policy of complete reticence, his actions did not always adhere to it. After the bitter election he clearly wanted to make known, although in a very oblique way, that he was as much a Christian as any of his opponents, in fact a better Christian because he adhered to the primitive religion of Jesus. Thus his tactics were somewhat devious and reflected at times his own ambivalence—a fear of popular disapproval and of controversy, but at the same time a near-missionary zeal to promote his reformed version of Christianity and to embarrass his critics.

Rush gave him the occasion. By 1800 Rush was a persuaded universalist, yet a Trinitarian and not as heterodox as Priestley. He too wanted to convert Jefferson to a very inclusive and generous form of Christianity, and at least half persuaded Jefferson that some version of Christianity was a necessary foundation of republicanism, of liberty and equality. In response to such pressures from his good friend, Jefferson noted that he was preparing a private confession, or what he would soon denominate his "Syllabus of an Estimate of the merit of the doctrines of Jesus, compared with those of others." The immediate stimulus for this had been a small book by Priestley in which he compared Jesus with Socrates, with all the benefits of the comparison going to Jesus. By then it was clear that Jefferson had begun a very serious reading of parts of the New Testament. Possibly for the first time since his youth, and his capitulation to Bolingbroke, he now read the gospels with a growing appreciation. In the midst of his busy years as president, he completed this small, rather innocuous, but quite revealing syllabus in 1803, and sent copies of it to his two daughters, to both Rush and Priestley, to two Cabinet members, and eventually to a few other close friends. He obviously wanted some of these confidants to communicate more broadly the positive religious views of a now avowedly Christian Jefferson, yet not reveal the minimalist details of his renamed but basically unchanged religious beliefs. [15]

What had changed was Jefferson's evaluation of Jesus. He had earlier agreed with Bolingbroke—that a system of morals drawn from the ancient philosophers (Tully, Seneca, Epictetus) would be "more full, more entire, more coherent, and more clearly deduced from unquestionable principles of knowledge" than one drawn from the teachings of Jesus. [16] His reading now persuaded him that Bolingbroke had been mistaken. The problem was in the texts, which contained the pure, simple, and sublime moral teachings of Jesus, but this content was buried within all the excess baggage, the claims of divine authority, the miracles, and the mysticisms added by superstitious authors. Without a shadow of a doubt, Jefferson believed that by a very careful reading, he could distinguish the true teachings of Jesus, the wheat from the chaff, the diamonds in the dunghill of abstractions. When he did this he found what he believed to be the most enlightened system of ethics ever developed.

His syllabus was his first brief for his Jesus religion. He wrote it as an outline for a book he wanted Priestley to write, one that would expand his comparison of Jesus and Socrates to a broader comparison of the moral teachings of Jesus with that of the ancient Jews and a much broader array of ancient philosophers, including Epicurus and the Stoics. At Jefferson's urging, the now aged and ill Priestley spent the last year of his life trying to complete such a book. Burdened by limited library resources, Priestley finished a book, one more nearly compiled than composed, in which he assessed the moral thought of a few classical philosophers. He did not sum up all the merits that Jefferson now found in Jesus's teachings and left out any comparison with the Jews. Despite his disappointment, Jefferson loaned or gave copies of this book to friends, probably nourishing a private hope that he could some day write the kind of book he wanted on this subject. Thus, the syllabus was an outline of the arguments he expected to prove when he could do the needed research and analysis. [17]

Jefferson's syllabus revealed more about himself than about Jesus. He began with the ancient philosophers and generously forgave their obvious corruptions of reason (idolatry and superstitions), even as he was willing to discount the corruptions of Christianity added by the overlearned. He still credited the ancients with a very useful private ethic, one that had sustained him in hard times, but now argued that even the Stoics and Epicureans were deficient in estimating a person's duties to others, particularly those beyond family, clan, or nation. In brief, their morality was not universal and not sufficiently rooted in the heart. These judgments were, quite simply, unfair. The aspects of worldly renunciation in Epicurus might give some credence to these harsh judgments, but not the ethical systems of several Stoics. Jefferson began with a stacked deck. This was even more clear in his dismissive treatment of the ancient Jews. Except for the theism, he found nothing praiseworthy in Judaism. The Jews had a degrading image of God and an irrational, parochial, exclusive, and antisocial morality, so corrupt that it cried out for the reforms of Jesus. Such sweeping judgments documented Jefferson's unwillingness to read the Jewish scriptures seriously or to make the same discriminating judgments about their diverse content that he was now willing to do for the Christian scriptures. Almost all the merits he identified in Jesus were present in the Jewish prophets, most centrally in Deutero-Isaiah (Isaiah, chapters 40–55).

In his much more extensive treatment of Jesus, Jefferson began with a sketch of his life. He noted the disadvantages Jesus faced as a moralist—obscure parents, poverty, little education, no surviving texts and inept scribes, bitter opposition from rulers and jealous priests, and an early and undeserved death. Compounding the problem, his teaching survived only in fragments, and even these were often mutilated and misstated because of the corruptions of schismatizing followers, who sophisticated and perverted his simple doctrines, and who added to them the mysticism of Greek sophists (i.e., Plato). These circumstances had led good men (he probably referred to Bolingbroke) to reject Jesus' teachings in disgust, or to view him as an impostor. They were wrong to do so, for hidden by its subsequent distortions was the "most perfect and sublime" system of morals ever taught by any man.

Jefferson celebrated three great contributions made by Jesus. First, he restated and confirmed Jewish theism but dropped the cruel conception of God present in the Jewish scriptures. In brief, Jesus clarified the benevolent character of God and the justice of his government. Second, he taught a truly universalist morality, one that mandated philanthropy, or love, charity, and peace, toward all humankind. He not only recommended generous actions but tried to purify the thought that lay behind such actions, to "purify the waters at the fountain head." Third, he emphatically taught the doctrine of a future state, something doubted by the historic Jews. Jesus used this doctrine as an incentive, supplemental to a purified heart, for moral conduct.

One can easily mock this syllabus. It is a transparent ascription to Jesus, in very loose and general language, of the foundational religious beliefs long held by Jefferson. As an interpretation of Jesus' teaching it is highly selective and almost completely lifted out of the ancient cultural context. Jefferson simply ignored, or muted, some of the tensions within the teachings present in the four not always consistent gospels. For example, he ignored the Jesus who asked his disciples to risk all for his sake, to have no cares about food and clothing, to pluck out an offending eye or cut off a foot, and who once announced that he came not to establish peace on earth but to bring the sword, fire and strife, and deep divisions. Such a harsh and demanding Jesus not only routed the money-changers in the Temple, or grew angry at an unbending generation, or killed the fig tree for not bearing fruit out of season, but pronounced a vindictive justice upon relatively innocent deeds (homeowners who would not welcome his disciples, towns that rejected his ministry).

In two related areas only did Jefferson probe issues that were novel to most Christians of his generation. The first was his, and Priestley's, contention that Jews in the New Testament period, and thus Jesus, still retained a holistic conception of humans and had not yet absorbed Greek beliefs about a separable soul or mind. In this contention Jefferson was at least close to the truth. In outlying areas such as Galilee, the traditional Jewish belief in a holistic human personality probably still prevailed, and this may have been the unself-conscious outlook of Jesus. Yet, among sophisticated Jewish intellectuals, those most influenced by Greek philosophy, including a school of Jewish scholars and philosophers at Alexandria, aspects of Greek dualism had already become deeply embedded.

The second novel argument was his crediting Jesus with the doctrine of future rewards, and thus implicitly denying it to the Jews. To an extent he had a valid point, for belief in a bodily resurrection was a late introduction into Judaism, one not accepted by the conservative Sadducees at the time of Jesus. Jefferson's claim for Jesus rested on a biblical understanding, borrowed from Priestley, that would not be widely accepted until the mid-nineteenth century—that the Book of Daniel, which clearly promises a resurrection for righteous Jews, dated from about 165 B.C.E., the Hellenistic era, and not from the time of the Babylonian captivity, as the text claims. Thus, Jefferson could attribute the certification and broad acceptance of this doctrine to Jesus. Here he claimed too much. The dominant Jewish religious groups, including the Pharisees, had fully accepted and integrated the idea of a resurrection well before the birth of Jesus, and by then a few Hellenized Jews were already flirting with doctrines of immortality.

Since Priestley did not do justice to the moral theory of Jesus, Jefferson decided to take a preliminary step toward a fuller explication. He compiled from the four gospels what he took to be the central teachings of Jesus, and by use of scissors and paste put them together as a small manuscript. He referred to this "Philosophy of Jesus" in the years after 1804, but no text survived. The editors of the *Papers of Thomas Jefferson* have reconstituted its probable content.[18] It included largely biographical episodes along with many of the sayings of Jesus, all lifted directly from the English (Authorized or King James) Bible. Jefferson was not satisfied with this effort, and for years planned to expand it. He did so after retirement, probably in 1820, and called the final product "The Life and Morals of Jesus." Although he made oblique references to the challenge of such a compilation, he secreted the manuscript until his death in 1826. It has subsequently become famous, often referred to as the "Bible of Thomas Jefferson."

The "Life and Morals" was a strange labor of love. Jefferson's exact purpose for compiling it is unclear. He resumed his scissors-and-paste technique and expanded it to Greek, Latin, and French versions as well as English. This seemed to be largely a scholarly affectation, for all that it proves is that Jefferson could still, in old age, read these languages well enough to locate homologous texts. It is difficult to envision any audience for the foreign language texts, and the parallel texts created some problems for Jefferson (the language differences conceal some problems of interpretation and of exact parallelism). At one level, he attempted an old task—the integrating and harmonizing of the gospels. He borrowed Priestley's *Harmony* and undoubtedly knew others. For what he included, he tried to draw from the four gospels (though including very little from John), and to end up with a coherent biography and ordered teachings. He eliminated most, but not all, the repetitions in the synoptic gospels, and grouped the teachings around unifying themes. To this extent he created as much coherence as most of his predecessors.[19]

It was not the harmonizing that distinguished this peculiar manuscript, but the careful selectivity. In more detail than in his earlier "Philosophy," Jefferson now tried to make good his claim that the authentic teachings of Jesus were easily identified among all the chaff. What he retained was a completely demystified Jesus. He included nonmiraculous biographical details, drawing more heavily on Luke than Matthew. He excluded all references to miracles or to a Holy Spirit, all ascriptions to Jesus of any special authority, and ended the biography with Jesus's death (no resurrection). For the teachings of Jesus he concentrated on his milder admonitions (the Sermon on the Mount) and his most memorable parables. What resulted is a reasonably coherent, but at places oddly truncated, biography. If necessary to exclude the miraculous, Jefferson would cut the text even in mid-verse. This curious exercise was consistent with Jefferson's mature religious views, but added nothing to them.

One might think Jefferson an early biblical scholar. This he was not. He did not question the integrity of the existing gospel texts, only the layers of interpretation added to them. As for the "authentic" teachings of Jesus, he was a biblical literalist in every way. Somehow, he believed that the actual, easily identifiable words of Jesus had been preserved in the texts, and on this issue was more credulous than most modern fundamentalists. It is true that he unintentionally anticipated some lines of nineteenth-century biblical criticism: later scholars would affirm one of his central claims—that the authors of the gospels read back into the life of Jesus some of the later doctrines of a developing and in Jefferson's perspective an already corrupted Church. In 1835, David Strauss, in the first frightful blast of German higher criticism, wrote a life of Jesus (*Das Leben Jesu*) in which he tried to prove that most of the gospel stories were mythological. This radical salvo began the long and doomed effort to find the historical Jesus. In one sense, Jefferson also sought the real historical Jesus, but his selective criteria fit his own religious bias, not any scholarly standard. In fact, the later problem of critics was how to find the presentist content read back into Jesus's life by his earliest biographers. From this perspective, one of the most clearly presentist interpretations of Jesus ever written, one that most ignored the religious culture in which Jesus lived, was this heavily expurgated gospel according to Thomas Jefferson.

IV

In his last years Jefferson changed none of his core religious beliefs. They had been amazingly constant from youth. He had changed his mind about Jesus and finally made him the greatest of all religious teachers, but he did this not by transforming his own religious doctrines, but by finding, or creating, a Jesus that matched these doctrines. In his years of retirement, plagued by the mounting debts occasioned by his expensive tastes, poor management, and terrible luck, he remained surprisingly irenic about religious developments. He and Adams noted the gains for evangelical and revivalistic Protestantism and lamented not the virtues it often engendered, but the intolerance it supported—in stronger blasphemy laws, in sabbatarian legislation, in nonlegal harassment of religious minorities. But accompanying this evangelical boom was a countertendency, not back toward the religious rationalism so widespread in their youth, but toward a humanistic Arminianism and then unitarianism in New England, and a benevolent universalism countrywide. Adams, to the envy of Jefferson, died in a Unitarian congregation in Quincy, a year after likeminded ministers formed the American Unitarian Association and thus marked their break from traditional or orthodox Congregationalism. Jefferson died on the same day as Adams, with no real church of his own but with soaring and, as it turned out, misplaced hopes for the Unitarian movement, which he observed and blessed from afar.

Organized Unitarianism poses the final questions about Jefferson's religious views and contributions. In time, American Unitarians would proudly claim Jefferson as one of their own, and the present Unitarian-Universalist Association has named one of its districts after Thomas Jefferson and another after his religious mentor, Priestley. In this tradition both have gained a type of beatification. Once again, as with almost all questions about Jefferson and religion, the fitness of this recognition requires careful clarification and then qualification.

For people who seemed on the right side, politically or religiously, Jefferson could be generous and forgiving. He easily ignored petty faults, smoothed over ideological differences, and gladly enlisted in their cause. He was just the opposite for his critics or enemies. In a stream of letters, written above all to Adams but also to five or six other religious confidants in these latter years, Jefferson indulged himself with scathing criticisms of all types of orthodoxy, in pithy and sharp and often cruel denunciations. These still charm religious sophomores, just breaking free from the repressions of childhood confessions, and provide ammunition for those who, for various reasons, resent or despise a professional clergy. In his last years the hopes and the laments balanced each other. Once again, as in his ready and full embrace of Priestley, Jefferson did not fully understand what lay behind the New England Unitarianism he so enthusiastically applauded.

The liberals in New England, out of Puritan roots, had little affinity for Priestley's brand of unitarianism. Jefferson never quite appreciated the differences. They had the right title, and at times they sounded like Priestley. Actually, the liberals in New England backed into doctrinal unitarianism largely as a response to critics. Most of the religiously liberal (by this self-chosen label they meant a broadly tolerant or inclusive or catholic outlook) ministers had moved only to an Arian position by 1825 (they believed in a divine Jesus but yet one begotten by and thus subordinate to God). The leaders of the movement were diverse, unified, if at all, only by a common rejection of some of the doctrines of Calvin, and by a very humanistic or benevolent conception of God. In this they clearly pleased Jefferson, who read sermons by William Ellery Channing and Jared Sparks, with whom he corresponded. But none of the ministers, so far as the record proves, accepted the corporealism of Priestley and Jefferson, and lurking among several of the young ministers was that apotheosis of idealism or spiritualism that we now label transcendentalism. Ironically, in that movement lay a much more radical critique of received Christianity than ever envisioned by Jefferson, for Ralph Waldo Emerson and Theodore Parker challenged the foundations of Jefferson's creator god, all doctrines based on the design argument, and any moral standards rooted in the authority of any god.

Jefferson died before he glimpsed this horrifying apostasy. Had he and Adams lived another decade, they might have despaired. Plato had won.[20]

Even though Unitarian sermons seemed congenial to Jefferson, they could not conceal the cultural gap that separated the preachers from Jefferson. Almost as much as the orthodox Congregationalists, they had voted Federalist, had joined in the denunciations of Jefferson in 1800, and had tried to counter infidelity and various beliefs they labeled deism. However much they humanized their god or subjected scripture to rational analysis, they still affirmed a religion based on revelation and confirmed by miracles. In other words, they were unitarian Christians, and much closer to most forms of orthodoxy than Priestley had been. The movement would change in time, and after the transcendentalist controversy move around or past Jefferson rather than in his direction. But even by 1818 the liberals at least fought the right enemies, and in one of his first commendations of the emerging Unitarians, Jefferson rejoiced at their attacks on Calvinism, but lamented even then their sectarian tone. He noted that Calvin introduced more new absurdities than Jesus purged from the old Jewish religion, and as usual lambasted sophistications, subtleties, and intellectualism in religion: "Our saviour did not come into the world to save metaphysicians only. His doctrines are levelled to the simplest understanding and it is only by banishing Hierophantic mysteries and Scholastic subtleties, which they have nick-named Christianity, and getting back to the plain and unsophisticated precepts of Christ, that we become real Christians."[21] He hoped the Unitarian reformers would complete the half-work of Luther and Calvin, and thus return to the original or primitive beginnings of Christianity. For a lonely old man at Monticello, dismayed by the problems of the new republic and haunted by the pitfalls of sectional division over slavery, there was solace in the fact that a unitarian form of Christianity was coalescing into an organized movement—one blessed by a great college, without creeds or clerical hierarchies, and clearly led by the most educated and sophisticated and tolerant clergy anywhere in the world. In fact, this was one of the few encouraging developments of his last decade of life.

Despite his enthusiasm, Jefferson characteristically refused to go public in his support of Unitarianism. He cited his usual reluctance to profess his religious views publicly and claimed the right, as an old man, to protect himself from further calumny.[22] But in friendly letters he offered his blessing and, as always, some advice. For example, he urged Unitarians to avoid all creeds, citing the Quakers, whom he usually admired.[23] In one of his more revealing late confessions, shared with Jared Sparks, he revealed what he wanted Unitarianism to be. This confession encapsulates so well his mature religiosity:

> I hold the precepts of Jesus, as delivered by himself, to be the most pure, benevolent, and sublime which have ever been preached to man. I adhere to the principles of the first age; and consider all subsequent innovations as corruptions of his religion, having no foundation in what came from him. The metaphysical insanities of Athanasius, of Loyola, and of Calvin, are to my understanding, mere relapses into polytheism, differing from paganism only by being more unintelligible. The religion of Jesus is founded on the Unity of God, and this principle chiefly, gave it triumph over the rabble of heathen gods then acknoleged. Thinking men of all nations rallied readily to the doctrine of one only god, and embraced it with the pure morals which Jesus inculcated. If the freedom of religion, guaranteed to us by law *in theory,* can ever rise *in practice* under the overbearing inquisition of public opinion, truth will prevail over fanaticism, and the genuine doctrines of Jesus, so long perverted by his pseudo-priests, will again be restored to their original purity. This reformation will advance with the other improvements of the human mind but too late for me to witness it. [24]

The problem with the Unitarians was that they had not proselytized in Virginia. Jefferson invited them to send disciples and, perhaps again more out of hope than realistic judgment, argued that the common folk, but not the priests, would welcome the liberating new faith, that emissaries from Boston would be greeted more avidly than Trinitarians from Andover (an orthodox Congregational seminary). The Unitarian missionaries would be "attended in the fields by whole acres of hearers and thinkers." Soon, they would drive away the foggy mists of Platonism. [25] Implicit in this hospitality was Jefferson's dream that the simple, creedless, primitive religion of Jesus would eventually prevail in America, that it was the logical counterpoint of political freedom, the only proper religion for a free republic. He expressed this hope to Adams: "But we may hope that the dawn of reason and freedom of thought in these United States will do away all this artificial scaffolding, and restore to us the primitive and genuine doctrines of this the most venerated reformer of human errors." [26]

Jefferson died before he could glimpse the limited appeal of Unitarianism. In 1824, two years before his death, he rejoiced in the new efforts to restore primitive Christianity, in the simplicity with which it came from the lips of Jesus. Finally, the metaphysical abstractions of Athanasius and the manic ravings of Calvin were under siege, and "our political reformation will extend its effects to religion." [27] Earlier, in 1822, he had marked the advance of Unitarianism in the east, and its advance toward the west and south. He then predicted that the present generation would see Unitarianism become the religion of the United States.[28] In a letter a month earlier, he had predicted that not a young man then living would not die a Unitarian, an unrivaled but, in the light of subsequent events, almost pathetic example of misplaced optimism.[29]

V

What is one to make of Jefferson's religion pilgrimage? His various religious views would never have a major impact on organized religion in America. As he once ruefully, or perhaps gladly, lamented, his church included only himself. No one shared his exact repertoire of beliefs. Earlier rationalists might seem closest, but they never mastered the stoic discipline of Jefferson, followed him in his apotheosis of Jesus, or joined him in his effort to restore his version of the primitive church, which was in fact hardly a church at all but a band of faithful disciples out to implement the pure ethics of Jesus. It is perhaps a commentary on the breadth of Christian assumptions among Americans that Jefferson, who uttered more scathing and sweeping diatribes against all the dominant forms of Christianity than even Thomas Paine, ended up professing that he was a true and pure Christian.

Jefferson's religious beliefs never cohered. Major tensions and ambivalence made it impossible for him to give them any systematic treatment. At the level of experience, what was most congenial to him, closest to his temperament, was the ancient philosophical cults—cerebral, materialistic, ordered, world-weary, renunciatory. His most compelling images of blessed happiness, of beatitude, did not involve victories on the moral battlefield or even a harmonious social order, but peace and tranquility in a beautiful, ordered garden. Monticello was his prototype of heaven, as he worked a lifetime planning and building but never really completing it. He yearned to retire, retreat, find solace in what Santayana aptly called a postrational moral stance, one that has appeal only after the moral battles are all over, and one has come to understand that these battles can only lead to two unwanted outcomes—defeat or the even greater emptiness of always meaningless victories.

At war with such renunciation and compassion was Jefferson's unrelenting moralism. Much more than he would have admitted, he was very much in the tradition of such enemies as Augustine and Calvin. He had no ease of conscience and felt guilty if he were not at the task of cleaning up this old world as much as it would submit. He wanted to make the city of man conform to the city of God, and at times was irenic enough to believe the task not impossible. It was his moralism that led him to search for authority, for a cosmology that would anchor our knowledge and our moral principles. Even his belief in life after death, however it may have consoled him privately, was most critical to him because it seemed a needed support of moral conduct. It was his moralism, and his hopes for a virtuous citizenry to sustain the American experiment in self-government, that led him to his strange and partial and always to some extent ill-fitted reconciliation with a demythicized version of Christianity and with the teachings of Jesus. One has to note that, in the most strict sense of the label, Jefferson was never a Christian, for he never believed that Jesus was the promised Messiah, the Christ, although at times he turned the word Christ (a status term) into a proper name. He never bestowed any special authority upon Jesus beyond the power of his message.

Along with these tensions, ironies abound. Later events so confounded Jefferson's expectations, and historic hindsight has clarified so many unnoticed tensions, that this story is largely one of irony. Jefferson expected the ephemera of Christianity, the varied and mythical embellishments upon Jesus' teaching, the various schemes of salvation, to give way, eventually, to the power of logical criticism and to the honesty and simplicity fostered by our free institutions. Then the pure distillate, the core doctrines that no one doubted, would survive—a creative and providential God and the hope of future rewards. In fact, the rich and varied ephemera has proved more durable, more enticing, than the Semitic foundations, and intellectual trends in the nineteenth century would be more subversive of this cosmology than of the distinctively Christian superstructure.

Jefferson never dreamed of the fate of some of his distinctive and positive doctrines. Today, the only widespread acceptance of his corporealism, his belief in a literal resurrection without immortality, and his hopes of rewards without the specter of eternal punishment is within Adventist and Mormon denominations, or some of the most conservative and sectarian denominations in America. The organized Unitarianism that coalesced just before his death, and which Jefferson foresaw as the future religion of America, never had broad appeal. Today the Unitarian-Universalist denomination is small, elite, and for the most part nontheistic, characteristics that would all dismay Jefferson, especially the widespread rejection of what he could never doubt—the existence of a god, for it was upon this foundation that he reared all his hopes for an ordered, disciplined, and virtuous society.

Jefferson, as a youth, was able to break from existing molds and come to his own conclusions about a series of issues that we conventionally call religious. Such a voyage of discovery was of vital importance to him. None of our founding fathers was more involved in religious issues, either at the level of personal meditation and devotion or as a practical problem of right conduct. He was eclectic, broadly but rarely deeply involved with a wide range of religious phenomena. As a result of the breadth, he came to know about more religions options than any but a few contemporaries. Yet because of his impressionistic and hasty evaluations of these options, and his dislike of dogma or philosophical complications, his critical judgments were of small value, usually a matter of caricatures and oversimplifications. In the same sense, his enthusiasms—for Bolingbroke, for Priestley, for the Jesus of the gospels—were more sentimental than rigorously grounded and much more selective than he ever realized. Such limitations should not conceal the fact that Jefferson was authentically religious. In his age, when so many people were indifferent to religion, not willing to devote the time and effort and thought that Jefferson gave to the subject, he stands with that small cadre of religious seekers, of innovative but warm and sentimental and not always rigorous thinkers, who have graced each period of human history.

NOTES

This essay overlaps with a lecture I delivered in 1988 at a symposium sponsored by the U.S. Capitol Historical Society: "Priestley and Jefferson: Unitarianism as the Religion for a new Revolutionary Age," in Ronald Hoffman and Peter J. Albert, eds., *Religion in a Revolutionary Age* (forthcoming).

1. TJ to J. P. P. Derieux, July 25, 1788, in *Boyd,* VI, pp. 418–19.

2. The story of his two teachers is in *Malone,* I, pp. 43–44. Much of the biographical detail throughout this essay is drawn from Malone's magisterial biography of Jefferson, although I will not cite the enormous volume of detail from which I draw my very brief sketches.

3. The actual evidence of such a religious crisis is very thin. Malone suspected such a crisis (p. 107) but cites only one letter as primary evidence for it. In this letter to Isaac Story, Dec. 5, 1801, in Dickinson W. Adams, ed., *Jefferson's Extracts from the Gospels: The Papers of Thomas Jefferson,* second series (Princeton, 1983), pp. 325–26, Jefferson noted youthful speculations about the realm of spirits, speculations that left him in the same ignorance as when he began. Thus he reported that he had stopped thinking about such hidden subjects—a nice way to extricate himself from the queries of a clergyman.

4. The Bolingbroke selections are in Douglas L. Wilson, ed., *Jefferson's Literary Commonplace Book: The Papers of Thomas Jefferson,* second series (Princeton, 1989), pp. 24–63.

5. Such a confusion does not characterize the two most detailed studies of Jefferson's

religion: Charles B. Sanford, *The Religious Life of Thomas Jefferson* (Charlottesville, Va., 1984); and the excellent introduction by Eugene R. Sheridan to Adams, ed., *Extracts from the Gospels*.

6. The fullest record of Jefferson's efforts to gain a complete disestablishment in Virginia in 1776 is in *Boyd*, I, pp. 525–58.

7. Wilson, ed., *Commonplace Book,* introduction, pp. 3–20, and selections from Cicero, pp. 56–63.

8. Jefferson added his syllabus of the doctrines of Epicurus to a letter to William Short, Oct. 31, 1819, in Adams, ed., *Extracts from the Gospels,* pp. 387–91; I was vastly influenced in this analysis of Epicurus by the work of a former graduate student, Carl J. Richard, whose work "The Founders and the Classics" is now in press.

9. The critical letter to Price, dated July 12, 1789, is in *Boyd,* XV, pp. 271–72; Jefferson had earlier ordered for his library a pamphlet by Priestley (*Boyd,* X, pp. 242–43), one which may have involved science rather than religion; in any case, Jefferson clearly had not yet read Priestley's views on unitarianism.

10. Jefferson's comments on his meeting with Priestley and on attending his sermons in Philadelphia are in a letter to John Adams, July 18, 1813, in *L&B,* XIII, pp. 319–22; Adams's more skeptical remarks about Priestley are in a letter to Jefferson, July 22, 1813, *L&B,* pp. 322–24.

11. The details about Priestley's early life are in Frederich W. Gibbs, *Joseph Priestley: Revolutions of the Eighteenth Century* (New York, 1965); a convenient, short summary of Priestley's mature religious views is in *Memoirs of Dr. Joseph Priestley, to the Year 1795,* 2 vols. (Northumberland, 1806), II, pp. 465–69; I used the third, American edition of Priestley's *History of the Corruptions of Christianity,* 2 vols. (Boston, 1797). This volume was published by a liberal minister who headed the unitarian-oriented King's Chapel in Boston, and despite Jefferson's earlier references to the corruptions, this may well be the edition that he read "over and over again."

12. Adams to TJ, July 22, 1813, *L&B,* XIII, pp. 322–24; TJ to Adams, Aug. 22, 1813, Adams, ed., *Extracts from the Gospels,* pp. 347–49.

13. Priestley aired his concerns in a letter to Jefferson on May 7, 1803, in Adams, ed., *Extracts from the Gospels,* pp. 338–40.

14. The other side of the controversy over the status of Jesus is reflected in Samuel Horsley, *Tracts in Controversy with Dr. Priestley, etc.* (Burlington, N.J., 1824).

15. Benjamin Rush to TJ, Aug. 22, 1800; TJ to Rush, Sept. 23, 1800, both in Adams, ed., *Extracts from the Gospels,* pp. 317–21.

16. This quotation from Bolingbroke is in Wilson, ed., *Commonplace Book,* p. 35.

17. TJ to Priestley, April 9, 1803, Adams, ed., *Extracts from the Gospels,* pp. 327–29; the copy of the Syllabus is in a letter from TJ to Rush, April 21, 1803, ibid., pp. 331–36.

18. This is in Adams, ed., *Extracts from the Gospels,* pp. 57–122.

19. This fascinating manuscript is printed in full, with abundant and helpful notes, in Adams, ed., *Extracts from the Gospels,* pp. 131–314.

20. The most detailed history of the origins of New England Unitarianism is in Conrad Wright, *The Beginnings of Unitarianism in America* (Boston, 1955).

21. TJ to Salma Hale, July 26, 1818, in Adams, ed., *Extracts from the Gospels,* p. 385.

22. Jefferson eloquently gives his reason for confidentiality in a letter to Timothy Pickering, Feb. 27, 1821, ibid., pp. 402–4.

23. TJ to Thomas Whittemore, June 5, 1822, ibid., p. 404.

24. TJ to Jared Sparks, Nov. 4, 1820, ibid., pp. 401–2.

25. TJ to Benjamin Waterhouse, July 19, 1822, ibid., pp. 406–8.

26. TJ to John Adams, April 11, 1823, ibid., pp. 410–13.

27. TJ to John Davis, Jan. 18, 1824, ibid., pp. 413–14.

28. TJ to James Smith, Dec. 8, 1822, ibid., pp. 408–10.

29. TJ to Benjamin Waterhouse, June 26, 1822, ibid., pp. 405–6.

CHAPTER 2

Jefferson and the Republic of Letters

DOUGLAS L. WILSON

A few months after he had retired from the presidency of the United States, Thomas Jefferson was approached about issuing a complete edition of his writings. Reviewing the categories of his official papers, he concluded that they "would be like old newspapers, materials for future historians, but no longer interesting to readers of the day" and "not likely to offer profit, or even indemnification to the re-publisher." And he offered what may have been an even more critical reservation: "I must observe that no writings of mine, other than those merely official, have been published, except the Notes on Virginia and a small pamphlet under the title of a Summary View of the rights of British America."[1] The former he intended to revise and enlarge and would defer publication until that was done, and the *Summary View,* he said pointedly, "was not written for publication." The upshot of this letter is that, apart from official writings only incidentally preserved in print as part of the public record, one of the most prolific and influential writers of his or any other time had, at the age of 66, offered but a single work for publication.

This is all the more remarkable when one considers the period in which he lived. During the course of the eighteenth century, perhaps nothing was more dramatic than the ascendancy of printing and publication and the tremendous importance they assumed. The spread of literacy, the rise of the newspaper, the increasing availability of printed books, and the consequent emergence of a broad reading public are well-known developments that contributed to notable transformations in virtually every field of endeavor. Becoming a community of readers, it has lately been argued, significantly changed the way people thought about themselves and the society they constituted.[2] According to another recent analysis, printing became so important during this period that it helped to change the way reality itself was conceptualized.[3] These are provocative claims, but what is beyond dispute is that the ideas and information seminal to that eventful age were promulgated in significant measure through printing and publication, which is why it is astonishing that Thomas Jefferson, who was closely identified with so many important developments, should have offered nothing for publication except *Notes on the State of Virginia* (1785).

Jefferson's reticence about appearing in print was undoubtedly genuine, though given his facility and remarkable productivity as a writer, it strikes us as not a little strange and somewhat paradoxical. His rise to public prominence, after all, came directly through his ability as a writer, having distinguished himself early with the spirited argumentation of the *Summary View* (1774). The impression made by this effort, together with his repute for drafting legislative resolutions and other documents—what John Adams called "the reputation of a *masterly pen*"—led directly two years later to his becoming the author of the Declaration of Independence. Jefferson himself was fully aware that he was prized by his Revolutionary colleagues and subsequently by his countrymen for his extraordinary abilities as a writer, and it was first and foremost as a writer, according to the inscription he devised for his own tombstone, that he wished to be remembered: "Author of the Declaration of American Independence / of the Statute of Virginia for religious freedom / & Father of the University of Virginia." Why, in these circumstances, he assiduously avoided writing for publication is part of the mystery of the man and the inscrutable personality that has baffled so many students of his life.

An indicative incident occurred when, as Secretary of State, one of Jefferson's private letters descrying Vice President John Adams's "political heresies" appeared in print without his knowledge. Properly horrified, Jefferson wrote to both the vice president and President George Washington to explain himself. In his letter to Washington, he said, "I certainly never made a secret of my being anti-monarchical, and anti-aristocratical; but I am sincerely mortified to be thus brought forward on the public stage, where to remain, to advance or to retire, will be equally against my love of silence and quiet, and my abhorrence of dispute."[4] In the same letter, Jefferson asked to borrow the letters he had written to Washington during his term as governor of Virginia so that he might replace the retained copies that had been destroyed by the British. Here is the true Jefferson: deploring the publication of some frank opinions he had willingly spread in private, even as he is diligently seeking to ensure that the file of his official letters not be lost to posterity.

I

The only American of his time whose distinction as a writer could be said to rival Jefferson's, at least from a modern point of view, was Benjamin Franklin, whose example affords an instructive comparison. Franklin began life as a printer, a trade of no high standing in the American colonies in the early years of the century, and developed his extraordinary talents as a writer in the pages of public newspapers. Though as a young man he practiced his writing assiduously, Franklin may be said to have conducted his literary education in public, contriving with versatility and imaginative innovations to make his workaday medium take on the classic aims of literature—to amuse and instruct. Franklin met with enormous success and thus not only took advantage of the rising importance of printing and the public press, but helped to bring it about. His writings and scientific discoveries eventually brought him a measure of international fame that was unprecedented for an American; he collected gold medals, honorary degrees, and the accolades of distinguished authorities. "America has sent us many good things, gold, silver, sugar, tobacco, indigo, etc.," the Scottish philosopher and historian, David Hume, wrote to Franklin, "but you are the first philosopher, and indeed the first great man of letters, for whom we are beholden to her."[5]

By contrast, Jefferson groomed himself as a writer entirely in private. The beneficiary of a superb classical education, he evinced a keen appetite for learning and developed a facility for written expression that is evident in his earliest surviving letters. Correspondence, school exercises, and commonplace books were the principal outlets for his writing up to the time he began to practice law at the age of 24. Though these would seem no match for the opportunities afforded the young Franklin, who was a successful newspaper proprietor at the same age, the surviving letters and commonplace books show that Jefferson was, like Franklin, a diligent student of style, displaying close attention to the special qualities of expressive language and to the importance of being concise. That he found many occasions to indulge his penchant for written expression other than the handful of surviving documents is certain, for when he was elected to the House of Burgesses at the age of 26, his abilities were immediately engaged, and his brilliant career as a draftsman of political documents was launched.

Jefferson's sense of himself as a Virginia gentleman no doubt contributed to his reticence about appearing in print initially, although there would have been few opportunities to do so in any event. In the case of his first notable paper, *A Summary View,* he does not seem to have objected that his friends had it printed, but he always wanted it clearly understood that the pamphlet had been published without his knowledge. He was certainly never ashamed of it, though its doctrines of political allegiance, parliamentary authority, and its rather far-fetched account of colonial history were, as he later conceded, radical and unrepresentative. Nor did he regret the notoriety and enmity the unauthorized pamphlet earned him in Great Britain. The reason he took pains to point out that he had no part in its publication seems to have been something else: the (for him) all-important consideration that he had not written it for the public but for his fellow delegates to the Virginia convention.

Nor was *Notes on the State of Virginia*—apart from the Declaration of Independence, Jefferson's most acclaimed literary achievement—written for the public. In its original form, it was compiled and composed in response to a series of routine questions posed by the secretary of the French legation, the Marquis de Barbé-Marbois, during the Revolutionary War. But so much did the project of assembling information on the geography and culture of his native country appeal to the young Jefferson that he continued to add to and revise his text for several years after sending his reply to Marbois in 1781. As the reputation of his remarkable manuscript grew and the demand for copies multiplied, Jefferson determined to have a few copies printed privately. By the time the printing was actually accomplished in Paris in 1785, the number of copies to be printed had risen to 200, and Jefferson was considering distributing copies not only to his friends but to the students at the College of William and Mary.

In spite of his specifically advising recipients to "put [the *Notes*] into the hands of no person on whose care & fidelity he cannot rely to guard them against publication,"[6] it was naive of Jefferson to think that such a valuable literary commodity, unprotected by any copyright, could long escape publication—and it did not. Within a year's time, a poor French translation had been issued, and Jefferson was faced with the prospect of that being translated back into English. Weighing this dismal prospect against both his extreme reticence about presenting himself before the public in print and his real fear of compromising the cause of progressive legislation in Virginia was not an exercise in false modesty but an agonizing, if self-created, dilemma. He prided himself on his candor: "I never had an opinion in politics or religion which I was afraid to own," he told a friend during his Paris years. "A costive reserve on these subjects might have procured me more esteem from some people, but less from myself." But at the same time he did not want his opinions aired in public. "My great wish," he went on, "is to go on in a strict but silent performance of my duty; to avoid attracting notice and to keep my name out of newspapers, because I find the pain of a little censure, even when it is unfounded, is more acute than the pleasure of much praise."[7] This candid admission tells worlds about its author and about what it cost him when, encouraged by his friends to believe his book could do much good, he finally decided in favor of publication.

II

There are many indications that the Revolution thoroughly disrupted the life Jefferson had envisioned for himself and consequently thrust him into uncongenial activities and pursuits. He repeated at many different times what he told Margaret Bayard Smith after his retirement: "The whole of my life has been a war with my natural taste, feelings and wishes. Domestic life and literary pursuits, were my first and my latest inclinations. . . . The circumstances of our country at my entrance into life, were such that every honest man felt himself compelled to take a part, and to act up to the best of his abilities."[8] Dutiful to a fault, he accepted the responsibilities and conditions imposed by the Revolution, which entailed the neglect of his farms and his family, giving up his legal practice entirely, and absorbing the devastating financial loss incurred in accepting worthless colonial currency from his debtors.

But beyond this, there may have been an even greater sacrifice, at least in Jefferson's eyes. In giving himself to the Revolution, he characteristically applied his powerful mind and imagination to the problems at hand, and these, being chiefly political, required a shifting of intellectual ground and a change in imaginative focus. As Merrill D. Peterson has put it, "His reading shifted from law and literature, which had predominated, to the theory and practice of government, and with it went a change in the contours of his mind."[9] To effectively engage the intellectual challenge of the Revolution he had to put aside more congenial activities. When he left the governorship of Virginia in 1781, he thought he was leaving politics and public service behind and resuming the life he much preferred. He wrote to Edmund Randolph: "I have taken my final leave of everything of that nature, have retired to my farm, my family and books from which I think nothing will ever more separate me."[10] But in less than a year, the dream was shattered by the death of his wife, and he wrote to his friend Chastellux: "Before that event my scheme of life had been determined. I had folded myself in the arms of retirement, and rested all prospects of future happiness on domestic & literary objects." [11]

One of the things that Jefferson seems to have had in mind for himself until the Revolution and the call to public life intervened, and again after he thought he had slipped its noose, was some sort of amateur literary vocation. His references to "literary objects" and "literary pursuits" undoubtedly refer to a life of reading and study, for Jefferson was among the most bookish of men. But he was also an irrepressible activist, a congenital doer, and there are indications that he had in mind at least one project that involved extensive research and writing. He says in his autobiography that when the request from the French government for information about the state of Virginia was passed on to him, he was not unprepared. "I had always made it a practice whenever an opportunity occurred of obtaining any information of our country, which might be of use to me in any station public or private, to commit it to writing. These memoranda were on loose papers, bundled up without order, and difficult of recurrence when I had occasion for a particular one. I thought this a good occasion to embody their substance, which I did in the order of Mr. Marbois's queries, so as to answer his wish and to arrange them for my own use." [12] This is, of course, the origin of the *Notes on Virginia*.

Jefferson implies here and elsewhere that he already had a project vaguely in mind that coincided with the purposes of the French diplomat's queries. [13] His initial work on the French questionnaire in the fall of 1780, which his correspondence shows he took up with great relish, was interrupted by affairs of state but was promptly resumed on his retirement from office in the summer of 1781. His beginning to revise the manuscript immediately after sending it off to Marbois was almost certainly prompted by his coming into possession of the great *Encyclopédie* of Diderot and D'Alembert. As governor, he had arranged the purchase of the work for the state of Virginia, and it was turned over to him for his inspection in December 1781, just as he was sending his completed questionnaire to Marbois.

Though he knew the *Encyclopédie* well by reputation, this was apparently Jefferson's first opportunity to peruse it extensively, and he forthwith became an enthusiastic user. The all-encompassing character of the *Encyclopédie*, which aimed at nothing less than the presentation of knowledge in all its dimensions, clearly captivated Jefferson, as did the philosophical aims and orientation of the compilers. "The Encyclopedists," writes Robert

Darnton, "identified their philosophy with knowledge itself—that is, with valid knowledge, the kind derived from the senses and the faculties of the mind as opposed to the kind dispensed by church and state." [14] Under the aegis of this stimulating encounter, and with solicited suggestions and information from Charles Thomson and others, Jefferson "corrected and enlarged" his own copy of the manuscript in the early months of 1782. [15] He became so absorbed in the *Encyclopédie* that a special resolution had to be passed by the legislature the following summer to remind him to return it. [16] He subsequently became a evangelistic promoter of its successor, the expanded *Encyclopédie méthodique,* which he told a correspondent "is really a most valuable work, and almost supplies the place of a library." [17]

Although it ultimately brought him fame and esteem as a philosopher and true man of science, Jefferson always considered his *Notes* as a preliminary unfinished essay on his subject. Using his leisure moments as a member of Congress in 1784 to review his manuscript, he "found some things should be omitted, many corrected, and more supplied and enlarged," until the original was "swelled to treble bulk," [18] and he continued to make changes and improvements up to the time he had it privately printed in Paris in 1785. In the "Advertisement" to the first published edition in 1787, necessitated by the threat of unauthorized editions, he advised the reader, "The subjects are all treated imperfectly; some scarcely touched on." This was partly due to the circumstances in which they were drafted, he explained, but "the great mass" of imperfections must be ascribed "to the want of information and want of talents in the writer." [19]

Much of his subsequent commentary on the *Notes* is of this kind, some of which may be attributed to conventional authorial modesty. But he did continue through life to make notes for a revision, and there is no reason to doubt that Jefferson regarded the published *Notes* as fragmentary and incomplete. Certainly his friend Charles Thomson believed that his work on the Marbois project was only a beginning, for he wrote Jefferson in 1782, "Though I regret your retiring from the busy and anxious scenes of politics, yet I congratulate posterity on the Advantages they may derive from your philosophical researches." [20] Merrill D. Peterson has observed that "the evidence, from notations in his author's copy, suggests that he viewed the published work as only the first installment of an ongoing enterprise." [21] These may all be regarded as indications that Jefferson's published notes on his native state had done but scant justice to a larger conception.

What was this larger conception? A more complete and satisfactory treatment of the state of Virginia, to be sure. But there are other indications that Jefferson had in mind a project with an even more ambitious scope: an encyclopedic depiction of America. Peterson suggests that thoughtful and cultivated Americans such as Jefferson were aware of the debate in Europe over the meaning of the New World: whether it represented a return to barbarism or a Lockean state of nature in which to begin anew. As they "began to think of themselves as Americans," Peterson says, they began to take stock of the native environment, "differentiating it from the European world they had fled, and to define its unique promise."[22]

One of the important things that a more comprehensive and more accurate account of conditions in the New World would accomplish, in addition to advancing the frontiers of natural history, would be a definitive refutation of the erroneous assumptions and beliefs of European scholars regarding the supposedly debilitating effects of the Western climate and physical environment. Some of the most vigorous and effective argumentation in the *Notes* is directed toward these, and Jefferson knew from first-hand experience that the great French naturalists such as Buffon and Raynal were not to be turned around so easily, for he found their views prevalent in Paris and the principals themselves, whom he met, quite unrepentant. Because the European savants were prepared to draw a significant correlation between the physical environment and the kind of human institutions that prevailed, Jefferson's scientific vindication of the natural environment of America over against the strictures of Buffon and Raynal would have had considerable philosophical and political meaning. Most important, it might demolish a plausible pretext for disparaging the Americans and their political experiments.

Having a larger project in prospect, something that attempted to do for the New World what the *Encyclopédie* had done for the Old, would accord with, if not account for, his extraordinary efforts at book acquisition abroad:

> While residing in Paris, I devoted every afternoon I was disengaged, for a summer or two, in examining all the principal bookstores, turning over every book with my own hand, and putting by everything which related to America, and indeed whatever was rare and valuable in every science. Besides this, I had standing orders during the whole time I was in Europe, on its principal book-marts, particularly Amsterdam, Frankfort, Madrid and London, for such works relating to America as could not be found in Paris.[23]

But Jefferson was not to have a career as the encyclopedist of the New World. His involvement in public affairs—as congressman, as a diplomat in France, as Secretary of State—occupied most of his time for some twenty years, and then, following a three-year respite dedicated to putting his plantation in order, he was preoccupied for another dozen years as vice president and president. With the sale of his great library to Congress in 1815, the means for the necessary research were permanently removed, and a chapter was effectively closed on the Jefferson's principal literary ambition.

III

The example of *Notes on Virginia* is not entirely anomalous. In fact, Jefferson initiated a number of literary projects he seems to have regarded in a similar light, as preliminary essays, or mere beginnings, for potentially larger and grander projects. To review some of these affords a glimpse of the literary career he may have been capable of, or wished for, but never had. Some were literally beginnings. For example, it was characteristic for Jefferson to become enthusiastic about a work in a foreign language and conceive the need for a translation. Occasionally he would actually begin the task himself and then persuade others to finish what he had begun, as with Destutt de Tracy's critique of Montesquieu or Volney's *Ruins*.[24]

As an avid student of Voltaire and Bolingbroke, the young Jefferson developed not only a profound skepticism about religious doctrines but a deep distrust of the traditional Church and the defenders of Christian orthodoxy. When he discovered, in reading law as a young man, that Christianity was considered part of English common law, he embarked on a program of research that took him far back in legal history to the earliest authorities. To almost the last year of his life, he delighted to share with select correspondents the triumphant results of these early labors, which he believed showed that the acceptance of Christianity as constituting part of the common law depended either on nothing but presumption, or else on a mistranslation of "ancient writing" for "Holy Scripture."[25] His researches were conducted "at a time of life when I was bold in the pursuit of knowledge," he told Thomas Cooper, "never fearing to follow truth and reason to whatever results they led, and bearding every authority which stood in their way."[26] Though the results were summarized in no more than two long entries in his legal commonplace book, such was his enthusiasm and aptitude for this research that it could very well have proved, in other circumstances, the subject of a book-length work.

Jefferson thought so well of this excursion into legal history that he included its findings ("a Disquisition of my own") as an appendix to a collection of law reports he assembled for the press before his death.[27] Published posthumously with the title "Whether Christianity is a part of the Common Law?" it presents his conclusions nearly verbatim from his commonplace book entries, but with two revealing excisions. He had originally concluded both entries with exuberant specimens of his incisive wit, but these testaments to his boldness, which he included for his correspondents, were both sacrificed, presumably in the interest of the sensitivities of a public audience, and milder sentiments substituted. The example given below protests the lumping of "the whole bible and testament" into the common law (the sentence in italics is the one Jefferson excised).

> And thus they incorporate into the English code, laws made for the Jews alone, and the precepts of the gospel, intended by their benevolent author as obligatory only *in foro conscientiæ;* and they arm the whole with the coercions of Municipal law. *In so doing this too they have not even used the Connecticut caution of declaring, as is done in their blue laws, that the laws of god shall be the laws of their land, except where their own contradict them.*[28]

That he felt constrained to suppress so fine an example of his gift for irony perhaps tells us something of significance about his disinclination to write for publication.

As with his translations, some of Jefferson's literary projects were possibly designed not so much for himself as for others. Jefferson's project to extract from the Bible the authentic sentiments of Jesus, so as to get at the essence of Christianity, is well known by virtue of the widely reprinted *Jefferson Bible,* a selection from the four gospels he called "The Life and Morals of Jesus of Nazareth Extracted textually from the Gospels."[29] But this fascinating document was a product of his old age and, in fact, something of a by-product of a much more ambitious project that he had tried to promote as president. Since his youth, Jefferson had been a relentless rationalist and had viewed the doctrines of Christianity with great skepticism, a philosophical stance that was readily construed by his political antagonists as atheism and hostility to religion, and for which Jefferson was pilloried in the campaign of 1800. Convinced by the scholarship of the British dissident Joseph Priestley that Christianity was originally the simple teachings of an inspired reformer that had been corrupted and made mysterious and unintelligible by later interpreters, Jefferson came to see his own beliefs as completely in harmony with uncorrupted Christianity.[30] Activated by the sense of himself as a true Christian, Jefferson conceived a work that would put Christianity in a new light before the world and at the same time vindicate the rationalistic principles he so resolutely embraced.

In 1803, Jefferson wrote to Priestley himself and outlined the important and potentially revolutionary work he had in mind:

> I should first take a general view of the moral doctrines of the most remarkable of the antient philosophers, of whose ethics we have sufficient information to make an estimate: say of Pythagoras, Epicurus, Epictetus, Socrates, Cicero, Seneca, Antoninus. I should do justice to the branches of morality they have treated well, but point out the importance of those in which they are deficient. I should then take a view of the deism and ethics of the Jews, and shew in what a degraded state they were, and the necessity they presented of a reformation. I should proceed to a view of the life, character, and doctrines of Jesus, who, sensible of the incorrectness of their ideas of the deity, and of morality, endeavored to bring them to the principles of a pure deism, and juster notions of the attributes of god, to reform their moral doctrines to the standard of reason, justice and philanthropy, and to inculcate the belief in a future state.[31]

Shortly thereafter, Jefferson sent to Benjamin Rush a more detailed outline of the same project, which he alternately described to family and friends as "my religious creed" and "a Syllabus, or Outline, of such an Estimate of the comparative merits of Christianity."[32] This expanded on the categories given in bare outline to Priestley, particularly with respect to the system of morals taught by Jesus, "which, if filled up in the true style and spirit of the rich fragments he left us, would be the most perfect and sublime that has ever been taught by man."[33]

But this grand project was not one that Jefferson actually proposed to undertake himself. As president, he had not the time to devote to it, and he sincerely believed that Priestley's talents and learning perfectly suited him for the task. Yet the idea of this work took dramatic possession of Jefferson's mind and imagination in the early years of the century, and he demonstrated a prospective author's enthusiasm and clarity of purpose. In his zeal for rescuing the authentic fragments of Jesus's moral teachings from the mass of later impositions that corrupted the gospels (which he later said were "as easily distinguishable as diamonds in a dunghill"[34]), he made in 1803 a scrapbook of forty-six pages into which he pasted clippings from the gospels of what he conceived as the true Christian teachings. It was this scrapbook, which he called "The Philosophy of Jesus," that was the prototype for the more extensive compilation performed many years later in his retirement, "The Life and Morals of Jesus." But even this expanded form, done strictly for his own personal use, was but a vestige of a larger project of Jefferson's literary imagination.

His activist temperament moved him no less in the intellectual realm than in the political to formulate solutions wherever he saw problems. He brooded, for example, on what he regarded as the baleful influence of Hume's history of England on youthful republican minds. "The elegant [history] of Hume seems intended to disguise & discredit the good principles of government, and is so plausible & pleasing in it's style & manner, as to instil it's errors & heresies insensibly into the minds of unwary readers."[35] To combat this insidious influence, Jefferson was full of schemes. The best way to deal with the "poisons" of Hume's history, he advised a publisher, would be to reprint the entire text and counter his "errors & heresies" editorially in collateral columns or notes, but he acknowledged that this "would make a work of great volume, and would require for its execution profound judgment and learning in English history."[36] Another method would be to edit Hume's text so as to correct its aberrations, a method that had already been attempted in an abridged and imperfect form by an English political dissident, John Baxter. Since both these methods required a large investment of time by a qualified editor and considerable financial risk for a publisher, Jefferson eventually contented himself with warning everyone who would listen about the dangers of Hume's history and urging an American edition of Baxter.[37] But one cannot read his animated letters on this subject (which became something of a hobbyhorse) without sensing that he would himself have liked to undertake the editorial task he worked out and described for others.

If his thoughts on the best means of countering Hume came to nothing, a friendly dispute with a member of the French Academy produced a substantial essay. Composed for the Marquis de Chastellux, "Thoughts on English Prosody" is an instructive specimen of Jefferson's literary mind at work. It is more than a mere beginning, and yet the form in which it comes down to us lacks the polish and coherence of a finished work. Written in Paris, it records the results of his attempts to refute Chastellux's contention that the basis of English verse was accent rather than quantity. Having opened the subject when Chastellux was a visitor to Monticello in 1782, the two men continued their amicable argument a few years later during Jefferson's diplomatic mission to Paris. Jefferson had taken the orthodox position, as espoused by Dr. Samuel Johnson and other authorities, that English prosody was like that of Greek and Latin, but he was unable to convince his learned companion, who was, in fact, well informed on poetics and the author of a comparative study of Italian, English, and German versification.[38] The letter that Jefferson drafted in 1786 to accompany his carefully worked-out findings is a model of philosophical capitulation. "Error is the stuff of which the web of life is woven: and he who lives longest and wisest is only able to wear out the more of it. I began with the design of converting you to my opinion that the arrangement of long and short syllables into regular feet constituted the harmony of English verse; I ended by discovering that you were right in denying that proposition." [39]

Jefferson's conversion to an accentual basis for English verse was, as with so much of his thinking, a harbinger of things to come, for the analogue with classical verse would eventually be displaced by the authority of accent. Finding that he could not reconcile his preconceived opinions on prosody with the hard realities of English verse, he turned his efforts to discovering "the real circumstance which gives harmony to English poetry and laws to those who make it." [40] Unfortunately, his results have been muddled and seriously marred in the only edition thus far to see print, but the manuscript shows perceptive insights into the nature of English poetry. In venturing that verses of five feet are "the longest the language sustains," Jefferson further observed, "it is remarkable that not only this length, tho' the extreme one, is generally the most esteemed, but that it is the only one which has dignity enough to support blank verse," which, he added, constitutes "the most precious part of our poetry. the Poet unfettered by rhyme, is at liberty to prune his diction of those tautologies, those feeble things necessary to introduce the rhyming word. with no other trammel but that of measure, he is able to condense his thoughts & images and to leave nothing but what is truly poetical." [41]

Jefferson crowns his paean to blank verse characteristically with an empirical demonstration of how the poet, "when enveloped in all the pomp and majesty of his subject . . . sometimes even throws off the restraint of the regular pause [at the end of the line]." After first citing the famous opening lines of Milton's *Paradise Lost,* he substituted instead (without attribution) some lesser-known lines from the same work, writing them out as prose:

> and in his hand he took the golden compasses Prepar'd in god's eternal store, To circumscribe this universe, and all created things: One foot he centr'd, & the other turn'd round through the vast profundity obscure, & said Thus far extend.

The purpose of this demonstration is to illustrate that there are only two pauses "in this whole passage of seven verses," and that these "are constantly drowned by the majesty of the rhythm & sense." [42] Like many other passages in the essay, this one has been so mangled by its editors as to be virtually meaningless in the printed edition, but in Jefferson's manuscript it serves to show that his understanding and appreciation of poetry went well beyond the technical aspects of versification. [43]

Although "Thoughts on English Prosody" was ostensibly written for the sole perusal of his friend Chastellux, Jefferson's draft letter leaves no doubt that he had given the matter considerable thought. One cannot be certain that the essay was actually completed to the author's satisfaction, so heavily revised and possibly fragmentary is the only surviving version, but the manuscript clearly shows that he expended a substantial amount of time and effort on the project—in research, in writing, and in extensive revision.[44] What, if not publication, had put him to all this trouble? He wrote it, he tells Chastellux in his draft letter, as a "tribute due to your friendship" and for "having recalled me from an error in my native tongue."[45]

The array of projects just reviewed—the research into Christianity and the common law, the comparison of the ethical teachings of Jesus with those of the ancient moralists, the "editio expurgatio" of Hume's history of England, and the demonstration that accent is the basis of English verse— show to advantage the range and color of Jefferson's intellectual interests. All but the last are projects that Jefferson clearly would have liked to pursue further, and, significantly, all are projects for the library. Brought to his subject by a problem encountered in experience, he was attracted to solutions that required study and research. "A patient pursuit of facts, and cautious combination and comparison of them," he observed in the *Notes on Virginia,* "is the drudgery to which man is subjected by his Maker, if he wishes to attain sure knowledge."[46]

IV

"During the entire length of his governorship," writes a biographer, "Jefferson wrote scarcely a letter in which he permitted himself to indulge his curiosity on literary, scientific, and artistic subjects."[47] Modern terms are employed here to suggest the variety of Jefferson's broad intellectual interests, but in the eighteenth century these were all subsumed under a single domain—the Republic of Letters. Apparently coined by the British essayist Joseph Addison at the beginning of the century, the phrase embraced a much wider field than "belles lettres." "Literature" was then used to designate virtually the entire corpus of written work. For Jefferson, the writings of "the three greatest men that have ever lived, without any exception"[48]—Bacon, Newton, and Locke—were literary, and their works crowning contributions to the Republic of Letters.

In one of Hume's essays, of which Jefferson was an admiring reader, the philosopher observes that the Republic of Letters consists of "the elegant Part of Mankind, who are not immers'd in the animal Life, but employ themselves in the Operations of the Mind," and that it may be divided into two classes:

> the *learned* and *conversible*. The Learned are such as have chosen for their Portion the higher and more difficult Operations of the Mind, which require Leisure and Solitude, and cannot be brought to Perfection, without long Preparation and severe Labour. The conversible World join to a sociable Disposition, and a Taste of Pleasure, an Inclination to the easier and more gentle Exercises of the Understanding, to obvious Reflections on human Affairs, and the Duties of common Life, and to the Observation of the Blemishes or Perfections of the particular Objects, that surround them.[49]

While Hume endorses closer relations between the "learned" and the "conversible" worlds and represents himself as an "Ambassador from the Dominions of Learning to those of Conversation," he clearly identifies himself with one side. But for Jefferson, the Republic of Letters was an undivided country, for he bridged the worlds of the learned and conversible in his own experience and example. Whereas in Hume's dichotomy there is a clear sense of writer and reader, scholar and layman, producer and consumer, it is doubtful that Jefferson saw his citizenship in the Republic of Letters as other than that of an active participant, whether learning from and discussing the works of others or contributing something of his own to the common store of knowledge.

Jefferson's own literary interests, in the eighteenth-century sense, were notoriously diverse. His most persistent and enduring interests were what we would call scientific, and he kept himself informed of the latest developments in chemistry, botany, anatomy, astronomy, zoology, and mineralogy, to name only a few. "The chemical dispute about the conversion and reconversion of air and water, continues still undecided," he wrote the president of Harvard from Paris. "Arguments and authorities are so balanced, that we may still safely believe, as our fathers did before us, that these principles are distinct."[50] In the same letter, at President Willard's request, he reviewed the latest European scholarly publications of note, ranging over a variety of subjects and in several different languages. His enthusiasm was perhaps greatest for the field of natural history (essentially botany, zoology, and geology), and he indulged this so far as to consent to the publication of a report on a fossil discovery he had presented to the American Philosophical Society.[51]

As a young man he was quite fond of poetry and belles lettres, and his tastes are suggested by the contents of the literary commonplace book he kept between the ages of about 15 and 30.[52] His attention was divided

between the English and classical poets, but his most passionate attachment was to Ossian. Like many readers of the day, Jefferson was smitten
by the verses disingenuously offered by James Macpherson as translations
of a third-century Celtic bard and characteristically tried to obtain the materials necessary to read Ossian in what he supposed was the original language. "I am not ashamed to own that I think this rude bard of the North
the greatest Poet that has ever existed. Merely for the pleasure of reading
his works I am become desirous of learning the language in which he sung
and of possessing his songs in the original form."[53] But as he grew older,
and as his public duties commanded his attention and guided his reading,
Jefferson's taste for poetry began to wane. At about the time he assumed
the presidency he confessed to a correspondent: "So much has my relish
for poetry deserted me that at present I cannot read even Virgil with
pleasure."[54]

Though he no longer read the poets for pleasure, Jefferson continued to
recommend them to students, principally for the salutary effect on the
development of their writing style.[55] As a young man he had urged that
"Shakespeare must be singled out by one who wishes to learn the full powers of the English language. Of him we must advise as Horace did of the
Grecian models, 'vos exemplaria Graeca Nocturna versate manu, versate
diurna.' [For yourselves, handle Greek models by night, handle them by
day.]"[56] Later in life he recommended the study of English prose writers
such as Sterne, Addison, and Hume for models of "eloquence of the pen."[57]

For Jefferson, the question of style was not one of language alone, but of
appropriateness and proportion. As there were different kinds of writing
for different occasions, there were different masters to follow. "No writer
has exceeded Paine in ease and familiarity of style, in perspicuity of expression, happiness of elucidation, and in simple and unassuming language."[58]
But this style, if it had important uses, had limitations. "Lord Bolingbroke's, on the other hand," he told his student correspondent, "is a style
of the highest order. The lofty, rhythmical, full-flowing eloquence of Cicero. Periods of just measure, their members proportioned, their close full
and round."[59] As this passage suggests, the classical writers were as valuable in the matter of style as their English counterparts. "I think the Greeks
& Romans have left us the present [purest?] models which exist of fine
composition, whether we examine them as works of reason, or of style &
fancy; and to them we probably owe these characteristics of modern composition."[60] The writer whose lean, spare style Jefferson most admired was
Tacitus. In justifying some deliberate liberties he took with the English
language, Jefferson pointed to the example of Tacitus, who, "by boldly

neglecting the rigorisms of grammar" succeeded in making himself "the strongest writer in the world." [61]

If Jefferson's best writing has a sharpness of line and a conciseness of content, it is no accident. One of the things he consciously worked at as a young writer was paring down the wordy prose of others, particularly the legal writers he read so extensively. Commonplacing such reading, he advised a student, "is doubly useful, inasmuch as it obliges the student to seek out the pith of the case, and habituates him to a condensation of thought, and to an acquisition of the most valuable of all talents, that of never using two words where one will do." [62] His commonplace books, most notably the one he kept for readings in the law of equity, bear testimony to his own success in such efforts. In serving as a reviser of the laws of Virginia, he deliberately attempted to offer an alternative to the notorious style of legislative prose. He told his mentor and fellow reviser, George Wythe, that he had "aimed at accuracy, brevity and simplicity" and that he sought "to exhibit a sample of reformation in the barbarous style into which modern statutes have degenerated from their antient simplicity." [63] A more familiar and accessible example is the case he makes for the moral utility of fiction in his letter accompanying a select list of books sent in 1771 to Robert Skipwith. This brief essay proves to be an incisive summary of a theory set forth at great length by Lord Kames in a work that strongly influenced the young Jefferson, *Elements of Criticism* (1762). [64]

The question of style was, for Jefferson, not merely one of ornament but of utility, just as the world of learning was not the preserve of the privileged. For him, the Republic of Letters was democratic. Though the eighteenth century was the age of Enlightenment, neither the learned nor the conversible were much interested in expanding the boundaries of their common domain and making it more inclusive. "Rightly or wrongly," Alvin Kernan has written of this period, "it was widely believed that the spread of reading, and writing, particularly among the lower classes, endangered the established order in polite letters, as well as in the more critical areas of politics and religion." [65] This was perhaps more true in England than in America, but few of Jefferson's colleagues in the founding circle shared his well-known enthusiasm for bringing literacy and the world of letters within the reach of ordinary citizens. The developments in printing and publication, as Kernan shows, "desacralized letters by expanding its canon from a group of venerable texts written in ancient languages known only to an elite to include a body of contemporary writing in the native language understood by all who could read." [66] This is a trend that Jefferson, who could himself read many of the venerable texts and ancient

languages, applauded and encouraged, and he claimed no superiority because of his advantages. In accepting the presidency of the American Philosophical Society, he allowed that his one qualification was "an ardent desire
to see knowledge so disseminated through the mass of mankind, that it
may at length reach the extremes of society, beggars and kings."[67]

V

Jefferson never seems to have seriously tried his hand at any of the standard literary forms of poetry, drama, fiction, or even the polite essay, but
his best prose exhibits a mastery of the distinguishing features of each:
rhythm, action, imagination, and grace. These, however, are almost never
on display in his writing for their own sake. Though enormously gifted
and undoubtedly aware of it, Jefferson was for the most part incapable of
showing off. This may indeed be a key to his reticence about publication,
which for him was too much like putting oneself on display. In private, of
course, one must still play roles, for it is impossible to address all in the
same voice, regardless of relationship and situation. But in private correspondence, it is possible to address one person at a time and to key one's
message and persona to a particular relationship and occasion. There can be
little doubt that Jefferson's finest literary form, and the one at which he is
virtually unexcelled, is the personal letter. For this reason, and because of
the sheer magnitude of his output (estimated at 19,000 letters), his richest
literary legacy is his correspondence.

Jefferson's talent for letter writing is already evident in his earliest surviving letter, written after he left college but before he was twenty. Writing
to his classmate John Page, he affects to complain about the drudgery of
reading:

> But the old-fellows say we must read to gain knowledge; and gain knowl-
> edge to make us happy and be admired. Mere jargon! Is there any such
> thing as happiness in this world? No: And as for admiration I am sure
> the man who powders most, parfumes most, embroiders most, and talks
> most nonsense, is most admired. Though to be candid, there are some
> who have too much good sense to esteem such monkey-like animals as
> these, in whose formation, as the saying is, the taylors and barbers go
> halves with God Almighty; and since these are the only persons whose
> esteem is worth a wish, I do not know but that upon the whole the advice
> of these old fellows may be worth following.[68]

Adolescent imperatives require that he scoff at the advice of elders, but as
the advice in this case is something the young Jefferson approves, he art-

fully works his way around to agreeing with them, using the fop and the joke about tailors and barbers as diversions.

As he grew older and became a man of consequence, Jefferson's correspondence became more circumspect, and he usually measured his words more carefully. But he could still be candid and caustic with his close friends, as when he wrote wryly to Abigail Adams in London: "I fancy it must be the quantity of animal food eaten by the English which renders their character insusceptible of civilisation. I suspect it is in their kitchens and not in their churches that their reformation must be worked, and that Missionaries of that description from hence would avail more than those who should endeavor to tame them by precepts of religion or philosophy." [69]

Jefferson's letters to women during his Paris years are prime evidence of his versatility and facility with language, for he could readily play the gallant, striking a bold figure of speech and wittily sustaining it, as in a letter to Lafayette's aunt:

> Here I am, Madam, gazing whole hours at the Maison quarrée, like a lover at his mistress. The stocking-weavers and silk spinners around it consider me as a hypochondriac Englishman, about to write with a pistol the last chapter of his history. This is the second time I have been in love since I left Paris. The first was with a Diana at the Chateau de Laye Epinaye in Beaujolois, a delicious morsel of sculpture, by Michael Angelo Slodtz. This, you will say, was in rule, to fall in love with a fine woman: but with a house! It is out of all precedent! No, Madam, it is not without a precedent in my own history. While in Paris, I was violently smitten with the hotel de Salm, and used to go to the Thuileries almost daily, to look at it. [70]

If the facade is one prescribed by the conventions of gallantry, there is also, as almost inevitably with Jefferson, another, more serious side. While the American tourist cheerfully portrays himself as playing the fool, he manages to communicate the fact that his eye has been busy and his mind much engaged.

Jefferson's style in his mature correspondence is not unvarying, and it is difficult to characterize, partly because it is often transparent. A careful and deliberate craftsman who often revised and rewrote his letters before sending them, his letter writing was artful in every sense of the word. But his is always the artfulness of engagement, of purpose. It bends our attention to what he is trying to convey, and thereby often obscures his means and methods. When John Adams pronounced one of Jefferson's letters as "the best letter that ever was written," [71] he was responding to the generosity and forbearance that his old friend had shown in dismissing as unimportant some harsh words that Adams had written about him privately and which had recently been published. But scrutiny of the letter itself reveals how much the manner in which the generosity and forbearance are manifested—the diction, the sentence structure, the imagery, and perhaps most important of all, the rhythms—contributed to the matter and to the effect that Adams acknowledges. No single sentence can do justice to a letter whose artistry is evident from the very outset, but consider, as representative, the artfulness of this sentence:

> And if there had been, at any time, a moment when we were off our guard, and in a temper to let the whispers of these people make us forget what we had known of each other for so many years, and years of so much trial, yet all men who have attended to the workings of the human mind, who have seen the false colours under which passion sometimes dresses the actions and motives of others, have seen also these passions subsiding with time and reflection, dissipating, like mists before the rising sun, and restoring to us the sight of all things in their true shape and colours.[72]

The sentence describes a trajectory of meaning that begins with forgetfulness and ends with the restoration of true sight. Ascending fairly rapidly to its grammatical climax, it then descends slowly to its resolution in looping syntactical spirals, finally coming to rest with the image of dawn. And here, as throughout the letter, the rhythms and intonations foster and enhance the residual theme of reassurance.

Jefferson's famous letter to Maria Cosway containing the dialogue between the Head and the Heart presents a special case. Ostensibly a letter that reveals the two opposing sides of his nature, his rational Head and romantic Heart, its central dialogue is conspicuously contrived and artificial, taking its cue from the same conventions and code of gallantry as his letter to Madame de Tessé. The Head and the Heart, at least in their basic opposition, seem to say just what one would expect them to say. Of getting involved with the Cosways (which one takes to mean Maria), the Head says, "Do not bite at the bait of pleasure till you know there is no hook beneath it. The art of life is the art of avoiding pain: and he is the best pilot who steers clearest of the rocks & shoals with which he is beset."[73] This seems like eminently good advice, but the Heart responds, "We have no rose without it's thorn; no pleasure without alloy. It is the law of our existence; and we must acquiesce. It is the condition annexed to all our pleasures, not by us who receive, but by him who gives them."[74] The Head regards the misery of Heart, bereft of its new-found friend, as the predictable price of entering into entangling alliances. The Heart, on the other hand, refuses to make friendship a matter of fine calculation and prizes above all else the effusive warmth of affection.

As the experience of most readers and commentators will attest, it is difficult not to see in this letter a strong subtext of self-revelation. But as to what is revealed, there seems to be no real agreement. There is little doubt that, except for his cold-bloodedness about taking on new friendships, the Head is much more like Thomas Jefferson than the Heart. But, it can be argued, this is because Jefferson took such pains to keep his personal feelings and passionate nature out of public view. Nobody doubted that Jefferson had a head; he is trying in this letter to prove to Maria Cosway that he has a heart. Putting his strong feelings for her on display, even by means of a literary convention, may thus be regarded a form of removing the veil.

Modern readers are regularly struck by the passion that Jefferson evinces for Maria in this letter and the sexual dimension that it portends. But it may be, given the preoccupations of the late twentieth century, that we are much too eager to see the dialogue solely as a love letter and Jefferson's undoubted infatuation with Maria Cosway as soap opera. It seems more in keeping with the author and his outlook to see the underlying (perhaps subconscious) purpose of the dialogue as conveying the idea or circumstance that the Heart, while not wanting in warmth, is obliged to occupy the same person as the Head. The Heart's key contention is that "Morals were too essential to the happiness of man to be risked on the incertain combinations of the head. She laid their foundation therefore in sentiment, not in science." [75] That this represents Jefferson's own belief is as certain as our knowledge of its source—Scottish common-sense philosophy. But Jefferson's belief that the promptings of the heart are implanted in human nature as a guide to right conduct is not to be equated with a philosophy of following wherever one's emotions lead. Such a philosophy of self-indulgence was anathema to Jefferson, and the opposite of what he believed happiness depended on, which was virtue and self-restraint. [76] Maria Cosway seems to have been surprised and disappointed by the coolness that subsequently developed in their relations, but the explanation may have been there in Jefferson's peerless letter all along.

VI

In spite of his inveterate reticence about appearing in print, Jefferson did actually publish one other book besides *Notes on the State of Virginia*. [77] A year after retiring from the presidency he was sued for an action he had taken as chief magistrate in ordering the removal of Edward Livingston, who had taken possession of a sandbar in the Mississippi River near New Orleans. For six months of the year, when it was above the surface, this extensive stretch of sand and alluvium adjoined his property, but it had been previously been considered and used, for as long as the older citizens could remember, as a public beach, or batture. Upon first learning of the suit, Jefferson had researched the legal aspects of the case in considerable depth and presented his findings to his lawyers in an extended brief. The suit was eventually dismissed on technical grounds (lack of jurisdiction), but Jefferson was concerned that the important substantive issues—such as whether, as president, he had acted properly and whether a private citizen could in fact be sued for actions performed as a public official—were thereby buried. Soon after the case was dismissed, he decided to take the extraordinary step of publishing at his own expense the brief he had written, and it duly appeared under the title *The Proceedings of the Government of the United States, in Maintaining the Public Right to the Beach of the Mississippi, Adjacent to New Orleans, Against the Intrusion of Edward Livingston* (1812).[78]

This unpromising work, in spite of its forbidding legalisms and long quotations in foreign languages, contains some surprisingly choice examples of Jefferson's dry wit and keen sense of irony. A routine rehearsal of facts is given heightened interest, for example, as Jefferson employs an allusion to one of Shakespeare's most hilarious scenes to point up an inconsistency. "But how these 7 arpents, like Falstaff's men in buckram, became 12 in the sale of the widow Pradel to Renard, 13 in Gravier's inventory, and nearly 17, as is said in the extent of his fauxbourg, the plaintiff is called on to show."[79] Though much of the exposition is necessarily given over to abstruse legal distinctions and colorless disputation, the brief is redeemed as prose and as the work of a writer who knows how to gain the attention of his reader by passages such as this:

> The batture alone is now estimated at half a million of dollars. But the truth is, that neither John Gravier, nor any one else, at that day, considered it but as public property. And for six years ensuing, he never manifested one symptom of ownership; until Mr. Livingston's arrival there from New York, with the wharves and slips of that place fresh in his recollection. The flesh-pots of Egypt could not suddenly be forgotten, even in this new land of Cannan. Then John Gravier received his inspiration that the beach was his.[80]

But why did Jefferson, with his notorious disinclination to appear in print, decide at the age of 69 to overrule a lifelong resolve and publish such a work? Jefferson's own answer to this question is given in the preface.

Having described the case and informed the reader of its having been dismissed, he explained, "My wish had rather been for a full investigation of the merits at the bar, that the public might learn, in that way, that their servants had done nothing but what the laws had authorized and required them to do. Precluded now from this mode of justification, I adopt that of publishing what was meant originally for the private eye of counsel."[81] That Jefferson is sincere in this can hardly be doubted, but there are other important elements in the equation that Jefferson can perhaps neither see nor say.

One is the uncharacteristically large measure of egoism that is betrayed in this gesture, for in publishing his own recondite legal brief written to exculpate himself, the admittedly thin-skinned ex-president appears as much concerned for his image as for his record. His conclusion is emotional and self-serving to an astonishing degree, and its strong and bristling qualities as prose only serve to bring out the most embarrassing aspects of its author's defensiveness. It begins on a sober note and builds steadily to a level of language and exhortation that comes close to being a tirade of self-justification. It concludes: "But I do say, that if human reason is not mere illusion, and law a labyrinth without a clue, no error has been committed: and recurring to the tenor of a long life of public service, against the charges of malice and corruption I stand conscious and erect."[82] Like another of Shakespeare's characters, he protests too much.

Jefferson's publishing his brief in the batture case bears, somewhat paradoxically, on the question of his reticence about appearing in print. Its self-justifying contents have the effect of placing him in an unaccustomed and ultimately unflattering light and go far to reveal the side of himself that Jefferson most wished to conceal: his thin skin with regard to criticism, his passionate and excitable nature, and his brooding self-consciousness and self-regard. As such, the contents of his brief in the batture case provide a telling clue to Jefferson's reticence.

Though he offered it for publication and wrote a preface addressed to the public, the brief itself is expressly represented as having been written for and addressed to his legal counsel. It appeals to the public for vindication, but it does so indirectly. This brings us to a crucial reflection about Thomas Jefferson as a writer—that his makeup was such that he could not bring himself to address the public directly. This does not, of course, mean that he was unable to reach the public with his ideas. He was able to communicate with the public as governor or as secretary of state or as president. Occasions of extreme urgency could prompt him to put his ideas before the public secretly, which he did in drafting the Kentucky Resolutions. He could address the public by proxy, as when he arranged for Philip Freneau's editorship of a partisan newspaper. He could conscript others to pseudonymous pamphleteering and newspaper writing, as when he urged Madison to take up his pen in the Republican cause, though he could not do it himself. He could even speak past his correspondents to an interested posterity, which he knew would eventually be reading at least some of his letters. But he seems to have found it next to impossible to direct his writing squarely at the public; to do so in his own persona, as Thomas Jefferson, was virtually out of the question.

Thomas Jefferson's literary career may have been the most unusual and distinctive in American letters, for in avoiding publication almost as assiduously as he wrote, he nonetheless became a writer of importance almost in spite of himself. Laboring most of his life in the turbulent sphere of politics, where contention was virtually continuous and acrimony the order of the day, he managed at the same time to inhabit just as meaningfully the absorbing world of science and letters, which, as he believed, "form a great fraternity spreading over the whole earth."[83] That this was not an imaginary or dream world but a realm of consequential realities is attested beyond doubt by the frequency with which his writings, in all their diversity, have been read and cited over the past two hundred years. "No republic is more real than that of letters,"[84] he told a correspondent, and no citizenship therein was more ardent or patriotic than that of Thomas Jefferson.

NOTES

I wish to gratefully acknowledge the assistance and advice of James S. Gilreath and Rodney O. Davis.

1. TJ to John W. Campbell, Sept. 3, 1809, *LofA,* p. 1210.
2. Michael Warner, *The Letters of the Republic: Publication and the Public Sphere in Eighteenth-Century America* (Cambridge, Mass., 1990).
3. Larzer Ziff, *Writing in the New Nation: Prose, Print, and Politics in the Early United States* (New Haven, 1991).
4. TJ to Washington, May 8, 1791, *Boyd,* XX, p. 222.
5. Carl Van Doren, *Benjamin Franklin* (New York, 1938), p. 290.
6. Quoted in Thomas Jefferson, *Notes on the State of Virginia,* ed. William Peden (Chapel Hill, 1955), p. xvii; hereafter cited as *Notes.*
7. TJ to Francis Hopkinson, Mar. 13, 1789, *Boyd,* XIV, p. 651.
8. Margaret Bayard Smith, *The First Forty Years of Washington Society,* ed. Gaillard Hunt (New York, 1965), pp. 80–81.
9. Merrill D. Peterson, *Thomas Jefferson and the New Nation* (New York, 1970), p. 37.

10. TJ to Edmund Randolph, Sept. 16, 1781, *Boyd,* VI, p. 118.

11. TJ to Marquis de Chastellux, Nov. 26, 1782, *Boyd,* VI, p. 203.

12. Autobiography (1821), *LofA,* p. 55.

13. See, for example, his Nov. 30, 1780, letter to D'Anmours: "I am at present busily employed for Monsr. Marbois without his knowing it and have to acknolege to him the mysterious obligation for making me much better acquainted with my own country than I ever was before." Quoted in *Notes,* xiii.

14. Robert Darnton, *The Business of Enlightenment: A Publishing History of the* Encyclopédie *1775–1800* (Cambridge, Mass., 1979), p. 7.

15. In the Advertisement to the 1787 Stockdale edition of the *Notes,* Jefferson wrote: "The following Notes were written in Virginia in the year 1781, and somewhat corrected and enlarged in the winter of 1782." *Notes,* p. 2.

16. *Boyd,* VI, p. 258n.

17. TJ to William Hay, Aug. 4, 1787, *Boyd,* XI, p. 685.

18. TJ to Chastellux, Jan. 16, 1784, *Boyd,* VI, p. 467.

19. *Notes,* p. 2.

20. Charles Thomson to TJ, March 13, 1782, *Boyd,* VI, pp. 163–64.

21. Merrill D. Peterson, "Thomas Jefferson's *Notes on the State of Virginia,*" *Studies in Eighteenth-Century Culture,* 7 (1978), p. 53.

22. Peterson, *Jefferson and the New Nation,* p. 66.

23. TJ to Samuel H. Smith, Sept. 21, 1814, *LofA,* p. 1353.

24. See E. Millicent Sowerby, comp., *Catalogue of the Library of Thomas Jefferson* (1952–59; reprint, Charlottesville, Va., 1983), nos. 2327, 1278.

25. See entries 873 and 879, in Gilbert Chinard, ed., *The Commonplace Book of Thomas Jefferson* (Baltimore and Paris, 1926), pp. 351–56, 359–63.

26. TJ to Thomas Cooper, Feb. 10, 1814, *LofA,* pp. 1321–29, and Major John Cartwright, June 5, 1824, in *LofA,* pp. 1490–96.

27. This was published posthumously as *Reports of Cases Determined in the General Court of Virginia* (Charlottesville, Va., 1829). Jefferson's "disquisition," an edited version of his commonplace book entries, is reprinted in *Ford,* I, pp. 453–64.

28. Chinard, *Commonplace Book,* p. 363.

29. Dickinson W. Adams, ed., *Jefferson's Extracts from the Gospels, The Papers of Thomas Jefferson,* second series (Princeton, 1983), p. 127ff. This edition contains a reconstruction of "The Philosophy of Jesus," a photographic reproduction of "The Life and Morals of Jesus," and a generous appendix of letters relating to Jefferson's religious beliefs and his gospel-extracting projects.

30. For a discussion of Priestley's influence on Jefferson, see Paul K. Conkin's contribution to this volume.

31. Adams, ed., *Extracts from the Gospels,* pp. 327–28.

32. TJ to Henry Dearborn, Levi Lincoln, and others, April 23, 1803; TJ to Benjamin Rush, April 21, 1803, ibid., pp. 336, 331.

33. "Syllabus of an Estimate of the merit of the doctrines of Jesus, compared with those of others," ibid., p. 333.

34. TJ to John Adams, Oct. 12, 1813, *LofA,* p. 1301.

35. TJ to John Norvell, June 14, 1807, *Ford,* X, pp. 416–17.

36. TJ to Mathew Carey, Nov. 22, 1818, in Sowerby, *Catalogue,* pp. 176–77.

37. See Douglas L. Wilson, "Jefferson vs. Hume," *WMQ,* XLVI (1989), pp. 49–70.

38. "Reflexions sur le Méchanisme de la Versification Italienne, Anglaise & Allemande," *Journal Étranger,* Paris (June 1760), pp. 3–58. Chastellux's authorship of this treatise is

acknowledged in another of his own, *Essai sur l'Union de la Poésie et de la Musique* (1765). For these references, I am indebted to the notes of Howard C. Rice on file at the office of the Jefferson Papers in the Princeton University Library, and to Ruth C. Lester and Charles T. Cullen for assistance in using them.

39. TJ to Marquis de Chastellux, c. Oct. 1786, *Boyd,* X, p. 498.

40. Ibid.

41. This is my rendering of the manuscript text that excludes stricken material. Jefferson Papers, Manuscript Division, Library of Congress.

42. Ibid.

43. See *L&B,* XVIII, p. 446.

44. Lacking a press copy, which he retained for virtually everything he wrote, the possibility exists that the letter and essay may never have been sent.

45. *Boyd,* X, p. 498.

46. *Notes,* p. 277n.

47. Peterson, *Jefferson and the New Nation,* p. 201.

48. TJ to John Trumbull, Feb. 15, 1789, *Boyd,* XIV, p. 561.

49. David Hume, "Of Essay Writing," *Essays Moral, Political, and Literary,* ed. Eugene F. Miller (Indianapolis, 1985), pp. 533–34.

50. TJ to Joseph Willard, Mar. 24, 1789, *Boyd,* XIV, p. 698.

51. The difficulties that attended this venture did nothing to encourage his reticence for publication. See Julian P. Boyd, "The Megalonyx, the Megatherium, and Thomas Jefferson's Lapse of Memory," *Proceedings: American Philosophical Society,* 102 (1958), pp. 420–35.

52. Douglas L. Wilson, ed., *Jefferson's Literary Commonplace Book: The Papers of Thomas Jefferson,* second series (Princeton, 1989).

53. TJ to Charles Macpherson, Feb. 25, 1773, *Boyd,* I, pp. 96–97. For a discussion of Jefferson and Ossian, see Wilson, ed., *Commonplace Book,* pp. 171–73.

54. TJ to John D. Burke, June 21, 1801, *Ford,* IX, p. 267.

55. See his letter to Nathaniel Burwell, Mar. 14, 1818, *LofA,* pp. 1411–12.

56. TJ to John Minor, Aug. 30, 1814, *Ford,* XI, pp. 424–25.

57. TJ to George W. Summers and John B. Garland, Feb. 27, 1822, *L&B,* XV, p. 353.

58. TJ to Francis Eppes, Jan. 19, 1821, *LofA,* p. 1451.

59. Ibid.

60. TJ to Joseph Priestley, Jan. 27, 1800, ibid., p. 1072.

61. TJ to Edward Everett, Feb. 24, 1823, *L&B,* XV, pp. 414–15.

62. TJ to John Minor, Aug. 30, 1814, *Ford,* XI, pp. 423–24n.

63. TJ to George Wythe, Nov. 1, 1778, *Boyd,* II, p. 230.

64. I have compared Jefferson's summary and Kames's text in "Thomas Jefferson's Library and the Skipwith List," *Harvard Library Bulletin* (forthcoming).

65. Alvin Kernan, *Printing Technology, Letters, & Samuel Johnson* (Princeton, 1987), p. 70.

66. Ibid., pp. 153–54.

67. Quoted in *Malone,* III, p. 341.

68. TJ to John Page, Dec. 25, 1762, *Boyd,* I, p. 5. The text of an earlier letter is known, but the document itself does not seem to have survived.

69. TJ to Abigal Adams, Sept. 25, 1785, *Boyd,* VIII, pp. 548–49.

70. TJ to Madame de Tessé, Mar. 20, 1787, *Boyd,* XI, p. 226.

71. John Adams to TJ, Nov. 10, 1823, *LofA,* p. 1570.

72. TJ to John Adams, Oct. 12, 1823, ibid., pp. 1479, 1480–81.

73. TJ to Maria Cosway, Oct. 12, 1786, *Boyd,* X, pp. 448–49.

76 Jefferson and the Republic of Letters

74. Ibid., pp. 451–52.

75. Ibid., p. 450.

76. See, for example, his letter to Thomas Law, June 13, 1814, *LofA*, pp. 1335–39, to William Short, Oct. 31, 1819, *LofA*, pp. 1430–33, and the discussion of Jefferson and Gassendi's Epicurism in Adrienne Koch, *The Philosophy of Thomas Jefferson* (New York, 1943), pp. 2–8.

77. I follow Jefferson's lead in excepting as a special case the famous parliamentary *Manual* he compiled for the United States Senate. See Wilbur Samuel Howell, ed., *Jefferson's Parliamentary Writings: "Parliamentary Pocket-Book" and A Manual of Parliamentary Practice: The Papers of Thomas Jefferson,* second series (Princeton, 1988), pp. 337–444.

78. The original edition was printed in New York by Ezra Sargeant in 1812. I have collated the passages cited here with the more accessible text reprinted in *L&B*, XVIII, pp. 1–132.

79. Ibid., XVIII, p. 2. I have edited this passage somewhat, principally to remove citation paraphernalia.

80. Ibid., pp. 12–13.

81. Ibid., p. lviii.

82. Ibid., p. 132. I have corrected the *L&B* text, which has "charge" where the original (at p. 80) has "charges."

83. TJ to John Hollins, Feb. 19, 1809, *LofA*, p. 1201.

84. TJ to Noah Webster, Jr., Dec. 4, 1790, *Boyd*, XVIII, p. 132.

CHAPTER 3

The First Monticello

RHYS ISAAC

In August 1771 a letter went forth from a hilltop house-in-construction that was coming to be called Monticello. The letter was from Thomas Jefferson, now nearing the successful completion of his courtship of Martha Wayles Skelton; it was directed to his future brother-in-law, Robert Skipwith, who had asked him for a short list of books suitable to form the basis of a small library. Jefferson broke off his explication of the categories in his list, in order to ask a question, and to deliver a summons:

> But whence the necessity of this collection [of your own books]? Come to the new Rowanty, from which you may reach your hand to a library formed on a more extensive plan. [In conjugal households] separated from each other but a few paces, the possessions of each would be open to the other. A spring, centrically situated, might be the scene of every evening's joy. There we should talk over the lessons of the day, or lose them in Musick, Chess, the merriments of our family companions. The heart thus lightened, our pillows would be soft, and health and long life would attend the happy scene. Come then and bring our dear [sister-in-law] Tibby with you; the first in your affections, and second in mine.[1]

Now I turn to a somewhat later mythologizing of that same place. The time is spring 1782, and Monticello is still the place of Jefferson's dreams of connubial bliss with Martha—a dream to be shattered in the late summer of that same year. The Marquis de Chastellux is describing a high point in his visit to the troubled ex-governor of Virginia on his mountaintop:

> I recall with pleasure that as we were conversing one evening over a "bowl of punch," after Mrs. Jefferson had retired, we happened to speak of the poetry of Ossian. It was a spark of electricity which passed rapidly from one to the other; we recalled the passages of those sublime poems which

had particularly struck us, and we recited them for the benefit of my traveling companions, who fortunately knew English well and could appreciate them, even though they had never read the poems. Soon the book was called for, to share in our "toasts": it was brought forth and placed beside the bowl of punch. And, before we realized it, book and bowl carried us far into the night.[2]

These two passages—one relating to the time just before the married and parenting life of Martha and Thomas Jefferson began at Monticello, and the other relating to what proved to be the closing months of that shared life—mirror a much deplored fact in Jefferson studies, the almost silent void in which the conjugal world of Monticello is historically engulfed. Nevertheless, both of the quoted passages show Monticello as a place of story. It is joined to the "new Rowanty" as the site of arcadian scenes of health-giving family merriment beside a mountain spring; or, it is on a peak charged by the lightning "spark of electricity" that brings the spirit of the wild Gaelic bard, Ossian, into the assembled company.

AN INVITATION

Let us explore the world that Thomas Jefferson was making as he moved up onto his mountaintop by examining both stories brought into that household and stories made during the time of its master's married life there. This special place during this special time I shall refer to as the first Monticello, distinguishing it thus from the second and subsequent ones that were rebuilt and more assiduously recorded after Jefferson's return from France and his retirement from the Presidency. We shall be concerned with the stocks of stories that entered into the young Thomas's formation, and with the stocks of stories he drew on as he carefully collected the extracts in his famous "literary commonplace book." The inscription of Monticello as a place in the world—in history and geography—through the momentous stories the young statesman wrote from his mountaintop will also require attention.

The general concern behind my enquiry here is the notion that we as humans, and the cultures to which we belong, are largely constructed in, and knowable through, the stock of stories we "possess" (or that "possess" us?). It is in that framework that we shall look at the world of Monticello as it was being constructed by the stories that its founder and others brought to it. In doing this we shall also be engaging with that most elusive topic—household.[3]

The household is the context in which a vast amount of adult experience occurs, especially in preindustrial times; it is also the first induction of all individuals at all times to the social world. Social historians generally need to pay more attention to this form of little community; certainly it cannot continue to be passed over in such cases as the Southern plantation, where the configuration of the household has been at once so complex and so enveloping. The concept of the "imagined family" has recently been taken up by John Gillis; adapting it to my own long-standing concern with "the imagination" and with "stories" and "storying," I mean to seek clues to the "imagined household" projected by Thomas Jefferson at Monticello, and to those of others more or less willingly caught up in his household formation.[4]

CHILDHOOD INDUCTIONS

It is in the nature of things that we cannot recall the earliest stories in our lives; these, haltingly learned at first, will be what have provided the forms for memory itself. Certainly we cannot know what the first stories were that entered into and organized the consciousness of the infant Thomas Jefferson. We know, however, that he was coming into consciousness in a richly complex, probably contested, world of stories. From the age of three, when the Jeffersons moved from Shadwell to Tuckahoe, until eight or nine, the family dramas of childhood were complicated by his growing up in a house that was not his father's but the property of a suddenly acquired older sibling cousin, Thomas Mann Randolph, to whom Colonel Peter Jefferson had become a resident guardian.[5]

Whatever familial dramas and direction-setting stories the years in a Randolph great house may have occasioned, we know that both the two households of the baby Thomas's first experiences sustained very varied stocks of stories. There were perhaps thirty African-Americans and an indeterminate number of Anglo-Americans at Shadwell, the household into which he was born; Tuckahoe had associated with it even greater numbers of slaves, overseers, and servants in and around its great house.[6]

The earliest memory of the old Thomas Jefferson was of his being taken to Tuckahoe on a cushion on the saddlecrupper of a mounted slave, whose arms supported him through the long journey. This physically intimate memory must put us in mind of the complex storied worlds of which he was by then certainly becoming aware. We do not know how much, if at all, little Thomas was involved in the life of the home quarters at Shadwell and Tuckahoe; we do know, however, from the reminiscences of Isaac Jefferson, a former slave at Monticello, that Thomas's younger brother, Randolph, did develop in his childhood sufficient rapport with the African-American folk to be able in later life to go away from the main house and mix "among black people; play the fiddle and dance half the night." Thomas's elder daughter, Martha, also had an ear attuned to the singing and storytelling of such occasions. Since she shared her knowledge with an interested traveler, who wrote down what she told him, a record survives of a few items from the repertoires of the slave families among whom Thomas had grown up. At the Monticello quarter they had, for instance, a song celebrating (perhaps mockingly) times gone by when "there was nothing but joy at Tuckahoe"; they also had a song telling of a lost key and a long search that continued "forty days and forty nights," until the seekers realized that they "were so far beyond the sun" that they "could see there blacks that [they] could not understand." There were also such very explicit spirit-world stories as the one recorded about Diah, a woman of power, whose magically obedient dogs came upon summons to rescue her by tearing an "evil genie . . . to pieces" as he was about to kill her. Because Martha was able to tell the tale of how Rabbit persuaded Fox to hide from the hounds in a chest, where he could be killed by Rabbit pouring in boiling water, we may be sure that these families shared among themselves—and perhaps had earlier with Thomas when he was a child—a rich stock of African trickster tales adapted to America.[7]

Concerning Thomas Jefferson we can only say with certainty, then, that whether or not he witnessed song, dance, and story in the circle of firelight at the quarter, his childhood world was undoubtedly suffused with the sounds of such performances, all communicating versions of the imaginative universe of the numerous African-Americans whose labor provided the wealth and sustained the routines of the Jefferson and Randolph households. We know, therefore, that those sounds around the house by day, and rising up to it on the night air, revealed to all who could truly hear them a world in which, as Albert Raboteau has summed it up, "The power of . . . the spirits was effectively present . . . for good or ill, on every level—environmental, individual, social . . . and cosmic." The boy Jefferson would have known the persons of power in this world and would have been at least dimly aware of spirit possession, of trance dances, and a whole distinctive set of ways of interpreting the world. Alas, we know too little of how sex, family, and household were told in these stories.[8]

In the persons of the overseers, white servants, artisans, and poorer neighbors, there were at Shadwell and Tuckahoe the bearers of another folk culture that was present in little Thomas's earliest household worlds. British Virginian folklore and the patterns of its stories must also have contributed to shaping his developing consciousness, by an involvement with an imaginative universe very different from the African one. Alongside the stories and cosmologies of the Bible, the great set of ballads told of a world of menacing familial dramas, of sibling murders, of violent courtship, and the pillaging by the suitor of the wealth of the males of the courted female's household. The ballads constantly told of doomed love and bloodily avenged betrayals. There is no record of these stories from Tuckahoe, but we know they were constantly sung among common folk a little way down the river in Devereux Jarratt's New Kent County. The stories of the ballads had such hold on Anglo-Virginian imaginations that they continued to be performed and passed down until well into the twentieth century.[9]

Two very different folklore mythologies, then, were powerfully present in the earliest formative years of Thomas Jefferson, even before the training in reading and writing opened to him the rich stocks of stories of ancient and modern literature.

COLLECTING STORIES

Some attention has been paid to the stories in the books that Thomas's father left to his elder son. It has been disputed whether Shakespeare was part of the legacy. Historians and biographers have, however, often speculated that Colonel Peter Jefferson had filled his son's head with tales of survey expeditions into the Western wilderness, and so given the youngster a lifelong fascination with the interior of the continent. Perhaps the explorer father did, but the path chosen by the son suggests a pattern of going in an opposite direction rather than simply following in his father's footsteps. Concern with the West was revealed in middle life, and then only in journeys of the mind. Jefferson never found himself, as he later put it, west of Augusta Courthouse. On the contrary, his first traveler's impulses took him toward the Atlantic shores and then over the ocean to France and the Mediterranean world. In these journeys, he seems to have been led by his most treasured stocks of stories.[10]

The earliest record of the young Thomas Jefferson's own engagement with stories certainly shows a classical Mediterranean orientation. It survives in the literary commonplace book. Here, in a thoroughly conventional genre of transcriptions, later rearranged and bound, the youthful Jefferson culled from his reading a storehouse of extracts from stories that he referred to and drew on for the rest of his life. (As will be seen, he later and poignantly shared this treasury with those closest to him.) The problem of dating a record so long in the making has complicated its use, but recently—through Douglas Wilson's careful sorting out in relation to a markedly changing handwriting pattern, as well as a systematic archaeology of the rearranged pages themselves—the entries have been shown to have a distinct stratigraphy.[11]

The earliest layer is a set of schoolboy and then college-student entries from the great classics—Virgil, Horace, Ovid, Cicero, and, since Greek had not been in the curriculum, Homer in Pope's translation. In this collection, dating from before 1763, when he turned twenty, the diligent student also transcribed extracts from Milton's great English epic poem, *Paradise Lost,* and from a collection of English poetic dramas, including some of Shakespeare.

The next layer dates from 1762 to 1766 and represents the cullings from the time when Thomas Jefferson had ceased to be a student at the College of William and Mary and had become an apprentice in law and affairs, working in his mentor George Wythe's Williamsburg law office. Since he was studying languages, the young scholar carefully collected a great number of short extracts from Euripides and Homer in the original Greek. The most extensive extracts made at this stage, however, were part of the thorough grounding in materialist philosophy that Jefferson was giving himself as he copied out long passages from Lord Bolingbroke's *Works.* Along with this materialist philosophy came a thoroughgoing skepticism toward the revealed religion of the Old and New Testaments.

There seems to have been a short interruption in the year or so around 1767 when Jefferson was admitted to the Bar and took up the practice of the law. In 1768, when he was turning from the low view of human nature presented by law practice in the courts, as he later told John Bernard, the young lawyer began a search for edification in poetry again. The next layer was thus made up of extracts in the learned languages and in English. At this time Jefferson included both classics and current literature, coming up to date with the then newly published works of Ossian and of Sterne. The collection of transcriptions was virtually complete by 1772, when Jefferson married and fully commenced housekeeping at Monticello. Only a tiny fraction of entries date unmistakably from that period and after.[12]

There is a problem in relating such an overview analysis of the literary commonplace book to our concern with discovering the stock of stories with which he was equipping himself for life. Onto the leaves of this book were copied out not stories but striking passages. Some of these—indeed, about a tenth overall, on a rough estimate—seem to be included mainly in order to record an admired turn of phrase; but the remainder do seem to indicate story-related topics, themes, or sentiments preoccupying the copyist. These have been analyzed in as systematic a way as I could devise. During the earlier schoolboy-and-student phase, from about 1758 to 1762, there is a strong concentration (20 to 30 percent) on the not unexpected themes (given the reading matter) of death, suffering, and stoic endurance. Equally unsurprising is a slightly smaller cluster (about another 20 percent) relating to honor, striving, comradeship, friendship, and betrayal. Much more noted by Jefferson biographers is a third group of transcriptions evaluating womankind—negatively in about four cases out of five! The collection of misogynous lines of poetry makes up nearly 20 percent of the whole. More striking, perhaps, is the low representation—only one or two in 163 entries—of the topos of love as an enthralling passion.

I shall analyze the next two "layers"—1762 to 1766 and 1767 to 1772—as a single phase. These were the years of Jefferson's young manhood when, school and college having been put behind him, he was finding his feet in the world. During this period the garnerings make thematic clusters of similar proportions to those of student days—except that themes of politics and justice edge in more certainly. It is also important to notice now a slight preponderance of positive evaluations of womankind and some probably significant images of conjugality in a household setting.

One literary sensation of the day—the works of the bard, Ossian—so caught Thomas Jefferson's imagination as to inspire a resolution to obtain and learn to read these epics in the original Gaelic. Ossian cannot be dismissed just because many have declared that the translations published by James Macpherson were a literary hoax. There are important questions to be raised: What kind of world was opened up by Ossian for the enraptured young Virginian? What led him to exclaim concerning these writings that "the tender, and the sublime emotions of the mind were never so finely wrought up by human hand"?[13]

The places invoked by the newly discovered and translated Celtic Homer were wild-Irish, Highland Scottish, and far Nordic scenes of "desart" heath and "shaggy mountains." Water was a powerful element there, whether "dark streams from high rocks" or "waves . . . on the deep," that "roll to the rocks." This rugged landscape probably contributed to Jefferson's very literary appreciation of Natural Bridge and was, it seems, later discovered by him in the drama of the confluence of the Shenandoah and the Potomac rivers, which he made the centerpiece of a famous chapter in his *Notes on the State of Virginia*.[14]

Since the imagery of Ossian had entered into Jefferson's sense of the mountain ranges beneath which he had been born, that same imagery may have played an important part in his most singular self-declaring, self-constructing actions—his building on a high summit. For a time rival mythologies vied in his imagination to supply the name of the place. "Monticello," the name that now stands uncontested, Jefferson apparently concocted on a trial basis. He probably adopted the form of the word from a usage found in his most revered model of classical correctness. Andrea Palladio had described his Villa Rotunda in the Vicenza as being situated on a rise that was washed by a little stream, or *fiumicello;* when the inventive young Virginian did what the Italian master could scarcely have imagined and built an estate house on a high, steep-sided eminence, he may have also taken this way of forming a diminutive and applied it to the Italian for mountain. But alternatives to this allusion to the Mediterranean still made claims on the imagination. In a visionary moment, Jefferson had proposed to associate the place with the Nottowa Indian name "Rowanty"; he had also been drawn toward the English romantic strain of landscape design with a proposed temple, grotto, and the designation "Hermitage" for his home. Because classicism ultimately, and perhaps predictably, prevailed, we cannot assume that Ossianic images of "light . . . when it shines thro' broken clouds, and the mist is on the hills" do not provide vital clues concerning Jefferson's unprecedented choice of a high and wild setting among "the oaks of the mountains" for his plantation house.[15]

The texts of Macpherson's Ossian worked more powerfully in their day because their language was both rhythmically and visually reminiscent of the King James Bible—somewhere between metrically lined verse and conventional prose. The epics themselves are introduced in frame narratives as told around the campfires of warriors and huntsmen; thence the stories move to fields of battle and to the hunting of the stags on moors and mountainsides. Only occasionally, and that mostly when the women appear, does action or narration move to the fortresses and feasting halls that are the homes of the heroes. "Fingal," the first of the epics, may be characterized as a story, woven of stories, of men's striving for glory at the cost of each others' lives—and so, of the widowing of their women. Like all these songs, "Fingal" comes from the harp of the old, blind Ossian, who has outlived his own sons and all the heroes of his epics. It is a sustained lament for a vanished age.[16]

In powerful allegories of an eighteenth-century North Atlantic world that combined heightened sensuality with an imperative toward individual competitive achievement, the heroes slay each other in combat with a gallant freedom from personal animosities. Thus there is consistently sustained the idealized ethos of male fraternity. The bards celebrate fallen foes equally with their own champions. (Enmity, jealousy and hate are found almost exclusively among the women—who may even fatally divide boon companions with their vindictive passions.) The hunt and the feast appropriately allow for shared companionship, a sacred setting aside of lethal contests. Significantly, women—"maids of the bow"—may partake of the hunt. But the women remain soft, "white bosomed" creatures; they seem to be needed in an ambiguous role, as strong givers of themselves. Thus the maid may don man's armor and even challenge a warrior, but her concealed feminine weakness will either be revealed by the wound she then sustains (sometimes in error, at her own lover's hand), or she may suddenly cast off the armor to reveal "the heaving of her breast." Love, in the world of this epic, is a fatal, phallic passion: if the maids are not mortally pierced by swords, spears, or arrows, they die of grief on the bodies of lovers slain in battle. Male potency is dependent on victory; the defeated warrior believes he may not go back to his wife.[17]

Thomas Jefferson's famous letter to the kinsman of James Macpherson, the celebrated discoverer and translator of Ossian—as well as the extracts in the commonplace book—suggest that Jefferson was strongly drawn to the nostalgia, to the renown that belonged to valiant contestants regardless of outcome, and to the instances of a tender passion kindled in the maiden's "secret soul." Perhaps above all he was drawn to the exemplification of the bardic art—the art of "the son of songs . . . of other years" that could call up such a romantically gendered world of content and companionship.[18]

A story fragment from the Roman poet, Horace, may also be quoted here. Significantly, in the period when he was approaching marriage and homemaking, the now-mature Jefferson transcribed the famous "Beatus ille . . ." verse of Horace that introduces the note of Georgic celebration of the rustic villa or "great-house" household. This confirmed classicist copied it all in Latin—except that he omitted the twist at the end that makes it a bitterly ironic story as told by a retired money lender! I abridge and quote it in English, because it is *such* a connubial household scenario for a young Southern gentleman:

> Happy the man who, far from business cares . . . works his ancestral acres with his steers, from all money-lending free. [He may idle in summer shade, or go hunting in winter.] But if a modest wife shall do her part in tending home and children dear, piling high the sacred hearth with seasoned firewood against the coming of her weary husband . . . and drawing forth . . . sweet vintage from the jar, prepare an unbought meal . . . what joy to see the sheep hurrying homeward . . . to see the wearied oxen [returning] . . . and the home-bred slaves, troop of a wealthy house, ranged around the gleaming Lares![19]

Thomas Jefferson not only practiced collecting stories in his young man-hood, he also preached the value of such an engagement. In the famous "new Rowanty" library-list letter of August 1771 with which this essay opened, he celebrated the moral value of stories: "Every thing is useful which contributes to fix us in principles . . . of virtue. . . . We never reflect whether the story . . . be truth or fiction. . . . The spacious field of imagination is thus laid open to our use, and lessons may be formed to illustrate and carry home to the mind every moral rule of life." [20]

CREATING STORIES

We receive stories before we can tell them. It would undermine the approach I am attempting here were I to make too sharp a distinction between the stories Jefferson collected for himself in a commonplace book, and those he set out actually to tell to others.

In my review of the few surviving writings of the young Thomas Jeffer-son before his marriage, I find about thirty stories told in some twenty-two personal letters surviving from the years up to 1771. (By lumping, split-ting, or discarding differently, another reader would certainly have a cor-respondingly smaller or larger tally, so I do not pretend to offer a hard statistic here!) Of the thirty, a little fewer than half, when categorized by theme and plot, turn on a self-mocking narration of disasters that have, it is laughingly suggested, threatened to overwhelm the "small hero" in some situation or another. In one case, where he has indeed contemplated the disaster of being rejected by the young lady who—so he has persuaded himself—is the love of his life, he offsets this self-mockery with a perhaps more serious story of life as a journey. "Perfect happiness," he suggests, was never intended by "the deity" to be the lot of any of his creatures, but, as this story-version philosophy continues, the Creator "has very much put in our [own] power the nearness of our approaches to happiness, by enabling us to fortify our minds against the attacks of . . . calamities and misfor-tunes." Understanding this, we should endeavor "to assume a perfect res-ignation . . . [so as] to consider that whatever does happen, must happen." In consequence we will be enabled to surmount . . . difficulties . . . to bear up with . . . patience . . . and to proceed with a pious and unshaken resignation till we arrive at our journey's end, where we may deliver up our trust into the hands of him who gave it, and receive such reward as to him shall seem proportioned to our merit." The solemnity of this stoic religios-ity is not out of character; but the jocularity of most of the treatment of mock-calamities was certainly revealing of the posture to the world that was adopted both by the storyteller at this stage of his life and by the group of companions with whom he shared prospects of what the world might hold for them.[21]

Thomas Jefferson's own story of himself and his chosen band of companions is even more tellingly declared in a smaller group of at least four implied narratives that project forward in time. It seems that this shy and awkward yet very sociable young man sought escape from present trials— including the uncertainties of courtship—through a kind of dream scenario. The vision evidently inspiring him was that he might so arrange things as to combine marriage with the continued close fellowship of at least one of the boon companions of his youth by forming a joint household that would extend the circle by including the wives in the company. Thus Jefferson wrote to his friend John Page, "Dear Page" (the form of intimate address they used and continued to use): "I think to build [in Williamsburg]. No castle though I assure you, only a small house . . . [with] a room for myself and another for you, and no more, unless Belinda [Rebecca Burwell] should think proper to favor us with her company, in which case I will enlarge the plan as much as she pleases." He developed the idea to William Fleming in a more comprehensive, evensided way a few months later: "You exchange your lands for Edgehill, or I mine for Fairfields [a Burwell estate], you marry S[uke]y P[otte]r, I marry R[ebecc]a B[urwel]l, [join] and get a pole chair and . . . keen horses, practise the law in the same courts, and drive to all the dances in the country together."[22]

Even after more than six years, this vision had not faded—although the nature of the activities that would give meaning to such a composite joint household had changed by the time Jefferson renewed the proposal. The renewal came in a letter of February 1770, with flirtatious words directed to John Page's wife, Frances, that seem to have gone unnoticed even by Jefferson's "intimate" biographer, Fawn Brodie. In this letter, shifting his address from John to Frances, Jefferson expressed the wish that he were not so committed in Albemarle as not to be able to set up near Rosewell— though he fancied that a divine prohibition has been placed, because "the gods . . . were apprehensive that if we were placed together we s[houl]d pull down the moon or play some devilish prank with their works." He regrets this denial of togetherness as he reflects "with pleasure on the philosophical evenings . . . passed at Rosewell." He "was always fond of philosophy," he teased, "even in its dryer forms, . . . [but] from a ruby [lip] it comes with charms irresistible." Historians and biographers—intimate and reverential alike—seem not only to have missed the flirtation here but also to have overlooked the announcement in Latin, a year ahead of the date for which they proclaim it in English, that, already in February 1770, Thomas Jefferson was once more in love. He had not only "become an advocate for the passion" as regards others, but was *coelo tactus*—"touched by heaven."

The next time he projected his recurrent story of the making of a place in the world—a place that will be an idealized commune of married companions—is in the invitation of August 1771, already quoted, that Robert Skipwith should come with his bride, Tibby, and join residence with the Jeffersons at a "new Rowanty" close by Monticello. Thomas, for his part, would bring Tibby's sister, Martha, as his bride; there they would all together pass evenings at the "centrically situated" spring on that mountainside![23]

Trying to understand the storying that made Monticello involves juxtaposing Jefferson's stories with those of others who helped make his world and who had different cultural imaginations of life. Where did the young Thomas Jefferson's recurrent aspiration for an extended communal household, made up of co-resident couples, come from? Since this kind of household was contrary to centuries-old English norms, may it not have come to him as a possibility unconsciously suggested by African stories, and indeed by the actual way of life in the slave quarters all around him? Certainly in this personal domestic vision, as in other matters of wider political implication, this singular Virginian seems to have begun to envisage a different future from the past that his ancestors had made, had known, and had storied.[24]

ENSLAVEMENT STORIES

Before we seek the larger meanings that situate Monticello, that storied mountaintop, in Thomas Jefferson's wider world, and before we seek the larger stories that he wrote in that world, there are two disturbing stories to be noted, projecting very different pasts and futures. Neither was in a personal letter. One he wrote probably without thinking to tell a story at all—though he paid for it to be printed on a page of the *Virginia Gazette* for September 7, 1769, and in subsequent weeks:

> Run away from the subscriber in *Albermarle,* a Mulatto slave called *Sandy,* about 35 years of age, his stature is rather low, inclining to corpulence, and his complexion light; he is a shoemaker by trade, in which he uses his left hand principally. . . . He is greatly addicted to drink, and when drunk is insolent and disorderly. . . . He carried his shoemakers tools,

and will probably endeavour to get employment that way. Whoever conveys the said slave to me in *Albermarle,* shall have 40s reward. . . .

—Thomas Jefferson[25]

The other story Jefferson produced only a little later. It appears within the narrative framework of his reports of cases in the General Court at Williamsburg. *Howell vs Netherland* was heard in April 1770. The story is of the begats, or rather conceptions, producing Samuel Howell, whose case, a freedom suit, Jefferson took without fee. Samuel's great-grandmother was a white woman who had a bastard daughter by a slave man. Under Virginia law this daughter was bound in servitude until the age of thirty-one; but, during her servitude she conceived and was delivered of Samuel's own mother, who in turn, during her own imposed thirty-one-year servitude, conceived and was delivered of Samuel Howell. Samuel was now suing his master for outright freedom without a requirement that he first serve out thirty-one years of bondage. Jefferson told this story in these terms: an "act of 1705 makes servants of the first mulatto, and that of 1722 extends it to her children"; but, he said, seeking to avert the story of enslavement that would otherwise be projected forward: "it remains for some future legislature, if any should be found wicked enough, to extend it to the grandchildren and other issue more remote." The court, scandalized perhaps by this impugning of the legislature, and by the preliminary reference to the "law of nature" under which "we are all born free," dismissed the case, leaving Samuel in servitude, and without hearing any further argument.[26]

These two Jefferson-engendered stories stand in the record in mute contradiction of each other. The story of Sandy the shoemaker, who meant to be free and to live by his trade in the kind of independence that Jefferson came to symbolize, was a story Jefferson told only incidentally as part of an attempt—in which he succeeded—to lock Sandy once more into servitude. (Sandy was sold three years later to the father of Jefferson's nephews, the terrible Isham and Lilburn Lewis.) The story of Samuel, on the other hand, Jefferson told only a few months later, with great rhetorical performance, in an attempt—which could *not* succeed—to release Samuel from a servitude he declared a violation of the law of nature itself. Both stories stand as contrasting stories to such delightful dream-narratives as charming philosophic evenings with gentlemen and ladies sharing sensibilities, or the nights of familial merriment by the fountain at "the new Rowanty." Jefferson had reason to know—though differently from the way we know and tell—that the stories that would actually shape Monticello on the mountaintop included those of the Sandys and the Samuels of his world.

MYTHOLOGIES OF PLACE

Meanwhile Monticello was already becoming a legendary place. Thomas Jefferson had scarcely moved up onto the hill and let it be known that he would marry and keep house there when the mythologizing by himself and others began. He evidently sent out, "in the Miltonic stile," a description—now lost—of his bride-to-be. This description induced Mrs. Drummond, a lively older woman friend in Williamsburg, to exclaim to Thomas in an animated letter: "Thou wonderful Young Man . . . I . . . think Spirits of an higher order, inhabits Yr Aery . . . Mountain." The same sense of the aura of the place soon became apparent in the recurrent calls from his male associates in statecraft for him to come down from his mountain. The questions return: What, we may ask, was the meaning of Jefferson's unprecedented and immensely costly move up and away from the river-system arteries of his world onto an uninhabited hilltop? What stories was he telling? What stories was he leaving and entering into with his successive namings of the place—Rowanty, The Hermitage, then Monticello? What were the stories for which the first Monticello was the architectural expression—the container, as it were? Already we see foreshadowed the recurrent, almost contradictory, attempts to create a place both of intimate domesticity and of more comprehensive sociability—attempts to project a place of contemplative retreat and of continuing resort.[27]

The making of Monticello as a place of story intensified as Thomas Jefferson took up residence at the site he was preparing up on the mountaintop. He felt celestial inspiration—being, as he had phrased it, *coelo tactus.* It had undoubtedly been in this state that Jefferson had, in August 1771, penned his "new Rowanty" letter. In the course of this same year Jefferson had written into the memorandum book, which he carried with him everywhere, an extraordinary outline of how he might imprint a rich design of stories upon the summit and slopes of his sacred mountain:

> Choose out for a Burying place some unfrequented vale in the park, where is, "no sound to break the stillness but a brook, that bubbling winds among the weeds; no mark of any human shape that had been there, unless the skeleton of some poor wretch, Who sought that place out to despair and die in." let it be among antient and venerable oaks; intersperse some gloomy evergreens. the area circular, abt. 6of. diameter, encircled with an untrimmed hedge of cedar, or a stone wall with a holly hedge on it in the center of it erect a small Gothic temple of antique appearance. . . . let the exit . . . look on a small and distant part of the blue mountains. in the middle of the temple an altar, the sides of turf,

the top of plain stone. very little light, perhaps none at all, save only the feeble ray of a half-extinguished lamp.[28]

He included also his thoughts about "the spring on the North side of the park" and its surrounds:

The ground above the spring being very steep, dig into the hill and form a cave or grotto. build up the sides and arch with stiff clay. cover this with moss. spangle it with translucent pebbles from Hanovertown, and beautiful shells from the shore at Burwell's ferry. pave the floor with pebbles. let the spring enter at a corner of the grotto, pretty high up the side, and trickle down, or fall by a spout into a basin, from which it may pass off through the grotto. the [statue] will be better placed in this. form a couch of moss. the English inscription will then be proper.

> Nymph of the grot, these sacred springs I keep,
> And to the murmur of these waters sleep;
> Ah! spare my slumbers! gently tread the cave!
> And drink in silence, or in silence lave![29]

As part of the same planning fantasy, he had written two epitaphs on the same page—a Latin one for his deceased sister Jane, and, in English, an "Inscription for an African slave," who yearns for his "Vanish'd shores . . . with golden fruitage crown'd," and rested with the assurance that "there the stern tyrant" will find fortunes reversed and himself a "suppliant," in a regained world that would be free of "raging strife."[30]

The grotto with fountain and statue was never made; the graveyard was in time prepared, but without a Gothic temple, a turf altar, or a half-extinguished lamp; and, as far as we know, no African slave was buried with the verse lament to mark the spot. The sensibility that had projected all these fantasies in the time of approaching marriage turned inward, with marriage itself, toward an intensely private devotion to domesticity—a devotion that set up in the young aspiring statesman a tension between public service and private retreat that has remained legendary from that time to this. With one poignant exception, noted below, written stories belonging to this marriage were systematically destroyed.

MEASURED IMPROVEMENT

The sense of place that had led the boy born at Shadwell to the mountaintop above and had sustained him there could not, however, be denied enduring forms of expression. That sense of place was declared supremely in the form of the house itself and in the landscape surround—including the ordered gardens that were both the sites of imposed grid-patterns and the object of intense series of recorded observations of seasonal rebirth in nature. There are implicit stories here of the Pythagorean mathematical-musical harmonies, renderable in pure architecture and measured forms. They had been brought from the Old World to this summit at the edge of "improved" America at a point where it came up to the ranges that marked off the unsubdued wilderness beyond. But the stories implicit in the first Monticello, and in its building and landscaping as actually executed, are deep-laid by comparison with the gaucheries of the projected templed and epitaphed graveyard or the grotto nymph speaking to the intruder through inscription.

There was, however, another kind of storying associated with the pre-paring of the ground and the building of Monticello. The creation of the actual burying place was, in time, told with what now seems startlingly prosaic factuality; this was so in spite of the fact that its construction was occasioned in 1773 by the death of young Thomas's companion from his school days, Dabney Carr. With Carr the mythologizing of the mountain-top as a place of destiny, the place of their shared last rest, had begun. Thomas Jefferson nevertheless wrote a cryptic calculus as he prepared to fulfill his boyhood pact with his friend: "2. hands grubbed the Graveyard 80 f. sq. = 1/7 of an acre in 3 1/2 hours so that one would have done it in 7 hours, and would grub an acre in 49 hours = 4 days."[31]

These measurings are stories of a kind that could easily be overlooked, they seem so prosaic to us. They certainly appear at odds with the overt plays of sensibility in the necromantic thematization of the projected bury-ing ground and in the personification of the hillside with the imagined nymph of the grotto. But there was an equally powerful imagination at work in the arithmetic as in the allegorical stories. Thomas Jefferson and his like-minded contemporaries were taking their places in a cosmopolitan world where gentry culture was becoming more bourgeois, and mercantile society was being increasingly gentrified. An age-old taboo against the involvement of elites in the productive activities that sustained them had broken down. There had opened to excited fantasies an enchanting prospect of a bountiful future. Many more or less leisured gentlemen—whose Latin education was deemed masculine precisely because of its discipline com-bined with the "hard" reasoning of logic and mathematics—now thrilled to the project of studying, measuring, and redesigning the work processes of women and men that had hitherto been shaped by the transmission of craft skills across countless generations.[32]

Thomas Jefferson was notable but not at all singular in his engagement in this great project of his age. His recorded measurements contained little workaday narratives that fascinated him on account of the precise form he gave them; they in turn told and foretold the encompassing story of mankind's "improvement." Thus there is, extending back to the time of the first preparations to build Monticello, a series of records of the observations and mechanical fantasies and projects of a kind that we would associate with a management consultant or engineer. We see repeatedly the work of a quantifying, rationalizing taskmaster; we see it in careful records and measurements, for instance, of how much earth could be dug per hour by women and men excavating a well or a cellar, or of how much more dirt could be carted away per hour using a two-wheeled rather than a single-wheeled barrow.[33]

As he made his dwelling on the mountaintop, Thomas Jefferson was indeed recording stories of progress—"improvement." He was doing this comprehensively in the proportions of his house, and in the notebooks that entered measurements of the building process, and in notes on the weather and the seasons in the garden. He was, at the same time, *not* writing lasting stories of the marriage relationship at the heart of the project. His most fulsome surviving declaration of his romantic passion for Martha came in the already quoted "new Rowanty" letter of August 1771 to his future brother-in-law. He sent greetings to his fiancée by asking the letter's recipient to "offer prayers for me too in that shrine to which, tho' absent, I pay continual devotion," and went on to declare, "In every scheme of happiness she is placed in the fore-ground of the picture, as the principal figure. Take that away, and it is no picture for me." Thereafter—upon his marriage— in his repeated declarations of his need to be at home giving care and company to his wife, and in all his reticences, he marked Monticello strongly as an example of the novel setting that was becoming increasingly prevalent in the North Atlantic world at this time—a household sentimentalized by the married couple at its center as the secluded domestic sphere of "home." This was indeed something new. Households from time out of mind before this had been the setting for the manifestation of the quality of the patriarch and for productive processes—including both the raising of offspring and the transacting of business—but as the special settings for a sanctified domesticity they were something new.[34]

A PLACE IN HISTORY

Other stories that came from the newly married Jefferson also defined Monticello as a place. These were very different from the stories of measurement, promising improvement, or of a withdrawal that signified domestic privacy. They were momentous writings coming down from the mountain that characterized Monticello by telling a story of the North American land and the repeopling of that land. When, in successive versions of increasing amplitude, Thomas Jefferson told of the settlement of Virginia and of British North America, he was implicitly indicating the kind of settlement—the kind of household—he too had made at his own place. He was scarce two years into his marriage, with Monticello still a cleared site, a pavilion and outhouses, when he first made public a story of the free settlement of the land by his British ancestors. The Albemarle "Resolutions," and then the Albemarle "Declaration of Rights," were drawn up by the master of Monticello, and were adopted by the freeholders at large of his county at courthouse meetings in 1774. By such stories Virginia patriots were rallying their countrymen in support of New England, where the "abominable" Acts of Parliament would close the port of Boston and overthrow the constitutional government of the Massachusetts Bay Colony.[35]

Convinced of the illegitimacy of the British Parliament's claims to exercise such powers over American places and institutions, Thomas Jefferson explained that, "from the origin and first settlement of these countries," the Parliament had no jurisdiction whatsoever. This was so, as he told it, because "our ancestors, before their emigration, were the free inhabitants of the British dominions in Europe, and possessed a right, which nature has given to all men . . . of going in quest of new habitation, and of there establishing new societies, under such laws as shall seem most likely to promote public happiness." All obligation to the government of their former homeland they left behind them, just as their own "Saxon ancestors" had done long before when they left "the North of Europe." Jefferson told his neighbors, his fellow patriots, and the world that "America was conquered, and her settlements made . . . at the expense of individuals, and not of the British public." This story was advanced in validation of the right of his peers to the land to which their ancestors had come, and where they had joined to establish new societies. "For themselves they fought, for themselves they conquered, and for themselves alone they have right to hold."[36]

From his elevated place on an outlier of the South West Mountains, Jefferson further told how "settlement having been thus effected in the wilds of America, the emigrants thought proper to adopt that system of laws, under which they had hitherto lived in the mother country." He went on to tell how they continued a union with that parent country only through "the same common sovereign." Thus Monticello was implicitly told to be a settlement on "conquered" land from out of "the wilds"—but held in legal title under the common-law system adopted in Virginia. On this account Thomas Jefferson, together with his fellow subjects, had still to address their sovereign king for remedies to the invasions of their rights, both natural and customary, made by the British Parliament. This was a story of his America—of Virginia and so of Monticello—which Jefferson set forth in 1774, and was one to which he strongly adhered despite his failure to get it adopted by his copatriots.[37]

Some two years later this story-telling lawgiver of Monticello came down from his mountain and traveled north to a meeting of delegates from the thirteen colonies in rebellion. There he developed with pathos a narrative of free settlers and their affectionate continuing association with the ruler and peoples of their former home country, until, after a long series of injuries and assaults, culminating in the invasions and provocations that were the "last stab to agonizing affection," the Americans were finally compelled "to renounce for ever these unfeeling brethren."[38]

REVEALING HIS STATE

Some five years after the Declaration, Thomas Jefferson wrote more fully the historical geography of Virginia. In the *Notes on the State of Virginia* he wrote a natural philosophy treatise that reviewed the place of America, and so of Monticello, in the world. The five years after 1776 at first brought honor and then crisis to the author of the Declaration as anguished choices about his commitments to household and state seemed in rapid succession to be forced upon and taken from him. From the very start of their keeping house together, Thomas and Martha's way of understanding marriage and the Monticello household as "home" set up a tension between public political engagement and private retired domesticity. But that tension was being racked to breaking point in the last months of the young governor's second term, as he both tried to cope with invasion and the military near-collapse of the Commonwealth, and to find philosophic solace in writing answers to a set of questions about Virginia that a French secretary of legation had sent him.[39]

Notes on the State of Virginia was the largest and most complex body of writings to come from the first Monticello household. As with the Declaration of Independence, the place in the world of the author on his mountaintop, and of his household, was powerfully suggested in the stories he told in the *Notes*. It is very hard, then, to know where to begin—with the epic natural philosophic panorama that Jefferson penned from his elevated observation point, or with the return of the repressed in the haunting of his pages by the peoples from whose destruction and from whose servitude his household and his Commonwealth had arisen.[40]

First let me broach the epic vision of the grandeur of a continent. The *Notes* were in part a defiant answer to the French naturalist, the Comte de Buffon, who had declared life to be on a shrunken scale in the Americas. Jefferson asserted the contrary: the continent was remarkable for the large size and the robustness of its natural "productions," most especially of the animal kind. Before Jefferson's proudly observant eyes, this great land was being opened for a fortunate posterity as determined explorers and settlers moved down the Ohio—"the most beautiful river on earth"—and out onto the great Mississippi.[41]

A vast hinterland was becoming available as thousands of British Americans crossed the Blue Ridge and Alleghany mountains. These were the very mountains upon one of whose outliers Jefferson had made his residence; these were the mountains that were made truly sublime by the great Natural Bridge to the south of him, and, to his north, by the awesome breach that brought the Shenandoah into the Potomac River and allowed both to issue onto the plains and to the sea. This was "one of the most stupendous scenes in nature" that he described with an adaptation of a passage from Ossian. Perhaps it was a commonplace theme about peasants, perhaps it was another sniper's shot in a little war of reprisal by the discomforted and outraged ex-governor against his own people in this aftermath of his seeming rejection, but he noted that "here, as in the neighbourhood of the natural bridge, are people who have passed their lives within half a dozen miles, and have never been to survey these monuments of a war between rivers and mountains, which must have shaken the earth itself to its center."[42]

RECALLING THE EXPELLED

In the *Notes,* Thomas Jefferson projected a story that, for him, legitimated the continued ruthless seizure of the great continent of North America. He foretold an inspiring future for the land as an expanded domain of virtue, guaranteed by the fact that it would be a farmers' republic, the vast inheritance of "those who labour in the earth the chosen people of God." Monticello, as a center of husbandry, was thus implicitly to be known as a certain kind of place, not just conquered but made wholesome. With all its like households, great and small, it was "the focus" in which God implants "substantial and genuine virtue," and "keeps alive that sacred fire, which otherwise might escape from the face of the earth."[43]

Within this mythos Monticello was an archetypal place in profound opposition to another archetypal place, the city that could never, for Jefferson, be on a hill. In consequence of the mercenariness of their sustaining manufacturers and commerce, cities and their "mobs" were like "sores" in the body of society. What Thomas Jefferson and countless like him saw as the limitless availability of land on the continent they were appropriating, sustained an imperative for him that America's "work-shops" must "remain in Europe." Farms and estate houses would be the centers of civilization in this new world.[44]

The continent, however, had been inhabited before the ancestors of Thomas Jefferson came. The boy from Shadwell had known of the sacred associations that the landscape of his birth had for the first people. In the *Notes* he told how, when he must have been about ten years old, a group of "Indians" had come "directly" to an old barrow, or burial mound, near the Rivanna River, "without any instructions or enquiry." It was remembered that they had "stayed . . . some time, with expressions . . . of sorrow," before they "returned to the high road, which they had left about half a dozen miles to pay this visit." A little later, as a student all agog at the experience, the young Jefferson had stored up the memory of the eloquence of the Cherokee chief, Ontasseté, making a farewell speech to his followers outside Williamsburg before embarking for England. Yet the same young man imprinted no lasting marks of remembrance of this past—still less attachment to it—in the planning, naming, and laying out of the first Monticello. His declared attachment there was to the Old World—a discovered realm of Italian music, art, and literature. Even in the new slave quarter down by the mill weir, which Jefferson named Lego after a fabled waterland in Ulster, it was not the speech of Ontasseté, but the epics of Ossian that Jefferson recalled.[45]

As he wrote in 1780–81, however, Governor Jefferson was wrestling both with an intractable situation in his war-torn state and with the already noted belittlement of his native continent by the Comte de Buffon, who was considered the greatest writer of his day on natural history. The patriotic American natural philosopher now needed to identify and make common cause with the same Indians whose conquest he had emphasized in the polemics of 1774 with the British. Jefferson now needed to declare these aboriginal inhabitants to be as emblematic of the vigor of the New World as the convulsed mountains, the great rivers, and the large animals among its natural productions.

Thomas Jefferson contested Buffon's account of the Indians. He denied they were physically and sexually deficient, undermotivated, brutish beings without real human sensibility. Instead, Jefferson advanced an epic portrait of the typical man of the indigenous race as so "brave . . . that he will defend himself against a host of enemies, always choosing to be killed, rather than to surrender." Furthermore, Jefferson asserted of the Indian, "He is affectionate to his children," and "his affections comprehend his other connections," so that "his friendships are strong and faithful," and "his sensibility is keen, even the warriors weeping most bitterly on the loss of their children." He went on to make famous, with all the pathos he could manage, the story of the Mingo chief Logan and his lament for his family, the victims of white American aggression.[46]

As Jefferson affirmed the sensibilities of the Indians, he was still assuredly painting the portrait of the savage. "The women," he asserted, unconscious of the irony made by Monticello work practices, "are submitted to unjust drudgery." The master of Monticello was here making an important declaration: he was telling a foundation story of the meaning of his marriage to Martha, and of what assuredly he told himself he did for her: "This [drudgery of women] I believe is the case with every barbarous people. With such, force is law. The stronger sex therefore imposes on the weaker. It is civilization alone which replaces women in the enjoyment of their natural equality. . . . [and] first teaches us to subdue the selfish passions, and to respect those rights in others which we value in ourselves." In a further, equally celebrated passage, Jefferson declared the moral superiority of Indians, living, as he believed, in almost crime-free societies without ever "having . . . submitted themselves to any laws, any coercive power, any shadow of government," in a way of life where "their only controls are their manners," that is, their customs. On the basis of observations and reflections, he pronounced this to be undoubtedly a mode of social existence preferable to that governed by "too much law, as among the civilized Europeans"; under the Indian scheme of things, "the sheep are happier of themselves, than under care of the wolves."[47]

But when Jefferson wrote the *Notes,* the Indians were long gone from the surrounds of Monticello, and the story that his text unfolded of the future greatness of America as a virtuous farmers' republic silently but relentlessly continued the story of these Indians' dispossession. The possibility, necessity, and thus legitimacy of continually expanding the farmers' territory lay in the blandly revealed assumption that—as he put it—"we have an immensity of land courting the industry of the husbandman." Thus was Monticello a place within the forward-directed story of an idealized Anglo-

Saxon future. That this vision was, however, haunted by a knowledge of the forcible dispossession of former inhabitants is shown both by Jefferson's earliest blunt references to "conquest" in the *Summary View* of 1774, and by his deletion in the draft for the *Notes* of a reference to the way the now-emphasized purchases from the Indians had admittedly been made "with the price in one hand, and a sword in the other." [48]

PLANNING AN EXPULSION

There arose another specter, however, far more troubling to the author on the little summit of the South West Mountains. Monticello, and all but the smallest farm households around it, lived more by the husbandry of Africans and the descendants of Africans than by the labors of Anglo-Saxons. This was not just a haunting memory but a massive reality in the everyday life of all these households. It is not surprising therefore that Jefferson told also in the *Notes* strong stories about African peoples. It is striking that, directing his gaze now upon what was and what should be, he did not retell the story with the pathos that he had written in Philadelphia about "the war upon humanity itself" that had caused the Africans to be violently seized, that had made them slaves, and that had led them to be brutally transported to America. Instead he shifted the pathos, and told as a story of the present his famous scenario of the "unhappy influence on the manners of our people produced by the existence of slavery among us." As we shall see, Jefferson denied the cultural enrichments available from growing up in such complex households as Shadwell and Tuckahoe; he told instead the fable of moral degeneracy that met the needs of his case. The African past with its violent seizures was avoided; the present locked-together condition of masters and slaves was told with terrible, knowing certainty; equally certain was the future that lay in store, if the destructive commerce of despotism and degradation could not be halted. The story foretold, if history were left to run its course, was for Jefferson the most terrible imaginable: it was of nothing less than the enslavement of the whites by the blacks. [49]

There was real urgency, then, in the story of what might yet be done and in the legitimating of the solution proposed. Here, however, Jefferson was confronted with his greatest uncertainties. The story he wanted to foretell of the only possible "resolution" may explain why he did not retell the story of the forceful seizure and expatriation of the African ancestors of the slaves. For all its professed benign intentions, the enforced resettlement of the African-Americans that Jefferson insisted upon for the future was a recapitulation of that original story of seizure, separation, and expulsion. The necessity for Virginia's natural and moral philosopher to explain and justify his proposal involved him in the great perplexities of a painful review of his slaves' attributes. These "blacks" or "negroes," it seemed, were not to be known by following them back to Africa to seek the analogues of the small societies whose functioning provided the conclusive evidence of the full human sensibility of "the Indians." The Africans were, alas, followed back to their origins in the notorious sexual fantasy of the "Oranootan," whose lust for black women was considered by Jefferson to be analogous to the lust of black men for white women.[50]

In the end, after much tortured reasoning from his own "observations" and from what he had learned out of the stories of slavery among the Greeks and Romans, Jefferson—as is notorious—decided, on the one hand, that there was a probability of an inferiority in "the negro" as to "the faculties of reason and imagination." On the other hand, he affirmed that he found among the African-Americans around him "numerous instances of the most rigid integrity, and as many as among their better instructed masters of benevolence, gratitude, and unshaken fidelity." On the grounds of this aptitude for benevolence, this moral responsiveness, Jefferson insisted on the humanity that the blacks shared with the whites and on their claim to moral equality. But his story of an imaginable future reflected vehemently his insistence that such equality be realized within a framework of segregation.[51]

In his review of the faculties of the slaves, Jefferson wrote a denial of the oral-cultural storied richness of the households of his upbringing. In the same narration, Jefferson gathered from his literary sensibilities the basis of a strong affirmation of the superiority of the matrimonial household he had constructed on his mountaintop. We have seen how the Indian women, like all "barbarians," were contrasted with the women of his own people, whom "civilization" had contrived to "replace in the enjoyment of their natural equality." This crucial contrast between whites and Indians was linked to a philosophic pronouncement quoted from Buffon. The Count held that "the most precious spark of the fire of nature" derived from an "ardor for females" that produced "the most intimate of all ties, the family connection," and ultimately, "by extension love for . . . fellow men." Jefferson quite evidently told the same story of the foundation of society but he vehemently asserted that the Indians had not been left out of this process.[52]

Such stories of society's fundamentals were commonplace, being almost the secular religion of the literate elite of Jefferson's day. We can only watch appalled as we see how he took them and adapted them to deny the African part of his upbringing and, at the same time, justify his proposed expulsion of the bearers of African dances, songs, and stories from his America:

> The Indians [he wrote] . . . astonish you with strokes of the most sublime oratory. . . . But never yet could I find that a black had uttered a thought above the level of plain narration. . . . Misery is often the parent of the most affecting touches in poetry—Among the blacks is misery enough, God knows, but no poetry. Love is the peculiar oestrum of the poet. Their love is ardent, but it kindles the senses only, not the imagination. Religion indeed has produced a Phyllis Whately, but it could not produce a poet.

In a few lines, Jefferson had denied their stories to the African Virginians of all his households. (Perhaps his dismissive reference to "Religion" shows that he had some inkling of the powerful presence of what he denied.) In the same lines he had written over the top of that repressed African imagination—over the remembered sounds indeed of his childhood—the compressed but unmistakable story of his cherished "inner" conjugal household. Refined and refining love were denied to the African Monticellans. Yet refined and refining love were what made Monticello an idealized center of all that was most civilized in the world—an estate house distanced from, and in moral opposition to, the city and its corruptions.[53]

ENDING AND LIVING ON

Let me now present two stories that both bring closure to what I have discerned as the first Monticello. As Martha Jefferson lay dying in September 1782, family tradition has it that she began to write out sentimental words to express a sense of the situation. She wrote, copying from her devoted husband's own literary commonplace book, these lines originally adapted from Laurence Sterne's *Tristram Shandy:* "Time wastes too fast: every letter I trace tells me with what rapidity life follows my pen, the days and hours of it are flying over our heads like clouds of [a] windy day never to return—more every thing presses on—"

Report has it that at this point she could write no more. The copying continues in Thomas's hand: "and every time I kiss thy hand to bid adieu, every absence which follows it, are preludes to that eternal separation which we are shortly to make!" Thomas kept that scrap of paper, wrapped around a lock of Martha's hair till the end of his days; it was almost the only writing by Martha he did not deliberately destroy.[54]

On November 26, 1782, Jefferson wrote to the Marquis de Chastellux, the same Frenchman whose recollection of his visit to Monticello in the spring of that year I quoted at the outset: "Your letter, for too long unanswered," he explains, "found me a little emerging from that stupor of mind which had rendered me as dead to the world as she was whose loss occasioned it." He went on, "Before that event my scheme of life had been determined. I had folded myself in the arms of retirement, and rested all the prospects of future happiness on domestic and literary objects. A single event [Mrs Jefferson's death] wiped away all my plans and left me a blank. . . . In this state an appointment from Congress found me[,] requiring me to cross the Atlantic. . . . I accepted the appointment and my only object now is . . . to hasten over those obstacles which would retard my departure." [55] Martha Jefferson's death had brought to a close the storying that sustained his first Monticello; it released Thomas Jefferson for a vigorous career as a statesman of two hemispheres and as the foremost politician in the emergent United States of his day. His return and long, last residence there would make Monticello supremely, but in a different way, a place in American history.

The story of the place had been intimated in the waverings over naming and the associations that would go with that. These names—for a moment "Rowanty," then, it seems, "The Hermitage," and then enduringly "Monticello"—evoked a sequence of identifications—fleetingly with a native American domain, then more substantially with English romantic landscaping, and at last, decisively, with a classicism that would be the mold Thomas Jefferson wanted to set for the agrarian republic he would commit his life to creating.

In the household that had been the first Monticello, we may see the contrarieties in the place and in the man who had ordained it. Looking into the future, Thomas Jefferson told a story, and inscribed its principles, to give direction to the American dream, the American quest for equality. But his story reflected the enduring injustices of his own and his nation's colonizing origins. His farmer's republic could only sustain itself in the South by continuing enslavement; it could only extend itself across the continent by the violent dispossession of the aboriginal inhabitants, the "Indians," whose nobility and customary forms of community Jefferson had celebrated. As regards the women at the heart of the kind of place he most needed Monticello to be—an anticity, a rural retreat enfolding refined familial love—he both insisted that they be accorded their "natural equality" and that they find their lives and their selves in serving men. His whole system was designed in the unexamined logic of his stories. [56]

The great extended-family household of the United States of America can best claim its Jeffersonian legacies by uniting the grand story Thomas Jefferson told with the stories of the "unequals" that he denied. Only in a new history, a great set of diverse and shared stories that bring all, acknowledged equally, into "the family," can the nation properly find in Monticello a shrine for itself as a whole. Meanwhile, Jeffersonian principles stand as a perduring expression of the highest collective aspirations of the nation, while the confounding inequalities of his own and our present times remain a constant admonition that the revolutionary struggle is always to be kept up. Thomas Jefferson commemorations will lose their occasion if they fall to praising or blaming the great proclaimer of the founding story and its projected vision. Rather, it must be avowed that his predicament is still the nation's: the predicament of being enmeshed in forms of systematic injustice that seem forever to require radical redress.

NOTES

I wish to thank La Trobe University, especially the history department and its current chairperson, Judith Richards, for the facilities that have enabled this essay to be prepared and completed. Laraine Dumsday in our office and Pat Bates in the Borchardt Library have also been most helpful, with unfailing generosity. I wish also to acknowledge the support of the Rutgers Center for Historical Analysis in providing an extended opportunity for the interdisciplinary exploration of issues of identity to which this essay relates. Colleen Isaac has read, searched, and enthusiastically discussed Jeffersonian and other documentation for this essay. Ms. Cinder Stanton of Monticello has taken time and trouble, well beyond any call of duty, to help me with records and to share her own insightful work on the worlds of Monticello with me. The following have read drafts and helped with encouragement and advice: A. L. Becker, Inga Clendinnen, Greg Dening, Lyn Isaac, Donna Merwick, Bernard Newsome, and Bill Taylor.

I first came to Virginia history through the commencement of a study of Thomas Jefferson in the Atlantic Revolution. In the late sixties I read the early volumes of the Julian Boyd edition of the *Papers* and Gilbert Chinard's editions of the two so-called Commonplace Books. I eagerly read Dumas Malone's first Jefferson volume and seized upon Merrill Peterson's single-volume biography, when it came out in 1970. I understood Bernard Bailyn's paradigm-making work on the ideology of the Revolution to be, above all, an explication of the political world view expressed in the Declaration of Independence. But I found myself drawn from a study of Jefferson to a study of his Virginia world through its religious and political revolutions. Now I have come back to Jefferson study, finding myself with much changed perspectives on Virginian, American, and North Atlantic history. How could it be otherwise? Have we not been through several undeclared wars and their politics, the long aftermaths of civil-rights and affirmative-action campaigns, and the spectacular rise of transformative new versions of what history might be? During the last twenty years, the new cliometric and ethnic-diversity cultural histories have put Jefferson studies in an entirely different set of frames. His world is quite differently known since we have had the works of

Alan Kulikoff and the Annapolis Hall of Records team, as well as of Albert J. Raboteau and all historians of the African-American cultural tradition. Spanning overview history and an individual's recorded experience, Garry Wills has displayed the philosophic literary culture of the age of Jefferson in a spell-binding exegesis of Jefferson's Declaration of Independence, while Douglas Wilson has shown new possibilities in the systematic editorial presentation of the documents that record Thomas Jefferson's early engagement with ancient and modern poets, playwrights, and philosophers.

I have tried to write this exploration of the ways that Monticello came to be imagined, sustained, and mythologized as a kind of place in the world, so as to declare in the presentation what have been my most immediate sources for the understandings of culture and folklore that I have drawn on, and the nature of the records that have allowed me to overhear something of what was being told in and from that chosen mountaintop. The notes that follow will particularize the references in the customary way.

1. Boyd, I, 78. "Rowanty" was a Native American name associated with Skipwith's own plantation. Andrew Burstein has traced its actual origins and shown that it can hardly relate to Mesopotamian mythology, as the editors of the *Jefferson Papers* had supposed (Boyd, I, p. 81). See Burstein, "The Well-Ordered Dreamworld," draft dissertation chapter, History Department, University of Virginia, pp. 12–13.

2. Merrill D. Peterson, ed., *Visitors to Monticello* (Charlottesville, Va., 1989), p. 13.

3. The concept that we *are,* in some sense, the stories we have, has been given important constructive use in feminist scholarship, especially by Carolyn G. Heilbrun, *Writing a Woman's Life* (New York, 1988). For a recent systematic review of the place of narrative in knowledge and an invaluable overview of the rapidly growing literature, see Jerome Bruner, "The Narrative Construction of Reality," *Critical Inquiry,* 18 (1991), pp. 1–21. I am grateful to Bernard Newsome for calling this essay to my attention.

4. John Gillis, unpublished paper, 1991.

5. Jefferson's major biographers have not reviewed the possible emotional disturbances arising from the baby Thomas's displacement as eldest son and his finding himself living in the house owned by his supplanter. The subject was, however, addressed decades ago in H. J. Eckenrode, *The Randolphs: The Story of a Virginia Family* (New York, 1946), p. 148; and more recently in Gisela Tauber, "Thomas Jefferson: Relationships with Women." *American Imago,* 43 (1988), pp. 440–42.

6. At the time of Peter Jefferson's death, sixty slaves were listed in his inventory, but no white indentured servants. ("Inventory and Appraisement of the Estate of Peter Jefferson Esqr. deceased lying in the Rivanna river and its branches," April 13, 1758, Albermarle County Will Book II, pp. 41–47.) I have assumed that he might have owned little more than half that number of slaves thirteen years earlier, when Thomas was born and the household building and capital accumulation were at an early stage.

7. The memory of the ride during infancy is recorded in Henry S. Randall, *The Life of Thomas Jefferson* (New York, 1858), I, p. 11. Isaac Jefferson's reminiscence of Randolph Jefferson is reprinted in James A. Bear, Jr., ed., *Jefferson at Monticello* (Charlottesville, Va., 1967), p. 22. For the songs and stories learned and recorded by Thomas Jefferson's daughter, see Elizabeth Langhorne, "Black Music and Tales from Jefferson's Monticello," *Folklore and Folklife in Virginia,* 1 (1979), pp. 60–67. Langhorne includes the translations I have used from the only surviving version of Martha Jefferson Randolph's collection of this material, as published in Eugene A. Vail, *De la litterature et des hommes de lettres des Etats Unis d'Amerique* (Paris, 1841). I am indebted to Mechal Sobel for sending me a copy of the relevant pages of this rare book.

8. Albert J. Raboteau, Jr., *Slave Religion: The "Invisible Institution" in the Antebellum South* (New York, 1978), p. 11 and passim.

9. I have been greatly helped in an appreciation of Virginia folklore, including that of white folk, by the readiness of Thomas Barden to share with me his work, *Virginia Folk Legends* (Charlottesville, Va., 1991), while still in manuscript form. I have also made preliminary analyses of the folk ballads published in Arthur Kyle Davis, ed., *Traditional Ballads of Virginia, Collected Under the Auspices of the Virginia Folk-Lore Society* (Reprint; Charlottesville, Va., 1969). For a recollection of the vitality of these traditions in Tidewater Virginia at the time of Thomas Jefferson's birth, see Devereux Jarratt, *The Life of the Reverend Devereux Jarratt* (Baltimore, Md., 1806; Reprint, New York, 1969), p. 16.

10. On the introduction to books that the young Jefferson may have had from his father see Randall, *Jefferson,* p. 14. This, the westward engagement of the imagination, and other subjects relating to Jefferson's early life are very effectively attended to in John Dos Passos, *The Head and Heart of Thomas Jefferson* (London, 1955), pp. 27–43.

11. Douglas L. Wilson, ed., *Jefferson's Literary Commonplace Book, The Papers of Thomas Jefferson,* second series (Princeton, 1989). I have made a preliminary analysis of themes and implied stories from which to calculate approximate percentage proportions of each found in the different time layers of the stratigraphy.

12. Ibid., p. 8. Wilson refers to John Bernard's report of Jefferson's recollection of the process by which he (Jefferson) incorporated literary stories in his make-up; it is worth quoting in full. "'I was bred,' said he, 'to the law; that gave me a view of the dark side of humanity. Then I read poetry to qualify it with a gaze upon its bright side; and between the two extremes I have contrived through life to draw the due medium. And so,' he continued, 'substituting history and biography for law, I would have every man form his own estimate of human nature, because it seems to me that precisely the same directing forces should subsist in the social as in the solar system; there should be the same attractive or concentrating power in our hearts to draw us together qualifying the repelling impulse which we gain from our experience and reading.'" John Bernard, *Retrospections of America, 1797–1811* (Reprint; New York, 1969), pp. 238–39.

13. TJ to Charles Macpherson, Feb. 25 1773, *Boyd,* I, pp. 96–97. Dumas Malone seems to have avoided discussion of the Ossianic epics because he believed them fraudulent. See *Malone,* I, 392. This is not the place to enter the continuing debates on Macpherson's celebrated publications, beyond an affirmation that he does seem to have had a powerful knowledge of Gaelic originals. See Fiona J. Stafford, *The Sublime Savage: A Study of James Macpherson and the Poems of Ossian* (Edinburgh, 1988).

14. The quotations are from Jefferson's transcriptions; see Wilson, ed., *Literary Commonplace Book,* pp. 144, 150, 142, 151, 143. On the dating of the earliest references to Monticello by that name and the inscribing and deletion of the alternative name, see Douglas Wilson, "Thomas Jefferson's Early Notebooks," *WMQ,* 42 (1985), p. 437.

15. Andrea Palladio, *I quattri libri dell' architettura* (Venice, 1570), II, p. 58. I was led to this passage by a reference in L. S. Goodwin, "Interim Report [on the name 'Monticello']," Research Department, Monticello, Charlottesville, Va. The Ossian phrases are from Wilson, ed., *Literary Commonplace Book,* pp. 151, 143.

16. On the diction of "Fingal" and the other epics see Stafford, *Sublime Savage,* pp. 89–92. "Fingal" was first published in 1763; I have only had ready access to it in William Sharp, ed., *The Poems of Ossian* (Edinburgh, 1926).

17. Sharp, *Ossian,* pp. 89, 74, 97. For an episode in which a spiteful woman makes comrades fight to the death, see pp. 57–59. For the castrated impotence of the defeated warrior unable to return to his wife, see pp. 84, 103.

18. Wilson, *Literary Commonplace Book,* p. 144.

19. Ibid., pp. 139–40.

20. TJ to Robert Skipwith, Aug. 3, 1771, *Boyd,* I, pp. 77–78.

21. TJ to John Page, July 15, 1763, *Boyd,* I, p. 10. The self-mocking reference to the "misadventures" of a "small hero" is taken, not surprisingly, from Lawrence Sterne, *The Life and Opinions of Tristram Shandy,* Book I, chapter V (1759).

22. TJ to John Page; Oct. 7, 1763; TJ to Fleming, [Oct. 1763], ibid., pp. 11, 12.

23. TJ to John Page, Feb. 21, 1770, ibid., p. 36. The letter began, "Dear Page," but an important switch is made early in the second paragraph when Jefferson, having scolded John for not writing, solicits a correspondence from "my friend Mrs Page," and then either switches his address to her or includes her in it, at least until the point where he writes: "I do not mean, madam, to advise him [Fons, or James Fontaine] against it [being in love]. On the contrary I am become an advocate for the passion: for I too am coelo tactus." A line or so later he switches back to a primary address to the husband, "Page." Incidentally, the alternation of address, now to gentleman, now to lady reader, is a whimsy that could also have been taken up from Sterne's *Tristram Shandy. Malone,* I, p. 157, cites a letter of Feb. 20, 1771, as though he takes it to be Thomas's first reference to his courtship of Martha. In *Thomas Jefferson and the New Nation* (New York, 1970), p. 27, Merrill D. Peterson refers to the fall of 1770 as the commencement of the courtship, presumably dating it back from the February 1771 letter. Fawn Brodie, *Thomas Jefferson: An Intimate History* (New York, 1974), p. 80, in a remarkably perfunctory treatment of the courtship, seems to date its beginning in the same way, and shows no indication of having searched the documents for earlier traces.

24. For a systematic exploration of African-American cultural input into the Virginia and Southern culture of whites and blacks both, see Mechal Sobel, *The World They Made Together: Black and White Values in Eighteenth-Century Virginia* (Princeton, 1987).

25. *Boyd,* I, p. 33, where the subsequent sale of Sandy to Colonel Charles Lewis, Jan. 29, 1773, is also noted. In 1811, in Livingston County, Kentucky, Colonel Lewis's sons, Lilburne and Isham, brutally murdered Lilburne's seventeen-year-old slave, George. For an account of this terrible story, which brought forth within his own close kin circle all of Thomas Jefferson's most fearful nightmares about slavery, see Robert Penn Warren, *Brother to Dragons: A Tale in Verse and Voices* (New York, 1953). See also Boynton Merrill, Jr., *Jefferson's Nephews: A Frontier Tragedy* (Princeton, 1976), pp. 256–302.

26. Howell v. Netherland, April 1770, in *Ford,* I, p. 481. For a brief account of this case see *Malone,* I, pp. 121–22.

27. Mrs. Drummond to TJ, March 12 [1771], *Boyd,* I, p. 65.

28. This passage and most of the succeeding plans for allegorical landscaping of Monticello were published in Edwin M. Betts, ed., *Thomas Jefferson's Garden Book, 1766–1824* (Philadelphia, 1944), pp. 25–27. Jefferson has quoted from Nicholas Rowe, *The Fair Penitent* (1703); he had also transcribed it into his literary notebook. See Wilson, *Literary Commonplace Book,* 141.

29. Betts, *Garden Book,* pp. 26–27. The verse—which had already been given by Jefferson in Latin—was translated into English by Alexander Pope. See James A. Bear Jr., and Lucia C. Stanton, eds., *Jefferson's Memorandum Books: Accounts with Legal Records and Miscellany, 1767–1826, The Papers of Thomas Jefferson,* second series (Princeton, N.J., forthcoming).

30. There are stories about the recovery of stories! For some reason, Betts silently omitted the "Inscription for an African Slave" from his reproduction of the landscaping text. I found it when I went to a microfilm of the original (which is held in the Massachusetts

Historical Society) in search for the drawing, which he noted but did not reproduce. Bear and Stanton, *Jefferson's Memorandum Books* identify the "Inscription" as from William Shenstone's "Elegy XX."

31. Betts, *Garden Book,* p. 40. On the boyhood pact, see *Malone,* I, p. 161.

32. For a fuller statement of the argument concerning the bourgeois character of production-improvement concerns among the Virginia gentry and in the Atlantic world at large, see Rhys Isaac, "Imagination and Material Culture: The Enlightenment in a Mid-Eighteenth-Century Virginia Plantation," in Anne Elizabeth Yentsch and Mary C. Beaudry, eds., *The Art and Mystery of Historical Archaeology: Essays in Honor of James Deetz* (Boca Raton, Fla., 1992), pp. 401–23. See also Garry Wills, *Inventing America: Jefferson's Declaration of Independence* (New York, 1978), pp. 111–31.

33. Betts, *Garden Book,* pp. 16, 17, 33. For deep insights into the significance of such measurement-orientation in relation to changing epistemes or paradigms of knowledge, see the very important Atlantic, Pacific, and American cultural history in Greg Dening, *Mr. Bligh's Bad Language: Passion, Power, and Theatre on the Bounty* (New York, 1992), pp. 133–40 and passim. Certainly anyone who wants to understand some of the 1770s significance of building a house as a point from which to view should read Dening on the dramatization of perspective; see especially pp. 295–96 and 372–74.

34. The rise in Virginia of the ethos that idealized busy, populous households as "homes" set apart as places of conjugal affection is richly traced and interpreted in Jan Lewis, *The Pursuit of Happiness: Family and Values in Jefferson's Virginia* (New York, 1983). See also Rhys Isaac, *The Transformation of Virginia, 1740–1790* (Chapel Hill, N.C., 1982), pp. 70–74; 302–5.

35. *Boyd,* I, pp. 117–120.

36. *Boyd,* I, pp. 121–22.

37. *Boyd,* I, p. 122.

38. The pathos and sensibilities that gave the "Declaration of Independence" its meaning and power for Thomas Jefferson are wonderfully expounded in Wills, *Inventing America.* The quotation will be found in *Boyd,* I, p. 427; it is from a part of Jefferson's draft for the Declaration that was, to his lasting regret, struck out from the official version adopted by Congress; see Wills, *Inventing America,* pp. 312–16.

39. I have used the standard scholarly edition: William Peden, ed., *Notes on the State of Virginia* (Chapel Hill, N.C., 1955).

40. The issue of the remembrance by invading settlers of the first people of a land has hounded me, too, as an Australian. I was further advanced in my understanding of this important subject by reading and discussing with its author, Gesa Mackenthun, "Captives and Sleepwalkers: The Ideological Revolutions of Post-Revolutionary Discourse," paper presented to the 6th Biennial Symposium of the Milan Group in Early U.S. History, Milan, June 19–23, 1992. I am grateful also therefore to Professor Loretta Valz-Minucci for arranging this wonderful conference on memory in history and inviting me to participate.

41. Peden, *Notes,* pp. 48–58; quotation, 10.

42. Ibid., pp. 19–20. I find that Douglas Wilson has already noticed the parallels between the "war between rivers and mountains," as here described by Jefferson, and Ossian's description of an attacking army that was among the first passages of the bard to be transcribed by Jefferson; Wilson, *Literary Commonplace Book,* p. 143.

43. Peden, ed., *Notes,* pp. 164–65.

44. Ibid. For Jefferson, Monticello was a distinctive kind of place—an "anti-city." Anglo-Saxon culture has entered perhaps reluctantly into the imagery of Jerusalem and of Rome, and has persistently seen cities as places of evil rather than of highest aspiration. In

this respect, as in so many others, Jefferson and Virginia were more prophetic of the U.S. culture that was to come than were John Winthrop and New England. (On the very different approach to the land of North America by Continental Europeans who strongly idealized city life, see the important work of Donna Merwick, *Possessing Albany, 1630–1710: The Dutch and English Experiences* (New York, 1990), especially pp. 3–7, 120–33, 139–45, 220–58, and passim.

45. Peden, ed., *Notes,* p. 100. For the young student Jefferson's strong impressions of Ontasseté, see *Malone,* I, pp. 60–61. On Lego and other place names on the Monticello estate, see Lucia C. Stanton, "The Research File: What's in a Name?" *Monticello Newsletter,* Spring 1992. I am grateful to Ms. Stanton for her help with this. In the later Monticello the entrance hall was turned into what Jefferson called an "indian Hall," on account of the conspicuous display of artifacts; see TJ to Meriwether Lewis, Oct. 20, 1806, in *Ford,* X, pp. 295–96.

46. Peden, ed., *Notes,* pp. 59–60, 62–63.

47. Ibid., pp. 60, 93.

48. Ibid., p. 164. The deletion of the phrase about violent enforcement of sales is noted on p. 281, n4.

49. Ibid., pp. 162, 163. On the story of King George III's war against humanity itself, see Wills, *Inventing America,* pp. 65–75. At the end of the twentieth century, we are well placed to see how well-founded were the fears that made Jefferson say, "Indeed I tremble for my country." Continued attachment to slavery occasioned a terrible blood-letting in the Civil War. In 1811 Jefferson himself, was forced to witness, in the atrocity committed by his own sister's sons, Lilburne and Isham Lewis—offspring of the recaptured Sandy's new master—a fearful demonstration of the brutalizing effects of slavery on the masters. There seems still no end in sight to the legacies of violence. See note 25, above.

50. Peden, ed., *Notes,* p. 138. The plan for expulsion, transportation, and resettlement is outlined on pp. 137–38.

51. Ibid., pp. 138, 142–43.

52. Ibid., pp. 58–59, 60.

53. Ibid., p. 140.

54. *Boyd,* VI, pp. 196–97.

55. TJ to Marquis de Chastellux, Nov. 26, 1782, *Boyd,* VI, pp. 203–4.

56. "It is civilization alone which replaces women in the enjoyment of their natural equality," Peden, ed., *Notes,* 60. For a clear outline of Jefferson's assignment of gender roles, see Jan Lewis, chapter 4.

"The Blessings of Domestic Society"

Thomas Jefferson's Family and the Transformation of American Politics

JAN LEWIS

Why would Thomas Jefferson's family be interesting to those who are reflecting upon the Jeffersonian legacy? When Jefferson wrote his epitaph, he nowhere mentioned his own family or the families of his fellow Americans: he wanted to be remembered as the "Father of the University of Virginia," as well as the author of the Declaration of Independence and the Virginia Statute for Religious Freedom.[1] He measured his worth in ideas and institutions, not human relationships. Moreover, Jefferson entrusted his legacy not to his family, but to his compatriot and closest ally, James Madison. A few months before his death, realizing that the end could not be far off, Jefferson told his friend of fifty years that it has "been a great solace to me, to believe that you are engaged in vindicating to posterity the course we have pursued for preserving to them, in all their purity, the blessings of self-government." He asked Madison to "take care of me when dead."[2]

To his immediate posterity, a family that had "blessed me by their affections, and never by their conduct given me a moment's pain," Jefferson bequeathed a debt of over a hundred thousand dollars and memories that would last them all the days of their lives.[3] Years after her grandfather's death, Ellen Coolidge would find herself haunted by the memory of Monticello. "When I dream it is mostly of long past times. Night after night I have been surrounded by the friends of childhood and early youth—my grandfather, mother, brothers, sisters, those whom I dearly loved and who dearly loved me, and who I hope in God's own time to rejoin."[4] So dearly did Jefferson's grandchildren love him that they willingly accepted the huge debt, renouncing in advance the property Jefferson had hoped to be able to leave them, and claiming as their only due a lifetime of love.[5]

That Thomas Jefferson's children and grandchildren loved him deeply we cannot doubt, nor could we question his attachment to them. The letters that they wrote each other bespeak a passion that words could barely contain. He closed his letters to his daughters "with unchangeable and tenderest attachment" and "never-ceasing love," and his daughters Martha and Maria responded "with tenderest and constant love," "with the tenderest love and reverence" and "ardent affection."[6] So strong was the love and so inadequate mere words for expressing it that with almost each letter, the conventional closing would be changed. Even after their marriages and the births of their children, both daughters assured their father that he was the one they loved best. Maria apologized for her "inability to express how much I love and revere you. But you are first and dearest to my heart." Martha used almost the same words, asking her father "to believe yourself *first* and unrivalled in the heart of your devoted child," and as she contemplated his retirement from public office she assured him that "I make no exception when I say the *first* and most important object with me will be the dear and sacred duty of nursing and chearing your old age."[7]

Jefferson cultivated this love by telling his daughters that his happiness depended upon it. In 1799 he told Maria that the "affectionate expressions" in one of her letters "kindled up all those feelings of love for you and our dear connections which now constitute the only real happiness of my life." A year later he reminded his other daughter "how essential your society is to my happiness." Such expressions became the refrain of his letters from the seat of national government. A year before the end of his second term as president, Jefferson told his only surviving child, Martha (Maria had died in 1804), "I long to be among you where I know nothing but love and delight, and where . . . I would be indulged . . . with the blessings of domestic society." "It is in the love of one's family only," he had once told Maria, "that heartfelt happiness is known."[8]

Jefferson loved his daughters and, in due course, their children, ardently and deeply. Perhaps that is reason enough for us to be interested in Thomas Jefferson's family: he towers so over the landscape of American history, and his legacy is so great, that anything that was of such great importance to him must be important to us too. Thomas Jefferson adored not simply his own family, but the very notion of family life. As he explained to Maria just before her marriage to John Wayles Eppes, the event "promises us long years of domestic concord and love, the best ingredient in human happiness."⁹ Jefferson believed that true and complete happiness—for him and for everyone—could be found only at home.

These were the sentiments he voiced to his family, but not, as a rule, to the world at large. His views on the family do not form a significant part of his political or social philosophy, yet clearly they were deeply felt beliefs, in some ways an expression of his essential character. Because Jefferson's pronouncement on happiness, which proclaimed its pursuit as one of mankind's unalienable rights, is so central a part of our national heritage, it is perhaps curious that he apparently never discussed the relationship between the happiness he found at home and the public happiness that was a staple of Enlightenment thought. Scholars who have debated what Jefferson meant by "the pursuit of happiness" suggest that it must have been either a social, public happiness, or a more private and individualist pursuit—a euphemism for property. While it seems clear that Jefferson had in mind a social happiness whose achievement was somehow enhanced by good government,¹⁰ his letters to his family indicate that he believed deeply in a sort of private happiness that was something other than the acquisition of property. His correspondence—indeed, his life—with his family reveals that Thomas Jefferson believed in a realm of happiness that his political philosophy did not engage.

It might therefore be argued that Jefferson's family life and the opinions he expressed about it bore no relationship to his public, political writings and actions, and that when he used the term "happiness" in writing to his daughters, the words he had written in the first paragraph of the Declaration of Independence could not have been further from his mind. It is possible that Jefferson segmented his life, drawing a sharp line between the part that was private and the part that was public. But "public" and "private" are always relative rather than absolute terms; they derive their meaning from each other. And at just this time, the relationship between these two realms was being redefined.¹¹ In rendering a vision of private life, Thomas Jefferson was necessarily constructing the public world, as well.

I

If we want to know what place the family occupied in the Jeffersonian vision of social and political life, we might begin by examining those passages in his letters where he wrote most passionately about the blessings of domestic society. The first time Jefferson said that his happiness derived from his family was in June 1791 when, writing his daughter Maria from Philadelphia, where he was serving as George Washington's Secretary of

State, he exclaimed, "Would to god I could be with you to partake of your felicities, and to tell you in person how much I love you all, and how necessary it is to my happiness to be with you." [12] It is not clear what, if anything, occasioned this declaration. All of his previous letters to his daughters[13] had been affectionate by any standard, but it was only after he had returned to the United States from Paris, where he had been serving as ambassador, and entered Washington's Cabinet, that he began linking his happiness to his family.

From 1791 on, however, virtually each of Jefferson's explosions of love for his family was so clearly part of an explicit contrast he made with the public world of politics, that we might reasonably surmise that his 1791 letter to Maria was occasioned by some disappointment in Philadelphia. In January 1792, for example, he wrote Martha that his "reveries" about the happy times they had spent together "in our wanderings over the world . . . alleviate the toils and inquietudes of my present situation, and leave me always impressed with the desire of being at home once more, and of exchanging labour, envy, and malice for ease, domestic occupation, and domestic love and society." Jefferson's biographer, Dumas Malone, reads this letter as Jefferson's first disclosure that he had decided to retire from office. He had grown weary of his conflict with Alexander Hamilton and the rancor of national politics. At the time of his 1791 letter to Maria, Jefferson had become embroiled—not for the last time—in a newspaper controversy about Thomas Paine, and it may well have triggered his longing for the "felicities" of home.[14]

Jefferson, of course, did not resign his office for another two years, and barely two years after that he was back in Philadelphia as vice president. He would not retire from public office until 1809, after two terms as president. Except for several extended visits, his daughters remained in Virginia, where they received their father's ardent letters. Barely had Jefferson returned to government before he was once again telling his daughters, "I feel the desire of never separating from you grow daily stronger, for nothing can compensate me with the want of your society. . . . Continue to love me as I do you." [15] Such expressions, whose effect surely worked to achieve the end that Jefferson explicitly designed—increasing his daughters' attachment to him—continued as long as he held public office.

This construction of public life as a burden and a deprivation had been foreshadowed in a letter Jefferson had written to James Monroe in 1782 when he declined the office of delegate to the Virginia legislature. With his young wife weak after just giving birth and apparently dying in perhaps the same room from which he wrote, Jefferson gave voice to the claims of private life: "I considered that I had been thirteen years engaged in public service, that during that time I had so abandoned all attention to my private affairs as to permit them to run into great disorder and ruin, that I had now a family advanced to years which required my attention & instruction." Here family was, like public service, also an obligation, if a private and inescapably countervailing one. "If we are made in some degree for others, yet in a greater are we made for ourselves. It were contrary to feeling & indeed ridiculous to suppose that a man had less right in himself than one of his neighbors or indeed all of them put together. This would be slavery & not that liberty which the bill of rights has made inviolable and for the preservation of which our government has been charged." [16] Jefferson pitted the claims of society against the rights of the individual; like others at the time, he connected the obligations of family to self-interest, which he believed he had neglected. [17] His conception of the polity, at least for the moment, was individualist.

Jefferson no doubt was disappointed that public life had not been more gratifying. His service as governor had been sharply criticized, and the wounds had not healed. "By a constant sacrifice of time, labour, loss, parental & family duties, I had been so far from gaining the affection of my countrymen, which was the only reward I ever asked or could have felt, that I had even lost the small estimation I before possessed." [18] Jefferson must have anticipated that his public service would bind him to his countrymen by ties of affection; he would willingly have sacrificed his personal interest for this form of love. In its absence, he would return to the pursuit of a private, Lockean sort of happiness. In his letter to Monroe, Jefferson implicitly contrasted a Scottish Enlightenment vision of society, bound together by affection, and a Lockean one, in which "we are made . . . in a greater degree for ourselves." [19] In this schema, the family is merely an extension of the self.

In the years to come, Jefferson would return to public service; he would also rework his ideas about the relationship between the self and society. No longer would he expect affection from his fellow citizens; he would plant and nurture it at home. By the 1790s he had decided that the political world was not simply cold, but downright hostile. In 1798 he told Martha, "For you to feel all the happiness of your quiet situation, you should know the rancorous passions which tear every breast here, even of the sex which should be a stranger to them. Politics and party hatreds destroy the happiness of every being here. They seem like salamanders, to consider fire as their element." He longed to be with her, "in the only scene, where, for me, the sweeter affections of life have any exercise." A few weeks later, he would render the contrast almost in a shorthand: the seat of government represented "every thing which is disgusting," and his "dear family," "every thing which is pleasurable."[20]

The bitterness of political life made Jefferson long for his family. In 1797, he was becoming "more and more disgusted with the jealousies, the hatred, and the rancorous and malignant passions of this scene," and added, "I lament my having ever again been drawn into public view."[21] In 1798, political life was "a dreary scene where envy, hatred, malice, revenge and all the worse passions of men are marshalled, to make one another as miserable as possible."[22] In January 1801, writing from Washington where he was waiting to learn if he had been elected president, Jefferson complained that "here . . . there is such a mixture of the bad passions of the heart that one feels themselves in an enemy's country."[23] A month later he described for Maria "the scene passing here" as "a circle of cabal, intrigue, and hatred."[24] By 1807, Jefferson was "tired of a life of contention, and of being the personal object for the hatred of every man, who hates the present state of things."[25]

Jefferson was willing to serve his country, ultimately at great personal cost,[26] but he no longer expected the affection of the public. Public service might yield the satisfaction of duty performed and perhaps even the esteem of his countrymen, but it would never prove emotionally fulfilling. So often and so passionately did Jefferson contrast the love of his family with the enmity of political life that it is evident that, at some level, he had expected that public service would prove more personally gratifying. Moreover, the two terms, *family* and *politics,* were so closely linked in his mind that he could barely mention one without invoking the other.

How easily Jefferson could slide back and forth between descriptions of the pleasures of family and the tribulations of politics is nicely illustrated by the letter he wrote Martha after learning of his other daughter's engagement to John Wayles Eppes, a young man he knew and esteemed. It was a match that not only would ensure Maria's happiness but would also gratify the entire family: "I now see our fireside formed into a groupe, no one member of which has a fibre in their composition which can ever produce any jarring or jealousies among us. No irregular passions, no dangerous bias. . . ." Jefferson shifted smoothly from imagining his daughter's pleasure to fantasizing about his own, and from there it was only one more quick move to railing against the miseries of a life in politics. "When I look to the ineffable pleasures of my family society, I become more and more disgusted with the jealousies, the hatred, and the rancorous and malignant passions of this scene." And from there, another shift to the unrealized emotional expectations of public service: "I have seen enough of political honors to know that they are but splendid torments; and however one might be disposed to render services on which any of their fellow citizens should set a value; yet when as many would deprecate them as a public calamity, one may well entertain a modest doubt of their real importance, and feel the impulse to duty to be very weak. The real difficulty," the then vice president explained, was "that being once delivered into the hands of others, whose feelings are friendly to the individual and warm to the public cause, how to withdraw from them without leaving a dissatisfaction in their mind, and an impression of pusillanimity with the public."[27] No wonder "the impulse to duty" was so weak: The most that the public could offer was friendliness, and once an individual gave himself over to others there was no quitting, lest he be thought a coward. Better, perhaps, not even to have entered into public service.

When we see how quickly Jefferson could slip from contemplating his daughter's future happiness to reflecting upon his own present misery we might be tempted to conclude that he was simply an enormously self-centered man. Certainly, his relationship with his daughters was sometimes manipulative; there was the implication, especially in his early letters to these motherless girls, that his love was contingent upon their fulfilling his expectations. "The more you learn the more I love you," he told Martha in 1786, "and I rest the happiness of my life on seeing you beloved by all the world." A year later, spurring her on to industry in her studies, he elaborated upon his hopes not so much for her, but himself: "No body in the world can make me so happy, or so miserable as you. Retirement from public life will ere long become necessary for me. To your sister and yourself I look to render the evening of my life serene and contented. Its morning has been clouded by loss after loss till I have nothing left but you."[28] Patsy and Polly, as the young girls were called, were designated not simply surrogate wives, replacements for their departed mother, but the handmaidens of their father's happiness: their primary function in life was to make him happy. No wonder both would later tell their father that they loved him above all else; that is exactly what he had trained them to do.

But even in his patently manipulative 1787 letter to Martha, Jefferson implied that public life might still offer its own rewards; it would be only after his retirement that he would look to his daughters to make his life "serene and contented." His daughters were supposed to compensate him for losses in the private, not the public realm. So even if we choose to consider Jefferson an emotionally needy man who throughout their lives burdened his daughters with the responsibility for his own happiness, we must also recognize that over the years, his thinking about the relationship between the private and public realms changed significantly. The variable in this equation is Jefferson's view of public life.

Even with his wife dying and the criticism he had received as governor still ringing in his ears, in 1782 Jefferson's greatest complaint about public service was that he had lost the "estimation" of the public and neglected his family. It was only after he entered Washington's Cabinet, beginning a period of government service from which he would not completely retire for two decades, that Jefferson voiced his most passionate complaints about the rancor and malignant passions of political life; it was not simply that he had lost the esteem of the public, but that a considerable portion of it seemed to hate him.

II

Like most of the Revolutionary leaders, Jefferson had anticipated that the reward for his disinterested service would be fame. This expectation was an article of the republican faith. Indeed, as Garry Wills has argued, "Fame was . . . a social glue, a structural element, for the republic in its early days." The expectation of fame stimulated leaders to the acts of self-sacrifice that the founding generation called public virtue. As James Wilson had explained it, "The love of honest and well earned fame is deeply rooted in honest and susceptible minds. Can there be a stronger incentive to the operations of this passion, than the hope of becoming the object of a well rounded and distinguishing applause? Can there be a more complete gratification of this passion, than the satisfaction of knowing that this applause is given—that it is given upon the most honourable principles, and acquired by the most honourable pursuits?"[29] A number of historians have noted that George Washington sought this sort of fame, consciously deliberating his actions and contemplating their effect upon his reputation. In this successful effort to secure his reputation Jefferson encouraged him, giving him pointers along the way.[30] Years later Jefferson would describe Washington as virtue incarnate: "His integrity was most pure, his justice the most inflexible I have ever known, no motives of interest or consanguinity, of friendship or hatred, being able to bias his decision."[31] This was the standard—and reputation—by which Jefferson would judge himself.

The republican standard of public virtue promised that if one sacrificed one's interest—which included, as Jefferson's 1782 letter to Monroe had suggested—that of one's friends and family as well—one might earn fame, "the affection of my countrymen." That was the reward for public service that Jefferson asked for and expected. He was confounded when it was not forthcoming. And while the source of his disappointment may in some part have been his own sensitivity to criticism and his emotional neediness, some of it surely must be attributed to the nature of politics in the 1790s.

A quarter of a century ago John Howe described the 1790s as a period of "political violence," one characterized by a "brutality both of expression and behavior." Jefferson, Howe suggests, spoke for many other political leaders when he complained to Edward Rutledge in 1793 that "the passions are too high at present. . . . You and I have formerly seen warm debates and high political passions. But gentlemen of different politics would then speak to each other, and separate the business of the Senate from that of society. It is not so now." Howe attributes the volatility of politics in this era to the republican belief that republican governments were inherently fragile. So great were the risks and so likely the prospect of failure that inevitably "politics was a deadly business, with little room for optimism or leniency, little reason to expect the best rather than suspect the worst of one's political enemies."[32] Political violence, then, was a manifestation of republican ideology.

It was also, of course, an expression of the structure of politics. As Jack N. Rakove has recently suggested, both the Constitution and the process of ratification brought about a politics that was less stable and more popular than its framers anticipated. Turnover in the first Congresses was high, as members left public service to pursue private interests. Newspapers that published the proceedings of Congress not only helped create a national politics, but public opinion and pressure, as well.[33] Anyone who entered service in the federal government expecting to find there a forum for the dispassionate discussion of the issues of the day, isolated from the whims and demands of public opinion, was sure to be disappointed.

And Thomas Jefferson surely was disappointed. He began his service in the new national government equipped with republican expectations of fame at a time when politics was becoming increasingly volatile and violent. In theory fame was supposed to be a manifestation of public esteem, but in practice, especially at a time when the mechanisms of public opinion were unformed, it was established by a gentleman's peers, not the promiscuous public. Jefferson said he craved only the "affection of my countrymen," but what he effectively meant was the esteem of the relatively small group of men who served with him in the public realm, for how could he possibly know what the mass of men thought?

We have already heard Jefferson complaining to his daughters about the malice and venom of politics. Public approbation, or even a secure sense of the public's esteem, was elusive. In comparison to that vague sense of a public whose feelings were warm to the cause, but merely "friendly to the individual," the "jealousies, the hatred, and the malignant passions" of those whom he encountered daily cut him to the bone. Less than five months from his death, Jefferson had "no complaint against the world which has sufficiently honored me," but it was only his family that had "blessed me by their affections, and never by their conduct given me a moment's pain."[34] Jefferson had won his family's love, not his nation's fame.

It was a bargain that the fierce politics of the first decades of the early republic prepared him to make. That public life at the time was violent was no mere figure of speech; in fact, politics could be decidedly dangerous, as the experience of Jefferson's great rival, Alexander Hamilton, abundantly illustrates. The duel that ended his life was but the last and most lethal of a series of violent encounters that punctuated Hamilton's public life. In 1778 and 1779, while serving as an aide to George Washington, he twice came close to dueling.[35] Charles Royster has observed that it was just at this time that dueling, a tradition among European army officers, came into vogue among the young officers of the Continental Army. He explains that dueling "increased because it settled questions of honor in a distinctive, gallant way for men newly self-conscious about their uniqueness and their proper public inviolability." The duel mushroomed in the dank soil of Valley Forge, where anxious and ambitious young men who were strangers to one another were thrown together and compelled to establish their worth and standing in each other's eyes. As Royster notes, the world of the Continental Army officer was intimate and intense; the duel was a product of the volatile attachments this environment nourished. "The opinion of a circle of friends might decide a man's self-respect or disgrace."[36]

The same held true in the political world of the new nation, where men from a variety of backgrounds, eager for fame and anxious to prove themselves the equal in honor to the most honorable members of the new government, were thrown together on terms of intimacy. Former officers such as Hamilton, who had learned the rituals of the duel in the army, or hotheads such as John Randolph of Roanoke, insecure about their status, might find themselves issuing or provoking challenges throughout their careers. On one Saturday afternoon in July 1795, while Hamilton was out strolling with friends along New York's Wall Street, his group encountered a party of Republican rivals, also out for a walk. Words were exchanged, then insults; Hamilton attempted to intervene, he himself was insulted, and then promptly issued a challenge. The stroll resumed; a few minutes later Hamilton and his friends met another knot of Republicans, and more arguments, more insults, and another challenge ensued. One dispute was resolved immediately, but it took a week of negotiations to avert a duel in the other case.[37]

When men such as Hamilton believed that their standing with the public, and hence, their capacity to win fame by serving it, rested upon their honor, "the potential for violence hovered around every public dispute." Robert Wiebe has recently noted that, in order to prevent politics from becoming a virtual bloodbath, gentleman politicians began to devise rules and customs that could channel aggressions yet still protect reputations. One tack was to attempt to identify and isolate a private realm, off-limits to both insult and the necessity of defending one's honor. Nonetheless, "anything that could be justified on grounds of republican principle, no matter how vicious or destructive to an individual's reputation, fell within a public realm and lent itself only to political or legal redress." And, conversely, any attack on a public man's character might be construed as sedition. As St. George Tucker would explain, "The right of character is a sacred and invaluable right, and is not forfeited by accepting a public employment. Whoever knowingly departs from any of these maxims is guilty of a crime against the community, as well as the person injured."[38] Until the line between public and private could be sharply drawn—effectively narrowing the perimeters of public virtue and, hence, reworking the assumptions of republicanism—any word or deed that seemed to call into question a man's public honor could lead to political violence.

Wiebe has suggested that the wars of words waged by pamphleteers and newspaper editors in this period were nothing less than sublimated duels, contests of honor by proxy. Jefferson, for example, who had no taste for physical and life-threatening encounter, did not hesitate to spur polemicists on. "A free press," Wiebe explains, "served deep emotional as well as broad public needs."[39] But as long as politics itself remained intimate and emotionally intense it would retain its capacity for violence, and even pamphlets or articles could provide the stimulus to duels. It was a pamphlet, for example, that led Hamilton to challenge James Monroe to a duel.

The "Reynolds affair" is of particular interest to us for what it tells us about the way in which private affairs could become matters of public interest. The story began in November 1792 when the comptroller of the Treasury sued James Reynolds and Jacob Clingman for attempting to defraud the government by filing false claims. While in jail and after his release—charges were dropped when the pair agreed to make restitution and supply certain information—Reynolds hinted darkly that he was in possession of certain information that reflected very badly upon the Secretary of the Treasury. Eventually this information found its way to Frederick Muhlenberg, a Pennsylvania Republican and Speaker of the House in the First Congress; he then brought it to the attention of two Virginia Republicans, Senator James Monroe and Representative Abraham Venable, who then sought confirmation from Reynolds. In mid-December the Republican delegation went to visit Hamilton; he denied Reynolds's allegations and claimed that Reynolds was blackmailing him for having carried on an adulterous affair with Reynolds's wife Maria. "The result," Hamilton would write later, after the whole sordid affair had become public knowledge, "was a full and unequivocal acknowledgement on the part of the three gentlemen of perfect satisfaction with the explanation and expressions of regret at the trouble and embarrassment which had been occasioned to me."[40] He thought the matter had been laid to rest.

Rumors, however, circulated, and in the summer of 1797 pamphleteer James Thomson Callender made them public. If Hamilton had sought to deflect the accusation of public impropriety—specifically, speculating in public funds—by admitting to the private vice of adultery, Callender would recognize no such distinction. Although Callender believed that Hamilton fabricated the story of an affair with Maria Reynolds to cover up his unseemly financial activities with her husband, the pamphleteer was happy to have it both ways, faulting Hamilton both for defrauding the government and committing adultery. Callender would later spell out his rationale for examining what some suggested were purely private matters: "The world has no business with that part of a public character, unless . . . it shall be connected with some interesting political truth."[41] In Hamilton's case, the relevant issue seemed to be his hypocrisy; "We shall presently see this great master of morality," Callender told his readers, "though himself the father of a family, confessing that he had an illicit correspondence with another man's wife."[42] Hamilton was driven to publish an extended and passionate defense, which would call forth another of Callender's tracts. Hamilton, he charged, "has published ninety-three pages to prove, that he was guilty of conjugal infidelity. . . . This is the man, who, at the same moment, has the hardiness to announce 'a conspiracy of vice against virtue.' Mr. Hamilton should speak with reserve as to the faults of others."[43]

It is worth examining Hamilton's defense in some detail so that we may be able to compare it with the response Jefferson would make when, five years later, Callender turned his acid pen against him. In his defense, Hamilton worked hard to erect a barrier between his private and public lives. The stakes, he argued, were high. The attack upon him was a manifestation of the "spirit of jacobinism. . . . Incessantly busied in undermining all the props of public security and private happiness, it seems to threaten the political and moral world with a complete overthrow." Hamilton assumed that his effectiveness as a political figure—that is, his power—rested on his character. His enemies were attempting to destroy "the influence of men of upright principles." They were engaged in a conspiracy "against honest fame," and their strategy was to "wear away the reputations which they could not directly subvert." One of their tactics was to "stab the private felicity" of the person under assault. "With such men, nothing is sacred. Even the peace of an unoffending and amiable wife is a welcome repast to their insatiate fury against the husband."[44] Invading Hamilton's privacy and upsetting his wife is the final and lowest blow.

Although Hamilton argued that his private life was "sacred," and that his enemies should honor its inviolability, his defense reveals that his primary concern was his "public character" and his fame. His focus was upon the public sphere, and it is clear from the argument he would make several years later in the Croswell case that he believed the press ought to be given wide latitude in discussing the character and behavior of not only public figures, but even "private persons." "If this be not done, then in vain will the voice of the people be raised against the inroads of tyranny." Republican principles legitimated "fair and honest exposure." Anything that was true might be published—except if it were "for the purpose of disturbing the peace of families."[45]

Hamilton recognized a small private sphere whose sanctity should be inviolable, not because it contributed something to the public realm, but, instead, because so clearly it did not. The private realm is without political meaning. It became relevant only when it affected the composure and happiness of the public man. In other words, Hamilton depicted his wife and his family as merely extensions of his self. It is as if Hamilton had said to Callender and his other enemies, "Let there be something of mine that you cannot use to hurt me." His concern for his wife was merely a reflection of his interest in his own "private felicity." Had her happiness been a central preoccupation, he would not so coolly have confessed (or invented, if one follows the alternate interpretation) the details of his adultery with Mrs. Reynolds: "After this, I had frequent meetings with her, most of them at my own house; Mrs. Hamilton with her children being absent on a visit to her father." When all is said and done, however, "There is nothing worse in the affair than an irregular and indelicate amour." If, in the schemes of things, Hamilton's adultery was such a trifle, then it was not so much his "indelicate amour" that must be upsetting to his wife, as public discussion of it, which merely ate at *her* peace, but threatened *him* with eternal shame.[46] Mrs. Hamilton was merely an auxiliary to her husband's happiness; in his mind, he apparently has very little bearing on hers. Hamilton would protect himself by sectioning off a private realm, but in comparison to the wide public arena in which his fame would be won, it was a very small space indeed.

And it was in the public arena that Hamilton attempted to defend his honor. Not only did he publish this extraordinary pamphlet, but he challenged James Monroe to a duel. Once Callender published his pamphlets, Hamilton anxiously sought affirmation from Muhlenberg, Venable, and Monroe that they had been satisfied with his defense five years earlier. Muhlenberg's and Venable's responses were adequately reassuring; Monroe's, however, was not. There was an interview and an extended correspondence. Hamilton issued a challenge; Monroe accepted it; Hamilton backed off. More letters ensued. Finally, Monroe enlisted Aaron Burr and John Dawson to help him either make arrangements for a duel or resolve the matter. Although a duel once again seemed imminent, it somehow—and the record is unclear on this point—was averted.[47]

Less than four years later, Hamilton's son Philip would be killed in a duel. Philip and a friend had been challenged when they loudly mocked a speech critical of the Federalists. Philip accepted the challenge and took a bullet in his side. His mother's grief, an observer at the young man's deathbed said, "beggars . . . description."[48] Just over two years after that, Hamilton himself would engage in his fatal duel with Aaron Burr.

Robert Wiebe has suggested that the first political parties functioned, much like the newspapers, as vessels for containing political violence by making a ritual of it.[49] That assessment is no doubt true for the long run, but for at least the first few years of the First Party System, factional conflict could just as easily stimulate as sublimate violence. Burr had apparently been nursing a grudge against Hamilton for the role he played in denying him the presidency in 1800 and the governorship of New York in 1804, but it was not until the summer of 1804 that Burr thought he had grounds for a duel. Finally Hamilton said something—exactly what is unknown—that "could . . . be taken hold of." Burr issued the challenge; Hamilton accepted, and, like his son, he took a bullet in his side. He had left a letter for his wife, to be delivered only in the event of his death. "If it had been possible for me to have avoided the interview, my love for you and my precious children would have been alone a decisive motive. But it was not possible, without sacrifices which would have rendered me unworthy of your esteem."[50] His honor took precedence over her happiness; or rather, Hamilton believed his honor, his reputation, and his fame were, even more than his love, his essential contribution to her happiness.

III

There is little evidence of Thomas Jefferson's reaction to the death of one of his rivals at the hands of another. It is rather evident, however, that he must have followed Hamilton's discomfiture in the Reynolds affair with some glee. James Monroe had kept him informed, and as early as December 1792 Jefferson made note, albeit cryptically, of "the affair of Reynolds & his wife."[51] A number of years later, however, when Jefferson reflected on Alexander Hamilton and his character, he was able—in a way that Hamilton himself never had been—to separate the public from the private man: "Hamilton was indeed a singular character. Of acute understanding, disinterested, honest, and honorable in all private transactions, amiable in society, and duly valuing virtue in private life, yet so bewitched & perverted by the British example, as to be under thoro' conviction that corruption was essential to the government of a nation."[52] In retrospect, Hamilton's flaws were all in his public and political actions.

Perhaps it was his own experience at Callender's hand that made Jefferson not only more charitable, but also more careful in distinguishing between public and private virtue. By 1802, for reasons that need not detain us here, Callender had moved to Virginia; he had begun editing the Richmond *Recorder,* and turned against Jefferson and the Republicans.[53] In September of that year he began publication of a series of articles attacking Jefferson's reputation. "It is well known," the first of these articles began, "that the man, *whom it delighteth the people to honor,* keeps, and for many years past has kept, as his concubine, one of his own slaves. Her name is SALLY."[54] The story that Jefferson maintained a sexual relationship with his slave Sally Hemings and fathered a number of her children has been in circulation ever since, never effectively proved or disproved. The veracity of the charges, however, is not what concerns us. Instead, it is the manner in which Callender framed the accusation and the way in which Jefferson and his friends responded to it.

In the Reynolds affair, Callender's ostensible rationale for discussing Hamilton's relationship with Mrs. Reynolds had been Hamilton's hypocrisy. Maria Reynolds's connection to the allegation that Hamilton had speculated in government securities should have been reason enough for examining her relationship with the Secretary of the Treasury. Callender, however, was incensed that a "great master of morality, though himself the father of a family," would commit adultery and confess that he had "an illicit correspondence with another man's wife." [55] Similarly, he accused Jefferson of violating the sanctity of the family. His original charge—later amended—was that Jefferson had brought Sally over to France along with his two daughters. "What a sublime pattern for an American ambassador to place before the eyes of two young ladies!" [56] Other Federalist newspapers would pick up and republish Callenders's allegations, elaborating on that theme. The Lynchburg *Virginia Gazette,* for example, judged Jefferson a failed father. "These daughters, who should have been the principal object of his domestic concern, had the mortification to see illegitimate mulatto sisters, and brothers, enjoying the same privileges of parental affection with themselves." [57] A good father protected his daughters and gave them all of his affection.

In focusing on the character of Jefferson's fatherhood, Callender and his followers shifted the ground on which the discussion of character took place. No attempt was made to suggest that Jefferson's relationship with Sally Hemings or his daughters directly affected his capacity for governance or had immediate bearing upon his public virtue. It was simply, as Callender put it, that "the public have a right to be acquainted with the real characters of persons who are the possessors or candidates for office." Hamilton's *New-York Post* would elaborate (somewhat disingenuously, perhaps, considering Hamilton's own experience): "We feel for the honor of our country—And when the Chief magistrate labours under the imputation of the most abandoned profligacy of private life, we do most honestly and sincerely wish to see the stain upon the nation wiped away." [58] Honor, then, was a reward for private, as much as public, virtue.

Several years later, when these and other charges became the subject of debate in the Massachusetts legislature, the committee charged with considering them reported that "the preservation of our Republican Constitutions, and the impartial and faithful administration of laws enacted in conformity to them, depend alone on the knowledge which the people may have of the *conduct, integrity and talents* of those of their fellow citizens, who have been, or may be called to offices of trust and honour." [59] What hitherto might have been defined as private virtue was of public interest. As Callender asked rhetorically, in defense of his revelations, "What virtuous character has been destroyed by this paper? If seduction, and hypocrisy, if the grossest breach of personal friendship, and of domestic confidence, form a department in the new code of morality," then, and only then, would the newspaper he published have been in the wrong.[60] The personal had been rendered political.

Everything in a man's life was relevant, and the Federalist press, in its attempt to discredit the president, cast a wide net. Most of the charges originated with Callender, and they eventually included allegations of both a clearly public and just as clearly a private nature: Jefferson's behavior during the Revolution was cowardly; he had paid back a debt in depreciated currency; he had attempted an affair with Betsey Walker, the wife of his neighbor and friend; he had paid Callender to slander George Washington; he was destroying the navy; he did not believe in God; the Louisiana purchase was unwise.[61] This promiscuous mingling of political and personal accusations served to break down the precarious wall that had separated the public and private realms. In the fall of 1802, as the Federalist papers were filled with allegations, and the Republican press attempted a defense, everyone's character became fair game. The *Richmond Examiner* devoted more space to defaming Jefferson's enemies than to defending the President. It recirculated the tale of the Hamilton-Reynolds affair and insinuated that John Marshall, whom it suspected of supplying information to Callender, himself kept a slave mistress. It alleged that Callender himself was consorting with a black prostitute. It even raised questions about the manhood of Charles Cotesworth Pinckney, a potential Federalist candidate for the presidency, dubbing him "Miss *Charlotte* Cotesworth PINCKNEY" and referring to him repeatedly as "she."[62] In the heated political climate, the sexual behavior of any partisan was grist for the mill.

At the same time that the Republican press was tarring Jefferson's enemies with the brush that had been used on him, it began to frame a different sort of defense, one that would attempt to make impregnable the wall between public and private. To be sure, the press was working at contradictory and self-defeating purposes. While one column was defending the sanctity of Jefferson's personal life, another was violating Hamilton's or Marshall's, without even a pretense to consistency. Yet out of this unstable combination of approaches to the question of a public man's sexual behavior, a new understanding of the relationship between the family and the public world would emerge.

The first element in this new configuration was the assertion that the family ought to be protected from political scrutiny. The *Richmond Examiner* charged, in language reminiscent of that which Hamilton had used in his "Reynolds Pamphlet," that because the opponents of Republicanism could find no fault with its policies or its leaders, "they are driven into the sacred recesses of privacy, to hunt up malicious falsehood and obloquy at the hazard of family repose." In response, the Federalist press repeated the standard republican defense that anything that had bearing on a man's public actions was relevant. Hence, a contributor to the *Boston Gazette* would recoil in horror at "the new principles recently advanced . . . that it is unfair to expose the private vices of a public man" and confess himself "unable to discover upon what basis of morals, or of policy, the axiom can be supported, that the most detestable crimes of which a human being can be guilty, must be overlooked and concealed, if committed by a public man, unless they were committed in his *official capacity*." [63] As in the Reynolds affair, the arguments circled each other warily, like equally matched opponents, neither one capable of winning the round.

IV

As long as the political press saw the family as nothing more than an extension of the man who was its head, there could be no effective defense of its privacy. The harm that came from disrupting a family's repose, after all, was imagined to fall most heavily upon the public man, who was distracted from his important endeavors. Moreover, the lines of influence led entirely in one direction, from a man and his family, through society to the nation. That the nation—as distinct from a tyrant who perverted its will—might harm the family was a novel thought. When the Jeffersonian press asserted the sanctity of the "private recesses" of the family and began to describe the family in ways that would make the preservation of its privacy a positive and necessary good, it was redefining both the family and its relation to the political world. In fact, the political press was not the only or the most important sector of society that was rethinking the family; as a number of historians have shown, at just this time, educators, essayists, and novelists (both male and female), ministers, and political theorists, as well as middle-class and elite men and women on both sides of the Atlantic, were beginning to think in new ways about the nature of family and its relationship to the wider public. [64] Indeed, because the redefinition of the family was hardly their central occupation, it seems more likely that the political newspapers were reflecting, and in the process, politically legitimating, changes that were taking place in both society and thought as they attempted to craft a defense for their slandered leaders.

And so it was that defenders of Thomas Jefferson began to offer his character as a family man as an argument in his defense. If Callender accused Jefferson of carrying on a sexual relationship with a slave woman "before the eyes of his two daughters," the *Richmond Examiner* would respond that the presence of Jefferson's daughters rendered such behavior unthinkable. That a man such as Jefferson, "who is daily engaged in the ordinary vocations of the family, should have a mulatto child" was not possible. "Mr. Jefferson has been a Bachelor for more than twenty years. During this period," the paper explained, "he reared with parental attention, two unblemished, accomplished and amiable women, who are married to two estimable citizens. In the education of his daughters, this same Thomas Jefferson, supplied the place of a *mother*—his tenderness and delicacy were proverbial—not a spot tarnished his widowed character" until Callender started spreading his lies.[65] "The ordinary vocations of the family" precluded the sort of behavior of which Jefferson was accused. The unblemished daughters served as proof of their father's virtue. Family life implicitly was virtuous, and, if anything, required protection from the contamination of politics. One Massachusetts legislator was disgusted by the newspapers' discussions of Thomas Jefferson's character. "He asked, whether any gentleman, who had a family, and whose females or daughters, were in the habit of reading the public papers, would permit a paper containing such matter to come into his house."[66] It was the public—not the tender father—that threatened the sanctity of the family.

And it was at home, and on the basis of his fatherhood, that Jefferson was willing to be judged. Hamilton accepted Burr's challenge because, in the end, he had no other choice. He could not go home because his wife, or so he imagined, would consider him dishonored. Jefferson's passionate letters to his daughters should be understood in this context. It was no exaggeration to say that political life was filled with cabal, hatred, and intrigue. When he told Maria that "it is in the love of one's family only that heartfelt happiness is known,"[67] He spoke from both experience and desire. Yet the family is not naturally or necessarily happy or warm, nor is it the opposite of political life. Jefferson, the tender and delicate parent, made it—or at least saw it—as he needed it to be.

And because he fell back upon the happiness of home, Jefferson offered no public response to the charges of his enemies. They were astounded, taking Jefferson's silence as proof of their charges. Some expected a public denial, perhaps his own version of Hamilton's "Reynolds Pamphlet." The *Boston Gazette* "waited in expectation either that Mr. Jefferson himself would deem it not beneath his dignity, to meet the accusation of a crime so deeply infamous, at least with a pointed denial, or that some of his numerous friends and admirers would have taken the task upon themselves." In 1805 a Massachusetts legislator would accept the charges as true, for after all, they "had been made and repeated for more than four years. . . . They had been published and republished again and again, at the seat of government; avowedly and before the face of Mr. Jefferson. . . . Yet, during this whole time, these charges had not been contradicted, either by Mr. Jefferson or his friends.—this . . . in his mind, amounted to at least a tacit confession." Others speculated about possible duels. The *Richmond Examiner* published a report, later retracted, that Light-Horse Harry Lee had carried a challenge from John Walker to the President.[68] Some sort of response was expected.

Jefferson, however, remained almost completely silent. In 1805 he confessed to his Secretary of the Navy that "when young and single I offered love" to Mrs. Walker. "It is the only one founded in truth among all their allegations against me." In 1803 he wrote out his religious creed, explaining to Martha, "I thought it just that my family, by possessing this, should be enabled to estimate the libels published against me on this, as on every other possible subject."[69] The allegations troubled him, of course, as did the general tenor of the Federalist press. He gave both direct and indirect encouragement to the states to prosecute for libel, telling Pennsylvania's governor Thomas McKean that he had "long thought that a few prosecutions of the most eminent offenders would have a wholesome effect in restoring the integrity of the presses." Although, as Leonard Levy has pointed out, Jefferson's willingness to use not only the state but the federal courts to prosecute seditious libel marked a retreat from the more libertarian theories of freedom of the press developed by Republicans in response to the Sedition Act of 1798,[70] Jefferson himself did not seem willing to pursue his policy vigorously or publicly. He wanted McKean to keep "entirely confidential" his recommendation for intimidating the press in Pennsylvania, and he ordered a halt to the prosecution of a Connecticut minister when he learned that a trial would require a public discussion of the Walker affair. Jefferson's later explanation for terminating the prosecution—"I had laid it down as a law to myself, to take no notice of the thousand calumnies issued against me, but to trust my character to my own conduct, and the good sense and candor of my fellow citizens"[71]—surely casts his motive in the most favorable possible light; undoubtedly he must also have wanted to avoid the embarrassment that a public airing of the allegation that four decades earlier he had attempted to seduce his friend's wife was sure to bring. If we consider Jefferson's prosecutions as yet another means of displacing political violence, it is striking that even in this sublimated version of the duel, Jefferson would try to hold his fire.

V

Certainly, Jefferson's attitudes were shaped by his personality. He was by nature sensitive to criticism and averse to direct conflict. Yet, as was his nature, he transformed his inclinations into maxims, and when they were applied to public affairs, they became part of an emergent political culture. We have already seen how smoothly Jefferson would change subjects in letters to his daughters; evocations of the pleasures of family life would quickly and almost inevitably be transformed into diatribes about the miseries of political life. The object of these letters, in fact, was to shape family life so that it would continue to be an effective counter to the ravages of politics. He would tell his daughters both explicitly and indirectly how to behave in a way that would foster peace and family love. In the letters he addressed to their husbands and sons, Jefferson also would discuss family and political life in tandem, but here his objective was to instruct them how to behave in public so that they would live to enjoy the pleasures of family life.

In 1808, as he was nearing the end of his last term of office, Jefferson wrote his grandson and namesake, Thomas Jefferson Randolph, then studying medicine in Philadelphia, a long and, as Dumas Malone put it, "excessively didactic" letter.[72] Clearly he was worried that his young charge, away from home for the first time in his life, would fall in with a bad crowd. The ostensible purpose of the letter was to inculcate in young Jeff, as the President's grandson was known, the personal habits that would enable him to resist the usual temptations of youth—gambling, drinking, and so forth. But along with injunctions about what not to do, Jefferson also told his grandson exactly how to behave. This advice constitutes Jefferson's political sociology, his doctrine about the way men in public ought to act. Thomas Jefferson wrote his grandson a primer on how to avoid the duel.

First of all, a man had to develop the proper frame of mind. Jefferson counseled "good humor as one of the preservatives of our peace and tranquillity." If he could not summon it naturally, he could always feign it: "In truth, politeness is artificial good humor, it covers natural want of it, and ends by rendering habitual a substitute nearly equivalent to the real virtue." Politeness, in Jefferson's view, was a scaled-down version of public virtue—self-sacrifice for the common good, not so much of the nation, as the society in which a man happened at the moment to be. "It is the practice of sacrificing to those whom we meet in society all the little conveniences and preferences which will gratify them, and deprive us of nothing worth a moment's consideration; it is giving a pleasing and flattering turn to our expressions which will conciliate others, and make them pleased with us as well as themselves."[73] It might well be true, as Jefferson would observe at another time, that "the Creator would have been a bungling artist, had he intended man for a social animal, without planting in him social dispositions," but those dispositions required cultivation and even conscious calculation.

In the context of his wider social philosophy, Jefferson seems to have considered anger and political disputation as variants on self-love, the "antagonist of virtue."[74] The self-sacrifice and self-control required to walk away from an argument, then, constituted virtue. And it was just this form of virtue that Jefferson passionately enjoined upon his grandson. He told him quite directly never to enter "into a dispute or argument with anyone." To make his point, he attempted a number of tacks: He invoked the example of the revered Benjamin Franklin, "the most amiable of men in society," whose rule was "Never to contradict anybody." He told Jeff that argument was always in vain anyway: "I never yet saw an instance of one of two disputants convincing each other by argument"; if anything, such disagreements only made matters worse. He resorted to philosophy, sharing with his grandson the secret of his own success: "When I hear another express an opinion, which is not mine, I say to myself, He has a right to his opinion, as I to mine; why should I question it. His error does me no injury, and shall I become a Don Quixot to bring all men by force of argument, to one opinion?" And he tried simple scare tactics. He had seen too many antagonists "getting warm, becoming rude, and shooting one another." Disputation, Jefferson warned, could lead to death.

Perhaps Jefferson had in mind the sad example of Philip Hamilton when he told young Jeff not to worry about defending his grandfather's reputation from the "puppies in politics" he was sure to encounter. Jefferson assured his grandson that his character was "in the hands of my fellow citizens at large, and will be consigned to honor or infamy by the verdict of the republican mass of our country, according to what themselves will have seen, not what their enemies and mine shall have said." A public man's reputation rested not on his willingness to defend it by force or even on what a small circle of gentlemen in Washington or Philadelphia conceived it to be. Jefferson's character was a matter of public opinion, not the debating or dueling skills of his kin.

When Jefferson instructed his grandson how to avoid political violence, it is even more probable that he had in mind the duel that Jeff's father had narrowly avoided only two years earlier. In 1806, much to his chagrin,

Thomas Jefferson's son-in-law almost entered into a duel with his even more volatile cousin, John Randolph of Roanoke. This was not the first time that there had been trouble between John Randolph and the Jefferson sons-in-law, two Congressmen whom the Speaker of the House seemed to regard as tools of the president. After one minor altercation, Jefferson attempted to mollify the Speaker. He explained that there were "no men on earth more independent in their sentiments" than his sons-in-law; nor would Jefferson even consider talking politics with them. In fact, Jefferson would barely risk political dispute with anyone, even members of his own party, "experience having long taught me the reasonableness of mutual sacrifices of opinion among those who are to act together for any common object."[75] Jefferson had little interest in establishing a political dynasty, let alone a family one, or so he led Randolph to believe.

Such reassurances, however, could not cool tempers that were inclined to inflame, and in 1806 Thomas Mann Randolph and John Randolph came close to a duel. The dispute began, as it so often did, over a trifle—a debate in the House about repealing a duty on salt. The proponents were accused of trying to embarrass the administration; their heated response elicited a counter-response from Jefferson's supporters, including Thomas Mann Randolph, who objected to an opponent's tone. John Randolph, then Chairman of the House Ways and Means Committee and increasingly hostile to Jefferson and his policies, took the floor, making one of his typical speeches, nasty yet somehow vague. Jefferson's son-in-law thought it was aimed at him; he took offense and rose in his own defense, effectively challenging the Chairman to a duel. The Chairman sent a second, the son-in-law chose a second and then backed down, issuing an apology for his insults from the House floor. Other Congressmen, however, assailed the Chairman's leadership, and the newspapers transformed this undoubtedly merited criticism into a conspiracy to ruin John Randolph. Thomas Mann Randolph's character was called into question, and it appeared as if the duel might once again be on.[76]

Jefferson was beside himself with anxiety. He was afraid to write his son-in-law at home, where he had gone after Congress had recessed, for fear his daughter would read the letter and learn of the impending duel. He entrusted his letter to a mutual friend, to whom he complained that the newspapers were encouraging the duel. Jefferson decried the custom of resolving disputes by duels. They were especially inappropriate for men with families, and he was certain that "the mass of men would condemn it in a husband and father of a numerous family." He underscored the point to Randolph himself in a letter written several weeks later when the threat of a duel, mercifully, seemed to have passed. "The young ones indeed would have gotten over it; but to two persons at least it would have ended but with life. This period might have been long with one; with the other short but unceasingly bitter. A sincere affection for you personally, a reliance on you for succeeding to cases which age is unfitting me for, sympathies with a beloved survivor, and tender anxieties for those who would have had to embark in the world without guide or protection, would have filled with gloom my remaining time."[77] In this light, fighting a duel would be an act of supreme selfishness, unforgivable for a man with a family.

The family, then, and not honor, was a man's primary obligation. As Jefferson explained it to his son-in-law, "unnecessary risk . . . indeed is the falsest of honour . . . a mere compound of crime & folly."[78] Hamilton had had it all wrong. It was attention to his familial responsibilities that made even a public man worthy of his family's esteem. And it was in the family that a man could find the certain and unchanging love that the public world denied him. In counseling complacency and coolness in public, Jefferson was attempting to alter the tenor of public life; he was struggling to make politics less personal and emotionally intense. Don't argue, he said; don't fight; do as I do, and think of home. Only by constructing the family as the sole realm where heartfelt happiness might be found could Jefferson divest politics of the passions that threatened always to push it over the edge into violence. Not only was political passion in this age displaced, as Robert Wiebe has suggested, into newspapers, political parties, and similar ritualized and less lethal forms of dispute, but it was also transmuted into the love that was experienced at home. Family life would become more intense as political life became cooler.

VI

This process was just beginning as Thomas Jefferson achieved his long-proclaimed desire to retire from politics, but its effects would be profound. Indeed, it might be argued that a viable, relatively modern politics would not be possible until it became less emotionally intense, that is, less personal. It would be a number of years, of course, before the code of the duel would be replaced entirely by less dangerous means of resolving political dispute, but after the War of 1812, the duel—like other forms of violence—became increasingly confined to certain regions and classes.[79] An effective politics would not be possible until a man could argue a position without risking its being construed as a reflection on another man's honor. By the same token, an orderly politics would have to offer men other sources for constituting their identities. A man accepted a challenge in order to maintain his reputation among a small circle of political intimates; these were the men who validated his identity. Jefferson sought to ground reputation in an even wider sphere, "the republican mass of our country." But this wider public could not be the guarantor of a man's fame until mechanisms of communication were developed for registering public opinion. The newspapers and party organizations that were coming into being while Jefferson served in government and that at first seemed only to exacerbate conflict would eventually bring into political being the sort of mass public to which Jefferson attempted to appeal.

Jefferson knew, however, that although this public might esteem him, it could never bathe him in the sort of affection that as a young man he had seemed to crave.[80] For that he would have to turn to his family. They would provide him with the emotional sustenance that would make his continued participation in public affairs possible, and he in turn would serve his family, first and foremost, by not getting himself killed. He would also endeavor to keep the violence that seemed endemic in politics from spilling over into the home. The wall separating the home from politics could be built higher and stronger, now that there was something to protect. This process, which would define the home and what took place in it as sacred and private would not be accomplished until a number of years later after the newspapers and pamphleteers had examined Andrew Jackson's marriage in the minutest detail, insinuating that his most intimate relationship had profound public implications.[81] And although politics would periodically—especially in the nineteenth century—attempt to scale the wall that was supposed to separate it from the private realm, it turned out that the republican mass of the people in whom Jefferson placed his faith would accept the notion that the public and private spheres were separate and distinct. In the long run, they would demonstrate that they cared relatively little about what their leaders did in "the sacred recesses of privacy."

The connection between public and private virtue was in the process of being severed. It was not so much that the meaning of virtue was feminized as that different standards of behavior for politics and the home developed. The notion of public virtue would still have a specific, if less encompassing content; the specter of corruption, for example, a central republican fear, would continue to haunt American politics in the decades to come.[82] And new standards of personal conduct, particularly for the genteel, would be applied to both men and women concerning their behavior at home. Jefferson, after all, would instruct both his sons-in-law and his daughters, his granddaughters as well as his grandsons, to avoid conflict and disputation at all cost. "Honesty, disinterestedness, and good nature are indispensable to procure the esteem and confidence of those with whom we live, and on whose esteem our happiness depends," Jefferson instructed one grandson.[83] He could easily have given that advice to a granddaughter, as well. Personal integrity and unfailing good humor were qualities that knew no gender.

That is not to say that the new political and familial order that Jefferson worked to achieve would affect men and women in the same way, or even that Jefferson had identical expectations of his male and female kin. If a man's primary responsibility was to provide for his family and to return to it in one piece,[84] a woman's was to create the environment that would sustain masculine identity. The sort of behavior Jefferson enjoined upon women and men was similar: avoid conflict at all cost. But because the primary focus of their endeavors was different, so also, would be the meaning of their actions.

Jefferson counted on women to make family life agreeable, just as he expected men of good sense to keep political life calm. In his expectations of family life, Jefferson shared one of the contradictions of republican thinking; it assumed at one and the same time that family life was inherently conflict-free and that it was only the self-effacement of women that made it so. Like republican theorists of the family, Jefferson believed that a peaceful society was founded in a harmonious marriage, and a harmonious marriage required a deferential wife.[85] When his daughter Martha married Thomas Mann Randolph, her father warned her, "Your new condition will call for abundance of little sacrifices but they will be greatly overpaid by the measure of affection they will secure to you. The happiness of your life depends now on the continuing to please a single person." Several years later, he would offer similar words of advice to Maria. "Happiness in the married state is the very first object to be aimed at. Nothing can preserve affection uninterrupted by a firm resolution never to differ in will and a determination in each to consider the love of the other as of more value than any object whatever on which a wish has been fixed." Married people should never argue or criticize, especially in public, no matter what the provocation. "Much better therefore," he advised, "if our companion views a thing in a light different from what we do to leave him in quiet possession of his view."[86]

Although the words were strikingly similar to those he would address to his grandson several years later, it must be remembered that Jeff Randolph was instructed on how to avoid disputes in public, not at home. It is clear from his letters to his daughters that Jefferson expected husbands to be almost naturally disputatious, and that he placed almost the entire burden of family happiness on women alone. Nor was it just the peace of their immediate families with which women were entrusted; women were responsible for the harmony of all domestic society, that is, of all the homes in which men and women mixed and met. Again and again Jefferson would tell his daughters to suppress their own feelings and spread the balm of affection wherever they went. When her sister-in-law was caught in a scandal of incest and infanticide, Jefferson advised Martha to be charitable. "Never throw off the best affections of nature in the moment when they become most precious to their object; nor fear to extend your hand to save another, less you should sink yourself."[87] Jefferson offered this advice in 1793, well before he himself became embroiled in lesser scandals, yet it suggests how he thought a family ought to respond to a scandal that touched one of its members.

Martha's response would show that she grasped her father's intent: to display affection, even in the face of error, in the interest of maintaining harmony. Several years earlier, not long after Martha's marriage, her widowed father-in-law remarried a much younger woman and gave signs that he would begin a new family, threatening his older children's expectations for inheritance. Jefferson told Martha not to contest the marriage settlement, but instead to conciliate not only her father-in-law and his bride, but the bride's mother, as well. He gave his daughter detailed instructions in how to manipulate her in-laws. "Be you my dear," Jefferson's advised, "the link of love, union, and peace for the whole family."[88] Not only the peace of the family, but her material well-being depended upon it. When women maintained domestic order, they were doing nothing less than securing the basis for their society's economic and political stability.

Martha learned her lesson well. If we read between the lines of her response to her father's letter recommending charity toward Nancy Randolph, we can see how she absorbed her father's philosophy and transmitted it to her husband. Martha told her father that under the pressure of the scandal, the "divisions" in her husband's family were increasing daily, but that her husband was succeeding in healing them. Her husband's "conduct," she reported, "has been such as to conciliate the affections of the whole family. He is the Link by which so many discordant parts join. . . . there is not one individual but what looks up to him as one, and the only one who has been uniform in his affection."[89] Under her tutelage, her husband, radiating affection, had become the center of his family. And that was the way it was supposed to be: by "sacrifices and suppressions of feeling,"[90] a woman would cultivate the affections of the family, flattering even its most difficult members like a master politician, but it was always to install a man at its head.

Here was the difference, finally, between the home and the world of politics. The methods for achieving harmony in each were similar: they required forbearance, deference to the wishes of others, flattery even, and the suppression of the will. Yet the rewards for men and for women were necessarily different. Jefferson told both of his daughters that the compensation for their self-effacement would be gratifying, but indirect. He promised Martha that "your own happiness will be the greater as you perceive that you promote that of others," and a decade later he renewed the pledge to Maria: "Go on then, my dear, as you have done in deserving the love of every body; you will reap the rich reward of their esteem, and will find that we are working for ourselves while we do good to others."[91] A woman's work was to promote others' happiness, thereby ensuring her own.

Women, in other words, had to earn love; it was the return for love freely given. For men, it was their due. When Jefferson rhapsodized about the happiness of home, he assumed that his daughters would always love him; he never had to worry about earning their love. He could speak with confidence about the blessings of domestic society because he believed its love was eternal. As he told Maria, "The circle of our nearest connections is the only one in which a faithful and lasting affection can be found, one which will adhere to us under all changes and chances." For women, however, love was contingent; it had to be earned. "Be good and industrious," he told Martha when she was fifteen, "and you shall be what I most love in the world."[92]

The letters that Jefferson wrote later, when he was in Philadelphia or New York or Washington, attending to his nation's affairs, with their affectionate closings and their protestations of never-ceasing love more than implied that his daughters had met his expectations. It should not be surprising that they took him at his word when he said that he despised the rancor of politics and longed for the harmony of home. That was another way of saying that he loved them best. How painful it must have been for Martha, then, in the summer of 1800 when her father returned to Monticello for one of his long-anticipated visits, and she could barely spend "one sociable minute" with him for the crowds of people who came in his pursuit. So distressed was Martha that it took her a full two months before she could write. She complained that her father was "allways in a crowd, taken from every useful and pleasing duty to be worried with a multiplicity of disagreeable ones which the entertaining of such crowds of company subjects one to in the country." It was worse for her than if he had been in Philadelphia, "for at least I should have enjoyed in anticipation those pleasures which we were deprived of by the concourse of strangers which continually crowded the house when you were with us."[93] If, as her father told her, it was only the duties of home that were useful and pleasing, why was he entertaining this disagreeable crowd?

Jefferson answered the letter immediately. He assured Martha, "Nobody can ever have felt so severely as myself the prostration of family society from the circumstance you mention." It was more painful for him than it could have been for her. "Worn down here with pursuits in which I take no delight, surrounded by enemies and spies, catching and perverting every word which falls from my lips or flows from my pen, and inventing where facts fail them, I pant for that society where all is peace and harmony, where we love and are loved by every object we see." No, she had not misunderstood him; yes, he would prefer to be at home. "But there is no remedy." As a public figure, however, he had to bring at least part of the public home. Customs were changing, however, and before long, perhaps, the public might intrude only during the day, leaving the family "to tranquility in the evening." Jefferson concluded by asking his daughter to look on the brighter side and "to consider that these visits are evidences of the general esteem which we have been able [*sic*] all our lives trying to merit."[94] But it was, of course, Jefferson, and not his daughter, that these crowds of strangers were coming to see, just as it was Jefferson who was the object of their esteem.

Jefferson was, after all, a public man, and his aspiration was to serve the public in a way that would win him, if not fame, at least esteem. That is the hidden text of all of his letters. The complaints about enemies and spies notwithstanding, Jefferson was not about to leave public life. Even when he retired from government service, the crowds would still come to his home.[95] And he enjoyed the public, but he wanted it on his own terms. When he became president, he implored his daughters to come visit. Maria was reluctant; she had lived in the country so long that she was fearful of the capital's more sophisticated milieu. Her father empathized. Between his retirement from Washington's Cabinet and his election as vice president, he too had "remained closely at home, saw none but those who came there, and at length became very sensible of the ill effect it had upon my mind, and of it's direct and irresistible tendency to render me unfit for society, and uneasy when necessarily engaged in it."[96] He had learned his lesson, and she should, too. Society was good.

In most of his letters home, Jefferson drew a stark contrast between the world of politics and home, but there was really a third realm, one that he always assumed but rarely discussed. "Domestic society" was but a smaller, more affectionate distillation of society at large, differing from it more in degree than kind. Indeed, contemporary political thought conceived the family as the smallest of the concentric circles of social organization to which a man belonged. As a man moved from his immediate family, through various degrees of his kin, he entered his neighborhood, and then society, and after that, the nation or government, beyond which extended the universe of mankind at large. Scottish moral philosophers such as Adam Smith believed that man was by nature affectionate and sympathetic; the sort of love that bound him to his family also knit him to everyone else.[97] This is what Jefferson also meant when he said that man was a social animal. Yet political life confounded Jefferson's expectations, or at least hopes, of a universalizing sympathy. It was out of this frustration that he turned back to his family, as well as to his friends. As much as he relied upon his friends, however, Jefferson never developed a vision of friendship that could compare to the one he crafted of the family. His hopes dashed at the political end of the social spectrum, he fell back upon the smallest and most comforting unit he knew, making of the family his model for social relations. Jefferson described the family so passionately that it is little wonder that his daughters thought their father considered it the only place where he could be happy.

Jefferson was no hypocrite; he loved his daughters dearly, and surely it was their love that sustained him in his darkest days. But he also shaped his family—and indeed, the idea of the family—to meet his needs. It was the family that made a modern politics possible, by divesting it of the emotional intensity that led all too often to violence and by giving men alternate sources of identity. On his deathbed, according to Jeff Randolph, his grandfather was still thinking about the rancor of politics. "In speaking of the calumnies which his enemies had uttered against his public and private character with such unmitigated and untiring bitterness, he said that he had not considered them as abusing him; they had never known *him*. They had created an imaginary being clothed with odious attributes, to whom they had given his name."[98] It was a man's family, not those he encountered in public life, who knew who he really was.

VII

We have suggested that the requirements of modern politics would define and erect a wall between itself and the family, but that is not to imply that the family occupied a small or inconsequential space. The family, instead, was the prototype of society, the vast domain where men and women met and mingled and behaved with virtue, good humor, and self-restraint. For the wall that protected the family encompassed society, as well; it was the world of politics—and perhaps that of business—that was isolated by this fictive wall. Anywhere that women went, affection might prevail. Responding to a female friend who had congratulated him on his election to the presidency, Jefferson replied, "The post is not enviable, as it affords little exercise for the social affections. There is something within us which makes us wish to have things conducted in our own way and which we generally fancy to be in patriotism. This ambition is gratified by such a position. But the heart would be happier enjoying the affections of a family fireside."[99] Jefferson had reinterpreted public virtue—patriotism—as ambition and will; it was the affections nurtured in the family that bound society together. These were the best affections of our nature, the fulfillment of the disposition that the Creator had implanted in mankind's breast.

Politics and governance were separate and distinct. But this was the arena in which Jefferson had made his mark, and this was where his legacy, he hoped, would be. He asked Madison to help preserve the blessings of self-government, not those of domestic society. The latter he entrusted to his family. And the wall between the two realms had been built so strong that it could not be breached; it was the wall, finally, that separated women from men. Half a year before his death, Jefferson commiserated with his granddaughter Ellen. She had married a Bostonian and moved north. The ship that was carrying her baggage had been lost, taking with it all of her letters and books. "And your life cut in two, as it were, and a new one to begin, without any records of the former." Moreover, a beautiful writing desk made by the talented slave carpenter John Hemings was also gone. It could never be replaced. Jefferson, however, offered a substitute "not claiming the same value from it's decorations, but from the part it has *borne* in history": the lap desk upon which he had written the Declaration of Independence. He surmised that such objects were beginning to "acquire a superstitious value because of their connection with particular persons" and events, and that in years to come, the desk might have a place in celebrations of the Fourth of July. With that purpose in mind, Jefferson entrusted his desk not to his granddaughter, but to her husband. "Mr. Coolidge must do for me the favor of accepting this. Its imaginary value will increase with the years, and if he lives to my age, or another half century, he may yet see it carried in the procession of our nation's birthday, as the relics of the saints are in those of the church."[100] Near death, Jefferson imagined himself a saint in his own religion. It was a faith that his female kin, too, had helped him create, but from whose rituals they were excluded.

NOTES

I would like to thank Norma Basch, Barry Bienstock, Rhys Isaac, James Oakes, and Peter Onuf.

1. Merrill D. Peterson, *Thomas Jefferson and the New Nation: A Biography* (New York, 1970), p. 988. See also *Malone*, VI, p. 499.

2. Feb. 17, 1826, *LofA*, p. 513.

3. TJ to Thomas Jefferson Randolph, Feb. 8, 1826, Edwin Morris Betts and James A. Bear, eds., *The Family Letters of Thomas Jefferson,* (Columbia, Mo., 1966), p. 470; *Malone,* VI, p. 511.

4. Undated autobiographical fragment, Ellen Wayles Coolidge Correspondence, Alderman Library, University of Virginia.

5. See, for example, Ellen Wayles Coolidge to TJ, Aug. 1, 1825; Francis Wayles Eppes to TJ, Feb. 23, 1826; and Thomas Jefferson Randolph to TJ, Feb. 3 [1826], Betts and Bear, *Family Letters,* pp. 454, 467, 471–72.

6. TJ to Mary (Maria) Jefferson Eppes (henceforth, before marriage, Mary Jefferson; after, MJE), April 11, 1801; TJ to Martha J. Randolph (henceforth, before marriage, Martha Jefferson; after, MJR), Nov. 7, 1803; MJR to TJ received July 1, 1798; MJR to TJ, Nov. 18, 1801; and MJE to TJ, July 2, 1802, in Betts and Bear, *Family Letters,* pp. 201, 249, 166, 213, 232. Martha Jefferson was born in 1772 and married Thomas Mann Randolph in 1790; she bore twelve children, of whom eleven survived to adulthood. Maria Jefferson was born in 1778 and married John Wayles Eppes in 1797; only one of her three children, Francis, survived to adulthood. Maria died in 1804 and Martha in 1836.

7. MJE to TJ, Nov. 18, 1801; MJR to TJ, April 16, 1802, and March 20, 1807, Betts and Bear, *Family Letters,* pp. 213, 223, and 303.

8. TJ to MJE, Feb. 7, 1799; TJ to MJR, Feb. 11, 1800; TJ to MJR, Nov. 23, 1807; TJ to MJE, Oct. 26, 1801, Betts and Bear, *Family Letters,* pp. 173–74, 184, 315, 210.

9. TJ to Mary Jefferson, draft, June 14, 1797, in Betts and Bear, *Family Letters,* p. 148. See, similarly, TJ to MJE, Jan. 1, 1799, p. 170.

10. For a summary of this debate see Jan Lewis, "Happiness," in Jack P. Greene and J. R. Pole, eds., *The Blackwell Encyclopedia of the American Revolution* (Cambridge, Mass., 1991), pp. 641–47.

11. See Jan Lewis, *The Pursuit of Happiness: Family and Values in Jefferson's Virginia* (New York, 1983). Consider also Ruth Bloch, "The Gendered Meanings of Virtue," *Signs,* 13 (1987), pp. 37–58.

12. TJ to Maria Jefferson, June 26, 1791, in Betts and Bear, *Family Letters,* p. 86. Jefferson's association of happiness with home was foreshadowed in the letter he wrote Chastellux on November 26, 1782. Before the death of his wife Martha several months earlier, Jefferson "had folded myself in the arms of retirement, & rested all prospects of future happiness on domestic and literary objects." *LofA,* p. 780.

13. Jefferson destroyed the letters he had exchanged with his wife Martha, who died in 1782. *Malone*, I, pp. 393–98.

14. TJ to MJR, Jan. 15, 1792, Betts and Bear, *Family Letters*, p. 93. *Malone*, II, pp. 431, 363–66.

15. TJ to Mary Jefferson, May 25, 1797, Betts and Bear, *Family Letters*, 145.

16. TJ to James Monroe, May 20, 1782, *LofA*, pp. 777, 779.

17. Hamilton thought that "private attachments" to the family could undermine loyalty to the republic and even lead to oligarchy if a man put the interests of his family ahead of those of the nation ("The Federalist No. 77," in *The Federalist*, ed. Jacob E. Cooke [Middletown, Ct, 1961], pp. 518–19). George Washington agreed. He told Hamilton that it was a blessing to the nation that he was childless: "The Divine Providence hath not seen fit that my blood should be transmitted or my name perpetuated by the endearing, though sometimes seducing, channel of immediate offspring. I have no child for whom I could wish to make a provision—no family to build in greatness upon my country's ruins" (Washington to Hamilton, Aug. 28, 1788, quoted in M. J. Heale, *The Presidential Quest: Candidates and Images in American Political Culture, 1787–1852* [New York, 1982], p. 14).

18. TJ to Monroe, pp. 777–78.

19. See Jay Fliegelman, *Prodigals and Pilgrims: The American Revolution Against Patriarchal Authority* (New York, 1982), especially pp. 9–29; Daniel Walker Howe, "The Political Psychology of *The Federalist*," *WMQ*, XLIV (1987), pp. 485–509; and Garry Wills, *Inventing America: Jefferson's Declaration of Independence* (Garden City, N.Y., 1978), especially part 4. Consider also Perry Miller, "The Rhetoric of Sensation," in *Errand into the Wilderness* (New York: 1956), pp. 166–83.

20. TJ to MJR, May 17, 1798; May 31, 1798, Betts and Bear, *Family Letters*, pp. 162, 161, 164.

21. TJ to MJR, June 8, 1797, Betts and Bear, *Family Letters*, p. 146.

22. TJ to MJR, Feb. 8, 1798, Ibid., p. 155.

23. TJ to MJR, Jan. 16, 1801, Ibid., p. 191.

24. TJ to MJE, Feb. 15, 1801, Ibid., p. 196.

25. TJ to MJR, Nov. 23, 1807, Ibid., p. 315.

26. See, for example, TJ to Thomas Jefferson Randolph, Feb. 8, 1826, Betts and Bear, *Family Letters*, p. 469.

27. TJ to MJR, June 8, 1797, Betts and Bear, *Family Letters*, p. 146. See, similarly, his letter to Maria, June 14, 1797.

28. TJ to Martha Jefferson, March 6, 1786, and March 28, 1787, Betts and Bear, *Family Letters*, pp. 30, 35.

29. Garry Wills, *Cincinnatus: George Washington and the Enlightenment* (Garden City, N.Y., 1984), p. 129; James Wilson, Law Lectures (1791), *The Works of James Wilson*, 2 vols., Robert Green McCloskey, ed. (Cambridge, Mass., 1967), I, p. 405. See also Douglass Adair, "Fame and the Founding Fathers," in *Fame and the Founding Fathers* (New York, 1974), pp. 3–26. See also Jack P. Greene, "Society, Ideology, and Politics: An Analysis of the Political Culture of Mid-Eighteenth-Century Virginia," in Richard M. Jellison, ed., *Society, Freedom, and Conscience: The Coming of the Revolution in Virginia, Massachusetts, and New York* (New York, 1976), pp. 32–34.

30. See, for example, Wills, *Cincinnatus*, chapters 7 and 8, and Gordon S. Wood, *The Radicalism of the American Revolution* (New York, 1992), pp. 205–10.

31. TJ to Dr. Walter Jones, Jan. 2, 1814, *LofA*, pp. 1318–19.

32. John R. Howe, "Republican Thought and Political Violence of the 1790's," *American Quarterly*, XIX (1967), pp. 149, 165; TJ to Edward Rutledge, June 24, 1797, *The Life and*

Writings of Thomas Jefferson, Adrienne Koch and William Peden, eds. (New York, 1944), p. 544. Howe excerpts this letter somewhat differently. See also Marshall Smelser, "The Federalist Period as an Age of Passion," *American Quarterly,* X (1958), 391–419.

33. Jack N. Rakove, "The Structure of Politics at the Accession of George Washington," in Richard Beeman, Stephen Botein, and Edward C. Carter II, eds., *Beyond Confederation: Origins of the Constitution and American National Identity* (Chapel Hill, N.C., 1987), pp. 261–94.

34. Jefferson to Thomas Jefferson Randolph, Feb. 8, 1826, Betts and Bear, *Family Letters,* p. 470.

35. Forrest McDonald, *Alexander Hamilton: A Biography* (New York, 1979), p. 20.

36. Charles Royster, *A Revolutionary People at War: The Continental Army and American Character, 1775–1783* (Chapel Hill, N.C., 1979), pp. 209–11.

37. McDonald, *Hamilton,* pp. 308–9.

38. Robert H. Wiebe, *The Opening of American Society: From the Adoption of the Constitution to the Eve of Disunion* (New York, 1984), p. 100; St. George Tucker, *Blackstone's Commentaries* (1803), pt. II, n. G, pp. 29–30, quoted in Leonard W. Levy, *Emergence of a Free Press* (New York, 1985), p. 327.

39. Wiebe, *Opening,* p. 103.

40. Alexander Hamilton, "Printed Version of 'The Reynolds Pamphlet,'" in Harold C. Syrett et al., eds., *The Papers of Alexander Hamilton,* 27 vols. (New York, 1961–1987), XXI, p. 258. The Reynolds affair is detailed on pp. 121–44, as well as in McDonald, *Hamilton,* pp. 227–30 and ff., and Broadus Mitchell, *Alexander Hamilton: The National Adventure* (New York, 1962), pp. 399–422. My account of this episode relies upon these works.

41. Quoted in Michael Durey, *"With the Hammer of Truth": James Thomson Callender and America's Early National Heroes* (Charlottesville, Va., 1990), p. 94.

42. [James Thomson Callender], *The History of the United States for 1796* (Philadelphia, 1797), p. 205. Callender made his original charges in a series of pamphlets that have not survived; he later published them in book form as *The History of the United States for 1796.* Hence, it is from the book, rather than the original publications, that subsequent histories have been written. Syrett et al., *Papers of Hamilton,* XXI, pp. 121–22.

43. James Thomson Callender, *Sketches of the History of America* (Philadelphia, 1798), p. 91.

44. "Reynolds Pamphlet," pp. 238–39.

45. "Reynolds Pamphlet," p. 239; "People v. Harry Croswell, New York Supreme Court, 1803–1804, in Julius Goebel, Jr. et al., eds., *The Law Practice of Alexander Hamilton,* 5 vols. (New York, 1964–1981), pp. 810, 809, 820.

46. "Reynolds Pamphlet," pp. 239, 251, 267. Hamilton charged that "jacobin newspapers and pamphlets" were "artfully calculated to hold up the opponents of the FACTION to the jealousy and distrust of the present generation and if possible, to transmit their names with dishonor to posterity" (p. 239). Hamilton places most of the blame for his affair on the seductive Mrs. Reynolds. In order to entice him, she presented herself as appealingly weak: affecting an "air of affliction," she had "appl[ied]" to his "humanity" with a tale of abuse and abandonment. But once the affair had commenced, Mrs. Reynolds became dangerously strong: "her conduct made it extremely difficult to disentangle myself. All the appearances of violent attachment, and of agonizing distress were played off with a most imposing art" (p. 252).

47. For a thorough account, see Syrett et al., *Papers of Hamilton,* XXI, pp. 133–38, 316–20; for the relevant correspondence, see pp. 146–346.

48. Mitchell, *Hamilton,* II, pp. 496–99; quotation on p. 496.

49. Wiebe, *Opening,* p. 101.

50. For a thorough description of the duel and the supporting documents, see *Papers of Hamilton,* XXVI, pp. 235–349. Burr is quoted on p. 236. Hamilton's letter to Elizabeth Hamilton [July 4, 1804] is on p. 293. See also Hamilton's "Statement on the Impending Duel with Aaron Burr," [June 28–July 10, 1804], pp. 278–80. Among the reasons not to duel were: "My wife and Children are extremely dear to me, and my life is of the utmost importance to them, in various views." Nonetheless, he had to accept Burr's challenge. "To those, who with me abhorring the practice of Duelling may think that I ought on no account to have added to the number of bad examples—I answer that my *relative* situation, as well in public as in private aspects, enforcing all the considerations which constitute what men of the world denominate honor, impressed on me . . . a peculiar necessity not to decline the call. The ability to be in future useful, whether in resisting mischief or effecting good, in those crises of our public affairs, which seem likely to happen, would probably be inseparable from a conformity with public prejudice in this particular."

51. "Notes on the Reynolds Affair," Dec. 17, 1792, *Boyd,* XXIV, p. 75. See also *Papers of Hamilton,* XXI, p. 136. Michael Durey has recently suggested that it might have been Jefferson who gave Callender the documents that he printed in his exposé of Hamilton. After he, Venable, and Muhlenberg had interviewed Hamilton in December 1792, Monroe had kept the originals, which he later claimed to have sent to a friend, whom Durey claims was Jefferson. (Durey, *Hammer of Truth,* pp. 98–101.) The evidence is circumstantial and inconclusive. Most historians have believed that Callender probably got the documents from John Beckley, the Republican Clerk of the House, to whom Monroe had passed on the originals for subscribing. Whether or not Jefferson saw the documents before Callender published them, it is evident that copies of them, at least, and reports of their contents were well known in Republican circles.

52. "The Anas," Feb. 4, 1818, in *LofA,* p. 671. My interpretation follows that of *Malone,* IV, p. 431.

53. For an account of Callender's career, see Durey, *Hammer of Truth,* esp. chs. 6 and 7; and Fawn M. Brodie, *Thomas Jefferson: An Intimate History* (New York, 1974), ch. 23.

54. Richmond *Recorder,* Sept. 1, 1802, quoted in Durey, *Hammer of Truth,* p. 158.

55. Callender, *History of the United States for 1796,* p. 205.

56. Richmond *Recorder,* Sept. 1, 1802, quoted in Durey, *Hammer of Truth,* p. 158.

57. Reprinted in the Richmond *Recorder,* Nov. 3, 1802, quoted in Brodie, *Intimate History,* p. 353.

58. "From Callender's Recorder," in *Boston Gazette,* Nov. 11, 1802; "From the Boston Gazette," *New-York Evening Post,* Dec. 8, 1802.

59. *The Defence of Young and Minns, Printers to the State, Before the Committee of the House of Representatives* (Boston, 1805), preface.

60. Richmond *Recorder,* Feb. 2, 1803, quoted in Durey, *Hammer of Truth,* p. 163.

61. In 1805 the *New-England Palladium* pulled these charges together in an article entitled "The Monarchy of Federalism" (Jan. 18, 1805). The focus of the article was Jefferson's public character (he was described as "a patriot regardless of his country's welfare, and entirely devoted to raize himself and his partizans upon the nation's ruin"); the editors assumed without explaining the relevance of the Sally Hemings and Betsey Walker stories. For a summary, see *Malone,* IV, pp. 206–35.

62. *Richmond Examiner,* Oct. 2, 1802; Nov. 6, 1802; and Sept. 22, 1802. Republican suspicions about Marshall are discussed in Durey, *Hammer of Truth,* p. 161. For the allegations against Callender, see *Richmond Examiner,* Sept. 22, 1802, and Oct. 2, 1802, and

Durey, *Hammer of Truth*, 161–62. The basis for this slur against Pinckney is not entirely clear. Since 1799, allegations had been circulating that, while serving as emissaries to France, he and Marshall had been intimate with a French woman, who bore the already-married Pinckney a child and followed him back to South Carolina, where either Pinckney and Marshall were supporting her or she had been cast off. It is not clear, however, how this story might have been construed as a reflection upon Pinckney's masculinity, unless the mere association with France and South Carolina (where he enjoyed "the Atlantic luxuries of a southern climate") somehow feminized him. The insinuation might have been that as Hamilton's puppet, Pinckney was, like a woman, weak. For the allegations against Pinckney, see Marvin R. Zahniser, *Charles Cotesworth Pinckney: Founding Father* (Chapel Hill, N.C., 1967), pp. 175–76, 208–9, 239–41.

63. *Richmond Examiner*, Sept. 25, 1802; *Boston Gazette*, Dec. 2, 1802.

64. The literature on this topic is vast. One might begin with Fliegelman, *Prodigals and Pilgrims;* Melvin Yazawa, *From Colonies to Commonwealth: Familial Ideology and the Beginnings of the American Republic* (Baltimore, Md., 1985); Jan Lewis, "The Republican Wife: Virtue and Seduction in the Early Republic," *WMQ*, XLIV (1987), pp. 689–721; Lewis, *Pursuit of Happiness*. Changes in the American family are summarized in Steven Mintz and Susan Kellogg, *Domestic Revolutions: A Social History of American Family Life* (New York, 1988), chs. 2 and 3.

65. Richmond *Recorder*, Sept. 29, 1802, quoted in Brodie, *Intimate History*, p. 352; *Richmond Examiner*, Sept. 25, 1802. This vision of Thomas Jefferson's family life was not entirely a creation of the political press; it was the way that his family saw it too. Half a century later, Jefferson's granddaughter would also use it to rebut Callender's charges: "Some of the children earnestly reported to be Mr. Jefferson's were about the age of his own grandchildren. Of course he must have been carrying on his intrigues in the midst of his own grandchildren. . . . His apartment had no private entrance not perfectly accessible and visible to all the household. . . . But I put it to any fair mind to decide if a man so admirable in his domestic character as Mr Jefferson . . . would be likely to rear a race of half-breeds under their eyes and carry on his low amours in the circle of his family." (Ellen Wayles Coolidge to Joseph Coolidge, Jr., Oct. 24, 1858, Ellen Wayles Coolidge Collection, Alderman Library, University of Virginia).

66. *Defence of Young and Minns*, p. 50.

67. TJ to MJE, Oct. 26, 1801, Betts and Bear, *Family Letters*, p. 210.

68. *Boston Gazette*, Oct. 21, 1802; *Defense of Young and Minns*, p. 53; *Richmond Examiner*, June 25, 1803, and July 2, 1803. For Lee's role in the Walker affair, see Charles Royster, *Light-Horse Harry Lee and the Legacy of the American Revolution* (New York, 1981), pp. 208–9. See, similarly, *New-York Evening Post*, Dec. 8, 1802.

69. TJ to Robert Smith, July 5, 1805, in Brodie, *Intimate History*, p. 375; TJ to MJR, April 23, 1803, Betts and Bear, *Family Letters*, pp. 243–44.

70. TJ to Thomas McKean, Feb. 19, 1803, in Ford, IX, pp. 218–19 (incorrectly cited as IX, pp. 451–52 in Levy, *Free Press*, p. 341); Levy, *Free Press*, ch. X. For Jefferson's views on freedom of the press see also Frank L. Mott, *Jefferson and the Press* (Baton Rouge, La., 1943), and Levy, *Jefferson and Civil Liberties: The Darker Side* (New York, 1973), ch. 3. For freedom of the press in Virginia see Steven H. Hochman, "On the Liberty of the Press in Virginia: From Essay to Bludgeon, 1798–1803," *VMHB*, 84 (1976), pp. 431–45.

71. TJ to McKean, Feb. 19, 1803, Ford, IX, p. 218; Jefferson to Wilson Cary Nicholas, June 13, 1809, Ford, IX, pp. 253–54.

72. *Malone*, V, p. 624; TJ to Thomas Jefferson Randolph, Nov. 24, 1808, in Betts and Bear, *Family Letters*, pp. 362–65. This and the following paragraphs are derived from this

letter. See, similarly, Jefferson's letter to his other grandson, Francis Wayles Eppes (May 21, 1816, p. 415): "Above all things, and at all times, practice yourself in good humor. This, of all human qualities, is the most amiable and endearing to society." See, similarly, TJ to Thomas Jefferson Randolph, Dec. 7, 1808, p. 369, and TJ to Charles L. Bankhead, Nov. 26, 1808, *L&B*, XVIII, pp. 253–54.

73. TJ to Thomas Law, June 13, 1814, *LofA*, p. 1337.

74. Ibid.

75. TJ to John Randolph, Dec. 1, 1803, *Ford*, VIII, pp. 281–82.

76. *Malone*, V, pp. 127–32; Peterson, *Jefferson*, pp. 839–40. For a different interpretation see William Cabell Bruce, *John Randolph of Roanoke, 1773–1833* (New York, 1922), I, pp. 261–65. See also Henry S. Randall, *The Life of Thomas Jefferson* (New York, 1858), pp. 164–67.

77. TJ to James Ogilvie, *L&B*, XVIII, pp. 247–48; TJ to Thomas Mann Randolph, July 13, 1806, *Ford*, VIII, pp. 459–60.

78. Ibid., p. 459.

79. Wiebe, *Opening*, pp. 327–32. Until that time, however, any dispute between gentlemen risked becoming the occasion for a duel. Although the absolute number of duels fought may have remained relatively small, the number of challenges must have been much greater, and the presence in politics of volatile men such as John Randolph of Roanoke ensured that any debate could easily be interpreted as a slur upon one's personal honor. See p. 186. Consider also the accounts of duels printed in the *Richmond Examiner* during the fall of 1803.

80. TJ to Thomas Jefferson Randolph, Feb. 8, 1826, Betts and Bear, *Family Letters*, p. 470.

81. Norma Basch, "Marriage, Morals, and Politics in the Election of 1828," paper presented to the American Studies Association, Anaheim, California, October 1992. I am indebted to Professor Basch for letting me see the expanded version of her paper and for her invaluable insights into the ways in which gender figured in early American politics.

82. Bloch, "Gendered Meanings"; Richard L. McCormick, "Scandal and Reform: A Framework for the Study of Political Corruption in the Nineteenth-Century United States and a Case Study of the 1820s," paper presented to the Shelby Cullum Davis Center for Historical Studies, Princeton University, 1982; Robert V. Remini, *Andrew Jackson and the Course of American Freedom, 1822–1832,* (New York, 1981), vol. II, esp. ch. 2; Rubil Morales, "The Cloudy Medium of Language," M.A. thesis, Rutgers University-Newark, 1992.

83. TJ to Francis Wayles Eppes, May 21, 1816, Betts and Bear, *Family Letters*, p. 415. For similar letters to female kin see TJ to Mary Jefferson, April 11, 1790, p. 52; and TJ to Ellen Wayles Randolph, Nov. 27, 1801, p. 214.

84. For Jefferson's view on proper gender roles, see TJ to Governor William H. Harrison, Feb. 27, 1803, *LofA*, pp. 1117–19; "To the Brothers of the Choctaw Nation," Dec. 17, 1803, pp. 559–60; "Travel Journals," pp. 651–52.

85. Lewis, "Republican Wife." This is not to say, however, that all of Jefferson's attitudes about women and marriage were republican. Jefferson retained a streak of misogyny that was characteristic of an earlier age. See Kenneth A. Lockridge, *On the Sources of Patriarchal Rage: The Commonplace Books of William Byrd and Thomas Jefferson and the Gendering of Power in the Eighteenth Century* (New York, 1992).

86. TJ to MJR, April 4, 1790, Betts and Bear, *Family Letters*, p. 51. Jefferson also instructed Martha that she must now put her husband ahead even of him; this advice, however, she was not able to follow. TJ to MJE, Jan. 7, 1798, pp. 151–52.

87. TJ to MJR, April 28, 1793, Betts and Bear, *Family Letters*, p. 115. Thomas Mann

Randolph's unmarried sister, Nancy, had been accused of bearing her brother-in-law Richard Randolph's baby; Richard Randolph was tried and acquitted of the murder of the baby, whose body had never been found, although slaves had reported seeing both it and blood stains at the house where Richard and his wife Judith and her sister Nancy had been staying. Richard Randolph was the brother of John Randolph of Roanoke, and it is possible that his animosity to Nancy and her family exacerbated the political tensions that would grow between him and Jefferson. For a full account of the "Scandal at Bizarre," see Bruce, *John Randolph*, I, pp. 107–23, II, pp. 273–77.

88. TJ to MJR, April 28, 1793, Betts and Bear, *Family Letters*, p. 60.

89. MJR to TJ, May 16, 1793, Betts and Bear, *Family Letters*, p. 118.

90. TJ to MJR, June 22, 1792, Betts and Bear, *Family Letters*, p. 102.

91. TJ to MJR, July 17, 1790; TJ to MJE, February 12, 1800, Betts and Bear, *Family Letters*, pp. 61, 186. See, similarly, TJ to Mary Jefferson, May 30, 1791: "To see you in short place your felicity in acquiring the love of those among whom you live, and without which no body can ever be happy" (p. 84).

92. TJ to Mary Jefferson, Jan. 1, 1799; TJ to MJE, May 21, 1787, Betts and Bear, *Family Letters*, pp. 170, 41–42. See, similarly, Nov. 28, 1783; Sept. 20, 1785; pp. 20, 29.

93. MJR to TJ, Jan. 31, 1801, Betts and Bear, *Family Letters*, p. 192.

94. TJ to MJR, Feb. 5, 1801, Betts and Bear, *Family Letters*, p. 195. As long as he lived, strangers would feel free to visit Jefferson at home; Martha never reconciled herself to this situation. See MJR to Ellen W. Coolidge, Sept. 18, 1825, Coolidge Collection.

95. MJR to Ellen W. Coolidge, Sept. 25, 1825; Ellen W. Coolidge to Henry Randall, 1856, in Sarah N. Randolph, *The Domestic Life of Thomas Jefferson* (1871; reprint, Charlottesville, Va., 1978), pp. 344–45.

96. TJ to MJE, March 3, 1802, p. 218.

97. See n. 19 above; see also Adam Smith, *The Theory of Moral Sentiments*, D. D. Raphael and A. L. Macfie, eds., (Indianapolis, Ind., 1982). In the *Notes on Virginia* Jefferson repeated the Comte de Buffon's charge that because native Americans did not love their women, they did not love their fellow men: "Il ne faut pas aller chercher plus loin la cause de la vie dispersée des sauvages & de leur éloignement pour la société: la plus précieuse étincelle du feu de la nature leur a été refusée; ils manquent d'ardeur pour leur femelle, et par consequent d'amour pour leur semblables."). In defending native Americans, Jefferson implicitly accepted the Comte's sociology: "he is affectionate to his children. . . . His affections comprehend his other connections, weakening, as with us, from circle to circle, as they recede from the center." *LofA*, pp. 183–85. Also see Rhys Isaac, "The First Monticello," in this volume, p. 100.

98. Randolph, *Domestic Life*, p. 369.

99. TJ to Catharine Church, March 27, 1801, *L&B*, XVIII, pp. 240–41.

100. TJ to Ellen Wayles Coolidge, Nov. 14, 1825, Betts and Bear, *Family Letters*, pp. 461–62.

CHAPTER 5

"Those Who Labor for My Happiness"
Thomas Jefferson and His Slaves

LUCIA STANTON

To give liberty to, or rather, to abandon persons whose habits have been formed in slavery is like abandoning children.[1]

On January 15, 1827, Monticello blacksmith Joseph Fossett may have left his anvil to watch the bidding begin. His wife Edith and their eight children were among the "130 valuable negroes" offered in the executor's sale of the estate of Thomas Jefferson. "The negroes are believed to be the most valuable for their number ever offered at one time in the State of Virginia," declared the advertisement placed by Thomas Jefferson Randolph, Jefferson's grandson and executor. Despite bitterly cold weather, a large crowd assembled for the five-day sale, and bidding was brisk. Surprising sums were paid for faded prints and old-fashioned tables, while the slaves brought prices averaging 70 percent more than their appraised values.[2]

By the terms of Jefferson's will, Fossett would become a free man in July. Now his wife, two infant sons, and two teenage daughters were sold to three different bidders for a total of $1,350. "Thank heaven the whole of this dreadful business is over," wrote Jefferson's granddaughter on January 25, "and has been attended with as few distressing occurrences as the case would admit." Her brother remembered that week over forty years later as "a sad scene" and likened it to "a captured village in ancient times when all were sold as slaves."[3]

The monumental debt kept in check by Jefferson's presence overwhelmed all the residents of Monticello, both black and white. In the three years after his death the black families were dispersed by sale and the white family left the mountaintop and put the house on the market. The plantation "family" that Jefferson had nurtured and controlled for sixty years was no more. In the end, he had abandoned his "children."

"MY FAMILY"

In 1776 Jefferson made a census of the "Number of souls in my family." His Albemarle County "family" numbered 117, including, besides his wife and daughter, sixteen free men (his overseers and hired workmen), their wives and children, and eighty-three slaves. Throughout his life Jefferson used the word "family" for both a group of people connected by blood and—according to more ancient usage—all those under a head of household, or, in his case, plantation owner. In 1801 he vaccinated "70 or 80 of my own family" against smallpox; in 1819 he spoke of the voracious appetite for pork of "our enormously large family." At times this usage required the addition of qualifying adjectives. Jefferson wrote that his son-in-law's "white family" had recovered from a prevailing illness in 1806, and, in 1815, he noted the surprising number of sick "in our family, both in doors and out"—making a neat spatial distinction between the Jefferson-Randolph family inside the Monticello house and the black men, women, and children living in cabins on the mountaintop and adjacent farms.[4]

Joseph Fossett joined this family in November 1780, born to Mary Hemings (b. 1753) and an unknown father. Mary was the oldest child of Elizabeth (Betty) Hemings (c. 1735–1807), who, with her ten children, became Jefferson's property on January 14, 1774, on the division of the estate of his father-in-law John Wayles.[5] On that date Jefferson acquired 135 slaves who, added to the fifty-two slaves derived from his inheritance from his father, made him the second largest slaveholder in Albemarle County. Thereafter, the number of slaves he owned fluctuated above and below the figure of two hundred—with increases through births offset by periodic sales that were part of an attempt to pay off the almost £4,000 debt that accompanied the Wayles inheritance. Between 1784 and 1794 he disposed of 161 people by sale or gift.[6]

Unlike his father-in-law, Jefferson never engaged in the commercial buying and selling of humans. His infrequent purchases were usually made to fulfill needs of the moment and selling was primarily a reluctant reaction to financial demands. As Jefferson wrote in 1820, he had "scruples about selling negroes but for delinquency, or on their own request."[7] Several known transactions were intended to unite families. The purchase of Ursula in 1773 involved buying her husband Great George from a second owner. In 1805, Jefferson "reluctantly" sold Brown, a twenty-year-old nailer, to unite him with his wife, the slave of a brickmason about to leave Monticello. On this occasion Jefferson declared himself "always willing to indulge connections seriously formed by those people, where it can be done reasonably."[8]

In 1807 Jefferson bought the wife of his blacksmith Moses when her owner emigrated to Kentucky. "Nobody feels more strongly than I do," he wrote at the time, "the desire to make all practicable sacrifices to keep man and wife together who have imprudently married out of their respective families." This final phrase, a telling indication of the dual nature of Jefferson's recognition of the importance of the black family, reveals his hope that his slaves would seek spouses only within their master's domain. "There is nothing I desire so much as that all the young people in the estate should intermarry with one another and stay at home," Jefferson wrote his Poplar Forest overseer. "They are worth a great deal more in that case than when they have husbands and wives abroad." His methods for discouraging romance beyond the plantation boundaries are not known, but he did use rewards to encourage "prudent" courtship. To the slave women, for instance, he promised an extra pot and crocus bed "when they take husbands at home."[9]

Jefferson realized the potency of family bonds for the African-American members of his extended household. In 1814, there is even a note of envy in his comparison of the lot of English laborers and American slaves. Slaves "have the comfort, too, of numerous families, in the midst of whom they live without want, or fear of it." This "comfort" was not always possible for whites. Jefferson all his life sought to draw to the neighborhood of Monticello both kin and kindred spirits, but with only limited success. The mobility of white Virginians separated parent from child and sibling from sibling. His sister emigrated with her husband to Kentucky, and his younger daughter's husband could not be persuaded to leave his Tidewater plantation. Jefferson's fatherly tenacity kept his elder daughter Martha always at or near Monticello, at considerable jeopardy to her marriage. His rosy picture of the "comfort of numerous families" was drawn at a time when Virginian society was progressively destabilized by westward migration. He must, therefore, have witnessed how frequently the ties within extended slave families were severed, and he would have heard constant expression of the "dread of separation" that Frederick Douglass called the "most painful to the majority of slaves."[10]

Jefferson's awareness of the slave's attachment to a particular spot on earth and the extended network of relations that lived on it played a significant part in his actions as a slaveholder. He could foster family ties through benevolent intercession, he could exploit them to control behavior, or ignore them in the interests of efficient management. These ties could even inhibit his actions toward improving the lot of his slaves through emancipation or removal to cotton country, where conditions were considered more favorable to their well-being. Even freedom was not, in Jefferson's mind, sufficient justification for uprooting whole families. In 1814, he wrote that "the laws do not permit us to turn them loose," evidently referring to the 1806 act declaring that freed slaves must leave the state within a year. When his son-in-law Thomas Mann Randolph launched a scheme in 1802 to take his slaves to "a mild climate and gentle labor" in Georgia, Jefferson did consider sending "such of my negroes as could be persuaded to it." But in 1822, Martha Randolph knew her father "would never listen . . . for a moment" to the family's latest plan to try their fortunes further south—"although moving [his slaves] in a body would occasion little or no distress to them." [11]

Slaves were both humans and property, and as the protector of a large household and the manager of a working plantation, Jefferson always had to play two roles. He was gratified when "moral as well as interested considerations" were in accord, as when prescribing lighter labors for women with infant children in 1819: "I consider the labor of a breeding woman as no object, and that a child raised every 2. years is of more profit than the crop of the best laboring man. In this, as in all other cases, providence has made our interest and our duties coincide perfectly." But he must have had daily reminders of the frequent contradiction between "interest" and "duty." [12]

In his role as plantation manager, Jefferson's efforts to maximize the utility of each man, woman, and child led to regular interference in the family lives of his slaves. The demands of productivity limited his respect for the integrity of the black family. Like many other enlightened Virginians, Jefferson always specified that slaves be sold in family units: husbands were not separated from wives, nor parents from young children. But once black boys or girls reached the age of ten or twelve and their working lives began, they lost their status as children and with it, the guarantee of family stability. Teenagers were often separated from their families through sale or transfer to other plantations. Four boys from Poplar Forest, aged ten to twelve, were sent to Monticello to work in the nailery in the 1790s, and in 1813 two fourteen-year-old girls left Bedford County to learn weaving and spinning in the Albemarle County textile factory. The privileged household servants were particularly vulnerable to teenage separation as their young masters or mistresses grew up and married. Betty Brown left her family to attend the newly married Martha Jefferson at age thirteen, and her niece,

Betsy Hemings, was fourteen when she was given to Jefferson's daughter Maria on her marriage in 1797.[13]

Dinah was sold in 1792 with "her younger children" to accomplish the double objective of paying off a debt and uniting her with her husband. When Jefferson purchased the weaver Nance Hemings from his sister, he listened to a mother's plea. Nance "wishes me to buy her children," he wrote, "but I would not purchase the boy; as to the youngest child, if she insists on it, and my sister desires it, I would take it." Fifteen-year-old Billy was left in Louisa County and twelve-year-old Critta only came to Albemarle because she was bought by Jefferson's son-in-law.[14]

Joe Fossett was also separated from his mother by sale. During Jefferson's five-year absence in France, Mary Hemings was hired out to Thomas Bell, a respected Charlottesville merchant. In 1792 she asked to be sold to Bell, the father of her two youngest children, Robert Washington and Sally Jefferson. Jefferson asked his superintendent to "dispose of Mary according to her desire, with such of her younger children as she chose." Bob and Sally remained with their mother and became Bells, and eleven-year-old Joe and nine-year-old Betsy were now on their own at Monticello.[15]

Joe spent his days in and around the Monticello house, one of nine house servants. He and three of his cousins were the fetchers and carriers, the fire builders, the table setters and waiters; they met guests at the east portico and ventured forth on errands. They were the "boys" that Martha Jefferson Randolph finally got "in tolerable order" during Jefferson's absence, after some accidents to the household china.[16]

In the house Joe was surrounded by members of his own family, all Hemingses. The household staff included his uncles James and Peter; his aunts Sally and Critta; his cousins Wormley, Burwell, and Brown; and his sister Betsy.[17] From their arrival at Monticello as part of the Wayles estate in 1774, the children of Betty Hemings assumed the primary roles in the Monticello household. Robert Hemings (1762–1819) replaced Jupiter as Jefferson's valet and traveling attendant; Martin Hemings (b. 1755) became the butler; Betty Hemings and her daughters were employed in cleaning, sewing, and in personal attendance on Martha Jefferson and her children. In the period of Jefferson's retirement to Monticello from 1794 to 1797, visitors who did not wander over to Mulberry Row or down to the cellar dependencies would have seen only Hemingses.

Jefferson's grandson Thomas Jefferson Randolph recalled a slightly later period, when the "entire household of servants with the exception of an under cook and carriage driver consisted of one family connection and their

wives. . . . It was a source of bitter jealousy to the other slaves, who liked
to account for it with other reasons than the true one; viz. superior intelligence, capacity and fidelity to trusts." Monticello overseer Edmund Bacon
spoke of the women of the household: "They were old family servants and
great favorites. . . . I was instructed to take no control of them." And more
than one visitor would have noted, as did the Duc de La Rochefoucauld-
Liancourt in 1796, that the slaves visible at Monticello were remarkably light-skinned. "I have even seen," he wrote at a time when Sally Hemings's children were not yet on the scene, "and particularly at Mr.
Jefferson's, slaves who have neither in their color nor features a single
trace of their origin, but they are sons of slave mothers and consequently
slaves." [18]

Betty Hemings was the daughter of an African slave and an English sea
captain. At least seven of her children had white fathers. Isaac Jefferson
(1775–c. 1850), former Monticello slave whose reminiscences were recorded in 1847, recalled that Betty's children Robert and James Hemings
were "bright mulattoes" and Sally was "mighty near white." [19] Many of the
third generation of Hemingses were even lighter. Without reviving the
debate over the paternity of Sally Hemings's children, it is sufficient to note
here that several and perhaps all of Betty Hemings's daughters formed relationships with white men. [20] In at least one case, that of Sally Hemings,
the children had seven-eighths white ancestry and thus were white by Virginia law, which declared that a person "who shall have one fourth part or
more of negro blood, shall . . . be deemed a mulatto."

Jefferson looked up this statute in 1815 and, after demonstrating its
effects in a series of algebraic formulas, stated that "our Canon considers 2.
crosses with the pure white, and a 3d. with any degree of mixture, however
small, as clearing the issue of the negro blood. . . . But observe," he continued, "that this does not reestablish freedom, which depends on the condition of the mother." If the issue of the third cross were emancipated, "he
becomes a free *white* man, and a citizen of the US. to all intents and purposes." [21] Thus, future citizens of the United States were being held in
bondage at Monticello.

Jefferson did free all of Sally Hemings's children. He allowed Harriet
and Beverly to "run away," providing Harriet money and stage fare to Philadelphia, and gave Madison and Eston Hemings their freedom in his will.
Overseer Edmund Bacon remembered Harriet's departure, when "people
said he freed her because she was his own daughter" (Bacon's own candidate
for paternity was deleted in the published version of his reminiscences), but
the reasons given by Jefferson's granddaughter Ellen Coolidge accord with

his racial formulas. In 1858 she stated that it was her grandfather's principle to "allow such of his slaves as were sufficiently white to pass for white men, to withdraw from the plantation; it was called running away, but they were never reclaimed."[22]

"It is almost impossible for slaves to give a correct account of their male parentage," wrote former slave Henry Bibb in 1849. The fathers of Betty Hemings's children and grandchildren can never be positively identified. The only certainty is that some of them were white men, and those implicated by their contemporaries ranged from overseers and hired artisans to sprigs of the local aristocracy, family kinsmen, and even the master himself.[23] Jefferson, thus, who often stated his "aversion" to racial mixture, lived surrounded by its examples.[24]

Little is known about miscegenation at Monticello beyond the Hemings family. The presence of two mulattoes in the legacy of Peter Jefferson suggests that the crossing of racial lines was nothing new on the mountain.[25] Nevertheless, the Hemings family—as Thomas Jefferson Randolph's statement indicated—seems to have been a caste apart.

All the slaves freed by Jefferson in his lifetime or in his will were members of this family. Two, Robert and Martin, were allowed a measure of mobility no other slave had—they often hired themselves out to other masters during Jefferson's long absences in public service. Only Betty Hemings and her daughters were spared the grueling weeks of the wheat harvest, when every healthy slave was drafted to bring in the crop. None of her twelve children, and only two of her more than twenty grandchildren, found spouses "at home." Known husbands were drawn from the local community, both free black and white, and wives from the household staffs of neighboring plantations.[26] Only Joe Fosset and Wormley, who married a niece of Isaac Jefferson, found wives at Monticello.

At the boundary between the black and white worlds at Monticello, the Hemings family has occupied the foreground of all accounts of the slave community there because we know more about them. Their domination of the documentary record derives from the positions they occupied in the household and Mulberry Row shops, under perpetual observation by their master and his family.

"TO LABOUR FOR ANOTHER"

In 1794 Joe Fossett's life took on a new dimension. He was one of "a dozen little boys from 10. to 16. years of age" whom Jefferson installed in a new nailery on Mulberry Row.[27] Retired to Monticello, Jefferson devoted most of his energies at this time to the reformation of his farms, impoverished by thirty years of the extractive rotation of corn and tobacco and the unsupervised management of stewards and overseers. Expecting the change from tobacco to wheat production and the inauguration of his complex crop rotation schemes to cause a temporary decrease in farm production, he had determined to find a new source of income. He chose the production of nails, because it required little capital outlay and was within the capacities of his own slave labor force.

In the first three years of the nailery's operation, Jefferson was a daily presence. His surviving accounts reveal that he must have risen at dawn to weigh out the nailrod given to the nailers and returned toward dusk to weigh the nails they produced. An "Estimate on the actual work of the autumn of 1794" summarizes the results of his daily balancing of the scales. "Moses wastes 15 lb. in the [hundredweight]," he began, writing down the name of each nailer and the average amount of iron he wasted in the nail-making process. Fourteen-year-old Joe Fossett was one of the most efficient, wasting only nineteen pounds of iron per hundredweight, while two ten-year-olds—Burwell and James—were predictably the least efficient, making only seventy-one pounds of nails from every hundred pounds of nailrod. Another ten-year-old, however, the future wagoner Davy, was the third of nine in efficiency.[28]

Here was a new scene for Joe, Wormley, and Burwell, who now divided their time between the Monticello house and the Mulberry Row nailery, where a dozen teenagers stood at their anvils around four fires, pointing and heading nails with heavy hammers until they had completed their appointed tasks. Because of his household duties Joe's daily task was about two-thirds that of the full-time nailers—250 to 350 nails depending on size. Two years later, when he left the house to pursue the ironworking trade full-time, his task was increased. One page of accounts shows Jefferson apparently calculating the average production of his nailers in order to set a new and higher daily task. In an analysis Jefferson made in April 1796, Joe Fossett was the third most profitable nailer, making 316 pounds of nails in three months and earning for his master an average daily profit of about sixty cents.[29]

The Mulberry Row nailery served as more than a new source of income. It allowed Jefferson to observe the abilities and attitudes of his young male slaves and to select their future careers. By the same token, in the nailery these young men had a chance to influence their future by their own actions. Many of them evidently chose to please their master by their performance and eventually occupied the most important artisan and household positions on the mountain. Several became blacksmiths, carpenters, and coopers; one became the head gardener and another the Monticello butler; a few were unable to avert the usual fate of farm labor; and at least one, Jame Hubbard—the most "wasteful" in 1794—chose the route of resistance.

The nailery was also an important part of Jefferson's perpetual effort to make the most efficient use of his labor force. His constant attempts to eliminate every pocket of idleness from his operation went beyond the ordinary profit-seeking of plantation managers. Neither youth, age, illness, nor weather were allowed to stop the plantation machine. There is even a note of pride in Jefferson's accounts of his successful efforts to provide for all his wants by harnessing the energies of children. In the summer of 1795 he wrote that "a nailery which I have established with my own negro boys now provides completely for the maintenance of my family." A few months earlier he had declared that "my new trade of nail-making is to me in this country what an additional title of nobility or the ensigns of a new order are in Europe."[30]

Twenty years later Jefferson's favorite project was the textile factory, which "only employs a few women, children and invalids who could do little in the farm." Appropriate tasks were found for slaves past the age for farm labor. "The negroes too old to be hired," Jefferson wrote his steward in 1788, "could they not make a good profit by cultivating cotton?" Some older women served as nurses or cooks in the quarters while others joined the older men on the vegetable gardening team, dubbed by Jefferson the "veteran aids" and "senile corps."[31]

The sick who were not bedridden were treated with gentle doses of alternative labor. When all hands were diverted to the digging of a canal in 1793, the "invalids" were to "work only when they shall be able. They will probably be equal to the hauling away the earth and forming it into a bank on the side next the river." Poplar Forest's former "head man" Nace was to be "entirely kept from labour until he recovers." Jefferson suggested, nevertheless, that he spend his days indoors, shelling corn or making shoes or baskets.[32]

So that neither climate nor circumstance could interrupt the hum of activity on his plantation, Jefferson gave his laborers a variety of skills. Barnaby and Shepherd, whose main trade was carpentry, were to join Phil when he "proceeds to the making shoes for the people . . . in order to perfect themselves in shoemaking." Carpenters and coopers were also charcoal burners. Nailers were dispatched to the woods with axes when there was an immediate need for clearing land. Poplar Forest blacksmiths, when there was no work, could fell wood for charcoal or work in the fields; Bess made butter "during the season" and worked in the spinning house when there was no dairy work.[33]

Male domestic servants, in particular, were trained in a trade they could pursue during Jefferson's long absences in public service. Jupiter was a stonecutter as well as manservant and groom. Burwell Colbert, butler at Monticello for many years, was a skilled glazier and painter. Israel, a waiter and postillion, worked as a carder in the textile shop when his services were not needed by the household and, as already mentioned, the young boys in the house filled their extra hours with nail-making. Although overseer Edmund Bacon wrote that the female house servants had "very little to do" when Jefferson was absent in Washington, later references reveal that some were expected to master textile skills and complete a daily carding or spinning task.[34]

Joe Fossett's own training probably began in earnest in 1796. In his *Farm Book* Jefferson had penned a script for the childhood of his slaves: "Children till 10. years to serve as nurses. From 10. to 16. the boys make nails, the girls spin. At 16. go into the ground or learn trades." In 1796 Fossett— now sixteen—was issued overalls instead of his usual house servants' clothing allowance, and for several years he divided his time between nail-making—becoming a foreman of nailers—and learning the blacksmithing trade. He first worked under Isaac Jefferson's brother Little George and in 1801 began his training under a remarkable new teacher, William Stewart. Jefferson found "the best workman in America, but the most eccentric one" in Philadelphia and employed him for six years—"several years longer than he would otherwise have done," wrote Edmund Bacon, "in order that his own servants might learn his trade thoroughly." Drink was Stewart's downfall and, when he got into "his idle frolics," Joe Fossett had to carry forward the work of the blacksmith shop on his own. When Jefferson's patience ran out at the end of 1807, Stewart was dismissed and Fossett became the head blacksmith, running the shop until Jefferson's death. Bacon described Fossett as "a very fine workman; could do anything it was necessary to do with steel or iron."[35]

The workmen hired to build and rebuild the Monticello house also imparted their considerable skills to their African-American assistants. Jefferson had friends in Europe and Philadelphia on the lookout for the best masons and woodworkers. Moses was to be the "disciple" of a stonemason expected from Scotland. John Hemings worked first with David Watson, who had deserted from the British Army in the Revolution, and then with a newly arrived Irishman, James Dinsmore. Together Hemings and Dinsmore crafted Monticello's beautiful interior woodwork, to which, in Jefferson's opinion, "there is nothing superior in the US." Hemings alone was responsible for the interior joinery work at Poplar Forest and he reigned in the Monticello woodworking shop for all the years of Jefferson's retirement.[36]

"To be independent for the comforts of life," wrote Jefferson in 1816, "we must fabricate them ourselves."[37] To enable his own slave laborers to produce both the necessities and some of the comforts of life, he imported to Monticello at various times a Scottish gardener, an English brewer, a German painter, and a French chef. He hired white masons, smiths, carriage builders, charcoal burners, and weavers for the length of time required to pass their skills on to men and women who practiced their craft and who in turn passed it on to others.

As an observant Madison Hemings remembered in 1873, Jefferson in the years of his retirement had "but little taste or care for agricultural pursuits. . . . It was his mechanics he seemed mostly to direct, and in their operations he took great interest." Jefferson was certainly most comfortable in the management of his artisans, with whom his methods of personal control and rational incentives to industry were so successful. His daily supervising presence in the nailery in its first three years made it both profitable and relatively tranquil. A sense of pride and esprit de corps was instilled through rewards and special rations. Isaac Jefferson remembered that Jefferson "gave the boys in the nail factory a pound of meat a week, a dozen herrings, a quart of molasses, and peck of meal. Give them that wukked the best a suit of red or blue; encouraged them mightily." The special clothing prize would have had particular appeal in a community that received the equivalent of uniforms twice a year, and the *Farm Book* confirms a larger meat ration.[38]

Financial incentives were reserved for adult laborers. The blacksmith Little George, manager of the nailery, received a percentage of its profits. The Monticello coopers were allowed to sell for their own benefit every thirty-third flour barrel they made. Jefferson gave his slave charcoal burners a premium for efficiency, not just productivity. He paid them according to the average number of bushels of charcoal they could extract per cord of wood.[39] John Hemings the joiner and Burwell Colbert, butler and painter, were given an annual "gratuity" or "donation" of fifteen or twenty dollars—equivalent to one month's wages.[40]

Joe Fossett and other artisans at Monticello carried on their work with a notable absence of supervision. In 1798 Thomas Mann Randolph wrote an absent Jefferson about the slave manager of the nailery: "George I am sure could not stoop to my authority and I hope and believe he pushes your interests as well as I could." Jefferson was willing to give his tradesmen a remarkable measure of independence. On his departure from Monticello at the end of 1797, he left written instructions with his carpenters, merely asking his son-in-law to keep them "to their metal" by occasional questioning "as to their progress." A few years later he directed that Wormley and Joe Fossett work on their own, with auger and gunpowder, blasting rock in the canal. Overseer Gabriel Lilly, however, could not bring himself to let them do this dangerous work out of his sight. Randolph, too, had doubts about Jefferson's wisdom in leaving his artisans "under no command." He was convinced they would become "idle and dissipated," but admitted Jefferson's confidence was "less abused than I expected" and "it confirms them in honesty."[41]

The power of Jefferson's personal control is apparent in an incident related by Edmund Bacon. About 1807, one of the nailers was discovered in the theft of several hundred pounds of nails. Brought before Jefferson, "He was mortified and distressed beyond measure. He had been brought up in the shop, and we all had confidence in him. Now his character was gone." Jefferson considered his shame sufficient punishment and, despite the expectations of the nailery manager, ordered no whipping. According to Bacon, the chastened offender found religion through this experience and was baptized soon afterward.[42]

After Jefferson's return to public life, nailery profits shrank as cheaper British nails came on the market and the cooped-up crowd of teenagers became unruly. William Stewart, the blacksmith from the north, was entirely unequal to their management. In Jefferson's opinion, "They require a rigour of discipline to make them do reasonable work, to which he cannot bring himself." Overseer Gabriel Lilly began to resort to the whip and had to be restrained: "It would destroy their value, in my estimation, to degrade them in their own eyes by the whip: This, therefore, must not be resorted to but in extremities; as they will be again under my government, I would chuse they should retain the stimulus of character."[43]

"I love industry and abhor severity," Jefferson wrote in 1805, and no reliable document portrays Jefferson in the act of applying physical correction.[44] Overseer Edmund Bacon recalled that Jefferson "was always very kind and indulgent to his servants. He would not allow them to be at all overworked, and he would hardly ever allow one of them to be whipped. . . . He could not bear to have a servant whipped, no odds how much he deserved it." His intercession in the affair of the nail thief was only one of a number of such incidents. In the case of Hercules, a runaway from Poplar Forest, Jefferson suggested to his overseer that, as "it is his first folly in this way," further punishment was inappropriate; his imprisonment in Buckingham County jail had been sufficient. Another Poplar Forest slave, Phill Hubbard, was not to be punished for running away to Monticello: "Altho I had let them all know that their runnings away should be punished, yet Phill's character is not that of a runaway. I have known him from a boy and that he has not come off to sculk from his work."[45]

In Hercules's case, Jefferson advised the overseer to let him "receive the pardon as from yourself alone, and not by my interference, for this is what I would have none of them to suppose." And he gave Thrimston, whose transgression is not specified, "a proper reprimand for his conduct," and assured him that punishment for any further misbehavior would be left to the discretion of the stonecutter for whom he worked.[46] Despite Jefferson's wish to remain hidden behind the cloak of his overseers' authority, it is apparent that first-time offenders especially turned to him frequently in expectation of leniency.

Jefferson's views on physical punishment no doubt reduced whipping on his plantations to levels well below those of many of his neighbors. The whip was, however, by no means eliminated. From the 1780s Jefferson employed on the Monticello plantation over twenty overseers with diverse temperaments and management styles.[47] Some were cruel, even by the standards of the day. William Page, "peevish and too ready to strike," spent four years in Jefferson's employ. When he later became overseer at John Wayles Eppes's neighboring Pantops, Eppes was unable to hire slaves in the neighborhood because of "the terror of Pages name." The "tyrannical" William McGehee, overseer at the Tufton farm for two years, carried a gun "for fear of an attack from the negroes." One of Monticello's white house-joiners deplored the cruelty of Gabriel Lilly, overseer there from 1801 to 1805. Lilly whipped Critta Hemings's seventeen-year-old son James three times in one day, when he was too ill to "raise his hand to his Head." Yet Jefferson considered it impossible to find "a man who fulfills my purposes better than" Lilly and would have kept him longer had he not demanded a doubling of his salary.[48]

The whippings that Jefferson himself ordered were mainly for the benefit of their witnesses. He had the chronic runaway Jame Hubbard brought to Monticello in irons and "severely flogged in the presence of his old companions."[49] And when the excuses of youth, sentiment, or special circumstances had been exhausted, Jefferson invariably rid himself of disruptive elements by sale. Overseer Bacon remembered his orders: "If there was any servant that could not be got along without the chastising that was customary, to dispose of him."[50]

In 1803, an unforgettable example was made of an eighteen-year-old nailer. The usual turbulence of the nailery boiled over into violence in May, when Cary nearly killed Joe Fossett's cousin Brown with his hammer. Jefferson wrote home from Washington, "Should Brown recover so that the law shall inflict no punishment on Cary, it will be necessary for me to make an example of him in terrorem to others, in order to maintain the police so rigorously necessary among the nailboys." He was to be sold either to "negro purchasers from Georgia" or "in any other quarter so distant as never more to be heard of among us." It would seem to Cary's companions "as if he were put out of the way by death." In the language of this letter, Jefferson became increasingly vehement in his determination to deliver a shock to the family sensibilities of the African-Americans who would continue to share his mountaintop. He continued: "I should regard price but little in comparison with so distant an exile of him as to cut him off compleatly from ever again being heard of."[51]

By all accounts Jefferson was remarkably successful in surrounding himself with artisans and house servants of the proper "character," who united industry with trust. Jupiter and other "trusty servants" traveled alone all over Virginia, carrying large sums of money. In 1811 Jefferson promised "a trusty negro of my own" a reward in exchange for information on the whereabouts of a runaway.[52] Whereas George Washington's letters abound with exasperation at the performance of his craftsmen, Jefferson's are surprisingly silent on this head. Since it is doubtful that his expectations were lower, this suggests both the talents of his tradesmen and the success of his management methods.

With his farm laborers, however, Jefferson was less successful. He was always wrestling with the overseer problem. As his son-in-law expressed it, an overseer "will either reject all restraint or use it as an excuse for making no profit." Jefferson stated the case in the usual two parts in 1792, when he was contemplating a novel solution: "My first wish is that the labourers may be well treated, the second that they may enable me to have that treatment continued by making as much as will admit it. The man who can effect both objects is rarely to be found." He sought that rarity in Maryland, where, because of the mixture of free and slave labor, "the farmers there understand the management of negroes on a rational and humane plan."[53] But the tenures of his Maryland overseers were short and, for reasons unknown, not happy.

In 1799 Jefferson wrote: "I am not fit to be a farmer with the kind of labour that we have." And in the same period he indicted the labor system that harmonized so imperfectly with the systematic agricultural reforms he tried to introduce on his plantations: "My latest revulsion from retirement has overshadowed me with despair when I contemplate the necessity of reformation in my farms. That work finds obstacles enough in the ignorance and unwillingness of the instruments employed, even in the presence of the master. But when he is obliged to be absent the half of every year no hope remains of that steady perserverence in a fixed plan which alone can ensure it's success." [54] After the overseer experiment of the 1790s, the "instruments employed"—the men and women who labored in Monticello's fields—had to take their chances with a long succession of local aspirants to their management.

In the summer of 1806 one of Jefferson's tradesmen stepped out of character. Joe Fossett startled him by running away from Monticello just five days after Jefferson returned from Washington. He sent his head carpenter "in pursuit of a young mulatto man, called Joe, 26. years of age, who ran away from here the night of the 29th. inst[ant] without the least word of difference with any body, and indeed having never in his life received a blow from any one." His disbelief at this insubordination from one of his most privileged slaves was soon modified by a glimmer of understanding. "We know he has taken the road towards Washington," Jefferson continued. "He may possibly trump up some story to be taken care of at the President's house till he can make up his mind which way to go, or perhaps he may make himself known to Edy only, as he was formerly connected with her." [55]

Fossett's uncharacteristic action forced Jefferson to consider, for a moment, that his slave had a life of his own. Fossett had not been running away from Monticello. He ran *to* the President's House, where Edy had been in training under a French chef since 1802. Fossett's desperate journey was evidently precipitated by something he heard from two hired slaves who had accompanied Jefferson from the President's House. The situation may have been similar to that of the wagoner Davy and his wife Fanny, as remembered by Edmund Bacon. Fanny, too, was a trainee cook in Washington and she and her husband "got into a terrible quarrel. Davy was jealous of his wife, and, I reckon, with good reason." Bacon was summoned to take them to Alexandria to be sold. "They wept, and begged, and made good promises, and made such an ado, that they begged the old gentleman out of it. But it was a good lesson for them." [56]

The pressures of separation had nearly destroyed the relationship of Davy and Fanny, who saw each other two or three times a year when he carted trees and plants or led horses to and from Washington. Joe and Edy, on the other hand, may have seen each other very little, if at all, between at least 1802 and Joe's sudden appearance in 1806. Any necessary repairs to their relationship were made quickly, for shortly after his arrival, Fossett was caught by Jefferson's Irish coachman leaving the President's House and put in jail. No record has survived of the reception the runaway met on his return to Monticello, where he waited three more years for Edy to return with the retiring President. There they renewed their connection and raised eight children.[57]

"IN THE MOUNTAINS WITH OLD MASTER"

The descendants of Joe Fossett and his relatives still tell stories about the starring roles played by their ancestors in the momentous events of the summer of 1781. The hero of one tale was the Monticello blacksmith who foiled the pursuing British dragoons by shoeing Jefferson's horse backwards. Other family members took part in the preservation of the family silver. In one version, the blacksmith's wife devised a scheme for hanging the valuables on iron hooks in the well. In another story a slave, in the act of secreting the silver, is trapped under the front portico by the arrival of Banastre Tarleton's troops. Joe Fossett, then actually only seven months old, is given the part of bringing this man food and water for two days, until the enemy leaves the mountain.[58]

These family traditions carried down through the generations memories of the skills and ingenuity that enabled slaves to participate in epic world events. They also reveal the slaves' consciousness of the larger stage on which their master moved. The dash southward along Carter's Mountain in 1781 may not have been Jefferson's finest hour, but the participants in the events of the first days of June knew the importance of preventing the governor's capture. Isaac Jefferson, taken to Philadelphia in the early 1790s to learn tinsmithing, actually saw his master in action as a public man in his many-windowed house on Market Street, and, in memory, promoted him to president. As Martha Randolph remembered, the Monticello slaves believed her father to be "one of the greatest, and they knew him to be one of the best men and the kindest of masters."[59]

Jefferson would probably not have been able to reciprocate with tales of those living around him on the much smaller stage of Monticello. To protect himself from the realities of owning human beings, he needed the same psychological buffers as other well-intentioned slaveholders. The constant tension between self-interest and humanity seems to have induced in him a gradual closing of the imagination that distanced and dehumanized the black families of Monticello.

His records demonstrate this limited view. In the infrequent descriptive phrases of his correspondence, his slaves are singled out for characteristics—trustworthiness or unreliability, intelligence or stupidity, sobriety or drunkenness—that bear entirely on performance.[60] In the *Farm Book* they are given only first names, and diminutives at that. The husband and wife known as Joseph and Edith Fossett to their family members were just Joe and Edy to Jefferson. If Israel Jefferson's reminiscences had not been recorded by an eager journalist in 1873, we would never have known that the Ned and Jenny of Jefferson's records knew themselves as Edward and Jane Gillett. A negative picture emerges from correspondence with overseers and family members. There are discussions of misbehavior rather than comments on craftsmanship. Illness fills many pages, along with descriptions of the death throes of several slaves. Even Jupiter, Jefferson's lifelong companion as manservant and coachman, passed from the scene accompanied by words that demonstrated the inextricable connection between his humanity and his value as part of the labor force. Jefferson wrote, "I am sorry for him as well as sensible he leaves a void in my administration which I cannot fill up."[61]

Jefferson lived long enough to become fully entangled in the net of slavery's realities. His unsuccessful early efforts to curb or end slavery were followed by years in which he uttered simultaneous protestations of the impracticability of emancipation and cries of alarm about the consequences of inaction. The man who in 1786 wrote of "a bondage, one hour of which is fraught with more misery" than ages of the tyranny that American revolutionaries had just thrown off, was not the man who in 1814 told Thomas Cooper that American slaves "are better fed . . . , warmer clothed, and labor less than the journeymen or day-laborers of England," living "without want, or the fear of it." His insights into the kinds of behavior caused by enslavement were forgotten and his suspicions of racial inferiority gained the upper hand, perhaps serving as a defense against stings of conscience. While Jefferson was shocked at the sight of French and German women driving the plows and hoeing the fields of Europe—it was "a barbarous perversion of the natural destination of the two sexes"—he never expressed misgivings about the long days of hard agricultural labor of the women he owned. His farms always were cultivated by "gangs of half men and half women." According to one visiting Englishman, Jefferson expressed the opinion in 1807 that the "Negro race were . . . made to carry burthens."

He appears to have convinced himself that those who were, as he suspected in print in the *Notes on Virginia,* "inferior in the faculties of reason and imagination," and whose griefs were "transient," might find happiness in a bondage mitigated by a benevolent hand.[62]

Jefferson's own efforts turned to reforming slavery rather than ending it. In 1787 he wanted to put his slaves "ultimately on an easier footing," and five years later his experiment with Maryland overseers was inaugurated in order to place his slaves "on the comfortable footing of the laborers of other countries." While in Paris he briefly contemplated importing Germans to settle on fifty-acre farms, "intermingled" with his slaves, and "all on the footing of the Metayers [tenants who pay in kind] of Europe" (he prefaced this proposal with his opinion that freeing slaves was "like abandoning children"). But the overriding demands of debt made even his reform efforts contingent on the impossible. The ultimate "easier footing" could be realized only after the slaves "have paid the debts" due from the Wayles estate. In 1792, when the Maryland overseer plan was aired, the improved treatment of the slaves was made contingent on their own exertions; they must "make as much as will admit" the continuation of better conditions.[63]

Neither Jefferson nor his slaves ever succeeded in clearing away his massive debts, which only grew with the years. It is impossible to know, partly because his exact intentions were not expressed, just how much he was able to carry out his wish to ameliorate the condition of his own slaves, to contribute to their happiness as he perceived it. There is plentiful evidence, however, that the Monticello slaves were made more "comfortable" in bondage than most of their fellows, even in Virginia.

Edith Fossett returned to these conditions in the spring of 1809. She probably moved into the cook's room—a ten-by-fourteen-foot space with brick floor in the stone-built south dependencies of the main house. Two other rooms there were occupied by slaves, but most slaves lived in log cabins on Mulberry Row or elsewhere on the mountain slopes. A visitor from Washington in 1809, although struck by "a most unpleasant contrast" between the slave dwellings and the neoclassical "palace" standing together on the leveled summit of Monticello, declared that "they are much better than I have seen on any other plantation." Their superiority could not have been due to their size or materials—they varied from twelve to fourteen feet wide and fourteen to twenty feet long and had wooden chimneys and earth floors. Perhaps they were more carefully built and maintained. In 1809 Peter Hemings was to remove to a cabin on Mulberry Row, fitted up "in an entirely comfortable and decent manner," and instructions to overseers regularly mention the winter "mending" of slave cabins.[64]

Despite the hours she spent each day in the main kitchen, Edy Fossett still received the normal weekly food rations—a peck of cornmeal and a pound of pork—but she was probably able to vary this monotonous fare for her family with kitchen leftovers and her own skills. Her clothing allowance was similar to that on other southern plantations—two outfits a year, cotton for summer and a mixture of cotton and wool for winter; a striped blanket was issued once every three years. From at least 1815, when raw cotton prices were high, the summer cloth for her children was woven from a mixture of cotton and hemp. [65]

During the years of Jefferson's final retirement to Monticello, Edy and Joe Fossett filled two of the most important positions on the mountain. Almost a century later, Peter Fossett remembered that his mother was "Mr. Jefferson's favorite cook" and his father "had charge of all mechanical work done on the estate." Edy took over the new kitchen and prepared meals for a mounting flood of guests. While visitors' accounts are disappointingly vague about the food, all agreed on the quality of the fare. "The dinner was always choice, and served in the French style," wrote Bostonian George Ticknor. Daniel Webster recorded in 1824 that "dinner is served in half Virginian, half French style, in good taste and abundance." [66]

Joe Fossett ran the Mulberry Row blacksmith shop, which served the neighborhood as well as the master of Monticello. He was allowed to keep a shilling in every dollar of shop income and earned additional money by making chain traces and plating saddle trees for a Charlottesville blacksmith in his free time. Fossett's work day, like that of most other Monticello slaves, lasted from dawn to dusk. Jefferson's chart of the daily tasks of his textile workers indicates that their labors grew from nine hours in the darkest winter months to fourteen hours in the longest days of June and July. Jobs that were tasked could provide early release for fast workers but, when the tasks were set by Jefferson the maximizer, could also lead to even longer work days. "Jerry says that you tell him that he is to bring a certain number of logs a day," wrote Edmund Bacon, "and that it takes him till after night to do it." Bacon drew this situation to Jefferson's attention for the sake of the mules, not the wagoner. [67]

It is apparent that for many of the Monticello slaves a second working day began after dark. Mothers had to attend to their households, preparing meals, repairing clothing, and caring for their children. Both men and women pursued activities to supplement the standard of living provided by their master. Every slave household at Monticello had a poultry yard, and most raised their own vegetables. A typical Sunday is revealed in the household account book kept by one of Jefferson's granddaughters. Slaves carried to the mountaintop their chickens and eggs, cabbages and watermelons to stock the Monticello kitchen, and took home dimes and half-bits in exchange. Some probably obtained passes so they could take their products into Charlottesville for sale as well.[68]

The nearby river and surrounding forests also provided opportunities for additional food or money. Hunting and trapping expeditions yielded raccoons, possums, and squirrels to add to the pot, as well as skins to be sold. Isaac Jefferson's brother Bagwell, a farm laborer, makes several appearances in Jefferson's accounts, selling him skins for a bellows, fish, ducks, hops, timothy seed, watermelons, cucumbers, and cymlin squash. Jefferson's grandson regaled his children with tales of midnight forays as a boy after possum and honey, in the company of the black men. After the dogs treed their quarry or a bee tree was felled, they returned to sit around the fire in a slave cabin. At "a little table covered with the best," one of the wives provided "a pot of hot coffee, fried meat and eggs, and a dish of honey."[69]

The pleasures of the quarters received little comment in the correspondence of Jefferson and his family. Apparently without curfews, his slaves took advantage of the freedom of the night. Jefferson observed, in *Notes on Virginia,* that "a black, after hard labour through the day, will be induced by the slightest amusements to sit up till midnight, or later, though knowing he must be out with the first dawn of the morning." He knew his gardener John as a "great nightwalker" and thus unsuitable as a guardian for the main house. Former slave Isaac Jefferson remembered that his master's brother Randolph would "come out among black people, play the fiddle and dance half the night."[70]

There are further suggestions of the solace of music. Three of Sally Hemings's sons were noted musicians. Her oldest, Beverly (b. 1798), played fiddle in the South Pavilion for the Saturday night dances of Jefferson's granddaughters and young men at school nearby. He may also have provided the single note of holiday spirit in the quiet Christmas of 1821. Mary Randolph wrote her sister: "I have not had a single application to write passes . . . and except catching the sound of a fiddle yesterday on my way to the smokehouse and getting a glimpse of the fiddler as he stood with half closed eyes and head thrown back with one foot keeping time to his own scraping in the midst of a circle of attentive and admiring auditors I have not seen or heard any thing like Christmas gambols."[71]

The most remarkable evidence of the vigorous music and storytelling tradition in the Monticello quarters survives because of an interested foreigner and one member of Jefferson's household. His daughter Martha, who at fourteen had written her father, "I wish with all my soul that the poor negroes were all freed," was primed by the tales and songs of her childhood nurse. Even late in life, she had not lost her sensitivity to both the conditions and culture of the slave community around her. She shared cornshelling and rowing songs and tales of Mr. Fox and Mr. Rabbit with interested visitors. In the year she died Martha Randolph worried about the fate of some of her slaves, hoping to protect them from the laxer morals of the vicinity of the University of Virginia: "I feel anxious that these poor uneducated creatures should be placed in situations as little exposed to temptation as possible."[72]

The female members of Jefferson's household made the only recorded efforts to enlighten those "poor uneducated creatures." Madison Hemings recalled learning his ABCs from Jefferson's granddaughters, who also gave "special advantages in training and education" to Joe Fossett's son Peter. Ellen Randolph wrote in 1819 that she was "anxious to have it in my power to befriend, and educate as well as I can" one of the motherless daughters of Monticello butler Burwell Colbert. In the absence of explicit statements on the subject, Jefferson's own attitude toward the education of his slaves is harder to determine. His missing response to Quaker activist Robert Pleasant's 1796 plan for instructing black children seems to have recommended delay. The only emancipation plan Jefferson considered feasible called for education, at public expense, in "tillage, arts or sciences, according to their geniusses," followed by deportation. This plan required the permanent separation of children from their parents, a necessity that Jefferson agreed would produce "some scruples of humanity, but this would be straining at a gnat, and swallowing a camel."[73]

Closer to home, Jefferson's never-executed tenancy plan called merely for bringing up the children "in habits of property and foresight." The blacks' apparent absence of foresight weighed heavily in Jefferson's mind as a stumbling block to emancipation. It colored his discussion of racial characteristics in *Notes on Virginia*, and he brought it forth in conversation with visiting foreigners. A bemused British diplomat listened in 1807 to Jefferson's favorite example of the lack of forethought demonstrated by his own slaves. At the approach of summer they cast off their blankets, "without a thought as to what may become of them, wherever they may happen to be at the time, and then not seldom lose them in the woods or the fields from mere carelessness." No slave in the upper South took blankets lightly, so it is possible that Monticello's blanket-tossers may have counted on Jefferson's willingness to replace their loss. It is even more likely that some of these apparently thoughtless slaves had discovered a way to acquire extra blankets for warmth or sale. Jefferson himself had noted, in 1806, that a recent

Monticello overseer had failed to distribute a single blanket during his five-year tenure. This experience may have caused the very opposite of what the master saw—an effort to prepare for an unpredictable future.[74]

Israel, a twenty-four-year-old postilion, overheard Jefferson tell the Marquis de Lafayette that slaves should be taught to read but not to write, as that would "enable them to forge papers, when they could no longer be kept in subjugation." The statement Israel recalled, almost fifty years after the event, is difficult to verify. A number of Jefferson's slaves could read *and* write. John Hemings's surviving letters report on his joinery work at Poplar Forest, his brother James left an inventory of the Monticello kitchen, and there is one letter from Hannah, a Poplar Forest household slave. Several others could at least read: Jefferson left written instructions in his absences for the carpenters John and Davy and Great George the overseer. Albemarle County records reveal that Mary Hemings Bell and Joseph Fossett could sign their names and probably could read and write, although they may have learned after they were freed.[75] It is not known how these slaves learned their letters, nor is there any direct evidence that Jefferson took an active role in educating the African-American children around him.[76] There is also no sign that he took up his own challenge in *Notes on Virginia* or emulated the example of his mentor George Wythe, by testing the intellectual powers of blacks through the cultivation of their minds in improved conditions. One clue to this vacuum appears in a letter Jefferson wrote questioning the educational aims of the African Institution of London: "I wish they may begin their work at the right end. Our experience with the Indians has proved that letters are not the first, but the last step in the progression from barbarism to civilisation."[77]

Religious instruction of slaves would, of course, have been completely un-Jeffersonian. The life of the spirit was pursued beyond the control of the master and thus escaped his commentary. Again it is the negative events that inspired the scattered references that can only suggest the vitality of religious beliefs in the Monticello slave community. Jefferson's grand-daughter Mary complained of having to watch a visitor's children one Sunday because "mammy is gone '*to meeting*.'" Her sister told of the death of Priscilla Hemings, longtime head nurse in the Jefferson-Randolph household, whose last hours included "a prayer meeting at her house" and a Bible reading before bedtime by her husband John. African traditional beliefs are also evident, mainly in discussions of the ill effects of the prescriptions of black doctors—almost universally labeled "poisons" in Jefferson's papers.[78]

There were two worlds at Monticello, where medicine and beliefs in one were perceived as poison and superstition in the other. Jefferson had no access to the hidden world of his slaves, but they were a constant presence in his, listening and watching. From the slave women in the house to Israel on the carriage horse, they attended to all words and actions that might play a part in shaping their future. Joe Fossett, in the blacksmith shop— the closest thing to a neighborhood gathering place—may have been a monitor for the mountain, listening for assessments of the state of Jefferson's finances, so critical to the stability of the Monticello slave community. One of Lafayette's companions talked to the slaves in 1824, when they told him they were "perfectly happy, that they were subject to no ill-treatment, that their tasks were very easy, and that they cultivated the lands of Monticello with the greater pleasure, because they were almost sure of not being torn away from them, to be transported elsewhere, so long as Mr. Jefferson lived." [79]

INDEPENDENCE

On July 4, 1827, one year after Jefferson's death, Joseph Fossett became a free man. Six months earlier Jefferson's granddaughter Mary had reported to a sister the results of the Monticello dispersal sale: "The negroes with one exception I believe, are all sold to persons living in the state, many of them in this neighbourhood or the adjoining counties, and most of them I believe also, are well and satisfactorily placed, as much to their own wishes as they could be in leaving our estate." No reference was made to the breaking up of families that this satisfactory placement entailed. Joe Fossett had watched his wife and children sold to at least four different bidders. Edy and their two youngest children William and Daniel were bought by Jesse Scott; twelve-year-old Peter's new master was John R. Jones; fifteen-year-old Elizabeth Ann was sold to Charlottesville merchant John Winn, and University of Virginia professor Charles Bonnycastle bought seventeen-year-old Patsy; the fates of three other siblings are unknown. [80]

Jefferson had described Fossett at the time of his 1806 escapade as "strong and resolute," characteristics greatly needed in his first years of freedom. The fragmentary records suggest that he worked at his trade with a steadiness demanded by his need to reunite his scattered family and prepare for removal beyond the boundaries of slavery. Spared the requirement to leave the state within a year by an act of assembly requested in Jefferson's will, he continued to pursue his blacksmithing trade in Albemarle County. He may even have remained in the Mulberry Row blacksmith shop until 1831, when Monticello was sold to James T. Barclay and Fossett bought a lot in Charlottesville with a shop on it. [81]

At some time before September 15, 1837, Joe Fossett became the owner of his wife, five of their children (two born subsequent to the sale), and four grandchildren, for on that date he manumitted them all. It is apparent that the key to family unity was Joe Fossett's mother, Mary Hemings Bell. She and her children by merchant Thomas Bell had shared in Bell's estate in 1800, and her daughter Sally had married Jesse Scott in 1802. Thus, it was probably the combined resources of Scott and the Bells that provided the $505 for the purchase of Edy and the two youngest children— and probably also the money for the purchase of the third child, Elizabeth Ann.[82]

It is evident that, beginning in the 1780s, when Mary Hemings was leased and then sold to Thomas Bell, the Monticello slave community had a toehold in the more complex free community of Charlottesville. Thomas Bell's house on Main Street, occupied by his "widow," and then her daughter and son-in-law Sally Jefferson Bell and Jesse Scott, and their children, was the residence of Hemingses for a century.[83] Jesse Scott, a free man of color said to be part Indian, and his sons, the "famous fiddling Scotts," enlivened dances at the University of Virginia, at the Hot and White Sulphur Springs, and throughout the state for a good part of the century. In 1888 Ora Langhorne paid a visit to the last surviving member of "the Scott minstrels, long famous throughout the South and well known to all visitors at the Virginia springs." Robert Scott reported that "the taste for music shown by his family had early attracted Mr. Jefferson's notice, as he dearly loved music himself, and he had taken much kindly interest in the family. . . . Mr. Jefferson had always been very kind to [Jesse Scott] and had encouraged him to have his children educated."[84]

Peter Fossett was not one of the children his father was able to purchase and free before the family left for Ohio about 1840. He remained a slave for over twenty years after Jefferson's death, making at least two attempts to run away. The learning he had gleaned from his years as "a sort of family pet" in the Monticello household was increased by enlisting the aid of his new master's sons. Then Peter Fossett passed his knowledge on to a fellow slave by the light of pine knots, stealing away to a deserted cabin long after everyone else was asleep. Finally, again by the combined efforts of members of an extended network of kin, he was able to purchase his freedom and join his family in Cincinnati.[85]

Peter Fossett's story demonstrates the extent to which identity is buried by the dehumanizing institution of slavery. In freedom his life is known, and becomes an expression of much that cannot be known about the rest of the Monticello slave community. Flourishing unrecorded in the Monticello quarters were singular skills, a hunger for education, powerful bonds of family, and deep religious beliefs. Peter Fossett became "the most prominent of the early caterers" in Cincinnati, worked with Levi Coffin in the Underground Railroad, and is credited with being the father of the Ohio black Baptist church. His flock at First Baptist Church helped him satisfy a desire, at age eighty-five, to return to his birthplace. In 1900, the "last surviving slave of Thomas Jefferson," who had abandoned him in 1826, was welcomed to the entrance hall of Monticello.[86]

NOTES

I would like to thank the Virginia Foundation for the Humanities and the Thomas Jefferson Memorial Foundation for their support of work on a related project. I could not have written this essay without those months spent considering the lives of Jefferson's slaves. I am also grateful to Peter Onuf for suggestions about structure that were vital to the final product.

The title of this essay is drawn from the following quote, "I have my house to build, my fields to farm, and to watch for the happiness of those who labor for mine," TJ to Angelica Church, Nov. 27, 1793, *LofA,* p. 1013. In my work on this subject I am following trails already blazed by others, notably James A. Bear, Jr., whose longtime interest in the Hemings family of Monticello has nourished my curiosity and informed far more of his work than the directly relevant "The Hemings Family of Monticello," *Virginia Cavalcade* 29, no. 2 (autumn 1979), pp. 78–87. Other useful accounts of the African-American residents of Monticello include "To Possess Living Souls," chapter four in Jack McLaughlin, *Jefferson and Monticello: The Biography of a Builder* (New York, 1988), pp. 94–145, and Elizabeth Langhorne, "The Other Hemings," *Albemarle Magazine* (Oct.-Nov. 1980), pp. 59–66, and "A Black Family at Monticello," *Magazine of Albemarle County History* 43 (1985), pp. 1–16. Note that in her discussion of the fate of Sally Hemings after Jefferson's death, in the latter article and in chapter 37 of *Monticello: A Family Story* (Chapel Hill, N.C., 1987), Langhorne mistakes her for another Sally at Monticello. Material on Jefferson and Monticello contributes to an excellent discussion of larger issues in Mary Beth Norton, Herbert G. Gutman, and Ira Berlin, "The Afro-American Family in the Age of Revolution," *Slavery and Freedom in the Age of the American Revolution,* ed. Ira Berlin and Ronald Hoffman (Charlottesville, Va., 1983), pp. 175–191. Beware, however, of Table 3 on page 184, which credits Jefferson with twice as many slaves as he actually had. More recently there is much fascinating new information mixed with an unfortunate number of errors in Judith P. Justus, *Down From the Mountain: The Oral History of the Hemings Family* (Perrysburg, Oh., 1990).

1. TJ to Edward Bancroft, 26 Jan. 1789, *Boyd,* XIV, p. 492.
2. Charlottesville *Central Gazette,* Jan. 13, 1827. Only fragmentary documentation survives for the January 1827 sale. Transactions are mentioned in occasional letters and in almost thirty sales slips, which note the purchase of only thirty-four slaves (Monticello

Dispersal Sale receipts, University of Virginia Library [hereafter ViU], 5291). Apparently all 130 slaves were not actually sold in 1827, as an account of a second sale of thirty-three slaves, Jan. 1, 1829, also survives (ViU:8937).

3. Mary J. Randolph to Ellen Coolidge, Jan. 25, 1827, ViU; Thomas Jefferson Randolph reminiscences, ViU:8937. Randolph actually attended the sale; his sister Ellen did not.

4. Edwin M. Betts, *Thomas Jefferson's Farm Book* (Princeton, N.J., 1953), p. 27; TJ to Henry Rose, Oct. 23, 1801, *Farm Book*, p. 18; TJ to Craven Peyton, Nov. 14, 1819, *Farm Book*, p. 145; TJ to James Madison, July 26, 1806, Library of Congress (hereafter DLC); TJ to M. B. Jefferson, Aug. 2, 1815, *Farm Book*, p. 39.

5. Because of his surname, it has been suggested that Joe Fossett may have been the son of William Fossett, a white carpenter working at Monticello from 1775 to 1779. See entries for Feb. 11, 1775, Aug. 5 and Sept. 12 1779, in James A. Bear, Jr., and Lucia Stanton, *Jefferson's Memorandum Books: Accounts, with Legal Records and Miscellany, 1767–1826* (forthcoming). Some of Joseph Fossett's descendants make the claim that Jefferson was his father (see Lerone Bennett, "Thomas Jefferson's Negro Grandchildren," *Ebony* 10 (Nov. 1954), pp. 78–80). Betty Hemings may actually have had eleven children at this time. Lee Marmon, researcher for Poplar Forest, makes the plausible suggestion that Doll (b. 1757), wife of Abraham, a carpenter, was her daughter ("Poplar Forest Research Report," part 3, Aug. 1991, p. 39).

6. Jefferson inaugurated his *Farm Book* with three lists of slaves at the time of the division of the Wayles estate: the first, a roll of his own fifty-two slaves in Albemarle County; the second, the 135 Wayles slaves and their locations; the third, a list of the combined total of 187, with new locations in three counties (*Farm Book*, pp. 5–18). In 1782 his Albemarle County total was 129, behind Edward Carter with 242 slaves and ahead of the estate of Robert Carter Nicholas, with 120 slaves; see Lester J. Cappon, "Personal Property Tax List of Albemarle County, 1782," *Magazine of Albemarle County History* 5 (1944–45), pp. 54,69,72. After the sale of his Goochland and Cumberland county lands in the 1790s, Jefferson's slave property was usually distributed in a ratio of three to two between his Albemarle and Bedford county estates—both about 5,000 acres. The combined totals for 1796, 1810, and 1815 were 167, 199, and 223 ("Jefferson's Slaves: Approximate Total Numbers," March 8, 1990, Monticello Research Department). Auctions accounted for the sale of seventy-one slaves from his Goochland and Bedford county plantations, fourteen more were sold to individuals, and seventy-six were given to his sister and daughters on their marriages ("Negroes alienated from 1784. to 1794," Feinstone Collection, David Library of the American Revolution, on deposit at American Philosophical Society; this document is no doubt the missing page 25 of Jefferson's *Farm Book*).

7. TJ to John Wayles Eppes, June 30, 1820, ViU. On this particular occasion, he was grateful for Eppes's offer to buy slaves without moving them from Poplar Forest. This kept them "in the family." Isaac Jefferson's mother Ursula was bought at the request of Martha Jefferson, because she was "a favorite house woman"; Jefferson purchased Nance Hemings, the weaver, on the resumption of textile production in 1795; and young men were needed for the digging of his canal in the 1790s (TJ to Archibald Thweatt, May 29, 1810, DLC; TJ to W. Callis, May 8, 1795, ViU; entries for March 26, 1797, May 6, 1805, in *Memorandum Books;* TJ to John Jordan, Dec. 21, 1805, *Farm Book*, p. 21).

8. Jordan to TJ, Dec. 4, 1805, Massachusetts Historical Society, hereafter MHi; TJ to Jordan, Dec. 21, 1805 and Feb. 9, 1806, *Farm Book*, pp. 21–22.

9. TJ to Randolph Lewis, April 23, 1807, *Farm Book*, p. 26; TJ to Jeremiah Goodman, Jan. 6, 1815, in Edwin M. Betts, ed., *Thomas Jefferson's Garden Book* (Philadelphia, 1944), p. 540. This letter also suggests that Jefferson instructed his overseers to make some efforts

to control behavior. Goodman, who interpreted the "home" rule too strictly, repeatedly "drove" Phill Hubbard from his wife Hanah's house and punished her for receiving him. Hubbard and his wife lived on different plantations, but both were part of the Poplar Forest estate. Jefferson intervened to facilitate their union.

10. TJ to Thomas Cooper, Sept. 10, 1814, *L&B*, XIV, p. 183; Frederick Douglass, *Life and Times* (1881; reprint, New York, 1983), p. 89.

11. TJ to Edward Coles, Aug. 25, 1814, *Farm Book*, p. 39; Thomas Mann Randolph to TJ, March 6, 1802, MHi; Martha J. Randolph to Nicholas P. Trist, March 7, 1822, University of North Carolina Library (hereafter NcU).

12. TJ to Joel Yancey, Jan. 17, 1819, MHi. Another statement expressing the value of slave women as producers of "capital" appears in TJ to John Wayles Eppes, June 30, 1820, ViU.

13. *Farm Book,* pp. 5, 52; TJ to Jeremiah Goodman, March 5, 1813, *Farm Book,* p. 483; "Negroes alienated from 1784. to 1794.," Feinstone Collection, American Philosophical Society.

14. TJ to Randolph Jefferson, Sept. 25, 1792, *Boyd,* XXIV, p. 416; TJ to Thomas Mann Randolph, Oct. 12, 1792, *Boyd,* XXIV, p. 473; "Negroes alienated from 1784. to 1794."; TJ to W. Callis, May 8, 1795, ViU; *Farm Book,* p. 24. Critta (c. 1783–1819) eventually came to Monticello as the wife of the butler Burwell Colbert.

15. TJ to Nicholas Lewis, April 12, 1792, *Boyd,* XXIII, p. 408; "Negroes alienated from 1784. to 1794." Bell, whom Jefferson called "a man remarkeable for his integrity," acknowledged paternity of Bob and Sally and left his property in a life estate to Mary Hemings Wells [Wayles?] Bell in his will (TJ to William Short, April 13, 1800, Swem Library, College of William and Mary; Albemarle County Will Book, IV, pp. 59–60).

16. Martha Randolph to TJ, Jan. 16, 1791, Edwin Morris Betts and James A. Bear, eds., *The Family Letters of Thomas Jefferson* (Columbia, Mo., 1966), p. 68.

17. *Farm Book,* pp. 41, 49.

18. Thomas Jefferson Randolph to [Pike County *Republican?*], 1874, ViU:8937; James A. Bear, Jr., ed., *Jefferson at Monticello* (Charlottesville, Va., 1967), pp. 99–100; author's translation of F. A. F. La Rochefoucauld-Liancourt, *Voyage dans les Etats-Unis d'Amerique* (Paris, 1798–99), V, p. 35. I use this in preference to the 1799 London edition, which, for instance, translates *quarterons* as "mongrel negroes." The Comte de Volney also observed at Monticello, in the same summer, slave children "as white as I am." Jean Gaulmier, *L'Idéologue Volney* (1951; reprint, Paris, 1980), p. 371.

19. Bear, *Jefferson at Monticello,* p. 4. Robert, James, Thenia, Critta, Peter, and Sally were allegedly the children of Jefferson's father-in-law John Wayles. In the words of Isaac Jefferson, "Folks said that these Hemingses was old Mr. Wayles's children" (Bear, *Jefferson at Monticello,* p. 4). Sally Hemings's son, Madison, stated the connection more emphatically in 1873 (Fawn M. Brodie, *Thomas Jefferson: An Intimate Biography* [New York, 1974], p. 472). No reference to the Wayles-Hemings relationship has been found in the papers of Jefferson or his family. John Hemings was said to have been the son of Joseph Neilson, a white joiner resident at Monticello from 1775 to 1779 (Brodie, *Jefferson,* p. 475; *Memorandum Books,* Jan. 28, 1775, Sept. 12, 1779).

20. The story that Jefferson was the father of slaves by Sally Hemings was first published by James Thomson Callender in the Richmond *Recorder* in the fall of 1802. It was carried through the nineteenth century in Federalist attacks, British critiques of American democracy, and abolitionist efforts to end slavery. Fawn Brodie's biography of 1974 revived the claim and suggested a romantic dimension—that the connection was not exploitative but a meaningful thirty-eight-year union. Oral traditions originating with the children of Sally

Hemings strongly support the connection; Jefferson's daughter and grandchildren believed it a moral impossibility and suggested Jefferson's Carr nephews as more likely suspects. Both sides gained contemporary support, and Jefferson himself seems to have privately denied the charge in an 1805 letter to Robert Smith. Sources on the controversy include Douglass Adair, "The Jefferson Scandals," in *Fame and the Founding Fathers*, ed. Trevor Colbourn (New York, 1974), pp. 160–91; Fawn Brodie's biography and her articles in *American Heritage* (23, no. 4 [June 1971], pp. 48–57, 97–100; 27, no. 6 [Oct. 1976], pp. 29–33, 94–99); Virginius Dabney, *The Jefferson Scandals: A Rebuttal* (New York, 1981); Dumas Malone, "Mr. Jefferson's Private Life," *Proceedings of the American Antiquarian Society*, 84 (1974), pp. 65–72; Minnie Shumate Woodson, *The Sable Curtain* (Washington, 1985), appendix. Michael Durey has recently somewhat refurbished Callender's image, demonstrating the likelihood that Callender took the story from what he considered reliable sources rather than making it up; Michael Durey, *"With the Hammer of Truth": James Thomson Callender and America's Early National Heroes* (Charlottesville, Va., 1990), pp. 157–63. Also, another birth date has come to light. Sally Hemings's daughter Thenia, who did not survive infancy, was born about Dec. 7, 1799; Jefferson returned to Monticello from Philadelphia on March 8, 1799 (TJ to John Wayles Eppes, Dec. 21, 1799, ViU; *Farm Book*, p. 56).

   21. Samuel Shepherd, *The Statutes at Large of Virginia* (Richmond, 1835) 1, p. 123; TJ to Francis Calley Gray, March 4, 1815, DLC.

   22. Bear, *Jefferson at Monticello*, pp. 102, 122; *Farm Book*, p. 130; Ellen Randolph Coolidge to Joseph Coolidge, Oct. 24, 1858, Coolidge letterbook, pp. 98–99, ViU. She cited the cases of "three young men and one girl" (Harriet Hemings). Besides Beverly Hemings, one of the three men was probably James Hemings (b. 1787), son of Sally's sister Critta. When he ran away from Monticello in 1804, only persuasion was exerted in an unsuccessful effort to bring him back. He briefly reappeared at Monticello in 1815, apparently as a free man (*Memorandum Books*, Oct. 13, 1815).

   23. Gilbert Osofsky, ed., *Puttin' on Ole Massa* (New York, 1969), p. 64. Ellen Coolidge in 1858 blamed the "Irish workmen" building the Monticello house, "dissipated young men in the neighbourhood," and—in the case of the Hemingses—her own Carr uncles (Coolidge letterbook, pp. 100–102, ViU). Edmund Bacon reported that Thomas Jefferson Randolph's schoolmates were "intimate with the Negro women" (Bear, *Jefferson at Monticello*, p. 88). Although no indictments of individual overseers have been found, the overseer class often took the blame, as the Duc de La Rochefoucauld-Liancourt reported after his visit to Monticello in 1796 (*Voyage*, V, p. 35).

   24. TJ to William Short, Jan. 18, 1826, *Ford*, XII, p. 434. See also TJ to James Monroe, Nov. 24, 1801, *Ford*, IX, p. 317; TJ to Edward Coles, Aug. 25, 1814, *Farm Book*, p. 38. The Duc de La Rochefoucauld-Liancourt observed, in an unpublished paragraph of his travels, that fear of mixture lay at the root of Jefferson's reluctance to act on the emancipation issue: "The generous and enlightened Mr. Jefferson cannot but demonstrate a desire to see these negroes emancipated. But he sees so many difficulties in their emancipation even postponed, he adds so many conditions to render it practicable, that it is thus reduced to the impossible. He keeps, for example, the opinion he advanced in his notes, that the negroes of Virginia can only be emancipated all at once, and by exporting to a distance the whole of the black race. He bases this opinion on the certain danger, if there were nothing else, of seeing blood mixed without means of preventing it" (author's translation, Library of Congress microfilm of original manuscript in Bibliothèque Nationale, Paris).

25. Jefferson's first slave, Sawney, bequeathed him by his father, was described as "mulatto" (Peter Jefferson will, July 13, 1757, Albemarle County Will Book, 2, p. 33). So was Sandy, a carpenter who ran away from Shadwell in 1769 (advertisement, Sept. 7, 1769, *Boyd,* 1:33).

26. Harvest rolls 1795–1800, *Farm Book,* pp. 46, 58. At the time of Jefferson's death, Critta Hemings was married to free black Zachariah Bowles (Albemarle County Deed Book, XXII, p. 412) and Mary was living in the property left her by merchant Thomas Bell. John Hemings's wife Priscilla was head nurse in the household of Martha and Thomas Mann Randolph. Peter Hemings's wife was also probably a Randolph slave, as she and her children lived at Monticello in 1810, after the Randolphs had moved there from Edgehill (*Farm Book,* p. 134).

27. The title of this section is adapted from Jefferson's *Notes on the State of Virginia,* ed. William Peden (Chapel Hill, N.C., 1955), p. 163: "A slave . . . is born to live and labour for another." The quotation on the nailery is from TJ to J. B. Demeunier, April 29, 1795, *Ford,* VIII, p. 174.

28. *Farm Book,* p. 111. Surviving nailery accounts are fragmentary. There are five pages of accounts, 1794 to 1796, bound with Jefferson's Ledger, 1767–1770, ViU, and a nailery account book, 1796–1800, in the William Andrews Clark Memorial Library, University of California at Los Angeles.

29. Nailery account book, Clark Memorial Library.

30. TJ to James Lyle, July 10, 1795, *Farm Book,* p. 430; TJ to J. B. Deumeunier, April 29, 1795, *Ford,* VIII, p. 175.

31. TJ to James Maury, June 16, 1815, *Farm Book,* p. 490; TJ to Nicholas Lewis, July 11, 1788, *Boyd,* XIII, p. 343; TJ to Mary Jefferson Eppes, April 11, 1801, Betts and Bear, *Family Letters,* p. 201; TJ to Thomas Mann Randolph, Jan. 29, 1801, DLC.

32. TJ to Thomas Mann Randolph, Feb. 3, 1793, MHi; memorandum to Jeremiah Goodman, Dec. 1811, *Garden Book,* p. 467.

33. TJ to Edmund Bacon, Oct. 6, 1806, MHi; Thomas Mann Randolph to TJ, Jan. 3, 1801, ViU; TJ to Randolph, Jan. 9, 1801, DLC; memorandum to Jeremiah Goodman, Dec. 1811, *Garden Book,* p. 466.

34. Bear, *Jefferson at Monticello,* p. 100; Ellen W. Randolph to Martha J. Randolph, Sept. 27, [1816?], ViU.

35. *Farm Book,* p. 77; TJ to George Jefferson, Dec. 3, 1801, *Farm Book,* p. 425; Bear, *Jefferson at Monticello,* p. 102; memorandum to Edmund Bacon, Oct. 1806, in Bear, p. 54.

36. TJ to Thomas Mann Randolph, May 19, 1793, DLC; TJ to Thomas Munroe, March 4, 1815, Henry E. Huntington Library, San Marino, California. Dinsmore's inventory of the Monticello joinery in 1809, listing over eighty molding planes among its tools, is further testament to the extraordinary work done on the mountaintop (inventory, April 15, 1809, MHi).

37. TJ to Benjamin Austin, Jan. 9, 1816, *LofA,* p. 1371.

38. "Reminiscences of Madison Hemings," Brodie, *Jefferson,* p. 474; Bear, *Jefferson at Monticello,* p. 23. In 1799, thirteen-year-old nailer Phill Hubbard got a weekly ration of half a pound of beef and four salt herring, while Ned, a farm laborer the same age, had to share three-quarters of a pound a beef and six herring with five younger brothers and sisters (*Farm Book,* p. 57; see also p. 135 for special meat rations for children working in both the nailery and the textile shop in 1810).

39. Nailery account book, Clark Memorial Library; *Memorandum Books,* March 17, 1813. Davy, for instance, burnt a kiln of 40 cords that yielded 1,276 bushels of charcoal, or 32

bushels to the cord; Jefferson therefore paid him a "premium" of 32 times $.05, or $1.60 (*Memorandum Books,* April 23, 1823).

40. *Memorandum Books,* passim; see, for example, April 11, 1811, Oct. 26, 1816, and April 14, 1826.

41. Thomas Mann Randolph to TJ, April 22, 1798, ViU; TJ to Randolph, Feb. 15, 1798, Jan. 29, 1801, DLC; Randolph to TJ, Feb. 7, 1801, ViU; Feb. 3, 1798, *Farm Book,* p. 152.

42. Bear, *Jefferson at Monticello,* pp. 97–99. Bacon names Jame Hubbard as the repentant thief. This is unlikely, however, as Bacon remembered that "he was always a good servant afterwards," whereas Hubbard was a chronic runaway throughout Bacon's tenure as overseer. His brother Phill is a more likely candidate for this incident.

43. TJ to James Dinsmore, Dec. 1, 1802, DLC; TJ to Thomas Mann Randolph, Jan. 23, 1801, DLC.

44. TJ to John Strode, June 5, 1805, DLC. The anonymous note in Jefferson's papers reporting the flogging of a slave woman, printed in McLaughlin, *Jefferson and Monticello,* p. 97, should be assessed with great caution. Jean Gaulmier, in *L'Idéologue Volney,* gives the erroneous impression that Jefferson was the farmer Volney observed encouraging the pea-planting of his slaves with an almost comic frenzy of whipping (p. 370). This man was actually a French settler elsewhere in Virginia. I am grateful to C. M. Harris, editor of the William Thornton papers, for sharing his knowledge of Volney's manuscript journal, now in a private collection.

45. Bear, *Jefferson at Monticello,* p. 97; TJ to Jeremiah Goodman, July 26, 1813, Jan. 6, 1815, *Farm Book,* p. 36, *Garden Book,* p. 540. Nineteen-year-old Hercules's escapade was only the beginning of a life of resistance. He was involved in a poisoning case in 1819 and the assault on an overseer in 1822, after which he was sold (Joel Yancey to TJ, July 1, 1819, *Farm Book,* p. 44; TJ to Charles Clay, Aug. 9, 1819, typescript in ViU; McLaughlin, *Jefferson and Monticello,* pp. 117–18).

46. TJ to Jeremiah Goodman, July 26, 1813, *Farm Book,* p. 36; TJ to John Gorman, Feb. 18, 1822, *Farm Book,* p. 46. Most examples are from Poplar Forest, but some of the same behavior may be assumed for Monticello, where no letters had to be written to restore harmony.

47. I use the term "Monticello plantation" to encompass Jefferson's entire 5,000-acre operation in Albemarle County. It included the farms of Monticello and Tufton south of the Rivanna River, and Shadwell and Lego on the north side.

48. Thomas Mann Randolph to TJ, Feb. 26, 1798, ViU; John Wayles Eppes to TJ, Feb. 10, 1803, ViU; TJ to James Madison, Aug. 16, 1810, DLC; *Memorandum Books,* Dec. 25, 1809, Nov. 17, 1811; James Oldham to TJ, Nov. 26, 1804, MHi; TJ to Thomas Mann Randolph, June 5, 1805, *Farm Book,* p. 153. Young James Hemings ran away because of Lilly's treatment (Oldham to TJ, July 16, 1805, MHi). For other harsh overseers, see TJ to Thomas Mann Randolph, June 24, 1793, DLC; TJ to Joel Yancey, Jan. 17, 1819, *Farm Book,* p. 43.

49. TJ to Reuben Perry, April 16, 1812, *Farm Book,* p. 35. Jefferson's grandson Thomas Jefferson Randolph continued this practice. One incident stuck fast in the memory of Randolph's six-year old nephew after a visit to Edgehill from his home in Boston. His uncle brought a slave guilty of a theft "before the house, in front of which all the slaves were assembled, and flogged him with a horsewhip." *T. Jefferson Coolidge 1831–1920: An Autobiography* (Boston, 1923), p. 3.

50. Bear, *Jefferson at Monticello,* p. 97.

51. TJ to Thomas Mann Randolph, June 8, 1803, *Farm Book,* p. 19. Jefferson's belief in the power of positive and negative example is apparent throughout his writings. He invoked the example of "terror" at least twice more in this period. In 1803 he thought a convicted slave trader should serve his term "as a terror to others." In 1809 he fervently hoped that a slave who had plundered his baggage on its way up the James River should be hanged: "Some such example is much wanting to render property waterborne secure" (TJ to Christopher Ellery, May 19, 1803, *Ford,* IX, p. 467; TJ to John Barnes, Aug. 3, 1809, DLC). I am indebted for these citations to Philip J. Schwarz, who generously shared his personal compilation of references to Jefferson and slavery.

52. TJ to John McDowell, Oct. 22, 1798, *Farm Book,* p. 437; TJ to Reuben Perry, May 10, 1811, Swem Library, College of William and Mary.

53. Thomas Mann Randolph to TJ, March 6, 1802, MHi; TJ to Randolph, April 19, 1792, *Boyd,* XXIII, p. 436, and Feb. 18, 1793, *Farm Book,* p. 165.

54. TJ to Stevens Thomas Mason, Oct. 27, 1799, *Ford,* IX, p. 85. TJ to William Strickland, March 23, 1798, DLC.

55. TJ to Joseph Dougherty, July 31, 1806, *Farm Book,* p. 22.

56. Bear, *Jefferson at Monticello,* p. 104. John Freeman and Jack Shorter, footman and groom at the President's House, had accompanied Jefferson to Monticello (see *Memorandum Books,* Sept. 20 and 21, 1806).

57. Edy was at the President's House from at least the fall of 1802 until the spring of 1809. She bore three children in that period: an infant that did not survive in Jan. 1803; James, born Jan. 1805; and Maria, born Oct. 1807 (*Memorandum Books,* Jan. 28, 1803; *Farm Book,* p. 128). Edy, who was only fifteen when she went to Washington, may have been considered too young by her parents for formal marriage. There seems to be no way of knowing whether Jefferson gave her the option of remaining at Monticello with Joe Fossett and her family, was ignorant of the depth of her connection, or knew it and chose to disregard it.

58. The section title is drawn from Isaac Jefferson's reminiscences, Bear, *Jefferson at Monticello,* p. 19. For the stories told by descendants of Joe Fossett and his relatives, see Lucy C. Williams to Pearl Graham, July 14, 1947, and c. Jan. 22, 1948; Charles H. Bullock account of Peter Fossett, c. Oct. 1949, Howard University Archives, Washington, DC (hereafter DHU). The silver under the portico story was also told by the Jefferson-Randolph family; butler Martin Hemings fended off the British search while Caesar shared the dark space with the silver for eighteen hours. Henry S. Randall, *The Life of Thomas Jefferson,* (Philadelphia, 1865), I, pp. 338–39. Isaac Jefferson told another story of silver saved by his father, when Benedict Arnold's forces invaded Richmond earlier in the year (Bear, *Jefferson at Monticello,* p. 8).

59. Bear, *Jefferson at Monticello,* pp. 13–14; Martha J. Randolph recollections, undated, *Boyd,* XVI, p. 168.

60. See, for instance, TJ to John McDowell, Oct. 22, 1798, *Farm Book,* p. 437; to John Hartwell Cocke, May 3, 1819, ViU; to James Madison, April 11, 1820, *Farm Book,* p. 420; to John W. Eppes, Oct. 13, 1820, The Huntington Library.

61. Brodie, *Jefferson,* p. 477; TJ to Thomas Mann Randolph, Feb. 4, 1800, DLC.

62. TJ to J. N. Demeunier, June 26, 1786, *Boyd,* X, p. 63; TJ to Thomas Cooper, Sept. 10, 1814, *L&B,* XIV, p. 183; "Memorandums on a Tour from Paris to Amsterdam," April 19, 1788, *Boyd,* XIII, p. 36 n. 29; TJ to Thomas Mann Randolph, July 28, 1793, *Garden Book,* p. 200; Richard Beale Davis, ed., *Jeffersonian America* (1954; reprint, Westport, Conn., 1980), p. 149; Peden, *Notes,* pp. 139, 143.

63. TJ to Nicholas Lewis, July 29, 1787, *Boyd,* XI, p. 640; TJ to Samuel Biddle, Dec. 12, 1792, *Boyd,* XXIV, p. 725; TJ to Edward Bancroft, Jan. 26, 1789, *Boyd,* XIV, p. 492; TJ to Thomas Mann Randolph, April 19, 1792, *Boyd,* XXIII, p. 436.

64. [Margaret Bayard Smith], *The First Forty Years of Washington Society,* ed. Gaillard Hunt (New York, 1906), p. 68; *Farm Book,* p. 6; memorandums to Jeremiah Goodman, Dec. 13, 1812, and Nov. 11, 1814, *Garden Book,* p. 493, and Princeton University Library.

65. TJ to Jeremiah Goodman, Jan. 6, 1815, *Garden Book,* p. 539; *Farm Book,* pp. 152, 165, 167.

66. Charlottesville *Daily Progress,* May 25, 1900; George Ticknor, *Life, Letters and Journals* (Boston, 1876), I, p. 36; Charles M. Wiltse and Harold D. Moser, eds., *The Papers of Daniel Webster* (Hanover, N.H., 1974), I, p. 371.

67. *Memorandum Books,* April 13, 1811, Dec. 24, 1822, Oct. 10–11, 1823, Feb. 12, 1824; *Farm Book,* pp. 116, 152; Edmund Bacon to TJ, Sept. 9, 1822, MHi.

68. "Record of Cases Tried in Virginia Courts, 1768–1769," DLC; Mary Rawlings, ed., *Early Charlottesville: Recollections of James Alexander 1828–1874* (Charlottesville, Va., 1963), p. 2. Jefferson's early legal notebook was later used for Monticello household accounts by his wife Martha (from 1772–1782) and granddaughter Anne Cary Randolph (from 1805–1808). In the three years of the latter's records, every adult slave (except Sally Hemings and the two cooks) sold chickens or eggs to the Jefferson household; more than half the adults sold garden produce.

69. *Memorandum Books,* May 24, 1795, Dec. 2, 1797, Jan. 20, Oct. 28, 1818; Nicholas Lewis accounts, Sept. 19, Nov. 28, Dec. 9, 1790, Ledger 1767–1770, ViU; "Record of Cases," DLC; Lucia Goodwin, "Two Monticello Childhoods," *Anniversary Dinner at Monticello,* (Monticello, Va., 1976), pp. 2–3.

70. Peden, *Notes,* p. 139; TJ to Richard Richardson, Feb. 10, 1800, private collection; Bear, *Jefferson at Monticello,* p. 22.

71. Eliza Trist to Nicholas P. Trist, June 30, 1819, Trist Papers, DLC; [Mary J. Randolph?] to Virginia J. Randolph and Jane Nicholas Randolph, 1819–1820, NcU; Bear, *Jefferson at Monticello,* p. 4; Justus, *Down from the Mountain,* p. 89; Mary J. Randolph to Virginia Randolph, Dec. 27, 1821, NcU.

72. Martha Jefferson to TJ, May 3, 1787, *Boyd,* XI, p. 334; Martha Randolph to Benjamin F. Randolph, Jan. 27, [1836?], ViU. Eugène Vail published six songs and two stories he heard from Martha Randolph in French in *De la Littérature et des hommes de lettres des Etats Unis d'Amérique* (Paris, 1841), pp. 321–33. I am grateful to Mechal Sobel for providing copies of the relevant pages of this rare text. Elizabeth Langhorne provided commentary and translations back into English in "Black Music and Tales from Jefferson's Monticello," *Journal of the Virginia Folklore Society* 1 (1979), pp. 60–67. See also Mechal Sobel, *The World They Made Together: Black and White Values in Eighteenth-Century Virginia* (Princeton, 1987), pp. 141–42.

73. Brodie, *Jefferson,* p. 474; Charlottesville *Daily Progress,* May 25, 1900; Charles Bullock to Pearl Graham, Oct. 10, 1949, and account of Peter Fossett, DHU; Ellen Randolph to Virginia Randolph, Aug. 31, 1819, ViU; Robert Pleasants to TJ, June 1, 1796, William L. Clements Library, University of Michigan, and Feb. 8, 1797, Missouri Historical Society, St. Louis; Peden, *Notes,* p. 137; TJ to Jared Sparks, Feb. 4, 1824, *LofA,* p. 1487.

74. TJ to Edward Bancroft, Jan. 26, 1789, *Boyd,* XIV, pp. 492–93; Davis, *Jeffersonian America,* p. 149; instructions to Edmund Bacon, c. Oct. 1806, Bear, *Jefferson at Monticello,* p. 54.

75. Israel Jefferson reminiscences, Brodie, *Jefferson,* p. 481; TJ–John Hemings correspondence, MHi; kitchen inventory, Feb. 20, 1796, MHi; Hannah to TJ, Nov. 15, 1818, MHi (there is a possibility this letter was written by an amanuensis); TJ to Thomas Mann Randolph, Jan. 25, and March 8, 1798, *Farm Book,* pp. 160, 243; Albemarle County Deed Book, 29, p. 492, 36, p. 122.

76. There is one ambiguous payment in the 1806 Memorandum Book, to Benjamin Snead "for 2 1/2 mo[nth]s tuition of George's son" (Sept. 24, 1806). Isaac Jefferson's brother George (1759–1799), a blacksmith, was always listed alone in Jefferson's *Farm Book.* His wife was probably either a free woman or a slave on a nearby plantation. Snead was a teacher at the neighborhood school attended by Jefferson's grandson and, if he was the same Benjamin Snead with whom Jefferson had dealings in the 1760s, he was also a weaver (Martha J. Randolph to TJ, May 12, 1798, Betts and Bear, *Family Letters,* p. 161; *Memorandum Books,* Oct. 2, 1769).

77. TJ to James Pemberton, June 21, 1808, DLC.

78. Mary J. Randolph to Ellen Coolidge, Sept. 11, 1825, ViU; Cornelia Randolph to Ellen Coolidge, May 30, 1830, ViU. For "poisons" and "poisoners" see, for instance, Thomas Mann Randolph to TJ, recd. April 25, 1800, ViU, and Joel Yancey to TJ, July 1, 1819, *Farm Book,* p. 44.

79. Auguste Levasseur, *Lafayette in America, in 1824 and 1825* (New York, 1829), p. 218. Fossett did pass on at least one overheard conversation to overseer Edmund Bacon. Bear, *Jefferson at Monticello,* p. 117.

80. Mary J. Randolph to Ellen Coolidge, Jan. 25, 1827, ViU; Monticello dispersal sale receipts, ViU:5921.

81. TJ to Joseph Dougherty, July 31, 1806, *Farm Book,* p. 23; *Acts Passed at a General Assembly of the Commonwealth of Virginia* (Richmond, 1827), p. 127; Justus, *Down From the Mountain,* p. 121; Albemarle County Deed Book, 29, pp. 491–92. The shop on Lot 30 on Main Street was reserved in this deed, but was probably purchased from its owner, Opie Norris, in a separate unrecorded transaction. The lot, bought for $325, was sold for $500 in 1844 (Deed Book, 42, pp. 9–10).

82. Albemarle County Deed Book 4, pp. 59, 62–69; 35, pp. 219–20; William L. Norford, *Marriages of Albemarle County and Charlottesville, 1781–1929* (Charlottesville, 1956), p. 181. Since John Winn sued Jesse Scott and the Bells for a debt, they may have bought Betsy Ann from him (Deed Book, 29, p. 442; 36, pp. 121–22).

83. See Charlottesville Deed Book, 3, p. 270 for sale of the building out of the family on July 15, 1892. Another probable link between Monticello and Charlottesville is Daniel Farley, whose house in the town may have been a Sunday gathering spot for Jefferson's slaves. In 1816 Moses broke his leg "in a trial of strength in a wrestle with one of his fellows" and was "at Farley's" (Frank Carr to TJ, March 18, 1816, *Farm Book,* p. 40). County records, which need further study, suggest that Farley is Mary Hemings's son and Joe Fossett's brother, Daniel (b. 1772), given in the 1780s to Jefferson's sister Anna (*Farm Book,* p. 24; "Negroes Alienated"; Albemarle County Will Book, 13, p. 44; Deed Book 36, pp. 27–28).

84. Orra Langhorne, *Southern Sketches from Virginia 1881–1901,* ed. Charles E. Wynes (Charlottesville, Va., 1964), pp. 81–83. Sally and Jesse Scott's children did, in fact, attend the white school in Charlottesville. This work and a number of other sources on the Scotts were kindly brought to my attention by the staff of the Albemarle County Historical Society. Olivia Summers Dutcher deserves credit for sparking my interest in Jesse Scott and the resultant discovery of his connection with the Hemingses of Monticello. She is the owner

of a delightful oil portrait of Scott with his violin, and she and her late husband assembled a great deal of information on the musician and his instrument.

85. Charlottesville *Daily Progress,* May 25, 1900; Justus, *Down from the Mountain,* pp. 122–24; Charles H. Bullock account of Peter Fossett, c. Oct. 1949, DHU.

86. Justus, *Down from the Mountain,* pp. 122–24; Fossett obituary, Cincinnati newspaper, 1901, Monticello archives.

CHAPTER 6

Jefferson and Slavery
"Treason Against the Hopes of the World"

PAUL FINKELMAN

His words ring true and strong more than two centuries after he wrote them. It is "self-evident" that all persons "are created equal, and that they are endowed by their Creator with certain unalienable Rights, that among these are Life, Liberty, and the pursuit of Happiness." The message is clear; it is a fundamental credo of American culture.

The author of these words has been called "the greatest champion of liberty this country has ever had."[1] Even historians who have concentrated on his faults argue that Jefferson, along with Lincoln, "is the central figure in the history of American democracy."[2] Yet, this "apostle of liberty" could never reconcile the ideals of freedom, expressed in the Declaration of Independence and his other writings, with the reality of his ownership of men and women and his leadership of a slaveholding society.

An understanding of Jefferson's relationship to slavery requires analysis of his statements on and beliefs about the institution and an account of his actions as a public leader and a private individual. Scrutinizing the contradictions between Jefferson's professions and his actions does not impose twentieth-century values on an eighteenth-century man. Because he was the author of the Declaration of Independence and a leader of the American Enlightenment, the test of Jefferson's position on slavery is not whether he was better than the worst of his generation, but whether he was the leader of the best; not whether he responded as a southerner and a planter, but whether he was able to transcend his economic interests and his sectional background to implement the ideals he articulated. Jefferson fails the test.

When Jefferson wrote the Declaration, he owned over 175 slaves. While many of his contemporaries freed their slaves during and after the Revolution, Jefferson did not. In the fifty years from 1776 until his death in 1826, a period of extraordinary public service, he did little to end slavery or to dissociate himself from his role as the master of Monticello. To the contrary, as he accumulated more slaves he worked assiduously to increase the productivity and the property values of his labor force. Nor did he encourage his countrymen to liberate their slaves, even when they sought his blessing.[3] Even at his death Jefferson failed to fulfill the promise of his rhetoric. In his will he emancipated only five bondsmen, condemning nearly two hundred others to the auction block.

On the fiftieth anniversary of the Declaration, Jefferson died, a monument to a giant chasm between his words and his deeds on the question of race and liberty. His slaves, and those of America, may have been endowed with a right to "liberty," but Jefferson had done nothing to secure that right for them.

Jefferson's ideas about slavery and his relationship to the institution were complex and contradictory. A proponent of legal reform and humane criminal codes, he advocated harsh, almost barbaric, criminal punishments for slaves or free blacks; known for expansive views of citizenship, he would have made freed slaves "outlaws" in the land of their birth; opposed to "attainders for corruption of the blood," he would have expelled from Virginia the children of white women and black men solely because they had "corrupt"—mixed—blood.[4]

The public Jefferson avoided the problem of slavery, foregoing opportunities to undermine the institution and its growing stranglehold on national politics. Throughout his life Jefferson tried to dodge discussions of slavery. When he did speak of the institution, as in his *Notes on the State of Virginia,* it was at the prompting of others, to serve his polemical purposes (most notably in denouncing British tyranny), or when his business dealings required it.[5] When unable to evade the issue, Jefferson sought to avoid confrontation and friction. When corresponding with other slaveowners he sounded just like one of them—which he was;[6] to opponents of slavery, Jefferson sounded like an abolitionist who would do anything to end slavery—if only the circumstances were right. Dumas Malone has noted Jefferson's "extreme distaste for personal controversy" and admits this habit of avoiding conflict "was a defect of his politeness and amiability which caused him to seem deceptive."[7] Nowhere is this deceptiveness more apparent than when he talked about slavery.

Jefferson opposed the circulation of his *Notes on Virginia* in part because his comments on slavery might "produce an irritation."[8] Together with David Brion Davis, we might well ask "how he expected to encourage the cause of emancipation without producing irritation."[9] This is exactly the problem. Ultimately Jefferson was more concerned with avoiding irritation than promoting emancipation. He was, in William Freehling's words, a "Conditional Terminator,"[10] never able to argue for an end to slavery without conditions that were always impossible to meet. For Jefferson any cost in ending slavery, however low, was too high.

Perhaps because he faced slavery daily in the management of his own slaves, Jefferson simply could not allow himself to reflect on their lack of liberty. Jefferson remained strikingly unconcerned about slaves as individuals. He barely saw those slaves who served him at home and in his fields— and who all too often served as ready forms of capital to pay his debts. But he knew slavery was wrong. It could not have been otherwise for an eighteenth-century natural law theorist. Many of his closest European and American friends and colleagues were leaders of the new abolition societies. Jefferson was part of a cosmopolitan "republic of letters" that was overwhelmingly hostile to slavery.[11] But, for the most part, he suppressed his doubts, while doing virtually nothing to challenge the institution. On this issue Jefferson's genius failed him. As David Brion Davis observes, "Jefferson had only a theoretical interest in promoting the cause of abolition."[12]

Jefferson could not live without slaves. They built his house, cooked his meals, and tilled his fields. In contrast to George Washington, Jefferson failed to carefully manage his lands and finances and lived beyond his means. Washington refused to traffic in slaves. Chronically in debt, Jefferson overcame his professed "scruples about selling negroes but for delinquency or on their own request," selling scores of slaves in order to make ends meet.[13] Jefferson could not maintain his extravagant life style without his slaves and, to judge from his lifelong behavior, his grand style was far more important than the natural rights of his slaves.

JEFFERSON, RACE, AND REPUBLICANISM

Even if he had put his financial house in order and been able to extricate himself from his role as master and slaveowner, a general emancipation posed other problems for Jefferson. Who would replace the slaves in the fields and in other menial positions? A permanent lower class of free, poor whites would threaten republican society.

Contemporaries of Jefferson, as well as historians, have understood the relationship between slavery and republicanism. During Jefferson's presidency Sir Augustus John Foster, an English diplomat, observed that in Jeffersonian Virginia planters could "profess an unbounded love of liberty and of democracy in consequence of the mass of the people, who in other countries might become mobs, being there nearly altogether composed of their own Negro slaves." Historian Edmund Morgan agrees: "Aristocrats could more safely preach equality in a slave society than in a free one. Slaves did not become leveling mobs." [14] The liberty of the white masses rested on the slavery of the black masses.

Even if all whites could somehow remain equal without slavery, race presented an insurmountable barrier to emancipation. Jefferson could not accept blacks as his equals. He believed blacks were swayed by emotion, lacked intellectual abilities, and were not equipped to participate in a free republican society. As John Hope Franklin insightfully notes, "It would seem hardly likely that anyone with such pronounced views on the inferiority of blacks, who, at the same time, believed blacks and whites could not live together as free persons could entertain a deeply serious belief that slaves should be emancipated." [15] Jefferson was not alone in excluding blacks from the vision of equality. William M. Wiecek persuasively argues that for Virginians and other southerners, Jefferson's "self-evident truths contain[ed] an implicit racial exception" and "the lines, properly read in the light of American social conditions of 1776, contain[ed] the word 'white' before the word 'men.'" [16] But in Revolutionary America "strikingly similar expressions" of equality "did not always mean the same things." [17] Many northerners considered blacks—even slaves—entitled to their self-evident rights. In 1780 the Massachusetts Supreme Judicial Court interpreted its state Constitution to have ended slavery in that Commonwealth. The language of the Massachusetts Constitution was almost identical to that Jefferson used in the Declaration. [18] Every Revolutionary-era northern state took steps to end slavery; most extended political rights, including the franchise, to free blacks. [19]

For Jefferson, political equality for blacks was impossible because he thought "the real distinction that nature has made" between the races went beyond color and other physical attributes. Race, more than their status as slaves, doomed blacks to permanent inequality. In *Notes on the State of Virginia* Jefferson asserted that a harsh bondage did not prevent Roman slaves from achieving distinction in science, art, or literature because "they were of the race of whites"; American slaves could never achieve such distinction because they were not white. Jefferson argued that American Indians had "a germ in their minds which only wants cultivation"; they were capable of "the most sublime oratory." But he had never found a black who "had uttered a thought above the level of plain narration; never seen an elementary trait of painting or sculpture." He found "no poetry" among blacks. Jefferson argued that blacks' ability to "reason" was "much inferior" to whites, while "in imagination they are dull, tasteless, and anomalous" and "inferior to the whites in the endowments of body and mind." Jefferson conceded blacks were brave, but this was due to "a want of fore-thought, which prevents their seeing a danger till it be present." [20]

Jefferson could assert the equality of mankind only by excluding blacks. He admitted some qualms at reaching a "conclusion [that] would degrade a whole race of men from the rank in the scale of beings which their Creator may perhaps have given them." He suspected blacks might be "originally a distinct race, or made distinct by time and circumstances" and that because of this they were "inferior to the whites in . . . body and mind." [21] If they had natural rights, and Jefferson seems uncertain on this point, they could only exercise them outside the United States.

Because Jefferson could not imagine living in a society in which blacks could claim equal rights, he could never comfortably consider emancipation or manumission. He never could overcome the "biases that made it impossible for him to conceive of a color-blind republic devoted to the rights of *all* men." [22] Because Jefferson believed free blacks could never be citizens—despite the fact they were citizens in the states immediately north and south of Virginia[23]—he assumed they would necessarily become an exploited and ungovernable mob. Jefferson also feared that former slaves would take revenge on their former masters for the "ten thousand . . . injuries they have sustained." He believed "Justice" was "in one scale, self-preservation in the other." He told a fellow Virginian and slaveowner that, "if something is not done & soon done, we shall be the murderers of our own children." [24] But he had no idea what that "something" might be. A man who fearlessly pledged his life to fight the king of England and his mighty armies trembled at the idea of black slaves acting as free men.

Jefferson's negrophobia was profound. A scientist and naturalist, he nevertheless accepted and repeated absurdly unscientific and illogical arguments about the racial characteristics of blacks, for instance that blackness might come "from the colour of the blood" or that blacks might breed with the "Oran-ootan." [25] His assertion that black men preferred white women was empirically insupportable. The reverse was more likely the case, as he surely knew. Many white men, including his late father-in-law, preferred black women for their sexual liaisons.

Confronted with examples of black achievement, be it Phyllis Wheatley's poetry, Benjamin Banneker's mathematics, or the "Literature of Negroes" compiled by Bishop Henri Gregoire, Jefferson found the evidence inconclusive or unpersuasive.[26] Faced with black accomplishment, he reiterated unsubstantiated claims about black biological inferiority.

More than the precursor of the antebellum abolitionists, Jefferson was the intellectual godfather of the racist pseudo-science of the American school of anthropology. William Lloyd Garrison may have learned his political theory from Jefferson, but Josiah Nott, Samuel Cartwright, and Samuel G. Morton apparently learned their science from him.[27] Jefferson's theories about race "became indisputable dogma within a decade after his death."[28]

A SOUTHERN PLANTER IN THE AGE OF ENLIGHTENMENT

Jefferson's attitude toward slavery and his lack of any serious commitment to emancipation reflects his upbringing, class origins, and lifelong status as a wealthy landowner, slaveowner, and southern aristocrat. At twenty-one he came into his inheritance, 5,000 acres and twenty-two slaves. His wife brought him more slaves and land. By the end of the Revolution Jefferson commanded a "miniature state," with some ten thousand acres of land and nearly two hundred slaves.[29] The only "citizens" in this "state" were Jefferson and his white family.

As a slaveowner Jefferson was neither sadistic nor vicious, but he bought slaves, punished them, and hunted them down when they escaped.[30] He advised his friends and relatives about purchasing slaves and gave them as gifts. He sold slaves away from their families to punish them and to make examples of them "in terrorem to others." Throughout his life he sold large numbers of slaves to raise cash.[31] In all these respects, Jefferson was an ordinary southern gentleman and master.

The traditional image of Jefferson is of a slaveholder valiantly trying to come to terms with the inherent contradictions between slavery and the philosophy of the American Revolution. This image will not hold up under careful scrutiny. It will not do to defend Jefferson on the ground that he was a southerner, a slaveowner, and a man of his times. We must compare him to his peers—the intellectual, political, and cultural leaders of his generation—and not to his neighbors. Robert McColley concludes that "Jefferson was not ahead, but rather far behind, such public advocates of emancipation as John Jay and Alexander Hamilton of New York, Anthony Benezet and Benjamin Franklin of Philadelphia, and Robert Pleasants and Warner Mifflin of Virginia."[32] To this list we might add James Otis of

Massachusetts, John and Henry Laurens of South Carolina, Jefferson's life-long friend Benjamin Rush of Pennsylvania, Jefferson's mentor at the College of William and Mary, George Wythe, and a host of others in Virginia, Maryland, and North Carolina.[33] After the American Revolution "European social evolutionists generally assumed that all people had innate abilities that would enable them eventually to ascend to the heights attained by Europeans and Euro-Americans—and it was with reference to this proposition that Jefferson harboured doubts as to the abilities of the Negro race."[34]

Criticism of Jefferson for his failure to act on slavery must be based on what his own generation expected from him and on comparing his actions with those of others in his generation. There was in fact "much support in the Chesapeake for abolishing slavery by one means or another, not only among leaders . . . but among the generality of people."[35] After the Revolution many Europeans and Americans turned to Jefferson for answers, encouragement, and moral support in the struggle against human bondage. They were usually disappointed. Jefferson told his correspondents to look to the future, wait for the next generation to take control, or hope that diffusion, population growth, or some other natural process would solve the problem.

Meanwhile, many of his contemporaries set standards for facing the challenge of slavery. Colonel John Laurens, for example, jeopardized his political career in South Carolina by strenuously urging the legislature to support a program whereby slaves would be freed and enlisted in all-black regiments while masters would be recompensed by Congress. Laurens believed this would benefit "those who are unjustly deprived of the rights of mankind" while simultaneously helping the patriot cause. Laurens died before he could liberate his own slaves, but his father, Henry, carried out the plan of manumission.[36] Jefferson never contemplated such a plan for his slaves.

The dramatic growth of Virginia's free black population after the Revolution suggests many masters took Jefferson's words about "self-evident truths" at face value. In 1782, when the state adopted a law allowing voluntary manumissions, about 2,000 free blacks lived in Virginia. By 1790 this figure had risen to 12,766, and it continued to rise to 20,124 in 1800 and 30,570 in 1810. In the three decades after the Revolution free blacks "were the fastest-growing element in the Southern population." Some of this growth was due to natural increase, but most came from manumissions.[37]

Voluntary manumission attracted leaders of the Revolution with large numbers of slaves as well as relatively unknown individuals with just a few.

Virginians with far more slaves than Jefferson freed their bondsmen and women. In the 1790s Robert "Councillor" Carter manumitted his more than five hundred slaves and provided them with land and housing.[38] John and Jonathan Pleasants, who together owned almost as many slaves as Jefferson, tried to manumit them in their wills and—through the persistent efforts of their heir Robert Pleasants—these wishes came to fruition. George Washington freed all his slaves in his will and "provided for apprenticeship and tenancy for the able-bodied and lodgings and pensions for the aged." Washington hated slavery and declined to participate in its most seamy aspects, refusing "either to buy or sell slaves, 'as you would do cattle at a market.'" In 1785 Joseph Mayo, an obscure planter from Powhatan, "astonished some of [Jefferson's] acquaintances" by bequeathing freedom to his 150 to 170 slaves. When Jefferson's kinsman John Randolph of Roanoke died in 1833, he manumitted all of his hundreds of slaves and provided money to purchase land for them.[39]

Had Jefferson freed his slaves he would have given great impetus to this manumission movement. Certainly his well-known condemnations of the institution led some of his contemporaries to believe that he would take action. Yet if Jefferson condemned slavery, he was far more concerned about what slavery did to whites than about what it did to blacks. He was fearful of miscegenation, the enslavement of whites, and violent conflict between the races. A closer look at his public career and private life illustrates these themes, and shows there is little substance to the antislavery Jefferson.[40]

A YOUTH WITH NOBLE IDEAS

Two events from his prerevolutionary career suggest Jefferson's early hostility to slavery: his support for a bill to allow voluntary manumission in his first term in the Virginia legislature, and his failed attempt as a young attorney to win freedom for a mulatto held in servitude.

In 1769, as a freshman legislator in the House of Burgesses, Jefferson supported a bill to allow private manumission of slaves. The slim documentation of this effort consists of a letter Jefferson wrote in 1814 and an autobiographical note from 1821. The first account came in response to a request by Edward Coles that Jefferson endorse Coles's plan to free his slaves. In a long and revealing letter, in which he ultimately urged Coles not to manumit his slaves, Jefferson wrote about his earliest public opposition to slavery: "I drew to this subject [manumission] the attention of Col. Bland, one of the oldest, ablest, & most respected members, and he undertook to move for certain moderate extensions of the protection of the laws to these people. I seconded his motion, and as a younger member, was more spared in the debate; but he was denounced as an enemy of his country, & treated with the grossest indecorum."[41] Seven years later, in his autobiography, Jefferson wrote: "I made one effort in that body for the permission of the emancipation of slaves, which was rejected."[42]

The incident shows Jefferson was troubled by slavery, but not that he opposed the institution. Bland's proposal was not radical: it would not have freed a single slave. In simply allowing masters to manumit their slaves, it was fully in accord with Revolutionary-era notions of slaveowners' property rights. Nor is it clear how, according to Jefferson's suggestion, it would have extended the "protection of the laws" to slaves. In fact, the law was designed to allow masters to dispose of their slaves as they wished. Only when their masters chose to free them would former slaves have been under the same laws as other free blacks in Virginia.

Still, in a society where manumission was illegal, the Bland proposal would have been a meaningful step toward freedom, and one that Virginians finally did take in similar legislation in 1782. Whether or not Jefferson took the initiative in 1769—and it seems likely that he exaggerated his role in retrospect—this would be the last time he stuck out his neck on slavery while holding public office. The lesson Jefferson learned in 1769 was to avoid discussions of slavery that might lead to unpleasant confrontations with his colleagues. However troubled he may have been by slavery, Jefferson would let others work for amelioration or reform.

The other "antislavery" incident of his early career was a legal case. In 1770 Jefferson represented Samuel Howell, a mulatto who was held in servitude until the age of thirty-one. His status was based on the fact that he, his mother, and his grandmother were born out of wedlock. A 1705 law declared that illegitimate mulatto children of white women would be bound out by the churchwardens until they also were thirty-one. A 1723 law further provided that if a female held to service under the 1705 law had children before her servitude ended, the children would be bound out under the same terms.[43]

Howell's grandmother was the bastard child of a white woman and a black or mulatto man and had been bound out according to the 1705 law. When she was no older than eighteen the grandmother gave birth to a female child, who in turn was bound out until she was thirty-one. At nineteen she gave birth to Howell, and the court bound him to Netherland. When he was twenty-eight years old Howell sued for his freedom. Using unpersuasive legal arguments and some natural rights theory, Jefferson vainly sought to convince the court that this man should be free.[44]

This case was neither about slavery, nor was it "the surest indication of his attitude [toward slavery] at this time." [45] Samuel Howell, the plaintiff, was not a slave and would eventually gain his freedom, no matter what the court decided. In his argument Jefferson clearly makes this point, reminding the court that the plaintiff and his ancestors were all born free, subject only to an indenture.

More important, Jefferson's arguments are about race and status, not slavery. We cannot know Howell's color. His great-grandmother was white and his great-grandfather may have been half-white. We do not know the race of his grandfather and father, but under the 1705 and 1723 laws Howell would have been in servitude until the age of thirty-one if all of his ancestors except the great-grandfather had been white. The plaintiff's mixed heritage may have affected Jefferson's willingness to take the case. This is a plausible inference from his argument that the defendant's interpretation of the case was dangerous "[b]ecause it would make servants of the children of white servants or apprentices, which nobody will say is right." [46]

It is true that in this case Jefferson articulated the notion that "under law of nature . . . we are all born free." [47] But the key issue in this case— as in so many of Jefferson's writings on slavery, race, and liberty—hinges on what Jefferson meant by the term "we." It is likely that Howell had predominantly white ancestry, appeared white, and was, in Jefferson's view, a white person. Jefferson's argument was that the children of white women should not be made into temporary slaves.

Jefferson's private actions regarding his own slaves' attempts to gain freedom further undermine his antislavery reputation for this early period. Because the proposed 1769 statute failed to pass, no master could, on his own, free a slave. But even without a statute there were ways a master could free his slaves. One was by not interfering with their determined efforts to become free by running away. But Jefferson chased after his slaves, even as he urged the legislature to allow other masters to free theirs. In September 1769 Jefferson advertised he would pay up to ten pounds for the return of Sandy, a runaway. Sandy was caught and Jefferson later sold him for one hundred pounds. [48]

THE DECLARATION OF INDEPENDENCE

Three years after he sold Sandy, Jefferson pledged his life, his fortune, and his "sacred honor" to the cause of American independence and liberty.

He also lent his brilliant rhetorical skills to the cause. Jefferson considered his paternity of the Declaration of Independence one of his three most important accomplishments, along with drafting Virginia's Statute of Religious Freedom and being the "Father of the University of Virginia." More than anything else, his drafting of the Declaration—and a clause on the slave trade deleted from that draft—has sustained the myth of the antislavery Jefferson.

The most obvious connection between slavery and the Declaration is in the preamble, a clarion call to liberty. Its sentiments undermine the morality of slavery and its legitimacy under natural law. For those who would make Jefferson an antislavery icon, the preamble is crucial. Antebellum opponents of slavery as diverse as William Lloyd Garrison, Frederick Douglass, and Abraham Lincoln relied on this language to bolster their opposition to human bondage. In dedicating the nation to the dismantling of slavery and to a "new birth of freedom" Lincoln hearkened back to the Declaration which "brought forth . . . a new nation, conceived in Liberty and dedicated to the proposition that all men are created equal." [49]

Before turning to the Declaration itself, it is necessary to examine a clause of Jefferson's left out of the final document. In his original draft Jefferson complained that the British king had "waged cruel war against human nature itself, violating its most sacred rights of life and liberty" by perpetuating the African slave trade. Calling the African trade "piratical warfare" Jefferson complained that "a CHRISTIAN king of Great Britain" was so "[d]etermined to keep open a market where MEN" were bought and sold that he used his "negative" to suppress "every legislative attempt to prohibit or to restrain this execrable commerce." [50] While condemning the King for supporting the African trade, Jefferson also denounced him for encouraging slaves to enlist in the British army, "exciting those very people to rise in arms among us, and to purchase that liberty of which he has deprived them, by murdering the people on whom he also obtruded them: thus paying off former crimes committed against the LIBERTIES of one people, with crimes which he urges to commit against the LIVES of another." [51]

Although this "vehement philippic against negro slavery," as John Adams called it, never made it into the final version of the Declaration, [52] it has made it into the public mind as proof of Jefferson's opposition to slavery. But Adams's characterization of the clause is misleading. Congress deleted this clause for a variety of reasons, including the complaints of Georgia and South Carolina, still active participants in the transatlantic trade. But, even without the specific complaints of those states, "The charge," as Merrill Peterson suggests, "simply did not ring true. And Jefferson's bloated rhetoric gave it away."[53] In any case, Jefferson was attacking the African slave trade, not the institution itself. The arguments against the African trade were humanitarian, economic, and prudential. Many Virginians opposed the trade for "selfish considerations, such as protecting the value of their property in slaves and securing their communities from the dangers of an ever-increasing slave population," especially when that population was made up of recent arrivals from Africa, who tended to be more rebellious than other slaves.[54]

Jefferson certainly fit this class of Virginians. Throughout his life Jefferson sold slaves: the African trade undermined the value of his slaves. Similarly, Jefferson always argued for curbs on the growth of America's black population. He almost always tied any discussion of manumission or emancipation to colonization or "expatriation." Ending the African trade would slow the growth of the nation's black population. Thus, the attack on the King dovetailed with Jefferson's negrophobia and his interests as a Virginia slaveowner and did not necessarily indicate opposition to slavery itself.

Jefferson's last charge against George III on the slavery issue—and the only one incorporated into the final document—was that "he has excited domestic insurrections against us." The meaning is unmistakable.[55] For southern slaveowners "domestic insurrections" had only one meaning: slave revolts. Jefferson's original draft of the Declaration complains that the King has enslaved people "against human nature itself"; he then proceeds to condemn the King for enabling those people to fight for their freedom. Jefferson failed to consider the irony of Americans rebelling against the King while complaining that slaves were rebelling against them.

For Jefferson, former slaves in uniform were far more threatening than the King's white army. British soldiers killed enemies in battle, but slaves in uniform, fighting for their own liberty, were "murderers." Like so many of Jefferson's writings on slavery, his draft of the Declaration reveals his self-deluding inability to see African-Americans as human beings. They are mere objects, in this case to be used in the propaganda war against the King. Not a few Englishmen read the Declaration and wondered, as did Samuel Johnson, "How is it that we hear the loudest *yelps* for liberty among the drivers of negroes?"[56] Few of the revolutionaries yelped louder, or with more eloquence, than the master of Monticello; few owned so many Negroes.

REVOLUTIONARY SLAVEHOLDER

Jefferson might have blunted the biting criticism of Johnson and others if he had taken some actions against slavery during the Revolution. But he did not. Certainly he could have used the Revolution to sever or diminish his personal ties to slavery. During the war many masters enlisted their male slaves in the Revolutionary army. The master got the slave's enlistment bounty and made an important double contribution to the cause of liberty by providing a soldier for the Continental line and giving freedom to a slave. The slave gained his freedom and earned a place in American society.

Thomas Jefferson did not enlist any of his slaves, thus forfeiting a singular opportunity to free some of his slaves, be recompensed for his loss, and, as a Revolutionary officeholder, take a lead in recruiting soldiers. At the time Jefferson had not yet accumulated huge debts. Although a young man with a great future and a chance to make a statement about liberty that went beyond parchment protests, Jefferson did not enlist any of his slaves.[57]

Jefferson's failure to act is all the more striking in view of his reaction to a wartime event affecting his slaves. In 1781 Lord Cornwallis occupied Jefferson's Elkhill plantation. In addition to taking animals and food and destroying property, the British troops carried off thirty or so of Jefferson's slaves. Jefferson later wrote to the English intellectual William Gordon, "Had this been to give them freedom he would have done right, but it was to consign them to inevitable death from the small pox and putrid fever then raging in his camp."[58] Jefferson's biographer notes that "[t]his, indeed, was the fate of most of the slaves, and Jefferson recovered only five of them."[59]

The important question is not what Cornwallis did with the slaves, or what he might have done had he won at Yorktown, but what Jefferson did. He vigorously sought to recover his slaves. Had Jefferson done this to give them freedom, then Jefferson "would have done right." But Jefferson chased down his slaves to consign them to lifetime bondage. The fact remains that many slaves—including some owned by Jefferson—gained their freedom by escaping to British lines; none gained it by remaining on the Jefferson plantations.[60]

REVOLUTIONARY LAWMAKER

Jefferson's failure to take any action to end slavery is underscored by the unique opportunity he had, from 1776 to 1779, to shape the laws of Virginia. Shortly after he signed the Declaration, Jefferson left the national Congress to serve in the Virginia legislature. He remained there until June 1779, when he became governor. A careful examination of Jefferson's role as a Revolutionary lawmaker raises further questions about his reputation for opposing slavery. It shows that Jefferson's support for independence and liberty for white America ironically made him less sympathetic to the natural-rights claims of blacks.

Jefferson's legislative career was one of the most satisfying and creative periods in his life. Early on he proposed a bill for a complete revision of Virginia's laws. As chair of the revision committee Jefferson was able "to set forth in due course a long-range program emphasizing humane criminal laws, complete religious freedom, and the diffusion of education, and thus to appear on the page of history as a major prophet of intellectual liberty and human enlightenment."[61] During and after Jefferson's service in the legislature Virginia adopted many of the committee's proposed laws, including bills on religious freedom, the abolition of primogeniture and entail, education, citizenship, and the criminal code. More than two centuries later these still stand out, "and the credit for all of these belongs to [Jefferson]."[62]

The committee provided Jefferson, who was "pre-eminently a political architect, looking to the future,"[63] with a unique opportunity to change the law of slavery in Virginia. Unlike 1769, when he was a freshman legislator, Jefferson was now a respected leader with an international reputation, chairing a committee to revise the laws of the largest and most important state in the new nation. Here was the moment and the man to strike at slavery. Instead, Jefferson struck at slaves and free blacks.

One of Jefferson's goals was to modernize Virginia's criminal code, incorporating the humane concepts found in the new criminology of Cesare de Beccari. He reduced the number of capital crimes for white offenders to two and removed various barbaric customs from the criminal code. But, "except for the privilege of knowing that their corpses would not rot on gibbets, the slaves profited little from the enlightened humanitarianism" of Jefferson's draft code. His proposed law tightened the slave code, increased penalties for slave criminals, and "retained most of the inhumane features of the colonial slave law."[64]

Jefferson was proud of his law liberalizing rules for white immigrants seeking citizenship. But this same law, adopted just before he became governor, prohibited free blacks from becoming citizens. Under another law Jefferson proposed, any slave manumitted in the state had to leave Virginia within a year or "be out of the protection of the laws." Any free blacks coming into the state, except seamen, were to be outlawed. Visiting seamen were given a twenty-four-hour grace period before they were outlawed. Another of Jefferson's proposed laws would have banished any white woman bearing "a child by a negro or mulatto." If she failed to leave the state the woman would be outlawed and her child would be bound out for an unspecified time before being banished from the state.[65]

The legislature rejected Jefferson's proposed legislation for free blacks, manumitted slaves, and white women who bore mixed-race children. Nevertheless, these proposals stand in stark contrast with his earlier support for a manumission law and his arguments against "mak[ing] servants of the children of white servants or apprentices"[66]—not to mention his endorsement of the natural rights of "life, liberty, and the pursuit of happiness." How can we balance Jefferson's support for the 1769 manumission law with the law he proposed a decade later? How do we interpret his arguments against punishing the children of white women in the Howell case in light of his law to exile white women and their mulatto children? Had Jefferson soured on black freedom in the preceding decade, or had he never favored manumission in the first place?

Only one explanation makes sense. During the Revolution Jefferson saw his republican theories about equality and citizenship come into their own. This forced him to confront the problem of race and free blacks in a republican society, without any royal government to intervene. During the colonial period blacks could not vote, and no one was likely to suggest they should.[67] In 1769 Jefferson thus could argue in favor of liberalized manumission laws; he did not have to worry about the role of free blacks in his society—under British rule they would have none. But by 1779 free blacks could invoke Jefferson's own stirring words to claim citizenship and the franchise. Jefferson approved of an expanded franchise after the Revolution, but he never envisioned free blacks as voters or citizens. Jefferson's dilemma was that the only alternative to black citizenship, a large nonvoting population of free blacks, was in his view equally dangerous to the republic. Blinded by negrophobia and notions of black inferiority, Jefferson therefore could not allow free blacks to remain in republican Virginia.[68]

The free blacks and slaves of Virginia would have been better off if the British had won the war. "From the perspective of the black masses," A.

Leon Higginbotham concludes, "the Revolution merely assured the plantation owners of their right to continue the legal tyranny of slavery."[69]

A MANUMISSION LAW THAT NEVER WAS

As chair of the committee to revise Virginia's laws Jefferson was in the ideal position to work toward gradual emancipation.[70] But he failed to take the lead. And when legislators approached Jefferson with draft legislation that would have brought gradual emancipation to Virginia, he declined to add it to the proposed revisions because, he later explained, it was "better that this should be kept back" and only offered as an amendment.[71] When confronted with a chance to work toward public emancipation or private manumission, Jefferson backpedaled.

In his *Notes on the State of Virginia* Jefferson wrote that a bill "to emancipate all slaves born after passing the act" was not "reported by the revisors," but that "an amendment containing it was prepared, to be offered the legislature whenever the bill should be taken up." Under this proposed amendment the children of slaves would be educated and then "colonized" out of the state.[72] If such an amendment was prepared, no copy of it has survived. The first appearance of the text of this amendment was in the *Notes.*

Jefferson wrote *Notes on Virginia* in 1781, revised it in 1783–84, and made a final revision in France, "before turning his manuscript over" to his French publisher "late in 1784 or early in 1785."[73] By the time Jefferson left for France it was clear that no one would introduce his proposed emancipation-colonization scheme. Nevertheless, Jefferson did not revise his account of the emancipation amendment.[74] There is no indication why Jefferson persisted in telling his European readers that this law would be introduced when he knew it had not been, and would not be, proposed.

Curiously, Jefferson never altered the *Notes* to reflect what Virginia *did* do at this time, which was to pass legislation allowing masters to manumit their slaves. Virginia passed this law in 1782, well before Jefferson left for France. Jefferson's silence may reflect the fact that the manumission law was not part of Jefferson's program, but instead resulted from the pleas of citizens seeking to free their own slaves.[75] Or perhaps in exaggerating the prospects for a general emancipation, Jefferson may have been telling his European friends what he thought they wanted to hear. His failure to revise the *Notes* created the false impression that Virginia was prepared to act boldly against the institution.

Jefferson later claimed that the amendment was not proposed by the revisors because "the public mind would not yet bear the proposition." [76] This account is diametrically opposed to his assertion in 1774 in *A Summary View of the Rights of British America* that "the abolition of domestic slavery is the great object of desire in those colonies where it was unhappily introduced in their infant state." [77] Yet it is clear that Jefferson was not seriously interested in ending slavery, whatever the state of the "public mind." He was far more concerned with ridding the state of free blacks and creating a criminal code to keep slaves in line.

Jefferson's understanding of the public mind is the critical issue. Before July 1776 most Americans were not prepared to declare their independence. When Jefferson penned the Declaration, public opinion needed to be shaped by argument and debate. The manumission movement faced similar obstacles. Many Revolutionary Virginians, although surely not close to a majority, were ready to consider some form of gradual emancipation. Jefferson might have helped shape the public mind on emancipation just as he had on independence. Even without Jefferson's lead, the legislature adopted a law allowing private manumission *without* expatriation. This suggests that the "public mind" on this issue may have been far in advance of Jefferson's.

Jefferson's actions on the committee contrast with those of two prominent Virginia judges, George Wythe and St. George Tucker. During the post-Revolutionary period Wythe, Jefferson's teacher at William and Mary, publicly attacked slavery in *Hudgins* v. *Wrights,* arguing that the Virginia Constitution prohibited bondage. [78] Tucker overturned part of Wythe's ruling, on constitutional grounds. But Tucker was on record as favoring a gradual emancipation law. In his *Dissertation on Slavery with a Proposal for the Gradual Abolition of It in the State of Virginia,* Tucker was "much bolder than Jefferson in advocating emancipation." [79] Tucker circulated his pamphlet throughout the state, hoping to attract support for his manumission scheme; Jefferson sought to limit circulation of *Notes on the State of Virginia* in order to avoid "irritation."

Jefferson's service on the committee to revise the laws of Virginia underscores his hostility to free blacks, his growing fear of miscegenation, and his persistent dodging of the slavery issue. In these crucial respects there was nothing revolutionary about Jefferson's lawmaking. To the contrary, his proposals concerning slavery and race were reactionary. Fortunately for Virginia's free blacks, masters who might want to liberate their slaves, white women who chose to have liaisons with black men, and slaves convicted of crimes in Virginia, the legislature rejected most of Jefferson's proposals on slavery and race.

EMANCIPATION SCHEMES

Despite his hostility to free blacks and his refusal to introduce a gradual emancipation proposal in the Virginia legislature, on two other occasions Jefferson went on record as favoring some sort of emancipation or curb on the spread of the institution. The common thrust of these two schemes, as well as the emancipation amendment described in the *Notes,* was to eliminate slavery in a jurisdiction (either Virginia or the Northwest) while at the same time preventing the growth of a free black population.

Gradual Emancipation and the Virginia Constitution

In spring 1783 Jefferson privately suggested a gradual emancipation program for Virginia. Anticipating a state constitutional convention, Jefferson wrote a draft constitution that provided: "The General assembly shall not . . . permit the introduction of any more slaves to reside in this state, or the continuance of slavery beyond the generation which shall be living on the 31st day of December 1800; all persons born after that day being hereby declared free."[80]

The draft constitution is an intriguing document, unfinished and ambiguous.[81] The slavery clause suggests that in the deepest recesses of his heart and mind, Jefferson *knew* that someone had to do something about slavery. Jefferson sent a copy of his draft to James Madison but asked him not to share its contents with his colleagues. The draft might instead "serve as a basis for your [Madison's] amendment, or may suggest amendments to a better groundwork."[82]

Jefferson's proposal is congruent with his other responses to slavery. Characteristically, Jefferson refused to publicly advocate abolition, instead expecting Madison or others in the convention to promote his program. Similarly, Jefferson sought to delay any direct or immediate confrontation with the institution. (His emancipation program would not go into effect until seventeen years after he wrote it.) Finally, the proposal itself was ambivalent. Even if his program succeeded in the convention, the clause, as Jefferson wrote it, was not self-executing. The draft constitution admonished the "General Assembly" to act. If the assembly did not act, the clause would not go into effect.

Jefferson's first provision, banning the importation of slaves, would not have required much new legislation. By the time he wrote this proposal Virginia had already passed legislation prohibiting the importation of any new slaves, except by bona fide immigrants.[83] The proposal would have changed this law only by preventing immigrants from bringing slaves into

Virginia. If there was a departure in this proposal from Jefferson's lifelong views on slavery, it was in the lack of any requirement of expatriation of former slaves. The precedent here was the 1782 act allowing masters to free their slaves *without* requiring expatriation.[84]

For Jefferson the 1782 law was problematic. He was opposed to the presence of free blacks in Virginia. How, then, could he propose an end to slavery if former slaves could remain in the state? Jefferson's draft gradual emancipation scheme offered at least a partial solution to this problem. The delayed implementation of the plan would give Virginia masters years to sell their slaves out of the state. After 1801 masters would have been able to move pregnant women out of the state, so their children would be born as slaves.[85] Jefferson may have hoped to achieve at least a partial expatriation of free blacks because individual masters would make the economic decision to sell their slaves elsewhere.

Slavery in the West

Whatever Jefferson's intentions, no convention was called and he was soon back in politics. In November 1783 Jefferson took his seat in Congress. Here he took one more shot at slavery. Even if this salvo had landed on the target—and it did not—it would have been at best a glancing blow. Jefferson's "Plan of Government for the Western Territory" would have banned slavery after 1800.[86] Congress rejected the antislavery proviso. At this time thousands of slaves were already in the West, and more were arriving daily in what later became Kentucky and Tennessee; slavery was also already established in what became Indiana and Illinois. It took nearly a half century to fully eradicate slavery in Illinois after the adoption of the Northwest Ordinance, in 1787, which flatly prohibited slavery. Given the large slave population already in the territories south of the Ohio, it seems unlikely that Jefferson's proposal, delaying emancipation for sixteen years, would have been successful.[87] As William M. Wiecek notes, the phrasing of Jefferson's proposed ordinance "was, in effect, a permission to the western territories and states to establish slavery and retain it to the year 1800."[88] Delaying abolition in the West until 1800 would have given slaveowners sixteen years to populate the region and to lobby Congress for a change in the law.

Calling for a ban on slavery in the West was nevertheless an attack on institution, if for no other reason than it would have put the government on record as opposing its spread. Had Jefferson's ban passed, and had it worked, he might have continued in the direction of chipping away at slavery at the margins. Whatever his motivations—to reserve the West for free whites, to circumscribe the domestic slave trade, or to strike a blow against an unjust institution—it was a step in the right direction. It was a step, however, that Jefferson would later retract. During the Missouri debates Jefferson argued against prohibiting slavery in the West: a "geographical line, coinciding with a marked principle, moral and political" would stir the "angry passions of men." If Jefferson was inconsistent on slavery restriction, he consistently promoted what he considered best for white southerners. Always fearful of a concentration of blacks—slave or free—in 1820 he argued that introducing slavery in the West would lead to "diffusion," which would mean fewer blacks in the older slave states.[89]

Emancipation and the Notes on the State of Virginia

The gradual emancipation program that Jefferson described in the *Notes on Virginia*—and that was never introduced in the legislature—was his most comprehensive scheme. He presented it to his French readers as one of the more "remarkable alterations proposed" in the revision of Virginia's laws.[90] Jefferson claimed that the proposal in the *Notes* was the same one that was to be introduced by amendment in the legislature. Since it was never introduced, we can never know if it was ever on the agenda. What is clear, however, is that this proposal has all the marks of Jefferson's mature views on slavery and race and emancipation; moreover, it was presented in the *Notes* in conjunction with the most complete elaboration of Jefferson's racial theories.

According to Jefferson's proposal, children of slaves would remain with their parents until "a certain age" when they would be trained "to tillage, arts or sciences, according to their geniuses." The males would be fully emancipated at twenty-one, the females at eighteen. Then they would be "colonized to such place as the circumstances of the time should render most proper." Meanwhile, ships would travel "to other parts of the world for an equal number of white inhabitants" to be induced to come to America as paid agricultural laborers.[91]

This program was extremely impractical. The cost of removing Virginia's 200,000 slaves would have been enormous; finding willing white workers to enter Virginia's tobacco fields would have been almost impossible. Had this proposal been brought before the assembly, it probably would have been rejected. Aside from the unlikely chance of making such a program work, Jefferson's other comments in the *Notes* raise doubts about his own support for the proposal. It is in the rest of this rambling five-page paragraph that Jefferson offers his harsh views on the abilities of blacks.

Here Jefferson describes blacks as lacking "imagination," "reason," "forethought," and talents in poetry, art, oratory, and science. According to Jefferson, they even lacked basic human emotions: "Their griefs are transient" and their love was more like lust, lacking "a tender delicate mixture of sentiment and sensation."[92] In contrast to white Roman slaves, black slaves lacked skills in the "arts and sciences" even though they had been "liberally educated" and "lived in countries where the arts and sciences are cultivated to a considerable degree."[93] Jefferson's message is mixed. Under his emancipation scheme, the children of slaves would be educated, trained for freedom, and set free when ready. But he believed as blacks they would never be ready for freedom because they were incapable of learning.

THE SLAVE TRADE, LOUISIANA, AND THE PRESIDENCY

As president, Jefferson signed a bill outlawing the African slave trade. Jefferson pushed for this bill. It is likely the trade would have ended in 1808 if almost any of the early national leaders had been in office. The swift passage of the law indicates the strong popular appeal of banning the trade. Opposition to the slave trade did not necessarily signify opposition to slavery.[94] There were significant economic reasons for opposing the trade. A cessation of the trade would preserve the market value of the excess slaves in Virginia. Some slaveowners opposed the trade on both humanitarian and racist grounds: It was one thing to inherit slaves or buy and sell people who had been raised as slaves, but quite another to enslave free people in Africa. Jefferson sympathized with "the unhappy human beings" who were "brought away from their native country, & whose wives, children & parents are now suffering for want of their aid & comfort."[95] He also opposed the trade because it increased the nation's black population.

In an elaborate bargain—a "dirty compromise"—over commerce and the African slave trade, the Constitution prohibited Congress from banning the African trade before 1808. The Virginia delegation at the Convention, led by Washington and Madison, opposed the slave trade provision, which did not *require* Congress to abolish the trade in 1808. Advocates of the trade, mostly from the Carolinas and Georgia, probably expected to have enough clout in the future to keep the trade open past 1808.[96]

In his annual message to Congress in December 1806, Jefferson recommended legislation to abolish the African trade "to withdraw the citizens of the United States from all further participation in those violations of human rights which have been so long continued on the unoffending inhabitants of Africa, and which the morality, the reputation, and the best interests of our country have long been eager to proscribe."[97] Congress soon passed a law ending the trade on January 1, 1808. Historians have rightly noted that the 1808 law was a significant event in the struggle against slavery. It prevented hundreds of thousands of Africans from being brought to America, even if it probably had little effect on ending slavery in the United States.[98]

Jefferson's successful opposition to the slave trade forces us to ask why Jefferson failed to put his prestige, congressional majority, and popularity behind other antislavery reforms. After acquiring Louisiana, he did nothing to ban slavery in that vast territory. He might have used his influence to prohibit slavery throughout the territory, or at least limit it to what became the state of Louisiana. Either approach would have prevented Missouri from becoming a slave state and thus would have preempted the divisive debates of 1819–21.[99] Jefferson also could have proposed a gradual emancipation bill for the District of Columbia. Similarly he might have given diplomatic recognition to Haiti, which declared its independence in 1804, thereby showing his support for ending slavery in the Americas and his commitment to self-determination for free blacks.[100] His failure to do any of these things highlights Jefferson's lack of commitment to ending slavery, limiting its growth, or improving the legal position of free blacks.[101]

MANUMITTING HIS SLAVES

While Jefferson could not, or would not, effect a general emancipation, he certainly could have effected personal manumissions. Here was one area where Jefferson had absolute control. Jefferson repeatedly proclaimed his willingness to give up slavery. There was "not a man on earth who would sacrifice more," he claimed, "to relieve us from this heavy reproach, in any *practicable* way." He was willing "to make any sacrifice which shall ensure their retirement from the State." Ending slavery, Jefferson claimed "would not cost me a second thought, if in that way, a general emancipation and *expatriation* could be effected."[102]

Throughout his life Jefferson had opportunities to free some or all of his slaves.[103] With a very few exceptions, he never took advantage of these opportunities. Jefferson believed manumitted slaves could not survive in the United States. "Deep rooted prejudices entertained by whites; ten thousand recollections, by the blacks, of the injuries they have sustained, new provocations; the real distinctions which nature has made; and many other circumstances" made freedom within Virginia impossible. The major "other circumstance" was Jefferson's almost paranoid fear of a "mixture of colour here." "Expatriation" was always part of Jefferson's notion of a proper manumission: "If a slave can have a country in this world, it must be any other in preference to that in which he is born to live and labour for another." Jefferson supported colonization even as he understood that the cost of moving so many people to Africa made it "impossible to look at the enterprise a second time." However, "expatriation to the governments of the W[est] I[ndies] of their own colour" was "entirely practicable and greatly preferable to the mixture of colour here." In 1824 gradual emancipation, combined with colonization in Santo Domingo, seemed like the best solution. It was a reaffirmation of the plan suggested in the *Notes* forty years earlier to ensure emancipated slaves were "removed beyond the reach of mixture." [104]

Even if colonization was impractical on the grand scale, it was practical on the private scale. But Jefferson never took advantage of this option. Jefferson could have freed any of his slaves by sending them out of the state, or he could have freed the slaves he took to Europe and the North. There were no bars to manumission when he lived in or visited Pennsylvania, Massachusetts, New York, the District of Columbia, Great Britain, and France. Manumission in France would have been the ideal solution for some of his slaves: under French law they were already free and welcome in that country's growing free black community. But Jefferson did not free Sally or James Hemings while they were in France. On the contrary, he carefully avoided any unpleasant encounter with French law that might have led these slaves to claim their liberty. Moreover, while in France he advised other Americans there how to retain their slaves in violation of French law. He wrote, no doubt from personal experience, of "an instance where a person bringing in a slave, and saying nothing about it, has not been disturbed in his possession." [105]

Dumas Malone claims that when Jefferson "freed a particular slave, that individual was prepared for freedom in his opinion, and had a good place to go to." [106] In fact he freed only three slaves in his lifetime, and only in one instance does this characterization seem even partially accurate. Another biographer wrote that at his death Jefferson freed "his ablest and most faithful slaves." [107] These scholars avoid saying how many "particular" or "faithful" slaves Jefferson actually freed. This is not surprising, because the numbers are so embarrassingly small. It would almost be better for Jefferson's reputation if he had freed none—then at least we might plausibly argue he consistently opposed manumission, or that he forgot. But he did not forget to manumit his slaves. He just did not do it.

Jefferson freed only eight slaves: two in the 1790s, one in 1822, and five by his will in 1826. This small number allows for an instructive, detailed examination of each manumission. These slaves were indeed "particular," since they represent less than two percent of the total slaves Jefferson owned in his lifetime.[108] Skills and fidelity were not the tests Jefferson used to free his slaves. What were the characteristics of these emancipated slaves? All were members of the Hemings family, and thus were Jefferson's own relatives by marriage, blood, or both.[109] Even for his family members Jefferson was never generous with freedom. Seven of the eight were male; Jefferson seems to have had little regard for the liberty of his female relatives in bondage. Moreover, the three manumissions during his lifetime—including the one woman he freed—were not a result of philanthropic and humane instincts.

In 1794 Jefferson manumitted Robert Hemings, Sally's older brother. Robert actually purchased his freedom for £60. His future employer, George Frederick Stras, "advanced the money."[110] Robert was in fact already living with Stras and working for him at the time of the sale. This is a manumission in only the most technical sense. Jefferson did not grant Robert his freedom for his faithful service or out of political conviction; Jefferson sold Robert his freedom. Jefferson apparently agreed to give up Robert only because he was convinced that Stras had already "debauched" Robert, and thus he "complied reluctantly with an agreement by which Stras in essence purchased a number of years of Robert's service and retained the deed of emancipation until Robert had reimbursed him by serving out his time."[111]

Although Jefferson sold him as a slave, Robert was probably entitled to his freedom. Robert had accompanied Jefferson to Boston in 1784, and therefore had a claim to freedom under Massachusetts law. The case *Pleasants* v. *Pleasants,* which led to the emancipation of more than a hundred slaves in Virginia, indicates the pro-freedom inclinations of Virginia's highest court at this time; that court might have upheld Robert's claim to freedom on the basis of his residence in Massachusetts.[112]

The case of James Hemings is similar. Like his sister Sally (who Jefferson never freed), James Hemings had lived with Jefferson in Paris and was clearly free under French law.[113] Malone invokes James as another example of Jefferson's judicious manumission policy: while in Philadelphia Jefferson "signed an agreement to free him after he had returned to Monticello and stayed there long enough to teach somebody else how to cook—presumably in the French manner."[114] Merrill Peterson describes the manumission agreement as a bargain that favored James, "who won his freedom upon

fulfilling the pledge to teach his art [of cooking] to a worthy successor." [115]
These assessments are implausible and do not comport with the defensive
and apologetic language of the agreement.

> Having been at great expence in having James Hemings taught the art of
> cookery, desiring to befriend him, and to require from him as little in
> return as possible, I do hereby promise & declare, that if the said James
> shall go with me to Monticello in the course of the ensuing winter, when
> I go to reside there myself, and shall continue until he shall have taught
> such persons as I shall place under him for the purpose to be a good cook,
> this previous condition being performed, he shall be thereupon made
> free, and I will thereupon execute all proper instruments to make him
> free. [116]

This is not the language of a benevolent manumission; it is the language
of a contract between Jefferson and a suspicious and hostile party. Indeed,
the very existence of the agreement undermines any notion of benevolence.
Had he been willing to free James he could have done so without signing
an agreement for future manumission. Jefferson would have simply taken
James back to Monticello and told him to train another cook, and that
when he did so he could be free. But Jefferson did not do that, because it
is clear that "having been at great expence" for his training as cook he was
unwilling to lose James Hemings.

Why then, did Jefferson sign this agreement? A possible answer is that
he did so to avoid a suit from the Pennsylvania Abolition Society or some
other group or person in Philadelphia. [117] Under French law James was free.
Once Society members or others opposed to slavery found out that James
had been in France, they may have threatened a lawsuit to vindicate the
right. Whatever the source or grounds for such an action, Jefferson surely
would have wanted to avoid the embarrassment of a lawsuit over the freedom of a slave who was his wife's half-brother. This "voluntary manumission" looks suspiciously like a bargain between Jefferson and whoever was
threatening to intervene on behalf of James. James, who remained in bondage an extra three years, was the short-term loser. It is possible he acquiesced in the agreement because it gave him an opportunity to see his
family once again before returning to Philadelphia. In 1796 Jefferson finally
freed James. [118] Although Virginia law allowed him to remain in the state,
James chose to return to Philadelphia and Jefferson gave him thirty dollars
for the trip.

The only woman Jefferson freed was Harriet Hemings, the twenty-year-
old daughter of Sally. In 1822 she ran away with her brother Beverly. Jefferson freed Harriet while she was on the run, but not her twenty-four-

year-old brother.[119] Perhaps he blamed Beverly for the escape. Given the circumstances of Harriet's emancipation, it can hardly be called voluntary. None of Jefferson's biographers discuss this manumission.

This brings us to Jefferson's posthumous manumission of five Hemings family members: Joe Fossett, the son of Sally's sister Mary; Burwell, the son of Sally's sister Bett; Sally's brother, John Hemings; and Sally's sons Madison and Eston Hemings. Jefferson gave money to Burwell and tools to the other two adults. He allowed the adults to live on his lands for free, giving them a log house and an acre of land for their own use. He asked his executor to petition the legislature to allow the former slaves to remain in Virginia.[120]

Yet even in Jefferson's benevolence much was lacking. He directed his executors to allow the three men to live on land "convenient to them with respect to the residence of their wives."[121] Jefferson owned Joe Fossett's wife but did not provide for her freedom. She would later be sold to pay the debts of Jefferson's estate. Jefferson's daughter owned the wife of John Hemings. He made no attempt to acquire her so that she might live in freedom with her husband.[122] John was more fortunate than Joe, since his wife remained at Monticello after most of Jefferson's slaves were auctioned off. While he provided for the freedom of the teenaged Madison and Eston Hemings when they turned twenty-one, Jefferson did not manumit their mother, Sally.

Jefferson could have provided for the freedom of more than the five "faithful" slaves manumitted in his will.[123] He might have asked that his slaves be sent to Liberia; the American Colonization Society probably would have assumed the costs, as it did for less famous masters. In the context of Jefferson's own opposition to slavery, colonization made sense. Providing for the colonization of his slaves would have fit perfectly with Jefferson's lifelong assertions that he would support emancipation with expatriation. Of course, some of his slaves might not have wanted to end their days in a foreign place. Jefferson could have given his slaves the opportunity to choose between slavery in Virginia or freedom in Africa or elsewhere. Only a month before Jefferson died Herbert Elder, a master in Petersburg, Virginia, provided just such an opportunity for his slaves. Thirteen of Elder's fourteen slaves chose freedom on the continent of their ancestors.

Like Jefferson, Elder died with many debts. Elder's executor rented the slaves out to pay the debts of the estate, then he made plans to send them to Liberia. In 1833 a Virginia court approved these transactions, including the provision that the slaves make the final choice between being sold for the benefit of the estate or going to Africa.[124] If an obscure master in Petersburg could devise such a solution to the problem of debt and freedom, one could reasonably expect as much from the Sage of Monticello.

While considering the role of property in society, Jefferson told Madison the "earth belongs to the living" and that "no man can, by *natural right,* oblige the lands he occupied, or the persons who succeed him in that occupation, to the payment of his debts contracted by him." Otherwise, "the lands would belong to the dead, and not to the living."[125] Late in life he reiterated the theme: "Can one generation bind another?" He answered, "The Creator has made the earth for the living, not the dead."[126] Jefferson was talking about land. Apparently he did not see the irony that by his extravagances he would "oblige" living slaves, perhaps for "several generations to come," for "the payment of his debts contracted by him."

In 1817 Jefferson had asserted he was "personally . . . ready and desirous to make any sacrifice which shall ensure their gradual but complete retirement from the State, and effectually, at the same time, establish them elsewhere in freedom and safety."[127] Yet he never made the economies in his life style that would have enabled him to free his slaves in his life or at his death. He even failed to bequeath his slaves to the Colonization Society, missing a chance to accomplished all this *without* any sacrifice. Jefferson was not, in the end, interested in freeing his own slaves, even outside the country. In his will he directed that his tombstone indicate his authorship of the Declaration of Independence. In death, as in life, Jefferson wanted to be remembered for his words, even while failing to act on them with respect to his slaves. We honor him for the words of the Declaration, even as we remember his lifelong failure to implement liberty at the most personal level.

THE TIME WAS NEVER RIGHT

The hallmark of Jefferson's proposals to end slavery was delay and avoidance. He often spoke of the need for abolition, but asserted that the time was not right. "Not here" and "not now" was his philosophy. In the Virginia legislature he refused to offer an emancipation bill and instead left the task to others, when the time might be right. While in France he refused to manumit his slaves. "No wonder," William Freehling has written, "that posterity scorns this procrastinator" who "mastered dissimulation" and "developed fantastic powers of avoidance"[128] when it came to dealing with slavery.

Always a colonizationist, Jefferson could not conceive of emancipation without expatriation, which he conceded was impossible on any significant scale. He trembled at the thought that God's "justice cannot sleep for ever," but he trembled more at the immediate prospect of free blacks in his community. He thought it was "impossible to be temperate" in discussing solutions to slavery, so he offered none at all: "We must be contented to hope they will force their way into every one's mind." Deluding himself and his reader, Jefferson deferred to the next generation: "I think a change already perceptible, since the origin of the present revolution. The spirit of the master is abating, that of the slave rising from the dust, his condition mollifying, the way I hope preparing, under the auspices of heaven, for a total emancipation, and that this is disposed, in the order of events, to be with the consent of the masters." [129]

This theme of hoping the future would take care of past sins emerged in Jefferson's post-Revolutionary correspondence with Richard Price, a "liberal-minded Englishman." [130] Price's letters reveal how people around the world expected Jefferson to be a leader in a post-Revolutionary emancipation. Jefferson's response demonstrates both his hatred of slavery and his persistent belief that others, or the next generation, would have to deal with the problem.

Price told Jefferson that "the friends of liberty and humanity in Europe" were disappointed that "the people who have been struggling so earnestly to save *themselves* from slavery are very ready to enslave *others*." Those in Europe who supported the Revolution were now "mortify'd" that "an event which had raised their hopes will prove only an introduction to a new Scene of aristocratic tyranny and human debasement." [131] Price clearly expected Jefferson to lead America in a different direction.

Jefferson responded to Price with a harsh attack on slaveowners and "the enormity" of slavery—and an overly optimistic analysis of the prospects for emancipation in Virginia. The struggle over abolishing slavery is "the interesting spectacle of justice, in conflict with avarice and oppression; a conflict wherein the sacred side is gaining daily recruits, from the influx into office of young men grown, and growing up" who had "sucked in the principles of liberty, as it were, with their mother's milk; and it is to them I look with anxiety to turn the fate of this question." [132] Ironically, in condemning slavery and those who would not move against it, Jefferson condemned himself.

A year later Jefferson wrote that emancipation would happen "at some period of time not very distant" because support for emancipation "is continually recruiting by the addition of nearly the whole of the young men as fast as they come into public life." [133] Yet Jefferson would offer no leadership or encouragement to the rising generation. A decade later, Jefferson remained fearful of slavery, but still unable to act. He told St. George Tucker, "We shall be the murderers of our own children": Jefferson feared that a conflagration similar to that in Haiti awaited Virginians, and "only a single spark is wanting." [134] Yet even Jefferson's obsession with slave revolts could not lead him to act. "Soon" would have to be when the next generation came into power.

Shortly after the Louisiana purchase Jefferson asserted that the national government was constitutionally precluded from trying to attract European immigrants to take the place of slaves. Only the states could take such action. Once again, coming to terms with slavery was someone else's responsibility. [135] But when others did take the initiative, Jefferson refused their requests for aid or moral support. Instead, he counseled delay.

In 1814 Edward Coles wrote Jefferson, asking for support and encouragement in his personal campaign against slavery. Coles had grown up on the "mother's milk" of liberty in the shadow of Monticello. Jeffersonian notions of natural rights, life, liberty, and equality were second nature to Coles. He had gone to Jefferson's alma mater, read *Notes on the State of Virginia,* and been inspired by Jefferson's antislavery rhetoric. Coles asked Jefferson to endorse his plan to take his slaves to Illinois and free them. Jefferson rebuffed his young neighbor.

Coles represented the future generation that Jefferson had said would bring an end to slavery. He reiterated this belief to Coles: "I had always hoped that the younger generation . . . would have sympathized with oppression wherever found, and proved their love of liberty beyond their own share of it." Coles's letter was a "welcome voice" from this generation, making Jefferson think "the hour of emancipation is advancing, in the march of time." [136]

But Jefferson favored only a gradual emancipation of the children of slaves and counseled Coles against freeing his adult slaves. People "of this color" were "as incapable as children of taking care of themselves." Free blacks were "pests in society by their idleness, and the depredations to which this leads them." Jefferson feared their "amalgamation with the other color." Refusing to endorse manumission, Jefferson implored Coles to continue to care for his slaves. Merging his lifelong affection for states' rights with his hostility to free blacks, he urged Coles to "reconcile yourself to your country and its unfortunate condition." [137]

Six years later, he told Congressman John Holmes that slavery should be abolished "gradually, and with due sacrifices." It would happen when "*expatriation* could be effected." In his most memorable statement on the subject, Jefferson proclaimed, "We have the wolf by the ear, and we can neither hold him, nor safely let him go. Justice is in one scale, and self-preservation in the other." [138] The image was striking, but misconceived. Jefferson's perception of danger from emancipation resulted from his inability to comprehend free blacks living in his republican society, his fear that manumission would lead to miscegenation, and his extreme dislike of blacks in general.

In old age, Jefferson could not endorse emancipation, even as he repeated the tired litany of his theoretical support for abolition sometime in the future. Confronted with a member of that younger generation doing just what he always claimed he wanted, Jefferson refused to lift a finger or write a word to encourage emancipation. He shrank from the implications of his own rhetoric. Pathetically he declared in the last year of his life, "On the subject of emancipation I have ceased to think because [it is] not to be a work of my day." [139]

"TREASON AGAINST THE HOPES OF THE WORLD"

The history of Jefferson's relationship to slavery is grim and unpleasant. His words are those of a liberty-loving man of the Enlightenment. His deeds are those of a self-indulgent and negrophobic Virginia planter.

Throughout his life, as he condemned slavery, Jefferson almost always implied that, however bad it was for slaves, the institution was somehow worse for whites. His concerns about the institution had more to do with its effect on whites and white society than on its true victims.

In *Notes on Virginia* Jefferson emphasized the dangers of slavery by describing how it affected whites. It produced "an unhappy influence on the manners of our people." "Our people" here clearly meant the whites. The "whole commerce between master and slave," he wrote, was "a perpetual exercise of the most boisterous passions, the most unremitting despotism on the one part, and degrading submissions on the other." Jefferson's concern was with the "children [who] see this, and learn to imitate it." Jefferson argued that setting a role model for a child was a reason for "restraining the intemperance of passion towards his slave." Significantly, Jefferson did not suggest manumission as an alternative. Jefferson's concerns were solely with the "morals and manners" of the master class. He was concerned that slavery leads to despotism by the masters; but he never expressed regret for the mistreatment of the slave. [140]

Similarly, throughout his life Jefferson expressed his fears of miscegenation and a weakening of white society through contact with blacks. He favored some form of colonization that would put blacks "beyond the reach of mixture." [141] As a key figure in formulating early American foreign policy, Jefferson was obsessed with the Barbary pirates, who were turning white Americans into slaves. Jefferson worried about slave revolts and what to do with rebellious slaves. "I tremble for my country when I reflect that God is just," he wrote. Jefferson's point is clear: slavery undermines liberty and republican government and might some day lead to a bloody slave revolt. [142]

Jefferson despaired at the end of his life. It was not because the slavery question remained unresolved: he had spent his whole life as a slaveowner and would die as one, and his slaves would live on, working to pay off his debts. Jefferson instead despaired because he feared that his countrymen would throw away what he had worked so hard to achieve—and that they would throw it away over slavery. The Missouri Crisis had "like a fire bell in the night, awakened and filled [him] with terror." This was not because he feared a slave rebellion, or because he saw the crisis leading to emancipation. No, Jefferson feared that the crisis would destroy the nation he had worked so hard to build. "I regret," he wrote Congressman Holmes, "that I am now to die in the belief, that the useless sacrifice of themselves by the generation of 1776, to acquire self-government and happiness to their country, is to be thrown away by the unwise and unworthy passions of their sons." [143]

How could white people "throw away" "the blessings" of liberty and republicanism for the sake of black people, who were, after all, unsuited for freedom? Why were the children of the Revolution wasting their passions on such an "unwise and unworthy" problem as the fate of slavery and black people in America? How could his fellow white men "perpetrate this act of suicide on themselves, and of treason against the hopes of the world," [144] over, of all things, the place in society of a people Jefferson believed were inferior?

Truly, Jefferson missed the point. He had proclaimed life, liberty, equality, and happiness were the natural rights of all. In half the nation a growing number of white people were coming to believe that "all" included nonwhites. Since the Revolution, the world had been looking to Jefferson to take the lead on this issue. All his life he had lived in personal and political denial: the problem wasn't there, the problem would go away, the next generation would deal with it, the inferiority of blacks made the problem insoluble. By 1820 some Americans, who had read Jefferson only too well, were beginning to confront the contradiction of slavery in the land of the free.

Yes, there had been "treason against the hopes of the world." The treason was by that generation which failed to place the nation on the road to liberty for all. No one bore a greater responsibility for that failure than the author of the Declaration of Independence—the Master of Monticello.

NOTES

I thank my research assistants Ronald Fischer, Andrea Hecht, Philip Presby, Renee Redman, and Tiffany Snidow for their help on this article. For their comments and critiques of this paper I thank John Hope Franklin, Charles Miller, Peter Onuf, Lucia Stanton and my Virginia Tech colleagues Woody Farrar, Larry Shumsky, Dan Thorpe, and Peter Wallenstein.

1. Edmund Morgan, *American Slavery—American Freedom: The Ordeal of Colonial Virginia* (New York, 1975), p. 376.

2. Leonard W. Levy, *Jefferson and Civil Liberties: The Darker Side* (Cambridge, Mass., 1963), p. 1.

3. TJ to Edward Coles, Aug. 25, 1814, reprinted in Merrill Peterson, ed., *The Portable Jefferson* (New York, 1975), p. 544.

4. "Revisal of the Laws," in *Boyd,* II, pp. 470–78, 503–4; Davis, *The Problem of Slavery in the Age of Revolution* (Ithaca, N.Y., 1975), pp. 174–75. He would have expelled white women bearing mixed-race children.

5. Certainly "after his return to America" in late 1789 "the most remarkable thing about Jefferson's stand on slavery is his immense silence." Davis, *Slavery in the Age of Revolution,* p. 179. Two other aspects of his discussions on slavery are striking. First, he sometimes refers to "God" in his discussion of slavery—especially a Calvinist, vengeful God, which was contrary to his personal religious beliefs. Second, after his retirement from the presidency, he claimed to be ignorant of public affairs when writing about slavery. Neither claim rings true. "I had little opportunity of knowing the progress of public sentiment here on this subject." TJ to Edward Coles, Aug. 25, 1814, Peterson, ed., *Portable Jefferson,* p. 545. "I had for a long time ceased to read newspapers, or pay any attention to public affairs." TJ to John Holmes, April 22, 1820, ibid., p. 567.

6. "Both in power, when the responsibilities of office might have affected his judgement, and in retirement, when he presumably had a free range of options, Jefferson was a loyal member of the planter class to which he belonged." Duncan MacLeod, *Slavery, Race, and the American Revolution* (Cambridge, U.K., 1974), p. 128.

7. *Malone,* II, p. xxiii.

8. TJ to Marquis de Chastellux, June 7, 1785, *Boyd,* VIII, pp. 174, 184; TJ to James Monroe, June 17, 1785, ibid., VIII, p. 229; and TJ to Charles Thomson, June 21, 1785, ibid., VIII, p. 245.

9. Davis, *Slavery in the Age of Revolution,* p. 177.

10. William W. Freehling, *The Road to Disunion: Secessionists at Bay* (New York, 1990), p. 142.

11. Examples of this communication in his correspondence include: James Madison to TJ, Oct. 17, 1784, *Boyd,* VII, p. 446 (the "hobbyhorse" of the Marquis de Lafayette is "the *manumission* of the *slaves*" which *"does him real honor,* as it is *proof of his humanity"*); G. K. van Hogendorp to TJ, May 22, 1784, ibid., VII, p. 284 ("I should wish to know whether Your

Negroes marry, or what proportion do."); John Adams to TJ, May 22, 1785, ibid., VIII, p. 160 ("The passages upon Slavery [in *Notes on the State of Virginia*], are worth Diamonds. They will have more effect than Volumes written by mere Philosophers."). See also letters in ibid., VIII, pp. 174, 184, 229, 245, and 667.

12. Davis, *Slavery in the Age of Revolution,* p. 178.

13. TJ to John W. Eppes, June 30, 1820, in Edwin Morris Betts, *Thomas Jefferson's Farm Book* (Charlottesville, 1953), p. 45.

14. Morgan, *American Slavery—American Freedom,* p. 380.

15. John Hope Franklin, *Racial Equality in America* (Chicago, 1976), p. 19.

16. William M. Wiecek, *The Sources of Antislavery Constitutionalism in America, 1760–1848* (Ithaca, N.Y., 1977), p. 51.

17. J. R. Pole, *The Pursuit of Equality in American History* (Berkeley and Los Angeles, 1978,) pp. 26–27; see also Donald L. Robinson, *Slavery in the Structure of American Politics, 1765–1820* (New York, 1971).

18. *Commonwealth* v. *Jennison* (unreported, Mass., 1783), reprinted in Paul Finkelman, *The Law of Freedom and Bondage: A Casebook* (New York, 1986), pp. 36–37.

19. See generally, Arthur Zilversmit, *The First Emancipation: The Abolition of Slavery in the North* (Chicago, 1967) and Paul Finkelman, *An Imperfect Union: Slavery, Federalism, and Comity* (Chapel Hill, N.C., 1981); Paul Finkelman, "Prelude to the Fourteenth Amendment: Black Legal Rights in the Antebellum North," *Rutgers Law Journal,* 17 (1986), pp. 415–82. By the end of the revolution only Rhode Island and Connecticut, among the northern states, prohibited free blacks from voting.

20. William Peden, ed., *Notes on the State of Virginia* (Chapel Hill, N.C., 1955), pp. 138–43.

21. Ibid., pp. 142–43.

22. Ralph Ketcham, *From Colony to Country: The Revolution in American Thought, 1750–1820* (New York, 1974), p. 238.

23. Free blacks could vote and own property in both Pennsylvania and North Carolina from the Revolution until after Jefferson's death. Theoretically they could have held office in both states, although none did.

24. *Notes,* p. 138; TJ to John Holmes, April 22, 1820; TJ to St. George Tucker, August 28, 1797, *Ford,* X, p. 157; VII, p. 168.

25. *Notes,* pp. 138, 139.

26. John Chester Miller, *The Wolf by The Ears: Thomas Jefferson and Slavery* (New York, 1977), pp. 74–78.

27. William Stanton, *The Leopard's Spots* (Chicago, 1960). Larry E. Tise, *Proslavery: A History of the Defense of Slavery in America, 1701–1840* (Athens, Ga., 1987), p. 231, writes that Jefferson's *Notes* "cast doubt on the equality of men and thereby on the common origin of the human species. Such notions pandered easily to growing beliefs that Negroes were of an inferior race."

28. John Hope Franklin, "Ethnicity in American Life," in John Hope Franklin, *Race and History: Selected Essays, 1938–1988* (Baton Rouge, La., 1989), p. 326.

29. Merrill Peterson, *Thomas Jefferson and the New Nation* (New York, 1970) , pp. 9, 27, quoted on p. 28; Noble E. Cunningham, Jr., *In Pursuit of Reason: The Life of Thomas Jefferson* (Baton Rouge, 1987), p. 9; Cohen, "Thomas Jefferson and the Problem of Slavery," *Journal of American History,* 56 (1969), p. 506.

30. See Betts, *Farm Book,* pp. 13–40 for numerous examples of Jefferson buying and selling slaves and hunting down runaways.

31. "Advertisement for a Runaway Slave," [Sept. 7, 1769] in *Boyd,* I, p. 33; TJ to

Thomas Mann Randolph, Apr. 7, 1791, *Boyd,* XX, p. 160 (advice on buying slaves); TJ to Thomas Mann Randolph, Sr., Feb. 4, 1790, *Boyd,* XVI, p. 154 ("I propose to give to my daughter . . . 25. negroes little and big."); "Marriage Settlement for Martha Jefferson," Feb. 21, 1790, *Boyd,* XVI, p. 189 ("Giving as a wedding present six slave families totaling 27 slaves"); "Jefferson's Deed of Gift of Certain Slaves," Nov. 6, 1790, *Boyd,* XVIII, p. 12; William Cohen, "Thomas Jefferson and the Problem of Slavery," p. 506. For examples of this see TJ to Francis Eppes, Oct. 31, 1790, *Boyd,* XVII, p. 657 ("I shall sell 1000£ worth of negroes this time twelvemonth."); TJ to Robert Lewis, Oct. 5, 1791, *Boyd,* XXII, p. 186 ("My attornies found it necessary in 1785 to sell negroes to answer these demands"); TJ to John Bolling, Oct. 7, 1791, in *Boyd,* XXII, pp. 198–99 ("I find myself obliged this winter to make a very considerable sale of negroes"). Mary Beth Norton, Herbert Gutman, and Ira Berlin, "The Afro-American Family in the Age of Revolution," in Ira Berlin and Ronald Hoffman, eds., *Slavery and Freedom in the Age of the American Revolution* (Charlottesville, Va., 1983), p. 185; Ronald Takaki, *Iron Cages: Race and Culture in Nineteenth-Century America* (New York, 1979), p. 44; TJ to Thomas Mann Randolph, June 8, 1803, in Betts, *Farm Book,* p. 19 (in order to "make an example of him in terrorem to others, in order to maintain the police so rigorously necessary among the nail boys," he directs that the slave Cary be sold to "negro purchasers from Georgia" or to "any other quarter so distant as never more to be heard of among us, it would to the others be as if he were put out of the way by death"); Daniel Bradley to TJ, Oct. 6, 1805, and TJ to Bradley, Jan. 19, 1806, Betts, *Farm Book,* pp. 21, 22 (correspondence about one of Jefferson's runaway slaves Bradley had captured); TJ to Joseph Daugherty, July 31, 1806, and Daugherty to TJ, Aug. 3, 1806, Betts, *Farm Book,* pp. 22–23 (correspondence about recapturing a fugitive blacksmith).

32. Robert McColley, *Slavery in Jeffersonian Virginia,* 2d ed. (Urbana, Ill., 1972), p. 131.

33. Gary B. Nash, *Race and Revolution* (Madison, Wis., 1990), pp. 12, 16; MacLeod, *Slavery, Race and the American Revolution,* p. 15.

34. Pole, *Pursuit of Equality in American History,* p. 119.

35. Nash, *Race and Revolution,* p. 12.

36. Robinson, *Slavery in the Structure of American Politics,* pp. 118–22.

37. St. George Tucker estimated there were 2,000 free blacks in Virginia in 1782, when the state legalized private manumission. Virginia's 200 percent increase in free blacks from 1790 until 1810 far outstripped the growth rate of slaves or whites. Similar growth rates occurred in other states. In Maryland free blacks grew to one quarter of the entire black population in this period. By 1810, free blacks outnumbered slaves in Delaware. Manumissions continued in Virginia in large numbers until at least 1805. This percentage growth in free blacks nationally occurred despite the fact that South Carolina imported more than 80,000 new African slaves between 1803 and 1808. Ira Berlin, *Slaves Without Masters: The Free Negro in the Antebellum South* (New York, 1974), pp. 46–50.

38. Gerald W. Mullin, *Flight and Rebellion: Slave Resistance in Eighteenth Century Virginia* (New York, 1972), p. 70. Berlin, *Slaves Without Masters,* 59; Norton et al., "The Afro-American Family," in Berlin and Hoffman, eds., *Slavery and Freedom in the Age of the American Revolution,* p. 176.

39. *Pleasants* v. *Pleasants,* 2 Call 319 (1799); Finkelman, *Law of Freedom and Bondage,* pp. 116–123; James Currie to TJ, Aug. 5, 1785, *Boyd,* VIII, pp. 342–43; Miller, *Wolf by the Ears,* p. 107. Russell Kirk, *John Randolph of Roanoke: A Study in American Politics* (Indianapolis, 1964), p. 189; Berlin, *Slaves Without Masters,* p. 59. Under his will Washington's slaves gained their freedom at the death of his wife. Jefferson showed interest in this example; see TJ to Dr. Edward Bancroft, Jan. 26, 1789. See also "An act concerning the

emancipation of certain slaves of Joseph Mayo, late of Henrico County," act of Dec. 13, 1787, 12 *Hening's Statutes at Large,* p. 611.

40. The persistence of this image is remarkable. Writing in 1968 Winthrop Jordan noted that "Many school books still say that Jefferson freed his slaves." Winthrop Jordan, *White Over Black: American Attitudes Toward the Negro, 1550–1812* (Chapel Hill, N.C., 1968), p. 431n. I do not know how many books still say this.

41. TJ to Edward Coles, Aug. 25, 1814, reprinted in Peterson, *Portable Jefferson,* 544.

42. Autobiography (1821), reprinted in Adrienne Koch and William Peden, *The Life and Selected Writings of Thomas Jefferson* (New York, 1944), p. 4.

43. *Acts of Virginia,* 1705, c. 49, sec. 18. "If any woman servant shall have a bastard child, by a negro or mulatto or if a free Christian white woman shall have such bastard child by a negro or mulatto; in both the said cases the churchwardens shall bind the said child to be a servant until it shall be of thirty-one years of age"; *Acts of Virginia,* 1723 c. 4, sec. 22.

44. *Howell* v. *Netherland,* Jefferson (Va.) 90 (1770); "Argument in the Case of Howell *vs.* Netherland" [April, 1770], in *Ford* I, pp. 373–81. *Malone,* I, p. 121.

45. *Malone,* I, p. 141n; Cunningham, *In Pursuit of Reason,* p. 13.

46. "Argument in the Case of Howell v. Netherland," *Ford,* I, pp. 378, 380. Throughout his life Jefferson's views of race were complex; but it is worth noting that the only slaves he liberated at his death were those of mixed ancestry.

47. "Argument in the Case of Howell *vs.* Netherland," *Ford,* I, p. 380.

48. *Boyd,* I, p. 33.

49. "Final Version, Gettysburg Address," in Roy P. Basler, ed., *The Collected Works of Abraham Lincoln,* 9 vols. (New Brunswick, N.J., 1953–55), VII, p. 23.

50. Autobiography, in Koch and Peden, *Life and Writings,* pp. 25–26. Jefferson similarly attacked the King in *A Summary View of the Rights of British America* (1774). He wrote, "The abolition of domestic slavery is the great object of desire in those colonies where it was unhappily introduced in their infant state. But previous to the infranchisement of the slave we have, it is necessary to exclude all further importations from Africa. Yet our repeated attempts to effect this . . . by imposing duties which might amount to a prohibition, have been hitherto defeated by his majesty's negative." *Boyd,* I, p. 130.

51. Autobiography, in Koch and Peden, *Life and Writings,* pp. 25–26.

52. Adams quoted in Robinson, *Slavery in the Structure of American Politics,* p. 82.

53. Peterson, *Jefferson and the New Nation,* p. 92.

54. Peterson, *Jefferson and the New Nation,* 91; Peter Wood, *Black Majority: Negroes in Colonial South Carolina from 1670 Through the Stono Rebellion* (New York, 1974); Mullin, *Flight and Rebellion.*

55. One of the few scholars to discuss this is Benjamin Quarles, *The Negro in the American Revolution* (Chapel Hill, N.C., 1961), pp. 42–43.

56. Quoted in Robinson, *Slavery in the Structure of American Politics,* p. 80.

57. During the Revolution a number of states, including New York, Pennsylvania, and Maryland, allowed masters to gain some financial compensation by manumitting and enlisting their slaves in the army. Virginia did not authorize this, but it happened so frequently that as the war wound down the Commonwealth declared that slaves who served "a full term" in any "continental or state [military] establishment" or had been legally discharged from service "shall be held and deemed free." This law "required" Virginia's attorney general to sue "in behalf" of any black soldiers who were subsequently reenslaved. "An Act Directing the Emancipation of Certain Slaves who Have Served as Soldiers in this State," *Laws of Virginia,* 1782–83, Chap. CXC.

58. Jefferson to William Gordon, July 16, 1788, in *Boyd*, XIII, pp. 363–64.

59. Peterson, *Jefferson and the New Nation*, p. 236, places the number of slaves taken at twenty-seven. In 1786 Jefferson told his Scottish creditor Alexander McCaul that "Ld. Cornwallis's army took off 30 of my slaves burnt one year's crop of tobacco in my houses" and destroyed other property "to the amount of three or four thousand pounds." TJ to Alexander McCaul, April 19, 1786, *Boyd*, IX, p. 389.

60. Even Jefferson admitted that some of the slaves that the British carried off eventually became free in Canada. Jefferson to William Gordon, July 16, 1788, in *Boyd*, XIII, pp. 363–64. On the escape of Virginia slaves to British lines during the war, see Sylvia R. Frey, *Water From the Rock: Black Resistance in a Revolutionary Age* (Princeton, N.J., 1991), pp. 141–242.

61. *Malone*, I, pp. 247–63, quoted on p. 247.

62. *Malone*, I, pp. 247–63, quoted on pp. 247, 251, 263.

63. *Malone*, I, p. 247.

64. Miller, *Wolf by the Ears*, p. 20; Davis, *Slavery in the Age of Revolution*, p. 174. The legislature eventually rejected some of the more vicious aspects of Jefferson's proposed criminal code for slaves.

65. "A Bill concerning Slaves," *Boyd*, II, pp. 470–73. "An act declaring who shall be deemed citizens of this commonwealth," 10 *Hening's Statutes at Large* 129 (May 1779). After Jefferson left the governorship, the legislature passed a liberal manumission law but rejected his harsh proposal for expelling free blacks. "An act to authorize the manumission of slaves," 11 *Hening* 39 (May 1782). The legislature also rejected the proposal to expel the white mothers of mixed-race children.

66. "Argument in the Case of Howell *vs.* Netherland," *Ford*, I, pp. 378, 380.

67. Jack P. Greene, *All Men are Created Equal: Some Reflections on the Character of the American Revolution* (Oxford, 1976), p. 16.

68. "A Bill Declaring Who Shall be Deemed Citizens of This Commonwealth," *Boyd*, II, p. 476. This stands in marked contrast with the changes in the states to the north and the south of Virginia that gave free blacks political rights. Finkelman, "Prelude to the Fourteenth Amendment"; on free blacks in North Carolina, see John Hope Franklin, *The Free Negro in North Carolina* (Chapel Hill, 1943).

69. A. Leon Higginbotham, *In the Matter of Color. Race and the American Legal Process: The Colonial Period* (New York, 1978), p. 371. At least one Virginia patriot understood this. When some of his slaves joined the British Army, Robert Pleasants wrote General William Phillips urging him to guarantee their freedom if they served in his army. Robert Pleasants to General William Phillips, May 14, 1781, reprinted in Roger Burns, ed., *Am I Not a Man and a Brother: The Antislavery Crusade of Revolutionary America, 1688–1788* (New York, 1977), p. 465.

70. Dumas Malone argues that Jefferson's "personal activities against the institution of slavery were greatest in the period of the American Revolution, when he vainly proposed a plan of gradual emancipation for his own commonwealth," and that "he strongly favored emancipation." In fact, while in the legislature he never did propose this plan; when others wanted to do so, he stopped them. *Malone*, III, p. 207; I, 246. Merrill Peterson explains "he would let [the slavery issue] lie rather than risk the loss of all power of accomplishment by untimely advocacy of so arduous a cause." Peterson, *Jefferson and the New Nation*, p. 152. Both Peterson and Malone assume that Jefferson wanted to do something about slavery, but there is no evidence for such a conclusion.

71. TJ quoted in Peterson, *Jefferson and the New Nation*, p. 153.

72. *Notes*, pp. 137–38.

73. Peden's introduction to *Notes,* pp. xiv–xvi.

74. Jefferson repeated this in his authorized edition published by John Stockdale in London in 1787. Peden's introduction to *Notes,* p. xi.

75. "An Act to Authorize the Manumission of Slaves," *Laws of Virginia,* 1782, Chap. LXI.

76. Autobiography, in Koch and Peden, *Life and Writings,* p. 51.

77. *Boyd,* I, p. 130.

78. *Hudgins* v. *Wrights,* 11 Va. (1 Hen. & M.) 133 (1806). Wythe also provided for the manumission of his slaves at his death.

79. McColley, *Slavery in Jeffersonian Virginia,* p. 132.

80. "Jefferson's Draft for a Constitution for Virginia," [May-June, 1783], *Boyd,* VI, p. 298.

81. Curiously, few Jefferson scholars mention the antislavery provision of the draft constitution. Neither Malone, Peterson, Boyd, nor Cunningham discuss the clause in their biographies. *Malone,* I, p. 400; Peterson, *Jefferson and the New Nation,* pp. 132, 267, 381; "Editorial Note," *Boyd,* VI, pp. 278–84; Cunningham, Jr., *In Pursuit of Reason,* pp. 84–85. Adrienne Koch, *Jefferson and Madison: The Great Collaboration* (New York, 1950), p. 13, noted the slavery provision should be considered "by all who remember him as a 'slave holding Virginia planter,'" but she refuses further "speculation" on the clause.

82. TJ to James Madison, June 17, 1783, *Boyd,* VI, p. 277.

83. "An Act for Preventing the farther importation of slaves," *Laws of Virginia,* 1778, pp. 471–72.

84. "An Act to authorize the manumission of slaves," 11 *Hening* 39 (May 1782).

85. Jefferson's draft constitution can be compared with the Pennsylvania Gradual Emancipation Act of 1780. The Pennsylvania law went into effect the day it passed. "An Act for the gradual abolition of slavery," Act of March 1, 1780, 1 *Laws of the Commonwealth of Pennsylvania* 492–96, reprinted in Finkelman, *Law of Freedom and Bondage,* pp. 42–45. The gradual emancipation laws of Connecticut (1784) and Rhode Island (1784), and later New York (1799) and New Jersey (1804), also went into effect immediately. Massachusetts, New Hampshire, and the fourteenth state, Vermont, abolished slavery outright rather than gradually.

86. "Revised Report of the Committee," March 22, 1784, *Boyd,* VI, p. 608.

87. Paul Finkelman, "Slavery and the Northwest Ordinance: A Study in Ambiguity," *Journal of the Early Republic,* 6 (1986), pp. 343–370; Paul Finkelman, "Evading the Ordinance: The Persistence of Bondage in Indiana and Illinois," *Journal of the Early Republic,* 9 (1989), pp. 21–52.

88. Wiecek, *Sources of Antislavery Constitutionalism,* p. 60.

89. TJ to John Holmes, April 22, 1820, *Ford,* X, p. 157; Drew McCoy, *The Last of the Fathers* (New York, 1989), pp. 268–74.

90. Jefferson also mentioned as "remarkable" a proposal "To make slaves distributable among the next of kin, as other movables." That Jefferson thought this was a "remarkable" suggests that his commitment to property was far greater than his opposition to slavery. Maintaining restrictions on the transfer of slave property would have made it less valuable, thereby encouraging manumission. Removing those restrictions enhanced the value of the property. *Notes,* p. 137.

91. *Notes,* pp. 137–38.

92. *Notes,* pp. 138–140.

93. *Notes,* pp. 138–42.

94. In 1740, following the Stono Rebellion, South Carolina restricted the trade, not out

of any antislavery conviction, but because of the fear that freshly imported Africans were dangerous. Wood, *Black Majority,* p. 325.

95. TJ to Christopher Ellery, May 19, 1803, *Ford,* VIII, p. 231.

96. Finkelman, "Slavery and the Constitutional Convention," pp. 209–223.

97. Thomas Jefferson, "Sixth Annual Message," December 2, 1806, in James D. Richardson, ed., *Messages and Papers of the Presidents,* (Washington, D.C., 1897) II, p. 306.

98. One might even construct a counterfactual argument that slavery would have ended faster if the nation had been flooded with slaves from Africa, thus driving down the value of slaves and undermining slavery in the border states, while at the same time leading to more slave revolts in the deep South. Jefferson's opposition to the slave trade dovetailed with his fear and hatred of free blacks.

99. Some slavery existed in Missouri in 1803 and would have probably lingered there, as it did in Illinois. See Finkelman, "Evading the Ordinance"; Freehling, *Road to Disunion,* p. 142.

100. John Hope Franklin, "The Moral Legacy of the Founding Fathers," in Franklin, *Race and History,* p. 161.

101. As President, Jefferson also signed a law which "excluded blacks from carrying the United States mail," even if these blacks were citizens and voters in the states where they lived. Franklin, *Racial Equality in America,* p. 25.

102. TJ to John Holmes, April 22, 1820; TJ to Thomas Humphreys, Feb. 8, 1817, *Ford,* X, pp. 157, 77.

103. Virginia manumission law changed rather dramatically during Jefferson's life. During the Revolution, Jefferson could have freed his male slaves by enlisting them in the army. From 1782 to 1805, Virginia law allowed masters to manumit their slaves within the state without requiring they leave the state. From 1805 until 1815, emancipated slaves needed permission of the legislature to remain in the state. After 1815, county courts could grant exemptions for "extraordinary merit." Courts appear to have interpreted this phrase quite loosely. The relevant statutes are found in Finkelman, *Law of Freedom and Bondage,* pp. 109–114.

104. *Notes,* Queries XIV, XVIII, 138, 163. TJ to John Holmes, April 22, 1820; TJ to Jared Sparks, Feb. 4, 1824; TJ to William Short, Jan. 18, 1826; TJ to Albert Gallatin, Dec. 26, 1820; *Ford,* X, pp. 157, 291, 362, 178. Also see TJ to James Monroe, Nov. 24, 1801, and June 2, 1802, *Ford,* VIII, pp. 105, 153. See also David Brion Davis, "American Slavery and the American Revolution," in Berlin and Hoffman, eds., *Slavery and Freedom in the Age of the American Revolution,* p. 279.

105. TJ to Paul Bentalou, Aug. 25, 1786, *Boyd,* X, p. 296.

106. *Malone,* III, p. 208.

107. Peterson, *Jefferson and the New Nation,* p. 1007.

108. No one have ever made an exact count of all the individual slaves Jefferson owned. At his death he had about two hundred. During the Revolution he lost over thirty, and after the Revolution he sold at least fifty. This means he held, over his lifetime at least 330 different people in bondage. Given births and deaths over the period from 1764, when he came into possession of his slaves, until 1826, it is likely that the total number exceeds four hundred.

109. *Malone,* VI, p. 513; Miller, *Wolf by the Ears,* p. 162. Sally Hemings and her siblings were the children of Jefferson's father-in-law, John Wayles, and thus the half-sisters and half-brothers of Jefferson's late wife. Peterson, *Jefferson and the New Nation,* p. 707; Freehling, *Road to Disunion,* p. 128. Who fathered Sally's children remains a mystery. James Callender, Fawn Brodie, Page Smith, and the oral traditions of the Hemings family have

argued that Sally's children were fathered by Jefferson. Other likely candidates are Jefferson's nephews Peter and Samuel Carr. If they fathered Sally's children, then the children were still doubly related to Jefferson—through marriage and blood.

There are two significant arguments against Jefferson's involvement with Sally. First is his lifelong hatred of miscegenation. Second is his own distaste for black people and miscegenation. In *Notes on the State of Virginia* he argued that blacks were less attractive than whites—"Are not the fine mixtures of red and white . . . preferable to that eternal monotony, which reigns in the countenances, that immovable veil of black which covers the emotions of the other race." Similarly, he disliked getting too close to them: "They secrete less by the kidneys, and more by the glands of the skin, which gives them a very strong and disagreeable odor." While thinking that black women were "more ardent" he doubted blacks capable of a serious relationship: "love seems with them to be more an eager desire, than a tender delicate mixture of sentiment and sensation" (*Notes*, pp. 138–39). Neither of these arguments is conclusive. Jefferson's words on slavery often conflicted with his deeds. Thus his hatred of race-mixing might not have stopped him from doing it, just as his hatred of slavery never prevented him from exercising all the privileges and duties of a master. Similarly, there is ample evidence that throughout the history of the South, white men who professed to be disgusted with blacks nevertheless maintained sexual relationships with black women. Furthermore, Sally Hemings was of mostly white ancestry, and may have appeared more white than black to Jefferson.

110. *Malone*, III, p. 208.

111. James A. Bear, Jr., "The Hemings Family of Monticello," *Virginia Cavalcade*, 29 (1979), pp. 80–81.

112. Under *Somerset* v. *Stewart*, 1 Lofft 1, 98 Eng. Rep. 499 (K.B. 1772), slaves became free the moment they entered a free jurisdiction. *Somerset* was part of American common law in all of the new states at the time of the Revolution. When cases arose on this issue in the 1830s, Chief Justice Lemuel Shaw expressed surprise that there was any doubt on the subject, because the law of Massachusetts had always been that slaves became free the moment they entered the state. Leonard W. Levy, *The Law of the Commonwealth and Chief Justice Shaw* (Cambridge, Mass., 1957); Finkelman, *An Imperfect Union*, pp. 20–25, 100–145. *Commonwealth* v. *Aves*, 18 Pick. (35 Mass.) 193 (1836). *Pleasants* v. *Pleasants*, 2 Call 319 (1799). For a discussion of that case, see Finkelman, *Law of Freedom and Bondage*, pp. 116–123; Robert M. Cover, *Justice Accused* (New Haven, 1975), pp. 67–75.

113. Finkelman, *Imperfect Union*, pp. 37–38.

114. *Malone*, III, p. 209.

115. Peterson, *Jefferson and the New Nation*, p. 535.

116. Agreement dated September 15, 1793, in Betts, *Farm Book*, pp. 15–16.

117. For examples of the activities of the Pennsylvania Abolition Society, see Finkelman, *Imperfect Union*, pp. 46–69, and Paul Finkelman, "The Kidnapping of John Davis and The Adoption of the Fugitive Slave Law of 1793," *Journal of Southern History*, 56 (1990), pp. 397–422. In the 1790s the Pennsylvania court freed a number of slaves based on residence in Pennsylvania, including one owned by Senator Pierce Butler, a former delegate to the Constitutional Convention.

118. Betts, *Farm Book*, pp. 15–16.

119. Bear, *Jefferson and Monticello*, Hemings family genealogical tables, after page 24. Jefferson did not chase after Beverly, and that might be seen as a *de facto* emancipation. But under Virginia law Jefferson's heirs, or perhaps his creditors, might have seized Beverly after his death. A fugitive slave *always* lived in fear of being seized; an emancipated slave, while concerned about kidnapping, was far more secure. The first fugitive slave case to

reach the U.S. Supreme Court, *Prigg* v. *Pennsylvania*, 16 Peters 539 (1842), involved a slave whose owner allowed her to run away, but who was later seized by an heir. See Paul Finkelman, "*Prigg* v. *Pennsylvania* and Northern State Courts: Anti-Slavery Use of a Pro-Slavery Decision," *Civil War History*, 25 (1979), pp. 5–35.

120. Jefferson's will, Ford, X, pp. 395–96. The Hemings family tree is found in Bear, *Jefferson at Monticello*, pp. 25–26. By that time Virginia no longer allowed manumitted slaves to remain in the state without the permission of the legislature.

121. Jefferson's will, Ford, X, pp. 395–96.

122. This could easily have been accomplished by making his daughter's legacy contingent on freeing this one slave. Benjamin Franklin, for example, made a legacy to his grandson Richard Bache contingent on Bache's manumitting "his Negro man Bob." Carl Van Doren, *Benjamin Franklin* (New York, 1941), p. 761.

123. According to Peterson, "neither the state of his property nor the state of the laws, he felt, permitted him to do more." Peterson, *Jefferson and the New Nation*, p. 1007. The law was but a minor impediment. Jefferson asked his heirs to petition the legislature to allow five of his manumitted slaves to remain in the state; he could have asked his heirs to petition the legislature to allow all of them to remain. It is inconceivable the Commonwealth would have denied this final request of one of its greatest citizens.

124. *Elder* v. *Elder's Ex'or*, 4 Leigh 252 (1833). Under Virginia law a creditor had a claim against any emancipated slave if the estate lacked sufficient assets to settle the debts of the deceased. "An Act reducing to one, the several acts concerning slaves, free negroes and mulattoes," Act of March 2, 1819, Sec. 54, 1 *Revised Code of Virginia* 421, at p. 434 (Richmond, 1819).

125. TJ to James Madison, Sept. 6, 1789, *Boyd*, XV, p. 395.

126. TJ to Major John Cartwright, June 5, 1824, in Peterson, *Portable Jefferson*, p. 580.

127. TJ to Doctor Thomas Humphreys, February 8, 1817, in Ford, I, p. 77.

128. Freehling, *Road to Disunion*, pp. 127, 128.

129. *Notes on the State of Virginia*, Query XVIII.

130. *Malone*, II, p. 95.

131. Richard Price to TJ, July 2, 1785, *Boyd*, VIII, pp. 258–59.

132. Jefferson to Price, Aug. 7, 1785, *Boyd*, VIII, pp. 356–57. In 1786 Jefferson presented a similarly overly optimistic analysis of the possibility of manumission to the French scholar Démeunier. "The disposition to emancipate them is strongest in Virginia. . . . I flatter myself it will take place there at some period of time not very distant." Here, as in his letter to Price and much subsequent correspondence, Jefferson asserted that the next generation would do the job, because support for emancipation "is continually recruiting by the addition of nearly the whole of the young men as fast as they come into public life." Answers to Démeunier's First Queries, Jan. 24, 1786, *Boyd*, X, p. 18.

133. Answers to Démeunier's First Queries, Jan. 24, 1786, *Boyd*, X, p. 18.

134. TJ to St. George Tucker, Aug. 28, 1797, Ford, VII, p. 168.

135. TJ to J. P. Reibelt, Dec. 21, 1805, Ford, VIII, p. 402.

136. TJ to Edward Coles, Aug. 25, 1814, reprinted in Peterson, *Portable Jefferson*, p. 544. This correspondence in brilliantly analyzed in Davis, *Slavery in the Age of Revolution*, pp. 180–83. Curiously, Jefferson's letter to Coles was not fully reprinted in the most popular and easily available edition of Jefferson's letters, *The Life and Writings of Thomas Jefferson*, edited by Adrienne Koch and William Peden in 1944, pp. 641–42. The editors ended the letter with this quotation about the "hour of emancipation." This would leave the reader with the impression that Jefferson favored what Coles was doing and endorsed it. This was not the case. The deleted material—more than half of the original letter—contains an

attack on the Haitian revolution, arguments against miscegenation, and Jefferson's advice to Coles not to emancipate his slaves. This is just one of many examples of historians trying to cover for Jefferson, trying to turn him into something he was not—an abolitionist.

137. TJ to Edward Coles, Aug. 25, 1814, in Peterson, *Portable Jefferson,* p. 546.

138. TJ to John Holmes, April 22, 1820, *Ford,* X, p. 157. Researchers at the Jefferson Papers have discovered that the original letter used the word "ear," not "ears." I am grateful to Lucia Stanton for pointing this out.

139. TJ to William Short, Jan. 18, 1826, *Ford,* I, p. 362. In contrast to Jefferson, Benjamin Franklin, who had once owned slaves, spent the last years of his life fighting slavery as the president of the Pennsylvania Abolition Society. His last public act was to petition Congress to end slavery, and then to write a brilliant satire demolishing the arguments of southern politicians who had denounced Franklin in Congress. Robinson, *Slavery in the Structure of American Politics,* p. 303; Zilversmit, *First Emancipation,* pp. 164–65.

140. *Notes,* pp. 162–63.

141. *Notes,* p. 143.

142. Jefferson even admitted such revolts might be "just," and that "the Almighty has no attribute which can take side with us in such a contest." *Notes,* Query XVIII.

143. TJ to John Holmes, April 22, 1820, *Ford,* X, pp. 157–58.

144. Ibid, p. 158.

PART II

JEFFERSONIAN VISIONS

CHAPTER 7

The Intellectual Reconstruction
of Virginia in the Age of Jefferson

JACK P. GREENE

Thomas Jefferson's relationship to his native Virginia has always been problematic. While historians have acknowledged the deep affection that underlay his frequent references to himself as "a Virginian" and to Virginia as "my own country"[1] and his pride in Virginia's many contributions to the American Revolution and its subsequent "enlightened" achievements, they have also emphasized the profound reservations implicit in his program for the social and political improvement of Virginia during the Revolution and his unflattering portraits of Virginia's old colonial regime during his later years.[2] These reservations seem to be thoroughly confirmed and made explicit by his many criticisms of Virginia society in his *Notes on the State of Virginia*. This chapter seeks to reexamine Jefferson's relationship to Virginia through an analysis of both the broad intellectual reconstruction of Virginia that occurred during his lifetime and his role in that reconstruction.

The primary premise underlying the analysis that follows is that each corporate entity is constructed both behaviorally and intellectually. It is behaviorally constructed by the recurrent actions of those who compose it, and intellectually constructed in the sense that those who undertake the daunting task of trying to render it comprehensible, both to those who belong to it and those who do not, do so by identifying and defining those common features of behavior and belief, of collective and individual experience, that give it personality or character and provide it with intellectual coherence. A secondary underlying premise is that the identities of such entities change in response to shifting temporal circumstances.[3]

From its very beginning, Virginia had been an enigma for those who sought to understand and identify it. From the early seventeenth century through the lifetime of Jefferson, commentator after commentator—resident and non-resident; writers of promotional tracts, descriptions, travel accounts, and histories; correspondents and diarists—pondered how a country rendered so fine by nature had turned out to be in so many ways a profound cultural disappointment. "The most general true Character of *Virginia,*" said Henry Hartwell, James Blair, and Edward Chilton at the close of the seventeenth century, was that it was at once "the best" and "the worst Country in the World." "As to all the Natural Advantages of a Country," these authors wrote, "it is one of the best, but as to the Improved Ones, one of the worst of all the *English* Plantations in *America.*"[4] In rendering this judgment, these writers were merely expanding upon a point made several decades earlier by observers such as John Hammond and Sir William Berkeley.[5] Robert Beverley's 1705 *History of Virginia* revolved around an elaborate exploration of this palpable and evidently intractable puzzle.[6]

Expanding wealth and population permitted the generation that came to maturity during the first quarter of the eighteenth century to develop a society that was in many respects far more improved and civil than Virginians of earlier generations could possibly have predicted on the basis of the colony's record during its first century. Still lacking the social and cultural density of metropolitan Britain, Virginia could nonetheless plausibly be depicted in Hugh Jones's *Present State of Virginia* as an example of that simple, tranquil, and uncorrupted rural society so frequently idealized in Georgian Britain, a place whose sociable inhabitants could scarcely avoid being contented and virtuous and, with care and diligence, might also become prosperous, independent, and polite.[7] Indeed, the worry of some members of this generation was that free Virginians were sacrificing their English ancestors' traditional devotion to liberty to their growing politesse and moderation. Thus, in his *History of the First Discovery and Settlement of Virginia,* published in 1747, William Stith sought to recall his countrymen to a proper dedication to this aspect of their English inheritance by emphasizing their predecessors' contributions to the establishment of liberty in English America during the first generation of the colony's history.[8]

But the behavior of many members of the generation that came to maturity in the 1740s and 1750s seemed—to both Virginians and visitors—to present a formidable challenge to the emerging conception of Virginia as an Anglophone Arcadia. Indeed, that behavior strongly suggested that the indolence, extravagance, dissipation, and degrading dependence that those vices brought in their train might soon become the most pronounced features of the Virginians' identity as a people. During the third quarter of the eighteenth century, at the very moment when people of the generation of Thomas Jefferson were reaching adulthood and Virginia was transforming itself from a colonial to an independent political society, the question of whether Virginians would be virtuous or vicious, a polite or an abandoned people, was still very much in doubt. The late colonial period was a critical time for Virginians as they sought to comprehend what kind of society they had created and what kind of people they had become.

During the American Revolution and the early national period, Virginia's experience operated to amplify and redefine these conceptions of the new state and its free white inhabitants. This process of intellectual reconstruction may be studied through an analysis of the principal texts that reflected and in turn helped to define contemporary understanding of Virginia and Virginians.

Three of these works were of special importance. First published in London in 1787, Thomas Jefferson's *Notes on the State of Virginia* was the most ambitious work describing Virginia since Hugh Jones published his book over sixty years earlier.[9] A four-volume *History of Virginia,* the longest and most comprehensive history of the colony produced up to that time, was mostly written by John Daly Burk, an Irish immigrant and follower of Jefferson who took up the subject under Jefferson's tutelage. Burk published the first three volumes of his work in Richmond in 1804–5. After he was killed in a duel in 1808, Skelton Jones and Louis Girardin, two of Jefferson's other clients, completed the last volume, which was not published until 1816. This work covered the history of Virginia from the beginning of the colony to the end of the War for Independence in 1781.[10] In much briefer form, Edmund Randolph's *History of Virginia* also treated the period from Jamestown through the Revolution. Scion of an old Virginia family and a relative of Jefferson's, Randolph himself had played a prominent role in the Revolution and had served with Jefferson in Washington's Cabinet as the first Attorney General of the United States. Randolph was gathering material for his history as early as the 1780s but probably did not write it until the years just before his death in 1813. The volume remained in manuscript until the 1930s and was not published in full until 1970.[11]

In addition to Jefferson, Burk, and Randolph, a variety of other observers produced analyses of the new state between 1775 and 1815. Except for the dissenter John Leland's "Description of Virginia," published in 1790,[12] the jurist St. George Tucker's *A Letter to the Rev. Jedidiah Morse* and *A Dissertation on Slavery, with a Proposal for the Gradual Abolition of it, in the State of Virginia,* issued respectively in 1795 and 1796,[13] and John Marshall's *Life of George Washington,* the first volume of which was published in 1805 and contained a brief history of Virginia down through the middle of the eighteenth century,[14] these were all written by outsiders from continental Europe, Britain, or other parts of North America.[15]

I

Some of Virginia's many outside observers during the Jeffersonian era praised the character and style of life of at least some members of the prominent gentry class and expressed an appreciation for the political capacities exhibited by many of the state's leaders during the Revolution. But most were sharply critical of both the state and its inhabitants. Collectively they limned an overwhelmingly negative picture. Complaining about the slovenly character of Virginia's rural landscape, agriculture, and housing, these writers decried its lack of urban development, economic enterprise, and investment of either time or money in religion and education, as well as its continuing commitment to chattel slavery. Denouncing the pride, selfishness, indolence, carelessness, extravagance, dissipation, and penchant for violence on the part of its white inhabitants, they argued that Virginia lagged far behind its bustling, more developed, and, many thought, far more enterprising, accomplished, and civilized neighbors to the north.

In the well-developed tradition of self-criticism displayed by Robert Beverley and many other earlier Virginians, analysts of the Revolutionary and early national eras contributed to reinforce this highly unflattering reputation; this observation applies with special force to Jefferson. No inhabitant at any time during the period considered in this chapter provided a more powerful social and cultural critique of the state than did Jefferson in his *Notes on the State of Virginia.*

As he evaluated Virginia by the standards of the cosmopolitan Western tradition with which he often sought to identify, Jefferson, like Beverley in his *History* eighty years earlier, found much to deplore. Implicitly contrasting the "enterprising temper of the Pennsylvanians" with the "indolence" of his countrymen, Jefferson in the *Notes* decried the "indifferent state" of Virginia agriculture, the "infinite wretchedness" produced by its heavy economic reliance on tobacco culture, the dilatoriness of Virginians in undertaking desirable public works such as the improvement of inland navigation, and the state's failure to develop major urban centers. Lamenting the absence of any system of public education, he complained about the ugliness and temporary character of most Virginia private housing and outbuildings, the paucity and indifferent architectural quality of its public buildings, and the scarcity of competent tradesmen; he chided his country-men for continuing to live in a formal condition of "religious slavery" with a state-established church.[16]

Writing the *Notes* while he was still licking his wounds from his inglo-rious governorship of 1779–81, Jefferson was particularly hard on Virgin-ia's republican state constitution. Worrying whether Virginians after the war might disregard "their rights in the sole faculty of making money," he condemned the mutability of a constitution that had been adopted by no greater authority than an act of the legislature without recourse to the people. He cited, among its several "capital defects," its failure to extend the franchise to all those who paid taxes and fought for the state, to provide for an equality of representation among the several political units of the state according to the size of their free populations, and to achieve a genu-ine separation of powers among the several branches of government so as to prevent the concentration of power in the hands of the legislature.[17]

In contrast to Beverley or any other earlier Virginian interpreter, how-ever, Jefferson reserved his most stringent criticism for the institution of chattel slavery. The sudden rise of antislavery sentiment throughout the enlightened world after 1750 powerfully called attention to what Edmund Randolph would later refer to as the great "pollutions and cruelties of slav-ery."[18] Not just Jefferson and Randolph but St. George Tucker, John Daly Burk, and many other contemporary Virginia interpreters agreed with out-side observers that slavery was a "blot in our country," a "great political and moral evil" that was "more portentous and afflicting" than any other imag-inable.[19]

Together, these Virginia writers took pains to point out the many ways by which slavery had "stained" the country. By requiring Africans to undergo the most "degrading submissions," it forced them into an "unnat-ural debasement" that reduced them almost "to the condition of brutes." "Among the blessings which the Almighty hath showered down on these states, there is a large portion of the bitterest draught that ever flowed from the cup of affliction," declared Tucker: "Whilst America hath been the land of promise to Europeans, and their descendants, it hath been the vale of death to millions of the wretched sons of Africa. The genial light of liberty, which hath shone with unrivalled lustre on the former, hath yielded no comfort to the latter."[20]

But the liberty to have slaves, several Virginians conceded to their crit-ics, had by no means been an unmixed blessing for whites. On the one hand, it had enabled the wealthy to cultivate a life style of ease and gentility and helped to nourish among all free whites that "habitual arrogance and assumption of superiority" that had in turn given rise to the "quick and acute sense of the rights of freemen" that Virginians had so amply exhibited during the American Revolution. The association of slavery with passivity, both Randolph and Tucker suggested, contributed to make men exceptionally jealous of their liberty and proud of the conditions—specifically their capacity for independent and self-directed activity and their white skins—that distinguished them from the dependent and passive servile black population all around them. In a slave society such as Virginia, even the poorest of the free whites thus had some basis for a sense of worth.[21]

But that sense of worth had to be tenaciously preserved. For any free white man not to make an active defense against even the slightest challenge to his capacity for action and self-control was to behave like a slave and thus to forfeit both self-esteem and respect of peers. For white Virginians, these writers suggested, fear of passivity thus underlay both their praiseworthy devotion to personal independence and an unattractive and inflammatory pride that expressed itself in what outsiders had long perceived as a hypersensitivity to insult and a too-eager readiness to defend their honor—and thereby demonstrate their capacity for activity—by fighting and dueling.

Nor were such pride and the indolence arising from the identification of work with slavery the only ways in which slavery was "baneful to virtue" among whites. Indeed, declared Jefferson in a famous passage in his *Notes on the State of Virginia,* the whole relationship between masters and slaves was little more than "a perpetual exercise of the most boisterous passions, the most unremitting despotism." By nursing and educating white children in the "daily exercise . . . [of] tyranny," he contended, slavery destroyed not just the industry and civility but the very "morals of the people." Finally, wrote Tucker, slavery introduced into a society of free people a discordant and dangerous element that gave rise to severe apprehensions among whites that "so large a number of oppressed individuals" among us might "one day be roused to an attempt to shake off their chains."[22]

To stress only the critical dimensions of Jefferson's *Notes* is, however, highly misleading. It is important to recognize that Jefferson, no less than Beverley and other earlier Virginia interpreters, intended for his criticisms to provide the foundations for reform. As Jefferson wrote his friend Chastellux in September 1785, well before he had arranged for publication of the *Notes,* he regarded it as "good" for a people to have "the vices of their character . . . pointed out to them [so] that they may amend them; for a malady of either body or mind once known is half cured," and his subsequent efforts to get his volume into the hands of "all the young men of Virginia" who were then, as students of the remodeled College of William and Mary, in "preparation for public life" demonstrated his deep conviction that Virginians were capable of undertaking and achieving fundamental reform.[23]

Again like Beverley in his 1705 *History,* Jefferson, in the *Notes,* affirmed commitment not only to the cosmopolitan tradition of the Enlightenment but also a profound respect for the provincial traditions of Virginia. In no sense was he one of those people who had "contempt for the simplicity of his own country." Indeed, in its totality, the *Notes* provides not a negative but an affectionate and highly positive reading of Virginia's experience and promise. Modern analysts of the *Notes* have rarely failed to recognize the profound appreciation revealed by Jefferson for the sublimity of Virginia nature, the richness and extent of the state's natural resources, its astonishing capacity to produce a wide range of agricultural and mineral products and to sustain a burgeoning population, and its enormous potential for economic development through navigational and other public improvements.[24]

A close reading of the *Notes* also reveals that it celebrated not just the promise but the achievements of Virginia and Virginians. Jefferson's impatience with the rate and extent of Virginia's development should be set against his quiet emphasis on its extraordinary population growth, the progress it had already made in exploiting its iron and coal deposits, and the virtual absence of poverty among its native free population. His lamentations about the evils of tobacco culture need to be considered together with his appreciation of the diversity of Virginia agriculture and of the openness to agricultural innovation revealed by the rapid strides the state's farmers were already making in the cultivation of wheat and the breeding of Arabian horses. His remarks about the absence of towns have to be juxtaposed against his well-known approbation for Virginia's continuing "attachment to agriculture" and his characterization of the "discreet farmers" who dominated Virginia society—those "worthy" men who, though "not rich," were "easy in" their "circumstances"—as "the most virtuous independent citizens" for republics. His complaints about the absence of public education were to some extent mitigated by his pride in the recent modernization and secularization of the curriculum at his alma mater, the College of William and Mary. His denunciation of the Virginia religious establishment must be put in the context of his insistence upon the "moderation" of the Anglicans and his faith that the "people of this country" never "would suffer an execution for heresy, or three years of imprisonment for not comprehending the mysteries of the trinity." Even Jefferson's condemnation of the inhumanity among whites produced by slavery was counteracted by his suggestion that the prolifigacy of the black population was the result of "mild treatment." Further, Jefferson sought to emphasize the underlying moderation of the Virginia social system by his denial that whites had ever taken lands from the Indians by conquest and his assertion that from early on they had been careful to reserve lands for those Indians who chose to stay within the bounds of white settlement.[25]

Perhaps most important, Jefferson's litany of criticisms against Virginia's new state constitution must be counterpointed against his profound appreciation for the virtues of the traditional political culture of Virginia. Praising that culture for the public-spiritedness of local magistrates, he lauded the commitment to "temperate liberty" on the part of the citizenry—epitomized by the lenient treatment of Tories and general obedience to laws during the Revolution, and low taxes and small bureaucracy. Further, in the *Notes,* Jefferson also emphasized Virginia's long tradition of self-government and its leaders' unswerving dedication to the preservation of their constituents' "most essential rights." That dedication, he noted, had repeatedly been made manifest in a series of actions stretching from their refusal to accede to the authority of the English republican regime in 1651 until representatives of that regime had acknowledged those rights through their inauguration of opposition to the Stamp Act in 1765 and the "frequent assertions of the public rights" that filled Virginia legislative journals thereafter. Although the adoption of the legal reforms he and two colleagues, George Wythe and Edmund Pendleton, had undertaken after independence to purge the legal code of all laws that were "inconsistent with republicanism" had been delayed by the war, Jefferson also expressed little doubt that they would be implemented with the "restoration of peace."[26]

II

In the *Notes,* Jefferson not only displayed a profound veneration for Virginia but also provided essential foundations for and made a significant contribution to its intellectual reconstruction during the following quarter century. Between 1780 and 1815, Virginia analysts, including especially Tucker, Burk, and Randolph, built on the optimistic portrait Jefferson presented to create a new and highly positive sense of corporate identity for Virginia and Virginians. Stressing the "conspicuous patriotism" and "great-mindedness" Virginians had so amply displayed during the American Revolution, these analysts seized upon Virginia's experience during the Revolution to help Virginians recast their conception of their past and enhance their sense of collective self-worth.[27]

The Virginians' interpretation of their own behavior during the Revolutionary years strongly reinforced their corporate self-esteem. As the "most ancient American possession" of Britain and as the "most extensive, richest and most commanding colony in America," Virginia, they proudly declaimed in elaborating a point made by Jefferson in the *Notes,* had naturally assumed the leadership of the opposition to Britain—and, to its credit, without "any parade or assumption of superiority." From the very "beginning of the disturbances," from the Stamp Act crises in 1765 on, Virginia, said Randolph, had "produced public agents suitable to every crisis and service." Such heroic figures as Patrick Henry, Richard Bland, Peyton Randolph, Thomas Jefferson, George Washington, Richard Henry Lee, Edmund Pendleton, George Wythe, and George Mason had "stepped forth willingly" in behalf of the American cause. Virginians had been "the first to offer assistance to the Bostonians" in 1774 following the Coercive Acts, "and the first also to set on foot a considerable body of troops"; when in the 1780s the new union had seemed on the verge of collapse, they again took "a leading, active, and influential part in bringing about the . . . grand revolution in our Federal Government."[28]

Such "generous attention . . . to the general interest of all the colonies, so distant from the selfish policy but too apt to influence rival states, produced every where" during the Revolution, John Daly Burk happily reported, "a sentiment of tender respect and just admiration." To Virginia "was every where allowed the honourable praise of having originated every capital measure since the commencement of the disputes, and having supported them all with a constancy and wisdom nowise inferior to the ardour with which they had been adopted." No state, suggested Tucker, had contributed a higher "quota of men of eminence on the political theatre of the United States."[29]

Nor did outsiders dispute these claims. Virginia, noted the French traveler, the Duke de La Rochefoucauld, in repeating a common observation, "was one of the first [colonies] to take a part in the revolution [against Britain]: and no one of the states made more vigorous efforts, expended greater sums, or displayed more signal energy, to accomplish that happy object." Virginia, wrote the geographer William Guthrie, also "had the honour of leading the way to" the "most important reform in the [national] government" in 1785–87. "Some of the most illustrious characters that America can boast, either of those who now guide her councils, or of those who live but on the records of history," he pointed out in the mid-1790s, "derive[d] their birth from this state." Virginia, as even the New England critic Jedidiah Morse acknowledged in 1791, had indeed "produced some of the most distinguished and influential men that have been active in effecting the two late grand and important revolutions in America. Her political and military character will rank among the first in the page of history." Thus reinforced by outside opinion, Virginia's local interpreters could plausibly conclude that the Revolution had finally provided an appropriate occasion for the full flowering of the true Virginia "genius."[30]

From the perspective of Virginia's actions during the Revolution, indeed, it had become abundantly clear that Virginians had always been "a jealous and high spirited people," and, taking a cue from Jefferson in the *Notes,* both Burk and Randolph searched Virginia's past for earlier instances of their resistance to attacks upon their liberty and for evidence that an absolute revulsion against all forms of "tractable" behavior had ever marked the Virginia character. In ways that were perfectly compatible with the interpretation offered by Jefferson in the *Notes,* these writers reinterpreted Virginia's earlier history in the service of the new corporate identity they were constructing.[31]

If the "noble and spirited resistance" to Cromwell's forces in 1651 that Jefferson had pointed to in the *Notes* by itself constituted an ample, "honorable and lasting record of the spirit . . . of Virginians," both Burk and Randolph found many others. "As far as they depended on constitutions and conventions," wrote Burk, the Virginians' liberties were "scanty and precarious" throughout the colonial period:

> But as they were practically enjoyed, they were ample and substantial: and they were principally indebted for them to their own spirit and intelligence. Not all their obsequiousness to sir William Berkeley; not even their unfeigned respect and affection for his person and government, induced the slightest concession of their privileges. And when, at length, the sense of colonial grievances, added to the pressure of parliamentary restrictions dissolved the charm, which bound them for so long a time to this extraordinary man, they displayed in their resistance [in Bacon's Rebellion] the same ardent and determined spirit by which they had ever been distinguished.[32]

Rooted in their situation as independent rural landholders, that spirit, Virginia's post-Revolutionary interpreters declared, had given Virginians "an honester and more manly pride" and encouraged them in "free, unprejudiced modes of thinking." "In point of abilities of manly spirit," they suggested, no one excelled "the real Virginian planter," who, to his enormous credit, ever disdained "any abridgement of personal independence." There had never been, perhaps, these post-Revolutionary writers agreed, "a community so high spirited and independent as that of Virginia." The absence of "the style, and splendor" of Europe or even of the growing cities of the north was thus far more than "amply compensated [for] by the simple manners" and the virtuous and "independent spirit"—the "native spirit"—of Virginians.[33]

"From the first moments of her existence," post-Revolutionary writers argued in direct contradiction to those of the previous generation, "the conduct of Virginia," as Burk asserted, was thus "exactly the opposite" from the "unjust," if "universally received opinion . . . that Virginia was distinguished for her invariable loyalty, and her submissive and tractable temper, during the greater part of her colonial existence," "her yielding policy" contrasting sharply "with the sturdy patriotism of New-England." Neither Burk nor Randolph denied that Virginia began under the auspices of a charter in which "a mass of despotism" darkened "the scene." But they argued that the establishment of a representative assembly in 1619, as the historian Stith had affirmed a generation earlier, had "put the colonists once more under the protection of the laws of England" and provided them with the means to protect themselves against "such invasions of liberty as they had been taught to dread from their own experience and from the small though sturdy advances toward sound principles which English theory had even then made."[34]

Throughout Virginia's first century, these writers insisted, Virginians had stood up on behalf of liberty. When in 1624 the Virginia Company, composed of many of the "most conspicuous asserters of liberty in parliament," fell victim to "that power in the constitution which had long menaced with annihilation, the privileges of parliament, and the rights of the people," Burk wrote, the Virginians' "noble and spirited resistance" managed to save colonial representative government from the early Stuarts' "native propensity to tyranny." Thereafter, Virginians had repeatedly demonstrated themselves to be "animated . . . by the ardor of liberty," exhibiting a "daring and determined resistance" to governors such as Harvey and Howard, who behaved like petty tyrants.[35]

Burk actually rewrote some of the central episodes in seventeenth-century Virginia history to demonstrate that, contrary to earlier historians, Virginians had never wavered in their commitment to liberty. Although he admitted that "a spirit of complaisance and accommodation was reciprocated between the different branches [of the legislature] during the greater part of sir Wm. Berkeley's administration," he insisted that "religious zeal alone," more specifically, hostility to the religious zeal of the Puritans, was "the principal cause of" the Virginians' "supposed attachment to the king" during the English Civil War. "Their political attachments," said Burk, "were obviously on the other side; and in the career of liberty and resistance, they had even anticipated and outstripped the parliament. They had the same pointed regard for their rights and privileges, as this illustrious body; they resisted with equal ardor, and for a long time with greater success, the encroachments and insolence of the crown. Their cause was palpably the same." [36]

To suggest that Virginians "would have sacrificed any thing so essential, so precious in their estimation, as their rights, or the principles of freedom to" the "mere influence of sir William Berkeley," as had been so often asserted by previous historians, was, for Burk, patently absurd and could not "be collected from any part of their history." Clearly, "nothing but the infatuation or phrenzy of [religious] superstition" could account for their not immediately rushing to the banners of Parliament and the Commonwealth. So "mild and liberal, and even popular" was "the government of the English commonwealth . . . in Virginia" that its overthrow in 1659–60, even before the Restoration in England, Burk was persuaded, had to have been "the work of a mob" and not reflective of the true wishes of the people at large. [37]

Also in the hands of Burk, Bacon's Rebellion was for the first time incorporated into the story of the Virginia struggle for liberty. Set off by a disagreement over Indian policy, as earlier writers had argued, that uprising was, in Burk's view, also the result of "that crisis in the political malady when all ranks and classes" were "equally affected with . . . public grievances and oppressions [under Berkeley], and impatiently longed for an occasion, by one great and violent effort, to burst their chains and assert their independence." [38]

For Burk, Nathaniel Bacon became a heroic figure, a man of "a sanguine temper, a bold and dauntless courage, great promptness and decision of character, added to a presence of mind that rarely deserted him." Bacon's great "ardor and enthusiasm of liberty," said Burk, impelled him to come to the aid of a people whose liberties were "in danger" from an oppressive political regime. In sharp contrast to Berkeley, who, when he regained control of the colony, "was daily executing men by mock trials," Bacon was "never reproached with shedding a single drop of innocent blood, save what was unavoidably spilt in the heat and hurry of battle." [39]

Burk transformed Bacon and the "intrepid" Robert Beverley, father of the historian—whose "noble ardor and constancy in opposing the encroach-

ments on the liberties of his country" by Berkeley's successors, Culpeper
and Howard, deserved a lasting "monument"—into suitable precursors to
the famous defenders of liberty in Virginia during the Revolution. The
exploits of these local heroes constituted a standing reminder that champions in the cause of liberty had never been wanting in Virginia. Received
"by the people at large with every demonstration of unfeigned joy and
exultation," the Glorious Revolution of 1688 had rendered "the principle
of resistance to arbitrary power," as represented by men like Bacon and
Beverley, "popular and even fashionable," albeit Burk lamented that the
"entire essence" of that Revolution had not been "universally imparted"
into the colony.[40]

If Burk rewrote the history of seventeenth-century Virginia to stress the
Virginians' continuous devotion to liberty, he also emphasized, with Randolph, the extent to which that devotion had usually been tempered by a
prudence, a moderation, an equanimity that appeared to be an integral
component of the Virginia identity. It was "the happiness of Virginia character," wrote Randolph, "hardly ever to push to extremity any theory [or
spirit] which by practical relations may not be accommodated." Agreed
Burk, "the conduct of the colonists was invariably marked by great order
and moderation."[41]

These historians found little difficulty in illustrating this point. Thus,
Burk wrote, in the uncertain days between the revocation of the charter of
the Virginia Company and the establishment of royal government, "habits
of rational submission and decent manners" proved to have been "so confirmed . . . that the ordinary operations of government, and the settled
regulations of laws and commerce, were carried on unembarrassed by riot,
and unstained by excesses." Similarly, Randolph noted, during the Interregnum and Restoration Virginians scrupulously avoided both the "fanaticism and hypocrisy of Cromwell" and the "licentiousness of the second
Charles," and he cited this same "principle of accommodation" to explain
Virginia's acceptance of the metropolitan monopoly of its trade; and many
other similar "claims of usurpation" by the home government that eventually "grew . . . into a metropolitan right upon a mere reluctance to quarrel
with the mother country."[42]

Within the colony, these writers affirmed, "a spirit of mildness" also
pervaded social relations. The Virginia aversion to excess was particularly
reflected in the "mildness of church government." Anglicanism was established by law; however, with the exception of a few zealots, its essential
spirit, as even Jefferson agreed, had very early, like all other aspects of life
in Virginia, "subsided into moderation." "Virginia soil," the Baptist John

Leland confirmed, had "never been stained with vital blood for conscience sake." Virginia, said Randolph, had received from the parent state "an original stamina, perhaps . . . something phlegmatic in her temper, which inclined her to regulated liberty by saving her from those ebullitions which teem with violence and subordination." That "original stamina," he was persuaded, had given Virginia "manners . . . a polish which without enfeebling courage" had moderated, even in the early decades of the colony's existence, "that ferocity which suspicion sometimes ascribes to the rough inhabitants of a newly cultivated desert." Happily for Virginians, they had repeatedly proven themselves to be "equally aloof from the frenzy of reform and the abjections of vassalage."[43]

Bacon's Rebellion was the single exception to the temperate character of Virginia public life after the Restoration, and the Glorious Revolution further encouraged this spirit of moderation by producing "a profound calm" in the colony. For the next seventy years, as Burk wrote, "the interior concerns of the colony were conducted with moderation, and blessed with content and tranquility." As George Chalmers had affirmed in the 1780s, from the early 1720s on "the love of order, the obedience to law, and the peacefulness of the province of Virginia [had] offered a striking contrast to the tumult, the refractoriness, and [the] anarchy of its . . . neighbors." Beginning with Edward Nott in 1705, Burk noted, royal lieutenant governors in the colony were "model[s] of virtue and excellence." Such "liberal conduct" and "mild" government proceeding from such an "apparent regard to justice and equity" on the part of the home government so intensified the deep loyalty Virginians had traditionally manifested for the mother country that they, said Burk, "looked back with a mingled pride and admiration on the land of their ancestors" as "the seat of arts, the sanctuary of liberty, terror of tyrants, like the Roman senate, the hope, the refuge, the consolation of the distressed." Having from early in their history been intent upon adhering "to those excellent and refined customs of their native land, as nearly as the capacity of the country would admit," Virginians were so proud of their connection with Britain, said Randolph, that "every political sentiment, every fashion in Virginia appeared to be imperfect unless it bore a resemblance to some precedent in England."[44]

Virginia interpreters also took pride in contrasting their "own loyalty with the turbulent spirit" of the New England colonists, and, they thought, the colony's common effort with the Crown to defend its western territories against the French and Indians during the Seven Years' War "still further cemented the bonds of nativity and attachment." But this "almost idolatrous deference to the mother country," these strong "ties of affection" and deep loyalty, were, Randolph stressed, "debased by no servile compliance" but were accompanied by that "patriotic watchfulness" that had always been so conspicuous in the Virginia character. Although that watchfulness never degenerated "into the mere petulance of complaint," Virginians, as Lieutenant Governor Robert Dinwiddie discovered when he tried to levy a fee upon land patents without authorization of the legislature in 1753–54, knew "when to complain with truth and how to complain with dignity." Among such "watchful patriots," asserted Randolph, there was obviously "an elevation of character" that would render them "incapable of being seduced by the artifices" of any set of men.[45]

This strong attachment to Britain and the powerful drive toward Anglicization that accompanied it were further strengthened, as Randolph phrased it, by a confident consciousness that Virginia had, perhaps, "more nearly approached the British model . . . of excellence" than any other American colony, a development that had been made possible by the extraordinary growth of the colony during the first six decades of the eighteenth century. Neither Burk nor Randolph challenged the assessment of George Chalmers that Virginia, "notwithstanding every possible natural advantage," had "remained for ages poor, inconsiderable, and feeble." But they noted that the "assurance[s] of freedom and security" provided by the Glorious Revolution had "introduced the concomitant blessings of industry and peace" while the "patient industry of the English character" thereafter had finally given "a direction to those natural benefits" that all earlier commentators had praised in the Virginia environment. From 1700 on, they observed, the "Virginians augmented their numbers, their commerce, their wealth, and their power . . . beyond the example of other colonies." By 1750, this populous and prosperous society of independent landowners with no beggarly poor had, in terms of tobacco exports alone, become of greater commercial consequence to Britain "than all the other continental settlements" in combination.[46]

Economic success, Burk proudly reported, had been accompanied even by some cultural advances, although he admitted that Virginia's "present high reputation in the arts" dated only from the era of the Revolution. Throughout the seventeenth century, that "dark age in Virginia['s history]," the colony had been "stationary, if not retrograde in her taste and acquirements," producing, said Burk, "not a remnant . . . of any moral disquisition, of the investigation of any problem; in any science," "no ode, no sonnet" to shine "even for a moment, thro' the gloom." With most of its inhabitants "actuated chiefly by the love of gain" and few who "could boast of any considerable acquirements or taste in literature," with no printing

press and few educational institutions, it was scarcely surprising, in Samuel
Miller's words, that Virginians in those early days "paid little attention to
literary institutions" and slowly sank into a kind of cultural degeneracy.[47]

In the early eighteenth century, however, Virginia, its interpreters contended, at last began to exhibit some "instances of honourable literary en-
terprize," principally in the histories of Beverley and Stith. The latter, Burk
insisted, was "little, if any thing inferior in execution to lord Clarendon's
history of the civil disputes in England." During the same period, the
College of William and Mary improved considerably, largely through the
appointment as professors of "men of erudition" from abroad; a newspaper
was established in Williamsburg in 1736, an event that finally roused "the
genius of the country" out of "its long and death-like sleep" and provided
a foundation for the subsequent flowering of the literary talents of Richard
Bland, Jefferson, and others during the 1760s and after.[48]

But it was in the field of politics that Virginia's development in this
period was most impressive. Under the long tutelage of Speaker John Robinson, who held office for thirty years before his death in 1766, the House
of Burgesses, Randolph explained, became a model of "decorum," equal in
every way to the British House of Commons under his contemporary the
great Onslow and drawing out of "a constellation of eminent lawyers and
scholars" a group of brilliant and patriotic political leaders.[49]

As the German traveler Johann David Schoepf would later observe, the
"impulse to political affairs" was the one thing, other than the prospect of
pleasure and money, that could rouse Virginians from their customary "in-
activity." "There is probably no College in the United States," Samuel
Miller observed in 1803, in "which political science is studied with so
much ardour, and in which it is considered so pre-eminently a favourite
subject" as at the College of William and Mary. Such a deep fascination
with politics, as well as the "perpetual political or legal discussions" of the
sort visitors repeatedly encountered in Revolutionary Virginia, had clearly
produced "an assemblage" of men whose political acumen admirably
equipped them to assume the leadership of the opposition to Britain beginning in the 1760s and to demonstrate beyond any possibility of contradiction that from "a political view [Virginia was] inferior to no other colony."[50]

The spirited exertions of these brilliant political leaders, Virginia's post-
Revolutionary apologists never tired of pointing out, won for Virginia the
"exalted opinion" of the other colonies before and during the Revolution:
the Virginians' "courage, intelligence and patriotism" made them and their
colony objects of "grateful panegyric" and willing "deferences" throughout
America. Through the whole of the long struggle with Britain, they had

exhibited a "steady adherence to the maxims of their ancestors" and in particular to what Jefferson referred to in the *Notes* as that "temperate liberty" for which, Virginians liked to think, they had always been famous. They were always both firm and "cool and deliberate" in their protests. During the Stamp Act crisis, their "spirited behaviour," which had had such "a wonderful effect in animating and confirming the zeal of the other colonies," had been accompanied by "no riots or popular excesses" to stain "the reputation of Virginia," and at no later point did they fail to keep "public dissentions within limits of moderation."[51]

Nor, both Burk and Randolph insisted, were Virginians hasty in abandoning efforts at reconciliation. Even after the Stamp Act, they continued to regard "England as a model of all that was great and venerable" and for the better part of the next decade remained "a people, devoted indeed to liberty, and ready to seal their attachment with their blood; but at the same time loyal, just, humane, disposed to affection, and won even by trifling kindness[es]" such as those displayed by Governor Norbonne Berkeley, Baron de Botetourt, during the late 1760s. Only after British attacks on Massachusetts in the spring of 1775 had "changed the figure of Great Britain from an unrelenting parent into that of a merciless enemy, whose malice was the more severe, as her affection had been the more earnestly courted"—only after, in Jefferson's words, "no alternative was presented but resistance, or unconditional submission"—were Virginian affections for Britain finally and irrevocably alienated. So deep had the loyalty of the colony run that independence, as Randolph averred, could only have been "imposed upon us by the misdeeds of the British government."[52]

Moreover, the Virginia commitment to "temperate liberty" had continued to serve Virginia well throughout the Revolution. Notwithstanding the "relaxation of law" during the transitional period from royal government to independence in 1775 and 1776, noted Randolph, "order was maintained, and licentiousness discouraged by general morality" all over the colony, which "glide[d] from monarchy into self-government, without a convulsion or a single clog to its wheels from its novelty or from disaffection" and with remarkable unanimity among its inhabitants. There were few Tories, and the Virginia government treated them with such leniency that, as Jefferson announced, there was not "a single execution for treason" in the state during seven years of war. "From the experience of nearly sixty years in public life," Edmund Pendleton, one of the foremost lawyers and judges in Virginia, wrote in 1798, "I have been taught to . . . respect this my native country for the decent, peaceable, and orderly behavior of its inhabitants." Even in the midst of revolution, he noted, justice had been "duly and diligently administered—the laws obeyed—and constituted authorities respected, and we have lived in the happy intercourse of private harmony and good will."[53]

The Revolution may have generated some modest social reforms in Virginia, including the abolition of the slave trade, primogeniture, and entail, and the disestablishment of the Anglican church. Moreover, the fragility of liberty was revealed by two separate efforts, one in December 1776 and the other in June 1781, to invest, in Jefferson's words, "a *dictator. . .* with every power legislative, executive and judiciary, civil and military, of life and of death, over our persons and over our properties." But the traditional moderation of the Virginia character, its post-Revolutionary analysts emphasized, always preserved the new state from rash changes in the political fabric that might, in a less prudent polity, have resulted from a too easy application of what Randolph referred to as "the pruning knife of reformation."[54]

The unanimity, moderation, generosity, patriotism, and political expertise repeatedly demonstrated by Virginians at every stage of the Revolution seemed to be a standing proof of the appropriateness of the state's claim, so vividly symbolized in the new state seal devised in mid-1776, that virtue was indeed, as Randolph put it, "the genius of the Commonwealth." There was obviously no truth in the "evil" insinuations, spread by the enemies of Virginia, that the "revolution was coveted only by those whose desperate fortunes might be disencumbered by an abolition of debt" to British merchants. Quite the contrary, Randolph argued; most of the leaders "had at stake fortunes which were affluent or competent and families which were dear to them," and to suppose that they would "have jeopardized" either "of these blessings . . . upon a political speculation in which their souls were not deeply engaged" was absurd. Nothing but the purest motives of patriotism and devotion to the preservation of the temperate liberty and independence of Virginia, he observed, could possibly have accounted for their behavior.[55]

III

For these Virginia interpreters, the one deeply disturbing flaw in the positive image they constructed for Virginia out of the state's Revolutionary experience was black slavery. Although they emphatically did not try to justify that institution, they found much to say to explain its rise and perpetuation. The initial settlers, they explained, had neither brought slavery with them nor deliberately sought to introduce it into Virginia. Rather, the institution had arrived by chance in 1619 when a storm had driven a Dutch ship loaded with slaves into the Chesapeake Bay. Just as "considerations of profit" had earlier induced English merchants, inhabitants of "the freest nation, at that time in the world, to embark in so nefarious a traffic, as that of the human race," so also had similar motives prevented early Virginians, "most of whom" had come to America because of "the allurement of amassing gold without toil," from resisting the temptation to purchase such productive sources of labor.[56]

No less motivated by economic considerations than Virginians, New Englanders, Tucker took pains to point out, had similarly begun to acquire slaves within five to ten years after their arrival in the New World. In contrast to the situation in New England, however, natural conditions "contributed extremely" to the proliferation of slavery in Virginia. The "violent heats of the summer," the "overwhelming indolence of white men" in such temperatures, and the "infatuation" of Virginians with tobacco as the surest way to satisfy their "eagerness for present gain" eventually combined to rivet the institution in the heart of Virginia. At the same time, the colony's climate proved to be "so congenial to the African constitution" as to cause blacks to multiply rapidly.[57]

By the early eighteenth century, as the Scottish historian Dr. William Robertson remarked, slavery had come to be seen, in Britain and Virginia, as "essential to the existence of the colony." Thus, with a few slave purchases in the colony's earliest years, Tucker lamented, "Our forefathers [had] sown the seeds of an evil, which, like a leprosy, hath descended upon their posterity with accumulated rancour, visiting the sins of the fathers upon succeeding generations" as slavery slowly but steadily "diffuse[d] itself in a variety of destructive shapes."[58]

Nevertheless, as Burk pointed out, Virginians derived much "honor" from the fact that they did not "pretend to justify" slavery. Rather, as Tucker endeavored to show at length, the Virginia legislature as early as 1669 had manifested a "disposition to check its progress," a disposition that gained strength over the following century. Had it not "been uniformly opposed" by British authorities, he contended, it would no doubt have resulted in prohibition of further slave imports well before the American Revolution. "A system uniformly persisted in for nearly a whole century, and finally carried into effect" soon after Virginia had declared its independence, he was persuaded, thoroughly evinced "the sincerity of that disposition which the legislators had shewn during so long a period, to put a check to the growing evil." More important in terms of their own self-esteem in a world in which slavery was more and more becoming an object of widespread condemnation, the legislature's persistence, Tucker was convinced, provided white Virginians with a "clear . . . vindication . . . from the opprobrium, but too lavishly bestowed upon" them, of "fostering slavery" at the same time as they boasted "a sacred regard to . . . liberty."[59]

"A very large proportion of" white Virginians thus both considered slavery "an evil of the most serious and afflicting nature" and professed "an entire willingness to apply a remedy, whenever it shall appear safe or practicable." "Is it not our duty to embrace the first moment of constitutional health and vigour," asked Tucker, "to effectuate so desirable an object, and to remove from us a stigma, with which our enemies will never fail to upbraid us, nor our consciences to reproach us?"[60]

But no Virginia analyst believed that the immediate prospects for abolition were very bright. Both Jefferson and Tucker, its most ardent proponents, took pains to explain to their readers the many extraordinarily powerful "obstacles" that stood in the way of such a measure. Especially from the perspective of the "recent history of the French West Indies" in the early 1790s, it appeared obvious that any sudden abolition would bring economic ruin to white slaveowners, misery to blacks, and destruction to the state, as ex-slaves, like the rebels of St. Domingue, would licentiously combine into ungovernable "hordes of vagabonds, robbers and murderers."[61]

Nor was gradual abolition without severe difficulties. Though Jefferson hoped that elimination of the slave trade would retard the spread of slavery "while the minds of our citizens" were being "ripened for a complete emancipation of human nature" within the state, he was concerned, along with Tucker and Burk, about the effects of such an eventuality upon Virginia society. Differences in skin color, culture, and intellectual ability, all of these writers feared, would prevent blacks from ever achieving full civic competence or being satisfactorily incorporated into the polity as a whole. If that turned out to be the case, if it was "true, as Mr. Jefferson seems to suppose, that the Africans are really an inferior race of mankind," Tucker worried, "sound policy" strongly advised against admitting them into free society either immediately or "at any future period," lest such a step "eventually depreciate the whole national character."[62]

In the face of such a dilemma, Virginians could only take solace in their belief that they were "with few exceptions . . . humane and liberal masters" and that Virginia slavery was comparatively benign. They did not deny that Virginia's early laws systematically degraded slaves "below the rank of human beings" and provided for a form of slavery "so malignant" that it did not "leave to its wretched victims the least vestige of any civil right, and even" divested "them of all their natural rights." But they did contend that the harshness of the law did "not proceed from a[ny] sanguinary temper in the people of Virginia, but from those political considerations indispensably necessary, where[ver] slavery prevails to any extent" and that the "rigours of slavery in this country were [n]ever as great" as the laws seemed to suggest. Indeed, Tucker argued, the legislature had significantly ameliorated slave laws beginning with the "dawn of humanity" in 1769. Since the Revolution, he asserted, "Our police respecting this unhappy class of people" had been "not only less rigorous than formerly, but perhaps milder than in any other country where there are so many slaves, or so large a proportion of them, in respect to the free inhabitants." [63]

Notwithstanding the "misfortune" of slavery, Virginia's analysts during the post-Revolutionary era had finally constructed a credibly positive—and, in many respects, satisfying—sense of corporate identity. In view of the political contributions of Virginians during the "new and more splendid aera" represented by the Revolution, the many other cultural and character deficiencies that had long worried earlier generations of Virginia interpreters no longer seemed quite so urgent. Unlike Burk and Randolph, earlier Virginians had, after all, as Randolph said, written "before the country could be said to have been explored in its political concerns with much accuracy, and," even more important, "before the era of Virginia luster" during the Revolution. [64]

To outsiders, however, Virginians still appeared, as the English traveler J. F. D. Smyth put it in the early 1780s, to be "a strange combination of incongruous contradictory qualities, and principles directly opposite; the best and the worst, the most valuable and the most worthless, elegant accomplishments and savage brutality, being in many of them most unaccountably blended." Indeed, for outsiders, such incongruities seemed to define the character of Virginia and Virginians. [65]

Deservedly known for their hospitality, politeness, and sociability, Virginians, visitor after visitor claimed, were among the most inactive and indolent people in the world. Inordinately fond of elegance, they permitted their houses to fall into disrepair and their agricultural lands to be slovenly worked. With a reputation for being good mates and tender parents, they frequently gave themselves over to jealousy and improvidence. Though "a taste for reading" was "more prevalant among the gentlemen of the first class than in any other part of America," "no state" seemed to be "so entirely destitute of all means of public education" nor exhibited such widespread ignorance among the "common people." With many "men of public spirit and extensive information, occupied with the welfare of the country and desirous of effecting it," Virginia had one of the "most imperfect" constitutions in the United States, and a growing number of its able men were forsaking public service in pursuit of more lucrative careers in private life. Having, "since the revolution, produced more men of distinguished talents than, perhaps, any other state of the Union," Virginia was filled with people who seemed to have fallen into total dissipation. "Equally distinguished for their valour and love of liberty" during the Revolution, the latter of which visitors found was "yet trembling alive among all classes of the [free] people," Virginians had not yet by any means sufficiently imbibed modern "sentiments of philanthropy" to be able to commit themselves to the emancipation of their slaves. Indeed, for people who had come from nonslave societies, the contrast between the Virginians' love of liberty and their "maintenance of slavery" seemed especially incongruous, "speeches on liberty and independence sound[ing] rather strangely from the lips of masters of slaves."[66]

At least in part because of the negative elements in these contradictory pairs of characteristics, visitors agreed that post-Revolutionary Virginia still fell considerably short of its potential. Despite the "influence which it is supposed to have over the Union," Rochefoucauld observed in 1799 after constructing a careful balance sheet of Virginia's desirable and undesirable features, its population was still too low, its agriculture too backward, its commerce and manufactures too undeveloped, its wealth too little and too unevenly distributed, and its leading inhabitants a little too complacent in their "pride of family" and too "contempt[uous] of the commercial spirit" to make it plausible for any impartial observer "to praise with any degree of justice the power of the state of Virginia."[67]

Rochefoucault did not dispute that the state had been "undoubtedly invited by nature to become the most powerful, or one of the most powerful, [members] of the Union." He even conceded that its "time of improvement may be near." But he insisted that that time had "not yet come" and could not be expected until its inhabitants' "manners [had been] . . . corrected, industry encouraged, and the bounties of nature turned to advantage."[68]

IV

Virginians were by no means impervious to negative reports by outside observers, as attested by Tucker's indignant defense of Williamsburg against Jedidiah Morse's "wanton aspersions" in his *American Universal Geography.* In response, they developed a series of apologies in which they claimed that many of the reputed flaws in the Virginia character could be dismissed as unworthy English inheritances, while others could be excused as in some respects beneficial.[69]

Carried out in behalf of virtue, as well as liberty, the Revolution could scarcely have failed to refocus the attention of Virginians on the adverse effects of their notorious tendency to bring "ruin upon themselves by their extravagance" and addiction to a "spirit of gaming." But such extravagance, Randolph explained, was the product of the Virginians' habit of sinking "too often . . . into . . . English vices," one of the most pronounced of which was "ostentatious hospitality." Similarly, the "fatal propensity to gaming," which, as Randolph granted, had "been often lamented . . . as breaking forth in Virginia in ways destructive to morals and estates," had been rendered especially "fashionable" in the decades just before the Revolution by the example of Francis Fauquier, a popular British governor, who, though he had many fine qualities, was an inveterate gamester whose bad habits were copied by many of "the most distinguished landholders" in the colony.[70]

Though Randolph liked to think that during the Revolution both extravagance and gambling had been largely confined to the "most worthless part of society," he had to admit that they had not yet "been extirpated." In any case, such behavior could be excused as the "natural offspring" of that laudable spirit of hospitality and liberality that had always "marked the character of Virginians." As Virginia had become more affluent during the middle years of the eighteenth century, the old "unaffected hospitality" of Virginians, Burk and Randolph suggested, had slowly—and unwittingly—slipped into an "ostentatious hospitality" characterized by extravagant display and the indulgence of "passions . . . to profusion and excess." "Amongst a class proverbial for their hospitality, their politeness and fondness of expence," the habit of spending lavishly and the "rage of playing deep, reckless of time, health, or money," they argued, had, once Fauquier had lent legitimacy to such behavior, quickly "spread like a contagion."[71]

Nor, they contended, was the situation with regard to education quite so lamentable as visitors and other outsiders suggested. Virginia had many private primary and secondary schools, and, in addition to the several new private colleges noted by outsiders, the College of William and Mary, Virginia apologists claimed, was slowly regaining the eminence it had begun to achieve in the decades just before Independence. The Revolution had deprived the college of three-fourths of its revenues and, through the dispersion of its faculty, left it wholly disorganized. But by the 1790s, William and Mary had two faculty members and fifty to sixty boys in the grammar school, and six professors and forty to fifty students in the college, a number that was "considerably greater" than at any time before the Revolution. It taught mathematics, classics, four modern languages, moral philosophy, and chemistry.[72]

Most students reportedly were attracted to natural philosophy or law, the two subjects in which the college took special pride. "Almost constantly growing in the number of its votaries, and in the degree of attention it has received," the former, which was "much more comprehensive than is usual in most colleges," had been developed by the president of the college, Bishop James Madison, and the latter successively by George Wythe, state chancellor of Virginia, and St. George Tucker, both of whom during their tenures as professor of law annually gave a celebrated course of lectures on the principles of law, civil government, and the constitutions of Virginia and the United States. A sharp rise in the number of students reading natural philosophy instead of law suggested, at least to Tucker, that science was "beginn[ing] to be more generally cultivated among the citizens at large." Having already produced a higher proportion of national political leaders than could possibly have been expected for such a small institution, as well as many "men of high professional character in law, physic, and divinity," the college, its defenders claimed, was "so far from being in a declining state" that its prospects were becoming infinitely "more favorable."[73]

If their claims to respectability in education were patently weak, Virginians now began to argue with far more conviction that their "fixed and unconquerable repugnance" to living in towns and their deep attachment to agriculture were not liabilities, as most earlier writers and many contemporary visitors had argued, but assets. Expanding on themes earlier writers such as Robert Beverley and William Byrd of Westover had only tentatively advanced, Jefferson, Burk, and Randolph agreed that, as Randolph put it, "Men who are occupied by labor in the country are more exempt from the vices prevailing in towns." "Those who labour in the earth are the chosen people of God, if ever he had a chosen people, whose breasts he has made his peculiar deposit for substantial and genuine virtue," wrote Jefferson in a much-quoted comment: "It is the focus in which he keeps alive that sacred fire, which otherwise might escape from the face of the earth. Corruption of morals in the mass of cultivators is a phaenomenon of which no age nor nation had furnished an example." People in towns depended "for their subsistence . . . on the casualties and caprice of customers"; the abject dependence that was necessarily so rife in urban areas, Jefferson insisted, begat "subservience and venality," suffocated "the germ of virtue," and prepared "fit tools for the designs of ambition" and unfit materials for the preservation of "a republic in vigour." It seemed obvious that the rural character of Virginia and the commitment of its inhabitants to agriculture were the primary sources of that "high sense of personal independence" that had been so laudably and so universally revealed in Virginia behavior during the Revolution.[74]

For Virginia's own analysts, the glorious contributions of the state and its inhabitants to the Revolution and the new American nation thus overshadowed any deficiencies in their own character and society. From the perspective of 1790 or 1815, the story of their country seemed, in Randolph's words, to have been one of its gradual rise to greatness, as it progressed "from infancy and a wilderness, through various fortunes, into wealth, a character, and an influence which largely contributed to the establishment of American independence and to the formation of that most illustrious among civil acts, the Constitution of the United States of America."[75]

"Being the earliest among the British settlements in North America, having been soon withdrawn from the humiliation of proprietary dependence to the dignity of a government immediately under the crown, advancing rapidly into wealth from her extensive territory and the luxuriant production of her staple commodities," and with "the sons of the most opulent families trained by education and habits acquired in England," Virginia, even before the Revolution, explained Randolph, had acquired a pride that "had so long been a topic of discourse in the other colonies that it had almost grown into a proverb."[76]

But it was not primarily the circumstances that underlay that growing pride and the unease it disguised, but "the public spirit and intelligence of her citizens" during the Revolution that gave Virginia such a "conspicuous" place as "the elder branch of a confederacy." Virginia, its protagonists insisted, had taken the lead in throwing down "the gauntlet to kings" and had become "the asylum of oppressed humanity; the faithful guardian and depositary of public spirit." These actions, they announced, amply confirmed their image of Virginia as a commonwealth of virtue whose independent and patriotic but prudent sons were ever watchful of public liberty and ever ready to defend it with manly, courageous, and wise exertions. With such glorious accomplishments behind them, who could possibly gainsay the proud boasts overheard by Schoepf in 1783 that Virginia was "superior to the other American states" and that no other American could possibly "count himself the equal" of the polished, the virtuous, and the genuinely "noble Virginian"?[77]

By providing, in the *Notes* and elsewhere, the positive reading of Virginia's past and future and by sponsoring or endorsing much of the literature in which other post-Revolutionary analysts rewrote the history of Virginia and constructed a positive sense of collective self for Virginia and Virginians, Jefferson both participated in and made a major contribution to that undertaking. In so doing, he revealed that his famous and cultivated cosmopolitanism always coexisted symbiotically with deep loyalties to the local and provincial peculiarities that gave Virginia its distinctive shape—including even slavery. No matter how urgent his pleas, in the *Notes* and elsewhere, for the reformation of many aspects of Virginia society, his relationship to his native state was ever defined by an abiding Virginia patriotism.

NOTES

The author wishes to thank Michael Holt, Rhys Isaac, Jan Lewis, and, most especially, Peter S. Onuf for their suggestions in revising this chapter.

1. See, for instance, TJ to D'Anmours, Nov. 30, 1780, in *Boyd,* IV, p. 166; TJ to James Monroe, Oct. 5, 1781, Boyd, VI, p. 127.

2. See TJ to William Wirt, Aug. 5, 1815, in *L&B,* XV, pp. 336–37; TJ, Autobiography, 1821, L&B, I, p. 54.

3. This problem is discussed at greater length in Jack P. Greene, *Imperatives, Behaviors, & Identities: Essays in Early American Cultural History* (Charlottesville, Va., 1992), pp. 13–16, 113–14.

4. Henry Hartwell, James Blair, and Edward Chilton, *The Present State of Virginia, and the College,* Hunter Dickinson Farish, ed. (Williamsburg, Va., 1940), p. 3.

5. John Hammond, *Leah and Rachel, or, the Two Fruitful Sisters Virginia and Maryland* (London, 1656), in Clayton Colman Hall, ed., *Narratives of Early Maryland 1633–1684* (New York, 1910); Sir William Berkeley, *A Discourse and View of Virginia* (London, 1663).

6. Robert Beverley, *The History and Present State of Virginia,* Louis B. Wright, ed. (Chapel Hill, N.C., 1947).

7. Hugh Jones, *The Present State of Virginia,* Richard L. Morton, ed. (Chapel Hill, N.C., 1956).

8. William Stith, *The History of the First Discovery and Settlement of Virginia* (Williamsburg, Va., 1747). See also Thad W. Tate, "William Stith and the Virginia Tradition," in Lawrence H. Leder, ed., *The Colonial Legacy: Historians of Nature and Man's Nature* (New York, 1973), pp. 121–45.

9. Thomas Jefferson, *Notes on the State of Virginia,* William Peden, ed., (Chapel Hill, N.C., 1955).

10. John Daly Burk, *History of Virginia,* 4 vols. (Richmond, 1804–16). On Burk, see Michael Kraus, *The Writing of American History* (Norman, Okla., 1953), pp. 80–81, and Joseph I. Shulim, "John Daly Burk: Irish Revolutionist and American Patriot," *Transactions of the American Philosophical Society,* new series, LIV (1964).

11. Edmund Randolph, *History of Virginia,* Arthur H. Schaffer, ed. (Charlottesville, Va., 1970), pp. xvii, xxxvii–xxxix, 3.

12. John Leland, "The Virginia Chronicle," in L. F. Greene, ed., *The Writings of John Leland* (New York, 1969), pp. 92–124.

13. St. George Tucker, *A Letter to the Rev. Jedidiah Morse* (Richmond, 1795), and *A Dissertation on Slavery, with a Proposal for the Gradual Abolition of It, in the State of Virginia* (Philadelphia, 1796).

14. John Marshall, *Life of George Washington,* 4 vols. (Philadelphia, 1805–07), I, esp. pp. 50–77, 188–94, 314.

15. These included new general histories of Britain's early colonizing efforts in America by George Chalmers and Dr. William Robertson, as well as an abundance of travelers' accounts: for the late 1770s, by Benjamin West, a New England lawyer; Ebenezar Hazard, a New York bookseller; Elkanah Watson, a Rhode Island merchant; J. F. D. Smyth, a British doctor; and August Wilhelm Du Roi, a German officer; for the 1780s, Baron von Closen, an officer in the French Army; Thomas Anburey, a British officer; the Marquis de Chastellux; Johann David Schoepf; Rev. Thomas Coke, the English dissenting minister; Noah Webster, a New England scholar; James Joyce, an Irish immigrant; Robert Hunter, Jr., a British merchant; and J. P. Brissot de Warville, a French savant: and, for the 1790s, William Loughton Smith, a prominent South Carolinian; Médéric Moreau de Saint-Méry, a French refugee; the Duke de La Rochefoucault-Liancourt, another French émigré; Benjamin Henry Latrobe, the architect; and Isaac Weld, another Irish immigrant. Finally, Samuel Miller's brief survey of eighteenth-century intellectual developments in 1803 and the geographies of Jedidiah Morse and William Guthrie contained descriptions of the state and its people.

16. Jefferson, *Notes,* pp. 85, 108, 125, 135, 146–49, 152–54, 158–59, 166; *Ford,* III, p. 100.

17. Jefferson, *Notes,* pp. 118–29, 161.

18. Randolph, *History,* p. 202.

19. Jefferson, *Notes,* p. 87; Burk, *History,* I, p. 211.

20. Randolph, *History,* p. 202; Jefferson, *Notes,* p. 162; George Chalmers, *Political Annals of the Present United Colonies, from Their Settlement to the Peace of 1763* (London, 1780), p. 49; Tucker, *Dissertation,* p. 9.

21. Tucker, *Dissertation,* p. 77; Randolph, *History,* p. 193.

22. Randolph, *History,* p. 193; Jefferson, *Notes,* pp. 162–63; Tucker, *Dissertation,* p. 41.

23. Jefferson to Chastellux, Sept. 2, 1785, in *Boyd,* VIII, pp. 467–69; Jefferson to Richard Price, Aug. 7, 1785, in *Boyd,* VIII, pp. 356–57.

24. Jefferson to John Banister, Jr., Oct. 15, 1785, in *Boyd,* VIII, p. 636; Jefferson, *Notes,* pp. 1–3, 13, 19, 24–25, 29–30, 45–46, 82–84, 169.

25. Jefferson, *Notes,* pp. 29–31, 45–46, 82–84, 87, 95–96, 133, 141–42, 151, 158, 161, 164–65, 168–69, 175; Jefferson to C. W. F. Dumas, Oct. 4, 1785, in *Boyd,* VIII, p. 582.

26. Jefferson, *Notes,* pp. 85, 113–17, 130, 137, 155, 172–73, 177–78.

27. Burk, *History,* III, p. 373; Johann David Schoepf, *Travels in the Confederation,* trans. Alfred J. Morrison, 2 vols. (Philadelphia, 1911), II, p. 92.

28. Burk, *History,* III, p. 373; Randolph, *History,* pp. 178, 251; Marquis de Chastellux, *Travels in North America in the Years 1780, 1781 and 1782,* trans. Harold C. Rice, Jr., (Chapel Hill, N.C., 1963), II, p. 435; Jedidiah Morse, *The American Geography,* 2d ed. (London, 1792), p. 400.

29. Burk, *History,* III, p. 373; Tucker, *Letter to Morse,* p. 15.

30. Duke de La Rochefoucault-Liancourt, *Travels through the United States of North America*

(2 vols., London, 1799), I, p. 53; William Guthrie, *A New System of Modern Geography* (Philadelphia, 1794–95), pp. 500, 506; Morse, *American Geography,* 387.

31. Burk, *History,* II, pp. 226, 299.

32. Ibid., II, pp. 11, 91, xxxi.

33. Ibid., I, pp. 5, 2: 83, 226; Edward C. Carter II, et al., eds., *The Virginia Journals of Benjamin Henry Latrobe 1795–98,* 2 vols. (New Haven, 1977), II, p. 304; Randolph, *History,* pp. 153, 178; Fred Shelley, ed., "The Journal of Ebenezer Hazard in Virginia, 1777," *VMHB,* LXII (1954), p. 414.

34. Burk, *History,* I, p. 203, II, p. 233; Randolph, *History,* pp. 19, 87.

35. Ibid., pp. 207, 231, 294, II, pp. 11, 33, 292.

36. Ibid., II, pp. 75–76, iv.

37. Ibid., II, pp. 76, 120. Contemporary examples of the traditional interpretation of Virginia's behavior during the English Civil War and Interregnum may be found in Dr. William Robertson, *The History of America,* 2 vols. (Albany, N.Y., 1822), II, pp. 325–27, and George Chalmers, *An Introduction to the History of the Revolt of the American Colonies,* 2 vols. (Boston, 1845), I, p. 75.

38. Burk, *History,* II, p. 192.

39. Ibid., II, pp. 193–94.

40. Ibid., pp. 298, 307, 333. Both Randolph and John Marshall challenged Burk's effort "to metamorphose" Bacon's Rebellion "into one of those daring efforts which gross misrule sometimes suggests, if it may not strictly vindicate." Reaffirming the traditional interpretation as recently reiterated by both George Chalmers and Dr. William Robertson, they insisted that Berkeley was guilty of no "palpable or . . . clearly meditated" tyranny (Randolph, *History,* pp. 153, 202; Marshall, *Washington,* I, pp. 188–93).

41. Randolph, *History,* p. 157; Burk, *History,* II, p. 10.

42. Burk, *History,* II, p. 10; Randolph, *History,* pp. 116–17, 153.

43. Randolph, *History,* pp. 147, 153, 158, 247; Burk, *History,* II, p. xxxi; Jefferson, *Notes,* p. 158; Leland, "Virginia Chronicle," p. 107.

44. Burk, *History,* II, pp. 328, 330, 334, III, pp. 280–81; Chalmers, *Introduction,* I, p. 101, II, p. 198; Randolph, *History,* p. 176.

45. Burk, *History,* III, pp. 122, 281; Randolph, *History,* pp. 160–61, 163, 176, 248.

46. Randolph, *History,* pp. 146, 177; Chalmers, *Political Annals,* p. 70; Burk, *History,* I, p. 203; Chalmers, *Introduction,* II, pp. 70–71.

47. Burk, *History,* III, pp. 333–35; Samuel Miller, *A Brief Retrospect of the Eighteenth Century,* 2 vols. (New York, 1803), II, pp. 334–35.

48. Miller, *Brief Retrospect,* II, p. 361; Burk, *History,* III, pp. 399–400.

49. Randolph, *History,* pp. 173, 179.

50. Schoepf, *Travels,* II, p. 92; Miller, *Brief Retrospect,* II, p. 504; Latrobe, *Journals,* II, pp. 304, 341; Randolph, *History,* p. 161.

51. Burk, *History,* III, pp. 299, 310, 331, 347; Randolph, *History,* pp. 177, 238, 248; Jefferson, *Notes,* p. 85.

52. Randolph, *History,* pp. 166, 227, 234; Burk, *History,* III, pp. 361–62; Jefferson, *Notes,* p. 117.

53. Jefferson, *Notes,* p. 85, 155; Randolph, *History,* pp. 199, 227; "Edmund Pendleton to Citizens of Caroline County," Nov. 1798, in David J. Mays, ed., *The Letters and Papers of Edmund Pendleton, 1734–1803,* 2 vols. (Charlottesville, Va., 1967), II, p. 650.

54. Jefferson, *Notes,* p. 126; Randolph, *History,* p. 255.

55. Randolph, *History,* pp. 195, 208–09, 276; Burk, *History,* III, p. 373.

56. Tucker, *Dissertation,* p. 15; Randolph, *History,* p. 96.

57. Tucker, *Dissertation*, pp. 13–14; Randolph, *History*, pp. 71, 96; Robertson, *History*, II, p. 310.

58. Robertson, *History*, II, pp. 310–11; Tucker, *Dissertation*, p. 13; Randolph, *History*, p. 96.

59. Burk, *History*, II, p. 212; Tucker, *Dissertation*, pp. 41, 46–48.

60. Tucker, *Dissertation*, pp. 11, 67; Burk, *History*, I, p. 212.

61. Tucker, *Dissertation*, pp. 79, 81, 86.

62. Jefferson, *Notes*, p. 87; Tucker, *Dissertation*, p. 89.

63. Burk, *History*, I, p. 212; Tucker, *Dissertation*, pp. 51–52, 54, 67.

64. Tucker, *Dissertation*, 67; Burk, *History*, III, p. 167; Randolph, *History*, p. 5.

65. J. F. D. Smyth, *A Tour of the United States of America*, 2 vols. (London, 1784), I, p. 67.

66. Rochefoucauld, *Travels*, II, pp. 112, 115, 117–18.

67. Ibid., pp. 111, 115; Chalmers, *Political Annals*, p. 69.

68. Rochefoucauld, *Travels*, II, pp. 115–16.

69. Tucker, *Letter to Morse*, p. 12.

70. Randolph, *History*, pp. 61, 147, 279; Burk, *History*, III, p. 334.

71. Randolph, *History*, pp. 147, 193, 279–80; Burk, *History*, II, p. 226, III, pp. 334, 402.

72. Tucker, *Letter to Morse*, pp. 14–15.

73. Miller, *Brief Retrospect*, II, pp. 337, 377–78; Tucker, *Letter to Morse*, pp. 14–15.

74. Burk, *History*, II, pp. 126–27, III, p. 404; Randolph, *History*, pp. 197, 257; Jefferson, *Notes*, pp. 109, 164–65, 175; Rochefoucault, *Travels*, I, p. 502.

75. Randolph, *History*, p. 3.

76. Ibid., p. 177.

77. Burk, *History*, I, p. i.

CHAPTER 8

Putting Rights Talk in Its Place
The Summary View *Revisited*

STEPHEN A. CONRAD

Talking about "rights" has been one of the most persistent phenomena in American history. But over the span of our history, the meaning of rights talk has hardly proved uniform, or even consistent, or, perhaps, even coherent. To say this about the putative American "rights tradition" is not necessarily to indict it but to attempt to understand it on its own ever-changing terms.[1]

During a career as exalted as any other for defining the public and private happiness of America, Thomas Jefferson talked often about "rights." And what he had to say about rights was evidently so important to him that it eventually approached dogma, despite Jefferson's justly celebrated, "tenaciously Enlightened" aversion to dogmatism. Two years before his death he wrote, "Nothing then is unchangeable but the inherent and unalienable rights of man." Such talk might suggest not only that Jefferson had a general concept of and concern for "rights," but that rights provided *the* guiding idea of his public career. In this view, Jefferson's conception of rights and of the need to secure them shaped his approach to civic discourse in general, embracing constitutionalism and law, political theory and economy, republicanism, liberty, and equality—even the pursuit of happiness itself. Rights talk, in other words, stood at the very center of the Jeffersonian vision for America; and "rights" promised to provide the Archimedean point for raising America (and eventually the world) to the fulfillment of that vision.[2]

There is no gainsaying that rights were recurrently very important to Jefferson, from his first to his last utterances of what he thought America should and could be. Nevertheless, there are good reasons for hesitating to *identify* his visionary civics with his recurrent emphasis on rights. There are good reasons not to *reduce* all Jefferson's civic discourse to his rights talk. For one thing, over the course of a long career Jefferson only talked about rights sporadically.[3]

But there are other, more pointed reasons for putting Jefferson's rights talk in its place in any attempt to reach the fullest possible understanding of Jeffersonian visions. The reasons I have in mind have nothing to do with the inconsistency between Jefferson's rights talk and his actions, or inaction, when it came to putting his talk into effect. That one of our most revered national spokesmen for the equal rights of all human beings lived and died "one of the largest slaveholders of his time" is only the most arresting fact in Jefferson's record of evident inconsistency. On another count, Leonard Levy has forcefully and repeatedly argued that Jefferson's record as a defender and an enforcer of positive civil rights, constitutional and legal, also evinces a "side" of Jefferson's statesmanship so "dark" that we must question carefully what and how much "rights" really meant to Jefferson.[4]

Setting aside, as I mean to here, the question of Jefferson's putative hypocrisy as a rights advocate,[5] I turn to the theme of my essay, to the chief reasons that I question any inclination to accord any idea of rights primacy in Jefferson's uniquely visionary mind. And I question, in particular, the tendency to reduce Jefferson's inevitably complex rights discourse to his eloquently avowed attachment to the doctrine of the "natural" rights *of individuals.*

I want to pursue these questions by turning back to Jefferson's first nationally significant statement about rights,[6] his *Summary View of the Rights of British America,* first published in August 1774, when he was thirty-one years old. In narrowing the focus of my essay to this single, early pamphlet from Jefferson's pen, I do not pretend to offer a comprehensive account of what Jefferson said and thought about rights, much less any judgment on his commitment to rights in practice. But in the text and contexts of the *Summary View* alone there is ample evidence to question how and how much Jefferson cared about rights, whether as an end in themselves or as a means to a higher end. In any case, the *Summary View,* even more than the Declaration of Independence or any of Jefferson's other public papers, affords an especially extensive and illuminating display of Jefferson's thinking about rights. Jefferson's ambivalence and ambiguity in the *Summary View* is itself sufficient reason to hesitate before rushing to any conclusions about Jefferson's vision—or, more accurately, his multiple, complex visions—of rights.

To be sure, there are in the vast scholarly and popular literature on Jefferson both closely argued and conventionally impressionistic characterizations of him as one of our greatest and most devotedly single-minded exponents and champions of the idea of "rights." But there have also been commentators who have suggested that such characterizations are too simple at best. In this essay I mean to endorse these more subtle commentators, because to conclude, for example, that Jefferson's visions for the American republic all "derived" from his so-called natural rights philosophy; that for Jefferson "the doctrine of rights, natural and civil . . . shaped the very task of political construction"; or even to label the *Summary View* simply as a "natural rights pamphlet" obscures as much as it reveals about the character and place of Jefferson's text in its own authentic contexts. It is, in other words, this essentialist approach, in pursuit of the chimerical one "authentic Jefferson," that I am in part questioning. This essentialist approach has given us an image of Jefferson so inextricably linked to the very idea of Americanism that distinguished scholars can feel—as I do not—a "sense of obligation to the symbol" entailing an "obligation" even to compromise "the historical truth" about the man behind the symbol.[7]

I

It was the publication of the *Summary View* as a pamphlet in the summer of 1774, together with its prompt republication elsewhere in the colonies, and then in London, that in a stroke transformed Jefferson from an eminent young lawyer and a highly regarded Virginia civic leader into a national and international voice during the climacteric of the coming of the Revolution. In some respects, however, his was an anomalous entrance onto the greater scene. For Jefferson had not written the piece for publication; the title that all the printed editions bore was not his at all, although there is no evidence that he was ever uncomfortable with it. Strictly speaking, the publication of the *Summary View* was, typically of the times, anonymous, with the author identified on the title page of the original Williamsburg edition merely as "a Native, and Member of the House of Burgesses."[8] By every account, however, the identity of the author was generally known all along.

It was "certain admirers of his thought" among Jefferson's fellow burgesses who saw to the initial publication, probably as much for reasons of politics as of admiration: the "manly firmness" of the posture Jefferson took on imperial relations in the *Summary View* made the official positions taken by the Virginia convention during 1774 and 1775 look, by contrast, generously moderate. The summer of 1774 could hardly have been a more delicate moment in terms of deteriorating imperial relations. There was not yet any pronounced public sentiment in Virginia or anywhere else in America in favor of independence from Britain; in fact, in the late summer of 1774 Jefferson himself was at least a year away from embracing that fateful step. And yet to Jefferson and many throughout the colonies, imperial relations had by the summer of 1774 already become "intolerable." The immediate provocation for the "intemperance of Jefferson's language" in expressing his "indignation" toward the British Parliament and the king in the *Summary View* was the so-called Intolerable Acts, which had in the spring of 1774 closed the port of Boston, altered the charter of Massachusetts Bay, and removed local jurisdiction in certain classes of judicial cases to the imperial metropolis of London thousands of miles away.[9]

It was in the highly charged atmosphere of the summer of 1774 that Jefferson assumed his role as a patriot of national stature. This was the critical moment when what had long been the distinctively harmonious conditions of imperial government in Virginia were so precipitously transformed. It was an acute crisis of conflicting inclinations, not only as to matters of official policy but also with respect to the individual views of nearly every engaged American Whig.[10]

Jefferson's views developed in the immediate context of a series of events that forced him not only to decide where he stood on the imperial question, but also to articulate his position in a conspicuous way. When word of the Boston Port Bill, the first of the Intolerable Acts, reached Virginia, Jefferson joined his fellow burgesses in resolving to observe a ceremonial "Day of Fasting, Humiliation, and Prayer" on May 24 to show solidarity with the "Sister Colony of Massachusetts Bay." This pious colonial protest was enough to provoke Lord Dunmore, the royal governor, to dissolve the assembly. Undaunted, the burgesses promptly reassembled in a Williamsburg tavern—without official sanction—in order to pursue their campaign of protest. That next phase of the campaign came on May 27, when thirty-nine members of the "Late House" signed an "association," or agreement, urging limited nonimportation restrictions against the East India Company. This deliberately moderate measure was taken, again, in solidarity with the "sister colony" to the north, but also from what the subscribers said was a concern for the "security of our just, antient, and constitutional rights." Very soon, however, word came down from Boston that a much more general scheme of nonimportation by all the colonies was considered "absolutely necessary." Having already considered but rejected measures so extreme, at least for the moment, the burgesses slowed the recent dramatic pace of events in Virginia by adjourning until August 1, by which time the members could better learn and shape the prevailing sense of their constituents.[11]

Jefferson took advantage of this hiatus. It was then, sometime during the following two months, that he conceived and drafted what became the *Summary View*. During this period he also helped compose several other notable documents.

With John Walker, Jefferson's fellow Albemarle County delegate to the upcoming Virginia Convention (the reconstituted House of Burgesses), Jefferson issued a printed call to his constituents for the "fast day" on which the former House had decided. And he and Walker couched their call in terms of anxious concern about "the dangers which threaten our *civil rights*, and all the evils of civil war."[12] But in another public document of about the same time, and almost certainly from Jefferson's pen alone, the rights talk became notably richer, more general, complex, and emphatic. In a set of "Resolutions," presented to and adopted by the freeholders of Albemarle County and effectively addressed both to the members of the upcoming August 1 Virginia Convention and to the upcoming Continental Congress, Jefferson embraced the thoroughgoing nonimportation measures at which Virginia had earlier balked. And Jefferson justified this advanced position by moving far beyond the "civil rights" he and Walker had recently invoked.

Jefferson's "Resolutions" were predicated on a sweeping congeries of "rights": "the common rights of mankind"; *both* "the natural and legal rights" of Americans; "the rights of the British empire in general"; and "constitutional rights." These categories of rights might be analytically distinct, but they were invoked in such a discursive way as to seem interdependent and mutually reinforcing. In similar fashion, Jefferson's brief draft, "Declaration of Rights," apparently "drawn up in order to give effect to the Albemarle Resolutions," invoked, as if in one breath, this same congeries of rights: "the common rights of mankind"; the Americans' "natural and legal rights"; "the rights of the British empire in general"; and the "constitutional rights" of all British subjects.[13]

In this respect, as in others, there is noticeable "similarity" between, on the one hand, the July 26 "Resolutions" and the companion "Declaration" and, on the other, the virtually contemporaneous but much more elaborate *Summary View*. For there is similarly a remarkable, albeit even greater, variety of rights claims in the *Summary View*, which Jefferson prepared for the

August convention in Williamsburg, but which illness supposedly prevented him from presenting in person. Nevertheless, thanks to the generous offices of convention chairman Peyton Randolph, Jefferson's document circulated informally among the convention delegates and was then laid on the table for consideration as a set of draft instructions to the Virginia delegates to the upcoming Continental Congress.[14]

In its broadest outlines, the document Randolph presented on Jefferson's behalf can be read as falling into five distinct sections. The first is a single paragraph stating, and undertaking to justify, the principal resolution in question: that the congressional delegates from Virginia be instructed to propose an address by the Congress to the king, to communicate not only the Americans' "united complaints," but also their growing sense of frustration, together with their "hope" that this first "joint address" to the monarch would bring redress of their grievances.

The second section of the document, more than four very long paragraphs, recurs to history, loosely culled and interpreted, to authenticate a wide ambit of colonial autonomy. This section touches on the ancient Saxon migration to England and the earliest British migration to America, as well as the vicissitudes of English imperial rule during the tumultuous seventeenth century and under William and Mary, Anne, and the first two Georges.

Having thus "hastened thro' the reigns which preceded" that of George III, in the third section Jefferson turns to a commentary on the conduct of the British Parliament in its governance of the empire during the current reign, when the new English orthodoxy of parliamentary supremacy had come to mean for America a regime of escalating parliamentary "tyranny," lately culminating in the "utter ruin" and "annihilation of the town of Boston."

At the beginning of the fourth and longest section of the document, Jefferson turns—and a momentous turn it was[15]—to "proceed to consider the conduct of his majesty, as holding the executive powers of the laws of these [American] states, and mark out his deviations from the line of duty." In its length, daring, emphasis, and conceptual complexity, this section—stating and explaining shared American "grievances" against the king himself—stands as the center of gravity of Jefferson's somewhat ungainly text.

Altogether consonant with this central fourth section, the fifth and final section, one long paragraph, is an implicit ultimatum in the form of an impassioned plea and "prayer" to the king that invoked "fraternal love and harmony" as the fundamental principle of imperial relations.

II

This overview of Jefferson's text is offered only by way of introduction. But it might already begin to suggest that the ambivalence and ambiguity that have, over the years, led to such widely different (and sometimes internally inconsistent) characterizations of the *Summary View.*

For example, in 1948 Anthony Lewis published a highly regarded essay that makes a sustained argument for the importance of the *Summary View* in the Jeffersonian canon. Among all Jefferson's public papers, Lewis writes, "only [Jefferson's] first inaugural address invites as broad a canvass of his political principles as does the *Summary View.*" Lewis sees the pamphlet as an "earnestly" drawn and submitted "plan for preserving" the imperial connection: "It was in the distribution of powers among agencies of [imperial] government—the real task of statesmen—that Jefferson made his distinctive contribution." At the same time, however, Lewis does not slight the importance of the pamphlet as a rights tract. He argues that Jefferson's "goal was a defense of all rights *of the individual* which alone could lend fullest expression to life in the new world." "*Essentially,*" says Lewis—in apparent contradiction to his claim that Jefferson's pamphlet should be read as a "Chart of Political Union"—"this manifesto of 1774 was a bulwark of personal rights."[16]

As striking as it might be to modern readers, this ambiguity in Lewis's reading of the *Summary View* might not have seemed important or even perceptible to many of Jefferson's contemporaries. If we recall, for example, the common ground in "custom—both English and local"—that American Whigs took *both* for their various rights claims *and* for their overall conception of federated imperial government, Lewis's variously formulated characterizations of the *Summary View* might amount to an authentic representation of its meaning, without the least trace of internal contradiction.[17]

Just as complex in approach, just as hesitant to reduce the *Summary View* to a single meaning, is the only other study of the pamphlet that, I believe, matches Lewis's in erudition and subtlety. I refer to the essay published in 1974 by the veteran editor of the *Jefferson Papers,* Julian Boyd, and entitled unabashedly in the essentialist mode, "Jefferson's Expression of the American Mind." Boyd takes a revisionist approach that paradoxically makes both more and less of the *Summary View* than anyone had ever made of it before. As his title indicates, Boyd finds in the *Summary View* an historic "expression of the American mind" in general—from 1774 to the present—an expression superseded only by the more "mature" Declaration of Independence two years later. To Boyd, the essence of what the two documents share is their articulation of the principle that any and all power of government is held exclusively as a matter of "public trust." [18]

Yet, even while Boyd ultimately characterizes the *Summary View* as nothing less than a visionary statement of the American public mind about the fundamental principle of government, his account of the pamphlet's genesis suggests that it was a calculated tactical maneuver by Jefferson, intended to give fuel to Patrick Henry's famously rousing oratory on behalf of the Whig cause.

For it is well established that the (ostensibly) indisposed Jefferson sent not one but two copies of his pamphlet to Williamsburg for the meeting of the August convention: one to Peyton Randolph, who, as I have said, made sure it got a thoughtful hearing; and the other to Henry who, for whatever reason, utterly ignored it, at least for the public purposes of the moment. In an ingenious but controversial formulation, Boyd concludes that what Jefferson had chiefly in mind never came to pass: Jefferson hoped that Henry, the great patriot orator, would use the hastily composed draft as a fund of information and argument for another of Henry's incendiary speeches before the most important assemblage of Virginia's leaders.

Thus ignored by Patrick Henry, mooted in a gathering of notables at Peyton Randolph's house, and presented to, but not surprisingly rejected by, the Virginia Convention, Jefferson's text nevertheless soon became so widely published that it took on a life of its own. To understand the *Summary View* we need to understand Jefferson's intentions and the circumstances in which he wrote; we also need to understand the assumptions and predilections of his American and British readers. But without disregarding those contexts—indeed, in light of them—an attentive reading of Jefferson's text not only supports complex interpretations, such as those by Lewis and Boyd. It also shows that Jefferson's ideas about rights defy simple characterization; they cannot be aligned with any single "tradition" whatsoever.

III

In a brief essay such as this, I can only begin to suggest some of the problems of ambivalence, ambiguity, and perhaps even expediency that characterize Jefferson's talk about rights in the *Summary View.*

To begin, however, I would point out that, however much or little Jefferson relies on the authority of history to advance his argument, his detailed attention to history in the *Summary View* reveals his sense of the manifest contingency of rights talk, indeed, its chronic ineffectiveness and feebleness. "Rights," in Jefferson's account, have proved over time to be a slender reed, often broken, in support of the freedom and happiness of those who have invoked them. This point is too often overlooked in the perennial debate over how and how much Jefferson "argued from history" in the *Summary View.*

As my brief review of Jefferson's text has already indicated, Jefferson did attend at length to history in these draft instructions to Congress. Dumas Malone warns us that Jefferson's historical data were sketchy at best, and in some respects inaccurate—as Jefferson himself later acknowledged—and even unfair to the British imperial position. But as Malone sees it, Jefferson's inaccuracies were beside the point, which is that Jefferson's "mind craved historical as well as philosophical authority, and that he could not be content without finding precedent somewhere [particularly in the ancient Saxon migration to England] for the freedom he was so sure was right." [19]

Morton White rejects this view, insisting instead that Jefferson's appeals in the *Summary View* to the authority of history were but a cannily assembled batch of what might be called "forensic facts." [20] White interprets a passage from Jefferson's Autobiography as a confession that while he was conceiving and preparing the *Summary View,* Jefferson "rummaged over" the historical record quite selectively, and entirely for self-serving, pretextual purposes. [21]

Merrill Peterson and Trevor Colbourn have taken a subtler, intermediate position on the extent to which Jefferson's rights claims rested on the authority of history. Peterson reminds us that it was "thoroughly characteristic of Jefferson" to "blend" an appeal to the authority of the "rational" and "universal" principles of "the natural rights philosophy" with an appeal to the authority of the real Whig version of English constitutional history. And Colbourn, noting Jefferson's special regard for the urbane "country" persuasion of its most influential English exponent, concludes that "Jefferson rather used the past as Bolingbroke prescribed—'philosophy teaching by examples'. . . . [Jefferson] was imbued with sufficient eighteenth-century optimism to believe that an awakened historical consciousness would be adequate in warning of encroachments of tyranny in all its predictable forms." [22]

However much Jefferson ultimately *relies* on his arguments from history in the *Summary View,* they do comprise a large part of his text. He goes on at great length to discuss the fortunes of rights, rights claims, and rights enforcement in Anglo-American history. And it is not an account that testifies strongly to the relation between "rights" claims and the security of property, freedom, or happiness. To the contrary, Jefferson's tells a story that emphasizes the historic ineffectiveness of rights talk. Indeed, in more than one place in his account, he suggests that mere act of claiming a right sometimes simply makes matters worse.

There is some irony here in the fact that the text of Jefferson's *Summary View* affords so much documentary support for James Madison's later assertion (soon recanted) that affirming rights, even in official declarations and bills of rights, does nothing more than erect repeatedly violated "parchment barriers" against abuses of power. Jefferson eventually helped persuade Madison to change his mind on this matter as the great debate was joined over whether to add a bill of rights to the proposed new federal Constitution of 1787. But the irony is even greater when we note that at the very moment Jefferson was composing the *Summary View,* "the young James Madison . . . was intrigued . . . by the possibility that [an American] Bill of Rights might be adopted by Congress and confirmed by the King or Parliament, such that America's liberties would be 'as firmly fixed, and defined as those of England were at the [Glorious R]evolution.'" And Madison was not alone at this moment in hoping to resolve the imperial crisis through an explicit agreement on "rights." Among others, Elbridge Gerry, Arthur Lee, and even Samuel Adams seriously discussed "a hypothetical 'American Bill of Rights,' looking back to the English Bill of Rights established in 1689." [23]

By contrast, Jefferson apparently never seriously considered such a squarely rights-based solution to the imperial crisis. And, as I have said, much of his *Summary View,* especially in its attention to history, both recent and distant, evinces little faith in the utility of such articulations of rights. Or, better to say perhaps, Jefferson's text suggests a marked ambivalence in the matter.

The theme of Jefferson's review of Anglo-American history is that rights can be and have been frequently "injured" and "invaded." As Jefferson portrays the historical record, such violations of American rights became the norm almost from the outset: "Not long were [the British emigrants to America] permitted, however far they thought themselves removed from the hand of oppression, to hold undisturbed the rights thus acquired at the hazard of their lives and loss of their fortunes." Here is Jefferson arguing for, or at least asserting, what has been aptly termed the rights of "emigration purchase": that Americans purchased a certain measure of autonomy from Britain by assuming the costs of emigrating to and settling an untamed land. [24]

But, again, I am not concerned here with the scholarly debate over the origins, originality, or authority of Jefferson's notion of rights created through emigration. John Phillip Reid argues that this was a right long familiar in the writings of European thinkers, and stated even more "absolutely" by Burlamaqui, for one, than Jefferson ever stated it. Nor am I interested here in cognate formulations of this notion of emigration rights espoused by some of Jefferson's American Whig contemporaries.[25]

Rather, my immediate concern is a theme or motif that Jefferson's own historical account in the *Summary View* manifestly emphasizes: the fragility, vulnerability, and manipulability of rights claims in the actual historical experience of the American colonists. According to Jefferson, during repeated episodes of Stuart tyranny, the crown was able to invoke rights talk quite effectively to justify carving up America into "distinct and independent governments" entirely for the crown's own selfish purposes. During the Commonwealth regime for a brief period, the rights of the American colonies were better respected. But "upon the restoration" of the Stuarts, colonial rights—for example the right Jefferson asserts to "free trade" for America—"fell once more victim to arbitrary power."[26]

And when Jefferson turns to more recent history, his sense becomes even more acute that the meaning and content of rights are a function of political contingency. Under George II, Parliament callously "sacrificed" American rights out of its own exorbitant "avarice."[27] Much worse still, violations of Americans' rights under George III became alarmingly more frequent than ever before; and these violations were effectively perpetrated in the very name of a right, through the assertion (generally accepted in Britain) of a "parliamentary right" to govern America.[28] Thus Jefferson faces up to the reality that the rights of British America are in prevailing English constitutional theory, and all too often in English imperial practice, hostage to the myopic and corrupt politics of the metropolis. If in principle "force cannot give right," in practice the British government has sought to enforce its "right" by sending "large bodies of armed forces" to America "from time to time." And if such an assumed "right as this" can be sustained in practice on the basis of the malleable language of "rights"—even though in truth "his majesty has no right to land a single armed man on our shores"—then the king is in a position to "swallow up all our other rights whenever he should think proper."[29]

Jefferson suggests in the *Summary View* that merely engaging in rights talk can have its costs, as the recent dissolution of the House of Burgesses showed. In more than one recent instance, rights claims have provoked retribution: "To declare as . . . [the] duty of [American legislatures] required the known rights of their country, to oppose the usurpations of every foreign judicature, to disregard the imperious mandates of a minister or governor, have been the avowed causes of dissolving houses of representatives in America." [30]

Nevertheless, the potential costs and dangers of claiming rights hardly deterred Jefferson from drafting a text replete with self-consciously provocative claims. Indeed, he begins his final paragraph, his closing plea and prayer, with assertions of rights bordering on outright defiance: "That these are our grievances which we have thus laid before his majesty with that freedom of language and sentiment which becomes a free people, claiming their rights as derived from the laws of nature, and not as the gift of their chief magistrate. Let those flatter, who fear: it is not an American art. . . . This, Sire, is our last, our determined resolution." [31] And although there is no evidence that Jefferson ever regretted his boldness, he did come to believe that it had put him in personal jeopardy. The London editions of the *Summary View,* together with notice of the work in several British periodicals, brought Jefferson's views to the attention of the metropolitan government. As Jefferson writes in his Autobiography, he "always believed" the report ("probably only a rumor") that his "authorship of *A Summary View* led to his being added to a list of persons named in a bill of attainder passed by the House of Lords but then dropped." [32]

IV

Earlier in this essay, I have pressed the question of Jefferson's *implicit* ambivalence about how much store to put in rights talk. But in the *Summary View* Jefferson goes even further, indicating that during the critical summer of 1774 he *explicitly* turned away from rights talk to an alternative discourse in order to advance the cause and principles dearest to him. For in what I have called the third section of the *Summary View,* which recounts the "facts" of parliamentary tyranny in preparation for the indictment of and appeal to the king, Jefferson expressly sets aside rights claims. After showing that the language of rights has so often been successfully used to "injure" and "invade" the rights of British America, his argument takes this crucial turn: "Let us for a while suppose the question of right suspended, in order to examine this act [the Boston Port Bill] on principles of *justice.*" [33]

Only several paragraphs before taking this turn, Jefferson, in reviewing some of the most egregiously unjust legislation during the reign of George II, had gone out of his way to say, "We do not point out to his majesty the injustice of these acts with intent to rest on that principle the cause of their nullity, but to shew that experience confirms the propriety of those principles which exempt us from the jurisdiction of the British parliament. . . . [P]arliament has no *right* to exercise authority over us." Thus Jefferson by no means abandons the Americans' rights claims. But as he moves toward the central and most distinctive part of the *Summary View*—his consideration of George III's conduct and capacity—Jefferson moves beyond arguments based on "rights" to arguments based on the larger, ultimate standard of "justice." And even where his rights talk has been most distinctive and emphatic, he has introduced it in terms of his concern that there is no equal "justice" in the governance of the British federal empire. "One of these conclusions must necessarily follow," he laments, "either that justice is not the same thing in America as in Britain, or else that the British parliament pay less regard to it here than there." In this way Jefferson moves beyond the strictly legal and constitutional niceties of "rights," and even the "higher" principles of "natural rights philosophy," in order to take account of the reality that rights as matters of politics—relationships of power—ultimately derive from the predominant, and historically contingent, expectations of each distinctive society: "An exasperated people, who feel that they possess power, are not easily restrained within limits strictly regular." [34]

Jefferson refers to the authoritative expectations of British Americans when he says at the outset of the *Summary View* that it has been "penned in the language of truth." Constitutionalism, law, and politics are much more shaped by the prevailing local view of what is "right" than by opinion on matters of "rights." Thus setting aside the "rights" question, Jefferson ascends to the ultimate issue of "justice," that is, the well-settled sense of justice that obtains in British America. Whatever the constitutional or legal arguments, or the precepts of natural rights philosophy, "the great principles of right and wrong are legible to every reader [not least, the king]; to pursue them requires not the aid of many counsellors." And thus Jefferson's ultimate appeal to the king is that the king do nothing more or less than "quiet the minds of [his] subjects in British America against any apprehensions of future encroachment" on what they have come to feel—no less than their fellow subjects in Britain—to be not only their "rights" but what is "right" and "just." This is the distinctive Jeffersonian voice that Charles Peter Hoffer has helped us hear: the Jeffersonian plea for equitable justice that grew out of, but ultimately outgrew, its source in English legal culture. [35]

After all, as Robert Webking remarks, "most of the grievances Jefferson offers against the king are not about actions of the king that directly violate colonial rights." Jefferson's appeal to the king is much broader than any legal, constitutional, or even natural rights claims could compass. When Jefferson pleads, "Open your breast Sire, to liberal and expanded thought," he is indeed pleading for "those who are asserting the rights of human nature." But his appeal is not by any means restricted to justification in terms of rights.[36]

And if there could be any doubt that in his hierarchy of values in the *Summary View* "justice" ranks even higher than his concern over "rights," Jefferson resolves the matter by making it clear that he is quite willing for the Americans not only to trade away but even to "sacrifice" some of their rights—as long as the "terms" of the sacrifice are "just":[37]

> We are willing on our part [says Jefferson] to sacrifice every thing which reason can ask to the restoration of that tranquility for which all must wish. On their part [in Great Britain] let them be ready to establish union on a generous plan. Let them name their terms, but let them be just. Accept of every commercial preference it is in our power to give for such things as we can raise for their use, or they make for ours. But let them not think to exclude us from going to other markets, to dispose of those commodities which they cannot use, nor to supply those wants which they cannot supply.[38]

Moreover, in pleading for the king to intercede, in the name of justice, between a victimizing Parliament and the victimized British American colonies, by means of the crown's veto over legislation, Jefferson is all but rejecting the fundamental premise of the prevailing English Whig theory of rights. According to that theory, the Revolutionary Settlement had guaranteed political stability to eighteenth-century Britain, leading to unparalleled prosperity at home and unprecedented power abroad. To ask a Hanoverian monarch in 1774 to thwart the will of Parliament would have struck many Englishmen as a request for the king to undo the Glorious Revolution, to turn Tory against his own Whig government and the Whig consensus of the English political nation itself. In this respect Jefferson's plea and prayer moves outside, beyond, above the "Glorious" British rights tradition of the time, even as that rights tradition had come to integrate constitutional and legal rights with natural rights.[39]

It is worth noting in this regard how much less emphasis there is on "rights" in Jefferson's composition draft of the *Declaration of the Causes and Necessity for Taking Up Arms,* written in the early summer of 1775, than there is in the *Summary View.*[40] In later years Jefferson more than once reconsidered and rather deprecated what he had written about rights in the 1774 pamphlet. "If it had any merit," he wrote in 1809, "it was that of first taking the true ground, and that which was afterwards assumed and maintained." In 1815 he explained his point more fully: the *Summary View*'s "only merit was in being the first publication which carried the claim of our rights their whole length, and asserted that there was no rightful link of connection between us and England but that of being under the same king."[41] Even this latter-day Jefferson, who had done so much to establish and preserve and expand the new American nation, viewed in retrospect the "rights" issue of the summer of 1774 largely in terms of the larger issue that Anthony Lewis sees in the text of the *Summary View:* What is the "rightful," the just relationship of power and authority within a federated empire?

Even making allowances for Jefferson's characteristic modesty and complaisance, such remarks raise questions about how much of the *Summary View* he fully endorsed in retrospect. There can be little doubt that Jefferson proudly stood behind a passage in the *Summary View* that he had formulated with distinctive emphasis: "The true ground on which we declare these acts [of Parliament] void is that the British parliament has no right to exercise authority over us."[42] But among Jefferson's more than 6,000 words there is a great deal of talk about rights that reaches beyond this central contention about the right to legislate. Jefferson ultimately seems to have discounted much of it.

v

What can look to modern readers like ambivalence and ambiguity in Jefferson's varied and shifting rights talk in the *Summary View* is better understood when we recall that in Revolutionary America, thinking about "rights" was undergoing a profound transformation. Perhaps the most important aspect of this transformation was the process by which less and less emphasis was coming to be placed on the meaning of rights "in the early modern sense[,] as restraints on arbitrary government," while at the same time rights were coming more and more to be "conceived of . . . in the modern sense, as instruments for liberating individuals."[43]

Much of the seeming ambivalence and ambiguity in the rights talk of Jefferson's *Summary View* can be resolved by placing Jefferson's text in the very midst of a transition that, according to one recent account, spanned the years from 1750 to the early 1790s. In accepting as I do such an account of the nature of this conceptual change and its timing, I join most contemporary students in rejecting the view of Clinton Rossiter (writing in

1953) and others who have concluded that in America the "Revolutionary thinkers were completely oriented to individualism in their discussions of the purpose of political community."[44]

The text of Jefferson's *Summary View* is a *locus classicus* of a complex rights discourse in America that combined a commitment to "individualism" as a fundamental political value with the concern for the communitarian values so prevalent in early modern Britain and America. Indeed, it might not be too much to say that Jefferson's rights talk of 1774 even harks back in some ways to the joint concern for individual and corporate, or group, rights that some scholars have detected in medieval and early modern political thought. In the *Summary View* there is at least as much talk about the "rights" of groups, and even the rights of institutions of government, as there is talk of the rights of individuals. From this perspective the *Summary View* can be said to exemplify John Murrin's overall judgment that in "Jefferson's public universe [the communitarian orientation of] moral sentiment and civic humanism *governed* his unmistakable fondness" for a Lockean conception of rights that sanctioned "the frank pursuit of economic self-interest."[45]

In any case, as one careful reader of Jefferson has quipped, "Jefferson's pamphlet might accurately have been titled 'A Summary View of the *Several Kinds* of Rights of British America.'"[46] I would go somewhat further: the *Summary View* includes talk about not just several but *many* kinds of rights; and they are rights so vastly different in basic conceptualization that, taken as a whole, the transitional rights talk of the *Summary View* evinces ambivalence and ambiguity to the point of incoherence. But, again, to say this is not to render a hostile judgment of Jefferson. Rather, it is to suggest that his was an exceptionally faithful and eloquent voice in representing the groping, transitional American Whig political thought of the moment.

After all, when we look at the text of the *Summary View,* we see express references to the rights not only of individuals, but also of all British Americans, and even more broadly of "the people." Broader and even more prescient are references to the rights of "human nature," which Jefferson daringly ascribes even to the chattel slaves "imported" from Africa. Yet there is recognition too, as we have seen, of the idea that the particular rights of more circumscribed groups or entities are to be respected in principle, even when the content of those rights is in dispute. The "rights of Englishmen" are of special importance to Jefferson, if only for their value as an "invented tradition"[47] of uniquely historical authority in both Britain and America. But Jefferson also recognizes as legitimate categories the rights of Parliament, of legislatures in general, and of the king. And he joins those think-ers in Europe and America who contend for recognition of "emigrants" as a distinct class of rights bearers.

My point is to emphasize that in the *Summary View* Jefferson hardly re-stricts his rights discourse to claims of natural rights, much less to the rights of individuals. The pamphlet, in fact, features more instances of talk about the rights of groups and institutions than about the rights of individ-uals. In future years and dramatically different contexts, Jefferson's ap-proach to defining categories of rights remained equally capacious. Fifteen years after drafting the *Summary View,* Jefferson wrote Thomas Paine from Paris about ideas under discussion there that Jefferson endorsed for realiz-ing the promise of the French Revolution; these included a constitutional plan for France that recognized not only the celebrated "rights of man," but also the "Rights of the nation. Rights of the king. Rights of the citi-zens . . . [and] rights of the national assembly."[48]

Indeed, if one is seeking an unambivalently, unambiguously, essentially "modern" rights theorist from among the many eloquent rights spokesmen of the American Revolutionary generations, Tom Paine fits the bill much better than does the Jefferson of 1774 or of any time thereafter. I endorse Jack P. Greene's suggestion that it was Paine more than anyone else in Revolutionary America who "modernized political consciousness," in this respect as in many others. But if Paine's rights discourse is in some respects more "modern" than Jefferson's, one might still trace contemporary Amer-ican thinking about rights to Jefferson's more complex and ambiguous con-ception. If America is today a predominantly liberal regime of self-regarding citizens who interpret the public interest in terms of private interest and who typically vote their pocketbooks, then the *Summary View* can look quite visionary in its rights talk. After all, the *Summary View* can be read—as it must have been by many Britons in 1774—as representing little more than "the determination of Virginia tobacco planters to repu-diate their large debts to British merchants." Some of our most knowledge-able historians continue to read the *Summary View* as a manifesto of purely economic self-interest, if not necessarily as a ploy to repudiate debts.[49]

Such is the reading of Joseph Ernst, who acknowledges that Jefferson's *Summary View* and other protests from the Chesapeake region in the summer of 1774 were integral to the emerging American "independence move-ment." But Ernst insists that during that pivotal summer, independence was "not a foregone conclusion"; instead, the Virginians were at that point simply seeking to achieve "economic sovereignty."[50]

Without speculating about the aims of Virginia's political leaders during the summer of 1774, and without denying Jefferson's primary identification as a Virginian, Dumas Malone concludes that Jefferson's interests had already become "far more than provincial; they had assumed a continental scope."[51] The title of Jefferson's pamphlet, referring to all of "British America," might not have come from his pen, but his text resonates with a sense of identification with distant sister colonies. Given this identification, it is appropriate to ask whether and how Jefferson's rights talk was intended to promote union and a shared American identity.

In raising this question, I do not mean to discount the importance of "justice" as Jefferson's overriding end. The two ends would hardly have struck a "strong unionist" like Jefferson as in the least incompatible. And if one wants to take the view that Jefferson's extraordinary farrago of rights talk in the *Summary View* was a response, a solution, intended or otherwise, to a "problem," then there is reason to ask, with respect to the crisis of the moment in imperial relations in the summer of 1774, wasn't the weak sense of shared "American" identity as much a problem as the "injustice" of imperial administration? Indeed, weren't the two issues, for all American Whig political purposes, inseparable?[52]

The contextual and textual evidence for Jefferson's anxious concern for the welfare of Virginia's sister colonies makes it difficult to disregard this question about the relationship between Jefferson's conceptually incoherent talk about rights in the *Summary View* and his possibly controlling aim to consolidate American Whig sentiment beyond Virginia. The pamphlet's publication history strongly suggests that Jefferson's loosely crafted but vehemently expressed performance was most immediately important for what it accomplished in fomenting an early, if still inchoate, feeling of national identity.

VI

The various questions that I have raised about the meaning and significance of Jefferson's *Summary View* might well go beyond this single text. They might extend to Jefferson's talk about rights far beyond 1774, or to "Jeffersonianism" more broadly conceived, or even to the way we talk about rights today.

At the very least, these questions go to 1776, to the Declaration of Independence. According to some Jefferson scholars, it was largely owing to the continental reputation Jefferson had earned by virtue of the *Summary View* that he was selected to draft what became the most historic rights manifesto of the nineteenth and twentieth centuries. The respective texts of the *Summary View* and of the Declaration invite us to consider the close-ness of their relationship, if only because of the way Jefferson in both cases focuses on the failure of the monarch, the Americans' last resort, to do justice—both to the crown's constitutional duties and to the broader "rec-titude" of the grievances of imperial subjects who would remain loyal were they not abandoned and betrayed by the crown.[53]

We have already seen, however, that some probing historians have read the *Summary View* on its own terms, without an eye to its eventual signifi-cance as a step toward the rhetoric of rights in the Declaration of Indepen-dence. I can only suggest some of the many ways the *Summary View* has been described. Jefferson himself, thirty years after its composition, called the pamphlet a "Remonstrance."[54] On its face it was a "Draft of Instruc-tions to the Virginia Delegates in the Continental Congress."[55] It was also a set of "resolutions" and a "petition" to the king. In historical perspective, it has looked like a "chart of [imperial] union," a legal "brief," or at least a preliminary memorandum for a brief about law (or equity), a device useful for political posturing on the part of the Virginia Convention of 1774, a declaration of "economic sovereignty" for Virginia, and even a set of speech writer's notes for one of the greatest American orators of the age—not to mention another historic step toward a consolidated American identity, or even a timeless "expression of the American mind."

Here I have meant to approach the relationship between Jefferson and the keyword "rights" in the way Joyce Appleby has approached the rela-tionship between Jefferson and "liberalism." I have dwelt on the complexi-ties of the relationship. Jefferson's rights talk was no simpler, no more "mindless" than was his liberalism. So that when it comes to scrupulous historical interpretation of Jefferson's visionary rights talk and its lasting significance, it is important to take into account as much of the textual and contextual record as possible. In Appleby's words, "The values and beliefs that informed Jefferson's 'Americanism' must be *located* and made more pre-cise."[56]

In trying to "locate" Jefferson's rights talk in the *Summary View* with some precision, I have found myself continually questioning the nature and centrality of his concern over rights. John Phillip Reid is surely correct that in the late eighteenth century "Americans took rights seriously," even if his conception of those rights is somewhat narrower than the American colo-nists and Revolutionaries would recognize as their own.[57] And Reid has a good point, when quoting Edmund Burke, that many Americans of that era were so anxious about threats to their rights that they tended to "snuff [i.e., sniff] the approach of tyranny in every tainted breeze."[58] Yet, on the evidence of Jefferson's most elaborate and extensive discourse on rights, there is reason to question whether Jefferson should be grouped among the "rights fetishists"[59] of his day. Rather than fixating on rights per se, in the "paranoid style" of the times, Jefferson in his *Summary View* economizes on rights talk, never relying on it exclusively. Indeed, I would argue that the basic thrust of his argument does not depend on rights talk at all.

Even in his most wide-ranging consideration of rights, Malone concedes, "Jefferson gave no general statement of the doctrine of natural rights"[60]— or, for that matter, of any other doctrine or theory of rights, constitutional, legal, or otherwise. Some modern scholars of Jefferson's ideas have regarded him as a true "philosopher."[61] But on the evidence of the *Summary View,* there is reason to question whether Jefferson ever formulated—or intended to formulate—a "philosophy" of "rights."

To question Jefferson's status as a "philosopher" of rights is, however, not to deny him a preeminent role in the history of the development of rights talk, in America and the world. Although Jefferson, a talented and accomplished lawyer, might not have ranked among the very best legal minds of the Revolutionary generations,[62] the forensic dimension of his rights discourse has inspired some of the best legal minds of later generations, not to mention political thinkers and leaders, and countless peoples thinking and acting on their own account.

It is interesting, then, and perhaps significant in more ways than have yet been appreciated, that when Jefferson wrote his *Summary View* he had been studying and then both studying and practicing law as his "principal occupation" for more than a decade. And although in 1774 he was in the process of retiring from law practice, he never turned away from the law altogether, as his tireless efforts at law reform in early national Virginia amply testify.[63]

But more to my point, Jefferson's historically resonant rights talk has never resonated more with American lawyers than it does today. In 1983, for example, Louis Henkin, our leading expert on the contemporary international significance of American conceptions of rights, delivered the "Thomas Jefferson Lectures" at the University of Pennsylvania Law School. In his recently published *The Age of Rights,* the book based on those lectures, Henkin not only proclaims both "Jefferson's time" and "ours" an age of rights, he looks particularly to Jefferson's "theory of rights" as the guide for what we should be trying to accomplish both in American constitutional law and in the greater domain of international human rights.[64]

It is, among other things, this sort of continuing talismanic significance of Jefferson in modern-day rights talk that obliges us to "locate" Jefferson's ideas, even his most visionary ideas, as "precisely" as we can. In doing so we encounter questions about how accurate—however ultimately salutary[65]—it is, after all, to invoke Jefferson as uncritically as Henkin and others do in order to legitimate a rights-based reform of American constitutional law and of international law.

Such questions, which I have portrayed Jefferson himself as raising, or at least prompting, encourage a critical reconsideration of the distinctively American penchant for formulating controversial discourse on legal, political, and social questions almost exclusively in terms of "rights"—as Jefferson did *not* in his *Summary View.* Thus, from the perspective I have been endorsing here, it is the thoughtfully ambivalent critics of our Anglo-American rights culture, of the civic capability of any idea of "rights," who sound the most "Jeffersonian," whether or not they happen to invoke Jefferson.

The legal scholar Mary Ann Glendon is only one of the most recent of such critics. In her book *Rights Talk: The Impoverishment of Political Discourse,* Glendon aims, she says, "to trace the evolution of our distinctive rights dialect, and to show it frequently works against the conditions required for the pursuit of dignified living by free women and men . . . to demonstrate how our simplistic rights talk simultaneously reflects and distorts American culture" in all its richness and complexity. Among her many criticisms of our rights talk today is a familiar point that Professor Reid has abundantly documented with respect to Jefferson's own day: that the very conception of "rights" is historically and functionally derived from the idea of "property."[66]

Decades ago Hannah Arendt asked us to consider the costs to "freedom" and "public happiness" and other superseding values we may have incurred on account of the American Revolutionary legacy. What Reid has called the essential "'propertyness' of rights" was well established in Anglo-American constitutionalism and law by the time of a Revolution, which may have entrenched "prosperity" as the controlling end of American government from the outset.[67] Arendt surmised, as well—specifically in the text of *Summary View*—that Jefferson was giving voice to a distinctive American "dissatisfaction" with the limited capability of conventional rights talk, at least in so far as talking merely about rights failed to express and promote Americans' "quest" for a felt sense of "public happiness."[68]

Sympathetic critics of the hypostatized American "rights tradition" hardly conceal their engagement with contemporary political concerns. In this there is nothing at all un-Jeffersonian.[69] Indeed, when we revisit the *Summary View* to consider what Jefferson said and intimated there about

rights, then contemporary critics of American rights talk would appear to
be redeeming an authentic Jeffersonian vision from one of Jefferson's own
most visionary moments.

NOTES

It would be impossible for me to thank here everyone who has helped me substantially
with this essay, but I cannot fail to mention Lance Banning, Saul Cornell, Peter Hoffer,
Rick Matthews, Chuck Miller, John Murrin, Peter Onuf, John Scanlan, and Avi Soifer.

1. Thomas L. Haskell, "The Curious Persistence of Rights Talk in the 'Age of Interpretation,'" in David Thelen, ed., *The Constitution and American Life* (Ithaca, N.Y., 1987), pp.
324–52; Lawrence M. Friedman, *The Republic of Choice: Law, Authority, and Culture* (Cam-
bridge, Mass., 1990); Joseph William Singer, "The Legal Rights Debate in Analytical
Jurisprudence from Bentham to Hohfeld," *Wisconsin Law Review* (1982), pp. 975–1059.
Also see the discussion in Morton J. Horwitz, "Rights," *Harvard Civil Rights–Civil Liberties
Law Review*, 23 (1988), pp. 393–406. Daniel T. Rodgers, *Contested Truths: Keywords in
American Politics Since Independence* (New York, 1987), pp. 3–16 and 45–79.

2. Henry Steele Commager, *Jefferson, Nationalism and the Enlightenment* (New York,
1975), p. 73; cf. Noble E. Cunningham, Jr., *In Pursuit of Reason: The Life of Thomas Jefferson*
(Baton Rouge, La., 1987), p. xv. TJ to Major John Cartwright, June 5, 1824, *LofA*, p.
1494.

3. At least this is the impression one can take away from scanning some of the standard
collections of his writings, not least the chronologically arranged *Papers of Thomas Jefferson*
in the authoritative modern edition so entitled, which thus far covers the years from 1760
through 1792. *Boyd*, I–XXIV. Others include *The Complete Jefferson: Containing His Major
Writings, Published and Unpublished, Except His Letters*, Saul K. Padover, ed. (New York,
1943); *The Jeffersonian Cyclopedia*, John P. Foley, ed. (New York, 1900); *LofA; L&B*, I–XX.

4. John Chester Miller, *The Wolf by the Ears: Thomas Jefferson and Slavery* (Charlottesville,
Va., 1991), p. xii. Leonard W. Levy, *Jefferson & Civil Liberties: The Darker Side* (Cambridge,
Mass., 1963); cf. Levy, "Civil Liberties," in Merrill D. Peterson, ed., *Thomas Jefferson: A
Reference Biography* (New York, 1986), pp. 331–47.

5. Cf. Judith N. Shklar, "Let Us Not Be Hypocritical," in Shklar, *Ordinary Vices* (Cambridge, Mass., 1984), pp. 45–86.

6. Cf. *Malone*, I, 182.

7. Michael P. Zuckert, "Republicanism and American Identity: Thomas Jefferson's Natural Rights Republic," 1991 unpublished essay, p. 2 (kindly shared by the author and
quoted with his permission). Michael P. Zuckert, "Thomas Jefferson on Nature and Natural
Rights," in Robert A. Licht, ed., *The Framers and Fundamental Rights* (Washington, D.C.,
1991), p. 166. Lawrence Henry Gipson, *The Coming of the Revolution, 1763–1775* (New
York, 1954; reprint, 1962), p. 228. Charles A. Miller, *Jefferson and Nature: An Interpretation*
(Baltimore, Md., 1988), p. 165; cf. John Dewey's view that Jefferson "developed . . .
uninterruptedly in one direction," a view quoted with approval in Julian P. Boyd, "Jefferson's Expression of the American Mind," *Virginia Quarterly Review*, 50 (1974), pp. 556–59.
Merrill D. Peterson, *The Jefferson Image in the American Mind* (New York, 1960), esp.
p. 447.

8. See the facsimile edition by Thomas P. Abernethy (New York, 1943), p. 1.

9. *Revolutionary Virginia: The Road to Independence,* comp. William J. Van Schreeven, ed. Robert L. Scribner, 2 vols. (Charlottesville, Va., 1973), I, p. 242. Cunningham, *In Pursuit of Reason,* p. 29. Marie Kimball, *Jefferson: The Road to Glory, 1743 to 1776* (New York, 1943), pp. 272, 275; cf. *Malone,* I, pp. 195–96; Merrill D. Peterson, *Adams and Jefferson: A Revolutionary Dialogue* (Athens, Ga., 1976), pp. 13–14. *Malone,* I, 182.

10. Jack P. Greene, "Society, Ideology, and Politics: An Analysis of the Political Culture of Mid-Eighteenth-Century Virginia," in Richard M. Jellison, ed., *Society, Freedom, and Conscience: The American Revolution in Virginia, Massachusetts, and New York* (New York, 1976), pp. 14–76, 191–201. George M. Curtis III, "The Role of the Courts in the Making of the Revolution in Virginia," in James Kirby Martin, ed., *The Human Dimensions of Nation Making: Colonial and Revolutionary America* (Madison, Wis., 1976), pp. 144–45.

11. *Boyd,* I, pp. 105, 107, 111.

12. *Boyd,* I, p. 116 (emphasis added).

13. *Boyd,* I, pp. 117, 120n.

14. *Boyd,* I, p. 119. Boyd, "Jefferson's Expression of the American Mind," pp. 556–59.

15. Ian R. Christie and Benjamin W. Labaree, *Empire or Independence, 1760–1776: A British-American Dialogue on the Coming of the Revolution* (New York, 1976), p. 206: "In his *Summary View* Jefferson became the first American directly and publicly to criticize George III."

16. Anthony M. Lewis, "Jefferson's *Summary View* as a Chart of Political Union," *WMQ,* V (1948), pp. 46, 50, 48, 46, 50 (in the order quoted here). Cf. Charles R. Ritcheson, *British Politics and the American Revolution* (Norman, Okla., 1954), p. 164 (on the problematic relationship between "the federal principle" and "the inconvenient question of right"); and Charles Howard McIlwain, *The American Revolution: A Constitutional Interpretation* (New York, 1923), 142.

17. See, e.g., Jack P. Greene, *Peripheries and Center: Constitutional Development in the Extended Polities of the British Empire and the United States* (Athens, Ga., 1986), pp. 37–40. And see the approach to this matter taken in Garret Ward Sheldon, *The Political Philosophy of Thomas Jefferson* (Baltimore, Md., 1991), esp. where, on p. 2, Sheldon credits Jefferson with "adapting" Lockean liberalism to "the contingencies of revolutionary colonies seeking independence from a federated empire constructed ideologically from the venerable Ancient Constitution of England"; cf. pp. 16, 17, and 31 (on Jefferson's positing the rights of "free, equal, and independent legislatures" and "free and independent states" within the federated British empire on the authority of an analogy to the Lockean idea of the rights of free, equal, and independent individuals in the "state of nature"); and see the elaboration of Sheldon's argument in this vein on pp. 25–41.

18. Boyd, "Jefferson's Expression of the American Mind," esp. pp. 342 and 362. Cf. Peter Charles Hoffer, *The Law's Conscience: Equitable Constitutionalism in America* (Chapel Hill, N.C., 1990), esp. pp. 70–71; Hoffer, "The Declaration of Independence as a Bill in Equity," in William Pencak and Wythe W. Holt, Jr., eds., *The Law in America, 1607– 1861* (New York, 1989), 189, 195.

19. *Boyd,* I, p. 160. *Malone,* I, p. 185; cf. p. 184. And see *Boyd,* I, p. 191n, on Jefferson's 1775 composition draft of the "Declaration of the Causes and Necessity for Taking Up Arms": "Jefferson [then] conceded that in the past the colonies had occasionally, from warmth and affection, acquiesced in some assumptions of power by Parliament in legislating for the colonies. The concession is a tribute to his historical accuracy and to his sense of justice, but forensically it was a serious admission."

20. John Phillip Reid, *Constitutional History of the American Revolution: [Volume I] The Authority of Rights* (Madison, Wis., 1986), p. 126.

21. Morton White, *The Philosophy of the American Revolution* (New York, 1978), pp. 80–81, n30. White may well have a good point, generally speaking, about Jefferson's selective and willful use of history, but White is patently inaccurate in saying that Jefferson confessed to such rummaging when preparing the *Summary View;* rather, it was in connection with the preparation of the May 24, 1774, Resolution for a day of fasting, humiliation, and prayer that Jefferson confessed that he and his friends did the rummaging in question; see *Boyd,* I, p. 106.

22. Merrill Peterson, "Thomas Jefferson: A Brief Life," in Lally Weymouth, ed., *Thomas Jefferson: The Man, His World, His Influence* (New York, 1973), p. 17. H. Trevor Colbourn, "Thomas Jefferson's Use of the Past," *WMQ,* XV (1958), pp. 68–69.

23. Madison to TJ, October 17, 1788, *PJM,* XI, p. 297. See Adrienne Koch, *Jefferson and Madison: The Great Collaboration* (New York, 1950), pp. 33–61; but see Paul Finkelman, "James Madison and the Bill of Rights," in Gerhard Casper, et al., eds., *1990: The Supreme Court Review* (Chicago, 1991), pp. 328–33. Pauline Maier, *From Resistance to Revolution: Colonial Radicals and the Development of American Opposition to Britain, 1765–1776* (New York, 1972), pp. 245 (quoting Madison to William Bradford, Aug. 1, 1774) and 229. On the Declaration of Rights that the Continental Congress passed in October 1774, see Jack N. Rakove, *The Beginnings of National Politics: An Interpretive History of the Continental Congress* (New York, 1979), pp. 58–59.

24. *Boyd,* I, pp. 121, 123. Reid, *The Authority of Rights,* pp. 114–23 ("The Authority of Migration"). Cf. Jefferson's 1775 "Refutation of the Argument that the Colonies Were Established at the Expense of the British Nation," *Boyd,* I, pp. 277–285.

25. Reid, *The Authority of Rights,* p. 119; cf. Reid, *Constitutional History of the American Revolution: [Volume III] The Authority to Legislate* (Madison, Wis., 1991), pp. 102, 421–422 n. 21). Also see Randolph G. Adams, *Political Ideas of the American Revolution: Britannic-American Contributions to the Problem of Imperial Organization, 1765 to 1775,* 3d ed. (New York, 1958), p. 78 ("Jefferson's position, though not as carefully worked out as [James] Wilson's, was quite similar."); Benjamin Fletcher Wright, *American Interpretations of Natural Law: A Study in the History of Political Thought* (Cambridge, Mass., 1931), pp. 86–87 ("And although Jefferson is by reputation more closely associated with the doctrine of natural rights than any other man of his time, this pamphlet makes rather less use of the concept than do those of most other writers who were espousing the theory of dominion status. This is not to say, however, that he does not rely upon it at all.").

26. *Boyd,* I, pp. 123, 123–124, 124.

27. "The British parliament . . . have indulged themselves in every exorbitance which their avarice could dictate," *Boyd,* I, p. 124.

28. "The East India company . . . step forth . . . [as] the asserters of parliamentary right," *Boyd,* I, p. 127.

29. *Boyd,* I, pp. 134, 133.

30. *Boyd,* I, p. 131; cf. pp. 126 and 136 n.16 for Jefferson's reference to the "act for suspending the legislature of New York."

31. *Boyd,* I, pp. 134, 135.

32. *Boyd,* I, p. 676n. Cf. Sheldon, *The Political Philosophy of Thomas Jefferson,* p. 19: "In the years immediately prior to the Revolution, Jefferson became increasingly interested in matters relating to treason and death."

33. *Boyd,* I, p. 127 (emphasis added).

34. *Boyd*, I, p. 125 (emphasis added). Gilman Ostrander, in "Communications," *WMQ*, 37 (1980), p. 533; cf. Hoffer, *The Law's Conscience*, p. 69; and Hoffer, "The Declaration of Independence as a Bill in Equity," pp. 188, 193. William A. Parent, "Constitutional Values and Human Dignity," in Michael J. Meyer and William A. Parent, eds., *The Constitution of Rights: Human Dignity and American Values* (Ithaca, N.Y., 1992), p. 50. *Boyd*, I, p. 127.

35. *Boyd*, I, p. 121. Hoffer, *The Law's Conscience;* Hoffer, "The Declaration of Independence as a Bill in Equity"; cf. Stanley N. Katz, "The Politics of Law in Colonial America: Controversies over Chancery Courts and Equity Law in the Eighteenth Century," in Donald Fleming and Bernard Bailyn, eds., *Law in American History* (Boston, 1971), p. 283. See also Jack P. Greene, "The Origins of American Constitutionalism," in A. E. Dick Howard, ed., *The United States Constitution: Roots, Rights, and Responsibilities* (Washington, D.C., 1992), p. 37. *Boyd*, I, pp. 134, 135; cf. Montesquieu's famous definition of political liberty: "Political liberty in a citizen is that tranquility of spirit which comes from the opinion each one has of his security," in Montesquieu, *The Spirit of the Laws,* trans. and ed. Ann M. Cohler, et al. (Cambridge, Mass., 1989), p. 157. *Boyd*, I, p. 122: "His majesty's subjects in Great Britain have too firm a feeling of the rights derived to them from their ancestors to bow down."

36. Robert H. Webking, *The American Revolution and the Politics of Liberty* (Baton Rouge, La., 1988), p. 98. *Boyd*, I, p. 134.

37. T. H. Breen, *Tobacco Culture: The Mentality of the Great Tidewater Planters on the Eve of the Revolution* (Princeton, N.J., 1985), p. 141; cf. Judith N. Shklar, *The Faces of Injustice* (New Haven, Conn., 1990), pp. 83–126, 135–138.

38. *Boyd*, I, p. 135; contrast the interpretation in Christie and Labaree, *Empire or Independence*, pp. 206–7: "Despite a pious suggestion that the Americans were willing 'to sacrifice everything which reason can ask to the restoration of . . . tranquility,' Jefferson in fact offered nothing but defiance."

39. Webking, *The American Revolution and the Politics of Liberty*, p. 123; cf. John M. Murrin, "Can Liberals Be Patriots? Natural Right, Virtue, and Moral Sense in the America of George Mason and Thomas Jefferson," in Robert P. Davidow, ed., *Natural Rights and Natural Law: The Legacy of George Mason* (Fairfax, Va., 1986), p. 39; Peterson, *Adams and Jefferson*, p. 13.

40. *Boyd*, I, pp. 193–99. Julian P. Boyd, "The Disputed Authorship of the Declaration on the Causes and Necessity for Taking Up Arms," *WMQ*, 7 (1950), pp. 51–73. *Boyd*, I, p. 192n.

41. TJ to John W. Campbell, Sept. 3, 1809, *L&B*, XII, p. 308. TJ to Governor William Plumer, Jan. 31, 1815, *L&B*, XIV, p. 238; cf. TJ to Judge John Tyler, June 17, 1812, *L&B*, XIII, p. 165.

42. *Boyd*, I, p. 125.

43. Jack P. Greene, "'The Ostensible Cause Was . . . The True One': The Salience of Rights in the Origins of the American Revolution," *Reviews in American History*, 16 (1988), p. 202.

44. John M. Murrin, "From Liberties to Rights: The Struggle in Colonial Massachusetts," in Patrick T. Conley and John P. Kaminski, eds., *The Bill of Rights and the States: The Colonial and Revolutionary Origins of American Liberties* (Madison, Wis., 1992), p. 92. Clinton Rossiter, *The Seedtime of the Republic: The Origin of the American Tradition of Political Liberty* (New York, 1953), p. 411. In the same paragraph Rossiter takes into account that "[James] Wilson, [James] Iredell, and Jefferson were among those who moved beyond Locke to proclaim, however vaguely, a more positive purpose for the political community." But in short order Rossiter moves nevertheless to his conclusion that the American Revolutionaries

were thoroughgoing individualists. Cf. the much more refined case for Jefferson as a Lockean individualist made by Isaac Kramnick, *Republicanism and Bourgeois Radicalism: Political Ideology in Late Eighteenth-Century England and America* (Ithaca, N.Y., 1990), p. 179; Joyce Appleby, "What Is Still American in the Political Philosophy of Thomas Jefferson?," *WMQ*, 39 (1982), pp. 287–309.

45. Murrin, "Can Liberals Be Patriots?," p. 56. Compare Murrin's comment on p. 57: "Southern planters probably occupied the most ambiguous position. As we have seen with Jefferson, they could often sound more liberal than they were, especially when they supported free trade or attacked the deferential hierarchy of the colonial era." As an example of Jefferson's close association of the term "rights" with the term "liberties," see *Boyd*, I, p. 134. On the complexity of medieval and early modern rights theory, see Brian Tierney, "Tuck on Rights: Some Medieval Problems," *History of Political Thought*, 4 (1983), pp. 429–41; Charles J. Reid, Jr., "The Canonistic Contribution to the Western Rights Tradition: An Historical Inquiry," *Boston College Law Review*, 33 (1991), pp. 37–92; Knud Haakonssen, "From Natural Law to the Rights of Man: A European Perspective on American Debates," in Michael J. Lacey and Knud Haakonssen, eds., *A Culture of Rights: The Bill of Rights in Philosophy, Politics and Law—1791 and 1991* (Cambridge, Mass., 1991), 19–61.

46. Miller, *Jefferson and Nature*, p. 165 (emphasis added).

47. Eric Hobsbawm, "Introduction: Inventing Traditions," in Eric Hobsbawm and Terence Ranger, eds., *The Invention of Tradition* (Cambridge, U.K., 1983), p. 9.

48. TJ to Thomas Paine, July 11, 1789, *Boyd*, XV, p. 269.

49. Jack P. Greene, "Paine, America, and the 'Modernization' of Political Consciousness," *Political Science Quarterly*, 93 (1978), esp. pp. 87, 90–92. Greene, "'The Ostensible Cause,'" p. 198, in light of *Malone*, I, 193: "There is no reason to suppose, however that he [Jefferson] welcomed the closing of the courts in order to escape his own debts to British merchants, as Dunmore and some of his partisans asserted that many planters did." Also see Breen, *Tobacco Culture*, pp. 158–59.

50. Joseph A. Ernst, "The Political Economy of the Chesapeake Colonies, 1760–1775: A Study in Comparative History," in Ronald Hoffman, et al., eds., *The Economy of Early America: The Revolutionary Period, 1763–1790* (Charlottesville, Va., 1988), pp. 242–43; also see Breen, *Tobacco Culture*, p. 203.

51. *Malone*, I, p. 190.

52. *Malone*, I, pp. 190, 191. Michael Zuckerman, "Identity in British America," in Nicholas Canny and Anthony Pagden, eds., *Colonial Identity in the Atlantic World, 1500–1800* (Princeton, N.J., 1987), p. 157.

53. *Boyd*, I, p. 676; cf. Cunningham, *In Pursuit of Reason*, p. 27; but see Garry Wills, *Inventing America: Jefferson's Declaration of Independence* (Garden City, N.Y., 1978), p. 78. *Boyd*, I, p. 432; cf. *Malone*, I, p. 224.

54. Nathan Schachner, *Thomas Jefferson: A Biography*, 2 vols. (New York, 1951), I, p. 528, n. 3.

55. *Boyd*, I, p. 121.

56. Appleby, "What Is Still American in the Political Philosophy of Thomas Jefferson?," p. 308 (emphasis added).

57. Reid, *The Authority of Rights*, p. 3. By "rights" Reid means only customary and positive constitutional, and perhaps legal, rights—not abstract and universal natural rights. See Stephen A. Conrad, "The Constitutionalism of 'the Common-law Mind,'" *Law & Social Inquiry*, 13 (1988), pp. 619–36.

58. From Burke's March 22, 1775, speech in the House of Commons, quoted by Reid, *The Authority of Rights*, p. 170.

59. I borrow this evocative term from Valerie Kerruish, *Jurisprudence as Ideology* (London, 1991), pp. 16–19.

60. *Malone*, I, p. 184. Also see Sheldon, *The Political Philosophy of Thomas Jefferson*, p. 146: "Jefferson's most explicit articulation of the rights of man was in his support of the American Bill of Rights."

61. For example, in *The Political Philosophy of Thomas Jefferson*, Sheldon states: "This study finds Jefferson blending many philosophical concepts into a comprehensive and coherent political philosophy" (pp. 2–3 and passim). Also see Adrienne Koch, *The Philosophy of Thomas Jefferson* (New York, 1943).

62. Reid, *The Authority to Legislate*, p. 271.

63. Frank L. Dewey, *Thomas Jefferson: Lawyer* (Charlottesville, Va., 1986), pp. 25, 107–21. Also note the significance attached to Jefferson's law study in helping to shape his approach to the worsening problems of imperial relations in Sheldon, *The Political Philosophy of Thomas Jefferson*, pp. 17, 27–36.

64. Louis Henkin, *The Age of Rights* (New York, 1990), pp. ix, 83–108, 181–93.

65. In an Oct. 16, 1992, symposium panel discussion on "Jefferson and Rights" at the University of Virginia, Richard Rorty eloquently made the case for setting aside questions of historical accuracy and philosophical justification in order to sustain the present-day cause of international human rights, a cause that has lately invoked the Jeffersonian tradition to profound effect. See Richard Rorty, "The Priority of Democracy to Philosophy," in Merrill D. Peterson and Robert C. Vaughan, eds., *The Virginia Statute for Religious Freedom: Its Evolution and Consequences in American History* (New York, 1988), pp. 257–282.

66. Mary Ann Glendon, *Rights Talk: The Impoverishment of Political Discourse* (New York, 1991), pp. xi–xii, 23–25. Reid, *The Authority of Rights*, pp. 27–33, 96–113.

67. Hannah Arendt, *On Revolution* (New York, 1963; rev. ed., 1965), pp. 136–37 and passim; Reid, *The Authority of Rights*, p. 111. Cf. James W. Ely, Jr., *The Guardian of Every Other Right: A Constitutional History of Property Rights* (New York, 1992); Jennifer Nedelsky, *Private Property and the Limits of American Constitutionalism: The Madisonian Framework and Its Legacy* (Chicago, 1990).

68. Arendt, *On Revolution*, p. 127. The more recent argument of Joseph Raz, in *The Morality of Freedom* (Oxford, 1986) is restated by John Gray in "The Tyranny of Rights-Talk," *Times Literary Supplement*, Feb. 1, 1991, p. 8: "That no plausible political morality can be rights-based, that rights are never fundamental in moral and political reasoning but instead are intermediaries between claims about interests central to well-being and claims about the duties of others in respect of those interests, and that the value of rights cannot be explained satisfactorily in the individualist terms of their role in safeguarding the legitimate claims of persons but must rather be understood as elements in a common or public culture that has itself intrinsic value."

69. See, e.g., Richard K. Matthews, *The Radical Politics of Thomas Jefferson: A Revisionist View* (Lawrence, Kans., 1984).

CHAPTER 9

"The Earth Belongs in Usufruct to the Living"

HERBERT SLOAN

꧁꧂

It is safe to assume that no government proper, ever had a provision in its organic law for its own termination.
—Abraham Lincoln, 1861[1]

Our Constitution is a covenant running from the first generation of Americans to us and then to future generations. It is a coherent succession.
—Planned Parenthood v. Casey, 1992[2]

Jefferson's letter of September 6, 1789, to James Madison, setting out the principle that "the earth belongs in usufruct to the living," is a key text in the Jefferson canon.[3] Yet unlike other texts with equal claims on our attention—the Declaration of Independence and the Virginia Statute for Religious Freedom, for example—this one is very much a legacy in the literal sense, a text made available to the public only after Jefferson's death.[4] No more than a handful of Jefferson's intimates knew of its contents during his lifetime, and it was not until 1829, when the letter appeared in Thomas Jefferson Randolph's edition of his grandfather's papers, that Jefferson's countrymen could begin to assimilate its lessons. Only in our own century would the letter achieve the central position it now claims in any effort to appreciate Jefferson.[5]

Appropriately enough, the letter itself is about legacies. In broad terms, it asks us: what can one generation leave to another? And on what terms and conditions? Jefferson's answer argues that each generation must leave its successors freedom—freedom from debt and freedom to make their own political choices. Yet, by making his principle universal, applicable to each and every generation in its turn, Jefferson places a significant limitation on both the present and the future. The earth, he insists, belongs to the living only "in usufruct"—in trust, to use lay language. Hence the freedom each generation enjoys is circumscribed by the duty to respect the rights of its successors. And so, in a curious way, Jefferson ends by proposing the equivalent of a universal entail. If at first glance this seems paradoxical, it will not be the least or the last of the surprises his letter contains.

Endlessly fascinating, Jefferson's letter to Madison demands exploration on a variety of levels, and it will be difficult to do it full justice here. In what follows, I shall say something about the circumstances of its creation and about its subsequent history; I shall also suggest some of the ways in which it faithfully reflects many of Jefferson's central concerns. The letter to Madison, as much perhaps as anything Jefferson wrote, constitutes a summa, a profession of faith that tells us what mattered most to Jefferson at a significant moment in his life. 1789—the year of the French Revolution, the year the new American Constitution went into effect—was filled with promise: Jefferson could almost touch the future, and with only a little more time, a little more effort, the dreams of liberty he cherished would be realities. But the possibility that events might turn out differently disturbed him greatly. Well aware of the forces working against progress in France, aware as well of those threatening the republican experiment in his own country, Jefferson sought to articulate principles that would protect and foster the promise of 1789.

Jefferson's letter, then, is about legacies, about the crippling effects they can have, and about the kinds of changes required to avoid those effects. It speaks equally to the private Jefferson and the Jefferson of high politics and high thought, to Jefferson the Virginia provincial and Jefferson the habitué of Paris salons. In our effort to understand his letter to Madison, it is impossible to isolate these different Jeffersons.[6] For if it breathes the spirit of the opening days of the French Revolution, the letter is also the heartfelt cry of a debt-ridden Virginian, of a man whose own experience with legacies had been anything but happy.

I

For months Jefferson had been thinking in one fashion or another about the rights of the living generation and about the powers of the dead hand of the past, and he was now prepared to offer Madison his solution to those questions. After explaining that he is writing "because a subject comes into my head which I would wish to develope a little more than is practicable in the hurry of the moment of making up general dispatches," Jefferson states his proposition—"that the earth belongs in usufruct to the living."[7]

He then observes that, though of the utmost importance, it has somehow been overlooked: "The question Whether one generation of men has a right to bind another," he claims, "seems never to have been started either on this or our side of the water." [8] Continuing by way of illustration, he argues:

> No man can, by natural right, oblige the lands he occupied, or the persons who succeed him in that occupation, to the paiment of debts contracted by him. For if he could, he might, during his own life, eat up the usufruct of the lands for several generations to come, and then the lands would belong to the dead and not to the living, which would be the reverse of our principle. [9]

This is as true for society as a whole as it is for the individuals who comprise it: no generation has a right to burden those who come after it with a public debt. "I suppose," he goes on to say, "that the received notion, that the public debts of one generation devolve on the next, has been suggested by our seeing habitually in private life that he who succeeds to land is required to pay the debts of his ancestor or testator." [10] But this impression is misleading, Jefferson insists, for "this requisition is municipal only, not moral." On the contrary, "by the law of nature, one generation is to another as one independent nation to another." [11]

Running through Jefferson's discussion of debt is a visceral repudiation of the present generation's responsibility for the misbehaviors of its predecessor: a generation that does not pay its debts within its own lifetime commits nothing less than a crime against the law of nature. And the example Jefferson provides—of the prodigal Louis XV, borrowing from the moneylenders of Genoa and squandering away the proceeds of the loans on riotous living and the worst forms of self-indulgence—offers us a version of the grasshopper and the ant, a morality tale intended to bring home the principle that debts are rarely if ever wise in the first place. [12] What bothers Jefferson, clearly, is the way in which the debts of the previous generation make it impossible for him to enjoy what by natural law should be his— the usufruct of the estate during his own lifetime. We can sense here the immense frustration Jefferson feels as he realizes that he is condemned to pay what others should have paid during their lives, as he discovers that he is forced to labor for others.

Jefferson then turns to the practical applications of his principle. But first—and this is a critical move—he defines a generation. Using data drawn from tables compiled by the French naturalist Buffon, he arrives at the conclusion that the period of a generation is "18. years 8. months, or say 19. years to the nearest integral number," which then becomes "the term beyond which neither the representatives of a nation, nor even the whole nation itself assembled, can validly extend a debt." [13] Here he reaches the heart of the matter, insisting that "every constitution . . . every law, naturally expires at the end of 19 years." [14] The argument that silence can imply consent to continuing validity is rejected out of hand. "Every practical man," he insists, is bound to agree "that a law of limited duration is much more manageable than one which needs repeal." [15] Sadly, men are not virtuous enough to be trusted in so critical a business: "The people cannot assemble themselves. Their representation is unequal and vicious. Various checks are opposed to every legislative proposition. Factions get possession of the public councils. Bribery corrupts them. Personal interests lead them astray from the general interests of their constituents." [16] Only automatic expiration at the end of nineteen years will do, he concludes.

Having explained his general notion and suggested in broad terms how it might operate, Jefferson proceeds to his specific illustrations. He begins, in effect, with the French National Assembly's actions of August 4 and 11, only a few weeks earlier, and provides Madison with a catalogue of the technical but hardly insignificant difficulties the French nobility's renunciation of its feudal prerogatives left unresolved. The problems, as he sets them out, are numerous, but the principle that the earth belongs in usufruct to the living is relevant to all of them:

> It enters into the resolution of the questions Whether the nation may change the descent of lands holden in tail? Whether they may change the appropriation of lands given antiently to the church, to hospitals, colleges, orders of chivalry, and otherwise in perpetuity? Whether they may abolish the charges and privileges attached on lands, including the whole catalogue ecclesiastical and feudal? It goes to hereditary offices, authorities and appellations; to perpetual monopolies in commerce, the arts, and sciences; with a long train of et ceteras: and it renders the question of reimbursement [of the crown's debts] a question of generosity and not of right. [17]

While the range of applications he specifies is impressive, it soon becomes apparent that for Jefferson the real issue is not what is to be done in the Old World, but rather what can be made of the opportunity America presents. [18] "Turn this subject in your mind," he urges Madison, "and particularly as to the power of contracting debts." [19] Now, at the outset of the American experiment, is the time to see that the principle becomes an established part of American law and constitutional practice. It would, Jefferson suggests, "furnish matter for a fine preamble to our first law for appropriating the public revenue; and it will exclude at the threshold of our new government the contagious and ruinous errors of this quarter of the globe." [20] And by "contagious and ruinous errors" Jefferson understands the linked phenomena of wars and national debts; limiting the ability of the American government to borrow, he implies, would reduce the likelihood of war and so help avoid the dreadful consequences of debt. "We have," he thinks, referring to the provisions of the new Constitution, "already given in example one effectual check to the Dog of war by transferring the power of letting him loose from the Executive to the legislative body, from those who are to spend to those who are to pay." [21] Even so, "a second obstacle held out by us also in the first instance" would be welcome; in matters such as these, Jefferson is convinced, we can never be too careful. [22] And he adds that America is in the fortunate position of being able to adopt his proposition without reserve: because we "do not owe a shilling which may not be paid with ease, principal and interest, within the time of our lives," no other country "can make a declaration against the validity of long-contracted debts so disinterestedly as we." [23]

In conclusion, and almost as though the thought had just occurred to him, Jefferson adds a final suggestion, that the principle of nineteen years' duration be applied to patents and copyrights, in place of the fourteen years secured by English law. "Besides familiarising us to this term, it will be an instance the more," he remarks, here invoking another favorite theme, "of our taking reason for our guide, instead of English precedent, the habit of which fetters us with all the political heresies of a nation equally remarkable for it's early excitement from some errors, and long slumbering under others." [24]

II

The letter to Madison was clearly more than a sudden flash of insight or a random collection of thoughts, and, just as clearly, it had deep roots in Jefferson's personal, political, and intellectual experiences. The doctrine Jefferson unfolds in the letter draws on a wide range of materials and brings together many of the concerns he had developed since the 1760s. Most of what he has to say in the letter can be found elsewhere, and this has led some scholars to suppose that the intellectual paternity of the letter can be traced to a particular work or set of works. But while it is undoubtedly useful to know that others before Jefferson had denounced the dead hand of the past or asserted the rights of the living generation, we are likely to err if we try too hard to identify the source for Jefferson's ideas. [25]

The immediate context for Jefferson's thoughts on debt was an ongoing conversation, begun late in 1788, with a number of his Parisian friends. [26]

That discussion grew out of the crisis provoked by Louis XVI's decision to call the Estates General, a decision taken with the greatest reluctance and only after all other possibilities of restoring the monarchy's finances had apparently failed. For Jefferson and his French friends—above all, Lafayette—there was suddenly and unexpectedly an opportunity to remake the French state, to "regenerate" it, in the patriotic language of the day, and place it on a constitutional basis.[27] Inspired in part by the American founding, French liberals set out to create a new foundation for the monarchy. "Every body here," Jefferson reported early in 1789, "is trying their hands at forming declarations of rights," precisely as he himself was then doing in his correspondence with Madison.[28]

Jefferson was as ready with suggestions for his French friends as he had been with advice for Madison. By mid-1789, Jefferson and Lafayette had arrived at the idea of a right inherent in each generation to revise the constitution at fixed intervals—"le droit des generations qui se succedent," the right of successive generations, they called it in a version worked out by Lafayette in consultation with Jefferson in late June and early July.[29] Lafayette formally offered that version to the National Assembly on July 11, only three days before events in the streets of Paris overtook the theorizing at Versailles. As the pace quickened after the fall of the Bastille, some twenty-seven or twenty-eight additional projects for a declaration were proposed in the Assembly, and a committee, the Sixième Bureau, was charged with working out an acceptable version.[30]

Two of the Assembly's actions the following month probably helped push Jefferson toward his formulation of September 6. First, on August 11, putting flesh on the promises made a week earlier by reforming members of the nobility—exactly the sort of men with whom Jefferson had been having his conversation that year—the Assembly abolished feudal privileges throughout France. If the immediate consequences of this step were more symbolic than practical, it nevertheless brought to the fore the debate over the dead hand of the past.[31]

Having thus "mowed down a whole legion of abuses," as Jefferson informed John Jay, on August 19 the National Assembly returned to the unfinished business of the declaration.[32] After several days of debate, on August 26 it adopted a final version of the *Declaration des droits de l'homme et du citoyen* that was silent on the right of each generation to revise the constitution. That right, of course, had formed part of the draft declaration composed by Lafayette and Jefferson and offered to the Assembly on July 11, and it or a similar right of constitutional revision had been widely urged both by leading members of the Assembly, the Comte de Mirabeau and Emmanuel-Joseph Sieyès among them, and by such publicists as the Marquis de Condorcet. In the end, despite last-minute efforts by Mathieu de Montmorency and others to insert the Lafayette-Jefferson language on the right of generations, the Assembly preferred to say nothing on this point, and the "droit des generations qui se succedent" was omitted.[33] For Jefferson and his friends, this must have been a sharp disappointment, though Jefferson did not say so, limiting his comments on the Declaration as adopted to the remark, "Their declaration of rights is finished."[34]

But if the Declaration was finished, Jefferson was not. The "droit des generations qui se succedent" was obviously much on his mind that summer, and it is hardly surprising that he should go on to tease out the wider implications of the generational principle. At the beginning of September, he was pondering them with the help of an elderly English physician attached to the British embassy, Dr. Richard Gem. A figure of some standing in Jefferson's circle, Gem had been an important participant in the constitutional conversation earlier that year, and no doubt he and Jefferson continued to talk over these matters in the intervening months.[35] Immobilized with one of his periodic headaches during the first days of September, Jefferson apparently called in Gem for medical advice. The two men soon found themselves discussing the rights of the living generation so recently omitted from the Declaration.[36]

The exchanges with Gem at the beginning of September seem to have forced the issue, allowing Jefferson to reach the conclusions recorded in the letter to Madison. That there was a breakthrough can be established readily enough by comparing Jefferson's letter with a slightly earlier proposal by Gem. Gem took it for granted that "one generation of men in civil society" did not have the right to bind another, calling it "a truth that cannot be contested." He then went on to make two brief points, each of which Jefferson discusses in the letter. First, Gem suggested that there was nothing to keep an individual or a generation from subjecting its property to the payment of debts; "no rights of posterity seem to be violated" by this, he concluded, "because the property of the present generation does not belong to [posterity]." Second, as a practical matter, he thought it might be wise, given "the interested, ambitious and corrupt conduct of the administrators of nations," to limit the duration of public debts "to a certain term of years."[37] Jefferson then responded to these propositions, rejecting the former and using the idea of a generation to fix a limit for the latter. His own debts must have helped him to see a connection that others, including Gem, had overlooked.

If the political context of the letter presents a reasonably reliable narrative of major events and Jefferson's response to them, the personal context requires more investigation. No one reading the letter to Madison can fail to notice what it says about the rights of the present generation to be free from the financial burdens of the past, or about the corresponding duty not to impose such burdens on its successor. This is the real heart of the letter. Much on Jefferson's mind both in 1789 and for the rest of his life, the themes of debt and the rights of the living generation are tied to his larger vision of an American society permanently liberated from the "contagious and ruinous errors" of the Old World; they are also—and perhaps just as importantly—tied to Jefferson's perception of his own financial situation. And though I do not want to imply that Jefferson's doctrines are simply the self-serving pleas of a debt-ridden Virginia planter, it is impossible to overestimate the significance of Jefferson's own indebtedness.

Debt, in fact, is where Jefferson begins the letter to Madison, literally as well as conceptually. He begins not simply with debt per se, but with a specific kind of debt—inherited debt, debt owed by an ancestor or a testator which then becomes a charge against the property left at death. This, I suggest, is a curious place to start an argument about the rights of the living generation, and within the context of late-eighteenth-century thinking about those rights it is a highly unusual one. Others who took up the cause of the living generation at this time—Condorcet and Thomas Paine, for example—hardly thought it necessary to refer to the laws of inheritance in establishing their versions of the principle.[38] But for Jefferson this was a subject of enormous personal importance, and it is by thinking through what it means for one generation to be able to impose on another the burden of paying its debts that Jefferson arrives at his conclusion about the rights of the living generation to political freedom. The logic that drives Jefferson in this direction, when all is said and done, is to be found in his unhappy experience as a debtor.

It is no secret that debts and the rights of the living generation preoccupied Jefferson in 1789. In early September 1789, Jefferson was preparing to take his long-deferred leave and return to Virginia for six months or so in order to sort out his increasingly problematic financial affairs.[39] His debts were considerable, and if forced to repay all of them at once, Jefferson would have to liquidate a substantial part of his property. For six years, since 1783, he had been holding his British creditors at bay with promises that, his best intentions notwithstanding, never translated into cash. But by the fall of 1789, thanks to the ratification of the Constitution and the creation of the lower federal courts, the Virginia laws barring suits by British creditors no longer protected him.[40] Unless Jefferson could reach agreement with his creditors, ruin was a real prospect.

Jefferson may have dreamed that, as he said of the debts of the French king, the payment of his own debts could be a matter of generosity and not of right, but he was sufficiently realistic to know that this was not the case. His realism did not, however, make him any less resentful, and in fact he had reason to complain about his burdens. His troubles in 1789 had their origin in his voluntary assumption of part of John Wayles's debts to British merchants at the time of his father-in-law's death. Rather than wait years until Wayles's estate was settled, Jefferson gambled in 1773–74 that he would gain by taking his portion of the land and slaves immediately, in return accepting responsibility for a share of the estate's debts—exactly the situation he describes to Madison when he speaks in the letter of the heir who succeeds to land being responsible for the debts of his testator.[41] But he had no way of foreseeing how badly the Revolution would upset his calculations, wiping out much of what he expected from the Wayles legacy. For the property he sold on credit to liquidate the debts he assumed returned little or nothing. Like a good many other Virginians caught up in the whirlwind of Revolutionary inflation, Jefferson found himself forced to accept depreciated paper money worth "but a shadow" from his own debtors, and when it was over all he could show for his sacrifices was a handful of state certificates discharging his British debts.[42] These in turn proved useless when the Treaty of Paris reinstated prewar obligations to British creditors, though the Virginia legislature did its best for Jefferson and the other British debtors to put off the day of reckoning.[43]

But there was nothing new about the problems Jefferson and other well-placed Virginians were having with debt in the decade after independence; by 1789, gentry debts were an old story. The planter elite's growing realization of its dependence on British merchants and British credit had helped to fuel pre-Revolutionary tensions in the Old Dominion, and debt remained a powerful issue for Virginians like Jefferson in the years after 1776, and particularly after 1783.[44] Whatever hopes he and those like him entertained when they decided to separate from Britain, the result had not brought financial relief. If anything, the role of debt in Virginia politics during the mid-1780s was greater than ever, and with Madison keeping him informed of developments, Jefferson was well aware of the trouble debt and debtors were causing at home.[45]

Like many of his gentry contemporaries, Jefferson was not yet at ease in a world where economic uncertainty was becoming the order of the day. Dependence on the vagaries of a market economy, particularly when combined with an appetite for the goods it offered, could induce considerable discomfort, and in Jefferson's case that discomfort achieved notable proportions.[46] In the 1780s—and for decades thereafter—he was the man caught in the middle. Never able to refuse himself the things he wanted and thought he deserved, even at the cost of running up substantial debts, at the same time he was forever extolling the Franklinesque virtues of thrift and self-restraint.[47] And Jefferson's comments about his debts in the 1780s suggest a remarkable level of distress. "The torment of mind I endure till the moment shall arrive when I owe not a shilling on earth," he said, "is such really as to render life of little value." Making his estate productive so that he could begin to reduce his debts would be his "only salvation," he told Col. Lewis, his Virginia manager; if this could be done, he assured his brother-in-law and fellow Wayles debtor Francis Eppes, he would feel "like a person on shore, escaped from shipwreck."[48]

But it is a passage from 1786—whose words foreshadow what he would say to Madison three and a half years later—that gives the best sense of what debt meant to Jefferson. Replying to questions posed by the French writer Jean Nicholas Démeunier, then composing the articles on the United States for the new *Encyclopédie méthodique,* Jefferson described the debts he and other Virginians owed to British creditors as "hereditary from father to son for many generations, so that the planters were a species of property annexed to certain mercantile houses in London" or, he could have added, annexed to houses in Bristol and Glasgow as well.[49] In suggesting that the debtor was the slave of his creditor, Jefferson exposed the rawest of raw nerves. To raise the prospect of slavery was a standard move in late-eighteenth-century Anglo-American political rhetoric, and one with particular resonance in slave-holding Virginia. That slaves had no independence went without saying, and without that independence, without control over one's own resources, there was no material basis for republicanism as the founding generation understood it.[50] Debt as a kind of slavery, debt as the practical negation of liberty—Jefferson could hardly have been more revealing.

Thus, as he prepared to leave Paris early in September 1789, Jefferson's feelings were mixed. It was, he felt, unfortunate that he would be away just at the moment when there were real possibilities for improving Franco-American relations, and if he looked forward to taking the pulse of American politics, he regretted that he would be unable to witness the regeneration of France.[51] But even more, he must have wondered how his affairs in Virginia would turn out. He knew all too well that a good deal of hard bargaining on his part would be required—especially now that his legal position was weaker than it had been in the mid-1780s. Once home, it took weeks of negotiating before Jefferson could reach agreement with the Virginia representatives of his British creditors, and if he finally got from them most of what he wanted, at times he found himself hard pressed.[52] That Jefferson was anxious as the date for his departure approached is beyond question, and the connection between that anxiety and the passionate denunciation in the letter to Madison of the debts left by one generation to burden the next is plain enough.

IV

The debts that one generation heaped up for others to pay were never far from the surface of his concerns in 1789, but they did not occupy all his waking thoughts. He could hardly ignore the questions raised by public debts, if only because he had in front of his eyes the eighteenth century's leading example of what happened when public debts got out of hand. Like later historians, Jefferson understood how important a part the financial collapse of France played in the political convulsions of 1788 and 1789.[53] But even without the French example, Jefferson would have been forced to think about the implications, practical and theoretical, of a public debt. He and John Adams, as the active American representatives in Europe after 1785, had frequently corresponded on the subject, and once Adams sailed for home in 1788, management of American finances in Europe was entirely in Jefferson's hands.[54]

Given the state of the Confederation's treasury—so empty that, to Jefferson's acute embarrassment, even the pensions for French officers who had served in the American army could not be paid—there was little he could do, except arrange further loans from the obliging bankers in Amsterdam and assure all who would listen that America would soon begin to pay.[55] That strategy resembled the one he employed in coping with his own creditors, and it cannot have been any more agreeable to Jefferson to have to resort to it in this case.[56] Still, the experience gave Jefferson some insight into the ways of international banking—if he never fully understood what was going on, he did acquire a working understanding of both the significance of public credit and the dangers it involved. Moreover, Jefferson knew that the empty treasury at home had been a principal reason for the

Philadelphia convention of 1787, and he fully expected that the new federal system would restore American finances, making it possible at last to begin redeeming the public debt.[57]

Jefferson had his own ideas about public debts, and this points us to a third level of analysis. For Jefferson brought to the letter's composition a full stock of late-eighteenth-century ideas and attitudes that make his text a compendium of the standard assumptions of his day, examined and unexamined alike, about politics and economics. This third level is exceedingly rich, and I shall only be able to suggest some of that richness. The surprises here will be found not in hitherto unheard-of notions or newly discovered principles, but rather in what Jefferson does with commonplace ideas. In this sense, it is probably best to think of Jefferson as a *bricoleur* rather than a deeply original mind. Like most of us, he made do with an available and culturally acceptable set of materials, fashioning the solutions he needed out of them as the occasion required.[58] What in the end distinguished him from the run of his contemporaries was a characteristic willingness to take matters literally, to press on after others would have stopped and draw the logical conclusions others might have rejected as too extreme.

Certainly there was not the least trace of originality in Jefferson's ideas about public credit. His was the conventional wisdom, codified in the works of Hume and Adam Smith and a hundred other commentators and capable of being summed up in the notion that a nation, like an individual or a family, cannot spend more than it takes in without risking bankruptcy and ruin.[59] Jefferson accepted this premise without question; it conformed to the teachings of history as he understood them and it was validated by his own experience as a Virginia planter. Debts were dangerous, and it was best to avoid them whenever possible. The thought that they could be made a lever of sound public policy was, as Jefferson might have put it, sheer "heresy."[60]

Moreover, it was beyond dispute for Jefferson and most of his contemporaries that public debts sooner or later turned into instruments of political corruption. This too was common knowledge, part of the received teaching of the country party, part of the working political vocabulary of Jefferson's generation in England and America.[61] Jefferson's conviction that legislatures are not really to be trusted—recall his earlier reference in the *Notes on the State of Virginia* to the assembly as an "elective despotism"—is an important theme in the letter to Madison, as its endorsement of Gem's remarks on "the interested, ambitious and corrupt conduct of the administrators of nations" suggests.[62] The people may not err, but their representatives err all too often, and not from the best of motives. As he was to insist again and again in the 1790s, public debts created a dangerous and separate interest in the legislature fundamentally at odds with the good of society as a whole. Designing ministers and faithless legislators, Jefferson knew, took advantage of public debts to put their private concerns ahead of the common welfare. Worse yet, monocrats like Alexander Hamilton made use of the debt to purchase acquiescence in antirepublican schemes.[63] Reducing debt to a minimum and limiting its terms thus served to remove temptation; reversing the inevitable tendency of those in office to abuse their power, it would help to arrest the decay of the republican experiment.

The letter to Madison reveals Jefferson's keen appreciation of the connections between public debts and the aggressive foreign policies pursued by eighteenth-century European powers. He was just as keenly aware of the connections between international conflicts and the taxes they necessitated.[64] Britain's efforts to extract a revenue from its American colonies had brought home to Jefferson and his American contemporaries the truth of the warnings repeated incessantly since the early years of the century in Britain, that the national debt and the taxes required to service it would end by destroying English liberties.[65] In a political culture whose bedrock value was the notion of propertied independence, taxation was bound to be among the most sensitive issues. Nothing could be more obvious than the deleterious consequences of debt and taxation, nothing more obvious than the propensity of governments in want of funds to trample on the freedom of subject or citizen. Given the moral, political, and social dangers of public debts, wise statesmen would do all they could to contain and avoid them.

As the question of the public debt suggests, much of what Jefferson had to say in the letter to Madison was commonplace. Nor was the idea that the earth belongs to the living at all extraordinary in late-eighteenth-century thought. When Jefferson observed in 1785 to the Rev. James Madison, president of the College of William and Mary, "The earth is given as a common stock for man to labour & live on," he simply echoed a theme that natural law writers had insisted on since at least the seventeenth century. By Jefferson's day, it was a cliché, though admittedly an important one. It had figured in the arguments of Robert Filmer's opponents, Algernon Sidney and John Locke, in the 1670s and 1680s; eighteenth-century commentators and philosophers had endorsed it. God, after all, gave the earth to mankind, and if Jefferson's presentation remained resolutely secular, the point was as well established among the religious as among those of a more philosophical bent. Indeed, it was so widely acknowledged that it could take on quite varied forms; in the 1770s and 1780s, for example, it served as the point of departure for the radical speculations of William Ogilvie and Thomas Spence, and at the same time for the more acceptable arguments of Archdeacon Paley. In turn, Paine and others found it highly useful in the 1790s.[66] Jefferson broke no new ground in this respect; he merely took up a theme in wide circulation.

Even in the criticism of the dead hand of the past, Jefferson's arguments were by no means novel in 1789. The late eighteenth century had to be reminded—vehemently reminded—by Burke in 1790 that the past, as well as the present and the future, had its rights, and with that commanding intervention the terms of debate would begin to shift decisively.[67] But in September 1789, Jefferson could assume that what he had to say about the dead hand of the past was accepted by all thinking men. The dead hand—*mortmain* in the literal sense—had few if any defenders among the enlightened and was under assault everywhere in prerevolutionary Europe. Turgot's championing of the living generation in his essay on endowments for the *Encyclopédie* set the tone for progressive opinion throughout Europe. Though Jefferson may have had little respect for the monarchs of his day, the feudal abuses his principle would help clear away were precisely those Joseph II and other modernizing rulers were correcting and abolishing in the 1770s and 1780s. The mid-century Scottish debate over entails—we know Jefferson followed it closely—took up this theme as well, so persuasively that even William Blackstone, for all his conservatism, accepted its critique in his Commentaries.[68] As for Jefferson's thoughts on inheritance as a creature of the municipal, not natural, law, those too were utterly conventional—again, Blackstone confirms it.[69] We would be hard pressed to find much on this score in the letter to Madison that had not been said by one or more of the authors whose works we know Jefferson carefully studied.

Nor was there any novelty to Jefferson's claim that a people ought to be free to make its own decisions about political arrangements. This was explicit in the contractarian views that underlay the Declaration of Independence, and few of Jefferson's Anglo-American contemporaries would have denied it as a matter of theory. The authors to whom Jefferson attributed the doctrines of the Declaration—Sidney, especially—would have endorsed this anti-Filmerian argument; the doctrine of popular sovereignty, recently reaffirmed in the Preamble to the American Constitution—and even more recently in the doings of the French National Assembly—certainly implied as much.[70]

As for the idea that constitutions ought to be revised, that, too, was not invented in 1789. Both the Articles of Confederation and the federal Constitution of 1787 had amending provisions, as did a number of the preceding state constitutions. Jefferson had been interested in amending procedures since at least the early 1780s, and had suggested various ways they might be implemented in some of his earlier constitutional projects for Virginia—though never in the drastic terms he now urged on Madison.[71] The need to correct abuses and take advantage of what in 1789 he and Lafayette would call the "progrès des lumières" had thus been apparent to him for several years.[72]

Enthusiastic for what he called the present "age of experiments in government," Jefferson believed it offered unparalleled opportunities to move beyond the traditional reliance on "force or corruption" as the basis of government.[73] The experiment in constitutional revision he proposed was certainly one way to avoid both "force" and "corruption," for the regular exercise of popular sovereignty ensured that force would play no part in government and, by curtailing the sources of corruption, reduced the probability that corruption would reach dangerous proportions. Here, too, Jefferson was working to a great extent within an established tradition. The inevitable decay of republics was a familiar theme in the late eighteenth century, and Machiavellian exhortations of "frequent recurrence to fundamental principles," as his colleague George Mason put it in the 1776 Virginia Declaration of Rights, were widely heard.[74] If Jefferson went beyond Mason, suggesting that it was as much "le progrès des lumières" as "l'introduction des abus" that mandated frequent and regular constitutional revision, his proposal would have guaranteed the implementation of Mason's injunction.[75]

In all of these respects, then, Jefferson was doing little more than repeating the standard arguments of late-eighteenth-century political thought. Yet in the end there is still something different about Jefferson's principle, and it is not simply that he goes to extremes others might have avoided, though that is a part of it. If it is difficult, two centuries later, to escape the impression of intense personal hatred of debt the letter to Madison conveys, to read the letter other than as the product of a particular moment in Jefferson's life, as the coming together of diverse strands of Jefferson's intellectual interests, his personal dilemmas, and the political situation in Paris, we are still obliged to ask why Jefferson thought he had arrived at something quite new—to consider, in short, his claim of originality.

V

Ordinarily Jefferson was careful not to assert intellectual priority, and his justifiable modesty in refusing to insist on it in the case of the Declaration of Independence is well known.[76] That reluctance, I think, points us in the right direction: what he tells us he did in 1776 is what, for the most part, we see him doing in the 1789 letter to Madison. But in this instance Jefferson chose to stress that what he—or rather "we," the plural meant to include Richard Gem and possibly others as well—had to say was new, "a question never before started on this or our side of the Atlantic."[77] If Jefferson is right, and there is something original in the letter to Madison, we will probably find it in two places. First, there is what Jefferson himself emphasizes through his calculations—the transformation of otherwise commonplace notions of uncertain extent and application into a law of nature, a law which, for Jefferson, has all the status and rigor of a scientific fact. Second, there is Jefferson's modification of the standard terms of reference, a modification that involves both his use of the word "generation" in place of the standard Anglo-American and French practice of referring to "the people/le peuple," and his addition of the qualification "in usufruct" to the otherwise familiar notion that the earth belongs to the living.

With respect to the first of these innovations, the establishment of a fixed limit on the duration of constitutions, laws, and debts, we find ourselves confronting one of Jefferson's crochets. The Jeffersonian love of numbers comes into play at this point: "Mathematics was ever my favorite study," he would tell Benjamin Rush in 1811; "All here is reason, demonstration, and certitude."[78] And despite Jefferson's initial mistakes in calculation, he was sure that he had reached a scientific demonstration of the span of a generation (though he promptly rounded off his figure in the interests of practicality). What will strike us here, of course, is Jefferson's willingness to take literally the notion of the living generation. Not content with the standard eighteenth-century measure of the span of a generation as thirty years or so, Jefferson went on to calculate how long generations really did last.[79] The result allowed Jefferson to be specific where others before had been vague, and it gave him the right to insist that he was saying something new. Claims for the living generation had been made before, but never with the precision Jefferson was now able to supply; thanks to the authority of numbers, he was able to reduce generalities to a practical and workable law.

Arguably, the first of the two linguistic shifts I have identified, the adoption of "generation" as the favored term, is even more significant than

Jefferson's use of mathematics. Political discourse in the late-eighteenth-century United States made little if any use of the word; it does not, for example, appear in the pages of *The Federalist*.[80] Normally one referred to "the people," and while that phrase certainly included the present genera-tion, it was somewhat different in emphasis and significance. To speak of "the people" is to speak abstractly; as Edmund S. Morgan has reminded us, "the people" is perhaps the ultimate fiction. "The people" never dies; it has the same corporate immortality and collective right of sovereignty that attached to the king's political body in earlier theory.[81] A "generation," on the other hand, and certainly a "generation" as Jefferson defined it, is spe-cific and identifiable. Unlike "the people," it has a limited duration, so that there will be a time after which it no longer has rights. That limitation is critical, for it allows Jefferson to establish with precision who can exercise rights and when. With "the people," rights are, in effect, inchoate; with a "generation," we know exactly what we are dealing with.

It may be that the French context explains at least some of Jefferson's decision to employ "generation." In an atmosphere where notions of "regen-eration" were on everyone's lips, and where prerevolutionary pamphleteers like Louis-Sebastien Mercier occasionally deployed generational arguments resembling Jefferson's, it is easy to imagine how the rights of "le peuple"— or "la nation," the other standard formula in 1789—might have become those of a "generation" without anyone's quite noticing, at first, the poten-tial implications of the change.[82] Yet even in France, it was far from cus-tomary in 1789 to stress the right of generations. There, too, claims were ordinarily made on behalf of "la nation" or "le peuple."[83] But once made— the early drafts for a declaration of rights had referred to "la nation," "gen-eration" first appearing at the end of June or beginning of July 1789—that shift had the momentous effect of beginning an argument that, for all it owed to the shop-worn notions of the late Enlightenment, did go off in a new direction.[84]

Given Jefferson's difficulties with the Wayles legacy, it is possible that what was at first a purely political "droit des generations qui se succedent" to revise the Constitution could gradually have led him to question his own position as a debt-ridden successor. He would, I think, have been drawn to consider the latent meanings of the phrase, "generations qui se succedent," which, after all, suggested his own relationship to the Wayles legacy. Once that connection between the literal wording of the July 11 proposition and his own situation had been made—and Gem's early September proposition shows that the subject of debt had come up in the conversations he and Jefferson were having—Jefferson would have come to understand that the principle embraced much more than the right of the living generation to constitutional revision. Again, drawing *bricoleur*-fashion on the other bodies of knowledge available to him, Jefferson would have recalled standard ideas about the law of inheritance as municipal rather than natural, and about the dead hand of the past, and then built them into his developing argument. And, with his penchant for calculation and his skill as a legal draftsman, Jefferson may at this point have asked himself how a generation was to be defined. Already familiar with Buffon, he would have turned to the tables, done the arithmetic, and arrived at his nineteen-year duration of a generation.[85]

If this is what happened, we can understand why Jefferson began his letter with the passages on the laws of inheritance, for in linking that theme to political rights, he was making what to him could well have seemed a novel connection. (He was also, I suspect, using Gem's proposition as an *aide-mémoire,* for the order of discussion in the early pages of Jefferson's letter parallels the order of discussion in Gem's brief note.) In fact there are linguistic hints in the letter to Madison that this may have been the case: "succeed" and its variants are used several times by Jefferson when describing heirs who come into property.[86] The personal and the political contexts clearly overlapped here; in late August and early September, as the issue of the "droit des generations qui se succedent" was raised once again in the Assembly, and as Jefferson would have been thinking about the return to Virginia and the negotiations with his creditors, these two strands must have come together, each reinforcing the other, with the language of succeeding generations providing a bridge to join them in an unusual way.

And, finally, there is the addition of "in usufruct." Unlike "generation," which comes into the picture midway in the process, "in usufruct" is the product of the final stages in the formulation of Jefferson's doctrine. It expressly appears only in the letter to Madison; conceptually, it is not there until the early September exchange of views with Gem. Yet it may be this late addition of "in usufruct" that most distinguishes Jefferson's doctrine from other versions in circulation. Here, it seems to me, we have Jefferson the lawyer and pupil of George Wythe to thank, for in thinking of ways in which the rights of the living could be protected, Jefferson would certainly have remembered what he had learned long ago in Williamsburg.[87] He would, of course, have recalled the traditional common law methods of protecting estates from abuse by limiting the rights of present occupants and ensuring those of their successors.

As Jefferson envisioned it in the letter to Madison, the estate any generation enjoys would be an estate for life only, an estate that must be passed on intact to the next in line of succession. Thus any generation would have only the limited interest and rights of a tenant for life. It could not commit waste or burden the estate with debts for the next tenant to pay; it could appropriate for itself only the current proceeds.[88] Like a trusted family counselor, Jefferson accordingly drew up a deed of settlement ensuring future generations their right to benefit from the common property, and the means he employed to effect this, the entail, is the one a good eighteenth-century Anglo-American lawyer might have chosen.[89] But "entail" was not a word that Jefferson could have used without raising eyebrows. As the leading American law reformer of his day, Jefferson was filled with hostility for anything and everything that smacked of the "feudal system." Entail was high on his list of undesirables, and it was in large part through his efforts that Virginia did away with it.[90] Hence his need to find a more acceptable way of putting the matter, and, in all probability, his resorting to "in usufruct," with its Roman, civil law overtones and its relative lack of connection to the common law tradition.[91]

Even if Jefferson was only speaking metaphorically in 1789, his willingness to revive an outmoded legal doctrine he had consistently decried must strike us as paradoxical. We might further note the almost Burkean cast of Jefferson's letter. A year later, in 1790, Burke, who saw society as a "partnership not only between those who are living, but between those who are living, those who are dead, and those who are to be born," would write passionately of the limits on the right of any one generation to do as it wished, of its duty to preserve and pass on unimpaired to the future the heritage entrusted by the past to the present.[92] To be sure, any suggestion of similarity would have outraged Jefferson, but authors are not always the best readers of the texts they create.

Thus, while we can only suggest the train of thought that may have led Jefferson to the final form of his principle, it is apparent from the eagerness with which he writes to Madison, the almost breathless quality of the catalogues of abuses and the visions of the future, that Jefferson knew that he had done something important, important enough that he was willing to assign to himself something he rarely claimed—priority. The principle that the earth belongs in usufruct to the living generation of nineteen years was thus something new, and it confirms what historians have long argued: the standard doctrines of the Enlightenment had a radical potential that made them far more incendiary than some of their authors intended. In the heady summer days of 1789, Jefferson drew just such explosive consequences from a set of commonplace ideas, ideas that were very much in the air but had never been put together in quite this way, or received so precise a definition. This was no metaphor, no vague injunction. He meant it to be taken literally, for only if it were taken literally would its benefits be realized, only if it were taken literally would it fulfill its prophylactic role.

The keys to Jefferson's principle are thus his use of "generation" and "in usufruct" and the fixed limit of nineteen years he assigns to a generation. Together, they help to make up something new and different and so justify the claims he makes for his principle. What makes Jefferson different from his predecessors and his contemporaries is the spin he puts on things, the way—to change the figure—he makes up his dish, reinterpreting the classic recipes, adding new touches, giving us, in the end, a composition *à la jeffersonienne.* Aware that he had done this, Jefferson took pride in his accomplishment, claimed priority in the letter to Madison for his way of seeing things, and was convinced that his principle would preserve and further the republican experiment.

VI

We can appreciate what must have been Jefferson's disappointment when James Madison politely but firmly told him that it would not work. Madison's February 4, 1790, letter says virtually everything that can be said about the problems the principle would cause if applied in the literal fashion Jefferson intended.[93] For unlike his older colleague, whose efforts at making constitutions had largely been in the realm of theory, Madison knew a thing or two about the practicalities. It had been hard enough to get the new federal Constitution adopted, and the prospect of having to repeat the process every nineteen years can only have filled Madison with alarm. But this was to be expected; only recently, after all, Madison had publicly criticized Jefferson's earlier proposals for constitutional revision in the pages of *The Federalist,* adding his own strong warnings against frequent constitutional changes.[94]

More interesting in the reply is Madison's objection to the notion that one generation cannot impose obligations on the next. Madison suggests that there are, in fact, some public undertakings—"improvements" is his term—significant enough to justify a burden on "the unborn," and the American Revolution is his case in point. Would it be better to have foregone the armed struggle out of deference to the burden of debt on "posterity?"[95] Madison cannot believe it; the addition to the estate was worth the cost, even if some of it was left to future generations. Nor is Madison at all sanguine about the prospects for what he calls Jefferson's "philosophical legislation." Congress, he wrote Jefferson later that month, was unlikely to welcome "so great an idea as that explained in your letter of September"; the defeat of his own more modest proposal to have an occupational schedule added to the census proved it.[96] And last, but not least, Madison raises the specter of what will happen if society dissolves itself every nineteen years. What security for property then, he asks? What guarantee that the outcome will not be a thousand times worse than existing arrangements? For Madison, and others, even the republic is still an "experiment"; it needs a chance to establish itself firmly—a chance the automatic expiration of the Constitution in 1807 would hardly supply.[97]

But Madison's rejection was not the end of the matter, and Jefferson did not consign his principle to the realm of discarded ideas. On the contrary, almost from the outset of his resumption of public life in America in the spring of 1790, the principle was relevant to the conditions Jefferson encountered. The man who had placed a nineteen-year limit on public debts and confidently predicted that America's would easily be paid within that term was not prepared to accept the gospel according to Alexander Hamilton, least of all the notion that public debts could be turned into public blessings. We might read Jefferson's political path in the 1790s as an extended defense of the principle contained in his letter to Madison, and the debt reduction policies his administrations favored as practical efforts to implement it.[98] The Jefferson who insisted in his second inaugural address of 1805 that even in times of war it should be possible to "meet within the year all the expenses of the year, without encroaching on the rights of future generations, by burdening them with the debts of the past," had surely not given up on the insights of 1789.[99]

And the sense of urgency that filled his letters to political intimates during the War of 1812—letters in which Jefferson repeated the message of 1789, insisting that his principle supplied the only sound basis for war finance—suggests as well that it lost none of its relevance in later years.[100] So, too, his correspondence with a new generation of Virginia politicians—men like Joseph Carrington Cabell and Samuel Kercheval—on constitutional revision in the Old Dominion, long one of Jefferson's dreams, is further proof that he continued to believe in the political rights of the living generation.[101]

Yet to note that Jefferson continued to advocate his principle in one way or another is not to suggest that it remained static, its meaning forever fixed in 1789.[102] Jefferson was to live nearly thirty-seven years after writing the letter to Madison, nearly the length of two of his generations, and it would be absurd to suggest that there was no change, no development. If there is a shift, we can find it in his emphasis on limiting and eliminating the public debt over the need for constitutional change. Constitutional revision, indeed, will be confined entirely to the Virginia constitution; Jefferson seems to have set the principle aside in the case of the United States Constitution, no doubt for reasons of prudence.[103] Thus, despite his willingness to make use of the principle in the case of the Virginia constitution, the practical weight of Jefferson's principle moves heavily in favor of the hostility to debt.[104]

But how could it have been otherwise, given the politics Jefferson found himself confronting after his return to the United States in 1789? The principle becomes one more weapon in Jefferson's arsenal, one more reason to remain active in politics until the monster created by Hamilton—that serpent in the Garden of Eden who had so successfully and, as Jefferson came to feel, fatally tempted the Virginians in June 1790—could be tamed and eventually destroyed.[105] In his long campaign to rid America of the menace of Federalism, I would argue, the principle had a critical role to play. It gave Jefferson a benchmark, a standard against which to measure progress or decay, and, even more important, it gave him a vision of the way in which American society might be ordered differently.

Understood in this fashion, the principle provides a bridge between the two rather different Jeffersons historians have created in recent years, suggesting that Jefferson could at once be the republican and the liberal, backward- and forward-looking.[106] For there can be no question that Jefferson's hostility to debt ties him closely to the most traditional of country party, civic humanist, and republican concerns.[107] At the same time, however, Jefferson can envision a world free of the burdens and corruptions the national debt creates, a world that can give birth to a political culture vastly different from the one he knew and operated in. Jefferson has imagined a world, it can almost be said, in which politics are permanently adjourned. Without the ability to contract lengthy debts and wage costly wars at the expense of the future and to indulge in the other forms of waste that occupied so much of eighteenth-century Anglo-America's practical political energies, there would be little left to do except promote the good of the community.[108] (Jefferson in fact sketches something of this in his final messages to Congress, particularly in conjunction with his request for an amendment that will permit Congress to legislate in matters of internal improvements.[109]) This liberation, achieved through the application of the principle that the earth belongs in usufruct to the living, will then permit the improvement of the common estate, the application of progressive enhancements of knowledge and science to the highest possible end.

None of it, however, is possible as long as politics remains mired in its traditional forms and patterns, as long as the unenlightened and corrupt are allowed the means to prevail. Jefferson cannot ignore the conditions of actually existing politics in the new nation; unless the debt-created instruments of corruption are removed, and removed forever, the advances he dreams of are blocked. Thus read, there is a continuum, not a break, in Jefferson. Consumed though he is by the fears of the eighteenth-century Virginia planter confronted with the forces of debt and the power of credit, which he both knows only too well and at the same time never really understands, Jefferson is also capable of creating his own form of utopia, debt-free, beneficent, and in keeping with the teachings of natural law.

All this is to propose, then, something of the extraordinary complexity and importance of Jefferson's text, seen across the pattern of his long career. It has its ironies and its ambivalences, and it points in more than one direction; this very flexibility enables Jefferson to continue to call it into service on occasion after occasion. If a single text were to be taken as the key that would unlock Jefferson in all his contradictions, surely this is it. He meant every word of it, and he meant it deeply.

VII

If the letter to Madison has roots in Jefferson's biography, as well as in a specific late-eighteenth-century setting, it may be worth asking, briefly, what it has to say in 1993. This is probably not the sort of thing historians are equipped to do, but the history of this legacy invites just such efforts.

Whatever else the principle may have meant to Jefferson, it was decidedly not an invocation of the "living constitution"—though the New Deal tried hard to make it appear so.[110] Jefferson did imagine that each generation should have its own constitution, but that is a rather different matter. For Jefferson's constitutionalism was decidedly of the strict constructionist variety, and the notion that the text could be interpreted other than through the "original intent" he rejected out of hand. Convinced that all constitutions become corrupt over time, Jefferson understood that limiting their duration was the best means of correcting the abuses that invariably creep in, of curbing the inherent tendency of judges and legislators to usurp the power that properly belongs only to the sovereign people. For Jefferson, frequent and regular recurrence to the sole legitimate source of power, the people themselves, was the ideal way to keep constitutions pure; allowing those whose powers are limited by the original grant to make fundamental decisions ran against the grain.[111] Even Jefferson's often-quoted insistence that he did not regard constitutions with "sanctimonious reverence" as latter-day arks of the covenant, "too sacred to be touched," was made in the course of a letter supporting a new constitutional convention in Virginia, not a latitudinarian reading of the existing document.[112]

If, on the other hand, Jefferson's hostility to public debts strikes a certain chord in late-twentieth century America, it can only impress us as an impossible dream, and probably not a very desirable one at that.[113] Madison was surely right to suggest that there were projects worth the burden on future generations, and while many of the current projects our descendants will be paying for may not appear worthy (Jefferson's Louis XV analogy frequently seems apt), the national debt is not going to disappear.[114] Environmentalists, I suspect, may have rather more use for Jefferson's notion, and it is surprising that they seem not to have made much of it—they could do so with only minor violence to Jefferson's intentions. The current republican revival among the constitutional lawyers and theorists may also offer fertile soil for this part of the Jefferson legacy. Yet these days the notion of the people's reinventing itself every nineteen years is more likely to frighten than invigorate; if there is a hero for the republican revivalists, it is Madison, especially the Madison who entrenches the rights of minorities, not the Jefferson who argues for regular and repeated exercises in majoritarianism.[115]

It would be impolite, in Charlottesville of all places, to suggest that there is nothing left of this Jeffersonian legacy, but of course the historian's province is to insist on the historically specific and the historically unique. Once in hands other than his, Jefferson's legacy, when it is not rejected outright (and that has happened often enough, even in the Virginia generation that followed his), becomes something rather different, and Jefferson's dream of being able to control the future by limiting the rights of the present proves illusory.[116] Perhaps, in the end, his legacy is simply to remind us, in a disturbing way, that it was once possible to entertain real hopes for the future, and to do so with an elegance and a style that, as the republic enters its third century, seem utterly lost.

NOTES

This essay draws on material I explore in greater detail in *Principle and Interest: Thomas Jefferson and the Problem of Debt* (forthcoming). I wish to thank Peter Onuf and Ned Landsman for helping me to clarify some of the points raised in the essay.

1. Abraham Lincoln, First Inaugural Address, March 4, 1861, in Don E. Fehrenbacher, ed., *Speeches and Writings,* 2 vols. (New York, 1989), II, p. 217.

2. *Planned Parenthood of Southeastern Pennsylvania* v. *Casey,* 112 S. Ct. 2791 (1992) at 2833.

3. For Jefferson's letter, see *Boyd,* XV, pp. 392–97.

4. Jefferson, it will be recalled, asked that his tombstone bear the following inscription: "Here was buried Thomas Jefferson / Author of the Declaration of American Independence / of the Statute of Virginia for religious freedom / & Father of the University of Virginia." It was, he said, "by these, as testimonials that I have lived, [that] I wish most to be remembered." Epitaph, [1826], *LofA,* p. 706.

5. The letter to Madison was first published in Thomas Jefferson Randolph, ed., *Memoir, Correspondence, and Miscellanies, From the Papers of Thomas Jefferson,* 4 vols. (Charlottesville, Va., 1829), III, pp. 27–31. A highly selective list of modern discussions of the letter might include the following: Hannah Arendt, *On Revolution* (New York, 1963), especially ch. 6; Daniel J. Boorstin, *The Lost World of Thomas Jefferson* (New York, 1948), pp. 204–13; Stanley N. Katz, "Thomas Jefferson and the Right to Property in Revolutionary America," *Journal of Law and Economics,* XIV (1976), pp. 467–88; Stanley N. Katz, "Republicanism and the Law of Inheritance in Revolutionary America," *Michigan Law Review,* LXXVI (1977), pp. 1–29; Adrienne Koch, *Jefferson and Madison: The Great Collaboration* (New York, 1950), pp. 62–96; Staughton Lynd, *Intellectual Origins of American Radicalism* (New York, 1968), pp. 67–86; Richard K. Matthews, *The Radical Politics of Thomas Jefferson: A Revisionist View* (Lawrence, Kans., 1984), pp. 19–29; Garry Wills, *Inventing America: Jefferson's Declaration of Independence* (Garden City, N.Y., 1978), pp. 132–48; and the works by Merrill D. Peterson cited in note 71, below.

6. This is one case where the standard assumption of a sharp distinction between the public and the private Jefferson does not work. That, it seems to me, is additional reason for seeing the letter to Madison as central in the Jefferson canon.

7. *Boyd,* XV, p. 392.

8. Ibid.

9. *Boyd,* XV, p. 393.

10. *Boyd,* XV, pp. 393, 395.

11. *Boyd,* XV, p. 395.

12. *Boyd,* XV, pp. 394–95.

13. *Boyd,* XV, p. 394.

14. *Boyd,* XV, p. 396.

15. Ibid.

16. Ibid.

17. Ibid.

18. Convinced that the letter was not addressed to American conditions, Julian Boyd thought it primarily addressed to conditions in France (Editorial note, "The Earth Belongs in Usufruct to the Living," *Boyd,* XV, pp. 387–90). Not, Boyd concluded, "an authentic letter to Madison," it was "in actual fact a thesis stated for a pressing need, being intended to provide an instrument of justification for constitutional reforms then under discussion" in France (*Boyd,* XV, p. 390). Given that on August 26, 1789, the National Assembly failed to include in the *Déclaration des droits de l'homme et du citoyen* the right of successive generations to revise the constitution and then on August 27 postponed examination of additional articles for the Declaration until the constitution was completed, Jefferson's letter may well have been intended in part as a brief for his French friends, to be used when it

came time to resume the struggle to secure the right. (On the Assembly's actions, see Marcel Gauchet, *La Révolution des droits de l'homme* [Paris, 1989], IX, pp. 192–97.) But this hardly excludes the possibility of its being genuinely intended for Madison. In a more general sense, while Boyd is right to link the letter's origins with the situation in France, it does not follow that Jefferson did not intend his principle to apply to America as well—it was, after all, framed in universal terms—nor does it follow that it was, as Boyd asserts, "irrelevant to the existing situation in the United States." *Boyd,* XV, p. 388.

It should be pointed out that Boyd's editorial notes, often idiosyncratic to begin with, have not always aged well. This one, for example, appeared in 1958, well before most students of the period had learned to think in "republican" terms. It is hardly surprising that Boyd should have missed much that is apparent to us thirty-five years later; it is also obvious that editorial efforts like Boyd's to fix the meaning of documents are bound to fail.

19. TJ to Madison, Sept. 6, 1789, *Boyd,* XV, p. 397.

20. Ibid. But he was too late. The "first law for appropriating the public revenue," the Appropriations Act of September 29, 1789, passed without such a clause long before his letter reached Madison. In any case, on September 21, 1789, the House of Representatives instructed the new Secretary of the Treasury, Alexander Hamilton, to prepare a report on the public credit, and with that the chance of Jefferson's principle's finding its way into legislation decreased dramatically. The first statute appropriating money for the national debt, the Funding Act of August 4, 1790, also ignored the principle, pledging instead that Congress would continue to pay no matter how long it took. Linda Grant De Pauw et al., eds., *Documentary History of the First Federal Congress,* 9 vols. to date (Baltimore and London, 1972–), III, p. 220; IV, p. 49; V, p. 720.

21. TJ to Madison, Sept. 6, 1789, *Boyd,* XV, p. 397.

22. Ibid.

23. Ibid. Jefferson's October 1788 calculations of the time it would take to extinguish the American debts to France and to the Dutch bankers had demonstrated to his satisfaction that France could be paid by 1803, and the Dutch by 1805. See "Jefferson's Plan," [Oct. 1788], *Boyd,* XIV, pp. 202–04, 206–08.

24. TJ to Madison, Sept. 6, 1789, *Boyd,* XV, p. 397. Given Jefferson's dislike of monopolies and his unfavorable view of patents (for which see TJ to Madison, July 31, 1788, *Boyd,* XIII, p. 443, and TJ to Isaac McPherson, Aug. 13, 1813, *LofA,* pp. 1291–93), it is odd that he would use his principle to lengthen the period of protection. But I think we can take this proposition—not apparently one to which he later returned—as evidence of his real enthusiasm for the principle. Only a few days before, he had urged Madison to add to the Bill of Rights a limit on "Monopolies" in the form of patents and copyrights, but without specifying the duration. TJ to Madison, Aug. 28, 1789, *Boyd,* XV, p. 368. Perhaps he simply remembers in this last paragraph the unfinished thought in his earlier letter and now fills in the blank without bothering to make the connection.

25. Among the better discussions of paternity and influence, see Lynd, *Intellectual Origins,* pp. 69–82, and Koch, *Jefferson and Madison,* pp. 75–88. Less satisfying are efforts to establish Thomas Paine as the sole inspiration, such as that in Alfred O. Aldridge, *Thomas Paine's American Ideology* (Newark, Del., 1984), p. 265.

26. For the background, see Koch, *Jefferson and Madison,* pp. 62–96; editorial note, *Boyd,* XV, pp. 384–91; Louis Gottschalk and Margaret Maddox, *Lafayette in the French Revolution: Through the October Days* (Chicago and London, 1969), pp. 80–99, 220–26; and, more briefly, *Malone,* II, pp. 223–25.

27. On regeneration, see Mona Ozouf, "Regeneration," in François Furet and Ozouf,

eds., *The Critical Dictionary of the French Revolution,* trans. Arthur Goldhammer (Cambridge, Mass., 1989), pp. 781–91.

28. TJ to Madison, Jan. 12, 1789, *Boyd,* XIV, p. 437, enclosing "Proposed Declarations of Rights Drawn by the Marquis de Lafayette and by Dr. Richard Gem," ibid., pp. 438–39. Historians have long debated the extent to which the American example inspired the French; for the claims and counterclaims, see Stephane Rials, *La Déclaration des droits de l'homme et du citoyen* (Paris, 1989), pp. 355–69. For the Jefferson-Madison correspondence on the Bill of Rights, see TJ to Madison, Dec. 20, 1787, Feb. 6, July 31, 1788; Madison to TJ, Oct. 17, Dec. 8, 1788; TJ to Madison, Mar. 15, 1789, Madison to TJ, June 30, 1789, TJ to Madison, Aug. 28, 1789, in *Boyd,* XII, pp. 440, 569–70, XIII, pp. 442–43, XIV, pp. 18–21, 340, 659–61, XV, pp. 229, 367–68.

29. For the draft, see *Boyd,* XV, pp. 230–31; for the joint effort, see Lafayette to TJ July 6, [July 9], 1789, ibid., 250, 255.

30. For a brief account of the progress of the Declaration after Lafayette's July 11 proposition, see Gauchet, *Révolution des droits,* pp. 60–64. Rials, *Déclaration,* pp. 590–91, prints the text offered by Lafayette; though its language varied somewhat, it did not differ materially from the late June-early July draft with respect to the "droits des generations."

31. The most thorough account is Patrick Kessel, *La Nuit du 4 août* (Paris, 1969); see chs. 7 to 10 for a minute-by-minute account of the events of the evening. As Colin Jones notes, *The Peasantry in the French Revolution* (Cambridge, U.K., 1988), pp. 81–85, the decrees were more sham than reality. But Jefferson would have been among the last to notice, nor is there any evidence that he ever did so.

32. TJ to John Jay, Aug. 5, 1789, *Boyd,* XV, p. 334.

33. In addition to Rials, *Déclaration,* which reprints the surviving contemporary proposals for a declaration of rights, see Gauchet, *Revolution des droits,* esp. pp. 192–94, on the omission of the right of successive generations from the version finally adopted. For the text of the Assembly's debates on this, see Antoine de Baecque et al., eds., *L'An I des droits de l'homme* (Paris, 1988), pp. 65–68, 128, 149, 194. For supporters of constitutional revision, see Rials, *Déclaration,* 748 (Mirabeau), 606, 621 (Sieyès), 550 (Condorcet). For the effort to restore Lafayette's language, see de Baecque, ed., *L'An I,* p. 194.

34. TJ to Madison, Aug. 28, 1789, *Boyd,* XV, p. 364. A day earlier Jefferson had written to the acting Secretary of State that the "assembly is just finishing their bill of rights." Jefferson to John Jay, Aug. 27, 1789, ibid., 358. Nor does he make the point in the letter to Madison that the right of generations had been omitted from the Declaration. He may have muted his disappointment in order to avoid giving the impression of playing an active role in events; this would be consistent with the general discretion of his 1789 letters to American correspondents. In contrast, Condorcet at once protested the omission in his letter to Mathieu de Montmorency of Aug. 30, 1789. See *Lettres à M. le comte Mathieu de Montmorency* (1789), in A. Condorcet O'Connor and M. F. Arago, eds., *Oeuvres,* (Paris, 1847), IX, pp. 367–68, 371–72. His second letter to Montmorency, interestingly dated Sept. 6, 1789, returns to this theme. Ibid., 389–90.

35. First emphasized by Koch (*Jefferson and Madison,* pp. 78, 84–88), Gem's significance was elaborated on by Boyd in the editorial note cited in note 19, above.

36. For the illness, see editorial note, and TJ to John Trumbull, Sept. 9, 1789, *Boyd,* XV, pp. 384, 407.

37. *Boyd,* XV, pp. 391–92, 392–93.

38. For Paine, see *Dissertations on Government, the Affairs of the Bank, and Paper Money* (1786) and *The Rights of Man, Part One* (1791), both in *The Thomas Paine Reader,* ed. Michael

Foot and Isaac Kramnick (Harmondsworth, 1987), pp. 186–88, 203–4, 248; for Condorcet, in addition to the *Lettres à Montmorency* cited in note 35, above, see also his *Declaration des droits* (1789), and *Sur la necessité de faire ratifier la Constitution par les citoyens . . .* (1789), in *Oeuvres,* IX, pp. 210–11, 415–16.

39. Steven Harold Hochman's 1987 University of Virginia dissertation, "Thomas Jefferson: A Personal Financial History," is a thorough account, confirming in detail the view of Jefferson's financial history Malone had earlier given in his volumes. See pp. 144–57 for the situation in 1789.

40. On the Virginia British debts in the 1780s, the effect of the Constitution, and the litigation that followed, including *Ware* v. *Hylton,* which involved the Wayles estate, see Charles F. Hobson, "The Recovery of British Debts in the Federal Circuit Court of Virginia, 1790 to 1797," *VMHB,* XCII (1984), pp. 176–200.

41. Hochman, "Jefferson: A Personal Financial History," 74–83, describes the settlement of Wayles's estate in 1773–74.

42. Jefferson to William Jones, Jan. 5, 1787, *Boyd,* XI, p. 16.

43. Hobson, "Recovery of British Debts," pp. 177–81.

44. See in particular T. H. Breen, *Tobacco Culture: The Mentality of the Great Tidewater Planters on the Eve of Revolution* (Princeton, N.J., 1985), the most convincing effort to reconstruct the dilemmas of Virginia's elite as it confronted the break with Britain—though note Jack P. Greene's caveats in his review, *VMHB,* XCIV (1986), pp. 477–80. It is important to add that Breen ends his story with the decision for independence and so does not consider what happens when the prospects of 1775–76 fail to materialize. Jacob M. Price, *Capital and Credit in British Overseas Trade: The View from the Chesapeake, 1700–1776* (Cambridge, Mass., 1980), is essential for the merchants' side of the story, a perspective too often overlooked.

45. These developments are chronicled in Norman K. Risjord, *Chesapeake Politics, 1781–1800* (New York, 1978), pp. 96–103, 109–16, 122–26, 132–38, 149–56, 160–66, 174–79, 181–84, the most thorough narrative of Virginia politics in the Confederation years. See also Myra L. Rich's "Speculations on the Significance of Debt: Virginia, 1781–1789," *VMHB,* LXXVI (1968), pp. 301–17, and her 1968 Yale dissertation, "The Experimental Years: Virginia, 1781–1789." In 1790, per capita exports from the South were about half what they had been in 1770; what this meant for the plantation economy can readily be imagined. John J. McCusker and Russell R. Menard, *The Economy of British America, 1607–1789* (Chapel Hill, N.C., and London, 1985), p. 375. Risjord's detailed picture (*Chesapeake Politics,* pp. 160–66) confirms the traditional impression of hard times in the mid-1780s.

46. Among the many recent efforts to address the market's psychological effects on eighteenth-century Anglo-America, see the useful survey by Julian Hoppit, "Attitudes to Credit in Britain, 1680–1790," *Historical Journal,* 33 (1990), pp. 305–22, and Michael Zuckerman's speculative account, "A Different Thermidor: The Revolution Beyond the Revolution," in James A. Henretta et al., eds., *The Transformation of Early American History: Society, Authority, and Ideology* (New York, 1991), pp. 170–93, esp. pp. 174–79. Richard Bushman's study of how Americans learned to be "genteel," *The Refinement of America: Persons, Houses, Cities* (New York, 1992), offers suggestive insights into the tensions engendered by the competing need to be at once a producer and a consumer.

47. For examples of Jefferson as Poor Richard, see TJ to Paul Clay, [July 12, 1817]; to Thomas Jefferson Smith, Feb. 21, 1825, *Ford,* XII, pp. 74n–75n, 405–6.

48. TJ to Nicholas Lewis, July 29, Sept. 17, 1787; to Francis Eppes, July 30, 1787, *Boyd,* XI, p. 640, XII, pp. 135, 654.

49. Answers to Démeunier's Additional Queries, [c. Jan.-Feb. 1786], in *Boyd,* X, p.

27. Jefferson, of course, was in debt to merchants in all three British cities. Hochman, "Jefferson: A Personal Financial History," 74, 86.

50. As Jack P. Greene has remarked, "Perhaps in part because their constant exposure to black slavery impressed upon them how miserable and abject slavery could be, Virginians took great pride, as Wou'dbe inferred in *The Candidates,* in thinking that a spirit of personal independence was particularly strong among them." "Society, Ideology, and Politics: An Analysis of the Political Culture of Mid-Eighteenth-Century Virginia," in Richard M. Jellison, ed., *Society, Freedom, and Conscience: The American Revolution in Virginia, Massachusetts, and New York* (New York, 1976), p. 53. For additional comments on the use Jefferson made of the slavery metaphor in describing his own position at this time, see John M. Murrin, "Fundamental Values, the Founding Fathers, and the Constitution," in Herman Belz et al., eds., *To Form a More Perfect Union: The Critical Ideas of the Constitution* (Charlottesville, Va., 1992), pp. 24–25, which takes Jefferson's July 29, 1787, letter to Nicholas Lewis (*Boyd,* XI, p. 640) as its text.

51. On the prospects for improved relations with France, see TJ to Madison, Aug. 28, 1789, *Boyd,* XV, pp. 366–67; for the interest in American politics, see TJ to George Washington, Dec. 4, 1788, ibid., XIV, p. 332.

52. For details of the settlements he reached, see Hochman, "Jefferson: A Personal Financial History," pp. 164–70.

53. Jefferson remarked on the connection, both in his correspondence at the time and, later in life, in his Autobiography. See his letters to John Jay, May 23, 1788; to James Monroe, Aug. 9, 1788; to Richard Price, Jan. 8, 1789, *Boyd,* XIII, pp. 189–90, 489, XIV, pp. 420–23; Autobiography, in *LofA,* pp. 63–65, 78–80. For the consensus of a range of twentieth-century historians, see Michel Vovelle, *La Chute de la monarchie, 1787–1792* (Paris, 1972), p. 92; William Doyle, *The Oxford History of the French Revolution* (Oxford, 1989), p. 85; and Simon Schama, *Citizens: A Chronicle of the French Revolution* (New York, 1989), p. 62.

54. The account in *Malone,* II, pp. 187–91, 470–71, provides an overview of Jefferson's financial activities for the United States in Europe.

55. For some of Jefferson's comments on these issues, see TJ to C. W. F. Dumas, Feb. 9, 1787; to the Abbé Morrellet, Oct. 24, 1787; to John Jay, Mar. 16, 1788; and, esp., to George Washington, May 2, 1788, *Boyd,* XI, p. 128, XII, pp. 286–87, 671–72, XIII, pp. 126–28.

56. For his distaste for the financial side of the mission, see TJ to Madison, June 20, 1787, *Boyd,* XI, 482.

57. TJ to Madison, May 3, 1788, *Boyd,* XIII, pp. 129–31; John Adams to Abigail Adams, March 14, 1788, quoted in *Boyd,* XIII, p. 129n; *Malone,* II, p. 161.

58. On the *bricoleur* (the concept is borrowed from the anthropology of Levi-Strauss), see Gerald Garvey, *Constitutional Bricolage* (Princeton, N.J., 1971). As Douglass Adair long ago pointed out in "The New Jefferson," *WMQ,* III (1946), 132–33, it may be safer to assume that Jefferson was "an intellectual middle-man" than to start from the proposition that he was an original thinker.

59. "For why," David Hume asked, "should the case be so different between the public and an individual, as to make us establish different maxims of conduct for each?" Hume, "Of Public Credit" (1754), in *Writings on Economics,* ed. Eugene Rotwein (Madison, Wis., 1970), p. 91. Adam Smith similarly compared the state that resorted to borrowing to "an improvident spendthrift whose pressing occasions will not allow him to wait for the regular payment of his revenue." Smith, *An Inquiry into the Nature and Causes of the Wealth of Nations* (1776), ed. R. H. Campbell and A. S. Skinner, 2 vols. (Oxford, 1976), p. 912.

60. "Heresy," as all students of Jefferson know, was his usual designation of doctrines with which he disagreed.

61. The standard account is Lance Banning, *The Jeffersonian Persuasion: Evolution of a Party Ideology* (Ithaca, N.Y., 1978), esp. ch. 2, "Of Virtue, Balance, and Corruption."

62. Jefferson, *Notes on the State of Virginia,* in *LofA,* p. 245; Proposition Submitted by Richard Gem, [c. Sept. 1–6, 1789], *Boyd,* XV, p. 392.

63. See Banning, *Jeffersonian Persuasion,* pp. 161–207, 226–47, for the responses of Jefferson and his friends to these developments.

64. Here, too, twentieth-century historians would tend to agree with Jefferson. See, e.g., Patrick K. O'Brien, "The Political Economy of British Taxation, 1660–1815," *Economic History Review,* 2d ser., XLI (1988), pp. 1–32; John Brewer, *Sinews of Power: War, Money and the English State* (New York, 1989); and J. V. Beckett and Michael Turner, "Taxation and Economic Growth in Eighteenth-Century England," *Economic History Review,* 2d ser., XLIII (1990), pp. 377–403.

65. As Richard Bushman has noted in *King and People in Provincial Massachusetts* (Chapel Hill, N.C., 1985), these themes were by no means the exclusive property of the political elite (pp. 247–48). What he found for the plain people of Massachusetts is probably true for their Virginia counterparts as well, though evidence is harder to come by in the latter case.

66. TJ to Rev. James Madison, Oct. 28, 1785, *Boyd,* VIII, p. 682; see also TJ to James Madison, Oct. 28, 1785, *Boyd,* VIII, pp. 681–82. Thomas A. Horne, *Property Rights and Poverty: Political Argument in Britain, 1605–1834* (Chapel Hill, N.C., 1990), provides an overview, to which this paragraph is heavily indebted. For the roots of the theme in the Christian Middle Ages, see Janet Coleman, "Property and Poverty," in J. H. Burns, ed., *The Cambridge History of Medieval Political Thought, c. 350–c. 1450* (Cambridge, 1988), pp. 617–25, 643–46.

67. On the reaction to Burke's *Reflections,* see R. R. Fennessy, *Burke, Paine and the Rights of Man: A Difference of Political Opinion* (The Hague, 1963), pp. 160–212.

68. Turgot's article is in *Encyclopédie, ou dictionnaire raisonné des sciences, des arts et des metiers,* 39 vols. (Lausanne and Bern, 1781–82), XIV, pp. 892–97. Jefferson, who owned a copy of this edition of the *Encyclopédie* (E. Millicent Sowerby, comp., *Catalogue of the Library of Thomas Jefferson,* 5 vols. [Washington, D.C., 1952–59], entry no. 4890), was probably familiar with Turgot's essay. For comments on monarchs, see TJ to John Langdon, March 5, 1810, *LofA,* pp. 1221–22. Owen Chadwick, *The Popes and the European Revolution* (Oxford, 1981), pp. 246–52, 391–444, chronicles the travails of the eighteenth-century Church at the hands of reformers in Austria, Italy, and Spain. For an introduction to the Scottish debate on entails, see David Lieberman, "The Legal Needs of a Commercial Society: The Jurisprudence of Lord Kames," in Istvan Hont and Michael Ignatieff, eds., *Wealth and Virtue: The Shaping of Political Economy in the Scottish Enlightenment* (Cambridge, 1983), pp. 215–19. Jefferson's interest in this debate is evident in the extracts in *The Commonplace Book of Thomas Jefferson: A Repertory of His Ideas on Government,* ed. Gilbert Chinard (Baltimore and Paris, 1926), pp. 107–10, 145–49. For Blackstone, see his *Commentaries on the Laws of England* (1765–69), 4 vols. (Chicago and London, 1979), II, pp. 358–61.

69. Ibid., p. 12.

70. See TJ to Henry Lee, May 8, 1825, *Ford,* XII, p. 409, on authorities. For Sidney, see Alan Craig Houston, *Algernon Sidney and the Republican Heritage in England and America* (Princeton, N.J., 1991), especially pp. 140–45, 185, 191. Houston's account of "Sidney's radical interpretation of consent theory" and rejection of Filmer's "strong theory of inter-

generational obligations" (ibid., p. 144) suggests the possibility that Jefferson, a devoted reader of the martyred Englishman's *Discourses,* recalled his arguments in 1789.

71. Merrill D. Peterson has illuminated this theme in several important studies: see *Jefferson and Madison and the Making of Constitutions* (Charlottesville, Va., 1987), especially pp. 11–13; "Thomas Jefferson, the Founders, and Constitutional Change," in J. Jackson Barlow et al., eds., *The American Founding: Essays on the Formation of the Constitution* (Westport, Conn., 1988), pp. 275–93; and "Mr. Jefferson's 'Sovereignty of the Living Generation,'" *Virginia Quarterly Review,* 52 (1976), pp. 437–47.

72. For the phrase, see Lafayette's Draft of a Declaration of Rights, [late June–early July 1789], *Boyd,* XV, p. 231.

73. TJ to John Adams, Feb. 28, 1796, Lester J. Cappon, ed., *The Adams-Jefferson Letters,* 2 vols. (Chapel Hill, N.C., 1959), I, p. 260.

74. Virginia Declaration of Rights, May 27, 1776, Brent Tarter, ed., *Revolutionary Virginia: The Road to Independence,* VII (Charlottesville, Va., 1983), p. 272. On republican decay, see, generally, J. G. A. Pocock, *The Machiavellian Moment: Florentine Political Thought and the Atlantic Republican Tradition* (Princeton, N.J., 1975), and Drew R. McCoy, *The Elusive Republic: Political Economy in Jeffersonian America* (Chapel Hill, N.C., 1980).

75. Lafayette's Draft of a Declaration of Rights, *Boyd,* XV, p. 231. The tensions evident in this phrasing—between Jefferson's confidence in the progress of human knowledge and his considerably less optimistic evaluation of man's ability to use power without abusing it—are characteristic.

76. For Jefferson's refusal to claim originality in the Declaration, see TJ to Lee, May 8, 1825, *Ford,* XII, p. 409.

77. TJ to Madison, Sept. 6, 1789, *Boyd,* XV, p. 392.

78. TJ to Benjamin Rush, Aug. 17, 1811, *L&B,* XIII, p. 75. On Jefferson's penchant for calculation, see Patricia Cline Cohen, *A Calculating People: The Spread of Numeracy in Early America* (Chicago, 1982), pp. 86, 112–14, and, in a more critical vein, Garry Wills, *Inventing America: Jefferson's Declaration of Independence* (Garden City, N.Y., 1978), pp. 111–24, 132–48.

79. Nor was this particularly easy to do: see Jefferson to Gem, Sept. 9, 1789, *Boyd,* XV, pp. 389–90, for Jefferson's efforts to get the numbers right. The conventional figure of thirty years was used by Paine, for example, in his 1786 *Dissertations on Government,* p. 186; the article on "Generation" in the *Encyclopédie,* XV, p. 890, suggested a figure of "trente-trois ans ou environ." Was Jefferson aware of the possibility that age distribution would change over time, requiring constant upward or downward adjustment of the nineteen-year figure? While he realized that the European population data probably did not fit the American case and once tried to obtain better information (see note 102, below), he apparently did not envision the gradual aging of the population that has taken place since his day.

80. A search of *The Federalist* using WordCruncher reveals that while the authors used "people" 527 times, they never so much as mentioned "generation."

81. Edmund S. Morgan, *Inventing the People: The Rise of Popular Sovereignty in England and America* (New York, 1988), pp. 82–83, 153–54, 267.

82. For "regeneration," see Ozouf, "Regeneration." For the pre-1789 French anticipation of Jefferson on generations, see Mercier's essay, "Generation nouvelle," in his *Tableau des empires, ou notion sur les gouvernements,* 4 vols. (Amsterdam, 1788), III, p. 63. As Robert Darnton points out in "The Forbidden Books of Pre-revolutionary France," in Colin Lucas, ed., *Rewriting the French Revolution: The Andrew Browning Lectures* 1989 (Oxford, 1991), pp. 14–15, 17, 24, Mercier's works were immensely popular in the 1780s. Jefferson does not

seem to have owned a copy of the *Tableau des empires*—it is not among Mercier's works listed in Sowerby, comp., *Catalogue,* entries no. 173, 174, 1351, 1352, 3890, 4593—but it is conceivable that Jefferson or others in his circle read Mercier's "Generation" essay. The idea was "in the air."

83. Of the forty-eight proposals for declarations of right offered, both in the Assembly and out of doors, that are reprinted in Rials, ed., *Declaration,* some nineteen contain, in one way or another, a right of constitutional revision. Of these nineteen, only two—Lafayette's late June–early July draft and his formal motion of July 11, 1789—ascribe the right of revision to successive generations. Rials, pp. 568, 591. For the other plans, see ibid., 529 (Lafayette), p. 550 (Condorcet), 563 (Brissot), 606 (Sieyès), 612 (Target), 612 (Mounier), 621 (Sieyès), 626 (anon.), 632 (anon.), 636 (Thouret), 640 (Thouret), 645 (Custine), 661 (Duport), 725 (Pison), 725 (Petion), 731 (Boislandry), 748 (Mirabeau). Also see Rolf Reichardt, "Revolutionäre Mentalitäten und Netze politischer Grundbegriffe in Frankreich 1789–1795," in Reinhart Koselleck and Rolf Reichart, eds., *Die Französische Revolution als Bruch des gesellschaftlichen Bewusstseins* (Munich, 1988), pp. 185–215; "generation" does not figure in Reichart's list of the Revolution's key words.

84. For this linguistic shift, see *Boyd,* XIV, p. 429; XV, p. 231.

85. For Jefferson's ownership of Buffon's *Histoire naturelle, generale et particulière* (Paris, 1774–78), from which the data were taken, see Sowerby, comp., *Catalogue,* entry no. 1024, and *Boyd,* XV, p. 398n.

86. Thus he says that "no man can, by natural right, oblige the lands he occupied, or the persons who succeed him in that occupation, to the paiment of debts contracted by him," and speaks of "Each successive generation," "another generation or society succeeds," and "he who succeeds to lands." He also refers, in a political context, to "the succeeding generation." *Boyd,* XV, pp. 393, 394, 395, 396.

87. Neither Paine nor Condorcet (for whose versions of the right of generations see note 38, above) had been bred to the law; neither was thus likely to have thought about the matter in these terms, which came so naturally to Jefferson.

88. In a later version of the letter, Jefferson does employ the language of the common law of real property I suggest he had in mind. As he put it to John Wayles Eppes on June 24, 1813, "The case may be likened to the ordinary one of a tenant for life, who may hypothecate the land for his debts, during the continuance of his usufruct; but at his death, the reversioner (who is also for life only) receives it exonerated from all burthen" (*Ford,* XI, p. 298).

89. On the entail in pre-Revolutionary Virginia, see C. Ray Keim, "Primogeniture and Entail in Colonial Virginia," *WMQ,* XXV (1968), pp. 545–68, and Robert E. and B. Katharine Brown, *Virginia 1705–1786: Democracy or Aristocracy?* (East Lansing, Mich., 1964), pp. 80–95. *Malone,* I, p. 253, describes Jefferson's own problems with entail.

90. On Jefferson as law reformer, see Ralph Lerner, "Jefferson's Pulse of Republican Reformation," in *The Thinking Revolutionary: Principle and Practice in the New Republic* (Ithaca, N.Y., 1987), pp. 60–90. Bernard Bailyn enters a mild dissent in "Political Experience and Radical Ideas in Eighteenth-Century America" (1962), in *Faces of Revolution: Personalities and Themes in the Struggle for American Independence* (New York, 1990), pp. 191–92.

91. "Usufructus," Sir Robert Chambers (Blackstone's successor as Vinerian Professor at Oxford) wrote, commenting on the nature of property under Roman law, "is a right to make all the use and profit of a thing that can be made without injuring the substance of the thing itself. . . . This estate regularly lasted for life." Chambers, *A Course of Lectures on the English Law, Delivered at the University of Oxford, 1767–1773,* ed. Thomas M. Curley, 2 vols. (Madison, Wis., 1986), II, p. 85. For Jefferson's lifelong familiarity with Roman law, see

Edward Dumbauld, *Thomas Jefferson and the Law* (Norman, Okla., 1978), pp. 61–65, 98, 110.

92. Edmund Burke, *Reflections on the Revolution in France* (1790), in *The Writings and Speeches of Edmund Burke*, VIII: *The French Revolution, 1790–1794*, ed. L. G. Mitchell (Oxford, 1989), pp. 146–47. Like Jefferson, Burke too would exploit the legal metaphor inherent in the idea of generational rights, remarking in 1791, "With regard to futurity, we are to treat it like a ward. We are not so to attempt an improvement of his fortune, as to put the capital of his estate to any hazard." *An Appeal from the New to the Old Whigs* (1791), in *Further Reflections on the Revolution in France,* ed. Daniel E. Ritchie (Indianapolis, Ind., 1992), p. 91.

93. Madison's reaction is in his letter to Jefferson of Feb. 4, 1790, *PJM*, XIII, pp. 18–21. Among the commentaries drawing attention to Madison's reply as marking out the boundaries between Jefferson and his more conservative colleague, Peterson's *Jefferson and Madison and the Making of Constitutions*, pp. 6–7, 16, and Drew McCoy's *The Last of the Fathers: James Madison and the Republican Legacy* (New York, 1989), pp. 53–60, 71, 83, are of particular interest.

94. Madison in *The Federalist*, No. 49, Feb. 2, 1788, *PJM*, X, pp. 460–63.

95. Madison to TJ, Feb. 4, 1790, *PJM*, XIII, pp. 19–20; in any case, Madison was less sure than Jefferson that the Revolutionary debt could be paid off in nineteen years (ibid., p. 20).

96. Ibid., p. 21; Madison to TJ, Feb. 14, 1790, ibid., p. 41.

97. Madison to TJ, Feb. 4, 1790, ibid., pp. 20–21. As Drew McCoy suggests, Madison's awareness of the need to build confidence in the institutions of the new nation and the critical role played by habit and "prejudice" in that process links him, once again, to Hume. *Last of the Fathers*, p. 55.

98. Such a reading would, of course, rely heavily on Banning, *Jeffersonian Persuasion*, and John M. Murrin, "The Great Inversion, or Court versus Country: A Comparison of the Revolution Settlements in England (1688–1721) and America (1776–1816)," in J. G. A. Pocock, ed., *Three British Revolutions: 1641, 1688, 1776* (Princeton, N.J., 1980), pp. 368–453, esp. pp. 405–28.

99. Jefferson, Second Inaugural Address, March 4, 1805; and his Eighth Annual Message, Nov. 8, 1808, *LofA*, pp. 519, 549.

100. Among those letters, that to Jefferson's son-in-law, Congressman John Wayles Eppes, of June 24, 1813 (*Ford*, XI, pp. 297–301), is particularly interesting. Here the presentation of the idea is much smoother and certainly more efficient than in the 1789 letter to Madison. Jefferson no longer needs to think out loud on paper and does not rehearse the steps that led to his conclusion; things can be put a good deal more succinctly, almost as though Jefferson were repeating a well-learned lesson.

101. Jefferson to Kercheval, July 12, 1816, *Ford*, XII, pp. 3–15; to Cabell, July 14, 1816, Nathaniel Francis Cabell, ed., *Early History of the University of Virginia, as Contained in the letters of Thomas Jefferson and Joseph C. Cabell* (Richmond, Va., 1856), p. 67. Here, too, Jefferson couples his pleas for constitutional revision with graphic depictions of the dangers of debt.

102. Jefferson tried on one occasion to have the federal census refined to shed light on the age distribution of the American population. In 1800, as president of the American Philosophical Society, he submitted a memorial to Congress urging a more calibrated age schedule for the census. Noting the usefulness of "dividing life into certain epochs, to ascertain the existing numbers within each epoch, from whence may be calculated the ordinary duration of life in these States," and "firmly believing that the result will be

sensibly different from what is presented by the tables of other countries," Jefferson suggested the census takers record "the following epochs, to wit: Births, two, five, ten, sixteen, twenty-one, and twenty-five years of age, and every term of five years from thence to one hundred." *Memorial of the American Philosophical Society, Jan. 10, 1800,* in U.S. Congress, *House Report,* 41st Cong., 2d sess., no. 3, Jan. 18, 1879, p. 35. Congress ignored the memorial, approving instead a schedule which, for free whites, recorded the population under ten years of age, from ten to under sixteen, from sixteen to under twenty-six, from twenty-six to under forty-five, and forty-five and over. This schedule was retained in the other censuses taken during Jefferson's life, those of 1810 and 1820. Carroll D. Wright, *The History and Growth of the United States Census* (Washington, D.C., 1900), pp. 18, 20–21, 26, 132–33.

103. Among the amendments Jefferson urged, the following is noteworthy: "I wish," he told John Taylor of Caroline, "it were possible to obtain a single amendment to our constitution"—one "taking from the federal government the power of borrowing." This, he added, would restore "the administration of our government to the genuine principles of it's constitution." Jefferson to Taylor, Nov. 26, 1798, *Ford,* VIII, p. 481.

104. Alternatively, we can say that in later years Jefferson tends to adapt his message to the targeted audience. If the letter deals with debt and national finances, he stresses the right of the living generation to be free of inherited obligations; if with constitutional revision, it will tend to stress that. Given the urgency of debt-related issues after 1812, it is not surprising that Jefferson came to emphasize that part of the principle; this does not mean, of course, that he abandoned constitutional revision.

105. On the primal scene of the dinner-table bargain, see Jefferson's c. 1792 account in *Boyd,* XVII, pp. 205–7. Also see TJ to Edmund Randolph, Feb. 3, 1794, *Ford,* VIII, p. 138, for the comment, made early in his first retirement, that his only politics was "declaring to my countrymen the shameless corruption of a portion of the representatives to the 1st & 2d Congresses and their implicit devotion to the Treasury." He intended his words to "produce exertions to reform the evil, on the success of which the form of government is to depend."

106. J. G. A. Pocock insists that "even Thomas Jefferson was not immune from this double vision, that his ideals were rooted in a past as well as in a future, and that he viewed the movement of history with one auspicious and one drooping eye." "Conservative Enlightenment and Democratic Revolutions: American and French Cases in British Perspective," *Government and Opposition,* 24 (1989), p. 99. From the other end of the spectrum, Joyce Appleby notes the "unresolved tensions of Jefferson's own thought," observing that "Jefferson has obligingly bequeathed to posterity statements supporting both sides of arguments formed along the democratic-liberal axis." "Historians, Community, and the Pursuit of Jefferson: Comment on Professor Tomlins," *Studies in American Political Development,* 4 (1990), p. 41. While this is by no stretch of the imagination a concession on her part that Jefferson straddles the republican-liberal divide, it does suggest that she, too, sees Jefferson as pointing in more than one direction. One might also want to take note of the argument in Isaac Kramnick, "The Discourse of Politics in 1787: The Constitution and Its Critics on Individualism, Community, and the State," in Belz et al., eds., *To Form a More Perfect Union,* pp. 166–216, which identifies a veritable cacophony of political languages in 1787–88, none of them emerging as dominant. Finally, for a slightly bemused look at the way in which our understanding of the Founding Era has become ever more complicated as the earlier either/or positions have begun to unravel, see Daniel T. Rogers, "Republicanism: The Career of a Concept," *Journal of American History,* 79 (1992), 11–38.

107. This view of Jefferson is not universally shared. For an exchange that lays out the

arguments for and against, see Lance Banning, "Jeffersonian Ideology Revisited: Liberal and Classical Ideas in the New American Republic," *WMQ,* XLIII (1986), pp. 3–19, and Joyce Appleby, "Republicanism in Old and New Contexts," ibid., pp. 20–34.

108. This is, of course, not entirely unlike the vision Joyce Appleby delineates in *Capitalism and a New Social Order: The Republican Vision of the 1790s* (New York, 1984).

109. Jefferson, Sixth Annual Message, Dec. 2, 1806; Eighth Annual Message, Nov. 8, 1808, *LofA,* pp. 528–30, 548–49. But the antilog-rolling provisos he attached after the War of 1812 to his endorsement of a constitutional amendment authorizing congressional spending for internal improvements suggest that the moment of optimism was brief. See, for example, TJ to Albert Gallatin, June 16, 1817; to Edward Livingston, April 4, 1823, *Ford,* XII, pp. 72–73, 350.

110. On the New Deal's use and misuse of Jefferson and his principle, see Merrill D. Peterson, *The Jefferson Image in the American Mind* (New York, 1960), pp. 355–76, esp. p. 356. Frank Whitson Fetter, "The Revision of the Declaration of Independence in 1941," *WMQ,* XXXI (1974), pp. 133–38, throws additional light on FDR's appropriation of Jefferson's principle.

111. Jefferson's dislike of judicial construction of the Constitution is well known, but both in the 1790s and again after the War of 1812 he recognized that Congress could be an equally dangerous source of constitutional usurpations. See David Nicholas Mayer, "The Constitutional Thought of Thomas Jefferson" (Ph.D. diss., University of Virginia, 1988), pp. 453–524 on Congress, and pp. 593–666 on the courts.

112. TJ to Kercheval, July 12, 1816, *Ford,* XII, p. 11.

113. Readers may recall the television spots sponsored some years ago by W. R. Grace & Co., in which a newborn infant was handed a bill for its share of the national debt. And those who have visited the New York Public Library at 42nd Street will have seen the national debt clock, ticking away at an alarming rate, on a nearby building—this courtesy of one of New York's major real estate developers, Harry Macklowe. Neither the ad nor the clock invokes Jefferson directly, but there is, I suspect, a level on which many Americans still adhere to a sort of popular—albeit debased—Jeffersonianism when it comes to the national debt.

114. Inflation offers a way of reducing or even wiping out the national debt, but if there was anything Jefferson dreaded as much as debt, it was inflation. See TJ to Nathaniel Macon, Jan. 12, 1819; to Richard Rush, June 22, 1819; to William C. Rives, Nov. 28, 1819, *Ford,* XII, pp. 112, 128–29, 149–50.

115. Bruce Ackerman, for example, pays considerable attention to Madison's *Federalist* no. 49, but does not mention Jefferson's alternative. *We the People* (Cambridge, Mass., 1991), pp. 176, 179.

116. Note, for instance, that neither of the two constitutions adopted in antebellum Virginia (those of 1830 and 1850) contained an amending clause, let alone a provision for automatic revision. As Robert P. Sutton remarks, "Not until 1870 did Virginia surrender the idea of a constitution as immutable law." *Revolution to Secession: Constitution Making in the Old Dominion* (Charlottesville, Va., 1989), pp. 103, 141.

CHAPTER 10

Thomas Jefferson and the American Democratic Experience
The Origins of the Partisan Press, Popular Political Parties, and Public Opinion

MICHAEL LIENESCH

Among the many legacies left by Thomas Jefferson, democracy may be the most lasting. Author of the Declaration of Independence, champion of the Bill of Rights, and a founder of the Democratic-Republican party, Jefferson has passed on to the American people his abiding faith in the ability of citizens to govern themselves. Of the assumptions that make American politics possible, none is more fundamental. Yet it must be said that the legacy left by this high-minded and idealistic philosopher, who was also a hard-headed and pragmatic politician—this egalitarian owner of slaves—is by no means simple. At the very least, as Charles Wiltse suggested almost half a century ago, Jefferson has left Americans with a divided conception of democracy. On the one hand, in advocating equality and popular sovereignty, he paved the way for a tradition of social democracy that extends from Albert Gallatin to Andrew Jackson to FDR and the progressive reformers of the twentieth century. On the other hand, as a believer in liberty and limited government, he can be seen as the source of a tradition of democratic individualism that runs from John Taylor to John C. Calhoun to contemporary conservatives who champion personal rights and advocate restrictions on the role of the state. "This double emphasis in Jefferson's thought," concludes Wiltse, "has left to American democracy a dual tradition." [1]

To understand this dual tradition, scholars have turned to an analysis of the origins of democratic politics. Important among their studies have been those that investigate the development of American democracy during the formative era of the 1790s. Two of these treatments have been especially significant. In *The Jeffersonian Persuasion,* Lance Banning described the development of American democracy in the 1790s through an analysis of Jeffersonian thinking. Concentrating on a group of thinkers and writers loosely connected to one another and to Jefferson, Banning described their ideology of opposition as the product of a classical republican theory containing three distinct elements: a commonwealth ideal that emphasized commitment to the public weal or common good, a country ideology that stressed the conflict between popular and party interests, and a radical constitutional conception of popular sovereignty that defined the people as sovereign in republican states. All of these strains contained an abiding fear of corruption. In contrast, considering the same decade and many of the same thinkers in *Capitalism and a New Social Order,* Joyce Appleby views their thinking as the product of a more modern liberal theory that assumed individual interests, considered politics to be a clash of competing parties, and described sovereignty as the product of a representative system of government. Implicit in this liberal theory was a progressive, or at least a hopeful, vision of the future. While both writers admit that each of these strains was present in the political thought of the time, neither can explain how the two could coexist. As Appleby puts it, "The liberal concept of liberty was everything that the classical republican concept was not. So at odds were these two liberties that it is hard to understand how they could have coexisted in the same political discourse. That is a puzzle yet to be solved."[2]

This essay attempts to provide at least a partial solution to the puzzle. Its purpose is to consider the place of Thomas Jefferson in the creation of an American democratic experience. Its focus, like that of Banning and Appleby, is on the 1790s, and particularly on the period from 1791 to 1793, the short but highly significant time during which Jefferson served as Secretary of State in Washington's first Cabinet. It treats three themes: the development of the partisan press, the creation of popular political parties, and the mobilization of one of the earliest campaigns of organized public opinion. Using his own words, especially those from his public and private correspondence, the essay considers the changing thinking of Jefferson during this time, describing the transition from republican to liberal principles and the resulting interconnection of republicanism and liberalism in his political thought. At the same time, it tries to tie these philosophical principles to political practices, discussing his thinking in the context of the part he played in several of the most significant political events of his time. In this way, the essay attempts to show how Jefferson's contribution to the creation of a democratic experience was highly ironic, the product of a troubled transition from republicanism to liberalism, and of a sometimes painful pilgrimage from eighteenth- to nineteenth-century political ways. Yet it contends that while Jefferson did not describe himself as a democrat, his commitment to democratic politics was firm and enduring, and must be counted among his lasting legacies.

I

Almost as soon as he arrived in New York in late 1790 to assume his duties as Secretary of State, Jefferson had become concerned about the place of the republican press in the new nation. As a believer in the eighteenth-century commonwealth assumption that the press was the best safeguard against the abuse of authority by people in positions of power, and as an avid reader of every available domestic and foreign newspaper, he was almost at once dissatisfied. Put off by the provincialism of the New York papers and angry at the antirepublican sentiments that seemed to be all too prevalent in them, he decided to do what he could to encourage the development of a national newspaper that would be committed to espousing republican principles. Predisposed in his new role as Secretary of State to think both nationally and internationally and armed with the authority to select publishers to print the new nation's laws and other public documents, he determined to make use of his public position to establish such a newspaper. His purpose, he explained, proceeded "from a desire of seeing a purely republican vehicle of news established between the seat of government and all it's parts."[3]

Thus he set to work to create a national republican newspaper. At first sight, his plans may seem partisan and politically self-serving. Yet to Jefferson, considering the press in commonwealth terms as a sentinel of the people against the abuses of their rulers, his efforts were not only nonpartisan but also highly public-spirited. It is indicative of his intentions that his first overtures, made within two weeks of his arrival in New York, were to John Fenno, editor of the *Gazette of the United States*. While Fenno's *Gazette* would later become the flagship of the Federalist press, it was at this time less Federalist than federalist in character, being staunchly supportive of the new federal Constitution. Moreover, among American newspapers it could best lay claim to national status by virtue of its wide circulation in the states. Providing Fenno with copies brought through

diplomatic channels of the republican *Leyden Gazette,* which he saw as providing an antidote to the aristocratic sentiments of the English press, and
passing on information contained in his own diplomatic correspondence,
Jefferson actively encouraged Fenno's *Gazette* for most of 1790. When the
paper's editorial stance changed sharply during the summer of 1790, turning in what Jefferson thought was an antirepublican direction, he shifted
his support to the *General Advertiser* of Benjamin Franklin Bache, whose
Revolutionary republican pedigree had been passed to him from his famous
grandfather. Within a matter of months, as Bache's paper began to fall
short in selling subscriptions, Jefferson sought a more dependable and more
efficient republican publisher. It was in this context that he came to consider recruiting the one-time Revolutionary poet Philip Freneau, now a
New York editor. Increasingly enthusiastic about Freneau, Jefferson wrote
to his son-in-law Thomas Mann Randolph about his plan "to get another
weekly or *half-weekly* paper set up excluding advertisements, so that it
might go through the states, and furnish a whig-vehicle of intelligence."[4]
    In attempting to attract Freneau, Jefferson used the patronage power
available to him as Secretary of State. While his efforts might suggest partisan purposes, he saw the situation in nonpartisan terms, as evidence of a
respectably republican desire to establish a channel of communication between the people and their government. While Madison had first recommended Freneau for a clerkship in the office of the Secretary of State, Jefferson needed no encouragement to offer him the position—which required
that he serve as a clerk and translator (from French, in which Freneau never
claimed to be more than moderately proficient)—but that also "gives so
little to do as not to interfere with any other calling." When Freneau declined the clerkship, preferring to begin a paper in his native New Jersey,
Jefferson entered into a last-ditch effort to change his mind, acting through
Madison to assure Freneau that along with the clerkship, with its access to
much of the public and private correspondence of the Secretary of State, he
was also being offered the contract for "the publication of all proclamations
and other public notices within my department, and the printing of the
laws." When Freneau relented in August 1791 and decided to establish the
National Gazette in the new capital of Philadelphia, the Secretary provided
what he had promised, including a steady stream of sources which he not
only delivered but also on occasion edited and even translated for the paper.
Although the extent of his editorial involvement is not entirely clear, Jefferson was active enough to know in advance what would be published in
the paper. "I need not write you news, as you receive Freneau's paper," he
would write to his friend Dr. George Gilmer. "In his next after this date

will be an interesting report of a committee of Congress on the causes of the failure of the last campaign."[5]

Jefferson supported Freneau's paper both privately and publicly. Again assuming commonwealth principles, Jefferson made no attempt at secrecy, considering his support to be above board and in the public interest. It was in this republican spirit that he entered into an active and highly visible campaign to assure the success of the *National Gazette*. Thus his private letters and public papers of this time show him deeply interested in issues such as the development of post roads, the placement of post offices, and the rates for postal delivery, especially of newspapers. Going even further, he repeatedly sought to secure subscriptions for the paper from friends and family members, acting as a kind of one-man advertising agent and customer service representative. At the same time, he was forwarding his own funds to Freneau to be paid back later. His letter to his neighbor Thomas Bell suggests the intensity of his involvement, while also capturing the complexity of some of the financial considerations. After listing subscribers in his area of Virginia, he explained the arrangements to Bell:

> Having learned by Mr. Randolph's last letter th[at the] post to Charlottesville is now regularly established, I ha[ve given] in to Freneau the list of subscribers you sent me . . . and have desired him to send off the [papers] by every Friday's post, so that you will receive them eight days afterwards. He is to give me a note of the advances necessary to be made, which I am to pay him for the subscribers, and must get you to settle with them for me. I am in hopes indeed that you will send forward five names more, and so be entitled to your paper gratis, for collecting the rest. In this manner the business can be done between them and Freneau by you and myself.

Throughout 1791, he remained an active and vocal advocate for the paper, endorsing it frequently to his correspondents. "I am in hopes his paper will give satisfaction," he told Bell: "it is certainly the best I ever saw published in America."[6]

Yet Jefferson's thinking, not only about Freneau's paper but also about the role of the press, had begun to take a turn. Throughout the summer of 1791, American newspaper readers had been treated to an extraordinary and unprecedented popular debate concerning the character of republican politics. The debate had been inspired in part by Jefferson himself—apparently unintentionally—when his endorsement of Thomas Paine's pamphlet *The Rights of Man,* along with an offhand criticism of certain antirepublican "heresies," had made its way into a number of newspapers. Responding to these remarks, which were widely taken to be a criticism of John Adams, were a bevy of anonymous critics led by "Publicola," later considered to be John Quincy Adams. Other writers responded to the responders in support of Jefferson, and the nation's newspapers began to fill with partisan rhetoric. By midsummer at least a few newspapers had begun to choose sides in the conflict; first among them was Fenno's. Already in late July, at a point at which he was actively recruiting Freneau, Jefferson was complaining to William Short in France of Fenno's turn away from republican principles, describing "the tory-paper of Fenno" as "rarely admitting any thing which defends the present form of government in opposition to his desire of subverting it to make way for a king, lords and commons." At the same time, he took heart that the people were refusing to subscribe to Fenno's aristocratic sentiments, remaining "to a man, firm as a rock in their republicanism." [7]

While his thinking was changing, Jefferson continued to conceive of the role of the press in commonwealth terms. He was realistic enough to see Freneau as offering a partisan political alternative to Fenno. At the same time he continued to describe the choice between the two in commonwealth terminology, as a conflict of principles rather than of parties or policies. Increasingly considering Fenno an advocate of some kind of American aristocracy, Jefferson assumed that Freneau would have no trouble in attracting loyal republican readers to the other side. Fenno's paper, he told Madison in July, was already "under general condemnation for it's toryism and it's incessant efforts to overturn the government." All that was needed, Jefferson assumed, was that the choice be put before the people. It was with this in mind that he wrote to David Humphreys that he should "soon be able to send you another newspaper written in a contrary spirit to that of Fenno. . . . The two papers will shew you both sides of our politics." At the same time, he held firm in his eighteenth-century faith that when presented with the choice, the people would roundly reject aristocratic principles and support republican ones. So it was that he regularly sent Thomas Mann Randolph copies not only of Freneau's paper, but also of Fenno's, allowing how the comparison "will enable our neighbors to judge whether Freneau is likely to answer their expectation." [8]

Nevertheless, Jefferson's conception of the role of the press was changing. Throughout the fall of 1791, he continued to be enthusiastic about the new national newspaper. Moreover, he continued to view the paper in the terms he had originally envisioned, as a nonpartisan source of impartial information. For its part, the *National Gazette* justified this enthusiasm by taking a nonpartisan stance, apparently at least in part to build circulation and establish a reputation for reliability. By early 1792, however, largely in response to Hamilton's economic program, a full-fledged newspaper war had broken out, and Freneau was in the thick of the fighting. For several months the *National Gazette* featured a series of anonymous attacks on Hamilton's aristocratic policies: several of these essays were almost certainly written by Madison, apparently with the approval and encouragement of Jefferson. Added to them were additional attacks, some quite vitriolic, by other anonymous writers. Freneau himself contributed columns expressing his own criticism, in no uncertain terms, of Hamilton and Vice President Adams. Jefferson seemed to approve of these developments, although he appeared somewhat uneasy about their direction. His letter to Thomas Barclay in April conveys a sense of worry: "With the present I send you the newspapers, which will inform you so fully of all transactions, public and private here, as to leave me little to add. You will perceive therein the state of the public mind, somewhat dissatisfied of late."[9]

Within a matter of months, he was thinking in altogether different terms. Throughout the early part of 1792, Republican essayists controlled the public debate over Hamilton's economic policies. Then, in July and August, writing as "T. L." and "An American," Hamilton struck back, seizing the initiative in a series of stinging attacks on Jefferson that called into question not only his public principles but also his personal motives. Arguing from liberal premises and drawing a clear distinction between public and private ends, Hamilton raised the issue of Jefferson's integrity. Thus he contended that Jefferson had recruited, paid, and consistently supported Freneau, using public funds and the power of his patronage to support a partisan newspaper whose only purpose was to advance Jefferson's own political ambitions by attacking the present administration and, by extension, the Constitution itself.

Jefferson was stunned by the assault on his character and replied to Hamilton's charges in a long letter to the president written from Monticello in early September 1792. Mixing angry self-righteousness with indignant self-defense, Jefferson proceeded to answer all charges point by point, justifying his relationship to Freneau and his newspaper in an excessively detailed way that suggested his own misgivings. In confronting and denying Hamilton's charges, Jefferson took on his enemy's assumptions and even his terminology. Thus in closing, after denouncing Hamilton for his lack of personal integrity, he defended his own: "I believe that, as far as I am known, it is not as an enemy to the Republic, nor an intriguer against it, nor a waster of it's revenue, nor prostitutor of it to the purposes of corruption, as the American represents me: and I confide that yourself are satisfied that, as to dissension in the newspapers, not a syllable of them has ever proceeded from me." [10]

The defense marks a turning point in Jefferson's thought. Though holding to commonwealth theory and considering himself somehow superior to political partisanship, still he found himself increasingly thinking in partisan terms as well as playing a more actively partisan political role. From the fall of 1792 on, the *National Gazette* assumed the character of a Jeffersonian newspaper, becoming ever more closely associated with Jefferson and those around him. At the same time, its criticism of Hamilton and his followers became increasingly predictable and shrill. By the end of the year the paper's rhetoric had become unrelentingly partisan, with Freneau's polemicists pounding out a steady drumbeat of denunciations, criticizing the Hamiltonians for their self-serving policies and, ironically, for their partisanship. Although worried about its changing character, Jefferson continued to encourage its publication, writing in a way that was both more circumspect and more politically calculating than before. Thus he confided in November 1792 to Thomas Mann Randolph: "Freneau's paper is getting into Massachusetts under the patronage of Hancock and Sam Adams, and Mr. Ames, the colossus of the monocrats and paper men, will either be left out or hard run. The people of that state are republican; but hitherto they have heard nothing but The hymns and lauds chaunted by Fenno." [11]

Jefferson's idealism did not disappear. Instead, as he applied it to an ideologically polarized political world, it began to seem more realistic, or at least more partisan. From early 1793 on, as American political divisions deepened in reaction to the French Revolution, partisan newspapers not only proliferated but also became even more ideological. Taking the lead was Freneau's *National Gazette,* which by midyear had become so vocal in its devotion to the cause of the French Revolution that it had begun to be politically embarrassing to Jefferson and those around him. By July he would be complaining to Madison that the paper's extreme views had made it impossible for them to use it to get their message to the public, leaving them "no channel of our own." Even so, when Freneau's newspaper began to fail later in the year, in part through a lack of subscriptions, Jefferson was writing to Thomas Mann Randolph, asking him to encourage subscribers to "send on their money." And when the president suggested to Jefferson that he act to curb Freneau's outbursts, Jefferson flatly refused. Ironically, almost unwittingly, the commonwealth philosopher, champion of the common good, had become also the liberal politician, defender of a free and partisan press. "His paper," he wrote in a passage that reveals his principled partisanship, "has saved our constitution which was galloping fast into monarchy, & has been checked by no means so powerfully as by that paper." [12]

II

In taking up his new position as Secretary of State, Jefferson brought with him a set of strongly held assumptions about public service. As a believer in the commonwealth principles of the British "country," or oppositionist, tradition, he assumed that politics consisted of a struggle between the people and the placemen, meaning the court politicians who were constantly conspiring to create parties of privilege that would subvert the liberty of the people. Furthermore, as the product of an eighteenth-century political culture, he saw the political world as consensual, deferential, and elitist, believing that citizens would choose, as a matter of course, to defer to legitimate republican leaders, men of talent and social standing who would protect the people from these parties of privilege. It was in these terms that Jefferson conceived of himself as a self-sacrificing servant committed to putting the interest of the people above that of any party or person. Arriving in New York, he sought to put theory into practice, calling on old colleagues and friends for advice and counsel and attempting to attract to the new government a set of virtuous and disinterested public servants. His earliest letters suggest his thinking; for example, when he wrote to William Short, then representing the new nation in France, asking that Short assist the tobacco merchant Andrew Donald in his attempts to establish business ties there. Describing Donald as a man of "integrity and honor," Jefferson observed that "I cannot do better than recommend him as my particular friend to you, and ask for him your counsel and recommendation to the proper persons so far as may be consistent with the general interests of our country which is the first object of your office, and the right of other individuals of it which may in justice claim your patronage also." [13]

Almost at once, Jefferson became aware that American politics in the 1790s were not to be so simple. Throughout the last session of the first Congress, which extended from December into the early months of 1791, Hamilton and his allies had been pressing, mostly successfully, for passage of a national economic policy. While Jefferson had supported parts of the program and had been active in bringing about the compromise that secured the assumption of state debts, he was deeply disturbed by proposals to create a national bank and a system of excise taxes that were particularly unpopular in the South and West. Moreover, as protests over Hamilton's programs appeared in Philadelphia, arriving especially from the South, he began to express concern about the state of political opinion beyond the halls of Congress. "There is a vast mass of discontent gathered in the South," he wrote to Robert R. Livingston in early February, "and how and when it will break god knows. I look forward to it with some anxiety." [14]

Looking for some sense of political opinion in the states, Jefferson began to reach out. These early efforts can be seen as attempts to create alliances that would later coalesce into a more coherent political party. It was, for example, at this time that he and Madison undertook an extended trip to New York and parts of New England, during which they collected botanical specimens and took political soundings. The political significance of the trip is debatable, but Jefferson's letters during this time reveal his intention of reaching beyond Congress and the new government in search of a broader political opinion. Thus he wrote to friends with increasing frequency during the early months of 1791. In all of the letters, he addressed his correspondents in traditional republican terms, confiding to them as friends and fellow gentlemen, and assuming without question that their views represented not only those of other people of rank and status, but also those of the citizens who looked to them for leadership. At the same time, he seemed increasingly interested in the perspectives of a wider public. For example, he sounded out Livingston about popular political views: "Are the people in your quarter as well contented with the proceedings of our government, as their representatives say they are?" Writing to George Mason in Virginia, he inquired specifically about Hamilton's economic plan: "What is said in our country of the fiscal arrangements now going on?" To Colonel James Innes, another Virginian, he asked again about Hamilton's program: "What is said with you of the most prominent proceedings of the last Congress?" The letters show a change in Jefferson's conception of parties; assuming a growing gap between government and the people, he sought to bridge it by bringing the decisions of a distant government before the bar of public opinion in the states. As Jefferson told Mason, "Whether these measures be right or wrong, abstractedly, more attention should be paid to the general opinion." [15]

At the same time, there appeared a subtle shift in Jefferson's conception of representation. Writing to a small and more or less like-minded group of gentlemen, he continued to invoke traditional assumptions about the role of republican leaders. At the same time, however, he began to suggest that officials speak not for all, but for a more specific republican interest. His letter to Colonel Innes, written in late March 1791, shows the shift in his thought. "I wish you would come forward," he wrote, "to the federal legislature and give your assistance on a larger scale than that on which you are acting at the present. I am satisfied you could render essential service, and I have such confidence in the purity of your republicanism, that I know your efforts would go in a right direction. Zeal and talents added to the republican scale will do no harm in Congress."[16]

In fact, Jefferson's thinking about the role of political parties in the new republic was in transition. Throughout late 1791, as Hamilton and his allies successfully carried their economic program through Congress, Jefferson came to consider politics less as a consensual gathering of gentlemen and more as a clash of conflicting parties. At this time he began to brand Hamilton and his supporters as antirepublicans, his letters bristling with references to American "aristocrats" and "monocrats." Moreover, tapping republican fears of faction, he began to portray Hamilton as a party leader, the head of a conspiratorial cabal that was attempting to use executive power to subvert legislative sovereignty. Increasingly during these months, as Merrill Peterson points out, he talked in terms of "we" and "they." By early 1792, his relations with Hamilton, always cool, had become conspicuously cold. Out of doors, in the increasingly partisan press, public debate was polarizing along party lines. By early summer, Jefferson was describing American politics as a battle between righteous republicans and cunning conspirators determined to destroy the Constitution. He wrote to Lafayette:

> While you are exterminating the monster aristocracy, and pulling out the teeth and fangs of it's associate monarchy, a contrary tendency is discovered in some here. A sect has shewn itself among us, who declare they espoused our new constitution, not as a good and sufficient thing itself, but only as a step to an English constitution, the only thing good and sufficient in itself, in their eye. It is happy for us that these are preachers without followers, and that our people are firm and constant in their republican purity.[17]

While changing, Jefferson's conception of parties was not changing rapidly enough to keep pace with American politics. Throughout the summer of 1792, as elections to the Second Congress approached, he seemed confused and divided. On the one hand, he was determined to check the power of Hamilton and his cabal and was deeply involved with Madison and Monroe in attempts to assure that friends of the republic were elected. He wrote to Lafayette, "Too many of these stock jobbers and King-jobbers have come into our legislature, or rather too many of our legislature have become stock jobbers and king-jobbers. However the voice of the people is beginning to make itself heard, and will probably cleanse their seats at the ensuing election." At the same time, Jefferson continued to see himself as above party politics, a representative of the people as a whole, or at least of the great republican majority, and not of any faction. Indeed, when Hamilton and his supporters portrayed him as the leader of a political party, Jefferson was affronted and outraged, and denounced Hamilton for "daring to call the republican party *a faction.*" Even while protesting, however, he continued to act like a party leader, seeking to attract friends into the ranks of republican officeholders. Thus he wrote in August to Edward Rutledge, "Would to god yourself, Genl. Pinkney, Majr. Pinkney would come forward and aid us with your efforts. You are all known, respected, wished for: but you refuse yourselves to every thing. What is to become of us, my dear friend, if the vine and the fig-tree withdraw, and leave us to the bramble and thorn?" [18]

Succeeding politically, Jefferson was struggling philosophically. By the end of the summer of 1792, as the republican cause seemed to be on the verge of victory in many of the coming congressional election campaigns, the Secretary was still attempting to reconcile his fear of factions with his increasing involvement in what to all appearances was active party politics. This ambivalence was most apparent in his responses to the disputed gubernatorial election in New York, where John Jay—running with the strong backing of Hamilton and John Adams—was defeated by George Clinton, Jefferson's clear choice, in an election in which Clinton's canvassers nullified votes in several counties sympathetic to Jay. While pleased at Clinton's election, which also constituted a defeat for Hamilton and his faction, Jefferson was troubled by the means used to secure victory. Writing to Monroe, he made clear his opinion that parties must operate according to the highest standards of public virtue. He wrote, "Upon the whole it seems probable that Mr. Jay had a majority of the qualified voters, and I think not only that Clinton would have honored himself by declining to accept, and agreeing to take another fair start, but that probably such a conduct would have ensured him a majority on a new election. To retain the office when it is probable the majority was against him is dishonorable." [19]

At almost the same time, Jefferson was on the defensive. Perhaps because he prided himself on his political virtue and partly because he continued to think of himself as a representative of the people rather than of any party, he was shocked when Hamilton denounced him in a letter to the Virginian Edward Carrington as the leader of a faction designed to overthrow the administration and the constitution. Of course, Jefferson should have been able to predict the assault, since he himself had been saying the same things about Hamilton in a series of letters and meetings with the president. Thus in a letter to Washington written in May 1792, at almost the same moment Hamilton was writing to Carrington, Jefferson was describing the division between "Monarchical federalists" who saw the new government "merely as a stepping stone to monarchy" and the "republican federalists, who espoused the same government for it's intrinsic merits." In a conversation with the president two months later, he warned of the "considerable squadron" in Congress, tied to the Treasury, that was "devoted to the paper and stockjobbing interest," and that was "legislating for their own interests in opposition to those of the people." When Washington responded in late August with an admonition to both Hamilton and Jefferson to set aside partisan differences, Jefferson answered defensively. Thus in his letter of September 9, in which he also denied Hamilton's allegations against him concerning Freneau, he defended himself against the charge that he was acting as leader of an anti-administration party. Condemning Hamilton for his "cabals with members of the legislature," he continued to denounce him and his Federalist followers as "deserters from the rights and interests of the people." As for himself, however, "no cabals or intrigues of mine have produced those in the legislature."[20]

Jefferson had become disillusioned. Throughout the fall of 1792, stung by Hamilton's charges and smarting at the president's admonitions, he continued to be troubled, as if trying to convince himself that he had done nothing to warrant the claims that he was acting as a party politician. Reiterating his opposition to party politics, he wrote to his friend Charles Clay, refusing to endorse his candidacy for Congress: "Your favor of Aug. 8. came duly to hand, and I should with pleasure have done what you therein desired, as I ever should what would serve or oblige you: but from a very early period of my life I determined never to intermeddle with elections of the people, and have invariably adhered to this determination." Jefferson was far from convincing. Instead of standing on principle—and stopping when he was ahead—he went on to make the implausible claim that he had little political influence. He wrote, "In my own county, where there have been so many elections in which my inclinations were enlisted, I yet never interfered. I could the less do it in the present instance, to a people so very distant from me, utterly unknown to me, and to whom I also am unknown: and above all, I a stranger, to presume to recommend one who is well known to them. They could not but put this question to me 'who are you pray?'" At the same time, referring to an earlier letter in which he had expressed support for Clay's candidacy, Jefferson went on to reinterpret its message: "In writing the letter to you on the former occasion I went further than I had ever before done; but that was addressed to yourself to whom I had a right to write, and not to persons either unknown to me, or very capable of judging for themselves."[21]

Jefferson had become what he had before consistently denied, a party politician. All that he believed as a matter of political principle, including every inch of his country ideology, led him to despise the role that he was now playing. Holding his tongue, relying heavily on Madison and Monroe, standing aside while an army of surrogates carried their common cause into the newspapers, he had become nonetheless a leader of the Republican party. Apparently he did not relish the task and seemed sometimes overwhelmed by it. Thus, still at Monticello in September, he wrote to John Syme, "The difficulty is no longer to find candidates for the offices, but offices for the candidates." When he returned to Philadelphia in the fall the situation seemed even worse, and he complained how old friends, now partisan enemies, crossed the street to avoid one another. "Party animosities here have raised a wall of seper[atio]n," he observed, "between those who differ in political sentim[en]ts." Looking back longingly to Monticello, trying to keep his promise to himself to resign his position as Secretary of State in the spring, he felt trapped, unable to leave under the cloud of Hamilton's charges, unwilling to give up the government to Hamilton's increasing influence. Again ironically, and almost in spite of himself, Jefferson the country ideologue, ardent enemy of factions, found himself playing the unlikely role of Jefferson the party politician, leader of a political party formed largely in his image. A December letter to Thomas Pinckney captures his distaste for politics, along with the pleasure he took in beating the Federalists at the polls in the fall elections: "They endeavored with as little success to conjure up the ghost of anti-federalism, and to have it believed that this and republicanism were the same, and that both were Jacobinism. But those who felt themselves republicans and federalists too, were little moved by this artifice; so that the result of the election has been promising."[22]

III

From the time he began his tenure as Secretary of State, Jefferson had proceeded to construct an American foreign policy based on the premise of popular sovereignty. As the product of an earlier era of colonial resistance and Revolutionary state-making, he was predisposed to believe in a radical republican constitutional theory that equated the voice of the people with the will of the state. Throughout his early days as Secretary he applied the assumption, thinking of himself and the diplomats to whom he wrote in Europe as representatives not only of the United States government but also of the American people. Thus in his diplomatic discourse he more or less indiscriminately used the terms "country," "government," "nation," and "people," substituting them for one another and seeing them in most contexts as synonymous. With the French Revolution, however, and particularly with the suspension of the monarchy in late 1792, he was asked for the first time to apply American assumptions to other revolutionary republics. The application was problematic, as the American representative to France, the staunchly conservative Gouverneur Morris, argued repeatedly at this time that the revolutionary French government not be recognized as the sovereign authority of the French state. Jefferson was firm in response, laying down the principle of popular sovereignty not only to Morris but also to American representatives to other European states as well. It was, he observed at this time, "the Catholic principle of republicanism, to wit, that every people may establish what form of government they please, and change it as they please. The will of the nation being the only thing essential." [23]

At stake was not only diplomatic principle, but also domestic politics. As diplomatic reports arrived in America announcing the creation of the French republic and the defeat of the aristocratic armies that had threatened it, Jefferson was jubilant, and he eagerly passed the news on to Freneau and the rest of the American press. Even more gratifying was the response of the American people, who greeted reports of French revolutionary successes with popular celebrations, public dinners, and countless toasts raised to the new fellow republic. Reporting to George Gilmer in December, shortly after receiving some of the first reports from France, Jefferson seemed surprised by the popular rejoicing: "We have just received the glorious news of the Prussian army being obliged to retreat, and hope it will be followed by some proper catastrophe on them. This news has given wry faces to our monocrats here, but sincere joy to the great body of citizens. It arrived only in the afternoon yesterday, and the bells were rung, and some illuminations took place in the evening." [24]

As the round of celebrations and dinners continued—John Adams would count twenty-two festivals, fifty-one celebrations, and 193 public dinners in late 1792 and early 1793 alone—Jefferson continued to seem surprised by the response, although his letters suggest that he was rapidly beginning to realize its political potential. "The Monocrats here still affect to disbelieve all this," he reported to John F. Mercer in mid-December, "while the republicans are rejoicing and taking to themselves the name of Jacobins which two months ago was affixed on them by way of stigma." By the first week of the new year, he had come to see the events in France as not only important but portentous for American politics. Thus he wrote on January 7 to his son-in-law Thomas Mann Randolph, "The event of the revolution there is now little doubted of, even by its enemies. The sensation it has produced here, and the indications of them in the public papers, have shown that the form our own government was to take depended much more on the events of France than any body had before imagined." [25]

In Jefferson's radical republican constitutional thinking, public opinion was closely linked to public policy. The connection was clearest in foreign policy, as he showed in a letter to William Short, who was acting as an American loan agent in France at this time. Responding to a letter in which Short had been strongly critical of some of the French revolutionary leaders, Jefferson was stern and almost patronizing to his republican protégé. Describing revolutionary events to Short—who had seen them himself at first hand—Jefferson declared the French Jacobin party to be the true representative of the French people: "And the Nation was with them in opinion, for however they might have been formerly for the constitution framed by the first assembly, they were come over from their hope in it, and were now generally Jacobins." Admitting that there had been excesses and deploring the loss of life and property, Jefferson went on to make it clear that such costs, presumably paid mostly by aristocrats, were small compared to the benefits derived by the people. He continued, in lines that would become famous and infamous: "My own affections have been deeply wounded by some of the martyrs to this cause, but rather than it should have failed, I would have seen half the earth desolated. Were there but an Adam & an Eve left in every country, & left free, it would be better than as it now is." Furthermore, Jefferson allowed that this opinion was not his alone, but that of "99. in an hundred of our citizens." Thus he underlined the connection between popular opinion and public policy. Describing a recent conversation with Washington in which the president expressed support for the French Revolution, and denigrating the few who were hostile to France while favoring England, he closed with a ringing defense of the republican cause, both at home and abroad. He concluded, "This country is entirely republican, friends to the constitution, anxious to preserve it and to have it administered according to it's own republican principles." [26]

Soon Jefferson was realizing that public opinion could play a significant role in partisan politics as well. Reports from France continued to generate widespread enthusiasm. To Jefferson's surprise, even the news of the king's execution did not seem to dampen popular support for the revolution. Aristocrats and conservatives were apparently appalled, but the tide of opinion was against them. "It is certain," he reported to Madison in March, "that the ladies of this city, of the first circle are all open-mouthed against the murderers of a sovereign, and they generally speak those sentiments which the more cautious husband smothers." [27] As the announcement of war between England and France arrived, American politics became more polarized than ever before. Yet, as Jefferson realized at once, the advantage was clearly on the side of France's supporters. As he wrote to Madison later in the spring of 1793:

> The line is now drawing so clearly as to shew on one side 1. the fashionable circles of Phila, N. York, Boston & Charleston (natural aristocrats), 2. merchants trading on British capitals, 3. paper men, (all the old tories are found in some one of these three descriptions). On the other side are 1. merchants trading on their own capitals, 2. Irish merchants, 3. tradesmen, mechanics, farmers & every other possible description of our citizens. [28]

Writing to Brissot de Warville in France, he was even more enthusiastic. "We too have our aristocrats and monocrats, and as they float on the surface, they shew much, though they weigh little. . . . Tho' they may harrass our spirits, they cannot make impression on our center.—A germ of corruption indeed has been transferred from our dear mother country, & has already borne fruit, but its blight is begun from the breath of the people." [29]

Policy and politics would soon merge. With the arrival in America of the new French minister Edmond Charles Genet, a radical supporter of the revolution and a zealous advocate for the revolutionary republic, American politics was thrown into confusion. Again Hamilton took the initiative within the Cabinet, seeking to convince the president that Genet, whose instructions came from a self-created revolutionary council, should not be received as the duly constituted diplomatic representative of France. Hamilton went on to argue that the American alliance with France was founded on treaties signed with the French king and therefore should be declared void. In a long and closely reasoned legal opinion written in his role as Secretary of State, Jefferson countered these claims, insisting on the basis of republican principles that Genet be received as representative of France and that the alliance be considered to remain in force. For his part, the president hesitated, seeking to steer a neutral course but seeming to list noticeably to Hamilton's side. In the meantime, Genet had landed in Charleston to be welcomed by huge crowds of citizens, and was cheered by continuing demonstrations of public support on his way to Philadelphia. Recognizing the power of this public display, Jefferson determined to offset Hamilton's initiatives in the Cabinet by encouraging the popular response out of doors. He wrote hopefully to Madison, "We expect Mr. Genest [*sic*] here within a few days. It seems as if his arrival would furnish occasion for the *people* to testify their affections without respect to the cold caution of their government." [30]

At the same time, however, Jefferson was rapidly becoming aware of the dangers inherent in his strategy. As reports arrived of Genet's tumultuous reception, detailing celebrations and feasts in his honor in towns and cities along his way to Philadelphia, he seemed pleased but worried. Particularly troubling were reports that Genet, acting under instructions from Paris, had begun to contract with captains of American vessels to attack and seize British merchant ships. Protests from the British minister came directly to the Secretary of State's desk. Jefferson's correspondence thus began to betray signs of unease. He confided to Monroe on May 5, shortly before Genet's arrival in the capital:

> All the old spirit of 1776. is rekindling. The newspapers from Boston to Charleston prove this; & even the Monocrat papers are obliged to publish the most furious Philippics against England. A French frigate took a British prize off the capes of Delaware the other day, & sent her up here. Upon her coming into sight thousands & thousands of the *yeomanry* of the city crowded & covered the wharves. Never before was such a crowd seen there, and when the British colours were seen *reversed,* & the French flying above them they burst into peals of exultation. I wish we may be able to repress the spirit of the people within the limits of a fair neutrality. [31]

As Genet approached, Jefferson was increasingly concerned. For weeks, Hamilton had been pressing the president for some statement about the American position on the war between England and France. In late April Washington acted, publishing a presidential proclamation, later known as the Proclamation of Neutrality, that set forth a strictly impartial position on the war and included a stern condemnation of any hostile acts carried out by American citizens. Although not completely pleased with the document, Jefferson supported it as the best possible means of maintaining an uneasy peace with England while continuing friendly relations with the French. Moreover, as Secretary of State, the official representative of the American government, and as a member of the Cabinet, he felt doubly obligated to carry out the president's policies. To Genet, now arrived in Philadelphia, the Secretary was cordial but clear about the American position. At the same time, he was becoming concerned that the French minister was driving a wedge between the American government and the American people. As Genet continued to carry out his instructions, urging American captains to harrass British ships, Jefferson described his worries to Thomas Mann Randolph: "The war between them [France] and England embarrasses our government daily & immensely. The predilection of our citizens for France renders it very difficult to suppress their attempts to cruize against the English on the ocean, and to do justice to the latter in cases where they are entitled to it."[32] Four days later, caught in the middle between Genet and his own government, and apparently feeling increasingly alienated from public opinion, he confided again to Monroe:

> I do not augur well of the mode of conduct of the new French minister; I fear he will enlarge the circle of those disaffected to his country. I am doing everything in my power to moderate the impetuosity of his movements, and to destroy the dangerous opinion which has been excited in him, that the people of the U. S. will disavow the acts of their government, and that he has an appeal from the Executive to Congress, & from both to the people.[33]

Only ten days later, in the midst of the diplomatic crisis provoked by the French seizure of the British ship the *Little Sarah,* and having been told only days before of Genet's plan to use American citizens recruited along the southern frontier to incite rebellion in Spanish Louisiana, the Secretary of State had come to the end of his rope. He wrote angrily to Madison,

> Never in my opinion, was so calamitious an appointment made, as that of the present Minister of F. here. Hot headed, all imagination, no judgment, passionate, disrespectful & even indecent towards the P. in his written as well as verbal communications, talking of appeals from him to Congress, from them to the people, urging the most unreasonable & groundless propositions, & in the most dictatorial style &c. &c. &c. If ever it should be necessary to lay his communications before Congress or the public, they will excite universal indignation. He renders my position immensely difficult.[34]

Once again Jefferson was on the defensive. Throughout the summer of 1793 he appeared to be balancing on a kind of tightrope, attempting to reconcile his sympathies toward France, along with those of the sizable part of the American population who supported the French revolutionary cause, with his loyalty to the president and the government he represented. The assaults seemed to come from all sides. Predictably, the first came from Hamilton, writing as "Pacificus" in a series of articles in Fenno's *Gazette.* In a highly ideological defense of the president's proclamation, he declared the French alliance to be null and void, denounced the French Revolution,

and, at least by implication, denigrated the patriotism of those who disagreed with him, including those in the government. Jefferson was incensed, and contacted Madison at once, imploring him to respond in what
would become the letters of "Helvidius:" "For God's sake, my dear Sir, take
up your pen, select the most striking heresies and cut him to pieces in the
face of the public. There is nobody else who can & will enter the lists with
him." By July, as diplomatic relations with France deteriorated, the Cabinet had come to the conclusion that Genet would have to be recalled. For
his part, Jefferson supported the recall, only to find that many of his supporters opposed it. Of particular concern to him was the support for Genet
expressed by members of the Democratic-Republican societies that had
sprung up in many American cities to champion the French and republican
causes. Encouraging Madison and Monroe to establish contact with these
groups, he made it clear to them that support for Genet had to be distinguished from support for France. Complicating the problem was Hamilton's threat to present the case to the public as a choice between Genet and
the president. Jefferson was quick to see the ominous possibilities, realizing
at once that public opinion could be an enemy as well as a friend. "We have
decided unanimously to *require* the *recall of Genet,"* he wrote to Madison.
"He will sink the republican interest if they do not *abandon him. Hamilton
presses eagerly an appeal i.e.* to the *people.* It's consequences you will readily
seize but *I hope we shall prevent it."* By late August the situation had become
even worse, as Genet's defiance threatened to wreak havoc not only on the
republican cause but on the emerging Republican party. A solemn Jefferson
wrote to Madison on August 25: "Genet has thrown down the gauntlet to
the President . . . and is himself forcing that appeal to the public, & risking that disgust, which I had so much wished should have been avoided."[35]
Jefferson felt defeated. In early September, the problem of Genet had
been solved, because the French minister fell out of favor with the new
Jacobin government in Paris. Residents of Philadelphia were fleeing the
epidemic of yellow fever that had struck the city suddenly, taking a terrible
toll in lives and effectively closing down the government. But the damage
had been done. Writing to Madison in September, Jefferson told of a meeting with his good friend Dr. James Hutchinson, a leader of the republican
cause in Pennsylvania: "Hutcheson [*sic*] says that Genet has totally overturned the republican interest in Philadelphia." Ever the optimist, Jefferson
predicted hopefully that the people will "right themselves if they always
see their republican advocates with them, [and] an accidental meeting with
the monocrats will not be a coalescence."[36]
Despite the setbacks, Jefferson did not despair. Determined to use his

final two months in office to set affairs of state in order, he buried himself in reports to Congress, including his long-delayed Report on Commerce in which he strongly advocated principles of free trade and open navigation. Even more acutely than before, he felt the irresistible pull of his private world in Virginia. In the wake of the Genet fiasco, politics had become an even more painful pursuit. Returning to Philadelphia in December he mourned the death of his friend Hutchinson, a victim of the fever. The final irony was that in opening American politics to the power of public opinion, Jefferson had seen that power turned against him, against his party, and against the republican cause. While remaining committed to the principle that the people's opinion should always be sovereign, he had come to consider the concept of public opinion in more practical and procedural terms, as being best expressed by regularly elected representatives. On December 30, 1793, the day before his term came to a close, he wrote to Dr. Enoch Edwards, "We have now assembled a new Congress, being a fuller & more equal representation of the people, and likely I think, to approach nearer to the sentiments of the people in the demonstration of their own." [37]

IV

From 1791 to 1793, Thomas Jefferson played a pivotal role in the creation of an American political experience whose most prominent features include a free and partisan press, a system of popular political parties, and an extensive role for organized public opinion. The act of creation was ironic, the product of a troubled philosopher making an uneasy transition from republican to liberal ways of thinking, and of a harried and sometimes overwhelmed politician seeking to find his way in a political world that was rapidly moving from eighteenth- to nineteenth-century practices. Yet however ironic, his commitment to these essential elements of the American democratic experience did not waver. Unlike others of his aristocratic age, Jefferson was not one to turn back. While not describing himself as a democrat, he embraced and encouraged democratic forces. Thus in 1794, in the wake of the Whiskey Rebellion, when Washington communicated in an address to Congress a series of not-very-veiled threats to Republican newspapers, Republican party politicians, and "certain self-created" Democratic-Republican societies, Jefferson wrote at once in defense of the democracy he had helped create. "The denunciation of the democratic societies," he told Madison, "is one of the extraordinary acts of boldness of which we have seen so many from the fraction of monocrats. It is wonderful indeed, that the President should have permitted himself to be the organ of such an attack on the freedom of discussion, the freedom of writing, printing & publishing." Yet Jefferson remained secure in his faith that the measures that had been threatened by Washington would fail to win the support of the people. "I have never heard, or heard of, a single expression or opinion which did not condemn it as an inexcusable aggression." Moreover, looking ahead, he seemed highly optimistic about democracy's survival. He concluded to Madison, "The time is coming when we shall fetch up the leeway of our vessel. The changes in your house, I see, are going on for the better, and even the Augean herd over your heads are slowly purging off their impurities. Hold on then, my dear friend, that we may not shipwreck in the meanwhile." [38]

NOTES

For their comments and suggestions, I wish to thank Saul Cornell, John L. Larson, Richard Matthews, Peter Onuf, and Patrick Rivers.

1. Charles M. Wiltse, *The Jeffersonian Tradition in American Democracy* (New York, 1935), p. 217.

2. Joyce Appleby, *Capitalism and a New Social Order: The Republican Vision of the 1790s* (New York, 1984), p. 21. Compare Lance Banning, *The Jeffersonian Persuasion: Evolution of a Party Ideology* (Ithaca, N.Y., 1978).

3. TJ to Benjamin Franklin Bache, April 22, 1791, *Boyd*, XX, p. 246. On commonwealth thought see Banning, *Jeffersonian Persuasion*, pp. 42–53. See also Caroline Robbins, *The Eighteenth Century Commonwealthman: Studies in the Transmission, Development, and Circumstances of English Liberal Thought from the Restoration of Charles II until the War with the Thirteen Colonies* (Cambridge, Mass., 1959).

4. TJ to Thomas Mann Randolph, Jr., May 15, 1791, *Boyd*, XX, p. 416. For background, see *Boyd*, XVI, pp. 237–47.

5. TJ to Philip Freneau, Feb. 28, 1791, *Boyd*, XIX, p. 351; TJ to James Madison, July 21, 1791, *Boyd*, XX, p. 657; TJ to George Gilmer, May 11, 1792, *Boyd*, XXIII, p. 492. For background, see *Boyd*, XX, pp. 718–53.

6. TJ to Thomas Bell, March 16, 1791, *Boyd*, XX, pp. 758–59. See Donald H. Stewart, *The Opposition Press of the Federalist Period* (Albany, N.Y., 1969), pp. 6–12, Merrill D. Peterson, *Thomas Jefferson and the New Nation* (New York, 1970), p. 446, and *Boyd*, XX, pp. 718–53.

7. TJ to William Short, July 28, 1791, *Boyd*, XX, pp. 692, 693. See *Malone*, II, pp. 351–70.

8. TJ to James Madison, July 21, 1791, *Boyd*, XX, p. 657; TJ to David Humphreys, Aug. 23, 1791, *Boyd*, XXII, p. 62; TJ to Thomas Mann Randolph, Jr., Nov. 20, 1791, *Boyd*, XXII, p. 310. See also Banning, *Jeffersonian Persuasion*, p. 167.

9. TJ to Thomas Barclay, April 9, 1792, *Boyd*, XXIII, p. 384. See Banning, *Jeffersonian Persuasion*, pp. 147–60.

10. TJ to George Washington, Sept. 9, 1792, *Boyd,* XXIV, p. 358. See *Malone,* II, pp. 443–77.

11. TJ to Thomas Mann Randolph, Jr., Nov. 16, 1792, *Boyd,* XXIV, p. 623. See *Malone,* II, pp. 478–88.

12. TJ to James Madison, July 7, 1793, *Ford,* VIII, p. 437; TJ to Thomas Mann Randolph, Nov. 2, 1793, *Ford,* VIII, p. 58; Jefferson, "The Anas," May 23, 1793, *Ford,* I, p. 274. For background on the partisan press in the 1790s, see Appleby, *Capitalism and a New Social Order,* p. 76, Banning, *Jeffersonian Persuasion,* pp. 231–33, and Stewart, *Opposition Press,* pp. 487–558.

13. TJ to William Short, Nov. 25, 1790, *Boyd,* XVIII, p. 75. On country ideology, see Banning, *Jeffersonian Persuasion,* pp. 53–69. See also J. G. A. Pocock, *The Machiavellian Moment: Florentine Political Thought and the Atlantic Republican Tradition* (Princeton, N.J., 1957), pp. 401–22. On eighteenth-century political culture, see Ronald P. Formisano, *The Transformation of Political Culture: Massachusetts Parties, 1790s–1840s* (New York, 1983), pp. 24–33.

14. TJ to Robert R. Livingston, Feb. 4, 1791, *Boyd,* XIX, p. 241. On early party development, see Noble E. Cunningham, *The Jeffersonian Republicans: the Formation of Party Organization, 1789–1801* (Chapel Hill, N.C., 1957), pp. 3–32.

15. TJ to Robert R. Livingston, Feb. 4, 1791, *Boyd,* XIX, p. 241; TJ to George Mason, Feb. 4, *Boyd,* XIX, p. 241; TJ to James Innes, March 13, 1791, *Boyd,* XIX, 542; TJ to Mason, Feb. 4, 1791, *Boyd,* XIX, p. 241. See also Peterson, *Thomas Jefferson and the New Nation,* p. 437 and *Boyd,* XX, pp. 434–53.

16. TJ to James Innes, March 13, 1791, *Boyd,* XIX, p. 543.

17. TJ to Lafayette, June 16, 1792, *Boyd,* XXIV, p. 85. See Peterson, *Thomas Jefferson and the New Nation,* p. 463.

18. TJ to Lafayette, June 16, 1792, *Boyd,* XXIV, p. 85; TJ to James Madison, June 29, 1792, *Boyd,* XXIV, p. 133; TJ to Edward Rutledge, Aug. 25, 1791, *Boyd,* XXII, p. 74. See Peterson, *Thomas Jefferson and the New Nation,* pp. 464–65.

19. TJ to James Monroe, June 23, 1792, *Boyd,* XXIV, p. 115. See also TJ to James Madison, June 21, 1792, *Boyd,* XXIV, p. 105. For details of the disputed election, see *Malone,* II, p. 457. See also Cunningham, *The Jeffersonian Republicans,* pp. 33–49.

20. TJ to George Washington, May 23, 1792, *Boyd,* XXIII, p. 538; TJ, "Notes of a Conversation with George Washington," July 10, 1792, *Boyd,* XXIV, p. 211; TJ to George Washington, Sept. 9, 1792, *Boyd,* XXIV, pp. 353, 358. See *Malone,* II, pp. 457–77.

21. TJ to Charles Clay, Sept. 11, 1792, *Boyd,* XXIV, pp. 367, 367–68, 358.

22. TJ to John Syme, Sept. 17, 1792, *Boyd,* XXIV, p. 387; TJ to Mrs. Church, October 1792, *Ford,* VII, p. 156; TJ to Thomas Pinckney, Dec. 3, 1792, *Boyd,* XXIV, p. 697. See Cunningham, *The Jeffersonian Republicans,* pp. 50–66.

23. TJ, "Notes on the Legitimacy of Government," Dec. 30, 1792, *Boyd,* XXIV, p. 802. See also TJ to Gouverneur Morris, Dec. 30, 1792, *Boyd,* XXIV, p. 800, and TJ to Thomas Pinckney, Dec. 30, 1792, *Boyd,* XXIV, p. 803. On radical republican conceptions of popular sovereignty, see Banning, *Jeffersonian Persuasion,* pp. 70–90. For background, see Edmund S. Morgan, *Inventing the People: The Rise of Popular Sovereignty in England and America* (New York, 1988), pp. 209–33.

24. TJ to George Gilmer, Dec. 15, 1792, *Boyd,* XXIV, pp. 744–45.

25. TJ to John F. Mercer, Dec. 19, 1792, *Boyd,* XXIV, p. 757; TJ to Thomas Mann Randolph, Jan. 7, 1793, *Ford,* VIII, pp. 206–7. For background, and on Adams's calculations, see Peterson, *Thomas Jefferson and the New Nation,* p. 479.

26. TJ to William Short, Jan. 3, 1793, *Ford,* VII, pp. 203–4. See *Malone,* III, p. 45.

27. TJ to James Madison, March 1793, *Ford,* VII, p. 251.

28. TJ to James Madison, May 12, 1793, *Ford,* VII, pp. 324–25.

29. TJ to Jean Pierre Brissot de Warville, May 8, 1793, *Ford,* VII, p. 322. See *Malone,* III, pp. 90–113.

30. TJ to James Madison, April 28, 1793, *Ford,* VII, p. 301. See Peterson, *Thomas Jefferson and the New Nation,* pp. 479–81.

31. TJ to James Monroe, May 5, 1793, *Ford,* VI, p. 238. See Peterson, *Thomas Jefferson and the New Nation,* pp. 479–81.

32. TJ to Thomas Mann Randolph, June 24, 1793, *Ford,* VI, p. 318.

33. TJ to James Monroe, June 28, 1793, *Ford,* VI, p. 323.

34. TJ to James Madison, July 7, 1793, *Ford,* VI pp. 338–39. See Peterson, *Thomas Jefferson and the New Nation,* pp. 482–97.

35. TJ to James Madison, July 7, 1793, *Ford,* VI, p. 338; TJ to James Madison, Aug. 3, 1793, *Ford,* VII, p. 464; TJ to James Madison, Aug. 25, 1793, *Ford,* VIII, p. 7. On the Democratic-Republican societies, see Eugene Perry Link, *Democratic-Republican Societies, 1790–1800* (New York, 1965), esp. pp. 3–18.

36. TJ to James Madison, Sept. 1, 1793, *Ford,* VIII, p. 12. See also Peterson, *Thomas Jefferson and the New Nation,* pp. 507–8.

37. TJ to Dr. Enoch Edwards, Dec. 30, 1793, *Ford,* VIII, p. 134. See *Malone,* III, p. 162.

38. TJ to James Madison, Dec. 28, 1794, *Ford,* VIII, pp. 156, 157, 158–59. For background, see *Malone,* III, pp. 261–72. See also Richard K. Matthews, *The Radical Politics of Thomas Jefferson: A Revisionist View* (Lawrence, Kans., 1984), pp. 119–26.

CHAPTER 11

Jefferson's Union and the
Problem of Internal Improvements

JOHN LAURITZ LARSON

Flush with a sense of opportunity, and a little chastened by their brush with disaster during the War of 1812, Jeffersonian Republicans in the 14th Congress seized a number of policy initiatives designed to reinvigorate the American experiment in republican government. After reestablishing a central bank and raising tariffs to encourage manufacturing, Henry Clay of Kentucky and John C. Calhoun of South Carolina directed the attention of their fellow lawmakers to an urgent threat to progress and prosperity: the problem of transportation and communication inside the sprawling United States. The situation seemed propitious. The United States, argued Calhoun, was now "at peace with all the world, abounding in pecuniary means," and enjoying for the first time in a generation relief from "party and sectional feelings." What could be "more important than internal improvements?" [1]

More than convenience and opportunity drove improvers such as Calhoun. Internal improvement promised to protect the young republic from the perils of disunion. From the beginning of the confederation, geographical isolation had inhibited energetic government, perpetuated local jealousies, nursed secessionist conspiracies, and sparked confrontations that in turn provoked bitter partisan divisions about how best to protect liberty and good order in republican society. Building on James Madison's hope (expressed in *The Federalist,* no. 10) that an extensive republic might withstand factions better than a small one, Jeffersonian Republicans by 1817 believed that geographic expansion guaranteed the survival of their liberties. In Calhoun's words, "much of our political happiness draws its origin from the extent of our Republic." And yet, this same condition exposed

Americans "to the greatest of all calamities, next to the loss of liberty, and even to that in its consequence—disunion." The nation was rapidly, fearfully growing: "This is our pride and danger—our weakness and our strength." Whatever impeded "the intercourse of the extremes with this, the center of the Republic," Calhoun concluded, "weakens the Union." Therefore, Congress lay under the "most imperious obligation to counteract every tendency to disunion," to "bind the republic together with a perfect system of roads and canals." [2]

Calhoun's diagnosis, his prescription, and the sense of urgency behind his appeal reflected a growing consensus, throughout the country and across party lines, that public works of internal improvement were indispensable to progress and prosperity. To be sure, all kinds of fears and qualifications encumbered the internal improvement idea, but few doubted the fundamental need for networks of communication. [3] Still, when a Congress dominated by Jeffersonian Republicans fashioned the Bonus Bill of 1817 to inaugurate a program of national internal improvement, President Madison vetoed the measure as incompatible with orthodox principles—the very principles that lawmakers thought compelled them to take the initiative. Something was wrong with the Republican persuasion that so many of its disciples should have so ardently promoted while others—including its leaders—stubbornly obstructed a program of national improvement.

The confusion lay not in differences of interest between commerce and agriculture, not in sectional ambitions, partisan intrigue, or even individual corruption and duplicity—although all these factors can be found at work. The confusion lay in the inability of latter-day Republicans to reconcile Thomas Jefferson's radical creed of liberal self-creation with a stable framework of constitutional government under rapidly changing conditions. The Union Calhoun wished to secure already bore little resemblance to the Union the Constitution was crafted to perfect; the Constitution itself designed a Union its framers could not perfectly describe; and the elusive principles of Revolutionary republicanism, supposedly embodied in the Constitution, commanded the government to protect the people's liberties while authorizing people to resist all perceived abuses of governmental power. Unable to obtain final definitions, Revolutionary leaders plunged ahead, more or less confident that experience would clarify right procedures and institutions. [4]

Such a contingent settlement naturally produced a scramble to control new institutions and mold them with greater precision. In the 1790s, Federalist efforts to establish effective and energetic government reignited Jefferson's most radical partisan energies. Mobilizing popular opposition in ways many founders thought to be dangerous, Jefferson sought to capture the federal establishment and abolish its "monocratic" features. Offering his own preference for low taxes, little government, state sovereignty in domestic affairs, maximum personal liberty, and easy access to the western frontier as the "true principles" of republicanism, Jefferson encouraged both the geographical explosion and the political disintegration that by 1817 were threatening Calhoun's Union, and with it, liberty.[5]

Thus Jefferson's attempt to rescue and redeem the new nation's republican experiment fixed upon the next generation of Republicans in Congress a jacket of orthodoxy that inhibited further innovation. With federal initiative proscribed by Jefferson's cleansing principles, Republicans who wished to perfect the Union by promoting internal improvement found their ambitions blocked by colleagues who invoked their own principles of party orthodoxy. Try as they might to argue that conditions had changed, that new dangers confronted the Union, or even that Jefferson himself had disregarded strict constructionist scruples in promoting and protecting the nation's interests, postwar leaders such as Clay, Calhoun, and John Quincy Adams found themselves disabled by their mentor's radical sentiments. Legitimate heirs to the Republican persuasion, these promoters of internal improvement discovered that the angry rhetoric of opposition, congealed into orthodoxy during Jefferson's presidency, stifled the spirit of amity and accommodation that the framers—and Jefferson himself—had understood to be the key to the success of the republican experiment. As a result, the world's most liberal self-governing people seemed absurdly incapable of providing for the urgent needs of their own political Union.[6]

A UNION OF ABUNDANT LANDS

What was Thomas Jefferson's vision of this American Union that he would rescue and also restrain? First, it was a geographical place in which experiments in human liberation might yield a natural, rational, egalitarian order and alter the course of history. Within this formula lay interlocking propositions that rendered Jefferson's vision more radically—and rigidly—ideological than that of other Revolutionary leaders. Equal rights and equal opportunity were essential conditions of genuine liberation; this he never seemed to doubt. Honest majorities, unmolested by priests, quacks, and selfish deceivers, necessarily would make good decisions; this seemed equally axiomatic. All that was required to release the virtuous energies that naturally motivated all individuals were conditions of peace, independence, freedom of expression, and popular republican government.

After 1783, the American Union seemed the most likely place on earth where such conditions might be secured for all time.[7]

Land sustained Jefferson's vision, both literally and figuratively. In a preindustrial agricultural society, land promised independence and therefore liberty for the heads of the freehold families. In Virginia abundant uncultivated land held out the possibility of enlarging the community of independent freeholders. Where others saw in the West a field for private speculations, Jefferson hoped for social experimentation. In 1776 he proposed a gift of fifty acres to every person not owning that amount, and two years later he urged a headright "for the Encouragement of Foreigners," extending to native Virginians a birthright of seventy-five acres. Jefferson's fellow Virginians disappointed him on this as on so many other issues, but he always considered land reform as essential to republican self-creation. He believed that social change was as much a goal of constitution-writing as the design of governmental structures.[8]

Frustrated by grandees in Virginia, Jefferson took his radical vision to Congress in a plan for disposing of the western lands. Virginia's deed conveying the backlands to the United States (also drafted by Jefferson) required that the region be formed into states with "the same rights of Sovereignty, Freedom, and Independence" as other members of the Union. To further his own goal of filling the West with freehold farmers, Jefferson pressed a committee of Congress to report a relatively democratic plan for governing these frontier territories. The resulting Ordinance of 1784, guaranteeing local self-determination, exceeded the committee's charge and the constitutional authority of Congress—transgressions Jefferson might logically have condemned. But the importance of enfranchising real settlers and minimizing the influence of great landlords and speculative companies justified for Jefferson a breach of delegated powers.[9]

Western lands made it possible to conceive of general liberation without disturbing the proprietary interests of Jefferson's own planter class. Many national leaders, including George Washington, believed that rapid and unregulated settlement would abandon the West to chaos, but Jefferson professed great confidence in liberated settlers. With "lands enough to employ an infinite number of people in their cultivation," he predicted, the new republic could anticipate a happy agrarian future. Cultivators made "the most vigorous, the most independent, the most virtuous" citizens, who were "tied to their country and wedded to its liberty and interests by the most lasting bands." These were inherent qualities, and Jefferson trusted them to determine the results of liberation. Therefore, where Washington and others proposed gradual, compact settlement under vigorous government control, Jefferson preferred to introduce democratic institutions and nurture bonds of friendly intercourse and mutual interest. [10]

This was not to say politics could not influence the development of the Union and, therefore, liberty. Bad policies might foster urban dependency, manufacturing, and vice, while inept government surely would frustrate any natural ties of friendship between the Atlantic and western people. For this reason (he seemed to notice no local prejudice), Jefferson urged a Potomac site for the federal capital as "the only point of Union which can cement us to our Western friends when they shall be formed into separate states." In a world of commercial empires, he argued, the path of safe development for the United States lay in fostering the natural preference of the people for self-government and agriculture, and then engaging Old Europe in mutually beneficial trade. To George Washington he explained, "Our citizens have had too full a taste of the comforts furnished by the arts and manufactures to be debarred the use of them. We must then in our own defence endeavor to share as large a portion as we can of this modern source of wealth and power." [11]

In this visionary letter, written as Congress debated the Ordinance of 1784, Jefferson identified both the "nature" of coming developments and the force that government might exert on them. Western commerce would be carried by the Hudson, Potomac, and Mississippi rivers. Down the last would pass "all heavy commodities"; but Jefferson believed that navigation through the gulf was "so dangerous" and up the Mississippi "so difficult and tedious," that it was "not probable" that European merchandise would "return through that channel." There would develop then a "rivalship between the Hudson and the Patowmac" for the rising trade of the West. Figuring shorter distances between Alexandria and the western waters (and imagining no significant change in transportation technology), he concluded that nature had "declared in favour of the Patowmac, and through that channel offers to pour into our lap the whole commerce of the Western world." [12]

Nature's preferences, however logical, apparently were not self-evident, for the inferior route by way of the Hudson was "already open and known in practice," while the better Potomac route needed "still to be opened." The hand of enterprise must intervene to keep the scene unfolding according to nature's implicit design. At this point Jefferson believed that the state of Virginia was competent to mount the required river improvements, and he urgently sought government action before the accidental course of events awarded all commerce to New York. For the next several years he pursued internal improvements with vigorous and steady enthusiasm, and while Jefferson sought the aid of the monied gentry, he firmly believed that such public works were "much better" done "at public than private expense."[13]

Abundant land, improved by wise government and enterprising people, framed the experiment in American liberation. By the middle of the 1780s, Jefferson had charted for the Union a "safe" and liberal course in the management of western lands, including a rectilinear survey system that eventually reduced the continent to marketable numbered squares. In Virginia, he had taken the lead in the Potomac River and other improvement projects designed to bind the old states together with their frontier offspring. At stake was not just valuable natural resources but the very survival of American republicanism. A chance encounter in 1785 with a pauper woman in France—the inspiration for a sermon to Madison—affirmed in Jefferson's mind the centrality of land to human happiness:

> The earth is given as a common stock for man to labour and live on. . . . It is too soon yet in our country to say that every man who cannot find employment but who can find uncultivated land, shall be at liberty to cultivate it, paying a moderate rent. But it is not too soon to provide by every possible means that as few as possible shall be without a little portion of land.[14]

For Jefferson, small landholders necessarily composed "the most precious part of a state." As long as the resource of land existed and republican government prevailed, there would be hope for the American experiment.

A GOVERNMENT OF LIMITS

The other defining characteristic of Jefferson's American Union was the practice of limited government. Only majority rule and a check on interference with the rights of the people could protect the experiment in liberation. Departing radically from the traditions of the Virginia country gentry, Jefferson rejected all notions of prerogative except the will of the whole people. Not content with well-crafted constitutions and popular processes of adopting them, he urged the people to scrutinize their governments perpetually and guard against encroachments on their rights. A consummate revolution maker, Jefferson found it harder to support and perfect the institutions of the new regime, partly because interested opponents distorted the workings of newly formed governments and partly because real majorities of liberated people sometimes favored policies or visions that he could not imagine were legitimate.

No statement better summarizes the extent of Jefferson's radical departure from tradition than the Declaration of Independence. There he proclaimed as self-evident a set of propositions that were as novel, abstract, and implausible as they were rhetorically powerful. According to Jefferson's formula, equal individuals endowed with "inalienable rights" instituted governments according to their fancy in order to "secure" their rights and "effect their safety and happiness." Order, privilege, tradition, presumption, national honor, and patriotic loyalty—all the customary attributes of government—were made subordinate to the "natural rights" of human beings. For this reason, Jefferson recognized the careful framing of new constitutions, delimiting the powers of government, as comprising the "whole object" of the revolutionary movement. [15]

Proper constitutions, however, proved hard to construct. Jefferson's first draft of a constitution for Virginia, written about the same time as the Declaration of Independence, outlined his model for republican government. Strictly separating the functional powers, Jefferson proposed an annually elected popular assembly with an upper house of senators selected from among the lower for life terms (later reduced to nine years). Executive functions devolved on a weak administrator chosen for one year, who was deprived of most prerogatives enjoyed by English governors and checked by an independent judiciary. Stepping beyond government structures, Jefferson wished to distribute land to the landless; to destroy the English inheritance system which protected great estates; to extend the suffrage to all genuine residents, subject to a minimal property requirement; to guarantee religious liberty, the right to bear arms, and freedom of the press; and to prohibit standing armies, bribery, and (in a second draft) slavery. [16]

Abuse of power, local partiality in legislation, long tenure in office, and pandering to local electors were the evils that worried Jefferson. Thus he wished to see governors stripped of their powers, representatives scrutinized annually, and senators protected from transient interests by long terms and indirect selection. Unlike most of his contemporaries among the Revolutionary elites, Jefferson did not "think integrity the characteristic of wealth." Rather, he believed that "the decisions of the people, in a body," would be "more honest and more disinterested than those of wealthy men." Alongside this confidence in popular majorities lay an abiding suspicion of power in the hands of the governors. Everything about the American "Whig" understanding of politics (derived as it was from English "oppositionist" traditions) pointed to the maxim that power corrupted the rulers. Constitutions should demystify government and so clearly delineate authority that every citizen could understand its limits. This conviction, laid down at the beginning of the Revolution, became the pole star of Jefferson's republicanism and would distinguish him as more democratic than many of his Revolutionary colleagues.[17]

This passionate commitment to majority rule and limited government, embedded in a dream of widespread land ownership and legal equality, helps explain Jefferson's vision of political and social change. Driven toward an ideal objective, one that coincided with his material interests but seemed not explicitly determined by them, Jefferson hesitated to alter (or even test) his fundamental propositions as the Revolutionary process unfolded. Yet experience predictably frustrated Jefferson's idealistic pursuit of republicanism. In Virginia, the established gentry rejected his guarantee of rights, broad suffrage, reapportionment, land distribution, inheritance reform, and the abolition of slavery. Soon he found himself trying to secure by ordinary legislation objects that he considered to be natural rights. After a particularly vexing term as governor in 1781, Jefferson began rethinking his model structures. Alerted in these years to the facility with which men could accommodate republican forms to the substance of bad old politics, Jefferson learned to play an expedient game in pursuit of higher principles. During the same period he began to display a habit of blaming disappointments in practical politics on the designs of conspiring men.[18]

Governing the Union posed a different set of problems for a man who usually saw Virginia as his country. Conceived primarily as a league of defense, the Articles of Confederation never had commanded the respect of the states. Most delegates to the Continental Congress conceded very limited powers to the Union; Jefferson especially had resisted vague grants of power over "mutual and general welfare." The postwar struggle to manage western lands, however, awakened Jefferson's interest in national authority. By 1785 he was condemning a proposal to distribute public lands among the states because it threatened to divide their interests, "which ought to be made joint in every possible instance in order to cultivate the idea of our being one nation, and to multiply the instances in which the people shall look up to Congress as their head." For certain purposes, Jefferson knew that the Union was important, even crucial.[19]

Jefferson's concern for the integrity of Congress increased dramatically during his diplomatic mission to France. When he arrived in Paris in 1784, he found that "all respect" for the American government had been "annihilated" among the great powers, "from an idea of its want of tone and energy." Lacking any "original and inherent power" in Congress to control the commerce of the states," Jefferson moved to construct one indirectly through the treaty-making power. His "primary object" in arranging treaties, he explained to James Monroe, was to take commerce "out of the hands of the states, and to place it under the superintendence of Congress, so far as the imperfect provisions of our constitution will admit, and until the states shall by new compact make them more perfect." Assuming that the need was self-evident and the remedy naturally forthcoming, Jefferson acted without hesitation.[20]

Here was another early example of creative or "broad" construction within the framework of a limited constitution that so often marked Jefferson's efforts (protests to the contrary notwithstanding) to solve real problems confronting his experimental republic. He took evident pleasure in the thought that Europe's insults were encouraging the states to "vest Congress" with "absolute power" over trade. Such a change would "consolidate our federal building very much," he enthused, "and for this we shall be indebted to the British." With similar approbation, Jefferson encouraged Madison and others at home to pursue reform of the federal constitution.[21]

Jefferson watched from Paris as the confederation government collapsed. Madison and others regularly informed him on the sequence of events leading up to the Philadelphia convention, but he did not experience the chaos and he never shared the founders' sense of urgency. In 1785, Madison warned him that the southern intransigence on commercial reform might drive "the Eastern and Middle States" to "some irregular experiments" (disunion). One year later, rumors that a treaty with Spain would close the Mississippi in return for Atlantic commercial concessions promised, in Madison's words, to separate the "interests and affection between the western and eastern settlements and to foment the jealousy between the eastern and southern states." By the winter of 1786–87, confronting commercial isolation on the seas, Indian wars on the frontier, social disturbances such as Shays' Rebellion in Massachusetts, and bitter jealousies among states, responsible leaders everywhere believed the Union lay in imminent peril. With its destruction would fall the American experiment in liberty.[22]

Jefferson offered a solution that quickly became for him the key to American federalism: "To make us one nation as to foreign concerns and keep us distinct in Domestic ones, gives the outline of the proper division of powers between the general and particular governments." From a distance the formula made sense, but the distinction between foreign and domestic government proved elusive in practice and would do nothing to relieve obstructions of national policy that commonly originated in state or local interests. Madison wanted more drastic cures for the "mortal diseases" that afflicted the confederation. There must be a new federal head "with a negative in all cases whatsoever on the local legislatures." Without this, Madison believed, no delineation of power "on paper" could survive against the

"Legislative sovereignties of the States." So armed, however, a new federal government could "guard the national rights and interests against invasion," restrain the states "from thwarting and molesting each other," and even prevent them from oppressing minorities "within themselves." Jefferson was startled by Madison's assault upon the states: "This proposes to mend a small hole by covering the whole garment." But his more urgent fear of losing the western states (and with them the field for liberation) sustained his interest in the work at Philadelphia.[23]

Jefferson welcomed the new Constitution with two important reservations. The lack of a bill of rights appalled him. People were entitled to such protection "against every government on earth, general or particular," and no "just government" would allow essential rights to "rest on inference." Also, he "greatly" disliked the reelection of the president. "Experience concurs with reason," he ranted, in an exceptional attack on the wisdom of the voters, that "the first magistrate will always be re-elected if the constitution permits it." Importantly, in light of Jefferson's later assault on federal consolidation, the fact that this Constitution dissolved the old confederation into "one general government" did not disturb him, even while Anti-Federalists at home raged against it. He watched the ratification progress with "great pleasure," not entirely happy with the document but "contented to travel on towards perfection, step by step." By June 1788 he was repeating what his friends so often told him: "It will be more difficult if we lose this instrument, to recover what is good in it, than to correct what is bad after we shall have adopted it."[24]

Jefferson grounded much of his optimism about the new Constitution on the ratification process (its worst flaws apparently escaped him) and on the promise of immediate amendments to incorporate a bill of rights. The whole exercise had set a "beautiful example of a government reformed by reason alone," and he covered further doubts with the faith that there was "virtue and good sense enough in our countrymen to correct abuses."[25] Such a process, more than the instrument, impressed Jefferson that the Revolution had survived. To the English radical Richard Price, he offered this extraordinary benediction (which surely would have struck Madison as ironical, if not naive):

> I did not at first believe that 11 states out of 13 would have consented to a plan consolidating them so much into one. A change in their dispositions, which had taken place since I left them, had rendered this consolidation necessary, that is to say, had called for a federal government which could walk upon its own legs, without leaning for support on the state legislatures. A sense of this necessity, and a submission to it, is to me a

new and consolatory proof that wherever the people are well informed they can be trusted with their own government; that whenever things get so far wrong as to attract their notice, they may be relied on to set them to rights.[26]

BEHOLD THE ENEMIES OF FREEDOM

Jefferson came home to Virginia at the end of 1789 fairly bursting with delight in the progress of American government. "Heaven has rewarded us with a happy issue from our struggles," he told a welcoming committee of Albemarle County residents, and now he hoped America would prove to the world that the will of the majority, "the Natural law of every society," was the "only sure guardian of the rights of man." Still, doubts seasoned his most optimistic moments, and while he urged others to build with confidence on the ground already gained, he never ceased to believe the enemies of freedom still coveted power. Thus he returned home and assumed the office of Secretary of State, full of hope for the new Constitution, yet expecting to learn its true virtues by its deeds.[27]

In principle Jefferson agreed with leading voices in the new administration that the urgent needs of the Union included restoring public credit, resurrecting foreign trade, perfecting government in the West, and harmonizing the interests of the states. When he arrived at New York in March 1790, Congress swelled with bitter debate over Secretary of the Treasury Alexander Hamilton's funding and assumption bills. Jefferson did not approve of Hamilton's plan to assume the debts of the states; nevertheless, "for the sake of union" and to ward off bankruptcy, he stood willing to "yield to the cries of the creditors in certain parts of the union." Declaring it "necessary to give as well as take in a government like ours," he proceeded in July to arrange a deal to break the southern opposition to assumption in return for a federal capital on the Potomac near Georgetown. Before long, however, Jefferson regretted his complicity in Hamilton's triumph. Dark suspicions accumulated around the relentless demands of the treasury chief, whose purposes, methods, and style all convinced Jefferson that enemies of freedom had resumed their calamitous advance. Ablaze once more with partisan zeal, Jefferson began to see the actions of the Federalists, not as alternative policies for national government, but as designs to reverse the Revolution.[28]

It was not the honest exercise of federal power, but the apparent usurpation of that power for counterrevolutionary purposes, that drove Jefferson into opposition to the Federalist regime. Secure in his own vision of the natural outcome of liberation and popular government, he found it practically impossible to imagine that Hamilton's British-style banking and stock-jobbing program promoted anything but "old corruption." Everywhere he turned he found Hamilton ahead of him, meddling in diplomacy, maneuvering congressmen, bending the ear of the president, and feeding lies and justifications to the press. With a sense of mounting emergency, Jefferson denounced the national bank as destructive of all limits in the federal Constitution: "To take a single step beyond the boundaries thus specifically drawn around the powers of Congress, is to take possession of a boundless field of power, no longer susceptible of any definition." Hamilton's *Report of Manufactures* (1792) verified Jefferson's worst fears, and he unburdened himself to the President: A treasury system had been contrived "for withdrawing our citizens" from "useful industry" into paper gambling. Bribery knit members of Congress into the scheme, who then assaulted the Constitution with "legislative constructions" designed to "keep the game in their hands." To perfect their usurpation, these enemies of popular government now proposed, by seemingly harmless bounties for encouraging manufactures, to take into the hands of Congress everything "which *they* should deem for the *Public welfare*." [29]

Hamilton's actions supplied the evidence, but Jefferson's assumptions completed the analysis in this hysterical assessment of the Federalist program. Begging Washington to stay in office and expose the conspirators, Jefferson insisted that their goal was to "prepare the way for a change" from republicanism to "monarchy." Perhaps the people would replace these usurpers in the fall elections, but what if the voters were deceived? Jefferson could "scarcely contemplate a more incalculable evil than the breaking of the union," but what else could be the result when "the owners of the debt" were in the South, the "holders of it" in the North, and the "Antifederal champions" had been strengthened "by the fulfillment of their predictions." Not content with such private efforts to rescue republican government, in fact, well in advance of his speaking to Washington, Jefferson stirred up public opposition through the pages of Philip Freneau's *National Gazette*. The resulting newspaper war set a bitter tone for the elections of 1792 and drew a sharp scolding from Washington, who disbelieved Jefferson's fantasies and condemned "exciting" editorial pieces, "particularly in Freneau's paper," as more likely than Hamilton's programs to yield anarchy and disunion. Unwilling to argue with Washington, but unshaken in his view of what endangered the Union, Jefferson retreated into brooding opposition. [30]

After 1792, nearly everything about the Federalist regime reinforced Jefferson's belief in an organized monarchist conspiracy. His rhetoric grew more desperate as Federalists continued to win elections and dominate the federal establishment. Early confidence that voters would throw the rascals out faded into charges that legislative corruption and Federalist propaganda swaddled the electorate in lies. The military build-up occasioned by hostilities between Britain and France confirmed in Jefferson's mind that "the monocrats & paper men in Congress" desired not war but "armies & debts"—the classical instruments of imperial tyranny. Washington's criticism of self-created "democratical societies" and his campaign against Pennsylvania's "whiskey rebels" hardened an already bitter heart. The 1795 Jay treaty astonished him for its bold disregard of the people's will: "The whole mass of your constituents," he wrote to Madison, "have condemned this work in the most unequivocal manner, and are looking to you as their last hope to save them from the effects of the avarice & corruption of the first agent [Jay], the revolutionary machinations of others [the Senate], and the incomprehensible acquiescence of the only honest man who has assented to it [Washington]." [31]

Guided by a Manichaean temper and radical assumptions that blended French political economy, English "country" thinking, and the "Whig" critique of modernization, Jefferson came to the conclusion that American liberty stood once more in mortal danger from an organized class of conspirators. "In place of that noble love of liberty & republican government," he explained in a 1796 letter to Philip Mazzei (which subsequently found its way into print!) "an Anglican monarchical, & aristocratical party" had "sprung up" to restore the substance and the form of British government. "The main body" of citizens remained "true to their republican principles" (the "whole landed interest" and the "great mass of talents"); against these stood the executive branch, the judiciary, all officers and would-be officers of government, all "timid men who prefer the calm of despotism to the boisterous sea of liberty," British merchants and their American debtors, and "speculators" in public funds. The greatest men of the Revolution had "gone over" to the British model. The "irresistible influence" of Washington "played off by the cunning of Hamilton" accounted for the first transformation of "republicans chosen by the people into anti-republicans." John Adams labored "with great artifice" to perpetuate the notion that his government represented the people; but such was not "the natural state." [32]

Electioneering and outdoor agitation belonged among the evils of factional politics, according to the wisdom of Jefferson's day. As early as 1795, however, Jefferson embraced partisan imperatives to action that rendered traditional independence ("the middle line") immoral. "Were parties here divided merely by a greediness for office," he explained, participation would

be "unworthy of a reasonable" person; but where "the principle of difference" was as pronounced as "between the parties of Honest men & Rogues,"
he felt obliged to play a "firm & decided part." As a party leader during the
Adams administration, Jefferson tried to shape the popular reaction to the
Alien and Sedition acts, the XYZ affair, and the Quasi-War with France.
Simultaneously he rallied opposition while seeking to curb its disintegra-
tive tendencies. To John Taylor in 1798 he praised the state governments
yet discouraged all talk of dividing the Union into new confederations. In
the 1798 Kentucky Resolutions, he proposed nullification as a local check
on the pretensions of federal authority while pledging to sacrifice "everything but the rights of self-government" to the cause of union. By 1800,
his objective was to win the presidential election and reestablish the Constitution in the "true sense in which it was adopted by the States." [33]

Jefferson defined this "true" republicanism in reaction to his vision of
Federalist crimes against the people's liberties. On the question of national
power they had tried to "seize all doubtful ground," and so he embraced a
more Anti-Federalist view of the Constitution than he had held twelve
years before. He transformed Madison's reluctant Tenth Amendment, re-
serving to the states "the powers not yielded by them to the Union," into
the centerpiece of his interpretation, and within the federal sphere he
wished to see Congress reclaim power usurped by the executive. He promised "rigorously frugal & simple" government, saving public revenue to pay
off debts and suppress taxes, minimizing public offices, trusting the militia
and minor naval forces to defend the homeland without grandeur. Convinced by the Federalists in power that institutions served only to rob,
cheat, manipulate, and oppress the people, candidate Jefferson described a
truly spartan federal establishment, more concerned with protecting the
people from their rulers than with pursuing programs of any design. Leave
the states "independent as to everything within themselves," he concluded,
and let the "general government be reduced to foreign concerns only," with
"simple" and "unexpensive" duties performed "by a few servants." [34]

Jefferson's horror at the exercise of power by the Federalists led him to
attack power itself. Forgetting how narrowness of interest had wrecked the
confederation government, and lacking firsthand experience of the disorder
of the later 1780s, Jefferson saw aggressive Federalist responses to the dis-
integrative tendencies in the Union as novel assaults on liberty. Because the
Federalist programs fostered a course of progress different from the one
Jefferson cherished, he assumed that such was their only—and sinister—
objective. He recoiled in anger, rejecting the bitter fruits of Federalist rule
as corrupt and illegitimate. Of course, all negotiations can be construed as

having generous or wicked intentions, and the defenders of Hamilton's design could (and did) just as reasonably argue that Jefferson's fantastic charges and reckless opposition undermined the new Constitution before its limits could be tested fairly.[35]

For the purposes of understanding Jefferson's approach to the practice of government, it matters less who was right or wrong than how one went about the business of deciding. The new federal government had been designed, debated, and ratified by the people expressly to conduct such negotiations within a national framework. Failing to block Hamilton's designs inside that framework, however, Jefferson attacked the new government itself—which directed debate once more to fundamental questions of power. Driven by his fears of monarchist conspiracies, Jefferson set out to rescue the national government. In the process he left profound and disabling marks on the practice of government under the Constitution, tending—intentionally or not—to perpetuate (perhaps forever) a contingent relationship between the people and their federal government.[36]

A UNION OF ORTHODOX REPUBLICANS

If Jefferson's election in 1800 rescued the Americans from the enemies of freedom, where did it leave the authority of government within the Union of states? The creed of opposition laid down by Jefferson since 1792 called for little government, strict construction, states rights, and above all majority rule. But would the Union in fact flourish in the hands of a "few servants" with simple duties? As the Federalists retreated, would real conflicts among the states and regions once more surface and demand resolution? The answer to this second question was a resounding "yes." The triumphant Jeffersonians remodeled the institutions of national authority according to their radical opposition doctrines, but the political life of the federal republic confounded their optimistic predictions. It remained to be seen how they would exercise the necessary power within the framework of their newfound orthodox republican principles.

The first task of Jefferson's government was to consolidate the support of the people and secure their fidelity to his definition of majority rule. "We are all republicans, we are all federalists," he told the inauguration audience. The same generous sentiments filled his correspondence with liturgical repetition, until he had constructed for himself an explanation of how the American republic had been saved. The people once were "hoodwinked," he told John Dickinson, but the "band is removed, and they see for themselves." After the "anxiety & alarm" surrounding the election, he informed James Monroe, the people once called federalists ("I always exclude their leaders") looked with "affection and confidence to the administration, ready to become attached to it," as long as it did nothing to "throw them off." To Joseph Priestley he penned an odd, extravagant report that his countrymen had "recovered from the alarm into which art & industry had thrown them." The "barbarians" [Federalists] had been repulsed, "science & honesty" had been replaced "on their high ground." The "order & good sense displayed in this recovery from delusion" left Jefferson "better satisfied" of the stability of the Union than before his campaign of opposition. To Nathaniel Niles he added that the size of the republic had been the key to its survival: "Had our territory been even a third only of what is, we were gone. But while frenzy & delusion like an epidemic, gained certain parts, the residue remained sound & untouched." In the end, all Americans really were republicans, "decoyed into the net of monarchists," but rapidly "coming back."[37]

Jefferson's denial of real party differences excused him from defending his partisan agenda or developing a program of accommodation. Real consolidation of public feeling would follow the restoration of good government, and in his first annual message to Congress Jefferson called for an end of internal taxes, reductions in expenditures and public offices, revision of naturalization laws, reform of the bloated judiciary, and a general scaling down of the old Federalist establishment. To Treasury Secretary Albert Gallatin he outlined a plan for retiring the public debt from the proceeds of import taxes freely paid by "the rich chiefly." Such good fortune accompanied Jefferson's arrival in office, that by the end of 1802 there was "nothing scarcely to propose" for action by Congress. Wags protested that Federalist taxes and fiscal policies made Jeffersonian frugality possible, but Jefferson dug in behind the bulwark of his original liberalism: "If we can prevent the government from wasting the labors of the people, under the pretense of taking care of them, they must become happy."[38]

Wedded to a vision of self-evident consensus among the republican majority out of doors, Jefferson failed to make the transition from the Revolutionary politics of 1798 to the regular practice of reconciling interests, sections, and classes within the framework of the national Union. Priests, lawyers, and opposition printers—all were condemned as schismatics. Ordinary legislative horse-trading among factions of his own Republican majority he blamed on the schemes of unreconstructed Federalists. He met with anger "malicious inquiries" from Congress for explanations of his presidential actions. Finally—astonishingly—he attacked self-created political societies (in particular, a Philadelphia ward committee): "As revolutionary instruments" they might be "indispensable," but "to admit them as ordinary & habitual instruments as a part of the machinery of the Constitution," would be to introduce "moving powers foreign to it." As the popular politics unleashed by Jefferson's campaign of opposition took root in fractious state and local organizations, Jefferson himself retreated toward a single principle of guidance: "Under difficulties of this kind I have ever found one, & only one rule, *to do what is right,* & generally we shall disentangle ourselves without perceiving how it happens."[39]

Strict construction of the federal Constitution, the second pillar of Jeffersonian orthodoxy, functioned as a necessary servant of the principle of majority rule and an antidote to government corruption. Yet this apparently rigorous guideline proved every bit as elusive as the search for consensus on just "what is right." Even as he condemned the process of "improving our constitution" by congressional interpretation, he yearned for a day when Republicans in both houses might pass a "Declaration of the principles of the constitution," explaining "all the points in which it has been violated." This ambivalence about who held the truth about the Constitution plagued Jefferson's thinking throughout his career. All three branches of the Federalist government upheld the 1798 Sedition Act, yet Vice President Jefferson, a sworn officer of that government, considered it "to be a nullity, as absolute and as palpable as if Congress had ordered us to fall down and worship a golden image." Once in the president's office, he ignored John Adams's judicial appointments on the grounds, privately construed, that an outgoing officer ought not exercise his legal authority. He hated Chief Justice John Marshall's "gratuitous opinion" that the Supreme Court should construe the Constitution. Instead, he claimed for each branch of government an equal right to interpret fundamental law within its proper sphere of action—an idea guaranteed to produce confusion but yielding "less mischief," he believed, than giving any one branch "control over the others." A potent slogan of opposition, strict construction as a governing principle melted to the touch; and while Jefferson invoked it often against projects he did not approve, he also did "what was right" in the absence of clear authorization.[40]

The outstanding example of Jefferson's violation of strict construction was the 1803 purchase of Louisiana. Spain's retrocession to France of the territory of Louisiana rekindled chronic fears in the American West about trade down the Mississippi River. Prodding Napoleon to sell New Orleans and West Florida, Jefferson's negotiators received an astonishing counteroffer: $15 million for the whole of Louisiana. The deal unquestionably was popular, even preferable to the war New England Federalists were demanding. It was just as unquestionably unauthorized within the letter of the Constitution. The general government, Jefferson freely confessed, had no "power of holding foreign territory, & still less of incorporating it into the Union." Accordingly, he drafted an amendment that indemnified his action and locked away from settlement all of Louisiana north of the 33rd parallel until further amendments established valid procedures for enlarging the Union. Good Republicans in Congress, however, doubted the need for Jefferson's amendment and they showed no interest in his conversion to a neo-Federalist plan of compact frontier management. Instead, by majority rule, they hurried Louisiana through the elastic fabric of the existing Constitution, with Jefferson's silent acquiescence.[41]

Louisiana was not the only example of quick and forceful action to achieve Jefferson's goals. Since Napoleon's transfer failed to include the coveted Spanish Floridas, Jefferson initiated a course of diplomatic threats and claims to hasten their "natural" incorporation into the American Union. Similarly, as the fortunes of war rose and fell in the Atlantic community, Jefferson pressed coercive commercial policies designed to manipulate European trade (however ineffectively) into fostering America's agricultural prosperity and expansion. The 1803 Lewis and Clark expedition, covered by a nominal objective of commerce with the Far West, belonged to a comprehensive system of government action that undermined Indian autonomy, broke down Indian resistance, and prepared the way for American settlers who would inevitably possess Indian lands and bring them into the empire of liberty. Subsidized commerce kept the peace and fostered dependency so much better than military power that Jefferson asked Congress in 1804 to enlarge the government capital employed in the Indian trade. Whether oblivious to the plight of the Indians or cynically committed to their ultimate destruction, he encouraged (with public money) such a "coincidence of interests" between those who had "lands to spare" and those who wanted lands as to guarantee American expansion. Expecting to overrun and absorb the Indians in the "natural progress of things," Jefferson decided it was "better to promote it than to retard it."[42]

The purchase of Louisiana, rising revenues from neutral trade, the reduction of debt, the suppression of taxes, reductions of the army and navy, and assaults on the Federalist judiciary—all went pretty well according to Jefferson's promises. Still, the actual consensus among his Republican followers disintegrated steadily during his presidency. The revolt of Virginia's John Randolph and the "Quids" in Congress, he explained to James Monroe (who knew much better), produced "momentary astonishment, & even dismay," but the "good sense of the house rallied around its principles, & without any leader pursued steadily the business of the session." The conspiracy of Aaron Burr and other Jeffersonians to stir up secession in the Southwest—precisely the kind of reckless adventurism Jefferson's Louisiana amendment would have contained—he dismissed with the tired old charge of Federalist conspiracy. Critics jeered at the impotence of Jefferson's stripped-down Republican government, but Jefferson reversed the moral of the story. By "proclamation alone" he had raised the "hand of the people" and given the "mortal blow to a conspiracy which, in other countries, would have called for an appeal to armies." Fortified by his own ideology, Jefferson raked from the ashes of this humiliation (including Burr's acquittal by the federal courts) an extraordinary posture of victory. Then tragically, in 1807, responding to a world of warring empires, Jefferson turned the coercive power of his government against his own commercial people, imposing an embargo of questionable wisdom, authority, or justice. Bitter protests rivaled Republican demonstrations against the Alien and Sedition acts; Connecticut hurled at Jefferson the language of state nullification cribbed from his own Kentucky Resolution.[43]

The point is not that Jeffersonians were hypocrites, but that "orthodox" republican principles—strict construction and majority rule—never yielded that simple clarity of right and wrong that Jeffersonians in opposition described. Majority rule disappointed various minorities, governors in office found it necessary to govern, and people with two sovereign governments sometimes played one against the other for advantage. In his haste to dismantle the edifice of empire thrown up by his Federalist enemies, Jefferson left himself precious little ground on which to build a national government; and by flattering the unerring wisdom of popular majorities, he undermined the institutional expression of majority rule in either Congress or the White House. The Revolution of 1800 democratized the practice of politics, resurrected the rights of states against the general government, and attached the allegiance of a liberated people to a rhetoric of radical principles rather than to habits of obedience to government. Long before the terms of this democratical dispensation found stable and enduring expression, new challenges confronted that government, produced by liberation itself, confusing national and local interests, engendering desperate jealousies and bitter competition, and falling under the seemingly harmless contemporary rubric of internal improvements.

THE CHALLENGE OF INTERNAL IMPROVEMENTS

The problem with internal improvements lay in the way they tangled together public authority and private interests—two things Jefferson sincerely wished to keep distinct. Roads, canals, and river improvements consumed great sums of investment capital, and hardly anyone denied that such facilities of public convenience fell within the proper sphere of government promotion. In America, the underdeveloped state of the country together with the urgent need for communication among the newly confederated states stimulated all kinds of public and private efforts to improve transportation. Almost immediately, local improvers discovered that ideal networks of communication crossed municipal and state lines, required cooperation (and contributions) from several taxing authorities, and scattered benefits in unfair patterns—often absolutely injuring citizens whose taxes supported the work![44]

Reasonable people assumed that natural geography favored no one, except insofar as individuals shrewdly picked better sites for their respective enterprises. However, public works to improve transportation, by their very nature, fostered general progress and prosperity by making particular men rich while consigning many others to marginal status within a new, government-directed system. In a republican regime, forbidden by principle to bestow unequal favors on its citizens, public works could be a treacherous business. In a confederated republic, where coextensive sovereign powers shared responsibility for the same public welfare, the potential for conflict in pursuit of undeniably benevolent objectives was enormous. Hardly anything a government could do more clearly proved that community infringed on private rights and that governments, no matter how liberally formed, must invade the estates of individuals in order to protect and promote the common good.[45]

Jefferson encountered this dilemma in the early 1780s, when he tried to win support from balky Tidewater planters for Potomac and James river improvements. "To remove the idea of partiality," he wrote to Washington in 1784, he had suggested "continuing this fund till all the rivers shall be cleared successively." Such a strategy of broadcasting government favors, while it quieted local opposition, invited limitless demands and raised extraordinary potential for corruption and the waste of public money—objections Jefferson readily acknowledged. What he did not admit—and what no politician ever honestly acknowledged—was that the real danger lay not in failure and waste but in successful works of permanent improvement.

The routes first improved enjoyed advantages over later "feeders." Economy in transportation required the concentration of effort along the most convenient and efficient routes, irreversibly building up those places and fixing in geographic space a framework that governed the prospects of all who followed. After all, Jefferson's stated objective in improving the Potomac was to bind the interior trade to Virginia before New Yorkers captured the prize. His less visionary Tidewater neighbors (not to mention New York merchants) wondered why the wilderness should profit from this tax on established Virginia property and enterprise. Equally jealous of the Potomac project were Maryland residents (especially in Annapolis and Baltimore), who shared legal jurisdiction over that river but whose own hopes for prominence would be diminished by the rising fortunes of Georgetown. It was the curse of internal improvements that every project could be opposed with equal vehemence by complacent interests, niggardly taxpayers, libertarians fearful of corruption, and ambitious self-interested rivals.[46]

In one sense, the federal Constitution of 1787 had been created to address just such a tangle of interests and authorities. The 1785 Mount Vernon Conference to discuss the Potomac River had produced the 1786 Annapolis Convention, which in turn called for the Philadelphia meeting the following spring. The forceful nationalism of Madison's original Virginia Plan and the willingness of most delegates at Philadelphia to abandon the Articles of Confederation suggested real frustration with the lack of a government that could compel obedience on matters threatening to the welfare of the Union. Yet the delegates would not include among the enumerated powers of Congress the right to make roads and canals in the states; fearing the loss of the whole instrument, improvers such as Madison acquiesced.[47]

Watching from a distance in Paris, and still confident that states could carry on improvements at home and on the western waters, Jefferson himself saw no compelling reason for national authority over roads and canals. After 1792, seeing everything through the lens of bitter opposition, he could not support any federal initiatives, justified by loose construction of the general welfare clause, that had the effect of raising taxes, distributing contracts, generating offices, and pressing down upon the people designs of the central authority. Therefore, in the 1790s Jefferson espoused a clear opposition to national public works. To James Madison, who strayed so far as to propose in 1796 a national Maine-to-Georgia post road, Jefferson responded with alarm: "I view it as a source of boundless patronage to the executive, jobbing to members of Congress & their friends, and a bottomless abyss of public money." On the eve of his own administration, he still denounced "making roads through the union as a money pit and the "richest provision for jobs to favorites that has ever yet been proposed." [48]

Jefferson seized the reigns of power in 1801, convinced that loose construction of the Constitution served only treasonous ends and committed to protecting the people in the states from their own national government. Once in office, however, his own partisans and the people at large called for more than mere restraints on the federal government, and the clear connection between popular liberty and government inaction blurred. Confident majorities in Congress experimented after 1802 with financing western roads from the proceeds of federal land sales, and Congress in 1806 ordered Jefferson to build a national road to Ohio. In 1804 the president had invited this spirit of initiative by asking lawmakers if anything could "be done to advance the general good" within "the pale" of their "constitutional powers." Surplus revenues continued to flood the treasury, and in his second inaugural address, Jefferson suggested an amendment to permit the "repartition" of these funds for improving "rivers, canals, roads, arts, manufactures, education, and other great objects within each state." Treasury Secretary Gallatin and others persuaded him that national control of internal improvements promised better, more harmonious results. In 1806, with the Burr conspiracy crashing into public view, Jefferson urged Congress to adopt an amendment authorizing federal internal improvements to cement the states together "by new and indissoluble ties." Still reluctant to embrace loose construction, but supported by Gallatin, Madison, and the irrepressible Robert Fulton, Jefferson now recognized a proper role for federal action in the "improvement of the country" and also "its Preservation." [49]

If Jefferson had always been an improver and now in 1806 acknowledged a role for the federal government, why was nothing accomplished? Jefferson took no steps to secure his amendment. One time he declared his intentions to lay "these enterprises" before the 10th Congress; but "the chance of war" raised an "unfortunate check," and anyway, there was a "snail-paced gait for the advance of new ideas on the general mind." This was an odd conclusion, for in the 10th Congress it was Jefferson, not the representatives of the "general mind," who balked at national public works. To the first session of that Congress, Albert Gallatin delivered his famous 1808 *Report on Roads and Canals,* which outlined a comprehensive network of projects possessing truly national importance. Admitting the possible need for a constitutional amendment, Gallatin nevertheless urged Congress to begin work wherever the assent of the states ("highly probable") could be obtained. The greatest problem, he knew, would come from patronizing actual routes (and by implication relegating others to merely local significance), but such was the natural duty of Congress. Only the "national legislature," he concluded in a striking articulation of the balance between national and state authority, "embracing every local interest, and superior to every local consideration," was "competent to the selection of such national objects." Neither Jefferson nor Madison dissented from Gallatin's important manifesto, while Republicans in Congress perceived it as a sign that the administration now supported public works. The high priests of Republican orthodoxy had discovered important work for the national government in the management of domestic affairs.[50]

Commercial depredations, embargo, and the immanent threat of war preoccupied Republicans in power for the next several years, but the unfortunate intrusion of foreign dangers does not explain the loss of the Gallatin Plan, national internal improvements, or the legitimacy of federal government action in the domestic affairs of the Union. Selfish maneuvering among the friends of particular roads and canals (especially New York promoters of the Erie Canal) plagued efforts to draft a national bill and proved anew the dangers of corruption in any program of public works. But renewed fear of legislative spoils does not explain the failure to press an amendment empowering the national government to sketch out a system that would put an end to competitive gambits in Congress. What killed national internal improvements was Jefferson's suggestion of such an amendment (without his own forceful endorsement) requesting more power from an electorate steeped in radical Jeffersonian republicanism.[51]

For fifteen years Jefferson had taught his partisans that the desire for central power was corrupt, that local governments ruled most appropriately, and that people served their liberties best by jealously guarding their own rights. Confident in the abstract faith that a free people would not endanger their own national community, Jefferson had pretty much ignored the possibility that honest conflicts could entangle the people and obstruct the government of the Union. Dishonest, stock-jobbing monarchists might disable the genius of the people, but honest laborers and agriculturalists knew the true shape of their rights and interests. Reluctant to test his hopes directly (and badly chastened by the disasters of his last year in office), Jefferson never asked for the grant of power that his constituents might refuse. His successor, James Madison, at first did not believe that the amendment was required. Later on, when the chaos of war and the bitter local jealousies which threatened his administration alerted him to a reckless attitude in Congress, Madison changed his thinking, vetoed the Bonus Bill, and called for an internal improvement amendment. By 1817, however, Jefferson's legacy had so altered the climate of politics that no amendment enlarging federal power could be secured.[52]

It was southern planters—"Old Republicans" led by Jefferson's one-time floor leader Nathaniel Macon and the renegade John Randolph—who sabotaged the claims of Republican nationalists during and after the War of 1812. Suspicious of northern and western ambitions, fearful of losing preponderance within the Union, and often personally discontented with the prospect of modernization, these sometimes reactionary characters seized every opportunity to retard and maybe reverse explosive growth and consolidation in the postwar American Union. Clinging to power as if by prerogatives they would not sanction in others, Old Republicans set out to obstruct internal improvements before change and integration further eroded the autonomy of their locales. To accomplish their ends they revived the acid rhetoric of 1798 and attached it to a perfectly Jeffersonian tactic—they espied ulterior motives in the desire to make internal improvements—this time a design to free the slaves! "Examine the constitution," Macon wrote to Bartlett Yancey as Congress attempted to override the Bonus Bill Veto, "and then tell me if Congress can establish banks, make roads and canals, whether they cannot free all the Slaves in the U.S." Macon never fired this torpedo in the Congress, but in 1824 John Randolph did, by which time many friends of slavery had become the ardent enemies of federal amendments and improvements alike.[53]

Of course, it was not a genuine threat of emancipation that killed the internal improvement amendment, for improvers in 1818 no more intended to free any slaves than did the Federalists of the 1790s intend to restore the British monarchy. Furthermore, revitalized Jeffersonian radicalism played as well in the North as in the South. Wherever partisan advantage or local interest might be secured by obstructing federal action, orthodox principles of strict construction, state rights, and local majority rule rallied voters as if invaders had laid siege to their homes. Oddly, for a people committed to change as a way of life, change in the structure of American republicanism became proscribed: "Add not to the constitution," Macon implored, "nor take therefrom." What prevented the enlargement of federal authority for the popular purpose of internal improvements was the deep suspicion that federal power cloaked hidden minorities who intended to sacrifice the rights of majorities for local or selfish advantage.[54]

Jefferson's rarefied vision of union and liberation, his abstract confidence in popular majorities, and his habit of dismissing serious opponents as enemies of the people all fostered a political temper that remained disinclined to accept the exercise of power with generosity, grace, or forbearance. Jefferson's practical campaign of opposition in the 1790s, and his articulation of Republican orthodoxy during his own administration, cemented in place a popular creed to which American voters and politicians became permanently attached. Ultimately, for Jefferson, republicanism prevailed "not in our constitution certainly, but merely in the spirit of our people." So effective was this hostile temper at discrediting power in government that Jefferson himself retired to Monticello and joined the ranks of "Old Republicans" in attacking the reformed national establishment he had labored eight years to erect.[55]

In the end, while Madison, Clay, Calhoun, John Quincy Adams, and other young Republican nationalists tried to meet popular demands for energetic government in the expanding American Union, Jefferson lent his prestigious aid and comfort to partisan critics of "consolidation" without much regard for the merits of their claims. This is the legacy of Jefferson's career as a democratic revolutionary in the early American republic: a kind of radical political temper that instinctively favored libertarian rhetoric and resented the exercise of power even in behalf of the interests of majorities. Jefferson's legacy set the stage for a style of politics that (ironically) required candidates to represent themselves as enemies of government, and once in office, to rule by deceptions and creative constructions—the very evils Jefferson despised. It transformed the promise of internal improvements into an intractable political problem for a generation that could not do without them nor find the political confidence to promote them according to any comprehensive, rational design. Finally, it established a union of states more loosely confederated than the framers of the Constitution desired and populated by individuals more truly liberated than almost anybody intended at the start of the Revolution. Unfortunately, it was a union that could not survive continued expansion and internal conflicts of interest— until the armies of a much different Republican party finally silenced the voices of states' rights radicals who thought they stood (with reasonable justification) at the center of Jefferson's original political tradition.

NOTES

My thanks to Michael A. Morrison and Peter Onuf for their editorial suggestions. This research was funded in part by a National Endowment for the Humanities summer fellowship.

1. *Annals of Congress,* 14th Cong., 2d sess., Feb. 4, 1817, p. 851.
2. Ibid., pp. 853–54; see Andrew R. L. Cayton, "'Separate Interests' and the Nation-

State: The Washington Administration and the Origins of Regionalism in the Trans-Appalachian West," *Journal of America History,* 79 (1992), pp. 39–67; Cayton, "'When Shall We Cease to Have Judases?': The Blount Conspiracy and the Limits of the 'Extended' Republic," in Ronald Hoffman, ed., *Launching the Extended Republic: The Federalist Era* (forthcoming); Malcolm J. Rohrbough, *The Trans-Appalachian Frontier: Peoples, Societies, and Institutions, 1775–1850* (New York, 1978); Robert W. Tucker and David C. Hendrickson, *Empire of Liberty: The Statecraft of Thomas Jefferson* (New York, 1990); and Thomas P. Slaughter, *The Whiskey Rebellion: Frontier Epilogue to the American Revolution* (New York, 1986).

3. For an example of truly anti-improvement thinking, see Harry L. Watson, "Squire Oldway and His Friends: Opposition to Internal Improvements in Antebellum North Carolina," *North Carolina Historical Review,* 54 (1977), pp. 105–119.

4. My understanding of the American founding era has been influenced most recently by Peter B. Knupfer, *The Union As It Is: Constitutional Unionism and Sectional Compromise, 1787–1861* (Chapel Hill, N.C., 1991), pp. 23–55; Cathy D. Matson and Peter S. Onuf, *A Union of Interests: Political and Economic Thought In Revolutionary America* (Lawrence, Kans., 1990); Michael Lienesch, *New Order for the Ages: Time, the Constitution, and the Making of Modern American Political Thought* (Princeton, N.J., 1988); and Gordon S. Wood, *The Radicalism of the American Revolution* (New York, 1992). The cornerstone of this scholarship remains Wood, *The Creation of the American Republic: 1776–1787* (Chapel Hill, N.C., 1969).

5. On Jeffersonian republicanism and its challenge to federalism see Lance Banning, *The Jeffersonian Persuasion: The Evolution of a Party Ideology* (Ithaca, N.Y., 1978); Banning, "Jeffersonian Ideology Revisited: Liberal and Classical Ideas in the New American Republic," *WMQ,* 43 (1986), pp. 3–19; Joyce Appleby, *Capitalism and a New Social Order: The Republican Vision of the 1790s* (New York, 1984); Appleby, "What is Still American in the Political Philosophy of Thomas Jefferson?" *WMQ,* 39 (1982), pp. 287–309; Appleby, "Republicanism in Old and New Contexts," *WMQ,* 43 (1986), pp. 20–34; Drew R. McCoy, *The Elusive Republic: Political Economy in Jeffersonian America* (Chapel Hill, N.C., 1980); Richard Buel, Jr., *Securing the Revolution: Ideology in American Politics, 1789–1815* (Ithaca, N.Y., 1972).

6. For a more detailed argument see John Lauritz Larson, "Liberty By Design: Freedom, Planning, and John Quincy Adams's American System," in Mary O. Furner and Barry Supple, eds., *The State and Economic Knowledge: The American and British Experiences* (New York, 1990), pp. 73–102; see also Larson, "'Bind the Republic Together': The National Union and the Struggle for a System of Internal Improvements," *Journal of American History,* 74 (1987), pp. 363–87; and George Dangerfield, *The Awakening of American Nationalism 1815–1828* (New York, 1965).

7. Three modern biographies sustain all students of Thomas Jefferson: Dumas Malone, *Jefferson and His Time,* 6 vols (Boston, 1948–81); Merrill D. Peterson, *Thomas Jefferson and the New Nation: A Biography* (New York, 1970); and Noble E. Cunningham, Jr., *In Pursuit of Reason: The Life of Thomas Jefferson* (Baton Rouge, La., 1987). A fourth body of scholarship rivals Malone's in magnitude; it is the editorial notes of Julian Boyd in the first twenty-one volumes of *The Papers of Thomas Jefferson.* I have drawn important insights from Richard K. Matthews, *The Radical Politics of Thomas Jefferson: A Revisionist View* (Lawrence, Kans., 1984); and from Forrest McDonald, *The Presidency of Thomas Jefferson* (Lawrence, Kans., 1976).

8. See TJ's 1776 drafts of a Virginia constitution, with editorial notes in *Boyd,* I, pp. 329–44; and TJ's draft of a Virginia land office bill, with notes in *Boyd,* II, pp. 133–40. See also A. G. Roeber, *Faithful Magistrates and Republican Lawyers: Creators of Virginia Legal*

Culture, 1680–1810 (Chapel Hill, N.C., 1981), esp. pp. 160–202, and Matthews, *Radical Politics,* esp. pp. 31–52.

9. See editor's notes in *Boyd,* VI, pp. 571–75 and 581–600; Boyd identifies five specific transgressions of constitutional authority in Jefferson's committee report, including one that significantly altered the terms of the Articles of Confederation itself. See also Merrill Jensen, "The Creation of the National Domain, 1781–1784,"*Mississippi Valley Historical Review,* XXVI (1939), pp. 323–42; Thomas P. Abernethy, *Western Lands and the American Revolution* (New York, 1937).

10. George Washington to William Duane, Sept. 7, 1783, quoted in editor's note, *Boyd,* VI, p. 582; TJ to J. P. G. Muhlenberg, Jan. 31, 1781, in *Boyd,* IV, p. 487; TJ to John Jay, Aug. 23, 1785, in *Boyd,* VIII, p. 426; TJ to Washington, March 15, 1784, in *Boyd,* VII, p. 25. See also Andrew R. L. Cayton, *The Frontier Republic: Ideology and Politics in the Ohio Country 1780–1825* (Kent, Ohio, 1986); Peter S. Onuf, *Origins of the Federal Republic: Jurisdictional Controversies in the United States, 1775–1787* (Philadelphia, 1983); Onuf, *Statehood and Union: A History of the Northwest Ordinance* (Bloomington, Ind., 1987), Onuf, "Liberty, Development, and Union: Visions of the West in the 1780s," *WMQ,* 43 (1986), pp. 179–213.

11. TJ to George Rogers Clark, Dec. 4, 1783, *Boyd,* VI, 371; TJ to John Jay, Aug. 23, 1785, *Boyd,* VIII, p. 426; TJ to George Washington, March 15, 1784, *Boyd,* VII, p. 26. For a particularly insightful discussion of how liberty, union, prosperity, commerce, and the West became interdependent in the minds of leading Virginia revolutionaries, see Charles Royster, *Light-Horse Harry Lee and the Legacy of the American Revolution* (New York, 1981), pp. 58–113.

12. TJ to George Washington, March 15, 1784, in *Boyd,* VII, p. 26.

13. *Boyd,* VII, pp. 26–27; TJ to Washington, May 10, 1789, in *Boyd,* XV, p. 117.

14. TJ to Madison, Oct. 28, 1785, in *Boyd,* VIII, p. 682.

15. Jefferson's draft of the Declaration of Independence, in *Boyd,* I, p. 429 (see pp. 413–33). See also editor's note on drafts of the Virginia constitution, *Boyd,* I, pp. 329–37.

16. See Jefferson's first draft of a Virginia constitution in *Boyd,* I, pp. 337–45. See also the editor's notes, pp. 329–36, and subsequent drafts, pp. 347–65.

17. TJ to Edmund Pendleton, Aug. 26, 1776, in *Boyd,* I, pp. 503–4. See Albemarle Instructions, [c. Sept. 1776], in *Boyd,* VI, pp. 286–87, with editor's notes, pp. 278–84, and supporting documents, pp. 284–316. On "Whig" and "oppositionist" traditions see Wood, *Creation,* pp. 3–45; J. G. A. Pocock, *The Machiavellian Moment: Florentine Political Thought and the Atlantic Republican Tradition* (Princeton, N.J., 1975); Forrest McDonald, *Novus Ordo Seclorum: The Intellectual Origins of the Constitution* (Lawrence, Kans., 1985), especially pp. 1–142; and Lienesch, *New Order,* pp. 17–65.

18. See Jefferson's proposed revisions for Virginia's constitution with editor's notes and documents in *Boyd,* VI, pp. 278–316. For narrative of Jefferson's frustrations during these years see Peterson, *Jefferson,* pp. 97–293, and Royster, *Harry Lee,* pp. 189–227. Patrick Henry early played the role of nemesis that was later identified with Alexander Hamilton.

19. TJ to Elbridge Gerry, Nov. 11, 1784, in *Boyd,* VII, p. 502; Jefferson's annotations on a copy of the Articles of Confederation in *Boyd,* I, pp. 177–82; TJ to John Adams, May 16, 1777, in *Boyd,* II, pp. 18–19. See Jack N. Rakove, *The Beginnings of National Politics: An Interpretive History of the Continental Congress* (New York, 1979), esp. pp. 133–240, and Onuf, *Origins,* pp. 3–20.

20. See TJ to James Monroe, June 17, 1785, in *Boyd,* VIII, pp. 228–31. See also Peterson, *Jefferson,* pp. 297–389.

21. TJ to James Monroe, June 17, 1785, in *Boyd,* VIII, pp. 228–31; Jefferson to G. K.

van Hogendorp, Oct. 13, 1785, in *Boyd*, VIII, pp. 632–33; see also TJ to David Hartley, Sept. 5, 1785, in *Boyd*, VIII, pp. 484–85.

22. James Madison to TJ, Aug. 20, 1785, *Boyd*, VIII, pp. 413–414; Madison to TJ, Aug. 12, 1786, *Boyd*, X, p. 233; see also John Jay to TJ, Dec. 14, 1786, *Boyd*, X, p. 597; Madison to TJ, March 19, 1787, *Boyd*, XI, pp. 219–20; and Matson and Onuf, *Union of Interests*, pp. 82–100.

23. TJ to James Madison, Dec. 16, 1786, *Boyd*, X, p. 603. See also Madison to TJ, March 19, 1787, *Boyd*, XI, pp. 219–20; and TJ to Madison, June 20, 1787, *Boyd*, XI, pp. 480–81.

24. TJ to James Madison, Dec. 20, 1787, *Boyd*, XII, pp. 440–42; TJ to William Carmichael, Dec. 15, 1787, in *Boyd*, XII, pp. 425–26; TJ to Edward Carrington, Dec. 21, 1787, in *Boyd*, XII, p. 446; TJ to Carrington, May 27, 1788, *Boyd*, XIII, p. 208; TJ to Moustier, May 17, 1788, *Boyd*, XIII, p. 174; and TJ to Carmichael, June 3, 1788, *Boyd*, XIII, p. 232.

25. TJ to Carmichael, June 3, 1788, *Boyd*, XIII, p. 232; TJ to Edward Rutledge, July 18, 1788, in *Boyd*, XIII, p. 378. See Patrick T. Conley and John P. Kaminski, eds., *The Constitution and the States: The Role of the Original Thirteen in the Framing and Adoption of the Federal Constitution* (Madison, Wis., 1988) and Michael Gillespie and Michael Lienesch, eds., *Ratifying the Constitution* (Lawrence, Kans., 1989).

26. TJ to Richard Price, Jan. 8, 1789, *Boyd*, XIV, p. 420.

27. "The Holy Cause of Freedom," TJ to the Citizens of Albemarle County, Feb. 12, 1790, *Boyd*, XVI, p. 179; see also TJ to Richard Gem, April 4, 1790, *Boyd*, XVI, p. 297. For examples of doubt see comments on the presidency in TJ to Edward Carrington, May 27, 1788, *Boyd*, XIII, pp. 208–09; and TJ to Alexander Donald, Feb. 7, 1788, *Boyd*, XII, p. 571.

28. TJ to Thomas Mann Randolph, April 18, 1790, *Boyd*, XVI, 351; TJ to James Monroe, June 20, 1790, *Boyd*, XVI, p. 537; TJ to George Mason, June 13, 1790, *Boyd*, XVI, p. 493. See also a memo of Feb. 1793, explaining Jefferson's role in the compromise, in *Ford*, VII, pp. 224–27; Jacob E. Cooke, "The Compromise of 1790," *WMQ*, 27 (1970), pp. 523–45; and Kenneth R. Bowling, "Dinner at Jefferson's: A Note on Jacob E. Cooke's 'The Compromise of 1790,'" *WMQ*, 28 (1971), pp. 629–48.

29. TJ memo to George Washington, "Opinion of the Constitutionality of the Bill for Establishing a National Bank," Feb. 15, 1791, in *Boyd*, XIX, pp. 275–80 (quotation on p. 276); TJ memo of conversation with Washington, March 1, 1792, *Boyd*, XXIII, pp. 186–87; TJ to Washington, May 23, 1792, *Boyd*, XXIII, pp. 535–40.

30. TJ to George Washington, May 23, 1792, *Boyd*, XXIII, pp. 535–40; see also editor's note and documents in *Boyd*, XX, pp. 718–59; and Jefferson's memo of a conversation with Washington, July 10, 1792, *Boyd*, XXIV, pp. 210–11. For contrasting narratives of the collision between Jefferson and Hamilton see Peterson, *Jefferson*, pp. 446–78; and Forrest McDonald, *Alexander Hamilton: A Biography* (New York, 1979), pp. 237–84.

31. TJ to Thomas Pinckney, Dec. 3, 1792, *Ford*, VII, pp. 191–92; TJ to Thomas Mann Randolph, March 3, 1793, *Ford*, VII, pp. 253–54; TJ to James Madison, May 12, 1793, *Ford*, VII, pp. 323–25; TJ to Madison, April 3, 1794, *Ford*, VIII, pp. 141–42; TJ to Madison, Dec. 28, 1794, *Ford*, VIII, pp. 156–58; TJ to James Monroe, Sept. 6, 1795, *Ford*, VIII, pp. 187–88; TJ to Madison, March 27, 1796, *Ford*, VIII, p. 231.

32. TJ to Philip Mazzei, Apr. 24, 1796, *Ford*, VIII, pp. 238–41; TJ to John Taylor, June 1, 1798, *Ford*, VIII, pp. 430–33 (quotation on p. 431). See Matthews, *Radical Politics*, pp. 1–52, 77–96.

33. TJ to William Branch Giles, Dec. 31, 1795, *Ford*, VIII, p. 203; TJ to John Taylor,

June 1, 1798, *Ford,* VIII, pp. 430–33; TJ to Taylor, Nov. 26, 1798, *Ford,* VIII, pp. 480–81; TJ to Wilson C. Nicholas, Sept. 5, 1799, *Ford,* IX, pp. 79–80; TJ to Elbridge Gerry, Jan. 26, 1799, *Ford,* IX, p. 17. See Ralph Ketcham, *Presidents Above Party: The First American Presidency 1789–1829* (Chapel Hill, N.C., 1984), pp. 3–99; and Noble E. Cunningham, Jr. *The Jeffersonian Republicans: The Formation of Party Organization, 1789–1801* (Chapel Hill, N.C., 1957).

34. TJ to Elbridge Gerry, Jan. 26, 1799, in *Ford,* IX, pp. 17–19; TJ to James Monroe, Sept. 7, 1797, *Ford,* VIII, p. 340; TJ to Gideon Granger, Aug. 13, 1800, *Ford,* IX, pp. 138–40.

35. The best brief for Hamilton's republicanism is Gerald R. Stourzh, *Alexander Hamilton and the Idea of Republican Government* (Stanford, Calif., 1970). See also McDonald, *Hamilton.*

36. See Matthews, *Radical Politics,* pp. 77–95, 119–26.

37. TJ, First Inaugural Address, March 4, 1801, in *Ford,* IX, pp. 194–99 (quotation on p. 195); TJ to John Dickinson, March 6, 1801, *Ford,* IX, pp. 201–2; TJ to James Monroe, March 7, 1801, *Ford,* IX, pp. 203–4; TJ to Joseph Priestley, March 21, 1801, *Ford,* IX, pp. 217–19; TJ to Nathaniel Niles, March 21, 1801, *Ford,* IX, p. 221; TJ to Thomas McKean, July 24, 1801, *Ford,* IX, pp. 282–83. See Noble E. Cunningham, Jr. *The Jeffersonian Republicans in Power: Party Operations 1801–1809* (Chapel Hill, N.C., 1963); Cunningham, *The Process of Government Under Jefferson* (Princeton, N.J., 1978); Leonard D. White, *The Jeffersonians: A Study in Administrative History, 1801–1829* (New York, 1951); Richard Hofstadter, *The Idea of a Party System: The Rise of Legitimate Opposition in the United States, 1780–1840* (Berkeley and Los Angeles, Calif., 1969), and Robert M. Johnstone, Jr., *Jefferson and the Presidency: Leadership in the Young Republic* (Ithaca, N.Y., 1978).

38. TJ, First Annual Message, Dec. 8, 1801, *Ford,* IX, pp. 321–42; TJ to Albert Gallatin, April 1, 1802, *Ford,* IX, pp. 358–60; TJ to Gallatin, Sept. 13, 1802, *Ford,* IX, p. 394; TJ to Thomas Cooper, Nov. 29, 1802, *Ford,* IX, p. 403.

39. TJ to Gideon Granger, May 20, 1803, *Ford,* IX, p. 468; TJ to Elbridge Gerry, March 29, 1801, *Ford,* IX, pp. 242–43; TJ to Thomas McKean, Feb. 19, 1803, *Ford,* IX, pp. 451–52; TJ to John Bacon, April 30, 1803, *Ford,* IX, pp. 463–64; TJ to Gideon Granger, April 16, 1804, *Ford,* X, pp. 75–76; TJ to William Branch Giles, April 6, 1802, *Ford,* IX, pp. 361–62; see also TJ to Albert Gallatin, Feb. 10, 1803, *Ford,* IX, p. 444; TJ to William Duane, July 24, 1803, *Ford,* X, p. 21; TJ to Wilson C. Nicholas, March 26, 1805, *Ford,* X, p. 138. For critical appraisals of the Jeffersonians see Leonard Levy, *Jefferson and Civil Liberties: The Darker Side* (New York, 1973) and Linda K. Kerber, *Federalists in Dissent: Imagery and Ideology in Jeffersonian America* (Ithaca, N.Y., 1970); see also Richard P. McCormick, *The Presidential Game: The Origins of American Presidential Politics* (New York, 1982), esp. pp. 41–163.

40. TJ to Edward Livingston, April 30, 1800, *Ford,* IX, p. 132; TJ to Philip Norborne Nicholas, April 7, 1800, *Ford,* IX, p. 128; TJ to Abigail Adams, July 22, 1804, *Ford,* X, p. 87n; TJ to George Hay, June 2, 1807, *Ford,* X, pp. 396–97n; TJ to Robert Brent, March 10, 1807, *Ford,* X, pp. 371–72; TJ to J. P. Reibelt, Dec. 21, 1805, *Ford,* X, pp. 205–6. On expounding the Constitution see Leonard Levy, *Original Intent and the Framers' Constitution* (New York, 1988), pp. 54–99.

41. TJ to Robert Livingston, April 18, 1802, *Ford,* IX, pp. 364–68; TJ to John Dickinson, Aug. 9, 1803, *Ford,* X, pp. 29–30. See Jefferson's message to Congress, Oct. 17, 1803, *Ford,* X, pp. 33–44; Peterson, *Jefferson,* pp. 745–800 (esp. pp. 773–75); and Tucker and Hendrickson, *Empire of Liberty,* pp. 108–35.

42. Jefferson, Fourth Annual Message, Nov. 8, 1804, *Ford,* X, p. 114; TJ to Benjamin

Hawkins, Feb. 18, 1803, *Ford,* IX, pp. 447–48. See Tucker and Hendrickson, *Empire of Liberty,* pp. 137–74; McCoy, *Elusive Republic,* pp. 185–208; McDonald, *Hamilton,* pp. 29–73; Reginald Horsman, *Expansion and American Indian Policy, 1783–1812* (East Lansing, Mich., 1967).

43. TJ to James Monroe, May 4, 1806, *Ford,* X, pp. 260–61; TJ to James Bowdoin, April 2, 1807, *Ford,* X, p. 382; TJ to Lafayette, July 16, 1807, *Ford,* X, pp. 463–64; TJ to H. D. Tiffin, Feb. 2, 1807, *Ford,* X, pp. 357–58; TJ to Dupont de Nemours, July 14, 1807, *Ford,* X, p. 461; TJ to William Branch Giles, April 20, 1807, *Ford,* X, pp. 383–87. See the discussions in Peterson, *Jefferson,* pp. 913–14, and Burton Spivak, *Jefferson's English Crisis: Commerce, Embargo, and the Republican Revolution* (Charlottesville, Va., 1979).

44. See Caroline E. MacGill, et al., *History of Transportation in the United States Before 1860,* Balthasar Henry Meyer, ed. (1917; reprint, New York, 1948); George Rogers Taylor, *The Transportation Revolution, 1815–1860* (New York, 1951).

45. Carter Goodrich, *Government Promotion of American Canals and Railroads, 1800–1890* (New York, 1960). See also Major L. Wilson, *Space, Time, and Freedom: The Quest for Nationality and the Irrepressible Conflict, 1815–1861* (Westport, Conn., 1974), pp. 3–72.

46. TJ to George Washington, March 15, 1784, *Boyd,* VII, p. 27; for Jefferson's long career as an improver see Joseph H. Harrison, Jr., *"Sic et non:* Thomas Jefferson and Internal Improvement," *Journal of the Early Republic,* 7 (1987), pp. 335–49.

47. See Max Farrand, ed., *Records of the Federal Convention of 1787,* 4 vols. (New Haven, Conn., 1911–37), II, pp. 615–20.

48. TJ to James Madison, March 6, 1796, *Ford,* VIII, p. 226; TJ to Caesar Rodney, Dec. 21, 1800, *Ford,* IX, p. 160.

49. Thomas Jefferson, Fourth Annual Message, Nov. 8, 1804, in *Ford,* X, p. 117; Second Inaugural, March 4, 1805, *Ford,* X, p. 130; Sixth Annual Message, Dec. 2, 1806, *Ford,* X, pp. 317–19. For the Burr conspiracy see Peterson, *Jefferson,* pp. 841–74; on Gallatin's political economy see John R. Nelson, Jr., *Liberty and Property: Political Economy and Policymaking in the New Nation, 1789–1812* (Baltimore, 1987), pp. 115–33.

50. TJ to Joel Barlow, Dec. 10, 1807, *Ford,* X, pp. 529–30; Albert Gallatin, *Report of the Secretary of the Treasury on the Subject of Roads and Canals* (1808; Reprint, New York, 1968), pp. 74–75. See Drew R. McCoy, *The Last of the Fathers: James Madison and the Republican Legacy* (New York, 1989), pp. 85–103.

51. See Harrison, *"Sic et non,"* pp. 341–44; Larson, "'Bind the Republic,'" pp. 374–77.

52. For Madison's administrations, see J. C. A. Stagg, *Mr. Madison's War: Politics, Diplomacy, and Warfare in the Early Republic, 1783–1830* (Princeton, N.J., 1983); for the Bonus Bill Veto see Larson, "'Bind the Republic,'" pp. 381–85.

53. Nathaniel Macon to Bartlett Yancey, March 8, 1818, in "Letters of Nathaniel Macon," Kemp P. Battle, ed., *Sprunt Historical Monographs* (Chapel Hill, N.C., 1900); Macon to Yancey, April 15, 1818, in Watson, "Squire Oldway," p. 118. See Noble Cunningham, Jr., "Nathaniel Macon and the Southern Protest against National Consolidation," *North Carolina Historical Review,* 32 (1955), pp. 376–84.

54. Macon to Yancey, April 15, 1818, in Watson, "Squire Oldway," p. 118. See Robert H. Wiebe, *The Opening of American Society* (New York, 1984), pp. 127–252.

55. TJ to Samuel Kercheval, July 12, 1816, *Ford,* XII, pp. 4–7.

CHAPTER 12

Jefferson and an American Foreign Policy

WALTER LAFEBER

Jefferson's policies illustrate some of the most important themes in American history, not least some of its central paradoxes and contradictions. An advocate of (and considered to be the spokesman for) an agrarian republic in the 1780s, Jefferson later argued for an equal role for manufacturers and commerce. The primary founder of the first opposition political party in the United States, he downplayed the role of parties during his presidency. An apparently eternal and relentless optimist about American prospects (the "Pollyanna" of the nation's history, as one historian has called him[1]), Jefferson ended his life embittered and frustrated when he witnessed the opening scenes of Jacksonian America. The author of the memorable phrase, "Entangling alliances with none," in the last years of his life he advised President James Monroe to make a highly entangling alliance with, of all peoples, the British, whom Jefferson had fought relentlessly from the 1770s through the War of 1812. A fervent believer in the manifest destiny of democratic government to overspread much of the world, he strongly advised that this destiny would be best realized by Americans staying at home—although his idea of home changed from state to continental to perhaps hemispheric proportions.[2]

In a larger sense, these are less contradictions and paradoxes than they are the story of a nation passing through the process of becoming a continental empire and having ambitions to become much more. Jefferson lived a long and active life, but his paradoxes and contradictions cannot be explained by the supposed fickleness of older people. Jefferson indeed changed, sometimes dramatically, as when he urged Monroe to make an alliance with the British in 1823 to protect the new Latin American revolutionary nations from the designs of the Holy Alliance. In the annals of American foreign policy, at least, his story is less that of an embittered old man, or a Pollyanna gone sour, than an encapsulation of the story of that foreign policy between the 1790s and 1820s when the United States became a continental empire, when an agrarian republic first showed signs of becoming a quite different kind of society, and when the nation initially glimpsed the possibilities of the modern presidency.

Of at least equal importance, it was during Jefferson's era that Americans had to come to terms with one of the most important problems they confronted during their two hundred years of independence: the ability of their government to order and control American expansion and foreign affairs—or, sometimes, the inability of the government, even in Jefferson's hands, to do so. The extension of power and the expansion of empire is not to be overestimated; even the least of totalitarian regimes have been capable of accomplishing those objectives. It is the transformation of that extension and expansion into a functioning, accountable, democratic republic that is more remarkable; and it is the mobilization of support for foreign policy in such a republic that, when it can be done, is especially noteworthy.

The dynamics of Jefferson's foreign policy ran as follows: his early belief in the virtues of, and need for, agrarian expansionism helped lead to a series of conflicts in the international arena that forced him to devise a set of stronger central governmental policies to protect both agrarian and, increasingly, more broadly defined national interests. These governmental policies included military action and a dominant presidency. The implementation of Jeffersonian foreign policies helps explain contradictions and paradoxes that turn out to be more apparent than real. For his faith in the virtues of agrarian expansion led Jefferson through a series of events that ironically ended in the acceptance of war and manufacturers, a call for an entangling alliance, an apology for slavery during the Missouri compromise debates, and deep personal frustration and bitterness in the last fifteen years of his life. These years, and pivotal events of his presidential terms, are explained less by seeing contradictions than by noting the logical results of his own belief in the need for agrarian expansionism. Or, to rephrase in the context of the ongoing debate over the nature of Jefferson's republicanism,[3] he began with a dynamic view of traditional republicanism and followed out its consequences in the context of the evolving United States of 1790 to 1820 until he had to accept a more mature capitalism, complete with the instability, central governmental powers, and international obligations that this capitalism required. A great revolutionary of the 1770s who transformed the nation's political relationships, Jefferson was finally frustrated by his encounter with a near-revolutionary capitalism that transformed economic and social relationships. The primary author of the Jeffersonian era, he was a first victim of the Jacksonian era.[4]

I

Jefferson's classic statement of the need for an agrarian republic is found in chapter XIX of his *Notes on the State of Virginia.*

> In Europe the lands are either cultivated, or locked up against the cultivator. Manufacture must therefore be resorted to of necessity not of choice, to support the surplus of their people. But we have an immensity of land courting the industry of the husbandman. . . . Those who labour in the earth are the chosen people. . . . Corruption of morals in the mass of cultivators is a phænomenon of which no age nor nation has furnished an example. It is the mark set on those, who not looking up to heaven, to their own soil and industry, as does the husbandman, for their subsistence, depend for it on the casualties and caprice of customers. Dependance begets subservience and venality, suffocates the germ of virtue, and prepares fit tools for the designs of ambition.[5]

In 1805, as he was about to begin his second presidential term, Jefferson wrote a friend that in any revision of the *Notes,* "I should . . . certainly qualify several expressions in the nineteenth chapter, which have been construed differently from what they were intended." He had feared that, at a future time, American cities would mirror the horrors of cities in Europe. But that time still seemed far off, Jefferson wrote some eighteen months after the Louisiana Purchase: "As yet our manufactures are as much at their ease, as independent and moral as our agricultural habits, and they will continue so as long as there are vacant lands for them to resort to; because whenever it shall be attempted by the other classes to reduce them to the minimum of subsistence, they will quit their trades and go to laboring the earth."[6]

Vacant lands and an ever-expanding frontier thus allowed not only independent and virtuous tillers of the soil, but unsubservient and virtuous manufacturers. Given the rapid natural expansion of the American population (to the calculation of which Jefferson devoted considerable attention, and which his close friend, and sometimes mentor, James Madison, put at the center of his political theory[7]), and given the rapid increase of immigrants into the United States (an increase that should be carefully limited, Jefferson wrote in his *Notes*[8]), the key to the continued independence and virtue of Americans would be ever more land. In 1776 Jefferson so fully believed that good citizenship depended on ownership of property that he proposed that Virginia grant fifty acres of land to every man who did not own that amount.[9] Within the next decade, however, he began to worry that without either control of population growth or more land, Virginia would, within the next century, have "nearly the state of population in the British islands."[10]

Before he became president, Jefferson had reconciled this need for a large (indeed, ever-larger) landed empire with his republican political theory. Madison played an important role in shaping Jefferson's mind on this problem of how a large landed empire could serve as the basis for a republic, even though classical theorists, from Aristotle to Montesquieu, had argued that such a reconciliation was impossible. Immediately after the Constitutional Convention, in an exchange of letters that reveals more about the assumptions of the new Constitution than any other documents except Madison's minutes of the Convention itself and *The Federalist,* Madison outlined for Jefferson how, contrary to Montesquieu, "in the extended Republic of the United States, The General Government would hold a pretty even balance between the parties of particular States, and be at the same time sufficiently restrained by its dependence on the community, from betraying its general interests."[11]

In a 1795 private letter to François d'Invernois, Jefferson rephrased the general theory: The idea of "Montesquieu and other political writers" that only small states are fitted to be republics can be replaced now by the theory that a "just republic . . . must be so extensive as that local egoisms may never reach it's greater part. . . . The smaller the societies, the more violent and more convulsive their schisms."[12] Perhaps Jefferson's most revealing statement on this subject of how large landed empires can be best suited for healthy republics occurred several weeks after he assumed the presidency in 1801. Looking back over the near-disasters of the 1790s—including foreign policy crises such as the Jay Treaty and the ensuing uproar, the undeclared war with France, the Alien and Sedition acts, and the response of the Virginia and Kentucky resolutions—Jefferson concluded that the nation's survival gave "new proof of the falsehood of Montesquieu's doctrine, that a republic can be preserved only in a small territory. The reverse is the truth. Had our territory been even a third only of what it is, we were gone."[13]

To acquire the necessary, ever-extending territory, the Virginian sent out government-supported expeditions, redefined international law, and stated in classic form the creed of American isolationism—that is, the creed of maintaining maximum freedom of action to obtain the maximum results in territory and commerce. In sending George Rogers Clark to secure the Illinois country during the Revolution, Jefferson urged him to accomplish the mission in such a way that there could be added "to the empire of liberty an extensive and fertile country, thereby converting dangerous enemies into valuable friends." Jefferson had the same "empire-of-liberty" goal in mind when he drafted the 1784 territorial government ordinance, sent out the Lewis and Clark expedition, supported the War of 1812, and, of course, when he bought Louisiana. The world, he had no doubt, was to be treated to the new sight of a "free and moderate government" presiding over "range after range" of new, equal states that covered the Mississippi Valley if not, ultimately, much of the Western Hemisphere. Such an empire required active government leadership, not mere acquiescence.[14] Such leadership, as Lawrence Kaplan has noted in his important studies on Jeffersonian diplomacy, included the redefinition of the Old World's international law. In 1792, for example, Secretary of State Jefferson flatly told Spain that American settlers on the upper portions of the Mississippi River Valley had a natural-law right to free navigation down the river to the sea. Spain, whose hold on what remained of its North American empire depended on controlling the giant spigot for trade at New Orleans, had never heard such a claim being seriously advanced. In Kaplan's phrase, "The claim of riparian rights under the rubric of natural law seemed to abuse not only the meaning of international law but also the practice of the time."[15]

Neither European-written international law nor the practice of the time, however, had been devised to meet the needs of a prolific agrarian community, spread over thousands of square miles, whose livelihood, indeed continuation within the union, depended on its access to giant river systems for the export of surplus product and import of needed goods. Madison had patiently explained the relationship amid the growing crisis caused by Spain's closing of New Orleans. He wrote privately to a fellow southerner who well understood the comparisons Madison made: "The Mississippi is to them [the multiplying U.S. settlers in the Mississippi valley] everything. It is the Hudson, the Delaware, the Potomac and all the navigable rivers of the Atlantic States formed into one stream."[16]

These expeditions and new interpretations of international law may be among the most significant results of Jefferson's belief that the American future must be largely agrarian, but they are not the best known, and certainly not the most discussed, of his foreign policies. Rather, the Jeffersonian belief in isolationism, in maximum freedom of action, has been at the center of the nation's debate over foreign affairs from the time of John Adams's abortive model treaty of 1776, through the Washington administration's stance in the 1790s toward the French Revolution, Jefferson's non-entangling alliances pledge of his first Inaugural and his sudden swerving away from the pledge in 1823, to the historic debates of the late 1940s (when its membership in the North Atlantic Treaty Organization became the most significant U.S. alliance since the French treaty of 1778), and the renewed debates over isolationism in the post-Cold War world of the 1990s. Taking his lead from Madison's leadership in Congress during 1790–1792, Jefferson came to agree with his friend that a closer relationship with France was necessary for both freeing U.S. commerce from British control and blocking Hamilton's financial programs. At no time, however, and particularly not during the heated debate over Washington's 1793 Proclamation of Neutrality in the growing French-British war, did Jefferson suggest tying American fortunes unalterably to those of France. By 1798, his early support of the French Revolution had been transformed by the insensitivity and foolishness of French Minister Edmond Genet, the Terror, and especially Napoleon's seizure of power, into the fear that even pro-French sympathy was misplaced and, certainly, corrosive for the politics of a republic. "Our countrymen have divided themselves by such strong affections, to the French and the English," he wrote Elbridge Gerry in June 1797, "that nothing will secure us internally but a divorce from both nations; & this must be the object of every real American, and it's attainment is practicable without much self-denial." [17] It has been too easy to confuse Jefferson's view of French culture and the early French Revolution with his views of French national interests in foreign affairs. In 1785, for example, he could admire French culture while, after learning of a French scientific expedition to the Pacific, asking John Paul Jones to find out if the expedition had any designs on the American West Coast (a coast to which, of course, the United States did not yet have any serious claim.)[18]

The best-known phrase that captures the principle of American freedom of action comes from the 1801 Inaugural. It is in that part of the speech in which Jefferson lists the "essential principle[s]" of the government. It is thus incorporated in what is probably the most concise litany available of the Jeffersonian principles for good government. "Peace, commerce, & honest friendship with all nations," the new president pledged, "entangling alliances with none." Eight principles later, he returned to the importance of commerce, but placed it in a different, highly revealing context: "Encouragement of Agriculture, & of Commerce as it's handmaid." [19] That the requirements of agriculture's "handmaid" might in turn require violating the principle of no entangling alliances only slowly became apparent to Jefferson. Meanwhile, as Albert K. Weinberg pointed out a half-century ago, "Jefferson used a pejorative term to describe his and other right-thinking Americans' view of foreign obligations: An entanglement, in international life as in the love life, is not a mere association," Weinberg concluded, "but a relationship so intimate that two destinies become intertwined—and by implication not for better but for worse."[20] Jefferson's agrarians and their "handmaid" were to maintain control of their own destinies.

Alexis de Tocqueville pinpointed Jefferson's seminal contribution to this debate over freedom of action when, more than three decades after the 1801 Inaugural, he wrote in *Democracy in America* that two men "imparted to American foreign policy a tendency that is still being followed today"—Washington, with his demand in the Farewell Address for what Tocqueville called "a perfect neutrality with regard to the internal dissensions of the European powers," and Jefferson, who "went still further and introduced this other maxim into the policy of the Union, that the Americans ought never to solicit any privileges from foreign nations, in order not to be obliged to grant similar privileges themselves."[21]

Tocqueville followed his analysis of Jefferson's "maxim" with the observation, "The foreign policy of the United States is eminently expectant; it consists more in abstaining than in acting." The first part of the observation was certainly true. The second part was certainly not true. Tocqueville believed that "the old nations of Europe" were confronted with the necessity "to make the best of the past and to adapt it to their present circumstances."[22] Europeans, in other words, were constantly confronted by the unfortunate need to come to terms with a distasteful past. Americans, Tocqueville concluded, had no such burdensome past with which they had come to terms. Jefferson, however, along with Madison and some others of this generation, indeed believed they had a past with which they had to come to terms. It was the past of those republics that grew corrupt, then despotic.[23] No guarantee existed that the American experiment would escape the cyclical fate that had destroyed earlier republics. But Jefferson believed that the present and future circumstances of the United States could, at least for a considerable time (and if the nation's foreign policies worked correctly), be brought into play to check that past while delaying, if not altogether preempting, the cyclical fate.

Jefferson wrote Madison (who was considerably more pessimistic about the nation's prospects for retaining an uncorrupted republic), that Americans would remain virtuous "as long as there shall be vacant lands in any part of America" and people were not "piled up on one another in large cities, as in Europe." Because of the nation's landed prospects, the crisis need not arise "for many centuries," Jefferson concluded optimistically.[24] By the 1790s and during his presidency, however, if not before, he moved to avert such a crisis not by "abstaining," (as Tocqueville would have it), but by acting, decisively and directly, on Spanish-held New Orleans, Louisiana, the Floridas, and even South America.

II

Tocqueville's misjudgment about Jefferson's, and beyond him the Americans', desire for "abstaining" rather than "acting" perhaps arose from the French visitor's next observation about the relationship, as he saw it, between "American democracy" and "the foreign policy of the country."

> I do not hesitate to say that it is especially in the conduct of their foreign relations that democracies appear to me decidedly inferior to other governments. . . .
>
> [A] democracy can only with great difficulty regulate the details of an important undertaking, persevere in a fixed design, and work out its execution in spite of serious obstacles. It cannot combine its measures with secrecy or await their consequences with patience.[25]

This formulation defined what can be called the Tocqueville problem in American history: how could a Jeffersonian democratic republic, whose vitality rested on the pursuit of individual interests with a minimum of central governmental direction, create the necessary national consensus for the conduct of an effective, and necessarily long-term, foreign policy? The two-century-long debate over the Tocqueville problem is as important, and even more complex, than the discussion of American isolationism, but the debate has not yet been studied in its full historical context. Indeed, it has been little studied at all.

Jefferson dealt with the Tocqueville problem with two general approaches. Consistent with the new federal principle of the Constitution, a principle that he and Madison discussed in some detail if not always in agreement during their extensive exchange of letters in 1787–1788,[26] Jefferson emphasized the need for state and local societies to be responsible for state and local affairs.[27] Jefferson's second approach involved the use of strong presidential powers in foreign policy. To argue, as scholars recently have, that Jefferson (rather naively in these authors' views), sought to break the European tradition of reason of state, with its assumption that foreign policy has a dominant role over domestic policy,[28] misses the central point of the Virginian's approach to both domestic and foreign affairs: given the nature of his agrarian republic, and given the proper working of the federal system in the necessarily large territorial sphere, Jefferson could rightly

assume that foreign and domestic policies were two sides of the same national interest. Europeans posited a distinction because their governments
were not sufficiently responsible to the welfare of their own people. The
American presidency was responsible—or, more accurately, in Jeffersonian
hands could be made responsible.

As Secretary of State between 1790 and 1793, Jefferson did not condemn
George Washington's exercise of the president's powers; he did criticize the
use of those powers for the purpose of achieving Hamilton's goals. Jefferson's early memoranda to the president argued, for example, that the Executive could limit the Senate's power over diplomatic appointments, and
that the president (not the Senate), could determine the nations with which
the United States should exchange ministers. Jefferson further argued that
to allow the Senate undue influence on these issues would set unfortunate
precedents for presidential power.[29] He was not unfriendly to the wide
exercise of executive power even before he became president himself.

Nothing, however, could increase that power as much as war, as Madison
and other authors of the Constitution perfectly understood.[30] Henry Adams
and more recent historians have emphasized that war was antithetical to
many essentials of Jeffersonianism because it required centralization of
power, increased taxation, mobilization of the society, and the copying of
discredited European techniques to settle disputes. As Adams phrased it,
"The party of Jefferson and Gallatin was founded on the dislike of every
function of government necessary in a military system."[31] A more recent
account elaborates Adams's thesis and repeatedly attacks Jefferson for being
unrealistically universal in his goals and pacifistic in his means.[32] A "dislike" of "military system" (to use Adams's phrase), however, should not be
confused with a rejection of the use of military power.

Jefferson, as Reginald Stuart has convincingly argued, viewed war and
the use of force as a necessary tool to assure the state's survival. In *Notes on
the State of Virginia,* Jefferson asserted that by avoiding folly, Americans
could escape half the wars that confronted them, but for the other half they
had to make "the best preparations we can." He believed that warring was
a part of human nature, and he did not see it as an aberration in human
activity. He only hoped, and worked, to keep war as limited, short, and
undestructive as possible. When, during the Nootka Sound crisis of 1790,
Great Britain threatened to move across U.S. land to seize territory from
Spain, Secretary of State Jefferson was prepared to accept "the general war
expected to take place should this be the only means of preventing the
calamity." He was also prepared to go to war with Spain over conflicting
U.S.-Spanish interests in the Southwest. Clearly, he thought the need for

American territorial expansion was worth both a war and the increase of central governmental (especially presidential) powers such a conflict could produce. As president, he waged a war against the Barbary Pirates to ensure an unencumbered American trade in the Mediterranean. That war was necessarily limited not because of Jeffersonian naïveté, but because of limited resources and vast distances. His reluctance to go to war against Great Britain between 1805 and 1809 was rooted less in his fear of how the conflict might affect American society (indeed, the requirements of that society seemed to demand the removal of British control over U.S. agricultural exports and the American carrying trade), than his fear of how it might turn out and how it might affect the union.[33]

Three of the most important parts of Jefferson's statecraft—his acceptance of strong presidential power, his willingness to use military force, and his skill in solving the Tocqueville problem by maintaining a strong consensus to support his policies—appeared with clarity in the Louisiana crisis of 1802–1803. These three characteristics of his foreign policy were not isolated or incidental, but integral to the achievement of his goals of ensuring the unhindered access of American agrarians to New Orleans after Spain closed the port in 1802, and then, in 1803 ensuring the acquisition (and, of equal importance, the control), of a vast territory that would indeed have "room enough for all descend[an]ts to the 1,000th & 1,000th generation," to borrow the phrase from his 1801 Inaugural.[34] The Louisiana Purchase is a case study of the necessary progression, a working out of the logic, of Jefferson's foreign policies. His agrarian empire depended on the reopening of New Orleans; as Madison observed, the Mississippi River was "everything" to the settlers along the 2,500-mile-long valley. The stakes were so great that, in Stuart's words, "the threat of war was an active weapon in the arsenal of American diplomacy, made more potent by Jefferson's hints at a possible British alliance." The President was not serious about allying with Great Britain, although the mere threat of such a rapprochement proved to be important; it haunted Napoleon after he forced Spain to sell Louisiana to him in 1800. Jefferson was serious about using force, if necessary, to protect U.S. entry to New Orleans. The president mobilized troops not only along the access routes to the port, but along strategic routes in the Northwest to help contain British forces stationed inside Canada. He also asked Congress in January 1803 to support an exploring expedition, led by Captain Meriwether Lewis and William Clark, to move into northern Louisiana to carry out military reconnaissance, find a route from the Mississippi to the Pacific, and "provide an extension of territory which the rapid increase of our numbers will call for."[35]

The already "rapid increase" of those "numbers" in the Northwest had pushed Jefferson into the crisis over access to New Orleans. When Napoleon offered to sell all of Louisiana for $15 million, his decision was only partly due to distress in Europe. He had also been unable to move enough troops out of ice-locked European ports to deal with the multiplying security problems in the New World—above all, to deal with the black revolt against French rule in his key sugar-producing country of Santo Domingo. Jefferson, and especially Madison, had purposefully compounded Napoleon's problems in Santo Domingo by stepping up aid to the rebels led by Toussaint-Louverture.[36] The president and the Secretary of State were not merely the lucky recipients of Europe's distresses when Louisiana fell into their hands in the spring of 1803. Jefferson had used his presidential powers, especially his prerogatives as commander-in-chief under the Constitution, along with shrewd diplomacy to acquire New Orleans and, beyond it, an area that he and Madison had assumed would someday become another, if distant, part of an American agrarian system. The settlers' demands for access to the most important outlet for their trade had led to crises in both the American West and relations with Europe; those crises in turn had required mobilizing troops, surreptitiously aiding African-American rebels (aid that Jefferson did not allow without much thought, given the presence of African-American slaves in his own country), and suddenly accepting without any explicit constitutional authority an incredible 828,000 square miles of landed empire.

Governing the new western empire seemed to hold as many dangers as had the negotiations leading to its purchase. In the last paragraph of *The Federalist,* no. 51, Madison had argued that the "larger the society, provided it lie within a practicable sphere, the more duly capable it will be of self-government." But the Louisiana territory was hardly a "practicable" sphere. It was sparsely settled with the Americans Jefferson and Madison believed had the necessary background and talents to make the constitutional system work. Jefferson discovered, in other words, that the need to quiet and stabilize the uproar of western agrarians over the closing of New Orleans had led to the more complex problem of how to govern an impracticable empire. The needs of Jefferson's agrarians had resulted not in stability and an easy working of the republican system, but a series of diplomatic, and threatened military, crises in 1802 and early 1803 that climaxed in yet another crisis for a constitutional system whose primary theorist assumed the system would work best in a "practicable sphere." The agrarians were working out their destiny as a "chosen people" not in a happily automatic Newtonian political universe, but in a dynamic, increasingly complex capitalist system where demands built upon demands, one crisis seemed to lead to another, and the role of government and presidential power became increasingly vital and complicated.

Jefferson and Madison finally made Louisiana a practicable sphere for governing by sharply modifying the territorial system put in place in 1787 and giving the president far more powers. They received bipartisan support, for both Democrat-Republicans and Federalists mistrusted the overly pluralistic population of the new area. Jefferson's Democrat-Republicans, who were not known for advocating the grant of extraordinary powers to the Executive before 1803, agreed with the president that the grant in this case was only temporary. One Federalist observed correctly and with appropriate sarcasm that if "such a bill had been passed by federalists, the Democrats would have denounced it as monarchical; but when enacted by the exclusive friends of the people, it is pure republicanism." Another Federalist concluded that the governing bill contradicted the Constitution because Jefferson became legislator and judge as well as executive in the territory.[37] For Jefferson, however, the risk was little risk at all, and the ultimate results were worth nearly any risk. "By enlarging the empire of liberty," he instructed the leaders of Indiana Territory in late 1805, "we multiply its auxiliaries & provide new sources of renovation should its principles, at any time, degenerate, in those portions of our country which gave them birth."[38]

The problem of governing the immense Louisiana territory and integrating it into the union, however, did not end with Jefferson's successes in Paris and Washington during 1803. In early 1806 the president began to receive numerous reports that Aaron Burr was planning at least the invasion of Spanish territory, and perhaps plotting the secession of western parts of the United States. Jefferson's vice president during the first term, Burr had become a political outcast after confrontations with the Virginian and the murder of Hamilton in the 1804 duel. Jefferson had used his powers of appointment to place loyal subordinates at strategic western points (such as William Claiborne, Governor of Louisiana, in New Orleans), and also used the patronage and other powers of his office to intimidate Burr's key associate, General James Wilkinson. It was Wilkinson who decided to break with Burr and send damning evidence about the conspiracy to Jefferson. Burr was captured just above New Orleans in early 1807 and returned to Richmond for trial. He was freed after the President's long-time political opponent, Chief Justice John Marshall, narrowly interpreted the Constitution's treason clause and ruled out evidence that might have incriminated the defendant. But Jefferson's decisive use of his executive powers, and the loyalty of his appointees in the West, destroyed whatever there was of the Burr conspiracy—the last important attempt to create an independent empire in the North American West. Moreover, in doing so Jefferson, in this and other instances, set significant precedents for the president's authority to withhold documents that he alone considered "private" or "confidential," thereby withholding possibly crucial evidence from the eyes of both Congress and the courts.[39]

Jefferson tried to follow up his success in doubling (and preserving) American territory during 1803 by further "enlarging the empire of liberty" through the purchase—or, if necessary, the seizure—of the Floridas. Again it was not mere territorial greed, but agrarian need that drove his policy. Settlers along the rivers that drained through the Floridas into the Gulf were growing as dependent on those waterways for their commercial survival as settlers in the Northwest had become on the Mississippi. The Floridas, moreover, were too loosely governed by a disintegrating Spanish empire that could not, and would not, control clashes between Indians and the advancing white settlers. A further danger loomed: If the United States did not quickly gain control of the Floridas, they would fall into the hands of either Great Britain or France. Jefferson tried to use secret congressional appropriations as an enticement for Napoleon to force Spain to surrender the territory. When that scheme failed, the President considered a military seizure. And Jefferson's plans for future expansion went beyond the Floridas. As Albert Gallatin explained to the French Minister in 1809, the taking of the Floridas was "Mr. Jefferson's hobby. . . . As for the possession of Cuba this was also a new idea of Mr. Jefferson." Gallatin disavowed any interest of the newly elected president James Madison in the Floridas, but within the next two years, Madison approved a covert operation that brought part of the Floridas under U.S. control.[40]

III

By 1807 to 1809, however, the agrarians' need for the Floridas became less important than their need for a freer trade with Europe. That commerce had become bound by the post-1805 restrictions imposed by British courts and orders-in-council on U.S. ships. The restrictions on American trade were not only pinching agricultural exporters. Important mercantile families had supported Jefferson since the late 1790s, including the Crowninshields of Salem, the Smiths of Baltimore, the Livingstons (and John Jacob Astor) in New York, and the Dallases of Philadelphia.[41] These were the commercial "handmaids" of the agrarian community, as Jefferson termed them in his 1801 Inaugural. They were as vital to the proper working of Jefferson's system, and more directly threatened by British and French attacks on U.S. commerce, than the agrarians themselves. Indeed, by 1807–1808, it became difficult to tell which was the "handmaid" or servant, and which was the master. The health of Jeffersonian America depended on its international trade.

Jefferson, in the American tradition that began with John Adams's treaty plan of 1776 and climaxed with the U.S.-directed international trade institutions established between 1944 and 1948, opposed any division of world commerce into blocs. The relative insignificance of American political leverage, and—of greater importance—the multiplying needs of American producers, permitted no alternative but to seek freer trade in the widest possible markets, rather than mercantilist-style competition between blocs. "I am for free commerce with all nations; political connection with none," Jefferson wrote Elbridge Gerry in 1799 while outlining his political and economic principles.[42] That principle, however, was directly challenged in a series of British and French efforts to control U.S. trade during the Napoleonic wars, until finally the efforts climaxed with the British attack on and seizure of sailors from the *Chesapeake* in 1807.

With ample evidence, historians have concluded that this was the point at which Jefferson might have most effectively taken an enraged and largely united country into war against Great Britain to protect U.S. rights on the high seas.[43] He refused to go to war for a number of good reasons: his belief that Great Britain would apologize and change its ways, renewed attacks by the French on U.S. shipping, the need to convene Congress to consider a war declaration, and the president's understandable reluctance to fight a British navy that had recently destroyed much of Napoleon's fleet. Especially important, however, Jefferson believed the United States possessed a better weapon than military force to change British policy: economic sanctions. Again, Jefferson's faith in such sanctions is an important link in the belief long held by many U.S. officials that American commerce, and especially the nation's agricultural trade, was so crucial for other nations that the imposition of economic sanctions would be a less bloody and costly, but equally effective, means of coercion than the use of force in the international arena. As Secretary of State Jefferson had phrased it in his historic "Report . . . on Commerce" in 1793:

> But should any nation, contrary to our wishes, suppose it may better find its advantage by continuing its system of prohibitions, duties and regulations, it behooves us to protect our citizens, their commerce and navigation, by counter prohibitions, duties and regulations, also. Free com-

merce and navigation are not to be given in exchange for restrictions and vexations; nor are they likely to produce a relaxation of them.[44]

In a letter to Thomas Pinckney of May 1797, Jefferson drew the explicit policy conclusion from his 1793 statement when he wrote, during a growing crisis with France, "War is not the best engine for us to resort to, nature has given us one in our commerce, which, if properly managed, will be a better instrument for obliging the interested nations of Europe to treat us with justice."[45] This statement was neither a naive belief or a view peculiar to Jefferson; it has been a working assumption of U.S. foreign policy since Thomas Paine's *Common Sense* of 1776, and at times (although not in 1776), it proved to be accurate and workable. Indeed, in the summer of 1812 Jefferson's and Madison's confidence in the diplomatic power of U.S. economic strength was proven to be well placed when the British finally did repeal their orders-in-council. They did so, however, less because they felt their people were dependent on U.S. agricultural products than because their merchants feared they would suffer if they did not have access to American markets.

This was a form of U.S. economic leverage that Jefferson had been reluctant to employ. In 1806 he had tried to formulate a nonimportation bill to coerce the British to lift their commercial restrictions, only to make the frightening discovery that Americans had grown heavily dependent on such British goods as medicines, fine cloth, and manufactured products. The 1806 bill was finally so laced with loopholes that John Randolph correctly derided it as "a milk and water bill, a dose of chicken broth."[46] Dependence on British goods, and the consequent loss of valuable specie to British merchants, seemed to form a weak base on which to build effective U.S. economic sanctions in either 1806 or 1812. And in 1812, with Jefferson's blessing, Madison took the nation into war despite the British repeal of some of their most onerous practices.

In 1807–1808, however, Jefferson did all he could to avoid war by imposing instead an embargo that prohibited the export of virtually any product overseas. It allowed only coastal trade. The embargo tragically distorted parts of Jeffersonian America and transformed others. Devised as a lever to make Great Britain suffer, it instead swept U.S. ships and goods off the seas and opened world markets to the one nation with the carrying fleet capable of exploiting those markets—Great Britain. American carriers, facing economic disaster, tried to break the embargo. Gallatin warned Jefferson that the Executive had to have "the most arbitrary powers and sufficient force" if the sanction was to be effective. U.S. ships were soon seized by Jefferson's agents, federal officials closely watched the loading of ships, goods suspiciously moving toward the border points were stopped by force, and the military was increased to enforce laws. Smuggling became so profitable that, according to local lore, one raft on Lake Champlain with an illegal cargo for Canadian trade stretched for a half-mile and held five hundred armed men on board to guard against federal seizure. In late summer 1808 Jefferson told Gallatin, "I did not expect a crop of so sudden and rank growth of fraud and open opposition by force could have grown up in the United States." Economic depression spread not only through the agrarian sections of the West and South, but in urban areas; in New York City alone over one thousand men were jailed for debt in early 1809, half of them for owing less than a week's wage of ten dollars.[47]

The president understood that the embargo was the "last card" he could play "short of war." As he left Washington in early 1809, he told Madison that while it was desirable to avoid war, and that while they had earned "credit with the world" for making the avoidance of war "our first object," war, nevertheless, "may become a less losing business than unresisted depredation."[48] By 1812, Jefferson fervently supported war against Great Britain. Even after the orders-in-council were rescinded, he believed that Americans "must sacrifice the last dollar and drop of blood" if necessary to roll back British power and, especially, force London to stop impressing men from U.S. ships. Again, it was not (contrary to some accounts[49]), that Jefferson had been too innocent to understand the consequences of his political and social assumptions, or that he was naive in believing that Europe was wrong to give the state and foreign policy primacy over domestic affairs. His willingness to go to war derived from his belief that the protection of agrarian interests was most essential for the survival of a virtuous and economically healthy republic; that those interests required the protection of their "handmaid," commerce; that this protection in turn required the use of state, especially executive, powers, first in trying to find a means of protection short of a costly war, and then, if necessary, in waging war itself. Indeed, as Reginald Stuart notes, for Jefferson "the issue [in 1812] was the political survival of the state,"[50] but it was a quite differently conceived state than those in Europe.

That war and increased executive powers were among the consequences of his belief in the need to protect agrarian interests did not surprise Jefferson. He was surprised, however, by the effect those governmental actions had on the rapid transformation of the nation's political economy. When the embargo encouraged the development of manufactures, Jefferson convinced himself that this was acceptable because they were household manufactures and limited to the making of items that Americans truly needed.[51] By 1816, however, Jefferson had realized that something more radical had occurred. A different kind of capitalism was replacing the agrarian republic, and it was doing so under the aegis of the embargo and the War of 1812.

By mid-1812, leading Jeffersonian editor Hezekiah Niles was no longer discussing the "chosen people," but supporting a war by promising that "during the war there will be ample employment for all." He emphasized that conflict could "seal the independence of the country" by establishing "a thousand [manufacturing] works, needful to the supply of our wants." This early form of military Keynesianism, as the term became known in the twentieth-century, was accompanied by demands from other Jeffersonians for such non-Jeffersonian policies as increased taxation and mandatory troop quotas that amounted to a conscription system. The war's drain on the U.S. Treasury was plugged in part with the issuance of huge amounts of Treasury certificates, a form of paper money that Jefferson had long attacked as inimical to the virtue and balanced prosperity of an agrarian republic.[52]

In January 1816 the Virginian wrote an often-quoted letter that admitted, "We must now place the manufacturer by the side of the agriculturalist." The context of that phrase is important, and less often noted; it provides Jefferson's rationale for his supposed change of mind:

> You tell me [he wrote Benjamin Austin] I am quoted by those who wish to continue our dependence on England for manufactures. There was a time when I might have been so quoted with more candor, but within the thirty years which have since elapsed, how are circumstances changed! We were then in peace. Our independent place among nations was acknowledged. . . . This was the state of things in 1785, when the "Notes on Virginia" were first printed; when, the ocean being open to all nations, and their common right in it acknowledged . . . by the assent and usage of all, it was thought that the doubt might claim some consideration. But who in 1785 could foresee the rapid depravity which was to render the close of that century the disgrace of the history of man? Who could have imagined that the two most distinguished in the rank of nations, for science and civilization, would have suddenly descended from that honorable eminence . . . and that under this disbandment of nations from social order, we should have been despoiled of a thousand ships, and have thousands of our citizens reduced to Algerine slavery.[53]

The statement imposes a historical interpretation on the 1780s that is misleading in view of the commercial discriminations that the United States, then under the Articles of Confederation, suffered repeatedly at European hands. It neatly ignores, moreover, Jefferson's own observations throughout the post-1785 era that the United States indeed needed to use the power of economic discrimination to survive in the jungle of the international marketplace. His frustration and anger resulted less from European attempts to reduce Americans "to Algerine slavery" than from the ever-accelerating demands of an American agrarian system whose security, as Jefferson himself defined it, required the use of centralized governmental powers to wage repeated clashes with European powers in order to acquire "an extension of territory which the rapid increase of our numbers will call for," as he instructed Lewis and Clark, and the ever-larger overseas markets that those "numbers" would, as producers, soon require.

Jefferson's attitude toward the Latin American revolutions after 1808, and especially after 1812, may have been a minor, but interesting, attempt to escape some of the problems he railed against in the January 1816 letter. He wanted little to do with the Latin American revolutionaries, even as he applauded their success in destroying European colonial controls and in establishing a new American system. Far from wanting to reform the region to the south by teaching its people how to be good republicans, he told Alexander von Humboldt in 1813 that "History . . . furnishes no example of a priest-ridden people maintaining a free civil government. This marks the lowest grade of ignorance, of which their civil as well as religious leaders will always avail themselves for their own purposes."[54] Jefferson, that is, wanted no democratic crusades, no attempt to teach Latin Americans to elect good men (as Woodrow Wilson once unfortunately phrased it during the Mexican Revolution). He did not want to reform Latin America but, rather, to people it with U.S. citizens. In 1801, he had written Monroe:

> However our present interests may restrain us within our own limits, it is impossible not to look forward to distant times, when our rapid multiplication will expand itself beyond those limits, and cover the whole northern, if not the southern continent, with a people speaking the same language, governed in similar forms, and by similar laws; nor can we contemplate with satisfaction either blot or mixture on that surface.[55]

If such thoughts passed through Jefferson's mind as he pondered the Latin American revolutions, there was an important precedent. In 1803–1804 he had taken exactly the same approach to the problem of Louisiana; the vast territory would be governable under republican institutions only after its overly variegated and too sparse population was replaced with, as Jefferson called it in 1801, "our rapid multiplication."

Jefferson's growing interest in Latin America after the 1800 election, and his understanding of the importance the region held for the expansion of both the North American people and their commerce, make more understandable his surprising advice to President Monroe in 1823 that the protection of U.S. interests in Latin America might well be worth an entangling alliance with Great Britain. After all, as Jefferson wrote, "The war in which the present proposition might engage us, should that be its consequence, is not her [Great Britain's] war, but ours."[56] That Jefferson did not see that the British would protect Latin America from the Holy Alliance even if Monroe did not join in a partnership with London is not surprising; neither did anyone else around President Monroe see this—except Secretary of State John Quincy Adams, who finally convinced the President that without any entangling alliance with Washington, the British would protect vital U.S. interests in Latin America (such as open markets), because these were also London's interests. (Apparently Jefferson, it might be noted in passing, did not accept the implications of Madison's argument in 1821 that the power of the Holy Alliance's largest member, Russia, might be overestimated because the "overgrown [Russian] empire, as in so many preceding instances, must fall into separate and independent states."[57])

IV

The apparent contradictions and paradoxes in Jefferson's foreign policy views and actions were less contradictory and paradoxical than the working out of his faith in, and his belief in the need for, an agrarian-based republic. By 1803 to 1807, the requirements of that republic were taking Jefferson into political realms which he finally accepted, if at times uneasily. By 1808 to 1816, he found himself confronting consequences he accepted, but neither liked nor—especially in the post-1808 appearance of early Jacksonian capitalism and politics—believed beneficial for his "chosen people" of the 1780s. That this early capitalism ran out of control, and headed even beyond the bounds of Jefferson's mind, is not surprising. The great historian of the Jeffersonian era, Henry Adams, defined the problem well in his autobiography, *The Education of Henry Adams,* when he outlined the major point of tension in the American system at the turn of the nineteenth to the twentieth century: "Washington was always amusing, but in 1900, as in 1800, its chief interest lay in its distance from New York. The movement of New York had become planetary—beyond control—while the task of Washington in 1900 as in 1800, was to control it. The success of Washington in the past century promised ill for its success in the next."[58] If the agrarian-based, commercial capitalism of Jefferson's era is substituted for

New York in Adams's account, it helps explain why Jefferson's post-1805 years were so full of anger and frustration.

Jefferson was less the victim of any supposed naïveté or pacifism in his conduct of foreign policy than he was a classic example of how the American domestic political economy is inseparable from its foreign policies, and how those policies in turn make demands on domestic political and economic institutions and ideology. The best example of Jefferson's need to move from his rather simplistic praise of his "chosen people" in the 1780s to a more sophisticated and complex view of how these people had to be protected was his diplomacy and use of presidential powers during the crises over Louisiana that lasted from its retrocession to France in 1800 to Burr's conspiracy in 1806–1807. In a new nation with a weak central state, Jefferson devised a powerful presidential authority to conduct diplomacy, move armies, and govern a freshly acquired empire. In an evolving democracy whose decentralization (as Tocqueville noted) made the conduct of foreign policy difficult, Jefferson, from at least the early 1790s, argued for a centralized power that could effectively use economic sanctions to protect the agrarians or, if necessary, wage war to defend them and their "handmaid" of commerce. In a fragmented country, where powerful factions and sectionalized political parties constantly threatened to arise, Jefferson used his control over foreign policy to strengthen and better balance the union by extending its sphere on both land and sea.

NOTES

I am greatly indebted to Peter Onuf, Drew McCoy, Melvyn Leffler, John Stagg, Norman Graebner, and participants in a seminar at the University of Virginia for comments on this paper.

1. Gordon Wood, "The Disappointments of Jefferson," *The New York Review of Books,* Aug. 13, 1981, p. 6.
2. James M. McPherson, *Abraham Lincoln and the Second American Revolution* (New York, 1990), p. 133.
3. Drew R. McCoy, *The Elusive Republic: Political Economy in Jeffersonian America* (Chapel Hill, N.C., 1980); Joyce Appleby, *Liberalism and Republicanism in the Historical Imagination* (Cambridge, Mass., 1992), especially pp. 277–339; Lance Banning, "Jeffersonian Ideology Revisited: Liberal and Classical Ideas in the New American Republic," *WMQ,* XLIII (1986), pp. 3–34.
4. Gordon Wood, *The Radicalism of the American Revolution* (New York, 1992), pp. 367–368.
5. *Notes on the State of Virginia,* William Peden, ed. (Chapel Hill, N.C., 1955), pp. 164–65.

6. TJ to Lithgow, Jan. 4, 1805, *Ford,* IV, 86–87.

7. *Notes,* Peden, ed., pp. 82–87; Drew McCoy, *The Last of the Fathers: James Madison and the Republican Legacy* (New York 1991), pp. 174–78.

8. *Notes,* Peden, ed., pp. 83–84.

9. Wood, *Radicalism of the American Revolution,* pp. 178–79.

10. *Notes,* Peden, ed., p. 83.

11. Madison to TJ, Oct. 24, 1787, *PJM,* X, p. 214.

12. TJ to D'Ivernois, Feb. 6, 1795, *Ford,* VIII, 165.

13. TJ to Nathaniel Niles, March 22, 1801, *Ford,* IX, p. 221.

14. Ralph Ketcham, *Presidents Above Party: The First American Presidency, 1789–1829* (Chapel Hill, N.C., 1984), p. 112.

15. Lawrence Kaplan, "Foreign Affairs," in Merrill Peterson ed., *Thomas Jefferson: A Reference Biography* (New York, 1986), pp. 311–12.

16. TJ to Charles Pinckney, Nov. 27, 1802, Gaillard Hunt, ed., *The Writings of James Madison,* 9 vols. (New York, 1900–1910), VI, p. 462.

17. TJ to Elbridge Gerry, June 21, 1797, *Ford,* IX, 405–6.

18. Kaplan, "Foreign Affairs," p. 317.

19. Inaugural Address, March 4, 1801, *Ford,* IX, pp. 197–98.

20. Albert K. Weinberg, "The Historical Meaning of the American Doctrine of Isolation," *American Political Science Review,* XXIC (1940), pp. 539–47.

21. Alexis de Tocqueville, *Democracy in America,* 2 vols. (New York, 1948), I, p. 233.

22. Ibid., I, pp. 234–35.

23. Madison's more detailed view of this problem is placed in the context of the early republics in *The Federalist,* nos. 18, 19, and 20; Jefferson is discussed in this framework in McCoy, *Elusive Republic,* pp. 313–14.

24. McCoy, *Elusive Republic,* pp. 189–95; Appleby, *Liberalism and Republicanism,* pp. 313–14 (where, it seems, Appleby's and McCoy's views are more in agreement than is made explicit in their texts.)

25. Tocqueville, *Democracy in America,* I, pp. 234–35.

26. *Boyd,* XII, pp. 270–79; pp. 439–40; *Boyd,* XIII, pp. 442–43.

27. Garrett Ward Sheldon, *The Political Philosophy of Thomas Jefferson* (Baltimore Md., 1991), pp. 13, 67–72, 83–88.

28. Robert W. Tucker and David C. Hendrickson, *Empire of Liberty: The Statecraft of Thomas Jefferson* (New York, 1990), p. ix.

29. Kaplan, "Foreign Affairs," pp. 320–21.

30. Especially important is the introduction to an analysis of the Jefferson presidency in Abraham D. Sofaer, *War, Foreign Affairs, and Constitutional Power* (Cambridge, Mass. 1976), pp. 25–38, 48–49.

31. Henry Adams, *History of the United States,* 9 vols. (New York, 1889–1891), IX, p. 226.

32. Tucker and Hendrickson, *Empire of Liberty.*

33. Reginald C. Stuart, "Thomas Jefferson and the Function of War: Policy or Principle?" *Canadian Journal of History,* XI (1976), pp. 160–64, 170–71.

34. *Ford,* IX, p. 196.

35. Alexander DeConde, *This Affair of Louisiana* (New York, 1976), pp. 121–31, has the references to the Anglo-American alliance possibility disturbing Napoleon; Stuart, "Jefferson and the Function of War," pp. 164–65. For another view, see Tucker and Hendrickson, *Empire of Liberty,* p. 124.

36. DeConde, *This Affair of Louisiana,* pp. 98–101.

37. Reginald Horsman, "The Dimensions of an 'Empire for Liberty'; Expansion and Republicanism, 1775–1825," *Journal of the Early Republic*, IX (1989), pp. 9–10.

38. Gerald Stourzh, *Alexander Hamilton and the Idea of Republican Government* (Stanford, Calif., 1970), p. 192.

39. Especially important is Sofaer, *War, Foreign Affairs, and Constitutional Power*, pp. 190–95, 225–27.

40. Adams, *History of the United States*, V, pp. 38–39; Stuart, "Jefferson and the Function of War," p. 165; Horsman, "Dimensions of an 'Empire for Liberty,' p. 11.

41. Charles Sellers, *The Market Revolution: Jacksonian America, 1815–1846* (New York, 1992), pp. 38–39.

42. TJ to Elbridge Gerry, Jan. 26, 1799, *Ford*, X, p. 99.

43. A recent study making this argument is Clifford L. Egan, *Neither Peace Nor War: Franco-American Relations, 1803–1812*, (Baton Rouge, La., 1983), pp. 73–76.

44. Report on Commerce, Dec. 11, 1793, *Ford*, VIII, p. 112; Merrill D. Peterson, "Thomas Jefferson and Commercial Policy, 1783–1793," *WMQ*, XXII (1965), pp. 584–610.

45. TJ to Thomas Pinckney, May 29, 1797, *Ford*, IX, pp. 389–90.

46. *Malone*, V, 476; Bradford Perkins, *Prologue to War: England and the United States, 1805–1812* (Berkeley and Los Angeles, Calif., 1961), pp. 316, 340.

47. Perkins, *Prologue to War*, pp. 164–65, 204; James Truslow Adams, *New England in the Republic, 1778–1949* (Gloucester, Mass., 1960), pp. 253–54; Sellers, *Market Revolution*, p. 25.

48. TJ to Madison, March 17, 1809, *L&B*, XII, p. 267; Stuart, "Jefferson and the Function of War," p. 166.

49. Tucker and Hendrickson, *Empire of Liberty;* the Jefferson remark to Madison is quoted in Stuart, "Jefferson and the Function of War," pp. 168–69.

50. Stuart, "Jefferson and the Function of War," p. 167.

51. Drew McCoy, "Political Economy," in Peterson, ed., *Reference Biography*, p. 115, contains a good, concise discussion.

52. Steven Watts, *The Republic Reborn; War and the Making of Liberal America, 1790–1820* (Baltimore, 1987), pp. xvi–xvii, 268–269, 277, 305–9; C. B. Luttrell, "Thomas Jefferson on Money and Banking," *History of Political Economy*, VII (1975), 172–73.

53. TJ to Benjamin Austin, Jan. 9, 1816, *Ford*, XI, pp. 502–3.

54. TJ to von Humboldt, Dec. 6, 1813, *Ford*, XI, p. 351.

55. TJ to Monroe, Nov. 24, 1801, *L&B*, X, pp. 296.

56. Manfred Jonas, "Isolationism," in Alexander DeConde, ed., *The Encyclopedia of American Foreign Relations*, 3 vols. (New York, 1978), I, p. 498.

57. James Madison, *Letters and Other Writings of James Madison* (Philadelphia, 1867), III, pp. 235–36, as cited in Norman E. Saul, *Distant Friends; The United States and Russia, 1763–1867* (Lawrence, Kans., 1991), p. 97n.

58. Henry Adams, *The Education of Henry Adams* (Boston, 1930), p. 436.

PART III

JEFFERSONIAN LEGACIES

CHAPTER 13

The Trials and Tribulations of Thomas Jefferson

GORDON S. WOOD

Jefferson scarcely seems to exist as a real historical person. Almost from the beginning he has been a symbol, a touchstone, of what we as a people are, someone invented, manipulated, turned into something we Americans like or dislike, fear or yearn for, within ourselves—whether it is populism or elitism, agrarianism or racism, atheism or liberalism. We are continually asking ourselves whether Jefferson still survives, or what is still living in the thought of Jefferson; and we quote him on every side of every major question in our history. No figure in our history has embodied so much of our heritage and so many of our hopes. Most Americans think of Jefferson much as our first professional biographer James Parton did. "If Jefferson was wrong," wrote Parton in 1874, "America is wrong. If America is right, Jefferson was right." [1]

As Merrill Peterson has shown us in his superb book published over thirty years ago, the image of Jefferson in American culture has always been "a sensitive reflector . . . of America's troubled search for the image of itself." [2] And the symbolizing, the image-mongering, the identifying of Jefferson with America, has not changed a bit in the generation since Peterson's book was published—even though the level of professional historical scholarship has never been higher. If anything, during these turbulent times the association of Jefferson with America has become more complete. During the past three decades or so many people, including some historians, have concluded that something was seriously wrong with America. And if something is wrong with America, then something has to be wrong with Jefferson.

I

Probably the opening blast in this modern criticism of Jefferson was Leonard Levy's *Jefferson and Civil Liberties: The Darker Side* (1963).[3] This was no subtle satire, no gentle mocking of the ironies of Jefferson's inconsistencies and hypocrisies; Levy's book was a prosecutor's indictment. Levy ripped off Jefferson's mantle of libertarianism to expose his "darker side": his passion for partisan persecution, his lack of concern for basic civil liberties, and a self-righteousness that became at times out-and-out ruthlessness. Far from being the skeptical enlightened intellectual, allowing all ideas their free play, Jefferson was portrayed by Levy and other historians as something of an ideologue, eager to fill the young with his political orthodoxy while censoring all those books he did not like. He did not have an open or questioning mind after all.

Not only did Jefferson not have an original or skeptical mind, he could in fact be downright doctrinaire, an early version of a "knee-jerk liberal." His reaction to European society and culture, says Bernard Bailyn, was "an eighteenth-century stereotype—a boldly liberal, high-minded, enlightened stereotype, but a stereotype nonetheless—a configuration of liberal attitudes and ideas which he accepted uncritically, embellishing them with his beautifully wrought prose but questioning little and adding little." In this respect he was very different from his more skeptical and inquisitive friend James Madison.[4] Jefferson could, for example, only understand the opening struggles of the French Revolution in terms of a traditional liberal antagonism to an arrogant and overgrown monarchy.[5] And he supported the addition of a bill of rights to the federal Constitution not because he had thought through the issue the way Madison had, but largely because a bill of rights was what good governments were supposed to have. All his liberal aristocratic French friends said so; indeed, as he told his fellow Americans, "The enlightened part of Europe have given us the greatest credit for inventing this instrument of security for the rights of the people, and have been not a little surprised to see us so soon give it up."[6] One almost has the feeling that Jefferson advocated a bill of rights out of embarrassment over what his liberal French associates would think. One sometimes has the same feeling about his antislavery statements, many of which seem to have been shaped to the expectations of enlightened foreigners.

It is in fact his views on black Americans and slavery that have made Jefferson most vulnerable to modern censure. If America has turned out to be wrong in its race relations, then Jefferson had to be wrong too. Samuel Johnson with his quip, "How is it that we hear the loudest yelps for liberty from the drivers of Negroes?" had nothing on modern critics. Who could not find the contrast between Jefferson's great declarations of liberty and equality and his lifelong ownership of slaves glaringly embarrassing? Jefferson hated slavery, it is true, but, unlike Washington, he was never able to free all his slaves. More than that, as recent historians have emphasized, he bought, bred, and flogged his slaves, and hunted down fugitives in much the same way his fellow Virginia planters did—all the while declaring that American slavery was not as bad as that of the ancient Romans.[7]

"Jefferson's attitudes and actions towards blacks are so repugnant these days," says historian William W. Freehling, that identifying the Sage of Monticello with antislavery actually discredits the reform movement. Jefferson could never really imagine freed blacks living in a white man's America, and throughout his life he insisted that the emancipation of the slaves had to be accompanied by their expulsion from the country. He wanted all blacks sent to the West Indies, or Africa, or anywhere out of the United States. In the end, it has been said, Jefferson loaded such conditions on the abolition of slavery that the antislavery movement could scarcely get off the ground. In response to the pleas of younger men that he speak out against slavery, he offered only excuses for delay.[8]

His remedy of expulsion was based on racial fear and antipathy. While he had no apprehensions about mingling white blood with that of the Indian, he never ceased expressing his "great aversion" to miscegenation between blacks and whites. When the Roman slave was freed, he "might mix with, without staining the blood of his master." When the black slave was freed, however, he had "to be removed beyond the reach of mixture." Although Jefferson believed that the Indians were uncivilized, he always admired them and made all sorts of environmental explanations for their differences from whites. Yet he was never able to do the same for the African-American. Instead, he continually suspected that the black man was inherently inferior to the white in both body and mind.[9]

It has even been suggested that Jefferson's obsession with black sensuality shared by so many other Americans was largely a projection of his own repressed—and perhaps in the case of his attractive mulatto slave Sally Hemings—not-so-repressed libidinal desires. The charge that Jefferson maintained Hemings as his mistress for decades and fathered several children by her was first made by an unscrupulous newspaperman, James Callender, in 1802. Since then, historians and others have periodically resurrected the accusation. In fact, in the most recent study of Jefferson's political thought, his "keeping of a black mistress" is treated as an established fact, a "common transgression of his class."[10]

In her 1974 psychobiography of Jefferson, the late Fawn Brodie made the most ingenious and notorious use of Callender's accusation, building up her case for the passionate liaison between Jefferson and his mulatto slave largely through contrived readings of evidence and even the absence of evidence. Brodie, for example, makes much of the fact that Jefferson in his journal of his travels in southern France in 1787 used the word "mullato" only twice in describing the soil. Then the fourteen- or fifteen-year old Sally joined the Jefferson household in Paris, and the result, says Brodie, was that the love-stricken Jefferson in his journal for a trip through northern Europe in 1788 mentions the word "mullato" eight times! Did Jefferson write to his supposed mistress during his trips? No letters have been found, but Brodie finds it significant that the letter-index volume for this year, 1788, has disappeared, the only volume missing in the whole forty-three-year record.[11] Having Jefferson's love affair be a secret one, of course, made it difficult for Brodie to find proof, but it did make it more exciting for our modern soap-opera sensibilities. That Jefferson dutifully recorded in his Farm Book the births of the offspring of this presumed love affair, along with all other slave births on his plantation, does, however, take the edge off the romance. Brodie's suggestion of a love match aroused a great deal of controversy, perhaps because a lot of people believed it or at least were titillated by it. A novel based on Brodie's concoctions has been written, and there was even talk of a TV production.

These may seem like small and silly matters, but they are not—not where Jefferson is involved; for the nature of American society itself is at stake. The relationship with Sally Hemings may be implausible to those who know Jefferson's character intimately. He was after all a man who never indulged his passions but continually suppressed them. But whether the Hemings relationship was true or not, there is no denying that Jefferson presided over a household in which miscegenation was taking place, a miscegenation that he believed was morally repugnant.[12] Thus any attempt to make Jefferson's Monticello a model patriarchal plantation is fatally compromised at the outset.

Everyone, it seems, sees America in Jefferson. So the shame and guilt that white Americans feel in their tortured relations with blacks can be best expressed in the shame and guilt that Jefferson must have suffered from his involvement in slavery and racial mixing. Where Jefferson for Vernon Louis Parrington and his generation had been the solution, for this recent generation he became the problem. The Jefferson that emerges out of much recent scholarship therefore resembles the America many critics have visualized in the past three decades—self-righteous, guilt-ridden, racist, doctrinaire, and filled with liberal pieties that under stress are easily sacrificed.

Wherever we Americans have a struggle over what kind of people we are, there we will find Jefferson. Jefferson stood for the rights of individuals, and the rights of individuals have been carried to extremes in recent years. So Jefferson and his Declaration of Independence are at fault.[13] Actually Jefferson's Federalist critics in the eighteenth century were even more harsh on Jefferson's obsession with rights. He talked endlessly of rights, said one typical Federalist satirist, and loved them so much that he even promoted the rights of weeds to flourish. And why not? Doesn't each plant have "an equal right to live?" "And why should wheat and barley thrive / Despotic tyrants of the field?"[14] (It's not so funny today, where many people are very serious about the rights of plants.)

But then others have raised the possibility that America was not always a liberal capitalistic society devoted to individual rights. If so, then our image of Jefferson as the representative American would have to change. Thus in the historiographical upheaval that has taken place over the past two decades, involving the recovery in Revolutionary America of a classical republican culture that emphasized virtue, corruption, and the public good rather than private rights and profit-making, Jefferson necessarily became a central bone of contention. In light of this classical republican tradition, Jefferson lost his reputation for being a simple follower of Locke concerned only with individual rights. Instead he became a stoical classicist frightened by cities, money-making, and corruption and obsessed with inculcating the proper social and moral conditions to sustain an agrarian republic of independent yeomen farmers who were free of the marketplace.

Some historians, namely J. G. A. Pocock, in their excitement over this discovery of a tradition of classical republicanism in early America, got carried away and declared that the American Revolution, far from being a progressive event moving America into a new liberal, capitalistic world, was in fact "the last great act of the Renaissance." Since America had been born in a "dread of modernity," its spokesman Jefferson had to be backward-looking and opposed to the great economic changes sweeping through the Atlantic world.[15]

This was too much for other historians who were eager to recover what was still living and progressive in the thought of Thomas Jefferson. When Garry Wills in his *Inventing America* (1978) argued that Jefferson's Declaration of Independence owed less to the possessive individualism of John

Locke and more to the communitarian sentiments of the Scottish moralist Francis Hutcheson, scholars were quick to reassert the influence of Locke.[16] After all, it was the character of America that was at stake. One critic even accused Wills, in emphasizing Jefferson's communitarianism, of aiming "to supply the history of the Republic with as pink a dawn as possible."[17] Several historians, especially Joyce Appleby, set about restoring some needed balance to our understanding of the Revolution and, of course, Thomas Jefferson. Others of the founding fathers may have been elitist, backward-looking, and pessimistic about the loss of virtue, but, said Appleby, certainly not Jefferson. Jefferson may have been a student of the classics, but he never accepted the antique notion that men achieved fulfillment only in the public arena. And he may have been an agrarian, but he was a modern one who accepted commerce. "More than any other figure in his generation," said Appleby, "Jefferson integrated a program of economic development and a policy for nation-building into a radical moral theory." He was "not the heroic loser in a battle against modernity," but the liberal progressive winner, confident of the future and eager to promote the individual's right to pursue happiness and further the commercial prosperity of America free from the deadening hand of government. The American people, argued Appleby, were less concerned with virtue, corruption, and community than with equality, private rights, and the selling of their produce all over the Atlantic world; in the 1790s they saw in Jefferson and his Democratic-Republican party the proper agency for their optimistic hopes and dreams. "Jefferson," wrote Appleby, "rallied his countrymen with a vision of the future that joined their materialism to a new morality" built on his sublime faith in the self-governing capacities of free individuals.[18]

So Jefferson was back leading Americans into their democratic commercial future—a symbol once again of liberal America. But if this means that Jefferson becomes too much a supporter of capitalism, then we have the work of Richard K. Matthews as an antidote. Matthews has discovered "a different, alternative Jefferson" for a different, alternative America: "a Jefferson who not only presents a radical critique of American market society but also provides an image for—if not a road map to—a consciously made, legitimately democratic American future." Matthews's Jefferson believed in permanent revolution, a kind of communitarian anarchism, and widespread political participation by the people. He was, concludes Matthews, an authentic American democratic radical.[19]

And so it has gone for much of our history—Jefferson standing for America and carrying the moral character of the country on his back. No historical figure can bear this kind of symbolic burden and still remain a real person. Beneath all the images, beneath all the allegorical Jeffersons, there once was a human being with every human frailty and foible. Certainly Jefferson's words and ideas transcended his time, but he himself did not.

The human Jefferson was essentially a man of the eighteenth century, a very intelligent and bookish slaveholding southern planter, enlightened and progressive no doubt, but possessing as many weaknesses as strengths, as much folly as wisdom, as much blindness as foresight. Like most people caught up in fast-moving events and complicated changing circumstances, the human Jefferson was as much a victim as he was a protagonist. Despite all his achievements in the Revolution and in the subsequent decades, he was never in control of the popular forces he was ostensibly leading; indeed, he never even fully comprehended these forces. It is the ultimate irony of Jefferson's life, a life filled with ironies, that he should not have understood the democratic revolution that he himself supremely spoke for.

II

It is true that much of Jefferson's thinking was conventional, though, as has often been pointed out, he did have "an extraordinary gift of lending grace to conventionalities."[20] He had to be conventional or he could never have had the impact he had on his contemporaries. His writing of the Declaration of Independence, he later correctly recalled, was "not to find out new principles, or new arguments, never before thought of . . . but to place before mankind the common sense of the subject, in terms so plain and firm as to command their assent, and to justify ourselves in the independent stand we are compelled to take."[21]

Jefferson's extraordinary impressionability, learning, and virtuosity were the source of his conventionality. He was very well read, extremely sensitive to the avant-garde intellectual currents of his day, and eager to discover just what was the best, most politically correct, and most enlightened in the world of the eighteenth century. It was his insatiable hunger for knowledge and the remarkable receptivity of his antennae for all that was new and progressive that put him at the head of the American Enlightenment.

The eighteenth-century Enlightenment represented the pushing back the boundaries of darkness and what was called Gothic barbarism and the spreading of light and knowledge. This struggle occurred on many fronts. Some saw the central battle taking place in natural science and in the increasing understanding of nature. Some saw it occurring mostly in religion with the tempering of enthusiasm and the elimination of superstition. Others saw it taking place mainly in politics—in driving back the forces of tyranny and in the creating of new free governments. Still others saw it in the spread of civility and refinement and in the increase in the small, seemingly insignificant ways that life was being made easier, politer, more comfortable, and more enjoyable for more and more people. In one way or another all of these Enlightenment activities involved the imposition of order and reason on the world. To contemplate aesthetically an ordered universe and to know the best that was thought and said in the world— that was enlightenment.

Jefferson participated fully in all these aspects of the eighteenth-century Enlightenment. He was probably the American Revolutionary leader most taken with the age's liberal prescriptions for enlightenment, gentility, and refinement. He was the son of a wealthy but uneducated and ungenteel planter from western Virginia and the first of his father's family to go to college. Like many of the Revolutionary leaders who were also the first of their family to acquire a liberal arts education in college, he wanted a society led by an aristocracy of talent and taste. For too long men had been judged by who their fathers were or whom they had married. In a new enlightened republican society they would be judged by merit and virtue and taste alone.

Jefferson was not one to let his feelings show, but even today we can sense beneath the placid surface of his autobiography, written in 1821 at the age of seventy-seven, some of his anger at all those Virginians who prided themselves on their genealogy and judged men by their family background. In the opening pages of his autobiography Jefferson tells us that the lineage of his Welsh father was lost in obscurity; he was able to find in Wales only two references to his father's family. His mother, on the other hand, was a Randolph, one of the distinguished families of Virginia. The Randolphs, he said with about as much derision as he ever allowed himself, "trace their pedigree far back in England & Scotland, to which let every one ascribe the faith & merit he chooses." [22] He went on in his autobiography to describe his efforts in 1776 in Virginia to bring down that "distinct set of families" who had used the legal devices of primogeniture and entail to form themselves "into a Patrician order, distinguished by the splendor and luxury of their establishments." We have often thought Jefferson exaggerated the power of primogeniture and entail and this "Patrician order." Not only was the docking of entails very common in Virginia, but the "Patrician order" does not appear all that different from its challengers. But

Jefferson clearly saw a difference, and it rankled him. The privileges of this "aristocracy of wealth," wrote Jefferson, needed to be destroyed in order "to make an opening for the aristocracy of virtue and talent," of which he considered himself a prime example. Such natural aristocrats, he said were "the most precious gift of nature, for the instruction, the trusts, and government of society." [23]

To become a natural aristocrat one had to acquire the attributes of a natural aristocrat—enlightenment, gentility, and taste. We will never understand the young Jefferson until we appreciate the intensity and earnestness of his desire to become the most cosmopolitan, the most liberal, the most genteel, and the most enlightened gentleman in all of America. From the outset he was the sensitive provincial quick to condemn the backwardness of his fellow colonials. In 1766 as a twenty-four-year-old making a grand tour up the Atlantic seaboard, he was contemptuous of the crude and barbaric behavior of the Maryland assembly he witnessed in what he sarcastically referred to as "this Metropolis" of Annapolis. The old courthouse the colonial assembly met in, "judging from it's form and appearance, was built in the year one," and its members made "as great a noise and hubbub as you will usually observe at a publick meeting of the planters in Virginia." "The mob (for such was their appearance) . . . were divided into little clubs amusing themselves in the common chit chat way." They addressed the speaker without rising, shouted out their votes chaotically, and, in short, seemed unaware of the proper or usual forms of conducting a legislature. [24]

Doing things properly and in the right manner was always important to Jefferson. At college and later in studying law at Williamsburg he played the violin, learned French, and acquired the tastes and refinements of the larger world. At frequent dinners with Governor Francis Fauquier and his teachers, William Small and George Wythe, Jefferson said he "heard more good sense, more rational and philosophical conversations than in all my life besides." Looking back, he called Williamsburg "the finest school of manners and morals that ever existed in America." Although as a young man he had seen very few works of art, he knew from reading and conversation what was considered good; and in 1771 he wrote a list, ranging from the *Apollo Belvedere* to a Raphael cartoon, of those celebrated paintings, drawings, and sculptures that he hoped to acquire in copies. [25]

By 1782, "without having left his own country," this earnest autodidact with a voracious appetite for learning had become, as the Marquis de Chastellux noted, "an American who . . . is at once a musician, a draftsman, an astronomer, a geometer, a physicist, a jurist and a statesman." Jefferson was the very model of an eighteenth-century republican gentleman—learned and genteel and possessing perfect self-control and serenity of spirit.[26]

In time Jefferson became quite proud of his gentility, his taste, and his liberal brand of manners. In fact, he came to see himself as a kind of impresario for America, rescuing his countrymen from their "deplorable barbarism" by introducing them to the finest and most enlightened aspects of European culture.[27] When Americans in the 1780s realized that a statue of Washington was needed, "there could be no question raised," he wrote from Paris, "as to the Sculptor who should be employed, the reputation of Monsr. Houdon of this city being unrivalled in Europe." No American could stand up to his knowledge. When Washington timidly expressed misgivings about Houdon's doing the statue in Roman style, he quickly backed down in the face of Jefferson's frown, unwilling, as he said, "to oppose my judgment to the taste of Connoisseurs."[28]

Jefferson's excitement over the sixteenth-century Italian, Andrea Palladio, whose *Four Books of Architecture* was virtually unknown in America, was the excitement of the provincial discovering the cosmopolitan and discriminating taste of the larger world. He became contemptuous and even ashamed of the "gothic" Georgian architecture of his native Virginia, and he sought in Monticello to build a house that would do justice to those models that harked back to Roman antiquity. In the 1780s he badgered his Virginia colleagues into erecting as the new state capitol in Richmond a magnificent copy of the Maison Carrée, a Roman temple from the first century A.D. at Nîmes, because he wanted an American public building that would be a model for the people's "study and imitation" and "an object and proof of national good taste." It was a building, he said, that "has pleased universally for near 2000 years." Almost single-handedly he became responsible for making America's public buildings resemble Roman temples.[29]

No American knew more about wine than Jefferson. During his trips around Europe in 1787–88 he spent a great deal of time investigating French, Italian, and German vineyards and wineries and making arrangements for the delivery of wine to the United States. Everyone in America acknowledged his expertise in wine, and three presidents sought his advice about what wine to serve at presidential dinners. In everything—from gardening and food to music, painting, and poetry—Jefferson wanted the latest and most enlightened in English or European fashion.

It is easy to make fun of Jefferson and his parvenu attitudes and behavior.

But it would be a mistake to dismiss Jefferson's obsession with art and good taste merely as a trivial affectation or as the simple posturing and putting on of airs of an American provincial who would be the perfect gentlemen. Jefferson may have been more earnest and enthusiastic about such matters than the other Revolutionary leaders, but he was by no means unique in his concern for refining his own sensibilities and those of the American people. This was a moral and political imperative of all of the founding fathers. To refine popular taste was in fact a moral and political imperative of all the enlightened of the eighteenth century.

The fine arts, good taste, and even good manners had political implications. As Shaftesbury had preached, morality and good taste were allied: "The science of virtuosi and that of virtue itself become, in a manner, one and the same."[30] Connoisseurship, politeness, and genteel refinement were connected with public morality and political leadership. Those who had good taste were enlightened, and those who were enlightened were virtuous.

But virtuous in a modern, not an ancient, manner. Such a new modern virtue was associated with affability and sociability, with love and benevolence. This affability and sociability were connected with good taste and with politeness, which James Wilson and his friend William White defined in 1768 as "the natural and graceful expression of the social virtues." Politeness and refinement tamed and domesticated the older, severe, civic humanist conception of virtue. Promoting social affection was in fact the object of the civilizing process. "What does the idea of politeness and refinement of a people suppose?" asked a writer in the *New York Magazine* of 1792. "Is it not this, that they cultivate intimate friendships; that they mutually sympathize with the misfortunes of each other, and that a passionate show of affections is promoted."[31] This new social virtue was less Spartan and more Addisonian, less the harsh self-sacrifice of antiquity and more the willingness to get along with others for the sake of peace and prosperity. Virtue became identified with politeness, good taste, and one's instinctive sense of morality.[32] As Lord Kames said, "A taste in the fine arts goes hand in hand with the moral sense, to which indeed it is nearly allied."[33]

To understand this new social virtue, this new mingling of politeness and morality, Jefferson did not have to read the works of Lord Kames, Francis Hutcheson, or any other of the Scottish moral sense school; the Englishmen Lord Shaftesbury and Bishop Butler were no less important in spreading the idea that politeness and refinement were natural social adhesives. But not just these great minds; there was hardly an educated person in all of eighteenth-century America who did not at one time or another try to describe people's moral sense and the natural forces of love and benevolence holding society together. Jefferson's emphasis on the moral sense was scarcely peculiar to him.

This modern virtue that Jefferson and others extolled was very different from that of the ancient republican tradition. Classical virtue had flowed from the citizen's participation in politics; government had been the source of his civic consciousness and public-spiritedness. But modern virtue flowed from the citizen's participation in society, not in government, which the liberal-minded increasingly saw as the source of the evils of the world. "Society," said Thomas Paine in a brilliant summary of this common enlightened separation, "is produced by our wants and government by our wickedness; the former promotes our happiness *positively* by uniting our affections, the latter *negatively* by restraining our vices. The one encourages intercourse, the other creates distinctions." It was society—the affairs of private social life—that bred sympathy and the new domesticated virtue. Mingling in drawing rooms, clubs and coffeehouses—partaking of the innumerable interchanges of the daily comings and goings of modern life—created affection and fellow-feeling, which were all the adhesives really necessary to hold an enlightened people together. Some even argued that commerce, that traditional enemy of classical virtue, was in fact a source of modern virtue. Because it encouraged intercourse and confidence among people and nations, commerce actually contributed to benevolence and fellow-feeling.

Jefferson could not have agreed more with this celebration of society over government. Indeed, Paine's conventional liberal division between society and government was the premise of Jefferson's political thinking—his faith in the natural ordering of society, his belief in the common moral sense of ordinary people, his idea of minimal government. "Man," said Jefferson, "was destined for society. His morality, therefore, was to be formed to this object. He was endowed with a sense of right and wrong, merely relative to this. . . . The moral sense, or conscience, is as much a part of a man as his leg or arm. . . . This sense is submitted, indeed, in some degree, to the guidance of reason; but it is a small stock which is required for this." All human beings had "implanted in our breasts" this "love of others," this "moral instinct"; these "social dispositions" were what made democracy possible.[34]

The importance of this domesticated modern virtue to Jefferson's and other Americans' thinking can scarcely be exaggerated. Unlike classical virtue, it was not nostalgic or backward-looking, but progressive and indeed radical. It laid the basis for all reform movements of the nineteenth century, and in fact for all subsequent modern liberal thinking. We still yearn for a world in which everyone will love one another.[35]

Probably no American leader took this belief in the natural sociability of people more seriously than Jefferson. His scissors-and-paste redoing of the New Testament in the early years of the nineteenth century stemmed from his desire to reconcile Christianity with the Enlightenment and at the same time answer all those critics who said that he was an enemy of all religion. Jefferson discovered that Jesus, with his prescription for each of us to love our neighbors as ourselves, actually spoke directly to the modern enlightened age. Jefferson's cut-up version of the New Testament offered a much-needed morality of social harmony for a new republican society.

Jefferson's faith in the natural sociability of people also lay behind his belief in minimal government. In fact, Jefferson would have fully understood the Western world's present interest in devolution and localist democracy. He believed in nationhood, but not the modern idea of the state. He hated all bureaucracy and all the coercive instruments of government; in fact, he sometimes gave the impression that government was only a device by which the few attempted to rob, cheat, and oppress the many. He certainly never accepted the modern idea of the state as an entity possessing a life of its own distinct from both rulers and ruled. For Jefferson there could be no power independent of the people, in whom he had an absolute faith.

Although he was not a modern democrat, assuming as he did that a natural aristocracy would lead the country, he had a confidence in the capacity and the virtue of the people to elect that aristocracy that was unmatched by any of the other founding fathers. Like the other founding fathers, Jefferson had doubts about all officials in government, even the popularly elected representatives in the lower houses of the legislatures ("173 despots would surely be as oppressive as one"); but he always thought that the people if undisturbed by demagogues or Federalist monarchists would eventually set matters right. He saw little potential conflict between what we today call positive and negative liberty, between the people and individual rights. He was one of those who paid no attention to what his friend James Madison called that "essential distinction, too little heeded, between assumptions of power by the General Government, in opposition to the will of the constituent body, and assumptions by the constituent body through the Government as the organ of its will."[36] It was never the people but only their elected agents that were at fault. The many were always being set upon and abused by the few, and that few included all the officials of government, even those elected by the people.

Not only did Jefferson thus refuse to recognize the structure and institutions of a modern state, he scarcely accepted the basic premise of a state, that is, its presumed monopoly of legitimate control over a prescribed territory. For him during his first presidential administration the United States was really just a loosely bound confederation, not all that different from the government of the former Articles of Confederation. Hence his vision of an expanding empire of liberty over a huge continent posed no problems for his relaxed idea of a state. "Who can limit the extent to which the federative principle may operate effectively?" he asked in his second inaugural address. In fact, Jefferson always conceived of his "empire of liberty" as one of like principles, not like boundaries. As long as Americans believed certain things, they remained Americans, regardless of the boundaries of the government they happened to be in. At times he was remarkably indifferent to the possibility that a western confederacy might break away from the eastern United States. What did it matter? he asked in 1804. "Those of the western confederacy will be as much our children & descendents as those of the eastern."[37]

It was Jefferson's contempt for the modern state and his extraordinary faith in the natural sociability of people as a substitute for the traditional force of government that made the Federalists, and especially Alexander Hamilton, dismiss him as a hopeless pie-in-the-sky dreamer. The idea that, "as human nature shall refine and ameliorate by the operation of a more enlightened plan" based on a common moral sense and the spread of affection and benevolence, government eventually "will become useless, and Society will subsist and flourish free from its shackles" was, said Hamilton, a "wild and fatal . . . scheme," even if its "votaries" like Jefferson did not always push such a scheme to the fullest.[38]

Jefferson and other Revolutionary leaders believed that commerce among nations in international affairs was the equivalent to affection among people in domestic affairs; both were natural expressions of relationships that needed to be freed of monarchical obstructions and interventions. Hence in 1776 and in the years following Jefferson and other Revolutionary idealists hoped to do for the world what they were doing for the society of the United States—change the way people related to one another. They looked forward to a rational world in which corrupt monarchical diplomacy and secret alliances, balances of power, and dynastic rivalries would be replaced by the natural ties of commerce. If the people of the various nations were left alone to exchange goods freely among themselves, then international politics would become republicanized and pacified, and indeed war itself would be eliminated. Jefferson's and the Republican party's "candid and liberal" experiments in "peaceable coercion"—the various efforts of the United States to use nonimportation and, ultimately, the Embargo of 1807–1809 to change international behavior—were the inevitable consequences of this sort of idealistic republican confidence in the power of commerce.[39]

Conventional as Jefferson's thinking may often have been, it was usually an enlightened conventional radicalism that he espoused. So eager in fact was he to possess the latest and most liberal of eighteenth-century ideas that he could easily get carried away. He, like "others of great genius," had "a habit," as Madison gently put it in 1823, "of expressing in strong and round terms impressions of the moment." So he alone of the founding fathers was unperturbed by Shays's Rebellion: "I like a little rebellion now and then," he said. "It is like a storm in the Atmosphere." It was too bad that some people were killed, but "the tree of liberty must be refreshed from time to time with the blood of patriots and tyrants. It is its natural manure." Similar rhetorical exaggeration accompanied his response to the bloody excesses of the French Revolution. Because "the liberty of the whole earth" depended on the success of the French Revolution, he wrote in 1793, lives would have to be lost. "Rather than it should have failed, I would have seen half the earth desolated. Were there but an Adam & an Eve left in every country, & left free, it would be better than as it now is."[40] Unlike Coleridge and Wordsworth and other disillusioned European liberals, Jefferson remained a champion of the French Revolution to the end.

He saw it after all as a movement on behalf of the rights of man that had originated in the American Revolution. And to the American Revolution and the rights of man he remained dedicated until his death. In the last letter he wrote, he expressed his lifelong belief that the American Revolution would be "the signal of arousing men to burst the chains under which monkish ignorance and superstition had persuaded them to bind themselves, and to assume the blessings and security of self-government."[41]

III

Yet these expressions of confidence in the future progress of the Enlightenment were fewer and farther between during Jefferson's final years in retirement. The period between Jefferson's retirement from the presidency in 1809 and his death in 1826 was a tumultuous one in American history, and not a happy time for Jefferson. To be sure, there was the Sage of Monticello relaxing among his family and friends and holding court on top of his mountain for scores of visiting admirers. There was his reconciliation with John Adams and the wonderful correspondence between the two old revolutionaries that followed. And there was his hard-fought establishment of the University of Virginia. But there was not much else to comfort him.

The world around him, the world he helped to create, was rapidly changing, and changing in ways that Jefferson found bewildering and sometimes even terrifying. The American Revolution was unfolding in radical and unexpected ways. American society was becoming more democratic and more capitalistic, and Jefferson was not prepared for either development. By the end of his life Jefferson had moments of apprehension that the American Revolution, to which he had devoted his life, was actually in danger of failing. In response he spoke and acted in ways that are not in accord with what we now like to think of as Jeffersonian principles. He turned inward and began conjuring thoughts, stirring up demons, and spouting dogmas in a manner that many subsequent historians and biographers have found embarrassing and puzzling.

After Jefferson retired from public life in 1809, he became more narrow-minded and localist than he had ever been in his life. He had always prided himself on his cosmopolitanism, and after Benjamin Franklin's death in 1790 he certainly had more European acquaintances and knew more about the world than any of his countrymen. Yet upon his retirement from the presidency, he returned to Virginia and never left it. In fact, he virtually never again lost sight of his beloved Blue Ridge. He cut himself off from many of the current sources of knowledge of the outside world and became, as one of his visitors George Ticknor noted, "singularly ignorant & insensible on the subjects of passing politics." He took only one newspaper, the *Richmond Enquirer,* and seemed to have no strong interest in receiving his mail. In all this he differed remarkably from his friend and neighbor, James Madison. Madison, said Ticknor, "receives multitudes of newspapers, keeps a servant always in waiting for the arrival of the Post—and takes anxious note of all passing events." [42]

Jefferson's turning inward was matched by a relative decline in the place of Virginia in the union. Decay was everywhere in early nineteenth-century Virginia, and Jefferson felt it at Monticello. Despite his lifelong aversion to public debts, his private debts kept mounting, and he kept borrowing, taking out new loans to meet old ones. He tried to sell his land, and when he could not he sold slaves instead. He feared that he might lose Monticello and complained continually of his debts, but he refused to cut back on his lavish hospitality and expensive wine purchases.

Unable to comprehend the economic forces that were transforming the country and destroying the Upper South, Jefferson blamed the banks and the speculative spirit of the day for both his and Virginia's miseries. It is true that he accepted the existence of commerce and, after the War of 1812, even some limited manufacturing for the United States. But the commerce he accepted was tame and traditional stuff compared to the aggressive commerce that was taking over northern America in the early nineteenth century. Jefferson's idea of commerce essentially involved the sale abroad of agricultural staples—wheat, tobacco, and cotton. His commerce was not the incessant trucking and trading, the endless buying and selling with each other, that was coming to characterize the emerging northern Yankee world. That kind of dynamic domestic commerce and all the capitalistic accouterments that went with it—banks, stock markets, liquid capital, paper money—Jefferson feared and despised.

He did indeed want comforts and prosperity for his American farmers, but like some modern liberals he had little or no appreciation of the economic forces that made such prosperity and comforts possible. He had no comprehension of banks and thought that the paper money issued by banks was designed "to enrich swindlers at the expense of the honest and industrious part of the nation." He could not understand how "legerdemain tricks upon paper can produce as solid wealth as hard labor in the earth. It is vain for common sense to urge that *nothing* can produce *nothing*."[43] As far as he was concerned, the buying and selling of stocks and the raising of capital were simply licentious speculation and wild gambling—all symptoms of "commercial avarice and corruption."[44]

The ultimate culprit in the degeneration of America, he thought, was the corrupt and tyrannical course of the national government. The Missouri Crisis of 1819–1820, provoked by northern efforts to limit the spread of slavery in the West, was to Jefferson "a fire bell in the night," a threat to the Union and to the Revolutionary experiment in republicanism. He believed that the federal government's proposed restriction on the right of the people of Missouri to own slaves violated the Constitution and threatened self-government. Congress, he said, had no right "to regulate the conditions of the different descriptions of men composing a state." Only each state had the "exclusive right" to regulate slavery.[45] If the federal government arrogated to itself that right, then it would next declare all slaves in the country free; "In which case all the whites within the United States south of the Potomac and Ohio must evacuate their States, and most fortunate those who can do it first."[46]

Jefferson despaired of stopping the spread of federal consolidation and commercial values and bemoaned "the degeneracy of public opinion from our original and free principles." He became a bitter critic of the usurpations of the Supreme Court and a more strident defender of states' rights than he had been even in 1798, when he penned the Kentucky Resolution justifying the right of a state to nullify federal laws. While his friend Madison remained a nationalist and upheld the right of the Supreme Court to interpret the Constitution, Jefferson lent his wholehearted support to the most dogmatic, impassioned, and sectional-minded elements in Virginia, including the arch states' rightists Spencer Roane and John Randolph. He became parochial and alarmist, and his zeal for states' rights, as even his sympathetic biographer Dumas Malone admits, "bordered on fanaticism."[47]

He was more frightened and fanatical than he had to be, and he went further backward to the principles of 1798 than he had to go, further certainly than his friend and fellow Virginian James Madison ever went. For someone as optimistic and sanguine in temperament as Jefferson usually was, he had a lot of gloomy and terrifying moments in these years between 1809 and 1826. What happened? What accounts for these moments of gloom and these expressions of fanaticism? How can we explain Jefferson's uncharacteristic but increasingly frequent doubts about the future?

Certainly his personal troubles, his rising debts, the threat of bankruptcy, and the fear of losing Monticello were part of it, but they are not the whole explanation. Something more is involved in accounting for the awkwardness of his years of retirement than these outside forces, and that something seems to lie within Jefferson himself—in his principles and outlook, in his deep and long-held faith in popular democracy and the future.

IV

No one of the Revolutionary leaders believed more strongly in progress and in the capacity of the American people for self-government than did Jefferson. And no one was more convinced that the Enlightenment was on the march against the forces of medieval barbarism and darkness and religious superstition and enthusiasm. In fact, so sure was he of the future progress of American society that he was intellectually and emotionally unprepared for what happened in the years following his retirement from public office. He was unprepared for the democratic revolution that he himself had inspired. In the end Jefferson was victimized by his overweening confidence in the people and by his naive hopefulness in the future. The Enlightenment, the democratic revolution he had contributed so much to bring about, and his own liberal and rosy temperament finally did him in.

None of the other major founding fathers was as optimistic and confident in the people as Jefferson was. All the problems of the present would eventually be taken care of by the people. This sublime faith in the people and the future is the source of that symbolic power he has had for succeeding generations of Americans. He was never more American than when he told John Adams in 1816 that he liked "the dreams of the future better than the history of the past."[48]

He was always optimistic; indeed, he was a virtual Pollyanna about everything. His expectations always outran reality, whether it was French aristocrats who turned out to be less liberal than his friend Lafayette, or garden vegetables that never came up, or misbehaving students at the University of Virginia who violated their honor code, or an American Revolution that actually allowed people to pursue their pecuniary happiness. He was the pure American innocent. He had little understanding of man's capacity for evil and had no tragic sense whatsoever.

Through his long public career, while others were wringing their hands, Jefferson remained calm and hopeful. He knew slavery was a great evil, but he believed his generation could do little about it. Instead he counseled patience and a reliance on the young who would follow. When one of those younger men, Edward Coles, actually called on Jefferson in 1814 to lend his voice in the struggle against slavery he could only offer his confidence in the future. "The hour of emancipation is advancing, in the march of time. It will come. . . ."[49]

It was the same with every difficulty. In one way or other he expected things to work out. In 1814 he saw his financial troubles coming at him and his household like "an approaching wave in a storm; still I think we shall live as long, eat as much, and drink as much, as if the wave had already glided under the ship. Somehow or other these things find their way out as they come in, and so I suppose they will now."[50] Was not progress on the march and were not science and enlightenment everywhere pushing back the forces of ignorance, superstition, and darkness? The future, he felt, was on his side and on the side of the people. A liberal democratic society would be capable of solving every problem, if not in his lifetime, then surely in the coming years.

But Jefferson lived too long, and the future and the coming generation were not what he had expected. His correspondence in the last decades of his life was punctuated with laments over "the rising generation, of which

I once had sanguine hopes."[51] Although he continued in his public letters, especially to foreigners, to affirm that progress and civilization were still on the march, in private he became more and more apprehensive of the future. He sensed that American society, including Virginia, might not be getting better after all, but actually going backward. The people were not becoming more refined, more polite, and more sociable; if anything, they were more barbaric and more factional than they had been. Jefferson was frightened by the divisions in the country and by the popularity of Andrew Jackson, regarding him as man of violent passions and unfit for the presidency. He felt overwhelmed by the new paper-money business culture that was sweeping through the country and never appreciated how much his democratic and egalitarian principles had contributed to its rise.

Ordinary people, in whom he placed so much confidence, certainly more than his friend Madison, were not becoming more enlightened. In fact, superstition and bigotry, which Jefferson identified with organized religion, were actually reviving, released by the democratic revolution he had led. He was temperamentally incapable of understanding the deep popular strength of the evangelical forces that were seizing control of American culture in these early decades of the nineteenth century, and became what we might call a confused secular humanist in the midst of real moral majorities. While in 1822 Jefferson was still predicting that there was not a young man now alive who would not die a Unitarian, Methodists and Baptists and other evangelicals were gaining adherents by the tens of thousands in the Second Great Awakening and transforming American society. In response all Jefferson could do was blame the defunct New England Federalists and an equally bewildered New England clergy for spreading both evangelical Christianity and capitalism throughout the country.

Jefferson's solution to this perceived threat from New England and its "pious young monks from Harvard and Yale" was to hunker down in Virginia and build a university that would perpetuate true republican principles.[52] "It is in our seminary," he told Madison, "that that vestal flame is to be kept alive."[53] Yet even building the university brought sorrow and shock. The Virginia legislature was not as eager to spend money for higher education as he had expected. The members were "a good piece of a century behind the age they live in"; they had "so many biasses, personal, local, fanatical, financial, etc. that we cannot foresee in what their combinations will result."[54] His support of the university actually became more of a political liability in the legislature than an asset. "There are fanatics both in religion and politics," he told Joseph Cabell in 1818, "who, without knowing me personally, have long been taught to consider me as a raw head and bloody bones." Even some in his own county were opposed to his promotion of higher education in Virginia.[55]

The people actually seemed more sectarian and less rational than they had been at the time of the Revolution. They did not seem to know who he was, what he had done. Was this the new generation on which he rested all his hopes? During the last year of his life, at a moment, says his biographer Malone, of "uneasiness that he had never known before," Jefferson was pathetically reduced to listing his contributions during sixty-one years of public service in order to justify a legislative favor.[56] No wonder he sometimes felt cast off. "All, all dead!" he wrote to an old friend in 1825, "and ourselves left alone midst a new generation whom we know not, and who know not us."[57]

These were only small cracks in his optimism, only tinges of doubt in his democratic faith, but for an innocent like him these were enough. Jefferson went further in states' rights principles and in his fears of federal consolidation than his friend Madison did because he had higher expectations of the Revolution and the people. Intellectually and emotionally, he had always invested so much more of himself in the future and in popular democracy than Madison had. Jefferson was inspired by a vision of how things could and should be; Madison tended much more to accept things as they were. Madison never lost his dark foreboding about the America yet to come, and he never shed his skepticism about the people and popular majorities. But Jefferson had nothing but the people and the future to fall back on; they were really all he ever believed in. That is why we remember Jefferson, and not Madison.

NOTES

1. Merrill Peterson, *The Jeffersonian Image in the American Mind* (New York, 1960), p. 234.

2. Peterson, *Jeffersonian Image,* pp. vii, 9.

3. Leonard W. Levy, *Jefferson and Civil Liberties: The Darker Side* (Cambridge, Mass., 1963).

4. Bernard Bailyn, *Faces of Revolution: Personalities and Themes in the Struggle for American Independence* (New York, 1990), p. 27.

5. R. R. Palmer, "The Dubious Democrat: Thomas Jefferson in Bourbon France," *Political Science Quarterly,* 72 (1957), pp. 388–404.

6. Jefferson to Francis Hopkinson, March 13, 1789, *Boyd,* XIV, pp. 650–51.

7. Robert McColley, *Slavery and Jeffersonian Virginia* (Urbana, Ill., 1964); William Cohen, "Thomas Jefferson and the Problem of Slavery," *Journal of American History,* 56 (1969), pp. 503–26. To get some historical balance in these critiques it is important to

remember that by the time of the American Revolution, slavery had existed in Virginia and in America for over a century without substantial criticism or moral censure. Therefore by condemning slavery and putting the institution morally on the defensive, Jefferson and many of his fellow revolutionaries did confront the slaveholding society into which they had been born and raised. It was an accomplishment of the Revolution that should never be minimized.

8. William W. Freehling, *The Road to Disunion: Secessionists at Bay, 1776–1854,* (New York, 1990), pp. 123, 127–28.

9. Jefferson, *Notes on the State of Virginia,* William Peden, ed. (Chapel Hill, N.C., 1955), pp. 138–43.

10. Garrett Ward Sheldon, *The Political Philosophy of Thomas Jefferson* (Baltimore, 1991), p. 126.

11. Fawn M. Brodie, *Thomas Jefferson: An Intimate History* (New York, 1974), pp. 229–30, 233–34.

12. Freehling, *Road to Disunion,* pp. 128–29.

13. Gary C. Bryner, "Constitutionalism and the Politics of Rights," in Gary C. Bryner and Noel B. Reynolds, eds., *Constitutionalism and Rights* (Provo, Utah, 1987), pp. 7–29.

14. Linda K. Kerber, *Federalists in Dissent: Imagery and Ideology in Jeffersonian America* (Ithaca, N.Y., 1970), p. 20.

15. J. G. A. Pocock, "Virtue and Commerce in the Eighteenth Century," *Journal of Interdisciplinary History,* 3 (1972), pp. 130–31, 134; Pocock, *The Machiavellian Moment: Florentine Political Thought and the Atlantic Republican Tradition* (Princeton, N.J., 1975), pp. 532–33.

16. Garry Wills, *Inventing America: Jefferson's Declaration of Independence* (Garden City, N.Y., 1978); Ronald Hamowy, "Jefferson and the Scottish Enlightenment: A Critique of Garry Wills's *Inventing America: Jefferson's Declaration of Independence,*" *WMQ,* 36 (1979), pp. 503–23.

17. Kenneth S. Lynn, "Falsifying Jefferson," *Commentary,* 66 (Oct. 1978), p. 66.

18. Joyce Appleby, *Liberalism and Republicanism in the Historical Imagination* (Cambridge, Mass., 1992), pp. 258, 300–301, 318.

19. Richard K. Matthews, *The Radical Politics of Thomas Jefferson: A Revisionist View* (Lawrence, Kans., 1984), p. 16.

20. Freehling, *Road to Disunion,* I, p. 123.

21. TJ to Henry Lee, May 8, 1825, in *LofA,* p. 1501.

22. Jefferson, Autobiography, 1743–1790, *LofA,* pp. 32, 3.

23. TJ to John Adams, Oct. 28, 1813, in Lester J. Cappon, ed., *The Adams-Jefferson Letters: The Complete Correspondence Between Thomas Jefferson and John Adams,* 2 vols. (Chapel Hill, N.C., 1959), II, p. 388.

24. TJ to John Page, May 25, 1766, *Boyd,* I, pp. 19–20.

25. Seymour Howard, "Thomas Jefferson's Art Gallery for Monticello," *The Art Bulletin,* 59 (1977), pp. 583–600.

26. *Malone,* I, p. 8; TJ to John Page, May 25, 1766, *Boyd,* I, pp. 19–20; Merrill D. Peterson, *Thomas Jefferson and the New Nation: A Biography* (New York, 1970), pp. 14, 15; Eleanor D. Berman, *Thomas Jefferson Among the Arts: An Essay in Early American Esthetics* (New York, 1947), p. 1.

27. TJ to Giovanni Fabbroni, June 8, 1778, *Boyd,* II, p. 196.

28. TJ to Benjamin Harrison, Jan. 12, 1785, *Boyd,* VII, p. 600; Washington to TJ, Aug. 1, 1786, *The Writings of George Washington,* John C. Fitzpatrick, ed., 39 vols. (Wash-

ington, D.C., 1931–44), XXVIII, p. 504; TJ to Nathaniel Macon, Jan. 22, 1816, *L&B*, XIV, p. 408.

29. Berman, *Jefferson Among the Arts,* p. 84; *Notes on Virginia,* p. 153; TJ to Madison, Sept. 20, 1785, in *Boyd,* VIII, p. 535.

30. Stanley Green, *Shaftesbury's Philosophy of Religion and Ethics: A Study in Enthusiasm* (Athens, Oh., 1967), p. 250; Lawrence Klein, "The Third Earl of Shaftesbury and the Progress of Politeness," *Eighteenth Century Studies,* XVIII (1984–85), pp. 186–214.

31. *New York Magazine,* II (1792), p. 406.

32. Stephen A. Conrad, "Polite Foundation: Citizenship and Common Sense in James Wilson's Republican Theory," in Philip Kurland et al., eds. *The Supreme Court Review—1984* (Chicago, 1985), pp. 361, 363, 365.

33. Berman, *Jefferson Among the Arts,* p. 18.

34. TJ to Peter Carr, Aug. 10, 1787, *Boyd,* XII, p. 15; TJ to T. Law, June 13, 1814, *L&B,* XIV, pp. 141–142.

35. For a fuller discussion of this radical celebration of politeness as a natural social adhesive see Gordon S. Wood, *The Radicalism of the American Revolution* (New York, 1992), 215–25. See also Richard L. Bushman, *The Refinement of America: Persons, Houses, Cities* (New York, 1992).

36. Drew R. McCoy, *The Last of the Fathers: James Madison and the Republican Legacy* (New York, 1989), p. 115.

37. TJ, Second Inaugural Address (1805); TJ to Joseph Priestley, Jan. 29, 1804, *LofA,* pp. 519, 1142.

38. Alexander Hamilton (1794), in Morton J. Frisch, ed., *Selected Writings and Speeches of Alexander Hamilton* (Washington, D.C., 1985), p. 415.

39. For the most recent critique of Jefferson's foreign policy see Robert W. Tucker and David C. Hendrickson, *Empire of Liberty: The Statecraft of Thomas Jefferson* (New York, 1990).

40. McCoy, *Last of the Fathers,* p. 144; TJ to Abigail Adams, Feb. 22, 1787, *Adams-Jefferson Letters,* I, p. 173; TJ to William Stephens Smith, *Boyd,* XII, p. 356; TJ to William Short, Jan. 3, 1793, *LofA,* p. 1004.

41. TJ to Roger C. Weightman, June 24, 1826, *LofA,* p. 1517.

42. McCoy, *Last of the Fathers,* p. 29.

43. TJ to Col. Charles Yancey, Jan. 6, 1816, *Ford,* XI, p. 494.

44. *Malone,* VI, 331, pp. 148–50.

45. TJ to John Holmes, Apr. 22, 1820, *LofA,* p. 1434; *Malone,* VI, pp. 336–37.

46. TJ to Albert Gallatin, Dec. 26, 1820, *Ford,* X, p. 177.

47. *Malone,* VI, p. 356.

48. TJ to Adams, Aug. 1, 1816, *Adams-Jefferson Letters,* II, p. 485.

49. TJ to Edward Coles, Aug. 25, 1814, *LofA,* p. 1345.

50. *Malone,* VI, p. 123.

51. TJ to Dr. Thomas Humphreys, Feb. 8, 1817, *Ford,* X, p. 77.

52. Robert E. Shalhope, "Thomas Jefferson's Republicanism and Antebellum Southern Thought," *Journal of Southern History,* XLII (1976), p. 542.

53. TJ to Madison, Feb. 17, 1826, *LofA,* p. 1514.

54. TJ to John Adams, Jan. 19, 1819, *Adams-Jefferson Letters,* II, p. 532.

55. *Malone,* VI, p. 275.

56. *Malone,* VI, p. 477.

57. TJ to Francis Adrian Van De Kamp, Jan. 11, 1825, *Ford,* X, p. 337.

CHAPTER 14

The Strange
Career of Thomas Jefferson
Race and Slavery in American Memory,
1943-1993

SCOT A. FRENCH AND EDWARD L. AYERS

For generations, the memory of Thomas Jefferson has been inseparable from his nation's memory of race and slavery. Just as Jefferson's words are invoked whenever America's ideals of democracy and freedom need an eloquent spokesman, so are his actions invoked when critics level charges of white guilt, hypocrisy, and evasion. In the nineteenth century, abolitionists used Jefferson's words as swords; slaveholders used his example as a shield. Deep into the twentieth century, white segregationists summoned Jefferson as the defender of local rights and limited government; advocates of black equality even more effectively summoned Jefferson as the author of the Declaration of Independence.[1]

The debates over Jefferson's legacy have become increasingly complex since 1943, when Americans proudly celebrated the 200th anniversary of his birth. Ambivalence and qualification now surround most writings on Jefferson, the willful innocence of the 1940s and 1950s yielding to skepticism and cynicism. Jefferson's life has come to symbolize America's struggle with racial inequality, his successes and failures mirroring those of his nation. The quest for a more honest and inclusive rendering of the American past has placed a heavy burden on Jefferson and his slaves. Generation after generation of Americans has sought some kind of moral symmetry at Monticello, some kind of reconciliation between slavery and freedom, black and white, past injustice and present compensation.

Those who have debated the Jeffersonian legacy on race and slavery since

1943 have spoken in vocabularies that sometimes seemed unintelligible to one another. Some have employed the cautious language of professional scholarship, in which written documentation serves as the true measure of the past. Others have placed their faith in oral tradition, finding in the words of former slaves and their progeny a kind of truth banished from the written record. Still others have insisted that we enter imaginatively into places where no record can take us, beginning with what we know with some certainty about Jefferson and Monticello but not stopping there.

At issue in these struggles is the cultural authority to shape the public memory of the American past. Audiences seem unsure about who has greater credibility: those who claim to speak from the disinterested perspective of the documentary record or those who lay claim to a more authentic oral tradition. The authority of white male scholars has been continually and increasingly challenged by women and African-Americans, both inside and outside of the academy. The authority of professional historians has been repeatedly tested by journalists, novelists, playwrights, and descendants of Monticello's slaves, with the question of whether Jefferson fathered children with one of his slaves, Sally Hemings, recurring as the major issue of contention. The struggle over cultural authority—taking on different forms in each decade since 1943—has become part of the Jefferson legacy on race and slavery.

I

On April 13, 1943, a crowd of five thousand people gathered on the blustery shores of the Tidal Basin in Washington, D.C., to witness the dedication of the new Thomas Jefferson Memorial. A towering likeness of Jefferson gazed out from the rotunda as President Franklin D. Roosevelt delivered a brief speech from the steps below. "Today, in the midst of a great war for freedom," Roosevelt began somberly, "we dedicate a shrine to freedom. To Thomas Jefferson, apostle of freedom, we are paying a debt long overdue." The significance of the occasion was not lost on Dumas Malone, a forty-nine-year-old historian who had just begun work on a multivolume biography of Jefferson. The Jefferson memorial, Malone observed in *The Saturday Review,* "signifies in a tangible way his recognition as a member of our Trinity of immortals." Exactly two hundred years after his birth and more than a century after his death, Jefferson had finally joined George Washington and Abraham Lincoln in the pantheon of American demigods.[2]

The bicentennial celebration of 1943 offered twentieth-century Americans an opportunity to reacquaint themselves with Jefferson and his world.

Americans were urged to learn as much as they could about Jefferson, whose democratic creed posed a sharp contrast to the "slave philosophy" of Hitler. With Americans enlisting Jefferson in the fight against Hitler, liberals saw an opportunity to attack racism on the home front. Gunnar Myrdal, a Swedish economist, sought to prick the conscience of white America in his 1944 opus, *An American Dilemma: The Negro Problem and Modern Democracy.* White Americans knew that blacks ought to be treated as equals, Myrdal argued, but they were paralyzed by fear and ignorance. As the author of the Declaration of Independence and a slaveholder, Jefferson felt that dilemma more acutely than anyone. Myrdal portrayed Jefferson as an open-minded social scientist, grappling with the Negro problem of his day. In his scientific treatise, *Notes on the State of Virginia,* Jefferson theorized that the "real distinctions" between blacks and whites were produced by nature, not by the conditions of slavery. "But he is cautious in tone, has his attention upon the fact that popular opinions are prejudiced, and points to the possibility that further scientific studies may, or may not, verify his conjectures," Myrdal wrote. "This guarded treatment of the subject marks a high point in the early history of the literature on Negro racial characteristics." Myrdal believed that social scientists of the twentieth century could pick up where Jefferson left off by demonstrating the environmental basis for racial distinctions. Once whites realized that segregation itself made blacks different, they would lift the remaining barriers to assimilation and live up to the American creed so eloquently espoused by Jefferson.[3]

Dumas Malone, the leading Jefferson scholar of the postwar era, fought the battle against southern white reactionaries on another front. Born in Mississippi and raised in Georgia, Malone abhorred the provincialism associated with the South in the early twentieth century. Malone cited Jefferson as the most conspicuous example of the great southern statesmen who loved their home region but who ruled the nation with an expansive, cosmopolitan outlook. "It is the largeness of these men that most impresses me," Malone wrote. "And it is certainly worthy of note that the leadership of Virginia and the South was most conspicuous when it was least sectional in view." The decline of southern leadership in the antebellum era coincided with "a narrowing of the Jeffersonian philosophy, an accentuation of its local emphasis and a repudiation of its larger implications." Love of locality became an "hysterical insistence on the theoretical rights of the states"; the flexible philosophy of Thomas Jefferson became the "rigid doctrine" of John Calhoun.[4]

Malone refused to concede Jefferson to southern segregationists who used

Jefferson to defend an unjust status quo. The Jefferson whom Malone admired was a fearless advocate of change who invoked states' rights to protect freedom of expression, not to defend slavery or racial subjugation. "There can be no question of the liberalism of the mind of Jefferson," Malone wrote. "In his own day, he was often described as a revolutionary, and his record of opposition to the vested interests of his time is clear." Unlike the civil rights activists of the twentieth century, however, Jefferson "favored a high degree of local control" and "feared the consolidation of power" in the national government. Malone attempted to strike a balance between these two positions in his own personal philosophy. Rather than condemn his fellow white southerners, Malone preferred to educate them, offering Jefferson as an example of enlightened southern leadership and Reconstruction as an example of what could happen when southerners failed to act responsibly.[5]

Malone saw history as an exercise in empathy. He did not hide his admiration for Jefferson, nor did he conceal his sympathy for white southerners of the antebellum era. He was less sympathetic toward the northern abolitionists and others whose "doctrinaire idealism" stirred sectional animosities. Malone applauded what he called the "pro-Southern" trend in American historiography, which had been dominant since the turn of the century. "Nothing irritates me more than the tone of moral superiority which was once assumed by Northern writers in connection with the great sectional controversy. I am glad to say that the participants in that struggle, on both sides of the line, are now generally regarded as human beings." Malone found nothing insidious in what others might call compensatory history; prosouthern historians were simply restoring balance to what had been a distorted view of the American past.[6]

C. Vann Woodward, the leading southern historian of the postwar era, was less enthusiastic about this prosouthern historiography, with its "distortions and perversions, of the past." In 1954, Woodward delivered a series of lectures at the University of Virginia in which he argued that segregation was a relatively recent phenomenon, not the time-honored tradition that southern apologists made it out to be. *The Strange Career of Jim Crow,* as his lectures were titled (and whose title we have borrowed), demonstrated that history was far more contingent, that stateways had changed folkways, even in the tradition-steeped South. Woodward, while a powerful advocate of racial justice, placed himself rhetorically in the center of the debate between segregationists and civil rights activists, arguing that a balanced view of the past was essential to an informed debate. "It has been my experience that impatient reformers are as surprised and incredulous as foot-dragging conservatives when confronted by some of the little-known history of Jim Crow," he wrote.[7]

Woodward dedicated his widely acclaimed lectures to "Charlottesville and the hill that looks down upon her, Monticello," an affectionate reference to Jefferson and his lofty ideals. Woodward noted that the lectures "were given before unsegregated audiences and they were received in that spirit of tolerance and open-mindedness that one has a right to expect at a university with such a tradition and such a founder." In summoning the spiritual guidance of Jefferson to challenge the racial hierarchy that Jefferson himself had bequeathed, Woodward bridged the gap between an older generation of Jefferson admirers and a younger generation of critics. Woodward sought to use whatever leverage he could get from the hallowed memory of Thomas Jefferson, southerner. While he was far more activist than Dumas Malone, Woodward shared with the older scholar a progressive vision of race relations in which white southerners had an important role to play. Jefferson was too useful to discard, too potent a symbol to concede to the states' rights advocates.[8]

II

In 1954, the same year that Woodward gave his Charlottesville lectures, *Ebony* magazine published an article entitled "Thomas Jefferson's Negro Grandchildren," in which readers learned about "a handful of elderly Negroes" who traced their ancestry to Jefferson. By far the most widely read publication among African-Americans, with a circulation of nearly half a million, *Ebony* generally spoke in moderate tones to a self-consciously respectable black audience. It was all the more telling, therefore, when the magazine abandoned its generally conciliatory posture and offered a bitterly ironic view of the Jefferson legacy. "In four generations," the unnamed author wrote, "these proud Negro descendants of America's third President have made the long and improbable journey from the white marbled splendor of Monticello to the 'Negro ghetto' in the democracy their forebear helped to found."[9]

Most of the "colored descendants" profiled by *Ebony* traced their roots to Sally Hemings, whose relationship with Jefferson reportedly began when she accompanied his daughter Maria to France in 1787. The partisan use of the stories did not diminish their standing as fact in the eyes of the *Ebony* author, who suggested that stories about Jefferson and his "slave concubines" were widely known and widely accepted within the academic community. "Many reputable historians concede that Jefferson fathered at least five Negro children and possibly more by several comely slave concubines who were great favorites at his Monticello home."[10]

While some historians may indeed have accepted the story as true, the leading Jefferson scholars of the day—all of whom were white—dismissed the charge as inconsistent with Jefferson's character. To their frustration, however, professional historians did not completely control public discussion of the past. Certain stories stubbornly refused to wither under their scrutiny. Most people, after all, took their view of history not from the monographs published by historians, but from dimly remembered schoolbooks, oral tradition, and whatever happened to come before them in newspapers or mass-market magazines.[11]

Douglass Adair, a white historian who had spent nine years editing the *William and Mary Quarterly,* worried over the renewed appeal of the Hemings story. The *Ebony* article, he wrote, "with its sensational modernized mixture of fact and fiction, is calculated to remind its Negro readers of one of the ugliest features of Negro-white relations in American history. Its printing is designed to stir up, to quote a phrase of Jefferson's, 'ten thousand recollections, by the blacks, of the injuries they have sustained.'" The appeal of the story was not limited to black militants; a white segregationist named W. E. Debnam had also revived the story to illustrate the dangers of integration. His book "is sold today in drugstores and newsstands all over the South," Adair wrote. "It has been widely reviewed and praised in southern newspapers." Adair did not deny the historical reality of miscegenation; few, if any, scholars did. Rather, he questioned the evidence used to implicate Jefferson and the motives of those who raised the subject in the racially charged atmosphere of the 1950s.[12]

Adair drafted a lengthy rebuttal entitled "The Jefferson Scandals," in which he argued that the Hemings story was being revived by militants, black and white, for its "usefulness as a weapon in current twentieth-century politics." In his view, the historically accurate Thomas Jefferson patiently recreated by careful scholars, the Thomas Jefferson who acted as an example of caution and good will in race relations, was in danger of being supplanted by a licentious and hypocritical Thomas Jefferson, dragged into politics once again. Adair claimed he could prove, using newly discovered documentary evidence, that Jefferson was not the father of Sally Hemings's children. Sifting through account books, letters, memoirs, and oral histories, Adair concluded that it was probably one of Jefferson's nephews, Peter Carr, who fathered the children. "The account of Jefferson and Sally Hemings, when one knows all the facts available in the new documents, is not a history that either whites or Negroes can use against each other with good conscience in our contemporary political battles." [13]

Adair sent a copy of his manuscript to Malone and others for comment. "It's been a damned hard thing for me to write," Adair confessed in a cover note to John Cook Wyllie, the University of Virginia librarian, "and I'm so closely involved that tho' I think the technical side will hold up O.K. I'm very unsure about the tone." Wyllie urged Adair to focus on "the history of the Jefferson menage" and leave the "contemporary politics" out. "I saw the *Ebony* article, and forgot about it. The Debnam book I never heard of, despite your implication that its widespread dissemination throughout the South is a primary reason for your writing." Adair agreed to revise the manuscript, but it remained unpublished until 1974, after his death, a private expression of a liberal scholar's fear that extremists would distort the past to achieve their divisive aims. The professional historians to whom Adair turned did not deem the present-day proponents of the Hemings story worthy of the recognition a scholarly rebuttal would give them. [14]

Still, the story refused to go away. In 1961, an amateur historian named Pearl M. Graham attempted to beat the professionals at their own game by mobilizing documentary evidence and adding footnotes—but that was a game the professionals could always win. Graham's scholarship, published in *The Journal of Negro History,* was superficial and her language intemperate: she praised Jefferson on the same page that she compared his ideas on race to Hitler's. Historians ignored the piece; even a scholar who did not reject the Hemings story out of hand later dismissed the article as "pseudo-scholarly." [15]

At about the same time, Merrill Peterson, who would soon succeed Malone in the Jefferson chair at the University of Virginia, published an award-winning book called *The Jefferson Image in the American Mind.* Peterson surveyed the ever-shifting ways in which Jefferson's legacy had been used and abused from his death until the bicentennial celebration of 1943. While not giving much attention to race, Peterson did pause to discuss the Sally Hemings case. In his view, "no serious student" of Jefferson gave the story credence. Peterson traced the genesis of the story, in part, to the "Negroes' pathetic wish for a little pride and their subtle ways of confounding the white folks, the cunning of the slave trader and the auctioneer who might expect a better price for a Jefferson than for a Jones, the social fact of miscegenation and its fascination as a moral theme, and, above all, the logic of abolitionism by which Jefferson alone of the Founding Fathers was a worthy exhibit of the crime." While noting that several recent books and articles had presented the story as true, Peterson concluded that the Hemings affair had long ago "faded into the obscure recesses of the Jeffersonian image." [16]

And there it remained throughout most of the 1960s, obscured by the Jefferson scholars who continued to shape the popular image and by the cultural boundaries that distinguished black consciousness from white. Black civil rights leaders, who were well aware of the Hemings story, saw no advantage in publicizing it, preferring to focus on the Jeffersonian ideals of freedom and democracy. In the academy, by contrast, the liberation struggle inspired scholars to take a closer look at the relationship between racism and slavery, using Jefferson as a representative figure. Meanwhile black activists were becoming increasingly disillusioned with white liberals who, like their hero Jefferson, seemed to say one thing and do another. In 1965, Malcolm X blasted the hypocrisy of Jefferson, calling him an "artful" liar. "Who was it wrote that—'all men created equal'? It was Jefferson. Jefferson had more slaves than anybody else." Malcolm saw no reason for black people to admire slaveholders like Jefferson. "When I see some poor old brainwashed Negroes—you mention Thomas Jefferson and George Washington and Patrick Henry, they just swoon, you know, with patriotism. But they don't realize that in the sight of George Washington, you were a sack of molasses, a sack of potatoes. You—yes—were a sack of potatoes, a barrel of molasses, you amounted to nothing in the sight of Washington, or in the sight of Jefferson, or Hamilton, and some of those other so-called founding fathers. You were their property. And if it was left up to them, you'd still be their property today." Where Martin Luther King, Jr., and other civil rights leaders portrayed Jefferson as a well-meaning white man caught on the horns of a moral dilemma, Malcolm X saw only a white slaveholder caught in a web of deceit. [17]

Other black social critics joined in the chorus of condemnation. Ishmael Reed, a poet and activist, questioned the sincerity of Jefferson and his white liberal disciples in a *New York Times* op-ed piece entitled "Gliberals." Referring to the leading liberal politicians of the 1960s, Reed wrote: "The Stevensons, Kennedys, and Humphreys are able to flit from one position to another without the modifying transitions, because they say it so pretty. Honeyed words, swiftly delivered like cats scurrying up a wet fence; liberally seasoned with anecdotes, catchy syntax, Biblical quotations, Shakespeare; writing techniques introduced by early political writers like Thomas Jefferson, the founding Gliberal, a slaveowner who insisted that the Bill of Rights be added to the Constitution." As white liberals came under attack for their gradualism, their patron saint suffered accordingly. [18]

In a 1972 article entitled "Mr. Jefferson and the Living Generation," Malone defended Jefferson against the charge of hypocrisy. "Contradictions there were, as indeed there are in all of us," Malone wrote, "but I am most impressed with his equilibrium—or, to use a musical rather than a physical term, with his polyphony." Malone defended the gradualism of Jefferson and his faith in the future. "To the fiery revolutionaries of our own time he probably seems a tame and timid creature. But no contemporary of his perceived more clearly the inevitability of change and the necessity that institutions keep pace with it." Unfortunately, Malone himself could not keep pace with the changes that were taking place in his own time. What Malone considered a balanced picture of Thomas Jefferson seemed increasingly unbalanced to his critics.[19]

III

As the civil rights movement, the New Left, and feminism pushed questions of moral commitment to the fore, the private life of Jefferson took on greater significance. Both professional historians and the general public seemed more interested in issues of consistency across the boundary between public and private than they had before. With varying degrees of sophistication, writers turned to psychology to bridge that gap, to explain apparent inconsistencies, to suggest causes for otherwise inexplicable behavior. Such a strategy quickly led to reevaluations of Thomas Jefferson and his tangled relationship with his slaves.

In 1968, Winthrop Jordan's *White Over Black* offered a thoughtful analysis of Jefferson and race. Jordan looked at Jefferson's writing on race unflinchingly, with the eye of someone who had studied some of the most inhumane things human beings had ever written about one another. He discussed the evidence of the Sally Hemings affair—noting that "despite the utter disreputability of the source, the charge has been dragged after Jefferson like a dead cat through the pages of formal and informal history"—only to declare that its truth did not matter much one way or another. Jordan went farther than earlier students, however, in emphasizing the recurring themes of miscegenation, black sexuality, and psychological repression in Jefferson's life and thought. Moreover, Jordan laid a considerable burden at his subject's feet: Jefferson's comments on black inferiority "constituted, for all its qualifications, the most intense, extensive, and extreme formulation of anti-Negro 'thought' offered by any American in the thirty years after the Revolution." Jordan turned Myrdal's Jefferson on his head.[20]

Fawn Brodie came at Jefferson's personal life from another angle. Brodie, a biographer and UCLA lecturer, had experimented with psychological models long before they became popular; her 1943 biography of Joseph Smith, written in this mode, led to her excommunication from the Mormon church. In the late 1960s, Brodie turned her attention to Thomas Jefferson, who was then—in her words—"under bombardment" from critics like Jordan. Brodie felt Jordan had overstated the racism of Jefferson; her Jefferson was far more ambivalent about racial differences, his comments on black inferiority offered as "a suspicion only." Still, those words were enough, she lamented, to destroy his "heroic image among black students and even some radical whites." Brodie also worried about the impact of the Hemings story on Jefferson's heroic image. She suggested that the Hemings story need not be considered a charge against Jefferson or a threat to his heroic stature. "It could be that Jefferson's slave family, if the evidence should point to its authenticity, will turn out under scrutiny to represent not a tragic flaw in Jefferson but evidence of psychic health. And the flaw could turn out to be what some of the compassionate abolitionists thought long ago, not a flaw in the hero but a flaw in society." By making these points in a lecture at the University of Virginia and an article in the *Virginia Quarterly Review,* Brodie was venturing into the lion's den, hoping to declaw her opponents before they attacked her.[21]

While Brodie continued to praise the work of Malone and Peterson, she made it clear that she was looking for something they had apparently overlooked in their otherwise exhaustive biographies. In a review of Peterson's biography, *Thomas Jefferson and the New Nation,* Brodie noted the absence of "any kind of probing into Jefferson's inner life for sources of his ambivalences toward blacks, which might explain his increasing apathy toward slavery." Here was a clue to her own evolving thesis: perhaps Sally Hemings held the key to Jefferson's thinking on slavery. In April 1971, Brodie delivered a paper entitled "The Great Jefferson Taboo" at the Organization of American Historians, with Peterson and Jordan serving as critics. According to *The Journal of American History,* Peterson "was especially critical of the psychological evidence presented by Brodie"; Jordan, by contrast, "stated that he had already been 60 percent on what might be called the Brodie side of the argument and described himself as having upped the percentage to eighty pro after reading her paper. He was impressed with the psychological evidence." The large audience—some 200 people—attested to scholarly interest in the topic; the publication of the paper, complete with footnotes, in *American Heritage* attested to its popular appeal.[22]

Brodie became increasingly critical of what she called "the Jefferson Establishment." In a 1971 article entitled "Jefferson Biographers and the Psychology of Canonization," she suggested that Malone and Peterson had succumbed to the impulse to sanctify without knowing it. "Both biographers teach at the University of Virginia, live virtually in the shadow of Monticello, and walk each day in the beguiling quadrangle Jefferson designed 150 years ago. Jefferson is so much a 'presence' in Charlottesville, and so omnipresent a local deity, that one cannot help wondering if this in itself does not exercise a subtle direction upon anyone who chooses to write about him." Brodie charged that the Jefferson biographers had focused almost exclusively on his public life, leaving his private life untouched. "There is important material in the documents which the biographers belittle; there is controversial material which they flatly disregard as libelous, though it cries out for careful analysis. And there is what one may call psychological evidence which they often ignore or simply do not see." Brodie concluded "that something is at work here that has little to do with scholarship," something that called for "speculation and exploration" and perhaps even Freudian analysis. Jefferson's male biographers could not seem to accept the possibility that Jefferson engaged in affairs of the heart outside of marriage; perhaps a female biographer could restore Jefferson's masculinity and accept the possibility that he had a sexual relationship with one of his slaves.[23]

Brodie seemed more intent on demystifying "the Jefferson establishment" than on debunking Jefferson, whom she clearly admired. She suggested, once again, that an intimate relationship between Jefferson and Sally Hemings could be seen in a positive light. Perhaps Jefferson, a lonely widower, "had turned to the 'dashing Sally' for solace" and she, in turn, found him attractive. "None of this has to be described as 'ruthless exploitation of the master-slave relationship.' And there is no man to whose character it could be genuinely unbecoming. He had then been for years a widower." Jefferson need not have been condemning his children to slavery, Brodie added, since they were, by his own definition, white.[24]

Brodie was not the only historian to criticize the Jefferson biographers as a group in the early 1970s. Eric L. McKitrick wrote that while "the view from Jefferson's camp, in the work of Peterson and Malone, is full as any such view can be," their perspective as biographers did not allow for alternative views. "If your host literally cannot imagine Thomas Jefferson as other than all that is finest and best not only in a gentleman but in the entire American tradition itself," McKitrick asked, "how can you?" McKitrick noted that Malone examined—and dismissed as unproven—the Hemings story in an appendix to his fourth volume. "If decorum and literal justice were to go hand in hand, we might leave it at that. Jefferson the individual has been 'cleared,' if that is the word. But what if, in the interest of speculation, such constraints were waived? It might then occur to us that the question of Sally Hemings went well beyond individuals, revealing about an entire society matters that are crucial to our understanding of the most portentous social fact of the age, black slavery." Like Jordan, McKitrick concluded that it "hardly mattered" whether Jefferson had a sexual relationship with Sally Hemings. What mattered was the psychosocial context in which Jefferson grappled with the related issues of slavery and miscegenation. "It is the psychosexual dilemma of an entire society, reflected in that undergone by the most eminent citizen of Virginia and one of the most enlightened men of his time."[25]

Brodie published her much-anticipated biography, *Thomas Jefferson: An Intimate History,* in 1974. Supplementing documentary sources with Freudian psychoanalysis, she concluded that Jefferson enjoyed a long-term, loving relationship with Sally Hemings, fathering several of her children. The book received favorable reviews in many publications, infuriating Malone and other Jefferson scholars, who considered its evidence inconclusive, its methodology questionable, and its thesis implausible. Supporters of Malone depicted Brodie as a woman obsessed with sex, a marginal historian who had made a "scholarly specialty of oddballs." Supporters of Brodie, on the other hand, depicted Malone as a hagiographer, a conservative defender of the national self-image.[26]

While Brodie discussed relationships between Jefferson and several women in his life, reviewers concentrated on the Hemings "scandal," shifting the focus from gender to race. *The New York Times* reviewer, Alfred Kazin, called it a "fascinating and responsible" book, "the most suggestive account we have of whatever there is to know about this slave, who belonged to Thomas Jefferson in all senses of the word." Kazin was impressed with the documentation offered by Brodie, but he seemed even more impressed with her imaginative reconstruction of events. Several letter writers took issue with Kazin, saying that he accepted the Brodie thesis without considering the more sober and scholarly views of Malone and Peterson. Kazin responded that the "understandably general and persistent" disbelief in the Hemings story represented a form of denial by white Americans, many of whom did not want to believe that Thomas Jefferson could have such a relationship with one of his black slaves. "I have the greatest respect for Dr. Malone," Kazin wrote, "but it is obvious that miscegenation itself affronts him even as a 'legend.'"[27]

Murat Williams, a white civil rights activist from Charlottesville, also commented upon the reluctance of "orthodox" Jefferson scholars to accept the possibility of a miscegenous relationship between Jefferson and Hemings. Writing in *The Daily Progress,* Williams argued that the truth or falsity of the Hemings story mattered less than the larger truths it revealed about racial attitudes and race relations in America. From the positive reviews of the Brodie book, Williams sensed that "justice was being done on a larger scale—not necessarily in the case of Jefferson, but rather in the case of all those Americans who are the sons and daughters of miscegenation. I felt that a veil was being lifted and that a barrier was being removed. All around us we in Virginia see the living evidence of miscegenation, but what kind of pretense are we guilty of to treat it as unmentionable?" Williams called the "indignant" reaction of "senior biographers" to the Hemings story an insult to "people of mixed blood." [28]

Malone was "surprised and pained" by the charges of racial insensitivity. "To me the story would be no more credible (and no more creditable) if the supposed object of Mr. Jefferson's amours had been white," he wrote in response to the Williams column. "So far as I am concerned," he added later, "the question of race is entirely irrelevant." On this matter, Malone agreed with Brodie: the issue was gender, not race. "From my understanding of his character, temperament, and judgment I do not believe that he would have done that with a woman of any sort. If I find the story unbelievable it is not because of Sally's color." [29]

Malone rarely mentioned Brodie or her book by name; as a highly respected scholar, he preferred to stay above the fray. Occasionally, however, he spoke out publicly against her. In May 1974, he wrote an op-ed column for *The New York Times* entitled "Jefferson's Private Life," in which he made public a letter written in 1858 by Jefferson's granddaughter, Ellen Randolph Coolidge. In the letter, Jefferson's granddaughter argued that he could not possibly have carried on a relationship with Sally Hemings at Monticello without raising the suspicions of his family. She suggested that the Hemings children allegedly fathered by Jefferson were actually fathered by his Irish workmen or his nephews, Peter and Samuel Carr. Here was a theory that could not be "dismissed lightly," Malone argued. [30]

A few months later, Virginius Dabney, a Pulitzer Prize-winning journalist and historian from Richmond, asked Malone for a public statement on the Brodie thesis, saying he wanted to quote Malone and the other leading Jefferson scholars in a Charter Day speech at the College of William and Mary. Dabney had personal ties to Jefferson and the University of Virginia: his fifth-great-grandmother was Martha Jefferson, sister of Thomas; his father was once the "one and only" professor of history at the university; and he earned both his bachelor's and master's degrees at the school. More significantly, he and Malone were old friends; they kept in close touch by mail throughout the Brodie controversy. Dabney wanted to go public against Brodie, but he lacked the stature to do it alone. "For me to say Brodie is nuts would mean little or nothing," he wrote to Malone in October 1974, "unless I could quote you, [Julian] Boyd [editor of the *Jefferson Papers* at Princeton], Peterson, and Adair. That would be a blockbuster!" Dabney also asked Malone to comment on *Burr,* a novel by Gore Vidal, in which Washington and Jefferson "are made out to have been the most despicable pair of incompetents and phonies ever heard of." Dabney cited the nation's upcoming Bicentennial celebration as a reason to respond quickly. "Since nobody has made any effective answer to Brodie and Vidal, and this is the beginning of the Bicentennial, it seems appropriate to me for someone to point out the disservice that these writers are performing in attacking the very people to whom we are indebted for the Bicentennial." [31]

Malone supplied Dabney with a three-page statement in which he called the Brodie thesis "highly objectionable." Jefferson was no "plaster saint," according to Malone, "but this author, in her obsession with sex, has drawn a distorted picture. In her zeal to demonstrate that Jefferson's sexual activity continued after his wife's death—until almost the end of his long life— this determined woman runs far beyond the evidence and carries psychological speculation to the point of absurdity." Malone took issue with the claim that Brodie had humanized Jefferson, saying her book "can be regarded as an attempt to drag an extraordinary man down to the common level—to show that he was no better than anyone else. That would be a perversion of the doctrine of equality." Malone closed with a metaphor. "Fawn Brodie and Gore Vidal cannot rob Washington and Jefferson of their laurels, but they can scribble graffiti on their statues. It is unfortunate that dirty words are so hard to erase, and it is shocking that the scribblers should be so richly rewarded." [32]

Dabney thanked Malone for his help with the speech, which "was received astonishingly well. I've never been so congratulated in my life." Malone asked Dabney if he had heard anything from Brodie or Vidal. "I haven't had time to hear from Brodie or Vidal," Dabney replied, "assuming that they pay any attention at all." Brodie apparently read about the speech in *Time* magazine; she responded angrily in a letter to the editor, calling the "graffiti" quote "a slap against black people." Dabney called the Brodie letter "extremely silly" and privately assured Malone that her charges could easily be answered if he chose to do so. "I have kept up with the references in *Time*," Malone replied, "and gain the impression that we are doing all right. I shall not give Mrs. Brodie the satisfaction of having a reply from me." [33]

Both Malone and Brodie were honored for their Jefferson biographies in 1975. He won the Pulitzer Prize for the first five volumes of his Jefferson biography; she was named "Woman of the Year" by *The Los Angeles Times*. Both were elevated to the status of celebrities. He was quoted along with Andy Warhol, Marilyn Chambers, and Jane Fonda in a tongue-in-cheek *New York Times* article on celebrity views of cottage cheese; she was teamed with Mary Tyler Moore and Helen Reddy at the *Los Angeles Times* awards ceremony. Yet both felt the sting of criticism from their peers, the professional historians and intellectuals who reviewed their books. [34]

The most daring critique came from Garry Wills, who suggested that Brodie—and, by extension, Malone—had glossed over the true nature of the Jefferson-Hemings liaison. Wills described a sexual relationship based on convenience, not love. He compared Hemings to a prostitute who was compensated by Jefferson for her services. "She was apparently pleasing, and obviously discreet. There was less risk in continuing to enjoy her services than in experimenting around with others. She was like a healthy and obliging prostitute, who could be suitably rewarded but would make no importunate demands. Her lot was improved, not harmed, by the liaison." Wills said the attempt to document a loving relationship between Jefferson and Hemings required "heroic feats of misunderstanding and a constant labor at ignorance. This seems too high a price to pay when the same appetites can be more readily gratified by those Hollywood fan magazines, with their wealth of unfounded conjecture on the sex lives of others, from which Ms. Brodie has borrowed her methods." Wills drew a line between what he considered well-founded conjecture and Brodie's uninformed speculation. [35]

Dumas Malone and his allies insisted they were not worried about Jefferson; his reputation was secure from attacks well informed or otherwise. "A bit of chipping around the edges of the alabaster isn't likely to be noticed," Edwin M. Yoder Jr. wrote in the conservative *National Review*. [36] Rather, they feared a lowering of scholarly standards. As they saw it, revisionists like Brodie valued ideology above accuracy. Julian Boyd, the editor of the *Jefferson Papers*, unleashed a blistering attack on Brodie and her supporters in a letter to the editor of the Princeton alumni newsletter.

> Mrs. Brodie's despairing, ambivalent, indecisive and guilt-ridden Jefferson may be soothing to those who so eagerly embrace the concept of collective guilt, who project our views of the rights of women and blacks

into the past, and who cast the new abolitionism, the new sectionalism, and the new attitudes toward sexual liberation into molds manufactured in our own time and in our own image, certainly not out of apodictic materials provided by the past. This, too, is understandable, but it assuredly is not scholarship, and the resultant Jefferson—unless I have wasted thirty of the best years of my life in studying all his recorded actions—is only an imaginative creature and, in my view, a rather repulsive one. [37]

Malone agreed that "the thing most to be deplored and feared" about the Brodie book was its disregard of historical standards of evidence. "That any real scholar could give serious consideration to such a book," Malone wrote to Boyd in a moment of exasperation, "is beyond my comprehension." [38]

Friends of Malone detected politics at work behind the popular acceptance of the Brodie thesis. "I wish that this matter might fade away but I suspect that there is more back of the promotion of Mrs. Brodie than meets the eye," Curtis Nettels, a history professor at Cornell, wrote to Malone. Dabney was more explicit. "*Ebony,* the black imitation of *Life,* is spreading the Hemings canard all over their bicentennial issue, and the blacks hereabout are reading it gleefully," he wrote to Malone. "We may as well resign ourselves to the fact that nothing anybody ever says, or proves, on this subject will shake their confident belief that TJ sired those mulattoes." Indeed, *Ebony* published an article entitled "The Dilemma of Thomas Jefferson" in its August 1975 issue, calling him "the slavemaster who railed against slavery, the miscegenator who abhorred race-mixing, the man of reason who spent a lifetime draped in the hairshirt of his own unresolved contradictions." The article quoted Fawn Brodie in the first paragraph. [39]

The popularity of the Brodie thesis reflected a changing attitude toward the American past and the people who shaped it. A new generation of historians began to question the motives and morality of men such as Thomas Jefferson, whose revolutionary ideology came to seem self-serving and sharply delimited. The eighty-three-year-old Malone sensed the shifting attitude. If Jefferson were to return, he sadly commented on the eve of nation's bicentennial, "the thing he'd notice most about the country today is the lack of faith, the widespread disillusionment, and the cynicism." [40]

Malone insisted that only a careful consideration of the entire record of Jefferson's life could allow us to understand any part of it. To him, that larger understanding emphasized Jefferson's democratic thought more than his failures on slavery; it ruled out any kind of sexual relationship between Jefferson and a slave on the basis of the consistency of Jefferson's character. For Malone, the political and personal ideals Jefferson embodied would have been violated, mocked, had he condemned his own children to slavery or banishment.

The people on each side of the debate assumed the worst about the other. Advocates of the Hemings story gave little credit to the scholarly biographers, making the academic works appear far more brittle and apologetic than they were. Critics of the Hemings story, in turn, ascribed petty and prurient motives to its proponents, making their charges appear less thoughtful and well intentioned than they were.

IV

The bicentennial anniversary of the Declaration of Independence in 1976 sent Americans in search of their nation's origins; for many, the home of the author of the Declaration of Independence seemed a natural destination. What visitors to Monticello found was a shrine to Thomas Jefferson, the architect of freedom; there was barely a mention of slavery, barely a hint that hundreds of black people had once lived, worked, and died there. The place in history assigned to slaves and slavery at Monticello was not lost on the relatively few black people who visited in the 1970s. Thomas A. Greenfield, a professor from historically black Virginia Union University, took Monticello to task in *The Crisis* for the guides' habitual use of the passive voice when it came to the work slaves performed: "Doors *were installed,*" "food *was brought,*" "nails and bricks *were* all *made* right here on the estate," and so on. Architectural features, Greenfield charged, received more attention than the people who built and worked with the elaborate machinery at Monticello, hiding the fact "black people were responsible for the construction, the operation, and the long-term survival of Monticello." Understandably, most black Americans continued to avoid the shrine in droves.[41]

When *Ebony* asked three black leaders whether blacks should celebrate the bicentennial, Jefferson appeared (though not always by name) in all three answers. Baptist church leader Dr. Joseph H. Jackson urged black Americans to follow the example of Benjamin Banneker, the black mathematician who demonstrated to Jefferson, through hard work, that he was qualified to "participate fully as a scientist and as a man of talent." Jackson believed this and other "lessons from the past" would lead and inspire black people "to participate in this historic celebration of the present." Vernon E. Jordan, Jr., the head of the National Urban League, saw the bicentennial as an opportunity to remind Americans "of the hypocrisy of many of the signers of the Declaration of Independence," but added that the Declaration "really was a revolutionary document, still relevant to our concerns and needs." Editor and historian Lerone Bennett, Jr., argued against the bicentennial celebration, calling for "national repentance" and "national action" instead. "Since Thomas Jefferson said goodbye to his slaves and went off to Philadelphia to write the Declaration of Independence, playing with freedom has become a national passion in America." Ever since, there had been only "betrayal of one of the greatest dreams mankind has ever known," "evasion," "mirage," "illusion," "nightmare." [42]

Ebony treated the Sally Hemings story as evidence of Jefferson's hypocrisy, contrasting his words against "race-mixing" with his deeds as a "miscegenator," his words against slavery with his deeds as a slaveholder who refused to free even the slave woman he loved. And it was love, according to author Carlyle C. Douglas, who cited the Brodie biography as his source. "Though nothing of a personal nature that Jefferson may have written about Sally Hemings has ever come to light (most of his biographers agree that much of his most personal correspondence was either destroyed or remains suppressed by his descendants), it seems clear that his relationship with Sally Hemings was closer in nature to a love affair than the casual debauchery of slave by master." Jefferson's feelings for Sally Hemings only heightened his dilemma, only intensified his hypocrisy. [43]

The rhetoric heated up on the other side as well. Dumas Malone, completing the final volume of his Jefferson biography, sought to debunk the 1873 memoir of Madison Hemings, whose mother Sally reportedly told him he was the son of Thomas Jefferson. In a journal article entitled "A Note on Evidence," Malone and his research assistant, Steven Hochman, dismissed the Hemings memoir as a piece of propaganda. Malone wrote that the Hemings memoir "reminds us of the pedigree printed on the numerous stud-horse bills that can be seen posted around during the Spring season. No matter how scrubby the stock or whether the horse has any known pedigree," owners invented an exalted lineage for their property. Horses could not know what was claimed for them, "but we have often thought if one of them could read and would happen to come across his pedigree . . . he would blush to the tips of his ears at the mendacity of his owner." [44]

John Chester Miller, whose 1977 study *Wolf by the Ears* was sharply critical of Jefferson's record on slavery, revealed just how much was at stake in the Hemings debate in his own strongly worded rebuttal. If the Sally Hemings story were true, he wrote, Jefferson "deserves to be regarded as one of the most profligate liars and consummate hypocrites ever to occupy the presidency. To give credence to the Sally Hemings story is, in effect, to question the authenticity of Jefferson's faith in freedom, the rights of man, and the innate controlling faculty to reason and the sense of right and wrong. It is to infer that there were no principles to which he was inviolably committed, that what he acclaimed as morality was no more than a rhetorical facade for self-indulgence, and that he was always prepared to make exceptions in his own case when it suited his purpose." Not even a deep and sincere love for Sally Hemings could "sanctify such an egregious violation of his own principles and preachments." David Brion Davis, author of a brooding and magisterial history of antislavery in Jefferson's era, agreed with Miller that "the consistency between Jefferson's words and deeds is precisely the point at issue," but argued that the evidence in the Hemings case was "highly inconclusive." Davis saw more important inconsistencies in Jefferson's record on slavery and suggested that Jefferson overcame whatever pangs of guilt he might have felt. "The absurdity of history's contradictions is matched only by humanity's capacity for rationalization and self-deception," he wrote.[45]

One important book went farther. Edmund S. Morgan's *American Slavery—American Freedom* suggested that the entire debate had been framed incorrectly. The supposed inconsistency and conflict between white democracy and black slavery was no inconsistency at all. In an elaborate and subtle argument, Morgan tried to show that the planter statesmen of eighteenth-century Virginia were able to envision broad-based white political rights precisely because slavery had solved the problem of a dangerous working class. With slavery holding the vast majority of the working poor in bondage and with race safely dividing poor white from poor black, men such as Jefferson felt free to adopt the most democratic ideals, to speak in the most democratic idiom. Morgan's Jefferson did not appear tormented or contradictory, but ruthlessly consistent. His was the most harrowing vision of all.

V

The debate over Jefferson and race took on renewed vitality in January 1979 when Malone and company learned of plans by CBS to develop a television miniseries based on the forthcoming book, *Sally Hemings: A Novel.* The author of the book, Barbara Chase-Riboud, did something no one had done before: she imagined the alleged affair between Jefferson and Hemings from the viewpoint of the female protagonist. In long interior monologues, Chase-Riboud explored the doubts and fears of the slave rather than the inconsistencies of the master. The author accepted the reality of the Hemings story and turned to fiction to supply what document-based history could not. Word of the novel distressed the Jefferson scholars, who did not want to see the story revived in any form. Still, it was word of the proposed miniseries, not the novel, that jolted them into action.[46]

According to an article in the Hollywood *Reporter,* a copy of which found its way to Malone, the miniseries would tell "the real-life story of the 35-year affair between Thomas Jefferson and his mulatto mistress," as depicted in the novel by Chase-Riboud. Distressed by the advance publicity, Malone and his allies decided not to wait until production of the miniseries or publication of the book to act. They mounted a letter-writing campaign aimed at stopping the miniseries and establishing the fictional content of the book. "I believe that CBS would render the American public a great service by abandoning the idea for a series based on a tawdry and unverifiable story," Malone wrote to Robert A. Daly, president of the CBS Television Entertainment Division. "If you *do* go ahead with the project, I would urge you to make it absolutely clear that you are presenting fiction." Malone claimed to speak for countless others who shared his concerns. "I do this not only on my own account, but in behalf of all persons who are concerned with the preservation and presentation of the history of our country." In a similar letter to CBS chairman William S. Paley, Merrill Peterson urged the network to "reconsider lending its name and network to mass media exposure of what can only be vulgar sensationalism masquerading as history." Peterson worried that a miniseries based on a novel based on the conclusions drawn by Brodie would "occupy the shadowy realm of 'docudrama' where it is impossible to distinguish between fiction and fact." He had little faith that television, commercial or public, would do justice to Jefferson. "I hope you will understand my concern," Peterson wrote plaintively. "I care very much for historical truth and also for the good name, reputation, and influence of Thomas Jefferson." The two goals, he believed, were not incompatible.[47]

Malone also objected to the way that Viking Press was characterizing the Chase-Riboud novel in its 1979 catalog, treating the "love story" as if it were undisputed fact. "Over three decades their passionate, complex love affair endured and flowered," the promotional blurb declared. "While most documents related to that passion were carefully destroyed by Jefferson's white family after his death, enough remained to substantiate the basic facts of the case. Using this historical premise and data, Barbara Chase-Riboud has fashioned a dramatic—and unashamedly romantic—novel." Malone dashed off a letter to the president of Viking Press, saying he was "appalled" by the promotional blurb. He called the assertion that family members had destroyed records "unsupported" and "utterly irresponsible." He also challenged the claim that existing documents substantiated the story. "To be sure, you are publishing a work of fiction," he wrote, "but it seems to me that you should make no claim that it has historical foundation." Alan D. Williams, the editorial director of Viking Press, apologized to Malone for "what might have been called catalog hype for the sales conference." He promised that "the statement about the non-destroyed or undestroyed documents re Thomas Jefferson and Sally Hemings" would not appear on the jacket of the book, but he gave no indication that Viking Press would stop stressing the historical foundations of the novel.[48]

On February 11, 1979, the *Richmond Times-Dispatch* published a front-page, tongue-in-cheek story about the book, the miniseries, and the "tremors" emanating from Monticello and Charlottesville. The newspaper identified the leading critics of the miniseries as Malone, Peterson, Dabney, and Frederick E. Nolting, Jr., president of the Thomas Jefferson Memorial Foundation—"Jefferson's first line of defense." Two days later, *The Washington Post* reported on efforts by "several of Virginia's more prominent historians" to "protect the good name" of Jefferson. The story quoted Malone, Dabney, and Robert Rutland, the editor of the James Madison Papers at the University of Virginia. "What bothers the Virginia historians," the *Post* reported, "is their fear that one woman's symbolism, as transmogrified by Hollywood writers, will become the definitive biography of Jefferson for the millions of Americans who learn their history from television." Malone was quoted as saying that a "gullible public" would believe the televised version of the novel, no matter how romantically it was presented. "What's the use of us trying to get history straight?" he asked.[49]

The hostile response of Malone, Peterson, and other Virginia historians to the popular revival of the Hemings story generated something of a backlash on the editorial pages of *The Cavalier Daily,* the student newspaper at the University of Virginia. "The Virginia historians seem less interested in scholarship than in the frenzied defense of their hero from imagined slurs," wrote Howard Brody, a doctor who had recently moved to Charlottesville. He accused the Virginia historians of ignoring the oral tradition passed down by Madison Hemings and focusing instead on "denials arising within the Jefferson family." An editorial in the student newspaper questioned the objectivity of the "local Jeffersonian scholars, who seem to view the book's publication and potential television adaptation as a personal affront." There was something unseemly, the editorial writer observed, about the way in which these supposedly detached scholars were defending their subject. "Chase-Riboud's work certainly is unscholarly; the author admits she gives 'free rein to her imagination' in recreating the love affair. But historians who say they hate to witness criticism of an old, familiar friend like Jefferson run the risk of appearing equally unscholarly." The editorial called for a more dignified response, one based on erudition rather than emotion.[50]

As the controversy escalated, Malone became increasingly uncomfortable with his role as a public defender of Jefferson; he refused to grant television interviews and only reluctantly agreed to speak with the print media. "I am a little sorry that this matter has received so much publicity," he wrote in March 1979 to Harold J. Coolidge, a Jefferson descendant who had participated in the earlier campaign against Fawn Brodie. "While every effort should be made to dissuade CBS from producing a mini-series, we don't want to give any more publicity to Sally Hemings and the forthcoming book than we have to." Dabney voiced similar concern. "The question is whether CBS will think this publicity makes it all the more desirable that they produce the mini-series. We'll just have to keep our fingers crossed." By April, CBS officials seemed to be distancing themselves from the project, saying they had "a commitment from an independent producer for a 'treatment' of the Jefferson story," but that they were "under no obligation to accept the treatment when and if delivered." In a letter to Harold Coolidge, CBS vice president E. K. Meade Jr. acknowledged the concerns of the Jefferson descendants and Jefferson scholars who opposed the miniseries. "As to the apprehensions you express and the objections of such eminent historians as Dumas Malone and Virginius Dabney, let me say that we are well aware of the controversy surrounding this particular work on Jefferson. More to the point, we assure you that those views will receive the most conscientious consideration in determining what, if any, decision we make in the matter." Unlike Warner Brothers, whose legal affairs director cited other "authorities" on the subject, CBS seemed ready to defer to the authority of the Jefferson scholars and Jefferson descendants who opposed the miniseries.[51]

Some critics who opposed the miniseries had no problem with Chase-Riboud or her book. "She is a poet, she calls her work fiction, and her agent says it is 'symbolic' of race relations in America," wrote Barbara Stanton, an editorial writer for the Detroit *Free Press.* "Race has been an open sore with us for more than three-and-a-half centuries; and it is the ordained function of a writer to poke our sores where they hurt, until we do something about them." Others considered the novel no less objectionable than the miniseries. In an article coauthored by Jon Kukla, assistant director for publications at the Virginia State Library, Dabney accused Chase-Riboud of manipulating historical fact to serve her own present-day purposes. "Her novel tells of an enslaved, black female being oppressed and intimately exploited by white, male America disguised as Thomas Jefferson." *Sally Hemings* was no love story; it was an angry polemic.[52]

Chase-Riboud denied that her book was a veiled attack on Jefferson or white America. "There isn't a bitter or angry word in the book," she told Flora Lewis of *The New York Times.* "Lots of people found rage in it, but it isn't mine. It's their rage which they're projecting." Chase-Riboud said the book was about "the metaphysics of race" in a "mulatto country," not about the plight of blacks in a white country. "'Sally' is by no means a black experience book," she said. "There's no such thing as 'black experience' except in relation to 'white experience.' I don't think we'll even be using those terms much longer." While the book received positive reviews in *The Black Scholar* and *The Journal of Negro History,* it was not universally applauded by blacks. The Baltimore *Sun* reported that "the black activists" were upset with Chase-Riboud "for suggesting that a white plantation owner and a black slave could have enjoyed a 38-year love affair."[53]

Chase-Riboud told interviewers that she found herself relating to her material not as a black person but as a woman. "I don't know who had the worse life. A woman was treated as property if she were white or black." She acknowledged that a streak of feminism ran through the book, "but I didn't introduce it purposely, it just came in the story of one woman and all her labels." Chase did not seem disturbed that she had been labeled a black activist or a feminist by critics of her novel; she said she had gained a sense of herself "without labels" while living in Paris, just like Sally Hemings some two hundred years before.[54]

When Chase-Riboud returned to Charlottesville in June 1979 to promote her book, she attempted to turn the tables on the Jefferson scholars, challenging them to prove that the affair between Jefferson and Hemings did not happen. "They just say that it couldn't have happened but they have to have the data to back it up," she told the local newspaper. "They just don't have it." Chase-Riboud said she hoped her book would inspire "younger" historians to "take up the investigation of, not just this incident, but other aspects of American history. We have been shown the straight, wide, white road of American history, and that's not necessarily the way it was." She said she thought the public was ready for her point of view, "especially as it in no way diminishes Jefferson's genius but increases the sense of his humanity."[55]

Apparently, the CBS executives disagreed. In December 1979, Dabney happily informed Malone that CBS had "dropped all plans" for the miniseries. His source was Frank McCarthy, "the Richmond-born Hollywood producer who turned down the idea himself years ago, and now sends glad tidings that CBS has lost all enthusiasm." Dabney did not know why CBS had decided to abandon the miniseries, but he was pleased nonetheless. "Enough damage has been done by Brodie and Chase-Riboud without TV also," he wrote. Malone congratulated Dabney on his efforts. "It seems to me that you deserve more credit for this fortunate result than anybody else." Still, Malone worried that the Hemings story might be revived by someone else. "As you say, we must keep our fingers crossed. Eternal vigilance will be necessary."[56]

In March 1980, Dabney wrote to Malone with "disturbing news" about a report he had seen in the *Amsterdam News,* the "Negro-owned" newspaper in New York City. Far from being a box-office flop, the Chase-Riboud novel had apparently sold 30,000 copies in hardcover, and a paperback edition was on the way. "I have seen an ad for the Avon paperback," Dabney wrote to Malone, "and it is lurid in the extreme." The publisher promised to promote the book "with a 30-second TV commercial to be seen by thousands of viewers in major markets, backed by print advertising in the June issue of Cosmopolitan." Meanwhile, another television network reportedly was reviving plans for a miniseries based on the Sally Hemings novel. Dabney saw little hope of changing the promotional strategy of Avon Books— "All they are interested in is making money, and who cares about the facts?"—but he did hold out hope for killing the miniseries. "CBS was talked out of the plan they had, and possibly this can be done with ABC." Dabney said he would ask Frank McCarthy, the Hollywood producer, for advice on how best to proceed.[57]

McCarthy confirmed that another network—actually NBC—was reviving plans for a miniseries based on the Chase-Riboud novel. He suggested that Malone enlist a member of the University of Virginia Board of Visitors to write a letter to the president of NBC, but Dabney insisted that Malone continue to lead the fight. "I am sure that you are the most important person of all to write the letter of protest because of your great prestige and the respect in which your views are held; and I should think Merrill Peterson should be enlisted for the duration." Malone cringed at the thought of writing another letter. "Let me say in the first place that I have no assurance that it would ever reach the president of NBC or be read by him. I never had the slightest acknowledgment to the letters I wrote to the CBS people. I must confess that I am completely worn out with this particular controversy and want to pass the buck if I can possibly do so." Malone asked Frank L. Hereford, Jr., the president of the University of Virginia, and Frederick Nolting, the head of the Thomas Jefferson Memorial Foundation, if they would be willing to write official letters of protest, but both declined. "I am as appalled as you at the prospect of what a national television network might do to the Hemings story," Hereford explained, "but I am a little reluctant to get in touch with anyone at NBC myself as President of the University. While we ought to encourage sound scholarship and scrupulous attention to the facts, in a case such as this, it worries me that any representation I might make would be taken to mean that the University is trying to act as a censor." Nolting, likewise, wanted to keep Monticello out of the controversy. "He is trying to find the name of somebody close to the president of NBC whom he can approach on a personal ground," Malone informed Dabney. "The point is that he does not want to involve the Foundation."[58]

While Malone was eager to pass the buck, Dabney was determined to fight to the finish. He informed Malone that he was writing a 35,000-word minibook on the Jefferson scandals for Dodd, Mead and Company. "Of course this will be no effective rebuttal to Brodie's Book of the Month and Chase-Riboud's Literary Guild selection and the vast amounts of publicity both works have received. But it seems desirable to have something on the record in hard covers." Published in 1981, *The Jefferson Scandals: A Rebuttal* allowed Dabney to repeat many of the points he had already made in newspaper and magazine articles. It also allowed him to challenge Brodie's claim that Malone and Peterson were members of a Jefferson Establishment, based in Charlottesville and dedicated to the "canonization" of Jefferson. Dabney stressed the diverse backgrounds of the two scholars, who were born, raised, and educated outside of Virginia. He said they were attracted to the University of Virginia by "the superb collection of Jefferson materials in the university's Alderman Library and at Monticello," not by their devotion to Virginia or Jefferson. Far from uncritical, they had written "scathingly" of Jefferson's conduct "in connection with the trial of Aaron Burr for treason and in ramming the embargo legislation through Congress." Malone and Peterson were united with other professional historians in their rejection of the Hemings story, Dabney acknowledged, but they were hardly canonizers or members of a Jefferson Establishment.[59]

Reviews of *The Jefferson Scandals* were decidedly mixed. *The New Yorker* called Dabney a "well-known journalist and historian" who "courteously yet firmly" presented the verifiable facts. *The New York Times* called him "a respected journalist with a long and strong record as a civil rights advocate," who, "despite a slight tone of protesting too much, is reasonable in his research." Others were more critical. *Commentary* reviewer Peter Shaw complained that Dabney "approached the subject as an apologist rather than a disinterested historian" and that he tended to "substitute a tone of sarcasm for a careful exposition of the flaws in Mrs. Brodie's book." In his zeal to defend Jefferson against the charge of miscegenation, Dabney missed "the broader implications of Sally Hemings's presence at Monticello—a matter of far greater import than the titillating question of her relationship to Jefferson." Dabney also shirked his responsibility by failing to explore the role of professional historians in promoting popular acceptance of the book. "The historians were obviously clear in their own minds about the factitiousness of Mrs. Brodie's account," Shaw wrote. "But they also knew that Mrs. Brodie had made something of a feminist issue out of her case. She had represented herself as entering a male bastion of Jefferson studies and bringing to a specifically feminine appreciation of 'feeling' and 'nuance.' To attack a book making such a claim in 1974 was to invite nothing but trouble." Shaw said historians were also reluctant, for similar reasons, to criticize Chase-Riboud's "novelization" when it came out in 1979. "At that point, to attack a novel that was at once a cry of outrage against male oppressors and an apotheosis of Sally Hemings as Jefferson's most intimate companion hardly made for an attractive prospect." Shaw concluded that the "true" Jefferson scandal lay in the "abrogation of scholarly responsibilities" by professional historians who held their tongues for fear of a feminist backlash.[60]

The debate over the Sally Hemings novel and television series taught Chase-Riboud something about the claims people made to the American past. "I have learned it is one thing to write a book and explore a character. But I have also learned about the presumed rights to interpret American history, even fictionally. Some people think this is a one-race, one-culture, one-sex country, or at least theirs is the only outlook. But I think they got more upset when they learned the vast public would see this story on television."[61]

In 1981, Malone himself was asked to serve as a consultant on a miniseries about Jefferson, an eight- to ten-hour production "ala *Masada* or *Roots.*" The producer, Clifford Campion, pitched the miniseries as "an opportunity to get the story of this great man out to the public." Malone was intrigued, but he had strong reservations about the mini-series format: "I am somewhat appalled by the prospect of a treatment of Jefferson's entire career since it took me a generation and six volumes to cover it." Malone would not consider lending his name to the miniseries unless he could review the contents and reject what he considered specious. Campion, for his part, was not about to let a scholar decide what should or should not go into a television movie. "A responsible producer lives and dies by his research support," he wrote. "Furthermore, the rules of docu-drama require accuracy and integrity. By the same token, I, as any producer in Hollywood, must have the latitude to express what might have happened given a set of facts and circumstances." Malone eventually begged off from the project, saying he could not sell his name. "You would not want me to do that." [62]

In 1984, two years before his death, Malone made a startling concession in an interview with *The New York Times*. "Gesturing with his big hands, Dr. Malone said that what struck him as most speculative and unhistorical in the Brodie version was not that Jefferson might have slept with Hemings but rather that he had carried on the affair with her in Paris and later as President for years on end. A sexual encounter, on the other hand, could neither be proved nor disproved, he conceded, adding, 'it might have happened once or twice.'" [63]

VI

In the early 1980s, the board of the Thomas Jefferson Memorial Foundation—the nonprofit organization that owns and operates Monticello—decided to delegate more responsibility to professionals. Daniel P. Jordan, a Virginia Commonwealth University professor of history who had studied with Merrill Peterson at the University of Virginia, took over as director in 1985. Jordan wanted Monticello to become less of a monument and more of an educational center. He began to build a larger staff, with departments of research, restoration, and education. Using information about Monticello slave life gathered from ongoing archaeological excavation and in-house research on the Hemings family, the staff attempted to give slavery a more prominent place in tours, the gift shop, and the new Visitors Center. Displays were created to acknowledge the presence and celebrate the skills of slaves at Monticello. House guides were instructed to discuss slavery during at least three (now four) of the nine stops on the tour; they were also urged to use anecdotes about members of the Hemings family, particularly John and James, and to avoid sounding defensive when answering questions about Sally. The education department developed a teacher resource packet on plantation life and an ambitious unit called "Finding Isaac Jefferson: A Monticello Slave." [64]

Despite the attempts of Monticello staff to provide a fuller and more balanced view of Jefferson and slavery, some visitors suspected the full story remained untold. They would often unnerve the guides—especially those who prided themselves on their candor—by suggesting that the subject of

Sally Hemings was still taboo. Yet, the subject *was* sensitive, even if it was no longer taboo. Some guides found the subject of miscegenation distasteful, especially when it involved Jefferson; others felt that to mention an unproven charge gave it a legitimacy it did not deserve. Officially, Monticello acknowledged the popular appeal of the story, but sided with the Jefferson scholars who discounted it. The first visitors' guide to Mulberry Row, prepared by research director Lucia Stanton in the late 1980s, discussed the Hemings story and its origins with matter-of-fact directness:

> Sally Hemings' name became linked to Jefferson's in 1802, when an embittered journalist published the allegation that she was Jefferson's mistress and bore him a number of children. This story, which Jefferson privately denied, continues to capture the public imagination. Although it is impossible to prove either side of the question, most Jefferson scholars discount the truth of such a liaison.[65]

The newly professionalized Monticello administration, self-consciously adopting the cautious standards of scholarship, hoped the pamphlet would finally put the charges of evasion to rest.

When African-American civil rights activist and politician Jesse Jackson visited in 1990 with three of his children, however, he told the local newspaper that the description of the Hemings relationship in the Mulberry Row pamphlet was inadequate, far too defensive, in fact, "a real propaganda sheet. I mean it's a very opinionated paragraph." To call the journalist "embittered," Jackson charged, "is a very political, prejudicial statement." Jordan responded that "since the story can't be proven, Monticello cannot arbitrarily proclaim it to be true."[66]

Jackson did not want the Hemings story to be featured as evidence of the hypocrisy and cruelty of Jefferson, the motive white scholars had so often attributed to African-Americans who publicized the story. Rather, Jackson saw the Hemings story as an example of the dilemma facing Jefferson and other white slaveholders who shared his racial beliefs and moral opposition to slavery. Jefferson's "exalted treatment" of Sally Hemings and her siblings reflected his uneasiness with slavery. While Jefferson "couldn't make the political break with the institution," Jackson was quoted as saying, "he made the personal break." The Mulberry Row pamphlet did nothing to ease his suspicion that Monticello was hiding the truth about Sally Hemings. What the Monticello staff saw as a balanced statement on the Hemings relationship, Jackson saw as "an attempt to pour sand over history."[67]

Despite its efforts to address the subject of slavery more openly, Monticello still seemed defensive on the subject of race. Several critics complained that Monticello viewed the past from a white perspective, and thus ignored the perspective of the blacks, both as historical figures and as present-day visitors. Leni Ashmore Sorensen, a local historical interpreter, argued that blacks were "invisible" at Monticello. "The continuing embarrassment over Sally Hemings and the various myths that have grown up around her seem to have paralyzed any effort to build a strong black interpretation into the program at Monticello," she wrote in *Off the Fence,* a local alternative newspaper. Noting the dearth of black administrators, guides, and researchers at Monticello, Sorensen argued that the museum missed "the encouragement and potential public support to grapple with the facts, the mythology and the impact of miscegenation in America." [68]

Mark Bograd, a white anthropologist at the National Museum of Natural History, also objected to the way in which slavery was presented at Monticello. From his point of view, Jefferson's moral opposition to slavery, so often stressed at Monticello, was "beside the point," even "offensive." The whole "wolf by the ears" approach focuses on "the moral discomfort of these slaveowners," defines "the experience of slavery from their perspectives, not from the perspectives of those they owned. Tourists are being told about metaphysical quandaries when they should be told about the physical reality of slave life." Bograd asked what critics had been asking since the 1960s: "Why do we need to purify our heroes, to justify or explain belatedly their actions when they do not meet with contemporary standards?" Such evasions at the shrines of the founding fathers "suggest a shallow faith in the greatness of these men. Are their achievements and images unable to take the tarnish of slavery?" [69]

Apparently. In 1990, the columnist George Will named Jefferson the "Person of the Millennium," declaring that Jefferson "is what a free person looks like—confident, serene, rational, disciplined, temperate, tolerant, curious." Jefferson, Will proclaimed, expressed the "American idea" not "only in stirring cadences, but also in the way he lived, as statesman, scientist, architect, educator." Slaveholding went unmentioned. [70] A new film shown at the Monticello Visitors Center describes slavery as a "shadow" over Jefferson's legacy, but is followed with former president Jimmy Carter explaining that Jefferson could not have "survived" as a "farmer" without slavery. Viewers who might be disturbed by the fact that Jefferson was a slaveholder are consoled by the message that Jefferson planted the seeds for liberation movements around the world, including the civil rights movement. The minute or so devoted to slavery is counterbalanced with more than half an hour on other aspects of Jefferson's life. None of the slaves who spent their lives on Monticello is mentioned by name. The film's focus on Jefferson's political ideas and public life is intended to complement the display on slave life at the Visitors Center, but viewers must make that connection themselves.[71]

It is not clear what visitors think about Jefferson, race, and slavery, or how deeply all the debates, articles, and books have penetrated. The administrators at Monticello do not find many angry notes in their suggestion box, nor do many of the tourists who trek to Charlottesville confront their guides or write letters of complaint when they get back home. Still, enough ask questions about Sally Hemings to suggest that the story has a firm hold on the American imagination.

A kind of schizophrenia surrounds Jefferson. On the one hand, opinion-makers, when the occasion seems to demand, sing the praises of Jefferson without reservation, celebrating the architect of freedom, and many people apparently agree. On the other hand, the public seems fixated on Sally Hemings, the subject of popular plays, novels, and even juvenile fiction. It is almost as if the public Jefferson and private Jefferson have gone their own separate ways, each embarked on a strange career of his own.[72]

The 250th anniversary of Jefferson's birth in 1993 inevitably calls for a reassessment of the man and his legacy. As was true with the recent bicentennials of the Revolution and Constitution, such reassessments are likely to be both inspired and provoked by celebratory and commemorative public events. The contrast between the current round of festivities and the somber and understated World War II commemoration could not be more striking. Monticello and a consortium of other historical organizations have planned more than two hundred activities spread out over more than a year. Many of these observances undoubtedly will evoke the usual patriotic hoopla. But it is a remarkable sign of these times that Monticello and the University of Virginia—the institutions most closely associated with Jefferson—have taken advantage of the anniversary to demonstrate their critical engagement with Jefferson's most problematic legacy, his record on race and slavery.

In 1943, on the bicentennial of Jefferson's birth, the university contented itself with installing some glass display boxes in its library. A much more elaborate program is now underway in commemoration of Jefferson's 250th birthday. The first major event, an ambitious academic conference, was scheduled for October of 1992, partly to permit the publication of this volume in April 1993 and partly to avoid overlapping with Monticello's larger celebration. A public television crew captured the events at the university, creating a verbatim record and collecting footage for future documentaries.

The Jeffersonian Legacies Conference was largely the work of Peter Onuf, who recently succeeded to Merrill Peterson's position in the history department. Having established his reputation not as a student of Jefferson himself, but as a student of Jefferson's era, Onuf hardly embodied the image of the "Jefferson establishment." As conference organizer, he struck a distinctly nonreverential air: sessions would consider the full range of Jefferson's legacies. As the brochure for the conference declared, "Our intention is to honor Thomas Jefferson by taking his ideas and his career seriously. But the conference will also explore the more ambiguous and, in the case of slavery and race relations, even tragic dimension of his legacy. Only by such an honest and open-ended accounting can the Jeffersonian tradition in American public culture be sustained and renewed." By and large, the scholars who were recruited to the conference were well known not so much for their specific knowledge of Jefferson as for their broader studies of the eighteenth and early nineteenth centuries. Merrill Peterson, retired from the university and hard at work on his study of the image of Abraham Lincoln in the American mind, chose to play only a limited role. It was time for another generation to reckon with the Jeffersonian image.

When conference participants convened in Charlottesville, a certain wary excitement provided the dominant tone. Few considered themselves Jefferson scholars in the distinguished tradition of Dumas Malone and Merrill Peterson. The days when biographies of great men ruled the academy had long passed. If many of these academicians clearly admired Jefferson, they were leery of becoming either banal and uncritical celebrants or anachronistic and ahistorical critics. Not surprisingly, complexity, ambiguity, and unanticipated consequences recurred as the conference's leitmotifs. It is perhaps also not surprising that positions on race and slavery became the measure of how "honest" speakers, sessions, the conference, the university—establishment America—were.

Despite the explicitly critical themes of the conference, the notion of a "Jefferson establishment" continued to cast a long shadow in the public perception. A member of the audience asked civil rights activist Julian Bond, who gave a glowing tribute to the power of Jefferson's words, whether the history department had given him any trouble about his comments. Even the academics half-jokingly commented on the risks of saying anything negative about "Mr. Jefferson" in Charlottesville. Yet the actual situation was quite different—perhaps, on race and slavery, even the reverse. No one stood up to defend Jefferson; those who insisted on putting his slaveholding in context took pains to make sure their comments were not taken as veiled defense of the indefensible. With the "establishment" thus neutralized, many of the discussions—especially the one on race and slavery—seemed unfocused and adrift. Instead of generating lively debate, Jefferson's record on race produced little more than the sounds of muffled agreement.

The press had a difficult time reckoning with this situation. The reporters who came to Charlottesville were looking for a story, a plot line that would sustain interest in the proceedings. Most of them focused on race and slavery, the issues that were sure to provoke the most debate. The Charlottesville *Daily Progress* began its preview of the six-day conference with this provocative question, "How did a slave-holding aristocrat, who believed blacks were inferior, come to inspire the civil rights movement and freedom-seeking revolutions through the world?" The reporter, Jim Denery, portrayed the invited scholars as myth-busters, out to destroy one-dimensional images of Jefferson. He noted that several of the papers prepared for the conference dealt with slavery. "There will be some sparks," he quoted Onuf as predicting, "because this situation hits close to home."[73]

The Washington Post was far more droll about the conference, portraying it as a scholarly sideshow to the 1992 presidential campaign, a public discussion of "the character issues" that still haunted "one of our greatest presidents." In a breezy article entitled "Thomas Jefferson, Tarnished Icon?" feature writer Joel Achenbach parodied the kinds of questions that twentieth-century scholars were asking of the nineteenth-century president. "Was he a hypocrite? Self-indulgent? A deficit spender? Did he take a slave, Sally Hemings, as his mistress? (*Sally,* they call her around here, as though she might walk in the door.)" The writer poked fun at the irreverent tone of the conference, quoting the words of one "dyspeptic professor," then declaring: "What tough times these are for icons!"[74]

After attending two days of seminars and lectures, Achenbach concluded that the Jefferson conference was not as radical or subversive as one might think, given its emphasis on race and slavery. "For the most part Jefferson has been lauded and praised; Jefferson scholars are hardly a spittle-spewing, stink-bomb–throwing bunch. But inevitably they have to deal with the not trivial problem of his attitudes toward blacks, women, Native Americans and just about anyone else who was not part of the white, male, property-owning elite." Achenbach characterized the scholars assembled for the conference as "a rather conservative group," hemmed in by the cautious standards of their own discipline. "An academic conference can be a tedious affair," Achenbach wrote. "There is a proliferation of nuance; scholars never met a nuance they didn't like. When things get slow, when the contextualization gets thick, it is easy to see the appeal of the screaming diatribe. It's exciting!" Achenbach proceeded to paraphrase the comments of Rhys Isaac, a white scholar who scolded his fellow conferees (most of them white) for ignoring the Jeffersonian legacy of inequality: "What about blacks? Women? Native Americans? What about the fact that we still haven't achieved reasonable equity among these groups?" Achenbach contrasted the present-minded concerns of Isaac with the more historically contextualized views of Gordon Wood, who called Jefferson "a man of his time—let's not ask him to be something he wasn't." Achenbach himself adopted the cool pose of the self-aware liberal, able to face the past without preaching or posturing: "The record shows that Jefferson had beliefs that are abhorrent to modern sensibilities," he wrote, suggesting that the record could—and should—speak for itself.[75]

The *Richmond Times Dispatch,* the only major newspaper to cover the much-hyped Saturday conference entitled "Jefferson, Race, and Slavery," focused on the dramatic appearance of a Hemings family descendant, Robert H. Cooley III, who informed the assembled scholars that the Hemings story was "not a story. It's true." Cooley offered himself and his family as "living proof that Jefferson had an affair with his slave," the newspaper reported. Cooley complained that the oral tradition of his family was not good enough for Monticello, which insisted upon documentary evidence. "We couldn't write then," he explained. "We were slaves." Cooley suggested that Jefferson's white children destroyed any records of his relationship with Sally Hemings after his death. "I doubt if there was any shred of a record remaining." The *Times-Dispatch* reporter contrasted the certainty of Cooley with the quibbling of the scholars, who "discussed the question" but provided no definitive answers. The only panelist to take a strong position on the matter was Bernadine Simmons, the community affairs director for a Richmond television station. She was quoted as saying that it was not difficult to imagine "a relationship between Thomas Jefferson and a comely quadroon on his plantation," despite the lack of definitive evidence. Both Simmons and Cooley spoke with the cultural authority of African-Americans speaking on African-American history, something the white scholars on the panel were loathe to challenge.[76]

The day after the panel discussion, both the Richmond and Charlottesville papers ran an Associated Press story about new archaeological evidence that tended to confirm the "strong connection" between the Jefferson family and the Hemings family. "After 13 years of digging around three Jefferson houses," the wire service reported, "William Kelso is considering more seriously the often-discounted stories that the United States' third president had children with Sally Hemings, one of his slaves." Both newspapers found it newsworthy that the chief archaeologist at Monticello, the last bastion of the Jefferson establishment, was willing to reconsider the plausibility of the Hemings story, based on new evidence. The Jefferson establishment no longer seemed able—or willing—to present the public with a pristine image of the founding father.[77]

It was left to Julian Bond, a black activist and veteran of the civil rights movement, to answer the question that the local newspaper had used to frame the conference: How did a slave-holding aristocrat, who believed blacks were inferior, come to inspire freedom-seeking revolutions throughout the world? Bond showed how Jefferson's words in the Declaration of Independence could be invoked to transcend—or overlook—Jefferson's bigotry. In Bond's interpretation, the true Jeffersonian legacy was the best one, the one that surmounted his own parochialism, racism, and slaveholding. It was, ironically, an interpretation reminiscent of Dumas Malone's, in which the real Jefferson is the one we want and need. Those who claimed descent from Jefferson and Sally Hemings spoke, too, from a hopeful vision, one in which a white man and a black woman transcended the social and cultural boundaries that separated them and bequeathed a proud, if complex legacy to their progeny.

When Thomas Jefferson died, he could not know with any certainty that his enduring legacy would be found in his noblest words rather than in his worst example. The inscription Jefferson wrote for his tombstone testified to his determination that he be remembered not for his entanglement in slavery but for his ideals of liberty and enlightenment. And he has been. But a different outcome on the battlefields at Antietam or Gettysburg might have rendered Jefferson's slaveholding and his racial theorizing more relevant to the twentieth century than his words in the Declaration of Independence. Thomas Jefferson's legacy might well have been other than the legacy we choose to remember in 1993.

NOTES

We would like to thank the following people at Monticello for answering our questions and for providing us with documents related to the evolving interpretation of race and slavery at the historic home of Thomas Jefferson: Daniel P. Jordan, executive director; Libby Fosso, public relations; Elizabeth Taylor, head guide; Cinder Stanton and Kristin Onuf, research; and Linda Lisanti, education. We would also like to thank our colleagues in the Corcoran Department of History and all those who participated in the Jeffersonian Legacies Conference. We are especially grateful to Peter Onuf, James Lewis, Charles Miller, Lee Quinby, Peter Kastor, and Michael Ackerman for their helpful comments on an earlier version of this paper. Our closest advisors, Ruhi Grover and Abby Ayers, encouraged us and inspired us throughout this project. Finally, we would like to thank the late Dumas Malone for trusting us with his papers.

1. The classic account is Merrill D. Peterson, *The Jefferson Image in the American Mind* (New York, 1960).

2. *The New York Times,* April 14, 1943, pp. 1, 16; Dumas Malone, "The Jefferson Faith," *Saturday Review,* 26 (April 13, 1943), p. 4. The black newspapers of Richmond and Baltimore did not cover the event.

3. Gunnar Myrdal, *An American Dilemma: The Negro Problem and Modern Democracy* (1944; reprint, New York, 1962), p. 90.

4. Dumas Malone, "The South in American Achievement," undated manuscript, Malone papers, Alderman Library, University of Virginia. For a published version of this thesis, see "The Geography of American Achievement," *The Atlantic,* 154 (December 1934), pp. 669–79.

5. Malone, "The Jefferson Faith," p. 6; Malone to John T. Caldwell, president of the University of Arkansas, Dec. 20, 1958. Malone loathed the idea of activist scholarship. Commenting on August Meier's dissertation, "Negro Thought on the Race Problem in America in the Age of Booker T. Washington," Malone wrote: "What most impressed me about this work, besides its thoroughness, was the balanced judgment of the writer. Dealing as he has with a very controversial topic, he showed the utmost fairness. He does not approach this problem as a propagandist but as a genuine scholar." (Malone to the American Council of Learned Societies, March 11, 1958.) Malone did not, however, object to political activism by scholars. As a member of the University of Virginia faculty in the early 1960s, Malone agreed to sign an ad pledging to boycott a segregated theater. "We wanted the list to be headed by some of the most distinguished members of the faculty," recalled Professor Paul Gaston, who helped to organize the boycott. "There weren't many in that category we could persuade to sign, but we knew we could count on probably the most distinguished— Professor Dumas Malone, the Jefferson scholar. I called him and asked him if he would have his name at the head of the list. And he said he would, but he felt a little hypocritical about that. And I said, 'Why, Dumas?' And he said, 'Well, you know, Elizabeth and I never go to the movies.' But I persuaded him, so his name went on the list, and several years later, he called me up and he said, 'Paul, Elizabeth and I want to go to the movies. Are we still boycotting?'" (Excerpted from "Sitting in in the Sixties," lecture by Paul Gaston, Charlottesville, Virginia, 1985.)

6. "The Way of the Scholar," undated manuscript (1934–1935?), Malone papers; "The South in American Achievement," undated manuscript, Malone papers.

7. C. Vann Woodward, *The Strange Career of Jim Crow* (New York, 1974), pp. xv–xviii. Woodward sided much more closely with the civil rights movement than he let on. In 1953, he agreed to write a monograph on the origins of the Fourteenth Amendment for the NAACP Legal Defense Fund, which was seeking historical evidence to buttress its argument in the landmark Supreme Court case *Brown* v. *Board of Education.* In agreeing to help, Woodward stressed that he would have to work within the constraints of his discipline, which adhered to strict standards of evidence and frowned upon advocacy. "You see, I do not want to be in a position of writing a gratuitous history lecture for the Court. And at

the same time I do not want to get out of my role as historian." John A. Davis, who headed the research task force, assured Woodward that he would have full autonomy: "Your conclusions are your own. If they do not help our side of the case, in all probability the lawyers will not use them. If they do help our argument, the present plan is to include them in our overall summary argument and to file the whole work in an appendix. No matter what happens, your work will be of real educational value to the men who must argue before the Court." Richard Kluger, *Simple Justice: The History of Brown v. Board of Education and Black America's Struggle for Equality* (New York, 1975), pp. 623–24.

8. Ibid., p. xvii.

9. "Thomas Jefferson's Negro Grandchildren," *Ebony,* 10 (November 1954), p. 78.

10. Ibid.

11. This became obvious to W. Edward Farrison, a black English teacher at North Carolina College, who interviewed several Hemings family descendants for a 1954 article on the origins of William Wells Brown's *Clotel,* a nineteenth-century novel based on the Hemings story. After surveying a variety of documentary sources, none of them conclusive, Farrison noted "the quiet stream of family history" that originated with Sally Hemings herself: "In September, 1948, in their modest home in Cambridge, Massachusetts, I talked at length with three sisters who were obviously far from being full-blooded Negroes, each of whom was more than sixty-five years of age, and who traced their lineage directly to Sally Hemings through her daughter Harriet, who was born in May, 1801, and whose father those sisters had been told was Thomas Jefferson. They had also been informed that Jefferson had once taken Sally Hemings to France 'to nurse his eight-year-old daughter.' Neither of those sisters had ever heard of Callender, Jefferson's plantation records, Mrs. Abigail Adams' letters, or any of the other references to Jefferson which I have cited. They had heard of Brown but knew practically nothing about any of his books." W. Edward Farrison, "The Origin of Brown's *Clotel,*" *Phylon,* 15 (1954), p. 354.

12. Trevor Colbourn, ed., *Fame and the Founding Fathers: Essays by Douglass Adair* (New York, 1974), p. 167.

13. Ibid., pp. 161, 169.

14. Douglass Adair to John Cook Wyllie, Aug. 28, 1960; Wyllie to Adair, Sept. 15, 1960, miscellaneous Adair papers ("The Jefferson Scandals" [1960]), Alderman Library, University of Virginia. Malone himself made an oblique reference to the Hemings story in a 1956 *New York Times Magazine* article: "In later years, political enemies spread wild stories, but there is no evidence that [Jefferson] was ever corrupted by the exercise of arbitrary power under a system he always deplored. His relations with his slaves were marked by no cruelty or sensuality. He was a responsible master in the best patriarchal tradition."

15. Pearl M. Graham, "Sally Hemings and Thomas Jefferson," *The Journal of Negro History,* 44 (1961), pp. 89–103; Winthrop D. Jordan, *White Over Black: American Attitudes Toward the Negro, 1550–1812* (Chapel Hill, N.C., 1968), p. 465n.

16. Peterson, *Jefferson Image in the American Mind,* pp. 186–87.

17. Malcolm X, *On Afro-American History,* 3rd ed. (New York, 1990), pp. 39–40; Martin Luther King, Jr., *Why We Can't Wait* (New York, 1964), p. 88.

18. *The New York Times,* March 31, 1973, p. 35.

19. Malone, "Mr. Jefferson and the Living Generation," *The American Scholar,* 41 (1972), pp. 587–98.

20. Jordan, *White Over Black,* pp. 465, 481.

21. Fawn M. Brodie, "The Political Hero in America," *The Virginia Quarterly Review,* 46 (1970), pp. 57–60.

22. *The Los Angeles Times,* May 31, 1970; Jack P. Greene, "The Sixty-Fourth Annual Meeting of the Organization of American Historians," *Journal of American History,* 58 (1971), p. 703.

23. Fawn M. Brodie, "Jefferson Biographers and the Psychology of Canonization," *The Journal of Interdisciplinary History,* 2 (1971), p. 161.

24. Ibid., p. 170.

25. Eric L. McKitrick, "The View from Jefferson's Camp," *The New York Review of Books,* 15 (Dec. 17, 1970), pp. 35–38.

26. For "oddballs" quote, see Edwin M. Yoder Jr., "An Unshaken Hero," *National Review,* 26 (May 10, 1974), p. 542.

27. *The New York Times Book Review,* April 7, 1974, pp. 1–2; ibid., May 12, 1974, p. 42.

28. Murat Williams, "Beyond the Story of Sally Hemings," *The Daily Progress* (Charlottesville, Va.), May 11, 1975.

29. Malone to the editor of *The Daily Progress,* undated, Malone papers.

30. "I generally avoid direct reference to her work in order not to exaggerate its importance," Malone to Edwin M. Yoder Jr., Oct. 11, 1976. *The New York Times Book Review,* May 5, 1974, p. 2; Malone, "Jefferson's Private Life," *The New York Times,* May 10, 1974, p. 31.

31. Virginius Dabney to Malone, Oct. 12, 1974. In the same letter, Dabney revealed that he had nominated Malone for a Pulitzer Prize. Noting that journalists sat on the board of trustees, Dabney said: "I find that ten of them are my personal friends, and I trust that will not ruin your chances. You should have had this and other awards years ago." Dabney himself won the Pulitzer Prize for editorial writing in 1948.

32. Malone to Dabney, Nov. 18, 1974, Malone papers.

33. Dabney to Malone, Feb. 14, 1975; Malone to Dabney, Feb. 12, 1975; Dabney to Malone, Feb. 14, 1975, Malone papers. *Time,* 105 (March 3, 1975), 67; Dabney to Malone, Feb. 28, 1975; Malone to Dabney, March 3, 1975, Malone papers.

34. For coverage of the Pulitzer Prize awards, see *The New York Times,* May 5, 1975, p. 1. For cottage-cheese story, see *The New York Times,* Aug. 6, 1975, p. 24; for coverage of the "Woman of the Year" ceremony, see the *Los Angeles Times,* March 11, 1975, section II, p. 1.

35. Garry Wills, "Uncle Thomas's Cabin," *The New York Review of Books,* 21 (April 18, 1974), pp. 26–28.

36. Edwin M. Yoder, Jr., "An Unshaken Hero," *National Review,* 26 (May 10, 1974), p. 542.

37. Julian P. Boyd, letter to the editor of the Princeton University *Alumni Weekly,* undated copy, Malone papers.

38. Malone to Boyd, July 23, 1974.

39. Curtis Nettels to Malone, Feb. 17, 1975; Dabney to Malone, Dec. 13, 1975, Malone papers. Carlyle C. Douglas, "The Dilemma of Thomas Jefferson," *Ebony,* 30 (August 1975), p. 61.

40. *The New York Times,* Oct. 14, 1975, p. 27.

41. Thomas A. Greenfield, "Race and Passive Voice at Monticello," *The Crisis,* 82 (April 1975), pp. 146–47; for a letter seconding his opinion, see the November 1975 issue, p. 370.

42. Douglas, "The Dilemma of Thomas Jefferson," *Ebony,* 30 (Aug. 1975), pp. 61–64, and "Should Blacks Celebrate the Bicentennial?" pp. 36–41. Also see O. C. Bobby Daniels, "The Bicentennial: Contradictions in American Democracy," *The Black Scholar,* 7 (1976),

pp. 2–6; Joseph Carpenter, "The Bicentennial and the Black Revolution: Is it a Myth or a Reality?" *Negro History Bulletin,* 39 (1976), pp. 496–99.

43. Douglas, "The Dilemma of Thomas Jefferson," *Ebony,* 30 (August 1975), p. 62.

44. Dumas Malone and Steven H. Hochman, "A Note on Evidence: The Personal History of Madison Hemings," *Journal of Southern History,* 61 (November 1975), pp. 523–28.

45. John Chester Miller, *The Wolf by the Ears: Thomas Jefferson and Slavery* (New York, 1977), p. 176; David Brion Davis, "Self-Evident Truths?" *The New York Times Book Review,* Nov. 13, 1977, p. 9.

46. Barbara Chase-Riboud, *Sally Hemings: A Novel* (New York, 1979). Chase-Riboud dedicated her novel "to the enigma of the historical Sally Hemings."

47. Dumas Malone to Robert A. Daly, Jan. 18, 1979, Malone papers. Merrill Peterson to William S. Paley, Jan. 16, 1979. Malone asked Julian Boyd and Virginius Dabney to write letters to CBS as well. "There seems to be a possibility that we can stop the series," Malone wrote to Dabney, "but even if we cannot stop it, we can certainly insist that it be presented as fiction." Malone to Dabney, Jan. 23, 1979, Malone papers.

48. Viking Press Catalog, 1979, p. 49; Malone to Irving Goodman, Jan. 19, 1979; Alan D. Williams to Malone, Jan. 24, 1979.

49. The *Richmond Times Dispatch,* Feb. 11, 1979, p. 1; *The Washington Post,* Feb. 13, 1979, p. C-1; *The Cavalier Daily,* Feb. 23, 1979, p. 2; *The Cavalier Daily,* Feb. 19, 1979, p. 2. Most press accounts of the controversy poked fun at the reaction of the Virginia historians: "Now, several historians in Virginia are fuming over the latest 'attack' upon the beloved native son." *Chicago Tribune,* July 3, 1979, section 2, p. 1.

50. *Richmond Times Dispatch,* Feb. 11, 1979, p. 1; *The Washington Post,* Feb. 13, 1979, p. C-1; *The Cavalier Daily,* Feb. 16, 1979, p. 1; Feb. 23, 1979, p. 2; Feb. 19, 1979, p. 2.

51. Malone to Harold J. Coolidge, March 8, 1979; Dabney to Malone, March 11, 1979; E. K. Meade Jr. to Coolidge, April 5, 1979, Malone papers.

52. The Detroit *Free Press,* April 1979; Virginius Dabney and Jon Kukla, "The Monticello Scandals: History and Fiction," *Virginia Cavalcade* 29 (Autumn 1979), p. 53.

53. *The New York Times,* Oct. 22, 1979, p. C-15; *The Black Scholar* 11 (1980); *The Journal of Negro History,* 65 (1980), p. 275; *The Sun* (Baltimore, Md.), July 10, 1979, p. B-1.

54. *Chicago Tribune,* July 3, 1979, section 2, p. 6; *The New York Times,* Oct. 27, 1979, p. C-15.

55. *The Daily Progress,* June 27, 1979, p. B-1.

56. Dabney to Malone, Dec. 2, 1979; Malone to Dabney, Dec. 5, 1979, Malone papers.

57. Dabney to Malone, March 14, 1980, Malone papers.

58. Dabney to Malone, March 22, 1980; Malone to Dabney, April 16, 1980; Frank L. Hereford, Jr., to Malone, April 3, 1980; Malone to Dabney, April 16, 1980, Malone papers.

59. Dabney to Malone, March 14, 1980, Malone papers; Virginius Dabney, *The Jefferson Scandals* (New York, 1981), pp. 113–19.

60. *The New Yorker,* 57 (Aug. 17, 1981), p. 107; *The New York Times,* Aug. 11, 1981, p. C-11; *Commentary,* 72 (Nov. 1981), pp. 100–102. The view of Dabney as a strong civil rights advocate was not shared by Paul Gaston, a University of Virginia professor who participated in the movement. In a 1979 review of Dabney's memoirs, *Across the Years,* Gaston commented on Dabney's "inability to accept—and therefore seriously probe—the most important transformation of southern society, the black liberation movement. There is no hint in his memoirs that he sees similarities between that movement and the struggles

for liberty of his white ancestors, including Thomas Jefferson. As an authentic patrician he is happy that 'our black citizens' are treated better than they once were, but he cannot truly admire the black and white people who made that circumstance possible." *The South Atlantic Quarterly,* 78 (Summer 1979), pp. 401–2.

61. *The Washington Post,* June 15, 1979, p. B-6.

62. Clifford Campion to Malone, Aug. 12, 1981; Malone to Campion, Oct. 23, 1981; Campion to Malone, Nov. 23, 1981; Malone to Campion, Dec. 11, 1981. Malone would have been paid handsomely for his name—between $25,000 and $40,000 for each two-hour segment. Roger Donald to Malone, Sept. 29, 1981, Malone papers.

63. *The New York Times,* July 4, 1984, p. C-9.

64. Some staff members say pressure for these changes came from the bottom up, with varying degrees of resistance. Others say the administration responded to pressure from outside, sometimes without a clear sense of purpose. A full history of the changes at Monticello is beyond the scope of this article.

65. "Mulberry Row: The story of Monticello's plantation industries and workers, both slave and free, with a self-guided tour," published by the Thomas Jefferson Memorial Foundation, 1990.

66. *The Daily Progress,* Nov. 25, 1990.

67. *The Daily Progress,* Nov. 25, 1990, p. 14.

68. Leni Ashmore Sorensen, "Are We There Yet?: Black Presence at Local Historic Museums," *Off the Fence* 1 (Fall 1991), pp. 1, 8–9.

69. Mark Bograd, "Apologies Excepted: Facing Up to Slavery at Historic House Museums," *History News,* 47 (1992), pp. 20–21.

70. George Will, "Winner of Person of the Millennium is . . ." *Daily Progress,* Dec. 16, 1990.

71. "Thomas Jefferson and the Pursuit of Liberty," videocassette of film shown at Monticello Visitors Center, Thomas Jefferson Memorial Foundation, Inc., 1991.

72. Garry Wills, "Uncle Thomas's Cabin," pp. 26–28; on "humanizing" Jefferson, see the introduction of Granville Burgess, *Dusky Sally,* a play (New York, 1987), p. xiii.

73. *The Daily Progress,* Oct. 4, 1992, p. 1.

74. *The Washington Post,* Oct. 17, 1992, p. D-1.

75. Ibid., pp. D-1, D-4.

76. *Richmond Times Dispatch,* Oct. 18, 1992, pp. A-1, A-10.

77. *Richmond Times Dispatch,* Oct. 18, 1992, p. A-10.

Afterword

MERRILL D. PETERSON

Americans have been assessing and reassessing and fighting over the legacy of Thomas Jefferson from the hour of his death on July 4, 1826, the fiftieth anniversary of the Declaration of Independence. Such an event could not but be seen as providential, more especially as his fellow revolutionary, John Adams, hundreds of miles away in Massachusetts, passed away on the same day. Providence had decreed, said Edward Everett in his eulogy of the departed sages, "that the revolutionary age of America be closed up, by a scene as illustriously affecting as its commencement was appalling and terrific."

It was the so-called one-party period of American politics. However, that one party, the Democratic-Republican party of which Jefferson was the honored founder, was splitting apart. A coalition of the politically aggrieved and ambitious who had adopted Andrew Jackson as their leader claimed the Jeffersonian mantle exclusively for themselves. They revived the spirit and tenets of the original party conflict of Republicans and Federalists and cast present-day issues in its terms. Their opponents, beginning with the president, John Quincy Adams, who wished to bury memories of that conflict, were perforce Hamiltonian Federalists in disguise. Calling themselves National Republicans, and later on Whigs, they repeatedly disputed the Jacksonian claim to the Jeffersonian tradition, but it proved a losing battle. According to their political mythology, the ascendant Jacksonian Democrats had returned the wayward government to the righteous foundations laid by Jefferson in 1800. He was their watchword, their polestar, their touchstone, "the highest democratic authority in America." His teachings and writings, gathered in four stout volumes and published in 1829, the year Jackson became president, were said to be "text-books of liberal political principles and axioms from which the modern politician deduces present applications and solutions." What principles and axioms? Individual liberty. Equal rights for all, special privileges for none. Let the people rule. Democratic simplicity. State rights and strict construction. In general, that "sum of good government" Jefferson epitomized in his first inaugural address: "A wise and frugal government, which shall restrain men from injuring one another, which shall leave them otherwise free to regulate their own pursuits of labor and improvement, and shall not take from the mouth of labor the bread it has earned." Political debate went forward in the shadow of the great conflict between Jefferson and Hamilton. To good Jeffersonian Democrats, their hero's highest claim to fame was that he established a political party which permanently fixed the character and destiny of the country.

With the coming of the Civil War, however, this tradition was discredited. Many in the North in 1861 held Jefferson's legacy responsible for secession, disunion, and bloodshed. They hailed the triumph of Union arms as a vindication of Alexander Hamilton's vision of a strong and supreme national government. Jefferson's fame went into eclipse. But it revived with the revival of the Democratic party near the turn of the century. Increasingly, as American democracy was challenged by a new and ruthless industrial order, the problem appeared to be one of adapting the Jeffersonian democratic legacy to new social and economic conditions. In an age of growing concentrations of power, when oppression was the consequence of too much rather than too little liberty, when the aggressions against the individual were likely to arise in the economic rather than the political order—in such an age the old Jeffersonian dogmas of state rights, individualism, and minimal government were incapable of renewing Jefferson's vision of democratic progress. How were the ills of the society to be remedied by recourse to the individualistic tradition whence they came? History had turned Jefferson's political universe upside down, and every liberal and progressive impulse ran toward making the national authority the overlord of certain rights, chiefly those touching property, previously reserved to the states or held to be private. The New Deal of Franklin D. Roosevelt facilitated this crucial transition in the career of the Jefferson symbol and legacy. National power and purpose grew without disturbing the axis of the democratic faith. For all practical purposes, the New Deal ended the historic Jefferson-Hamilton dialogue in American history. It was no longer possible to polarize the traditions; and while political debate might continue to resound to the clashes of old symbols and slogans, they no longer served the old purposes.

During the last half-century or so, the image of Jefferson the Renaissance Man, the multifaceted hero of civilization, has largely eclipsed the political hero. President Roosevelt dedicated the Jefferson Memorial in 1943 to the surest and truest image, Apostle of Freedom. But he realized that the man enshrined in the pantheon transcended politics. Jefferson had come to stand for ideals of beauty, science, and learning enriched by the heritage of the ages, yet distinctly American in outline; and so the president lauded him as one who had "led the steps of America into the paths of the permanent integrity of the Republic." This Jeffersonian legacy had been rediscovered in the twentieth century. The establishment of Monticello as a national shrine in 1923 played an important part in the rediscovery, for the man it disclosed was not the Great Democrat, but the Olympian humanist. Jefferson emerged as a major American prophet of public education in the writings of such democratic-minded educators as John Dewey and James Bryant Conant. As working scientists, they became curious about the American beginnings of inquiry in their fields, and encountered Jefferson at every turn. And so they wrote articles on "Jefferson the Naturalist," "Jefferson the Vaccinator," "Pioneer Botanist," "Pioneer Student of American Geography," "Father of American Paleontology," and so on. Probably the most important discovery made about Jefferson in this century lay in the field of architecture. Fiske Kimball, the premier student, crowned him "the father of our national architecture," and by underscoring his indebtedness to the Renaissance Italian, Andrea Palladio, contributed to the growing appreciation of him as an American Leonardo. Jefferson was a man of parts. Even if his political legacy should fall into disuse, the legacy of the Renaissance Man seemed likely to keep his memory alive.

The papers in this volume treat a variety of subjects. Several of them offer sweeping interpretations of major themes in Jefferson's life. Joyce Appleby directly addresses the question of Jefferson's legacy and finds it complex and even confused by the jangled elements of liberalism and democracy in its composition. Although an unabashed admirer, she wishes Jefferson's unique philosophy of personal freedom had not worked to fragment the community and deprecate and diminish the role of government. Paul Conkin's paper is especially notable for arguing the constancy and authenticity of Jefferson's "religious pilgrimage" over a lifetime. His intense secularism, his hostility to religious establishments and priestly authority of all degrees, has so often been interpreted as hostility to religion itself that one is both pleased and enlightened by this examination of Jefferson's personal pursuit of religious truth. Douglas Wilson's essay offers a

discriminating overview of Jefferson as a man of letters and, at the same
time, provides valuable insights about aspects of his personality: his self-
esteem, his sensitivity to criticism, his extreme reticence before the public.

Jefferson's private world at Monticello, and its implications for his public
life, is the focus of several papers here. Rhys Isaac bravely attempts to
penetrate the mind of the child and the young man for clues to the development of Jefferson's life, a theme first highlighted by the work of a great-
granddaughter, Sarah Nicholas Randolph, *The Domestic Life of Thomas Jefferson,* in 1871. As Jan Lewis observes, Jefferson measured his worth in the
contribution he made to ideas and institutions, not human relationships,
and so has posterity; but this does not gainsay the importance of better
understanding him in relation to family, friends, and slaves. Lucia Stanton's
paper on Jefferson as the slaveholding master of Monticello is, quite simply,
the most authoritative account yet written on that subject. Paul Finkelman
follows with a highly critical assessment of the public side of Jefferson's
involvement with slavery.

Another group of papers treats aspects of Jefferson's political thought
and practice. Jack P. Greene shows how Jefferson's thinking was shaped by
his identity as a Virginian, concerned with reforming and promoting his
state; Stephen A. Conrad offers a fresh reading of Jefferson's first published
work, *Summary View of the Rights of British America* (1774), that questions
the centrality of "rights talk" in his political philosophy. Herbert Sloan, in
his expert examination of Jefferson's radical idea, "The earth belongs in
usufruct to the living generation," argues persuasively that the burden of
private debt under which Jefferson groaned helped shape his theoretical
views on public debt. Michael Lienesch revisits the origins of political parties in the 1790s and concludes that by opening politics to the forces of
public opinion Jefferson was, indeed, the Father of American Democracy.
John L. Larson renders a more equivocal verdict in his treatment of the
problem of the constitutionality of internal improvements: Larson argues
that Jefferson's constitutional scruples, grounded in his "hysterical" fears of
the Federalist corruption, did not advance democratic government, but
disabled it at the start. Walter LaFeber offers an insightful and sympathetic
discussion of Jefferson and foreign affairs.

Two final papers round out the volume. One by Gordon Wood looks at
various facets of the image and puzzles over the problem of identifying the
historical figure behind the Jefferson symbol; but the paper is most illuminating on the disappointments and detachments of the aging Sage of
Monticello. Scot French and Edward Ayers explore several of the themes,

particularly those associated with the civil rights revolution, introduced into the evolving image of Jefferson during the last thirty years.

Among the larger questions that recur in a number of these papers is that of relationship between the public and the private Jefferson. For instance, one might ask what was there about Jefferson's religious quest that caused him to take such a firm stand on separation of church and state? Perhaps nothing, for he might have reached the same position as a Baptist instead of as a Deist. Yet that does not dispose of the question. The conjecture that the private debt Jefferson inherited fueled his theory of generational sovereignty is provocative as well as plausible, but is there evidence that he put the two things together either in moral or political terms? Biographers have found it difficult to subsume the public man and the private master of Monticello under a single set of characteristics. His political enemies, mainly the Federalists and their heirs, believed he was morally corrupt. They denounced him as a blaspheming infidel, a Jacobin visionary, a ruthless demagogue, and a traitor to George Washington. He was incapable of telling right from wrong. Duplicity was his consuming vice, and it originated, said John Quincy Adams, "in his overweening passion for popularity, and his consequent desire to be all things to all men." As a consequence, his political conduct and opinions were tattered tissues of contradiction. Because his character was bad, Jefferson's principles and policies could not be virtuous, and he was unfit to be president of the United States. Occasionally, though not often, the assault invaded Jefferson's well-guarded privacy. The chief instance was the allegation of a miscegenous relationship between Jefferson and a Monticello slave, Sally Hemings. Originating in the political heats generated by the election of 1800, the story had but a brief half-life until it was revived by abolitionists and British travel-writers after Jefferson's death as a telling exhibit of American democracy's complicity in the crime of slavery. It was revived again by a latter-day abolitionist, Fawn Brodie, in her *Thomas Jefferson: An Intimate History,* in 1974, which led many readers to suppose the hoary legend was, in fact, historical truth. By casting a romantic glow over a relationship that on Jefferson's own terms was absolutely abhorrent, Brodie attempted to lift from it the burden of opprobrium it has always carried and allow it to stand as a luminous metaphor of "the American dilemma." But this was fiction, possibly politics, certainly not history. Jefferson's public record with regard to slavery has been repeatedly scrutinized. He believed that he left posterity a legacy of antislavery consonant with his core principles; and many who came after him, including Abraham Lincoln and Martin Luther King, were inspired by that legacy. Yet the record was full of doubts and evasions which, while subject to historical explanation, nevertheless suggested flaws in Jefferson's armor.

Jefferson was a constitutionalist as well as a democrat, and a crucial question about his legacy concerns the nexus between them. Setting forth his theory of "the sovereignty of the living generation" in 1789, Jefferson made it applicable not only to public debt but also to written constitutions. Constitutions—his thinking on the subject developed with regard to state constitutions—rooted in "the consent of the governed" were fundamental instruments of popular government. Jefferson was perhaps the first of the founding fathers to call for popular ratification of constitutions framed in conventions and also for amendment articles to ensure that they embodied the ongoing will of the people. This was a matter on which he differed with his political friend and collaborator, James Madison. In Madison's opinion, too frequent appeals to the people needlessly disturbed the public tranquillity and deprived government of that veneration essential to its stability. But Jefferson castigated "sanctimonious reverence" for constitutions and declared that "laws and institutions must go hand in hand with the progress of the human mind." To this end he recommended provision in a new constitution proposed for Virginia in 1816 giving to each generation, that is by his own calculation every nineteen years, the opportunity to revise the fundamental law. With respect to the United States Constitution, Jefferson advocated regular employment of Article V—the amendment article—and rejected the Hamiltonian doctrine of "implied powers" as a means of accommodating constitutional change. He rejected as well, of course, the authority of the Supreme Court to twist and turn the Constitution to keep it current with changing needs and conditions, for such an approach sapped the foundations of free government in the sovereignty of the people. In retrospect, it has often seemed that Jefferson's "strict constructionism" has crippled the government and, indeed, kept it from responding to the will of the people. Democracy and progress were frustrated by too literal an understanding of the Constitution as a civil contract founded on the "consent of the governed." Thus, as Joyce Appleby remarks, "His way of approaching problems is getting in the way of solving our own." But one had supposed that bridge was crossed with finality fifty years ago when the Roosevelt New Deal accepted the modern resolution of the Jefferson-Hamilton conflict: Hamiltonian means for Jeffersonian ends. This became the formula that was at once capable of dramatizing traditional democratic principles while at the same time strengthening the hand of the national government. The formula solves nothing, yet it continues to offer an approach to problems that is on speaking terms with the political tradition.

This, of course, leads to the larger question of the relevance of Jefferson's legacy 250 years after his birth. Repeatedly during the conference at the University of Virginia, to which the papers in this volume were submitted, panelists spoke of the difficulty of translating Jefferson's ideas and values into an idiom intelligible to the modern mind. Daniel J. Boorstin underscored the problem forty-five years ago in his pathbreaking book, *The Lost World of Thomas Jefferson* (1948). The text of Nature that had confirmed Jefferson's values had, since the Darwinian dispensation, eroded that faith; and the boundlessness of human opportunity afforded by a virginal continent had been succeeded by a densely compacted and collectivized society that controlled and diminished Jefferson's sovereign individual. John Dewey essayed a revision of the Jeffersonian philosophy in the 1930s. In it he reformulated the text of Nature as a text of moral values and goals rooted deeply in the beliefs and aspirations of humankind; and he reformulated freedom, which Jefferson had identified with the state of being an individual, in ways that took account of the organizational imperatives of modern society. This was useful. However, the task of keeping Jefferson's legacy serviceable to the nation as it approaches the twenty-first century remains a challenge to all Americans who remain committed to his vision. Every nation gains strength from a sense of continuity with its past, and the vehicle for that is the symbolism from the past that evoke its ideals. "The art of free society," Alfred North Whitehead wrote, "consists in the maintenance of the symbolic code; and secondly in fearlessness of revision, to see that the code serves those purposes that satisfy an enlightened reason. Those societies which cannot combine reverence to their symbols with freedom of revision, must ultimately decay either from anarchy, or from the slow atrophy of a life stifled by useless shadows." Obviously, Jefferson has been a paramount symbol of the code. Moreover, as one who declared, "Nothing is unchangeable but the inherent and inalienable rights of man"—the maxim that Dewey thought "the heart of his faith"—he invited continuous revision and reconstruction.

James Madison, after the death of his great friend, attempted to sum up Jefferson's genius, and in doing so he anticipated the judgment of posterity. He was, said Madison, a man of generous learning and versatile industry who left "the philosophical impress" of his mind "on every subject which he touched." But what especially informed all this activity, he continued, was "an early and uniform devotion to the cause of liberty, the systematic preference of a form of government squared in the strictest degree to the equal rights of man." In Madison's judgment, clearly the ironies, paradoxes, and contradictions in Jefferson's life and thought, so much dwelled upon by scholars, mattered little in the light of this fundamental harmony and consistency.

There are many Jeffersonian legacies, but unquestionably the greatest is the philosophy of human rights so eloquently stated in the Preamble of the Declaration of Independence. Abraham Lincoln named those principles "the definitions and axioms of free society." They have done more to define the meaning and purpose of the nation than any other act or statement. But this "American Creed," as Gunnar Myrdal called it, was framed as an enunciation of the rights of all mankind. The universalism of the philosophy has made it one of the fountainheads of the international human-rights culture of our time. Jefferson is rapidly becoming a world citizen. In the correspondence of their old age, John Adams liked to twit Jefferson on the exploded hopes of the Enlightenment and the age of the democratic revolution through which they had lived. Jefferson admitted the horizon was clouded, yet could not share Adams's pessimism. "I shall not die without a hope that light and liberty are on steady advance," he declared. "And even should the cloud of barbarism and despotism again obscure the science and liberties of Europe, this country remains to preserve and restore light and liberty to them. In short, the flames kindled on July 4, 1776, have spread over too much of the globe to be extinguished by the feeble engines of despotism. On the contrary they will consume those engines, and all who work them." If, as Gordon Wood suggests, Jefferson went to his death somewhat disenchanted with what he had wrought, he seems to have suffered no failure of nerve. His intellectual commitment, together with his optimism, was unimpaired.

Contributors

JOYCE APPLEBY is Professor of History, University of California at Los Angeles

EDWARD L. AYERS is Professor of History, University of Virginia

PAUL K. CONKIN is Distinguished Professor of History, Vanderbilt University

STEPHEN A. CONRAD is Professor of Law, Indiana University, Bloomington

PAUL FINKELMAN is Visiting Associate Professor of History, Virginia Polytechnic Institute and State University

SCOT A. FRENCH is a doctoral candidate in history, University of Virginia

JACK P. GREENE is Andrew W. Mellon Professor in the Humanities, Johns Hopkins University

RHYS ISAAC is Professor of History, La Trobe University, Australia

DANIEL P. JORDAN is Director, Thomas Jefferson Memorial Foundation

WALTER LAFEBER is Noll Professor of History, Cornell University

JOHN LAURITZ LARSON is Associate Professor of History, Purdue University

JAN LEWIS is Associate Professor of History, Rutgers University, Newark

MICHAEL LIENESCH is Professor of Political Science, University of North Carolina, Chapel Hill

PETER S. ONUF is Thomas Jefferson Memorial Foundation Professor of History, University of Virginia

MERRILL D. PETERSON is Thomas Jefferson Memorial Foundation Professor of History, Emeritus, University of Virginia

HERBERT SLOAN is Assistant Professor of History, Barnard College, Columbia University

LUCIA C. STANTON is Director of Research, Thomas Jefferson Memorial Foundation

DOUGLAS L. WILSON is George A. Lawrence Professor of English, Knox College

GORDON S. WOOD is University Professor and Professor of History, Brown University

Index